Urban Planning and Real Estate Development
Second Edition

John Ratcliffe, Michael Stubbs
and Mark Shepherd

Spon Press
Taylor & Francis Group

LONDON AND NEW YORK

First published 1996 by UCL Press
Reprinted 1999, 2001

Second edition published 2004 by Spon Press
11 New Fetter Lane, London EC4P 4EE

Simultaneously published in the USA and Canada
by Spon Press
29 West 35th Street, New York, NY 10001

Spon Press is an imprint of the Taylor & Francis Group

© 2002 John Ratcliffe, Michael Stubbs and Mark Shepherd

Typeset in Goudy by Steven Gardiner Ltd, Cambridge
Printed and bound in Great Britain
by TJ International, Padstow, Cornwall

British Library Cataloguing in Publication Data
A catalogue record for this book is available from the British Library

Library of Congress Cataloging in Publication Data

ISBN 0-415-27262-9 (pbk)
ISBN 0-415-27261-0 (hbk)

Urban Planning and Real Estate Development

Second Edition

This second edition of **Urban Planning and Real Estate Development** is a comprehensive treatment of the twin processes of planning and development and the only book to bring the two fields together in a single text. Updated to reflect current practice, the case studies included in this text provide a clear understanding of the symbiotic relationship of these activities.

The student is guided through the procedural and practical aspects of developing land. Town planning subject matters are explored from both development control and property development angles. Town planning content deals with planning law and process, planning appeals and specialist areas such as historic buildings, conservation areas, planning obligations and sustainable development. Revisions include new work on urban regeneration, dispute resolution, probity in Local Government, best value and reforms to the system post 2001 Green Paper.

The development section deals with the whole development process from inception, through appraisal, valuation and finance to disposal of the completed project. There are specific sections dealing with the key issues affecting the retail, office, industrial and residential sectors. Revisions include new work on joint ventures and the private finance initiative, sustainability, PPG3 and PPG11, urban regeneration and design quality. The book is an invaluable text for all students of planning and real estate and all related courses.

Professor John Ratcliffe is Director of the Faculty of the Built Environment, Dublin Institute of Technology, Honorary Visiting Professor at the University of Salford, and a Chartered Planning and Development Surveyor with over 35 years in practice as a consultant. **Dr Michael Stubbs** is a lecturer, researcher and Chartered Town Planner with 15 years' experience as an academic, local government officer and consultant. **Mark Shepherd** is a Chartered Surveyor at Salford University, where he teaches the theory and practice of property development.

The Natural and Built Environment Series

Editors: Professor John Glasson
and Professor Michael J. Bruton

Methods of Environmental Impact Assessment: 2nd edition
Peter Morris and Riki Therivel

Introduction to Environmental Impact Assessment: 2nd edition
John Glasson, Riki Therivel and Andrew Chadwick

Public Transport: 4th edition
Peter White

Landscape Planning and Environmental Impact Design: 2nd edition
Tom Turner

Controlling Development
Philip Booth

Partnership Agencies in British Urban Policy
Nicholas Bailey, Alison Barker and Kelvin MacDonald

Planning, the Market and Private House-Building
Glen Bramley, Will Bartlett and Christine Lambert

British Planning Policy in Transition
Mark Tewdwr-Jones

Development Control
Keith Thomas

Forthcoming:

Urban Regeneration: A Critical Perspective
Sue Brownill and Neil McInroy

For our families

Contents

Part One
Introduction

1 Urban planning and real estate development: the context

Town planning: an introduction

The modern-day planning system is a post-war invention, with roots that may be traced to the enactment of the Town and Country Planning Act 1947. The notion of 'planning' land use goes back further still, arguably as far back as ancient Greece when Piraeus was laid out following a 'grid-iron' street plan. Consistent throughout an examination of such urban history is that society affords a measure of regulatory control to the state (i.e. the government) to supervise the use of land. What best distinguishes the 1947 legislation is its scope, principally that it established a comprehensive and universal system of land use control.

Then, as now, the system served the key function of balancing public and private interests. The creation of the post-war planning system effectively 'nationalized' the right of private individuals to develop land by stipulating that planning permission would be required for certain types of development. In return these 'applicants' were afforded the automatic right of appeal (to a planning inspector or to the Deputy Prime Minister) should consent be refused. This newly created system of town and country planning would exist to secure the interests of the community, in cases where amenity would be harmed. Amenity itself was never defined and since 1947 to the present it has been interpreted (usually by virtue of legal interpretation in the Courts) in many ways.

The public interest would, therefore, take precedence over the private right to develop land and property (Grant 1992). Nevertheless, the private interest should not be unduly restricted and in a variety of circumstances various freedoms, such as the right to extend a dwelling within a certain volume, would be deemed to fall outside planning control. Today, such freedoms from the need for planning permission are granted by subordinate (i.e. laid before Parliament) legislation, such as contained in the General Permitted Development Order and Use Classes Order (which permit certain building works and changes of use without planning permission).

What has changed since 1947 are the policy outcomes that the system is designed to secure. In 1947 this meant post-war reconstruction. In the first decade of the twenty-first century, it means 'sustainable development', so that by way of example, government policy seeks (by 2008) that 60 per cent of new housing will be built on brown (i.e. previously developed) land or by conversion of existing stock.

A growing awareness of sustainability on an international stage has followed from work by the United Nations in hosting global summits in Rio de Janeiro (1992), Kyoto (1998) and the World Summit on Sustainable Development in Johannesburg (2002). At its most fundamental this subject area sets out to 'make less last for longer' (RICS Foundation 2002), so that future generations would still be able to use and benefit from environmental resources. One key area of environmental threat comes from global warming as the production of carbon dioxide (by burning fossil fuels) traps some of the sun's energy and produces a rise in global temperature. Global consequences involve dramatic changes to weather patterns, melting ice caps and rising sea levels. At the 1998 Kyoto Agreement (Framework Protocol on Climate Change), the UK government committed itself to reducing the national production of such gases by 12.5 per cent. This would mean that by 2012 the volume of such emissions would be reduced to 1990 levels, in an attempt to arrest climate change. Today worldwide carbon emissions amount to 3 billion tonnes released annually into the environment. Yet, how can the planning system affect sustainability or, to be more precise, climate change? This is *the* policy challenge for the system today and in the future.

Sustainability, as a distinct discipline or component of town planning, is only some 15 years old. The 1987 World Commission on Environment and Development (The Brundtland Commission) provided the first and still most enduring definition:

> Development that meets the needs of the present without compromising the ability of future generations to meet their own needs.

While recent research by the RICS Foundation (ibid.) reveals considerable disagreement over how to measure sustainability, there is overwhelming scientific and demographic evidence in favour of action now. Statistical evidence is compelling. For example, the United Nations has estimated that by 2030 60 per cent of the world's population will live in cities (United Nations 2001). In England today 90 per cent (or 47 million) of the population live in urban areas, accounting for 91 per cent of total economic output and 89 per cent of all employment. Government land use change statistics reveal that during the 1990s, England's urban area grew by 0.29 per cent annually. This statistic may on the face of it appear of little consequence until you convert it into hectares, amounting to 39 000 lost from rural to urban use annually.

The planning system is well placed to deliver 'compact' cities, based upon efficient land use in which integration with public transport and promotion of mixed-use development discourages dependence on the private car. By promoting and implementing more efficient land use, reflected in density, layout, design, and mix of uses in close proximity, the planning system can make a tangible contribution to climate change and thus affect environmental sustainability.

The need, therefore, to address matters of urban density and layout is pressing. Demographic (i.e. population) change means that over the next generation there will be a significant rise in the number of one-person households, especially amongst younger people. This significant rise in demand for housing presents an opportunity as well as a potential threat for the system. A 'spectre' emerges in which planning control is overwhelmed by this volume of development in the following 20 years, a prospect neatly encapsulated by Lord (Richard) Rogers and Anne Power writing in 2000:

> We know that in this country [England] alone we may have to accommodate nearly four million extra households over the next twenty years . . . we can sprawl further round the edges of existing suburbs in predominantly single person households or we can make cities worth living in for those who like cities but do not like what we are doing to them.
>
> (Rogers & Power 2000)

So this potential threat can be made into an opportunity in which such development pressure is used to 'heal' the city by 'retrofitting' a new model of development into the existing urban fabric. The prevailing density of development in our cities must be raised and increasing amounts of urban land recycled. National planning policy sets a headline objective of building 60 per cent of new homes on previously developed land by 2008. National land use statistics reported that in 2003 64 per cent of housing was built on such recycled land, five years ahead of schedule. This encouraging statistic conceals the fact that it was achieved on the lowest number of housing completions for some 50 years.

How best to create procedural systems that will deliver a renaissance of our urban areas while maintaining many past principles governing the system (such as public participation)? The UK government, in 2001, began a review of the system with such reform very much in mind. Before considering the implications of such anticipated reforms, it is necessary to understand the context within which the town planning system operates. An examination of the past assists in understanding the future because the evolution of urban planning from the late Victorian period exhibits a number of policies, principles and environmental challenges analogous to the present day.

A history of urban planning

> Town planning, by its nature, is essentially concerned with shaping the future.
>
> (Ward 1994)

Today, control over land use is increasingly viewed as (one) means of influencing both urban and environmental change. In many policy areas planning is currently regarded as a reaction against environmental degradation/decay and global warming. For example, if the design and layout of a town reduces reliance upon the private car, then, albeit crudely, planning reduces carbon emissions and (in turn) global warming. By contrast, early planning legislation can be traced to the Public Health Acts of the period 1848 to 1875.

The genesis of such legislation was the work of people such as Sir Edwin Chadwick. Chadwick made a study of urban sanitation and by implication the conditions of the urban working classes in 1842.[1] The findings were themselves instrumental in the establishment of a Royal Commission on the Condition of Towns (1844) and subsequent legislation, albeit rudimentary, to establish minimum standards for urban sanitation. The 1875 Public Health Act increased the levels of control so that local government bodies could pass and implement 'by-laws' to regulate the layout of dwellings as well as acquiring the power to implement their own schemes following acquisition of urban land. The nineteenth century witnessed rapid urbanization that affected enormous change across society, economy and environment, and brought with it disease and ill health as a result of insanitary and overcrowded slum housing. Ward (1994) reports that 'In 1801 the urban population of England and Wales had been 5 million . . . by 1911 the figure was 36.1 million'.

Industrialization sucked the (rural) population into these new towns and cities. As these industrial urban areas expanded they also merged, giving rise to the new phenomenon of the 'conurbation'. Pressure mounted to introduce some measure of regulation and increasingly urban local government took control over matters of water supply, sewerage and urban layout. A series of local regulations (introduced under powers granted by the Public Health Act of 1875) afforded local control over housing layout to rule out the 'very cheap and high-density back-to-back building' typical of the Victorian slum. The grid-iron pattern of late Victorian inner suburbs (at 25 dwellings per hectare) characterised and gave physical form to this newly established regulation. Yet it was not an attempt to 'plan' whole districts and to integrate land uses but rather essentially a further attempt to prevent the disease-ridden slum dwellings of the previous 75 years by provision of sanitation within and space around individual dwellings.

The notion of planning entire areas is perhaps best traced to the Garden City movement of the turn of the twentieth century. The Garden City was something of an umbrella term, encapsulating many planning and property development principles in the quest for an environment based upon amenity or quality. Further, the Garden City represented a reaction against the squalor of the Victorian city, just as today the planning system strives to create sustainable environments as a reaction against environmental degradation.

> The Garden City idea and the movement it spawned were crucial precursors to the town planning movement in Britain.
>
> (Ward, 1994)

Howard published his 'theory' of the Garden City in 1898.[2] This was based on the notion that a planned decentralised network of cities would present an alternative to the prevailing Victorian system of urban concentration. The Garden City was created on the development of four key principles. First was the finite limit to development: each city would grow by a series of satellites of 30 000 population to a finite limit of around 260 000. A central city of 58 000 would provide specialist land uses like libraries, shops and civic functions. Each satellite would be surrounded by a greenbelt. Second, 'amenity' would be of fundamental importance so that open space and landscaping would provide valuable recreational and aesthetic benefit. Third, this pattern of development would create a topography based on the notion of a 'polycentric' (many-centred) social city with a mix of employment, leisure, residential, and educational uses within close proximity. Finally, all land would be under 'municipal control', so that the appointed Garden City Company would acquire land, allocate leasehold interests and collect rents. Initial capital to create the company would be raised from the issuing of stocks and debentures. In effect a development company would be created that would be managed by trustees and a prescribed dividend would be paid (a percentage of all rental income to the company). Any surplus accrued would be used to build and maintain communal services like schools, parks and roads. Howard's theory has been encapsulated as a kind of non-Marxist utopian socialism (Miller 1989) seeking at the time a reform of land ownership without class conflict.

Such a theory was itself derived from a combination of sources, in particular the concept of land nationalization in the late nineteenth century. This involved the creation of social change through land ownership. Further, Howard was affected by the aesthetic ideas of socialists such as William Morris and the 'model communities' of Victorian philanthropists such as Sir Titus Salt (Saltaire, Bradford 1848–63), George Cadbury (Bourneville 1894), William Lever (Port Sunlight 1888), and Sir Joseph Rowntree (Earswick, York 1905). All these projects conceived the notion of the utopian industrial suburbs to improve the conditions of the workers. Saltaire was noted for its communal buildings (schools, institute and infirmary), Bourneville its extensive landscaping and large plot size, Port Sunlight for its good-quality housing, and Earswick for its spacious layout.

In 1903 Howard embarked on the development of Letchworth in Hertfordshire, with Welwyn Garden City to follow in 1920. A Garden City company was established and remains today. The town plan showed a group of connected villages, linked to a civic centre and separated from an industrial area. The concept of 'planned neighbourhood' was born.

> Letchworth was probably the first English expression of a new town on a large scale.
>
> (Smith-Morris 1997)

Two architects previously employed at Earswick, Raymond Unwin (1863–1940) and Barry Parker (1867–1947) added design to Howard's theory, producing a medium-density (30 dwellings per hectare) low-cost cottage housing in tree lined cul-de-sacs (a layout first created at Bourneville). The vernacular design exhibited strong Arts and Crafts influences of William Morris (1834–96), C. F. A. Voysey (1857–1941), Richard Norman Shaw (1831–1912) and Philip Webb (1831–1915). Morris had viewed 'the home as a setting for an enlightened life and projected its virtues outwards to embrace community' (Miller and Gray 1992). Arts and Crafts architecture emphasised the picturesque, using gables, chimneys and reviving traditional construction, including timber framing. Raymond Unwin developed the 'local greens' (or

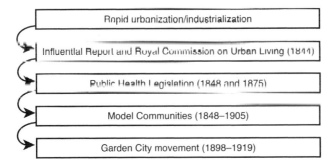

Figure 1.1 Development of the Garden City.

village greens) and cul-de-sacs used in Letchworth and also in Hampstead Garden Suburb.

Other schemes were to follow, notably Wythenshawe (Manchester) and Hampstead Garden Suburb (North West London). Howard had taken the rudimentary public health legislation of 1848 and 1875 and produced the 'master planning' of an entire area, based upon design innovation, affordable housing, mixed use, and social ownership. Such principles are of great importance today as government policy sets out to engender an urban renaissance. A summary of developments leading to the establishment of the Garden City movement is set out in Figure 1.1.

The key principles upon which the 'model communities' of late nineteenth- and Garden Cities/suburbs of early twentieth-century England were based are set out in Table 1.1. When considering the density as displayed (dwellings per hectare), it is worth comparing these data with the 1875 by-law figure of 25 dwellings per hectare and the post-war norm of between 15 and 20 dwellings per hectare. Historically, housing densities have fallen progressively over the last 125 years or so. What is perhaps most interesting is that they have fallen from the Victorian city where over-crowding prevailed to the low-density postwar suburbs of volume (i.e. mass-market) housebuilders. In other words they have fallen from the insanitary to the inefficient. Up to 2000, new housing layouts were wasteful in their use of land. By comparison Letchworth and Welwyn Garden City, as originally built, involved densities in excess of 30 dwellings per hectare yet maintained a leafy environment in which open spaces and amenities predominated. Much can still be learnt from examination of environments like this in the building of pleasant medium- to high-density housing without the need for a return to the high rise schemes of the 1960s.

So at the beginning of the twentieth century a series of urban planning experiments pointed the way forward. A statutory system lagged very far behind. The first town planning legislation (the Housing, Town Planning, etc. Act 1909) introduced 'town planning schemes',[3] which allowed councils to plan new areas, mostly for future urban extensions or suburbs – although a poor take-up resulted in only 56 schemes being drawn up in the first five years (by 1914). Yet in the inter-war years '. . . the town extension policies which

Table 1.1 Principles of early town planning

Place	Years	Size	Housing or population	Density (dwellings per hectare + key features
Bourneville	1895–1900	133 hectares	313 houses	• Density = 24 dwellings/hectare • Provision open space + sunlight to dwellings
New Earswick	1902–1903	61 hectares	24 cottages	• First scheme designed by Parker and Unwin
Letchworth	1903–1933	1546 hectares	5000 population	• Density = 30 dwellings/hectare • Open layout of roads + houses • Cottage design of red tiles + rough cast bricks
Welwyn Garden City	1920–1934	1000 hectares	10 000 population	• Density = 30–35 dwellings/hectare • Distinct neighbourhoods
Hampstead Garden Suburb	1907–1914 & extension of 1920–1930s	96 hectares	120 houses (by 1908)	• Density = 20 dwellings • Parker and Unwin design • Enclosed spaces to create village atmosphere • Use of closes + cul-de-sacs

had been embodied in the 1909 Act were now being implemented on a vast scale' (Ward 1994). Further legislation was enacted in 1919 with the Housing, Town Planning, etc. Act. This legislation incorporated a series of design space and density standards recommended by a government committee the previous year (the Tudor Walters Report) that importantly endorsed a housing model based upon Garden City densities of 12 houses per acre (30 per hectare). The Act imposed a duty on all towns in excess of 20 000 population to prepare a town planning scheme, albeit that take-up was again poor.

The 1930s witnessed a rapid growth in private speculative development on the urban fringe. Four million dwellings (some estimates are as high as 4.3 million) were constructed in the inter-war years, peaking at over 275 000 in 1935 and 1936 alone. Of all inter-war dwellings, 58 per cent were built by private speculators. By the 1930s the 'erosion' of land from agricultural to urban use stood at some 25 000 hectares per annum. This boom contains lessons for the present day. Such a volume of development was itself spurred on by a combination of factors. Social and economic trends involving a low cost of living (the 1930s depression suppressed prices to the benefit of those in employment). Interest rates were low and personal finance was made available in the growth of the newly created building societies. Cheap labour and building costs were combined with a social preference to buy one's own home. Expanding public transport infrastructure and cheap agricultural land on the urban fringe (Ward 1994) made suburban development a reality for developers and a saleable commodity for urban workers. This heady combination of factors led to rapid suburban growth. While the 1909 and 1919 Acts were powerless to really thwart this trend (many town planning schemes of the time merely served to assist suburbia by reserving road lines into the suburban area), it would be unfair to conclude that inter-war suburbia was 'unplanned'. As Ward (1994) argues, the early planners assisted in what was, in most part, an orderly pattern of development. A new landscape was created, with dormitory suburbs built at low densities of around 12–15 dwellings/hectare and relying less on a community infrastructure and more on home-based leisure and newly available consumer durables like radios and motor cars. Indeed, as suburbia grew so did private car ownership, as people became more isolated from shops and services and thus more dependent on private transport.

This pattern of development presents a powerful lesson for the present. Property development has an inextricable link to town planning. In the 1920s and 1930s vast tracts of agricultural land were lost to housing because development factors (finance and costs) were combined with planning ones (new infrastructure). Inter-war suburbia may be viewed as inefficient in its use of land, giving rise to low-density, mostly residential development. A stark parallel can be drawn with the present-day challenges confronting the planning system, in which 3.8 million dwellings are required (between 1996 and 2021). This amounts to a similar number to the 4 million dwellings delivered during the inter-war years of the 1920s and 1930s. Such inter-war suburbia covered an estimated 360 000 hectares, at a prevailing average density of 12 dwellings per hectare. The Urban Task Force led by Lord Richard Rogers countenanced the spectre of replicating such a model when dealing with current housing needs, thereby resulting in an additional urban area for England over the next 20 years the size of the West Midlands conurbation (Urban Task Force 1999).

The work of Le Corbusier provided a radical departure from the Garden City or indeed the inter-war suburban model of development. His work was influential in two principal areas. First, he developed the concept of 'open-plan' housing based upon a series of linked spaces. Second, he developed an urban plan (his 1922 scheme) that radically challenged the arcadian low-density cottage and Garden City layouts of Howard, Parker and Unwin. This 'city for 3 million people' comprised skyscrapers of 50–60 storeys separated by parkland and ringed by Green Belt (an idea taken from Howard), and criss-crossed by a grid of roads that fed into an elevated urban 'motor-way'. Such principles were applied to central Paris (the Plan Voisin) in 1925, comprising 15 apartment dwellings of 20 storeys, resulting in high-density living per block and around 60 dwellings per hectare (although the vast expanses of encircling parkland reduces the overall density). This urban vision for Paris was not realized and many of his urban redevelopment plans for Rio de Janeiro, São Paulo, Antwerp, Stockholm, and a second (1937) scheme for Paris travelled no further than the drawing board. His most significant implemented schemes comprised several high-rise apartment blocks (the Unité d'Habitation) in France and Berlin and the creation of the new city of Chandigarh in India. Perhaps less tangibly he also influenced some inter-war and post-war British architects in their fashionable adoption of high-rise architecture (such as at Roehampton in South West London). Yet as Smith-Morris (1997) reports 'sadly most of the other examples, some 384 towers built in Britain between 1954 and 1974, were cheap partial imitations of Le Corbusier's ideas, with devastating consequences'.

The urban vision promoted by Le Corbusier is, therefore, in stark contrast with that of Howard. It is easy to misinterpret his work. Le Corbusier is erroneously associated with the many failures of post-war high-rise flats. His ideas promoted a concept of well-designed, mixed-use, high-rise living (each block combining community functions like schools and roof-top recreational space) within spacious urban parkland. Each block would be orientated to achieve maximum natural light, in order to increase the sense of spacious-ness. What followed was a poor copy of that concept. In England such post-war high-rise building was often of poor construction, badly designed and located. Each block was confined to residential use only and often housed the most inappropriate residents for such a lifestyle, such as families with children. Ironically these tower blocks replaced low-rise housing as politicians embraced high-rise as a 'quick fix' solution to the rehousing of many inner-city communities. Yet the stigma so rightly levelled at these schemes should not detract from the fact that medium- to high-rise development still has a role to play in modern urban planning. The Urban Task Force (1999) themselves countenanced medium-rise urban redevelop-ment. The key issue as acknowledged by the Task Force is the use of mixed use/ownership urban space to create a well-designed and 'connected' urban place. The quality of design promoted by Le Corbusier is therefore of much relevance even if his ideas for civic renewal (such as the comprehensive demolition and rebuilding of central Paris) amount to no more than megalomania.

The work of a number of other key figures must also be acknowledged in providing orientation to the challenges of the present. Patrick Geddes (1854–1932), through his book *Cities in Evolution* (1915), promoted the idea of 'survey–analysis–plan', in effect the gathering of physical, economic and social survey information as the basis of devising all planning policy. Today it is vital that planning decisions are based upon a full grasp of all relevant information. Clarence Perry (1872–1944) developed the notion of a 'neigh-bourhood unit' (in 1939) as first introduced by Howard, in which a series of locally based functions (schools, community facilities and shops) are grouped within new housing layouts to create an identity and neighbourhood. This model has been widely copied ever since and is perhaps best illustrated in Milton Keynes (developed 1967 to 1992), where the neighbourhood unit provides the foundation stone for the construction of an entire new town. Walter Groupius (1883–1969) promoted high-rise housing, linked by walk-ways, to provide maximum light and air to each residential unit. Groupius was instrumental in the Bauhaus School of Design in Germany, which collectively developed higher-density mixed-use apartment blocks that included community facilities (such as public open space) and sought to separate pedestrians from traffic (by use of raised walkways). Provision of mixed uses is key to the creation of sustainable communities.

The Second World War provided the necessary genesis for the modern planning system, in respect of both physical reconstruction and the desire for more control to be exercised by government. This post-war land-use agenda was formulated during the war years with the publication of three influential reports. First, the Barlow Report (1940) on the regional distribution of population and employment, followed two years later by both the Uthwatt Report on the role of compensation and 'betterment'¹ in any planning system and the Scott Report on protection of the rural economy and countryside. Each report would bear fruit in the future in the form, respectively, of regional policy, taxation of development profit, and protection of national parks, the countryside and green belts.

A number of key developments in the creation of the current system can be traced to the 1945–51 Attlee Labour Government. Three 'towering' pieces of legislation were enacted in the New Towns Act 1946, the Town and Country Planning Act 1947 and the National Parks and Access to the Countryside Act 1949. A new era was heralded. In this era planned decentralization of new towns was to be peppered around the major conurbations of England. Comprehensive control was imposed over the right to develop land and recreational access to the countryside was assured by the formation of National Parks and Areas of Outstanding Natural Beauty. New legislative mechanisms were set in place to implement this legislation. Key amongst these was the 'New Town Development Corporation' who were vested with sweeping power to 'acquire, hold, manage and dispose of land and other property'. Subsequently 28 such New Towns were built between 1949 and 1970. Further, the 1947 Act introduced development planning (to establish land-use blueprints) and development control (consent required to build on or change the use of land). The 1947 Act, in effect, took away the private landowner's right to develop land (which was reasonably unfettered by the 1909 and 1919 Acts) and replaced it with the need to obtain planning consent.

Such legislation remained largely untouched for the remainder of the century. After the watershed of the millennium the Government heralded in a reform of the system that would affect widespread change. Following such reforms the central question to address would be whether or not the key foundations of 1947 would be undermined, namely the role of the state (i.e. government) in the regulation of property development.

Reforming the planning system

In December 2001, the Secretary of State for Transport, Local Government and the Regions (whose responsibilities were passed to the Deputy Prime Minister in May 2002) announced a major review of the planning system in England and Wales. The current system was considered to be 'complex, remote, hard to understand and difficult to access' (DETR 2001). Local Plans (i.e. locally produced planning policy) were deemed to be overly complex, often inconsistent with regional or national policies, too lengthy, inflexible in content, and slow and expensive to produce. A new framework was required. Development Control (the process by which decisions are made on planning applications) was considered slow and highly variable in speed measured across councils, as well as being unresponsive to the needs of business/investment and the community. A fundamental change in culture was required. While the Secretary of State upheld the guiding principles of 'good planning', he felt that the present-day system was failing to deliver this in that it was slow, obscure (at times) and, notwithstanding much formal consultation with the public, it failed to engage communities, leaving them 'disempowered'. Such criticisms were directed at achieving fundamental structural change. Yet the government was not proposing to alter the public (i.e. state) regulation of private property interests. As such, the government implicitly rejected the case for private land-use planning (Pennington 2002) but argued that many principles built up since 1947 needed drastic review. The Secretary of State felt that the public needed to be more 'engaged'. Such a critique was not unique. Five years earlier, Lord Nolan, in his report into Standards in Public Life (1997), reported that 'Public satisfaction with the planning system does not seem to be particularly high'. The government set out, in the 2001 Green Paper, to make the system more open and engaging (to the public), flexible (in production of local planning policy) and faster (in speed of determining planning applications). Further, a new ethical framework, governing the conduct of councillors, was put in place (operative since May 2002) and a 'best value' regime was established seeking continuous service improvement (operative since April 2000).

Direction of the 'reformed' planning system

Since the publication of the 2001 Green Paper it has become evident that the 'system', i.e. the procedures involved in the determination of an application, will be the subject of much change during the period 2003 to 2007 (as new planning documents are rolled out and reforms in the Planning and Compulsory Purchase Act 2004 are enacted). Alongside this the policies the system is vested to deliver (i.e. sustainability) are themselves rapidly changing to accommodate a more environmentally aware agenda. In assessing the most likely direction of future reforms, both will be considered.

In policy matters, the most significant issue has been the promotion of an 'urban renaissance' (Urban Task Force 1999). This aspiration is by no means an easy one. Past drift away from urban areas (especially amongst more affluent groups) alongside the creation of 'bland' car-dependent environments in suburban or fringe housing developments and out-of-town retail and campus-style office/business parks, must be reversed. Standards of urban development and design require significant improvement and the private sector must be encouraged (and supported) to recycle urban land that may be derelict, vacant and even contaminated. A reassessment of policy priorities was thus required; otherwise existing urban areas would sprawl further. Such an option would be not only environmentally unacceptable but also politically damaging as local people expressed their fury at seeing new development envelop the countryside by voting local politicians out of office. New development is nowadays viewed as something inherently bad, giving rise to the acronym NIMBY (not in my backyard). To compound matters further, as of 2000 700 000 homes were empty in England, of which 250 000 were vacant for in excess of one year (Urban Task Force 1999).

The Urban Task Force gave a great deal of consideration to the physical and (urban) design means by which the planning system may 'repair' the city. Four issues were identified for consideration. First, that past reliance on rigid planning standards stifled creativity. Adherence to highway standards (such as road widths and radii and visibility at junctions) predominated in post-war urban layouts and this 'roads first, houses later' priority produced bland civic design. Streets should be seen as places and not transport corridors. Second, the Urban Task Force promoted the notion of a 'compact city', to foster both sustainability and urban quality. Sustainability would be achieved by linking urban density to a hierarchy of urban centres/local hubs providing shops and services within well-connected public transport and walking routes. An appropriate integration of density and the 'connected compact city' will reduce the reliance on the car. Third, it should be acknowledged that density alone is not an indicator of urban quality, although it is an important factor. The Urban Task Force argued that higher densities (and not necessarily high-rise developments) contribute to urban sustainability. Previously in England half of all land used for housing has been at prevailing densities of 20 or fewer dwellings per hectare, equating to 54 per cent of all land used providing just one quarter of all housing units completed (DETR 1998a). Not only is this form of housing highly inefficient but it is no longer a viable means of providing housing when confronted with the dual priorities of satisfying 3.8 million units while stemming the annual flow of people who continue to leave urban areas and protecting the urban hinterland. Finally, greater attention should be paid to urban design, to facilitate mixed-use/mixed-tenure development and to foster sustainability. Good urban design will repair past mistakes and make cities more attractive places to live. The London Plan of 2003, produced by the Mayor of London, is the embodiment of this vision in its strategic attempt to accommodate population growth of 700 000 in the capital by 2016 while making London a sustainable world-class city.

A year after the Urban Task Force reported its findings, the government issued an Urban White Paper (DETR 2000b). This document laid down a vast array of policy initiatives dealing with the social, economic and environmental dimensions of urban life. The government took forward many ideas to promote the recycling of urban land, the improvement of urban design and architecture, and the employment of taxation and fiscal policy to encourage developments in deprived areas, to name a few. New thinking was emerging in many quarters, ranging across the private sector, regeneration agencies and the research community.

The Urban White Paper estimated that (as of 2000) 58 000 hectares of brown-field land is vacant, derelict or available for redevelopment and that 'more becomes available every year' (DETR 2000b). Indeed the White Paper (which by definition signals forthcoming legislation) set out a series of strategies. Much attention was devoted to bringing brown-field sites and empty properties back into use. A number of strategies were deployed including taxation (reform of VAT and tax breaks for conversions of property into residential use) and land assembly (creation of a national land-use database to monitor brown land across England). Between 50 000 and 200 000 hectares of land was estimated to be contaminated in England. The White Paper proposed tax relief for the clean-up of contamination, promoted new technologies of remediation and the creation of a database of such land and the nature of its contamination. Additionally it heralded the creation of 12 new 'urban regeneration companies' (such as Liverpool Vision or Sheffield One) to create local partnerships between public and private sectors in an attempt to bring greater levels of investment to such areas. By way of example, Liverpool Vision published an urban design appraisal of central Liverpool, in 2002 which identified a series of physical 'townscape' improvements to create urban spaces and places. A series of new cultural quarters and squares would be created to improve the 'sense of place' and encourage investment to bring residential and commercial (re)development back into the city core. Interestingly, Liverpool city centre contains the highest concentration of listed (i.e. heritage) buildings outside London but lacks any centrally located park or major public space.

Another important policy area was that of the mixed-use and mixed-ownership 'Urban Village' (also sometimes referred to as 'new urbanism'). A concept originally devised by private sector developers in the early 1990s, the Urban Village set out to raise urban density and to mesh different land uses within close geographic proximity and within buildings (Urban Village Group 1995). Such new pockets of development could be 'retrofitted' into existing urban areas, connecting and revitalizing neighbouring areas.

Research published by the DETR (in 1998) similarly looked at ways of realizing the potential of urban areas. This could be achieved by 'nodal' development (or 'ped-shed') that made people less reliant on private car use and served to make cities more attractive places in which to live. The node or ped-shed created an urban 'module' in which a node (bus/tram/train stop, shop, school, play space or park) is located within a walking distance of 5 minutes or 500 metres radius of a cluster of dwellings. A consequence of this model (similar to the Garden City in many ways) is the fact that residential environments are built to higher densities and of a human scale (on a medium rise not exceeding three or four storeys) to sustain shops, public transport, schools, and amenities. The chosen layout gives priority to urban design because careful use of urban public spaces can physically 'knit' these land uses together. By way of example, one key urban design principle deals with 'permeability' or pedestrian choice across the environment (Bentley *et al.* 1985). A permeable urban village, module, ped-shed, or node, call it what you like, will by use of pedestrian access increase the linkage to the node and thus promote less reliance on the private car, especially for short distances.

Government policy has, since 2000, become increasingly aware of this new policy agenda. Statements of national planning policy (in Planning Policy GuidanceStatement) and 'best practice' reports (e.g. *By Design*, issued by DETR in 2000g) have set out to raise the quality of design, reduce car parking provision and increase residential density. Past adherence to rigid planning standards in locally based planning policy is to be discouraged in an attempt to promote innovation. A much applauded example is the Poundbury development on the edge of Dorchester in Dorset. On land owned by the Duchy of Cornwall and under the direction of master planners such as Leon Krier, HRH the Prince of Wales created a sustainable urban extension with reduced parking (1.1 places per dwelling), raised density (40 per hectare) and relaxation of 'back-to-back' distances between dwellings. Poundbury has become the physical manifestation of a new approach in which much previous planning orthodoxy was ditched in favour of innovation in design. Further, the Prince of Wales and others (Wates 1999) have promoted new techniques of 'stakeholder' participation, in which members of the local community, developers, planners, and other interested groups sit down to devise plans and strategies for such developments through interactive workshops (The Prince's Foundation 2000). This often referred to concept of 'Planning for Real' represents a radical departure from traditional consultations involving letters sent to neighbouring occupiers seeking comment on a planning application.

Contemporaneously with this new approach, the Commission for Architecture and the Built Environment published research (2001) that challenged many previously held ideas on the cost of 'quality' urban design. The work set out to quantify what was meant by quality in urban design and to appraise the financial consequences of pursuing such provision in new development projects. After analysing a series of case studies the researchers concluded that

> Gradually, the case is being made across the development industry that good urban design brings better value.
>
> Good urban design does add economic value . . . high quality urban design is attractive to key sections of the rental, investment and owner/occupier market, who are prepared to pay extra for better quality design.

By way of example, one of the case studies dealt with Barbirolli Square in central Manchester. This involved a one-hectare redevelopment of former railway land to create a cultural and office district with a concert hall, two office blocks and a café/bar. A public space was created, linking and opening up a former canal basin. The site was considered by the researchers to be reasonably well connected and created '. . . a new landmark gateway to Manchester' (CABE 2001). Subsequently, the offices have commanded high rents and an economic 'ripple effect' is evident, in which new restaurants have opened up in the surrounding area.

Similarly, to build in a sustainable way is also viewed as a matter of commercial advantage for the developer, as reinforced by another research project published by the RICS Foundation (2002).

A new policy agenda has therefore emerged in town planning, directed at achieving both better design and more sustainable development. Over the last four or so years, practitioners and students have had to assimilate vast quantities of new policy, 'best practice' documents and research findings. Such material has come thick and fast. The challenge ahead is to create a new planning system able to deliver this policy effectively.

Turning to consider procedural matters, the 2001 Green Paper and the Planning and Compulsory Purchase Act 2004 led the way in establishing a blueprint for the future direction of the planning system. Alongside these key documents the government issued an array of new consultation papers dealing with the future of planning obligations (2001), the Use Classes Order (2002) and protection of heritage (2003). The government was intent upon seizing the moment and introducing an array of new initiatives.

Planning obligations, sometimes colloquially referred to as 'planning gain', refers to the practice of developers contributing (in cash or kind) towards infrastructure necessary to facilitate their development. Traditionally this system has been used to finance roads and other physical infrastructure as generated by planning applications (such as open spaces, schools and sewerage facilities). More controversially, albeit in the minority of cases, it has been used for matters unrelated to the development in question. The government was perhaps swayed into action by the Nolan Report, which reported the perception that this amounted to 'planning permissions being bought and sold' (*Standards in Public Life* 1997). Even if erroneous, this perception is damaging because it is harmful to public confidence in the system. The consultation paper argued in favour of scrapping this negotiated system in favour of standardized set tariffs. Public comment on the consultation paper endorsed this idea. These tariffs would be prescribed in local planning policy. When submitting planning applications, developers would see in 'black and white' the tariffs to be levied towards infrastructure (such as the total or partial cost of a road, school or children's play space necessitated by the development) (DETR 2001). This system represents the government's preferred reform, other options being stoutly dismissed in the consultation paper. Reform is to be rolled out between 2004 and 2006.

New systems of plan monitoring and production will also be introduced in the present decade. Government will seek a reduction in the volume of both nationally and locally produced planning policy and will create streamlined 'Local Development Frameworks and Documents' that involve more flexible (by virtue of being frequently updated) statements of local planning policy objectives. These will replace the current somewhat cumbersome system of Structure/Local/Unitary Development Plans produced by local authorities (since the early 1990s). Regional planning policy will be given more 'teeth' as a Regional Spatial Strategy is prepared by elected Regional Assemblies. County Councils will lose their strategic planning responsibilities from 2004.

It is intended that the speed of processing planning applications will be increased as fewer applications go before the elected planning committee for their deliberation. Conversely, the public will become more involved as 'stakeholders' as new participation techniques are introduced. One of these, 'Planning for Real' (mentioned above, p. 16) seeks greater community involvement in the design of planning applications (Wates, ibid.). The principal objective is that people become more engaged in the formulation of projects/development proposals and feel less cut off from the system. The existing model involves the public principally in that they are 'consulted' on a planning application, i.e. they are permitted to respond to advertisements about a planning application. This provides them with one solitary avenue for voicing opposition to be considered by the local planning committee. Certain initiatives by bodies like The Prince's Foundation (2000) and a number of local authorities have set out to enable the public to become more pro-active in their dealings with the planning system. Yet the government's aspiration that as few as 10 per cent of all applications go before the (locally elected) planning committee (to save time) are, arguably, contrary to the principles of participatory democracy.

The proposal (of December 2001) that objectors will not be able to appear and be heard before a Local Plan (to become the Local Development Document) Inquiry challenged one of the tenets of the 1947 system, namely that the public may participate in just about every stage of the planning process. It is often forgotten that the planning system is built on a democratic base. Any attempt to change or possibly erode this foundation will be viewed with suspicion and many planning pressure groups criticized the government for countenancing an arguably undemocratic threat to civil rights. Friends of the Earth (in a press release 12 December 2001) deemed the proposal to take away the right of the public to be heard in this way as the . . . 'biggest removal of rights ever seen in the British planning system'. In fairness to the government, their 2001 consultation paper proposed that such democratic and participatory input be dealt with at an earlier stage, in effect the local community getting involved in formulating the policies as opposed to commenting on them when formally published. Nevertheless, this concern demonstrates the strength of comment involved and sensitive nature of this important issue. The bulk of the 16 000 objections submitted against the Green Paper dealt with this issue. Seven months later (July 2002) the government dropped the idea.

While not explicitly stating as much in their reasoning behind this change of position, the government must have been mindful of the new legislative protection over rights of participation and consultation that followed the enactment of the 1998 Human Rights Act (operative from 2000). Any reforms to 'streamline' decision-making by diminishing this democratic right would have collided with such legislative protection. Inevitably the system will become more litigious as individuals and groups mount legal challenges to planning decisions and actions on the ground that their human rights have been infringed. The Planning and Compulsory Purchase Act 2004 creates the new system. The government announced with this new legislation that it was still committed to the 'plan-led' system. In other words, while the titles and content of planning documents would change, there would still be a presumption in favour of the 'plan' (or whatever it is to be called) when determining planning applications. The new system will be rolled out over a three-year period from 2004 to 2007 and greater emphasis than previously will be placed upon regional spatial planning.

To study planning and its relationship to property development presents many challenges. One of the most demanding of these is that of remaining conversant with the vast amount of documentation cascading from national and local government. Combine this with the volume of proposed reforms to the system and the enormity of the task soon becomes apparent. The Urban Task Force itself identified the importance of built-environment courses in creating inter-disciplinary graduates:

> The main emphasis should be on broader-based courses that bring the skills together with a strong emphasis on problem-solving and multi-professional teamwork.
>
> (Urban Task Force 1999)

The Task Force listed studies in property finance, urban design, environmental planning, and urban management as being key foundations for all built-environment education. The inter-disciplinary and indeed multi-disciplinary nature of planning and development makes for exciting times ahead when applied to the task of achieving sustainable development and/or reviving our urban environments. The planning system, vested with the responsibility of delivering this change, is itself the subject of review and reform. While sustainability is the key issue, we must not lose sight of the issues of democracy and public participation, which have been the hallmark of the 1947 system. Future reforms must deliver sustainability (i.e. in the control of out-of-town and low-density housing), but must also maintain public confidence through adequate consultation and participation.

Part Two

Urban planning organization

2   Policy and implementation of urban planning

Since 1948 a highly regulated system of land-use control has been gradually introduced by successive legislative reforms. Today, the implementation of urban planning controls is exercised under two distinct but interconnected subject areas, dealing first with the production of planning policies and then how those policies feed into the development control system, whereby decisions are made on individual planning applications. Both of these subjects form the bedrock of the planning system. Attention will be focused upon the context of planning policy, together with a detailed study of the processing of a planning application, including the formulation of the decision whether to grant or refuse such an application. Reference is also made to illustrative (but not exhaustive) case law on matters that constitute issues relevant to the determination of a planning application. The chapter is organized as follows:

- the development plan process
- the development control process.

The post-war planning system involving both the production and implementation of locally produced planning policy was first introduced by the Town and Country Planning Act 1947. All previous town planning statutes were repealed and the new legislation heralded the introduction of a major shift in public policy, from which we may trace the evolution of the current system. The new Act came into force on 1 July 1948 (the appointed day).[1] This legislation introduced the modern system as it exists today. The very need to apply for planning permission became nationalized. Private landownership would remain, but thenceforth permission would be required to change the use of buildings or to erect new structures. Planning policy would be prepared by local councils (city, district or borough) and county councils. Such locally produced policy would shape the patterns of development across the country. However, the overall organization of town planning would be the subject of a highly centralized system of control, whereby central government would determine the function of local government. As local government is responsible for the implementation of planning functions, this meant that the national government dictated the nature of town planning powers and their institutional structures. Today, central government departments, in particular the Office of the Deputy Prime Minister[2] (or Scottish Executive and Welsh Assembly [Planning Division]), have responsibility for the policy outcomes of the planning system. The Office of the Deputy Prime Minister, Scottish Executive and Welsh Assembly (Planning Division) issue PPSs and Circulars containing the views of the Secretary of State on a wide variety of policy areas. These documents constitute important material considerations and must be taken into account in decisions on planning applications and appeals. Other government departments, notably the Department of Culture, Media and Sport and Department of Environment, Farming and Rural Affairs (DEFRA) also influence the system.

The Town and Country Planning Act 1968 introduced a significant reform to the system of plan preparation with the introduction of structure plans and local plans. The structure plan was to be prepared by a county council or the Greater London Council and was to comprise a statement of strategic and longer-term planning objectives such as major housing allocations or green belt identification. The local plan was to be prepared by the city, district or borough, providing a more detailed and short-term list of policies to be applied specifically to individual sites. The local plan would need to be in conformity with the structure plan, and with central government advice. At first, county councils were encouraged to incorporate economic and social, as well as land use, policies in structure plans. However, in recent years central government has sought to exclude wider social policy objectives in an attempt to emphasize land-use strategies. This stance has been followed by councils, although they have not excluded considerations of issues such as transport[3] and sustainable development.

The reforms of 1968 were subsequently consolidated into the Town and Country Planning Act 1971. This statute remained the principal planning statute until the introduction of new planning legislation in the Town and Country Planning Act 1990 and Planning and Compensation Act 1991. The only other significant statutory reforms introduced between 1971 and 2000 dealt with the delivery of the planning function in the reform of the local government structure. The Local Government Act 1972 created a new system in England and Wales (which came into force in 1974), except for Greater London, which had been reorganized in the early 1960s under the Local Government Act 1963 (which came into force in 1965). In Scotland similar reforms to local government structure were introduced by the Local Government (Scotland) Act 1973 (which came into force in 1975).

The reforms to local government structure are shown in Table 2.1. The reforms of 1973 and 1974 increased the number of local government bodies (counties and districts) from 177 to 454 in England and Wales (Redcliffe-Maud Report 1969), whereas in Scotland it reduced them from 430 to 65.[4] Across Britain new structure involved a two-tier basis whereby the county/region (metropolitan or non-metropolitan) would be responsible for strategic planning matters and the district or city council, and London boroughs would be responsible for day-to-day matters, especially dealing with planning applications. In the metropolitan areas of and surrounding Manchester, Liverpool, Newcastle, Sheffield, Leeds and Birmingham, a two-tier system of metropolitan counties and districts was established. The objectives of the Local Government Act 1972 and Local Government (Scotland) Act 1973 were to introduce reforms to simplify and streamline

Table 2.1 Local government, 1974–94

England (except Greater London)	39	County councils.
	296	District and city councils.
	6	Metropolitan councils
	36	Metropolitan districts and borough councils.
Greater London	Greater London Council	
	32	London boroughs.
	+	City of London (special status being excluded from local government reforms).
Wales	8	County councils.
	37	District and city councils.
Scotland	9	Regional councils and three island authorities.
	53	District or city councils.

the structure of local government and implementation of local services, including town planning controls.

Today that two-tier system has been replaced by a confusing mix of two-tier and single-tier structures, a consequence of reforms introduced in 1986 and 1995. In 1986 the Greater London Council and six metropolitan counties were abolished, with their powers being passed on to the London boroughs and the metropolitan district councils. Therefore, in each of these urban areas only one body would be responsible for the implementation of local government including the town planning function, so the London borough or metropolitan district would be responsible for both structure and local plan policy. Policy would reflect an amalgamation of both objectives and would be called a unitary development plan. In 1995 and following a widespread review of local government structure undertaken by the Local Government Commission for England, the Scottish Office and the Welsh Office, the government announced further reforms, whereby some county and regional councils would be abolished, with their powers passing to the districts. Again, these councils would be responsible for producing a unitary development plan.

During the late 1990s the government's appetite for further structural reform of local government remained undiminished. The creation of devolved government within the United Kingdom (the Welsh Assembly, Northern Ireland Legislative Assembly and Scottish Parliament) were not matched by elected regional government within the English regions, albeit that such reforms are anticipated by 2005.[5] Instead a high-profile reform of the government of London heralded a partial re-introduction of the Greater London Council with the birth, in 2000, of the Greater London Assembly (GLA) and a mayor for London. The mayor would take a strategic lead in a number of areas (transport, economic development, spatial development, sustainability and the environment), with the Assembly responsible for

Table 2.2 Local Government post-2000

England (conurbations)	36 Metropolitan Borough Councils in Greater Manchester, West Midlands, Merseyside, South and West Yorkshire, Tyne and Wear
England (London)	Mayor and 32 London Boroughs and The Corporation of the City of London.
England (Non-Metropolitan)	47 Unitary Authorities. 34 County Councils, linking with 238 'shire' District Councils.
Wales	22 Unitary Authorities.
Scotland	32 Unitary Authorities.

Notes:
(i)   Most councils are unitary (i.e. responsible for both strategic and local functions) except in English non-metropolitan areas.
(ii) In English non-metropolitan areas powers are geographically divided between Unitary Authorities (mostly cities outside the big conurbations like Nottingham) and the County (Strategic) and District (Local) Councils in rural or 'shire' areas.
(iii) Town or Parish Councils are omitted. They are optional for District Councils to establish and do not have planning powers.
(iv) From 2004 County Councils will lose strategic planning powers.
(v)   From 2005 Regional Assemblies will produce Regional Spatial Strategies.

scrutiny of and comment upon the performance of the mayor's office. The London Development Agency (LDA), as the regional development agency for the capital, became responsible for delivering the mayor's economic development strategy. In 1999 the government created eight other Regional Development Agencies, vested with powers of economic development/ regeneration, promotion of business/employment, skills training, and promotion of sustainable development. If English regional government should become a reality then these bodies will provide powerful institutions directed at achieving inward investment, economic redevelopment and sustainable development.

In the realm of town planning the mayor and Assembly enjoy an array of strategic functions as allocated by the Mayor of London Order 2000 and Spatial Development Strategy Regulations. The mayor produces a Spatial Development Strategy (SDS) to provide a framework for all mayoral responsibilities over land-use matters. This was published as 'The London Plan' in 2003. While the mayor has a broad remit of policy areas, including housing, leisure, natural environment, and urban quality, the London boroughs remain in control of the development control functions and production of their own Unitary Development Plan policies. The mayor enjoys limited, albeit important, powers of intervention over strategic matters and is required to issue a certificate of conformity to establish that a UDP complies with the London Plan. In limited circumstances the mayor must be consulted on applications that raise matters of strategic importance, and if an appeal is lodged by the developer, will be required to defend that decision. One other significant area covers power over heritage, with the mayor responsible for framing conservation policies (working with English Heritage and London boroughs), although the boroughs retain control over individual Conservation Areas and Listed Building Consent applications.

Outside the domain of the London mayor, therefore, strategic planning remains the preserve of the (mostly rural) county councils. This is likely to change by 2005 as, first, the government appears committed to abolish strategic planning policy input by county councils (see the paragraph in the 2001 Green Paper) and second the creation in 2000 of Regional Development Agencies (to deliver economic regeneration) provides, together with regional assemblies/chambers, the perfect organizational structure to deliver regional planning.

The development plan process

The development plan is an 'umbrella' expression that covers all statutory planning policies produced by local planning authorities (Healey 1983). These policies are found in three principal documents:

- the structure plan produced by regions or non-metropolitan counties
- the Local Plan produced by district or city councils (to become the Local Development Framework/Document)
- the unitary development plan produced by the London boroughs, metropolitan districts or metropolitan districts with no county tier (also to become the Local Development Framework/Document)

Sometimes the LPA will introduce Supplementary Planning Guidance, policy that is used in decision-making on applications, but has not been included in the Local Plan/Framework. Such policy should supplement the plan and not seek to replace it. This practice is best used on technical guidance such as car parking standards or visibility splays from road junctions. It does not carry the same status as the plan and should be clearly cross-referenced to the local policy. If it is not related to such policy and has not been the subject of any public consultation, it will be considered as a 'bottom drawer' policy that carries little weight as a planning consideration. Refusals based solely on such 'bottom drawer' policy guidance will stand little chance of being supported by an Inspector when considering any subsequent planning appeal.

These Plans/Frameworks 'guide' development proposals by establishing a series of rules that may shape future development proposals and influence the chances of gaining planning permission (Bruton & Nicholson 1987, Healey *et al.* 1988). They also provide a 'starting point' for the consideration of various development proposals. Satisfying development plan policy does not guarantee that planning permission will be granted; however, the various development plan policies form an important and significant material consideration. These policies should always be examined in the first instance before submitting planning applications as they constitute an important material consideration in the decision whether to grant or refuse planning permission. The 'weight' attached to such policy increases as it proceeds through the various stages of its production. When policy has completed these stages, it will be 'adopted'. This will mean that:

> Where in making any determination under the planning Acts, regard is
> to be had to the development plan, the determination shall be made in
> accordance with the plan unless material considerations indicate other-
> wise.[6]

The local Plan/Framework produced by the district council (or city
council) deals with more detailed and local issues identifying specific land
uses suitable for individual sites and detailed policies for particular development proposals. Some local plans are also called action area plans (specific
sites, usually town centre development) or subject plans (dealing with specific
policies that cross district boundaries, usually green belts), although they
carry the same status as local plans. After 2004 the principal local policy
documents will be a Framework statement of key policies and a series of
regularly updated area-and topic-based policies (e.g. on greenfield development or heritage issues). The Framework will thus comprise a core strategy
proposal map (landuse design actions) and a series of Action Area plans. The
period 2004–7 will be transitional, with the most recently updated Structure
Plans and UDP/ Local Plans being 'saved' (i.e. still in force until the new
documents are rolled out by their respective councils). The core strategy
must contain a 'Statement of Community Involvement', demonstrating that
public participation has been involved in the process.

In 1991, the introduction of reforms resulted in greater weight to the legal
status of development plan policy within the decision-making process.[7] It is
therefore important that landowners and developers monitor the production
of planning policy and become involved in that process to influence the final
outcome (Table 2.3). Once policies have completed this process, they become
'adopted' or approved; resulting in considerable influence over the outcome
of future planning applications. These reforms also made the production and
adoption of district-/borough-wide local plans (or unitary development
plans) a mandatory requirement across England and Wales (this had been a
requirement in Scotland since 1973). In spite of DoE (up to 1997), DETR
(1997–2001), DTLR (2001–2) and Office of the Deputy Prime Minister (from
2002) targets seeking total plan coverage for England, delay in the production
of Development Plan policy and lengthy duration of Local Plan Inquiries (see
Stage D in Table 2.3) has meant this objective has been severely obstructed
in its achievement. As a consequence the original intention of having all
Development Plans in place by 1996 will not be complete until several years
into the new century. This failure to deliver has been acknowledged by
government in PPG12 (1999), and has largely contributed to wholesale
revision of the system anticipated in 2003/4 (see the paragraph in the 2001
Green Paper).

Groups interested in the planning process such as landowners, developers
and local or national interest groups, are advised to monitor the production
of plan policy, especially in the early stages (Stages A, B and C). Structure
plan revision and alteration should take place every 10–15 years and local
plan/UDP every 5–10 years. Any person or group who disagrees with a
particular policy should submit objections following the deposit stage

Table 2.3 The production of development plans policy

Structure Plan/Local Plan/Unitary Development Plan process (Local Development Frameworks after 2004)

Stages	What happens
A – Survey	Council gathers data on land use and other relevant information (e.g. transport patterns and population trends).
B – Prepare draft	Council formulates policies and supporting information.
C – Deposit	Plan is 'deposited' for a formal period of publicity and for the submission of objections against individual policies in the plan. After 2004 there will be only one formal opportunity to object to a local policy.
D – Review	Review by Inspector at Public Local Inquiry. Each will publish a report with recommended amendments.
E – Modification	Council must modify in line with the report. After 2004 the Inspector's report will be binding.
F – Notice to adopt	Council submits a notice to adopt to Secretary of State, who has a 28-day period to 'call-in' the plan and approve plan in whole or part.
G – Adoption	If no 'call-in' plan becomes adopted and now carries full statutory weight.

* Full details of all procedures can be found in Sections 10 to 54A of the Town and Country Planning Act, 1990 and also refer to PPG12: Development Plans (1999) Chapters 1–3 and the Town and Country Planning (Development Plan) (England) Regulations 1999 (No 3280). It is normally the case that plans are reviewed once every five years.

(Stages B and C). If they do not object, and the policy becomes adopted, it will carry the full weight of section 54A, making it unlikely that it could be ignored when dealing with a planning application or appeal. Objection to local plan or unitary development plan policies can be made in writing or in person before the Inspector.

In the Local Development Framework Inquiry, any objector has the right to appear before the Inspector to explain their case. At this point the Inspector will consider objections and all written representations or oral evidence submitted at the Inquiry. Such a review is conducted against the deposited plan (Stage C) and after it has been revised in light of negotiations between the local authority and objectors (designed to narrow the volume of contentious policies and sites and thus speed the task of the Inspector). In future years such negotiations may be productively helped by mediation (see Chapter 5). Anyone doing so is open to cross-examination by the LPA. Legal representation is allowed in similar format to a planning appeal submitted by way of public inquiry. Similarly, it is common for many objectors to instruct planning consultants to prepare proofs in support of their objection and to appear at the local plan Inquiry. For more depth see Sections 36–45 of TCPA 1990 and commentary in Grant (2002). The structure plan Examination in Public allows the 'panel'[8] to select issues and invite certain participants to make a contribution. No one who objects to a policy has the automatic right to appear before the panel. The examination takes the form of a discussion led by the chairman between panel members, representatives of the county council and the invited participants. Planning consultants and legal representatives are allowed to appear. Structure Plan examinations in public will be scrapped from 2004, but this method will be retained for discussion of proposed Regional Special Strategies.. A report is sent, in either case, to the relevant district/city/borough council or Regional Assembley. The Inspector/Panel may recommend modifications that the respective council must consider. The Secretary of State enjoys powers to object to policies in the plan, to direct the regional authority to modify a policy or to 'call-in' a Local Development Framework and direct that a policy be modified or altered.

The development control process: a definition?

> Development control is a process by which society represented by locally elected councils regulates changes in the use and appearance of the environment.
>
> (Audit Commission 1992)

The development control function is of itself difficult to define. It has been referred to as the Cinderella of the planning system in that it deals with the day-to-day administration of planning control. In many ways this function operates at the 'sharp end' of the system, as it deals with decision-making on planning applications, representations at appeal, and the enforcement of planning control. This all takes place within a political system whereby locally elected politicians make decisions within a planning committee or delegate such decision-making powers to officials, principally the chief planning officer of a local authority. To understand how this system operates, it is necessary first to examine the historical background of development control, as well as the debate surrounding the quality and service delivery of this function. The basis of today's planning system can be found in the reforms introduced by the Town and Country Planning Act of 1947. This legislation introduced a system of comprehensive control over development. What constituted development was defined by statute and would require planning permission by means of an application to a local authority. The system would be overseen by a government department (initially the Ministry of Housing and Local Government and today the Office of the Deputy Prime Minister), although the emphasis was on local control.

The Dobry Report, 1975

The first comprehensive review of the development control system took place in 1973, led by George Dobry QC (Dobry 1975). The review was

---

Case study 2.1: Local plan objection

Prefabricated Engineering Ltd owns a hectare of land occupied by a series of single-storey light engineering buildings.

The local council proposes in its Action Area plan that the site be identified for industrial use for the plan period (ten years). The owners wish to vacate in the next two years and consider that the site is better suited to residential redevelopment. They lodge an objection to the local development framework policy and instruct a town planning consultant to appear at the Plan Inquiry. The Inspector considers the objection and reports that the land is suitable for residential redevelopment and should be so designated. The local council must modify the plan to delete this site from industrial allocation and include it in residential allocation.

---

established to consider the current arrangements for planning appeals as well as appraising whether the development control system adequately met current needs, with a view to advising on areas for improvement. The report was commissioned against a background of dramatic increases in the numbers of planning applications and appeals submitted between 1968 and 1972. By 1972 the number of planning applications submitted had increased by more than 67 per cent over 1968 levels. Dobry concluded that, although the system was very good, its procedures did not adequately meet current needs, and he criticized them for being slow and cumbersome. A series of detailed recommendations were designed to speed the administrative and procedural side of the development control function, rather than the quality of the decisions made (a recurrent theme in subsequent reviews of development control).

The most significant recommendation, which the government considered to be too radical to enact, proposed that all planning applications be split into two categories with differing procedural requirements. Category (A) would be 'simple' applications of a small-scale nature or non-contentious (i.e. those in accordance with the development plan). Category (B) would be large-scale proposals or contentious proposals (i.e. not in accordance with the development plan). The planning authority would be required to issue a decision on (A) applications within 42 days of submission and on (B) applications within three months of submission. Failure to issue a decision on Category (A) within 42 days would result in a deemed grant of planning permission. No such deemed consent would apply to Category (B).

Although Dobry's major recommendation of Category (A) and (B) was rejected by the government, several of its minor recommendations were to be incorporated into various administrative reforms, notably the use of a standard application form when applying for permission, greater delegation of decisions to officers, publicity and public consultation for planning applications, and the introduction of a charge for submitting a planning application. The Dobry Report dealt with areas for improvement of efficiency within the system and it is important to distinguish between the desire to improve the efficiency of the development control process and the quality of the decisions made. Dobry dealt almost exclusively with seeking to improve the speed of decisions without affecting their quality.

This philosophy has been followed through more recently with the publication of three reports into the operation of development control, as follows.

The Royal Town Planning Institute Report 1991

In identifying the strengths and weaknesses of the current system, this report dealt with the problems surrounding an examination of 'effectiveness' within that system. The report stated: 'Attempts at defining an effective planning service can easily open up a debate on the ideology and philosophy of planning itself' (Royal Town Planning Institute 1991).

It was acknowledged that statistics could be employed to measure procedural issues (for example the percentage of planning applications determined within a particular time period). However, such methods could not be used to measure the quality of decisions made, as this was a largely subjective matter. It is a paradox of the system that the more carefully a planning officer negotiates to improve an application, the less likely it is that a decision will be made within the eight-week week statutory period that constitutes the only measure of quality control. The study therefore found that 'effectiveness' in the planning service does not necessarily equate with speed. With regard to development control, the study identified the following as the key attributes that contribute towards an effective planning service: clarity, speed, user involvement, openness and certainty. Recommendations were made, including several designed to improve service delivery, such as the need for concise reports to planning committee, encouragement to hold pre-application meetings, and greater delegation of decisions by planning committee to the Chief Planning Officer.

In conclusion, the report emphasized that, for a planning service to operate effectively, a 'service culture' must be built upon the concept of customer care. In development control, such a concept of care requires the process to be both 'accessible' to developers and the public, in that decisions are clearly and easily explained, as well as procedurally efficient in that administrative targets are set for the speedy despatch of decisions or responses to enquiries.

The Audit Commission: building in quality 1992

Like the Dobry Report, the Audit Commission's report (Audit Commission 1992) was concerned with the speed and efficiency of the development control function, but, unlike Dobry, its principal terms of reference were defined as improving the quality and effectiveness of the system. The report focused upon the attainment of quality outcomes. The Audit Commission had considered the views of both developers and consultants, as well as existing statistical performance indicators, such as the net expenditure per application by the local authority, or the percentage of applications considered under delegated authority. These quality outcomes were similar to the RTPI (1991) study in that they identified a series of administrative areas of concern as follows:

• Service objectives need to be established – encompassing all the publications or policy documents of the LPA.
• Pre-application discussions and advice – should be encouraged and guidance published on applications, as well as the existence of an accessible planning department reception.
• Efficient administrative backup – to register applications upon receipt and pass promptly to a planner.
• Consultation and notification – encouraging the notification objectives to be clearly set out in correspondence, together with guidance on the relevance of particular responses to avoid replies with no planning relevance.
• Assessment and negotiation – following any negotiation it must be necessary to demonstrate the achievements gained from this process. LPAs should utilize the services of specialist in-house staff to ensure consistency and quality in specific areas (e.g. economic development, design, traffic or ecological matters).
• Documentation – written reports to committee upon a case, dealing with the merits or otherwise of the case; jargon is to be avoided.
• Decision-taking and committees – potential for greater delegation to Chief Planning Officer and a frequent committee cycle.
• Decision notification – to ensure speedy delivery of decision reached.

Confederation of British Industry (CBI)/Royal Institution of Chartered Surveyors (RICS) (1992)

This report was the result of a CBI appointed task force of 21 business leaders and planning professionals, charged with examining the planning system and identifying areas where improvement would help the successful operation of businesses (CBI & RICS 1992).

The most far-reaching recommendation was for the creation of a National Framework of Strategic Guidance, with relevant central government departments producing a policy framework covering land use and infrastructure, over a projected five-year period and with the most immediate priorities identified for the next year, together with a funding commitment from the Treasury. This represented a call for greater direction by central government over strategic planning issues, together with associated financial commitment. The business community identified the need for a greater degree of direction regarding major land-use and transport proposals to ensure greater certainty for the property investment industry. Such a call was seemingly at odds with government philosophy, which in 1983 had proclaimed that strategic planning was an outdated concept of the 1960s and 1970s, followed in 1985, by the abolition of the Greater London Council and six metropolitan county councils (HMSO 1983).

Perhaps not surprisingly, the then Secretary of State for the Environment, Michael Howard, soon dismissed any possibility of the government adopting such a strategic framework.[9] The report considered that pre-application discussion should be made a statutory requirement and that the business community should seek to make a more cohesive and systematic input into plan preparation to ensure that planning policy adequately dealt with the needs of the business community.

Appraising quality within development control

These reports have all sought to appraise the development control function. It is far easier to identify quality within the system by examining administrative and procedural matters such as the frequency of committee meetings or the time taken to issue a decision notice. It is harder to examine the concept of quality when dealing with the actual quality of the decision. To appraise whether or not a particular local planning authority has issued a 'good' or 'bad' decision would be fraught with problems, as many planning decisions rely on professional judgement, based on policy and other material considerations. Appraisal of the quality of decisions made is further complicated by the fact that planning officers, committee, developers or the public may all hold differing views on the desirable outcome of the whole process and, therefore, what is a good decision to one group may not be a good decision to another group. The Audit Commission did attempt to link service delivery with the assessment of, and negotiation on, a planning application. This would be achieved by utilizing specialist contributions to the appraisal of a planning application (e.g. for conservation, landscape, economic development issues) and ensuring that the development control service is guided by the local authority's overall objectives. However, in the vast majority of recommendations in all of these reports, the overriding concern is service delivery and how it can be made more open and apparent to the public, quicker in dealing with administration and able to establish targets and guidelines. This is not to say that the current system is wholly inefficient, but that, in the past, little real attention has been paid towards a review of targets and performance. Some authorities have subsequently published Service Charters[10] setting out mission statements and targets for performance, and in some cases attention has been paid to improving public perception by allowing greater access for the public, on particular cases, to speak in committee meetings.[11]

When appraising development control, it is easy merely to associate quality with speed of decision-making. The eight-week statutory period encourages this,[12] as the Office of the Deputy Prime Minister will release annual statistics on the percentages of planning applications decided within eight weeks or in excess of eight weeks. This measure does allow for a crude indication of quality in that the more minor applications should be decided within such a period. However, for anything more complex, involving the consideration of many technical issues, the eight-week period is unreasonably short. In effect, to stay within it encourages LPAs to avoid negotiations seeking amendment, as the submission of amended plans (and associated requirement to go back to public consultation), will take the application outside the statutory period. It may be of benefit to their statistical returns for the LPA to refuse an application and pursue discussions prior to resubmission of a revised, fresh planning application. This would delay the developer, but would reflect a more efficient approach by the LPA. The Dobry recommendation of a two-tier system based upon Category A and B applications would reflect the workings of the system more accurately. Both the RTPI and Audit Commission reports have criticized the statutory period as not providing a measure of quality. As long as it remains, it provides a benchmark to assess the speed of decision-making, but it is necessary to acknowledge that caution should be exercised when using it to assess the effective delivery of the development control service.

Planning Paper 2001

In December 2001 the Secretary of State (then, for Transport, Local Government and the Regions) published a Green Paper (i.e. proposals for consultation and discussion) on the planning system. The government's reforming zeal was based on the premise that the system over the last 55 years has evolved into a . . . 'set of inflexible legalistic and bureaucratic procedures . . .', arguably harmful to business productivity because of cumbersome and slow decision-making. While many professionals working in the system agree that reform is timely, they do not always share the underlying premise. It is possible to demonstrate delay in the system, for instance that in 2001 only 30 authorities determined 80 per cent of planning applications within eight weeks, while on average nationally only 65 per cent of applications are dealt with in this period. As to whether delay demonstrably harms commercial competitiveness or productivity is quite another matter. No substantial research exists to demonstrate this. Friends of the Earth subsequently argued that the government have placed too great an emphasis on lobbying by pro-business groups like the Confederation of British Industry (CBI). In any event reforms will follow. New legislation and its implementation is expected by 2004. This will herald a new planning system.

The single most important area of continuing reform relates to the production of local planning policy. In the new system the government promotes the notion of a less-detailed structure comprising fewer documents of less complexity. Structure Plans (produced by County Councils), Local Plans (produced by district councils) and Unitary Development Plans (produced by unitary councils) will all be scrapped. They will be replaced by 'Local Development Frameworks', which combine a short statement of strategic and long-term planning objectives, combined with more detailed and site- or topic-specific 'action plans'. These action plans would deal with council-wide topics (say, green belts or design matters) or specific areas (say, those identified for major development or renewal). The core statement of strategic objectives would be regularly updated to avoid any conflict with statements of Government Planning Policy (PPGs and Circulars). The Action Plans would be reviewed and replaced as circumstances dictated, for instance to deal with housing projections or when new development or renewal policies are identified.

Such a more-focused and streamlined system would come at a cost, principally that of public participation. The Green Paper comes to no firm conclusions here but hints that the less time or energy spent in a Local Plan Inquiry the better. Removal of such an administrative tribunal (as exists in the pre-Green Paper regime) would require a different form of democratic input to the system. This would be achieved by a statement of Community Involvement, detailing how the public have been involved in the production of local planning policies. The government's aspiration here is that the public become more engaged in formulating policy, instead of having to oppose it in the formal and adversarial setting of a Local Plan Inquiry. It remains to be seen whether this will work. Such a model assumes that the public can become engaged in the planning system, helping shape and structure new development. If, as in past years, the public continues to view new development as a threat and not an opportunity, then it is difficult to see how such involvement at an earlier stage will make community involvement more meaningful. The real losers in these reforms will be the County Councils, who are effectively stripped of all town planning policy-making responsibilities. Alongside this, regional planning policy will be enhanced with a 'Regional Spatial Strategy', to be produced by a host of regional agencies (including Regional Development Agencies); local Development Frameworks would need to be in conformity with these regional strategies.

The Green Paper was not solely confined to policy formulation. Development control was also identified for something of a shake-up. A key objective of the Green Paper is that development control become more 'service-orientated and responsive to customers'. Initiatives in this area encompass greater use of pre-application discussions (which councils may charge for), greater employment of E-planning to facilitate applications and appeals, new target periods for determination of applications,[13] reform of planning obligations (see Chapter 5), business planning zones,[14] and reforms of the General Permitted Development Order and Use Classes Order (see Chapter 3). The key themes underlying such reforms were to make the system more open, fair and less bureaucratic. Achieving this will be a major task. Nevertheless, reform in such areas is overdue. For example, the government proposes that public speaking be extended across all planning committees, that consultation with the public is more engaging and that access to planning papers be both free (or a low cost) and available by web access. Yet this more-open process based on greater public involvement must not be achieved at the expense of jeopardizing increased speed in decision-making. However, the reverse may apply as the Green Paper sets out to make the planning system more 'efficient'. It promotes greater delegation in planning authorities, in other words allowing the Chief Planning Officer to make the decision on an application, instead of it going before the Planning Committee. By 2004 the government will set a target that 90 per cent of applications be determined this way. A tension is evident here because in such cases the application will never progress to Committee, thus precluding any opportunity for the public to speak and having the potential to alienate public objectors who may perceive this as the loss of a democratic right. The Green Paper is silent on this possible dilemma.

Taken overall, the 2001 Green Paper provides a template for reform. It contains many initiatives, some conflicting (as just identified). During the period 2004–7 it is anticipated that many new reforms will be introduced, with the creation of Local Development Frameworks being the most far-reaching. To keep on top of these reforms it is recommended that relevant government web-pages[15] be reviewed periodically and subscription to the monthly bulletin to *The Encyclopaedia of Planning Law and Practice* be maintained (Grant 2003).

'Modernizing' local government

During the late 1990s and into the new century the government issued a raft of new policy initiatives under the umbrella of modernizing local government or the planning function within local government. These initiatives have dealt with a broad range of topics from dispute resolution (such as mediation, see Chapter 5) to value for money (see 'best value' below). To accept the notion of modernization is to accept a preconception or premise, namely that the planning or local government system is itself dated and obsolete. This has clearly not been the case in past years and the system has undergone successive reforms since its post-war introduction. Nevertheless, the modernizing agenda has afforded a valuable opportunity to appraise many areas of the system, especially the impacts on businesses, to permit reforms to be based on a clear understanding of existing problems in service-delivery.

Two areas are of particular importance. First, the new constitutional arrangements in local government following the introduction of the Local Government Act 2000, and second, the Beacon Council Scheme, which has affected many areas of local government, including planning. Until 2000 the key constitutional framework of local government was a system of subject/responsibility-led committees (composed of around 10–15 elected councillors) and a full council (composed of all councillors). The planning function would normally be vested in one or more committees, with planning applications usually determined by a development control sub-committee. Fundamental reform to this structure was introduced in 2000 with the Local Government Act, allowing councils to adopt one of three broad categories of new constitution. They could restructure to include either an elected mayor, a cabinet with a leader or an elected mayor with a council manager. The first two models give pre-eminence to elected politicians who would run council affairs, while in the third a considerable amount of responsibility would be delegated to the most senior council officer (Chief Executive).

In the pre-2000 arrangement decision-making was diffuse, with many councillors taking an active part by sitting on one or several committees. With the post-2000 situation, by contrast, most key decisions would be taken by a cabinet and/or mayor. The remaining councillors outside this executive would be responsible for scrutinizing the actions of these key individuals as well as representing the interest of their local (ward) electorate. The impact on the planning system will be mixed. However, a cabinet/mayor will decide certain strategic matters, such as housing allocations or Local Development

Framework policy. The determination of individual planning applications is unlikely to be affected. However, a cabinet or mayor would be soon inundated by the sheer volume of work that this would entail and it seems inevitable that, notwithstanding the new constitutional framework established in 2000, the role of a planning applications committee or sub-committee will endure for some considerable time to come.

Now to consider Beacon Councils. The government promoted in the 2000s, alongside 'best value', the notion of 'Beacon status' to reflect good practice and innovation. Such innovation placed considerable weight on new ways of achieving both efficiency (in the delivery of a service) and effectiveness (in, say, involving people in participation in local decisions). In town planning this is particularly important, as decisions may be scrutinised against their speed and process (i.e. involving people by means of participation and consultation). Further, that planning decision-making must be based on relevant and up-to-date information in the Development Plan. A number of planning 'beacons' were identified, combining both qualitative and quantitative indicators. For example, Copeland Borough Council (in Cumbria) was praised for an efficient service delivery based upon speedy processing of applications and low number of appeals (quantitative indicators) combined with established partnership dialogues with representatives of the local industries, traders and developers (qualitative indicator). In Halton Borough Council (North Yorkshire) a series of internal procedures (such as wide powers of delegation from Committee to Officers) resulted in considerable efficiencies in the processing of applications, sufficiently so that in excess of 80 per cent of all business-related planning applications were decided within the eight-week statutory period. To progress this further the council produced a business 'help pack', to assist companies in their submission of a planning application. An important component of the beacon concept is the wider dissemination of such good practice, in order to promote similar initiatives across all planning departments. This links with the best-value regime and the work of the Improvement and Development Agency, an agency of government appointed to facilitate the work of the Beacon Councils (between 40 and 50 chosen annually) and organise and spread best practice. By 2002 four individual rounds of identifying Beacon status had been completed. Different topic areas are selected for each round. The (then) Local Government Minister[16] stated of the scheme: 'Beacon status is much more than a trophy . . . Beacon Councils can help to raise standards of public services across the country'.

The planning application process

Once it has been established that: the proposal constitutes development, in that it represents either a material change of use or operational development,[17] and that it would not otherwise be exempt from control by provisions within the General Permitted Development Order or Use Classes Order, then it is necessary to apply for planning permission by submission of a planning application to the local planning authority.

Two specific topics must be considered: the processing of the application, and how one arrives at the decision to grant or refuse planning permission.

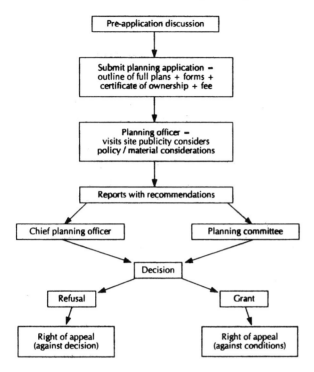

Figure 2.1 The planning application process.

Processing the application (Fig. 2.1)

Pre-application discussions

Before the application is submitted, the developer may wish to approach the LPA to seek either the informal views of the planning officer on the likelihood of permission being granted, or to clarify whether permission is required for the proposal in the first place.[18] The developer would be well advised at this stage to check the planning history of the site or its surroundings (previous application approvals or refusals and appeal decisions, i.e. whether these were allowed or dismissed, and any Inspector's comments).

The planning history constitutes an important material consideration.[19] The developer may leave the meeting in the knowledge that the proposal would be acceptable subject to certain issues or details being amended or that the proposal is unacceptable in principle (i.e. contrary to policy) and that the likelihood of a recommendation for approval by officers is unlikely. These meetings may also help the developer to decide whether to submit an application at all.

Which application?

The application can be made in either full or outline. In both cases it is necessary to submit the following documents:

- *Plans*   The exact detail or type of plan will depend largely on the proposal and whether the application is made in full or outline. Common to both will be an Ordnance Survey extract showing the site outlined in red and any other adjoining land also owned by the applicant outlined in blue. Full applications will require detailed elevational drawings and floorplans together with a siting drawing (showing proposed access, parking, relationship of proposal to adjoining land and, possibly, landscaping). Outline applications may only require the Ordnance Survey extract, although a siting plan may also be submitted, depending upon which matters are to be reserved for subsequent approval.
- *Forms*   The application must be made on standard forms issued by the LPA.
- *Certificate of ownership*   A certificate that only the applicant owns the land or has given notice of his application to all relevant landowners, and whether or not the land is on an agricultural holding, must be signed by the applicant or agent. It is therefore possible to make a planning application on land that is not within the ownership of the potential developer.
- *Fee*   Charges for planning applications were first introduced in 1980, the government's view being that some part of the cost of development control should be recovered from the applicant and not solely borne by the LPA. The fee structure changes approximately every two or three years. Reference should be made to the current Town and Country Planning (Fees for Applications and Deemed Applications) Regulations to ascertain the current charges.

Outline applications (Statement of Development Principles)

An outline planning application seeks to establish the principle of operational development on a particular site (applications for changes of use cannot be made in outline). The outline planning permission is one that is made subject to a condition requiring the subsequent approval by the LPA of reserved matters. These reserved matters cover five key areas of development control, namely siting, design, external appearance, means of access, and landscaping. The application form requests that the applicant nominates which matters are to be considered at the outline stage and which 'reserved' for subsequent approval. It is possible for all of the five matters to be reserved, although it is common practice for the applicant to request (and supply necessary information) that siting and means of access are considered at the outline stage.

The LPA has powers to request that further details are required and that the application will not be considered until such details are received. However, it is rare for this request to go beyond the details required for access and siting.

Once outline planning permission has been granted, any application for the approval of reserved matters must be made within three years of the outline approval, and the development must be started within five years of that date, otherwise the permission will lapse.

The distinct advantage of outline planning permission is that it establishes certainty within the development process, namely that a particular scheme is acceptable, subject to reserved matters. This allows the developer the guarantee of a scheme without recourse to an appeal. Thus, outline approvals may enhance the value of land by establishing the principle of redevelopment without needing to draw up full plans. The government has indicated this may be replaced by a certificate to be called a Statement of Development Principles.

Full applications

An application for full planning permission is for detailed approval. Full planning applications will therefore require submission of elevational drawings and floorplans, together with site plans showing access, landscaping and other treatment, such as car parking or servicing areas. It is usually the case that, although a good deal of detail will be submitted, the full planning permission may be granted subject to some conditions. These conditions may, similar to reserved matters on outline approvals, permit the proposal, while reserving for future consideration certain technical matters (e.g. details of internal matters such as soundproofing between converted flats). Conditions may also limit specific land-use matters, for example hours of operation, or maintenance of an approved landscaping scheme.[20] The full planning permission must be begun within a period of five years from the date of the approval or it will lapse. (After 2004 this will be reduced to three years.)

Formal submission of a planning application

When the application is made to the LPA it will be checked to ensure that all the documentation is correct and the necessary fee has been submitted. The application will then be acknowledged by the LPA and the date of the application's receipt will constitute the starting date for the two-month statutory period within which the LPA is required to issue a decision.

Following acknowledgement, it will be normal practice for most LPAs to undertake consultations with and publicity to various bodies or individuals.

Call-in powers

The Secretary of State for the Environment enjoys wide ranging powers to call-in any planning or listed building consent application for his own determination. These powers are rarely employed. Around 1000 planning applications are called in every year by the Secretary of State in England and of these some 151 will be formally determined, with the remainder referred back to the LPA. Most of these applications involve large-scale or controversial applications or applications that involve a departure from development plan policy, such as residential development within a green belt.

Table 2.4 Specified publicity for planning applications

Application	Publicity
1. Major development – 10+ dwellings, 1000+ m² floorspace, waste processing or working of minerals.	Advertisement by applicant in local newspaper and on site.
2. Developments affecting a conservation area and/or a listed building.	Advertisement by LPA in local newspaper and site notice.
3. Applications that depart from the development plan.	Advertisement by LPA in local newspaper and site notice.
4. Applications involving submission of an environmental statement.	Advertisement by applicant in local newspaper and site notice.
5. Minor development such as changes of use or extensions.	Site notice or neighbour notification.

The key criterion is that the application 'called-in' raises planning issues of more than local importance. If the LPA proposes to grant planning permission to such a 'departure application' it must consult with the Secretary of State to allow for 'call-in' to be enacted if the DoE considers the matter worthy of greater scrutiny or refusal. The Secretary of State also enjoys the power to give directions to the LPA that he must also be consulted on specific types of application, whereby he may then consider the use of 'call-in' powers, an example being in circumstances where the LPA wishes to grant planning permission for green-field housing development in excess of 5 hectares or 150 dwellings. In 2000 the Secretary of State issued a direction requiring consultation in such cases. If it were deemed that such a proposal raised matters of national policy importance, say an erosion of the 60 per cent brown-land housing threshold, then the Secretary of State would be entitled to call in the matter for determination, even refusal.

Publicity for planning applications

Publicity surrounding planning applications can be taken to mean advertisements in local newspapers, on site or by neighbour notification.[21] Examples are shown in Table 2.4

Third parties

Until 1991, LPAs were only encouraged to notify local residents who were neighbours considered to be affected by a proposal. However, it became increasingly apparent that different LPAs adopted different internal practices towards such consultation. An RTPI report (RTPI 1991) discovered that over three-quarters of all authorities undertook discretionary publicity and notification of planning applications. Yet, considerable differences existed between councils, with some only contacting immediately neighbouring occupiers, and others would contact widely within a set radius around the proposal site. Third parties did not enjoy any direct redress against the

Council for failure to consult them, as no statutory duty existed for notification to take place at all. Out of anger, or frustration, or both, many people lodged complaints with the Commissioner for Local Government Administration ('Ombudsman') on the grounds that the councils had been procedurally unfair in not consulting them.

In May 1991 the government accepted that all planning applications in England and Wales should receive some publicity, and regulations came into force in 1992.[22] Despite this, a problem still exists over the exact purpose of neighbour notification and publicity for planning applications. The Audit Commission (1992) identified a desire in many authorities to use neighbour notification as a public relations exercise, without informing the public about the exact purpose of such consultations. This devalues the process.

Third parties may draw the conclusion that the entire process is a waste of time if their comments are deemed irrelevant by the Chief Planning Officer in the report to planning committee. The Audit Commission recommended that authorities focus greater attention on providing the public with realistic expectations on both the process by which views will be taken into account, as well as the relevance of a particular type of response. Increasingly LPAs do provide guidance to the public over the form and content of planning objections. A number of local branches of the Royal Town Planning Institute provide voluntary services of qualified planners for groups or individuals unable to afford professional fees. West Midlands Planning Aid Service and Planning Aid for London provide, arguably, the most well-known examples of such assistance for community groups and individual residents in their respective areas. This work was praised by the 2001 Green Paper, the government indicating it may contribute resources in the future to achieve a better funding of the service.

Consideration by planning officer

The application passes to a case officer who will also deal with the results of the publicity and consultation exercise. The case officer will visit the site and consider planning policy and other relevant planning matters not covered by policy. The consideration of these issues is not the consequence of a haphazard interaction of factors but the discharge of a particular statutory duty imposed upon the decision-maker by planning legislation. This duty affects all decision-makers within the planning process, namely the local planning authority (i.e. planning committee or Chief Planning Officer), the Secretary of State (as regards called-in applications or appeal decisions) and Inspectors appointed by the Secretary of State to decide planning appeals. This duty will be considered below. As a consequence of such considerations, the planning officer may seek amendments to the proposal. The desire for amendment usually results in some element of discussion and negotiation between the officer and applicant (or agent appointed to deal with the application).

What emerges from this consideration is a recommendation from the case officer to the Chief Planning Officer either to grant planning permission subject to conditions[23] or to refuse permission, stating a reason or reasons in both instances. The consideration of the application may be deferred to allow for further information to be brought to a subsequent meeting (e.g. for amendments, details of proposed use or additional consultations). The planning committee may accept or reject (overturn) the recommendation of the Chief Planning Officer. If it rejects a recommendation to grant permission, and refuses the application, this must be a decision based upon sound planning judgement. The introduction of the award of costs in planning appeals means that any unreasonable refusal of planning permission may result in the 'punishment' of the LPA by an award of costs. However, overturning the recommendation of the Chief Planning Officer does not automatically constitute unreasonable behaviour from which costs will follow. Circular 8/93 on costs states 'While planning authorities are not bound to follow advice from their officers . . . they will be expected to show that they had reasonable planning grounds for a decision taken against such advice'.[24]

Delegated applications (i.e. decision-making delegated by committee to officers) will usually be considered by the Chief Planning Officer; the criteria that determines suitability for delegation will vary from authority to authority. In most cases such delegated powers apply to small-scale proposals (e.g. household extensions), usually with little or no third-party objection.

The use of such delegated authority benefits the development control function in that, by avoiding the need to report the matter to committee, the decision time can be reduced. The officer simply reports, verbally or by a short written summary, to the Chief Planning Officer. If this is accepted, then a decision notice can be prepared and dispatched. When dealing with committees it must be remembered that such bodies function on a cycle of meetings throughout the year. To report, an application requires considerable administration, as draft reports must be prepared and circulated to senior officers and then placed upon the agenda for the forthcoming meeting. With most committees on a cycle of one meeting every three to four weeks, to miss one committee would take the decision period to between six and eight weeks, greatly increasing the chances of it falling outside the statutory period. The further complication of awaiting consultation and publicity responses before reporting to a committee provides additional procedural problems in determining applications within the eight-week statutory period. LPAs can improve their performance by increased use of delegated powers and shorter committee cycles.

The decision-maker's duty – how the decision to grant or refuse is made: Section 54A

The decision-maker in arriving at a decision on a planning application must discharge a legislative duty. Under the provisions of Section 29 of the Town and Country Planning Act 1971, which became incorporated into Section 70(2) of the Town and Country Planning Act 1990, this duty was that the decision-maker 'shall have regard to the provisions of the development plan so far as material to the application and to any other material considerations'.

In 1991 this was significantly changed by the introduction of Section 26 of the Planning and Compensation Act 1991, which introduced a new Section 54A into the 1990 Act as follows: 'Where in making any determination under the Planning Acts regard is to be had to the development plan, the determination shall be in accordance with the plan unless material considerations indicate otherwise'. This provision has been carried over into the Planning and Compulsory Purchase Act 2004.

This legislative change resulted in a considerable flurry of debate among planning professionals regarding its implications for decision-making. The previous system was based on a clear 'presumption in favour of allowing applications for development'.[25] The courts had held that the words 'shall have regard to' did not mean slavish adherence to the contents of development plan policy.[26] The development plan was but one of possibly many material considerations. Certainly, on first impression, Section 54A gave greater weight to planning policy than was previously the case. In introducing the new section, the then Planning Minister, Sir George Young, said in the House of Commons:

> . . . if the development plan has something to say on a particular application the starting point would be that the plan should be followed unless the weight of the other considerations tell against it. In other words, there would be a presumption in favour of the development plan.

Section 54A has meant that:

- Greater attention needs to be paid to development plan policy. Although Section 70(2) was not repealed, the new Section 54A gives more weight to the contents of the development plan.
- Greater importance is given to adopted policy rather than emerging policy in the course of preparation. Both Section 70(2) and Section 54A apply to adopted policy. Emerging policy passing through the adoption process does not benefit from these provisions, although policy is said to 'gather weight' as a material consideration as it moves through the various stages towards adoption (refer to PPG1).
- A greater degree of certainty in the development process as developers/ LPAs realize that, if a proposal is in conflict with policy, a presumption exists that permission will be refused and, if the proposal is in accord with policy, a presumption exists that permission will be granted.
- Greater attention will be focused towards the procedures by which policy is formulated, as developers and other interested parties realize that the weight attached to policy warrants greater attention to its content. Policy formulation will need to be monitored so that objections may be considered at the appropriate stage.
- Material considerations will still be of importance in the development process and capable of outweighing policy, yet where policy is adopted and up to date it will carry considerable weight in influencing the decision-making process.

Section 54A has undoubtedly introduced changes to the perception of the role of planning policy by developers, planners and consultants.[27] Fundamentally, it seeks to steer the decision-makers towards examination of policy, unless for some reason a material consideration outweighs such policy. Consider the example in Case study 2.2 from the employment policies in the Oxford City Council local plan, regarding the former North and South Rover car facilities at Cowley.

Case study 2.2: Applying local plan policy

Policy EM5   Any land released for development on the Cowley Works site
will be retained primarily for B1 and B2 uses and some limited
B8 uses, together with ancillary uses such as an hotel. Any other
uses will only be considered if it can be demonstrated that they
will assist in achieving the rapid development of the site in an
acceptable manner . . .

The emphasis of this policy is to secure B1 (Business) and B2 (General
Industry) and B8 (Storage) redevelopment on the former Cowley Works site.
The consequence of Section 54A is that any proposal outside the terms
of EM5 will be required to demonstrate that it will bring benefits that will
outweigh these employment-related objectives.

What are material considerations?

Any consideration which relates to the use and development of land is
capable of being a planning consideration.[28]

The courts have provided detailed interpretation as to exactly what can be
considered to be a material consideration. A useful starting point in this area
is *Westminster City Council* vs *Great Portland Estates* (1985), in which Lord
Scarman stated that a material consideration was a consideration that served
a planning purpose and that a planning purpose was one that related to the
development and the use of the land.

So although the term 'material considerations' may throw a wide net with
a vast array of issues potentially of material importance, it is important
to remember that the key test is whether it serves a planning purpose. For
example, the developer's desire for profit would not be material.

Several key material considerations that have emerged from the courts can
be summarized as follows:[29]

Precedent: the granting of permission and its influence on adjoining land.

Case Law	Issues
Collis Radio vs *Secretary of State for the Environment* [1975] 29 P&CR 390.	**Held** that there is no error of law if an application is judged according to its consequences of the development of other sites.
Poundstretcher Ltd, Harris Queensway plc vs *Secretary of State for the Environment and Liverpool City Council* [1989] JPL 90.	**Held** that where precedent was relied upon some form of evidence must be required. Mere fear of precedent was not sufficient.

Comment: Every planning application and appeal site must be considered on
its own individual merits; however, this does not exclude concern regarding

the cumulative impact, whereby in granting permission on site A it will probably follow that permission will be granted on sites B, C and D. This logic is influenced by the fact that the decision-making must be consistent and that the grant of development on site A would influence similar decisions on sites B, C and D, unless distinguishing reasons can be shown. So, precedent can be material, yet caution is required here, as it refers to consistency of decision-making or the cumulative impact of decisions. It is not some kind of binding legal principle where the LPA must grant permission on comparable sites.

Planning history: previous granting of permission on proposal site.

Case Law	Issues
Spackman vs *Secretary of State for the Environment* [1977] 1 All ER 257. *South Oxfordshire District Council* vs *Secretary of State for the Environment* [1981] 1 WLR 1092.	**Held** in both cases that a previous planning permission is capable of being material even if it has expired (i.e. over five years old and not implemented).

Comment: The history of previous decisions on the site in question is a matter of some importance. Unimplemented and expired (i.e. more than five years old) permissions will be material yet, as with precedent, the LPA or Inspector on appeal is not automatically obliged to renew such permissions and must consider the merits of the case, which will include whether any change in circumstances has occurred.

Financial considerations: economic viability of a proposal.

Case Law	Issues
Sosmo Trust vs *Secretary of State for the Environment, London Borough of Camden* [1983] JPL 806. *R* vs *Westminster City Council, ex parte Monahan* [1989] 3 WLR 408 and 2 All ER 74 sometimes referred to as 'Covent Garden Royal Opera House case'. See below.	**Held** that it was material to consider the financial viability of a proposed scheme where it would have planning consequences.

Comment: The desire of the developer to make a profit from development is not a material consideration and never will be. However, the financial and economic viability of a proposal may have planning consequences and this, perhaps, may be the key determining factor. So, the developer's plea during negotiation, that not permitting a certain amount of additional floorspace will result in a proposal being economically unviable, can be a material consideration. LPAs may be sceptical about such arguments, although they will need to give them some attention. In such instances as the Covent Garden Royal Opera House case, issues of financial viability were material and considered sufficient to outweigh local plan policy, which would have otherwise resisted any commercial proposal on that site. The Opera House had argued that some commercial redevelopment (offices/shops) were required on its site in Covent Garden to fund and maintain the future existence of the theatrical use. This was accepted by Westminster City Council, the LPA and, following a legal challenge of the decision by a local Community Association, was held to be the correct approach.

Objections by third parties: residents or other people affected by a proposal.

Case Law	Issues
Multi Media Productions vs Secretary of State for the Environment and Islington London Borough Council [1989] JPL 96.	**Held** that it was perfectly correct for an Inspector to dismiss an appeal on issues raised by third parties and not by an LPA.

Comment: Objections by third parties are all capable of being material, provided that these objections are based upon sound planning considerations. In many ways it is not so much the sheer quantity of objection letters submitted in relation to an application or appeal but instead their quality in the extent towards which they deal with planning matters.

The development plan: combination of Local Development Framework documents and policies.

Case Law	Issues
St Albans District Council vs Secretary of State for the Environment [1993] 1 PLR 88.	**Held** that Section 54A of the T&CP Act 1990 meant that the policies in the plan shall prevail unless material considerations indicate that it should not.

Comment: It must be remembered that the Local Development Framework itself is a material consideration, as it is a matter concerned with the use and development of land. It is convenient to consider the development plan policies separately from material considerations, as town planning statutes tend to distinguish between the two when stating 'unless material considerations indicate otherwise'. All planning decisions will involve a balancing of issues. Section 54A attaches greater importance to the development plan as a matter of law. It follows that, after the introduction of this revision, the existence of a relevant and up-to-date development plan policy will be the strongest indicator of whether planning permission is likely to be granted or refused.

Government planning policy: combination of PPGs/PPSs, Mineral Policy Guidance Notes (MPGs), Regional Policy Guidance Notes (RPGs) and government Circulars.

Comment: Central government departments issue guidance to local government in the form of various policy guidance notes and Circulars. Such documents provide important, if broadly based, advice upon a range of development control issues and areas. Such information constitutes an important material consideration in determining applications and it establishes the broad direction in which the government wishes the development plan and development control system to progress. Although local planning authorities are not duty-bound always to follow this advice, they will need to show good reasons for any decisions that run counter to the government's view. It must also be remembered that if a matter proceeds to an appeal, the Inspector will take such guidance into consideration. Each of these documents carries the same weight; the principal difference between PPGs/PPSs and Circulars is that the latter tend to deal with technical guidance, whereas the former provide more general advice on the operation of the system. During 2003–5 all PPGs will be reviewed and if replaced or revised will become Planning Policy Statements (PPSs). The most widely used statements of government planning policy can be found in the following documents:

Document	Year issued	Topic
PPG1	1997	General Policy and Principles
PPG2	1995	Green Belts
PPG3	2000	Housing
PPG6	1996	Town Centres and Retail Developments
PPG13	2001	Transport
PPG25	2001	Development and Flood Risk
PPS11	2004	Regional Planning
PPS12	2004	Local Development Frameworks (replaces PPG 12)

Source: Grant (2003).[30]

Advertisement control

Control over outdoor advertisements is made under town planning statute and regulations.[31] Such control is self-contained from the rest of the planning system, with the creation of a separate category of advertisement control instead of planning permission. In addition to this, a series of exclusions and deemed consents are established, which reduce the need to seek consent for certain types of advertisements.

What is an advertisement?

An advertisement is defined by statute as meaning:

> any word, letter, model sign, placard, board, notice, or device or representation whether illuminated or not in the nature of, and employed wholly or partly for the purposes of advertisements, announcement or direction . . . and includes any hoarding or similar structure.[32]

In addition, an awning or blind (usually a 'canopy' outside a shop front) has been added to this definition. Examples of advertisements include a painted shop fascia or illuminated shop sign, projecting box sign, 'For Sale' or 'To Let' sign, and a canopy or blind to a shop.

The need for advertisement consent

The 1992 regulations divide advertisements into three broad groupings:

Grouping	Examples
Exclusions, i.e. no control is exercised	Traffic signs, national flags, those on a moving vehicle or displayed within a building
Deemed consent, i.e. would require consent, but this is granted by the regulations, so no application is required	14 specific categories including: • Sale/letting of a building • On business premises (relating to size, number and siting) • Flag adverts, on house-building sites during construction, and temporary hoardings (1–3 months)
Express consent, i.e. Advertisement Consent is required from LPA and an application is made on standard forms together with a fee to LPA.	Most illuminated signs or non-illuminated, which are above first-floor window level

If the LPA wishes to refuse permission for an application for express advertisement consent, it should only do so if it is considered that the advertisement will harm the visual amenity of the area (for example, because of its proximity to a listed building or its location within a Conservation Area) or the location will be detrimental to public safety (for example, it may obscure visibility of a highway or traffic signal). A right of appeal exists against such refusals. If the LPA wishes to grant permission for an application for express consent, it may impose a set of standard conditions as set out in the 1992 Regulations (for example, requiring the advertisement to be maintained in a clean and tidy condition).

Powers over contraventions

Display of an advertisement in contravention of the regulations is a criminal offence and if found guilty may be punished by a fine. The LPA has three distinct powers in respect of such matters. First, it may serve discontinuance proceedings that require discontinuance of an advertisement or use of a site for the display of an advertisement, whether or not it enjoys deemed consent. A right of appeal exists against such a notice. Second, it may seek an order to create an area of special control in which various restrictions of classes of deemed consent may apply, subject to the exact area to be protected. Such orders are commonly used to protect the appearance of conservation areas. Approval and consent must be given by the Secretary of State. Finally, it may seek special directions to be issued by the Secretary of State to limit specific areas of deemed consent. An example in recent years had been where such a direction excludes Class 3 ('for sale' and 'to let' temporary advertisements) in conservation areas and locations of predominantly flatted accommodation. Some LPAs had approached the Secretary of State following concern over the visual impact of many such boards in streets where former town houses were subdivided into flats.

Maladministration and town planning

> Maladministration refers to faulty administration resulting in some form of injustice to a person or group of people.

In 1974 the government created an Office of Commissioner for Local Authority Administration, commonly, referred to as the Local Government Ombudsman,[33] with powers to investigate maladministration in all areas of local government. A Parliamentary Ombudsman had been created in 1967 to investigate complaints about central government departments.

Maladministration is not defined by statute. Examples include bias, delays, neglect, carelessness, or failure to observe procedure, which have all resulted in injustice. Separate Ombudsman offices have been established for England, Scotland and Wales. Once a complaint is received, it will be investigated to see if the matter falls within their jurisdiction and that some maladministration is evident before a final investigation will be undertaken. The services of the Ombudsman are free and the staff is independent and impartial. If they find that maladministration has occurred, they may recommend a remedy to the matter, usually compensation paid to the complainants by the local authority. If the local authority decides to ignore the recommendation to pay compensation, no legal power exists whereby the Ombudsman may enforce payment.

Town planning matters often constitute the second most common area of complaints to the Ombudsman.[34] The lodging of a complaint does not mean that maladministration has occurred or been proven. It may be of little surprise that town planning does encourage complaints, because not all local people, some of whom may have been consulted on the application, will agree with a decision to grant permission. Although the system encourages public participation, such comment on applications is but one of the many material considerations. Frequently, public comment avoids planning matters and raises non-planning issues. Yet although some people feel aggrieved by planning decisions they consider 'unpalatable', this does not of itself constitute maladministration. Around 96 per cent of all complaints received do not proceed to a formal investigation. Matters found to constitute town planning maladministration have included a council's failure to enforce compliance with a landscaping scheme on a site; a delay of ten years to deal with unauthorized tipping of soil in an Area of Outstanding Natural Beauty; delay and conflicting advice by a council in deciding whether to save a tree protected by a Tree Preservation Order; and failure to take account of town planning history on a site and incorrectly informing the owner that a matter was permitted development when it was not.

A finding of maladministration in town planning is rare. Around 500 000 planning applications are dealt with every year in England, around 4000 planning related complaints are submitted to the Ombudsman. The Local Government Ombudsman Annual Report for 2003 revealed that 59 complaints were investigated and in only 24 cases the Ombudsman concluded that maladministration causing injustice had occurred.[35] The Ombudsman plays a limited role in town planning, albeit an important one, in providing a mechanism for the investigation of bad practice and the ability to expose procedural problems. This may result in not just financial compensation to the complainant, but it also allows the local authority the opportunity to introduce reforms to its working practices to prevent a repeat in the future.

Probity

The planning system involves governmental regulation over the 'private' right to develop land, in the wider public interest of environmental and amenity protection. Since the late 1990s the system has increasingly been the subject of review and reflection with respect to matters of probity. Probity refers to qualities of uprightness and honesty. In public life, such as in land use planning control, a high standard of probity is necessary to carry public confidence. This confidence is needed to give legitimacy to the precedence of public regulation over private interest in property development.

The UK planning system places the responsibility for decision-making on planning applications squarely on the shoulders of local elected politicians (councillors) who are not required to have any expertise in planning in order to take office. This key principle gives a powerful democratic endorsement of decisions. However, many tensions arise, as councillors on planning committee must make decisions based exclusively on planning reasoning yet must also serve their constituents and reflect local opinion. Such local opinion may not be based on planning-related argument, and in the last decade or so development has increasingly been viewed negatively by local people as representing something undesirable and to be resisted. Since the economic boom period of the 1980s such tensions have become acute as 'nimbyism'[36] has spread among local residents, who in turn will lobby their local councillors to help them in opposing development proposals.

This administrative duty on councillors is tempered by much planning law and locally produced policy. The Chief Planning Officer and his professionally qualified colleagues advise the committee and make recommendations on individual applications. Clearly additional tension exists here as officers may make recommendations, based on policy and other material considerations, that councillors find unpalatable in the face of strong local opposition. It is acceptable for a Planning Committee to overturn Officer recommendations to grant permission, although this must be on the basis of sound planning argument and not, for example, the volume or vociferousness of local opposition.

Since the 1970s the system has been monitored by the Ombudsman[37] with respect to maladministration. During the mid 1990s, however, two major scandals received widespread media coverage and promoted tougher regulation in the policing of the system. While these two cases were numerically insignificant in terms of the total number of decisions made by the respective councils, the ramifications that followed had wider consequences in denting public confidence and influencing changes in respect of probity.

Regulation of the planning system has traditionally been threefold. First, the behaviour of officers and councillors has been shaped by codes of conduct dealing with the competence, honesty and integrity of officers[38] and their duty to serve the local community and to act within the law for councillors.[39] Second, statutory duties[40] are imposed to establish a series of moral and ethical standards. Third, that officers and councillors must declare any interest that may affect their duty to determine a planning application. Such interests cover both financial (pecuniary) or other gains (such as the promotion of a private or personal interest). The division between pecuniary and non-pecuniary interest was established in the 1970s. The Local Government Act 2000 introduced a new system of ethical conduct in which any personal interest must be declared (including those of a relative, friend or employer). If that interest would be considered to be prejudicial to public confidence in the system, a councillor should play no part in consideration of the relevant planning application.

Reference to direct, indirect or remote pecuniary interest is therefore historic as a much wider test now applies.

Type of interest	Definition	Example
Direct pecuniary	Personal and financial position will be directly affected by a decision.	To grant a pp on land you own or refuse on land which adjoins yours.
Indirect pecuniary	Personal and financial interest of a person or body in close relation to decision maker (matrimonial or professional).	As above with benefit to a company in which the decision maker has some interest.
Remote pecuniary	Interest to include a wider remit of sons, daughters, siblings, parents of members.	Some benefits to these interests.

In North Cornwall District Council a number of decisions made by the planning committee in the late 1980s and early 1990s were questioned by journalists, culminating in a television documentary screened in 1991. It was alleged that a high number of planning permissions were granted to councillors sitting on planning committee (or their close family) and further that inappropriate development was granted in either the open countryside or Areas of Outstanding Natural Beauty, both against officers' guidance to refuse consent. Coincidentally, complaints to the Ombudsman from residents of North Cornwall rose to 39 in 1990–91, compared to six complaints three years earlier. In 1992 the (then) Secretary of State, Michael Howard, appointed an independent expert to conduct an administrative enquiry into the control of planning in North Cornwall. In her report the following year (Department of the Environment 1993) Audrey Lees made 18 recommendations, dealing mostly with the conduct of councillors. In particular, the enquiry dealt with how public confidence had been deeply damaged in circumstances where officer recommendations were ignored and councillors appeared to have acted unfairly by granting a large number of planning applications to fellow councillors. Audrey Lees clearly drew a line between such bad practices and any allegation of corruption. She explicitly stated that such matters fell outside her jurisdiction, although she did conclude that '. . . I cannot state categorically that there was no criminal corruption or conspiracy, only that I found no indication of it'. Nevertheless, in dealing with the conduct of the planning committee she set out guidance that '. . . it is not only the actual conduct of affairs which is important but also the *appearance* to the public . . .' (her emphasis). The detailed recommendations made plain the fact that elected councillors had a wider responsibility to their local community and extreme caution was required when voting on planning applications submitted by fellow councillors or when acting as a result of lobbying from applicants or constituents. While councillors may, quite legitimately, disagree with the recommendations of their officers, they would need good reason based upon sound planning judgement. One criticism levelled at officers in North Cornwall was that their reports on planning applications lacked sufficient detail on matters of planning policy. Councillors would need more guidance in these areas in the future.

In Bassetlaw (North Nottinghamshire) allegations of impropriety by their planning committee surfaced in 1995 and culminated in an independent inquiry at the instigation of the council.[41] The allegations centred on planning permissions, all granted against the professional advice of officers and all benefiting, in some way, the same developer. It was estimated that the total increase in land value on these sites was in the region of £6 million. Mr Phelps, the appointed investigator, drew the damning conclusion in his report that . . . 'a reasonable outside observer must conclude that the Committee has been manipulated in some way'. As with North Cornwall his conclusions avoided any direct charge of corruption, although he did state that 'whether or not there was any corrupt wrong doing, some persons stand to gain several million pounds through increases in land values by the granting of outline planning permission on sites against a whole range of professional advice and considerations'. His central recommendation was that, in the interests of public confidence, 'the present Planning Committee should resign en bloc as soon as practicable'. Beyond such a dramatic reform, itself subsequently accepted and implemented by Bassetlaw, Mr Phelps called for the revocation of several previous planning permissions and reversals of local plan allocations. The council would need to introduce a new code of conduct as well as provide better training to councillors in the workings of the planning committee.

Both North Cornwall and Bassetlaw represented *ad hoc* or 'one-off' attempts to deal with, thankfully rare, cases of impropriety in the planning system. In both cases it appears that councillors failed to understand their responsibilities as imposed in codes of conduct or in statute. This situation was compounded by an ignorance of town planning law and a failure of council procedures to establish good practice, such as requiring councillors to provide detailed reasoning when departing from officer recommendation to refuse permission. Cases like North Cornwall and Bassetlaw were themselves perhaps indicative of other, more structural, problems in the planning system. The relationship between councillors and officers was sometimes poorly defined and some councillors on planning committee did not have much knowledge of planning policy or process.

Research undertaken by Oxford Brookes University for the Royal Town Planning Institute (Royal Town Planning Institute 1997) uncovered wide disparities in councillor training, with some councils providing regular seminars and other events for their planning committee and others none whatsoever. One of the report's recommendations was that . . . 'members serving on planning committees have the opportunity to participate regularly in training events'.

The problem for the wider system was that public confidence in the planning process was diminished by such incidences, which were the subject of coverage in national press and television media. Such attention, combined with the occasional reporting of other high-profile cases of alleged inappropriate behaviour by councillors, such as in the London Borough of Brent (1991), Warwick (1994) and Doncaster (1997), served to keep this issue regularly in the public gaze. Such cases, albeit few and far between, contributed to a general malaise of public confidence in the system

In October 1994, the (then) Prime Minister, John Major, established a Committee on Standards in Public Life under the chair of Lord Nolan. The committee produced three reports between 1995 and 1997, *Standards of Conduct in Parliament, the Executive and Non-departmental Public Bodies* (covering the activities of members of parliament, government ministers and their civil servants), *Local Public Spending Bodies* (covering school and higher education and training/enterprise councils) and *Standards of Conduct in Local Government in England, Scotland and Wales* (covering activities of councillors and officers and the planning function at a local government level). The first report did not establish that standards of behaviour in public life (for example in Parliament) had declined but it did assert, however, that codes of conduct were not always clear and enforcement of standards sometimes inadequate (Committee on Standards in Public Life 1995). The Committee established seven principles to guide the behaviour of those in public life (see the table below) and laid down that maintenance of high standards should be achieved by the adoption of independent scrutiny of decision-making, the drawing up of codes of conduct, and education to promote and reinforce standards.

Seven principles	
Selflessness	Decisions made in the public interest
Integrity	Avoid any financial or other obligation to an outside body
Objectivity	Make a decision on merit only
Accountability	Open to scrutiny
Openness	Provide reasons
Honesty	Declare private interests
Leadership	Promote these principles by example

The third report (Committee on Standards in Public Life 1997) dealt extensively and, on occasion, contentiously with the planning system. The

Committee had invited representations from the public and professionals. Planning produced the highest volume of letters drawn from any local government area and the Committee reported, somewhat anecdotally, that . . . 'public satisfaction with the planning system does not seem to be particularly high'. The report itself was critical of the planning system. Training of councillors was patchy, the allocation of duties and responsibilities between officers and councillors was not always clear, planning gain amounted to the 'buying and selling' of planning permission, and there was insufficient scrutiny of planning decisions, especially when local authorities grant themselves planning permission. The Committee examined the responsibilities of councillors, concluding that it was acceptable for them to disagree with their officers, where appropriate, and that it is a duty of such elected people to listen to their constituents but to act properly when determining applications. Planning decision-making was viewed as an administrative and not a legal or judicial process.

Councillors were, therefore, free to balance community interests with other matters, while remaining within the constraints of planning law. The 39 detailed recommendations of Nolan divided themselves into three distinct areas, comprising the creation of a new ethical framework, clear reporting regarding declaration of interest and achieving best practice in planning. Under the provisions of an ethical framework, councils would write their own codes of conduct (with a framework approved by Parliament), establish a standards committee and be accountable to a new tribunal with powers to arbitrate on disciplinary matters (for instance, to clarify interpretation of the code of conduct or deal with appeals when councillors sought to challenge any assertion that they had acted improperly). Councils would therefore benefit from a regime of much tighter internal self-regulation than had existed previously.

The third Nolan report focussed on a desire for greater openness and accountability in local government, with new statutory penalties and the creation of a culture of more effective 'whistle-blowing' in cases of misconduct. It would be wrong to conclude from Nolan that the system prior to this report (in 1997) lacked such accountability. Indeed, the Nolan Committee in drafting best practice guidance did not claim originality for such ideas, as these recommendations were drawn from existing procedures already in place in many councils. Nolan, however, did crystallize these ideas and heightened awareness of them by seeking to raise the profile of local government generally and the town-planning function in particular. Such reforms have been viewed as 'far reaching'[42] and . . . 'the vital tonic which the planning process requires in order to re-establish its authority and reputation' (Winter and Vergine 1997). The report's findings established an agenda for change. Nolan's call for a new ethical framework in local government was incorporated into Part III of the Local Government Act 2000. Each council would be required to adopt a code of conduct for councillors and a Standards or Scrutiny Committee and tribunal to uphold such standards and investigate allegations of failure to maintain the expected ethical behaviour.

Once adopted all councillors must sign an undertaking to comply with the code and complete a register of their financial and non-financial interests (for example, employment or company interests). All codes must comply with a nationally set 'model code' issued by the Secretary of State, ensuring a degree of consistency across authorities. Any interest in a planning application must be declared. The decision as to whether a councillor should withdraw from the Committee (i.e. has a prejudicial interest) is determined by the hypothetical test that a member of the public with knowledge of the relevant facts would consider this personal interest to be prejudicial. Further, the Code imposes a high moral standard on councillors such that in both their official and private capacity their actions must not bring local government into disrepute. Regulation of the potential misconduct is a matter for the independently established Standards Board in England and Ombudsman in Wales. Sanctions available to the Standards Board include suspension or disqualification.

The third Nolan report raised awareness of probity in planning. Its sometimes critical stance must be tempered by the report's own acknowledgment that in its examination of local government it . . . 'found an enormous number of dedicated and hardworking people. . . . We are of course well aware of the relatively few, but highly publicised, cases where things have gone wrong or people have behaved improperly. But it is important to set such cases in the context of more than 20 000 councillors and 2 000 000 employees in local government.'

It is of fundamental importance that the planning system carries public confidence. Nolan and subsequent legislation maintained vigilance in this area, as evidently more can and should be done to promote openness and raise standards in planning decision-making. An important principle must be established by which even if people disagree with the granting or refusing of a planning application, they accept that the decision was made openly and fairly after due consideration of all relevant issues.

Best value

The best-value regime that emerged in 2000 was a by-product not of probity considerations but instead of compulsory competitive tendering (CCT). CCT had been introduced in the early 1990s to 'market-test' a whole raft of local government services. Existing services were assessed against value for money following comparison against services provided by external contractors or consultants. As a consequence some local government functions were run by outside agencies (such as refuse collection, road maintenance and legal services). Town planning development control was not directly affected by such reforms, acknowledging the 'market-sensitive' nature of this service, where it would be deemed inappropriate for planning departments to be staffed by external contractors who may also be involved in consultancies who submit planning applications to the same authority.

Best value replaced the CCT model, although it did not completely scrap the notion of market testing, in which current provision of services are compared with cost and performance of such duties by other bodies (either other councils or consultancies). Town planning is very much a part of this system.

Table 2.5 Superstore size and share

Event	Frequency	Key topics	Relevant criteria
(a) Best value performance plans	Every year	Performance targets Performance indicators	All set by Secretary of State
(b) Best value review		Review to improve function	Economy and effectiveness and efficiency of function
(c) Best value inspection	Five yearly	To report back to local people on services	To focus on services as users experience them

Best value came into force in 2000, implemented by means of primary legislation,[43] statutory instrument[44] and circular.[45] Each local government authority in England and Wales becomes a 'best-value authority' and thereby is duly accountable for its provision of services. The purpose of best value is established in broad terms in which a best value-authority . . . 'must make arrangements to secure continuous improvement in the way in which its functions are exercised having regard to a combination of economy, efficiency and effectiveness.' This notion of continuous improvement is viewed by national government as providing both a considerable challenge and a major opportunity. Yet these improvements in service delivery must be achieved against a shrinking financial base, with an annual efficiency improvement (or cutback) of 2 per cent to be achieved by every best-value authority. So best value exerts two significant changes: services must first improve year on year while second and contemporaneously budgets must be reduced.

The aspiration of the national government is clearly stated. Best value is not just about creating a statutory framework to 'impose' a better service culture on local government. It is about implementing real change to local communities, reflected in the fact that the local government bodies themselves shall be responsible for delivering those changes. To appreciate such a stance it is necessary to understand some of the language used, in particular best-value plans, best-value reviews and best-value performance indicators.

A sequence of events to illustrate how this review process works is set out in Table 2.5. Over a typical five-year period a total of five plans will be produced followed by a review of function. Each performance plan will deal with a record of delivery of local services and a statement of plans for future improvement. In 2002 the government scrapped the requirement that a review be conducted every five years. While a review would still be required, its timing would be at the discretion of the individual council.

Each best-value authority is expected to achieve a 2 per cent 'efficiency gain' year on year, so the review document will contain a summary of past activities and an action plan for the future. While local factors and circumstances are taken into account, the plan must satisfy various targets,

Table 2.6 Planning best-value performance indicators

Title	Key indicator
Strategic objective	Percentage of new homes (including conversion) built on previously developed land in accord with Planning Policy Guidance Note 3 (2000).
Cost/efficiency	Cost of planning service per head of population.
Service delivery outcome	(a) Percentage of all planning applications determined in eight weeks.
Land searches	(b) Percentage of Standard Land Searches carried out in 10 working days.
Delegation powers	(c) Number of planning applications delegated to Chief Planning Officer as a percentage of all decisions.

indicators and standards laid down by the Secretary of State. Guidance issued by national government has been keen to ensure that, whether a national standard (from the Secretary of State) or a local standard (from the local authority) they should be monitored against 'measurable milestones'. In town planning the Secretary of State published five such milestones (or best-performance indicators) in 1999 (Audit Commission 1999); these are set out as Table 2.6 and were re-stated for 2002/3 (Office of the Deputy Prime Minister 2002).

Each local planning authority service would be judged against such statistics as contained in its performance plan. Some criteria, like the brown-land target (60 per cent new homes/conversions to be on previously developed land) are 'policy driven', seeking to focus on the desire for a more economic use of urban land and consequential reduction of green-field development. Others focus upon crude measurements of efficiency, taken as the period within which an application is determined. Such statistics allow the national government to build a national profile of planning efficiency, measured in terms of time taken to determine applications or the volume of applications dealt with under delegated authority (in other words, those which did not go to the Committee).

In the periodic review of functions the local authority is charged with a duty to improve its service delivery. The national government's model of 'continuous change' dictates that two principal areas be addressed in this review. First, that improvements are directed towards economy, efficiency and effectiveness (the three 'E's). Second, that in conducting a review local authorities challenge how and by whom a service is provided, secure comparison with the service of others, consult with local taxpayers, and use fair and open competition to secure efficient and effective services (the four 'C's). In practice such guidance means that in, say, the exercise of town planning a local authority will need to consider whether development control or development planning can be more effectively performed by 'other' bodies, notably by consultants on a contractual basis. The underlying ethos of challenge, compare and compete is that local authorities must justify their own in-house provision of planning control against a raft of indicators dealing with speed and cost. In other words, that they will provide a *cheaper* and *quicker* service than anyone else, as opposed to providing a more *effective* service measured against the more subjective assessments of ensuring quality in decisions made.

Arguably other measurements could be applied to planning, such as the achievement of tangible improvements in the built environment. However, the government has settled for a more hard-nosed accountancy-led appraisal of the system based on notions of speed (of decision-making) and efficiency (of cost to the public purse). Local authorities, in working within the constraints of this system, must identify in their reviews how Best Value Practice Instructions might be improved upon, how the 2 per cent efficiency gains might be achieved and how this service might be better provided in-house and not by consultants. Past arguments that planning services must be performed in-house due to the sensitivity of the development process undertaking (i.e. the desire to be independent and distanced from consultants) are no longer applicable. The key issue for local authorities to address will be whether planning services would be more efficiently performed by consultants. If the answer is 'yes', then a best-value review will have little alternative to embracing the market and employing them. A seismic shift in attitudes will be felt over the next decade as planning control moves outside its traditional public-sector base.

Conclusions

The creation of a policy for future land-use control and the implementation of that policy by development control represents the central component of the entire planning system. This system is highly regulated, yet has evolved from the premise that the implementation of planning decisions should be subject to a degree of flexibility. This flexibility means that a local planning authority does not have to follow slavishly all that is written down in planning policy (see Case Study 2.3 for an extreme example of this). It is possible to weigh the policy implications against other planning (or 'material') considerations. Policies provide valuable guidance and not a rigid code. This distinguishes the British system from other planning systems (notably continental western Europe) based upon a zoning principle in which the zone stipulates what type of development must be implemented in a particular location. However, the inbuilt flexibility in the British model exacts a particular price, in that the outcome of the decision-making process will be less certain than under a zoning system. In spite of legislative reforms in the early 1990s, which place greater weight on the status of planning policy, the local planning authority still is afforded the opportunity to examine a broad range of material considerations in reaching a decision on a planning application. Examination of policy must always be the key starting point in any assessment of a development proposal. Any relevant guidance will be important but not always decisive in the outcome of a planning application. The UK system of planning policy and development control has been the subject of varied criticisms, based on the apparently negative stance

Case study 2.3: Planning and property development in the City of London

The ancient heart of London, 'The City of London', comprises one square mile in area (2.6 km^2) and incorporates the capital's financial sector. The Great Fire of London in 1666 destroyed approximately 75 per cent of the medieval City and bombing during the Second World War destroyed approximately 30 per cent (Marriott 1989).

The City Corporation is the local planning authority for this area. In the immediate post-war years the City Corporation was subject to the newly introduced planning regulations of the Town and Country Planning Act 1947. A statutory development plan was approved in 1951 under the guidance of Charles Holden and William Holford, who were themselves previously responsible for development of the London transport system (Holden) and for the redevelopment of the Paternoster district within the City (Holford).*

Since the early 1950s the city has been the subject of two property booms, those of the 1960s and the 1980s. The nature of each boom and its influence upon commercial development was shaped by the town planning system, and the buildings resulting from each boom may be distinguished by their contrasting architectural styles.

In the 1960s the demands for new office accommodation in the financial heart of London fuelled a building boom that was able to use newly acquired building methods involving concrete and steel construction to build high-rise office blocks. Architects such as Mies Van der Rohe (1886–1969) considered that concrete used in construction should be 'seen and not screened' (Ross-Goobey 1992). Redevelopment around London Wall and Paternoster Square provides good examples of the style of the age, notably external concrete facings and curtain walling, whereby the external walls are hung like curtains from the concrete floors.

Town planning policies were an influence, mostly by the imposition of plot ratio controls. These controls restricted the amount of lettable floorspace as a portion of every square metre of land within the plot. This would restrict the resulting height and bulk of a building, so that a common ratio of say 5:1 or 3:1 would allow 5 or 3 m of lettable floorspace for every 1 m of site area. Conservation area controls were not introduced until the late 1960s and the City Corporation made few design-related decisions during this period. The architect and developer were allowed a free reign to design the fashionable brutalistic-looking tower blocks of the age, so long as they satisfied the plot ratio criterion.

During the 1980s the City of London was to experience a second boom, yet one whose impact upon development was to be far more dramatic than that experienced during the 1960s. The growth in information technology, increased levels of economic activity, financial deregulation, a reaction by many people against the architectural style of the previous boom, and a relaxation of town planning controls, were all to contribute towards a second boom in commercial development. The rate of property development is largely controlled by the town planning system, because the amount of floorspace permitted will influence the level of market activity. During the 1980s the City Corporation relaxed the application of its own planning policies and increased plot ratios to permit more floorspace on a site in an attempt to encourage developers to come forward with redevelopment schemes. It was hoped that a relaxed town planning regime would be perceived by many developers as a positive move. In 1986 the City Corporation made provision for an increase in office floorspace. At that time the City accommodated around 2 694 000 m² (29 million ft²) office floorspace. Taking the development cycle between 1986 and 1994 2 276 050 m² (24.5 million ft²) office floor space was completed. At June 1994 a further 1 263 440 m² (13.6 million ft²) was the subject of unimplemented planning permission.

This almost relentless drive by the City Corporation planners and Planning Committee to permit new offices was not motivated by some desire to accommodate the needs of property developers but instead was a reaction to the threat posed by massive office development in the London Docklands, only a few kilometres to the east. Canary Wharf, the 244 m high tower on the Isle of Dogs created 929 000 m² (10 million ft²) of new offices alone, and the London Docklands Development Corporation created a total of 13 million ft² (1 208 000 m²) of new office floorspace between 1981 and 1994. The London Docklands Development Corporation (LDDC) and the Enterprise zone within it, were established by the Conservative Government in 1981 to redevelop the designated 2226 ha (5500 acres) of derelict former docks to the east of the City of London. The LDDC saw office redevelopment as a key part of its strategy. The new office floorspace could offer cheaper rents than the City, and new floorspace incorporating all the necessary information technology and modern services. The City, fearing an exodus of office occupiers, fought back by granting as many office planning permissions as it could. The LDDC itself was a deregulated planning body whose planning powers overrode the existing London boroughs. The City Corporation, although not a deregulated planning body, merely served to throw away many of its own development plan policies to achieve the same effect. With the following economic slump in 1989, the permissions of the 1980s created a massive oversupply in the 1990s, resulting in both much empty floorspace and a considerable drop in rents. Some of this new office floorspace may never be let. In 1994 (Williams and Wood 1994), it was estimated that in Docklands some office floorspace has a vacancy rate of 50 per cent with rents as low as £0.92 m achieved in the late 1980s. LDDC's[†] own statistics put this figure at 418 050 m² (4.5 million ft²) or 35 per cent of all floorspace being vacant. No comparable figure is available for the City.

In the City itself some of the new office floorspace may also never be let. Before market demand can be found, new technology may render obsolete some of the schemes of the 1980s. Their glittering architectural styling incorporating post-modern hi-tech and classical revival styles[‡] may serve as a monument to the inability of the planners to predict an oversupply and to apply a braking mechanism to the ferocious activity of the property developers combined with the planning policies pursued by the London Docklands Development Corporation to permit large-scale office redevelopments such as Canary Wharf.

---

* Refer to Study on Paternoster.
† London Docklands Development Corporation Property Facts Sheet, updated periodically and available from LDDC Information Centre.
‡ **Hi-tech** buildings are characterized by exposed steel structures, use of glass and external siting of piping and ducting, a good example being the Lloyds Building in London, by Richard Rogers.

Classical revival employs plentiful use of Greek and Roman decoration, sometimes called 'fake Georgian', a good example being Richmond Riverside, London, by Quinlan Terry.
Postmodern employs a mix of historic detailing with 'symbolism', where the building incorporates unusual shapes and forms, a good example being Alban Gate on London Wall by Terry Farrell.

of council planners towards development proposals, or delay in the determination of applications. The vast majority of planning applications are granted. However, performance measured against speed of decision-making is the subject of wide fluctuations across different local planning authorities, and, so far, this crude measurement is the only widely utilized quality standard within the system. Indeed, it is unlikely that the concept of quality will ever be the subject of universal agreement, as appraisal of what is 'good' or 'bad' in development control is so subjective. However, local planning authorities are looking increasingly at ways to improve administrative efficiency and they involve the public more fully in the policy-making process so that their views on environmental issues can be incorporated at an early stage in the development control process.

3 Town planning law and regulation

A system of comprehensive control over all development was introduced by the TCPA 1947, which required that all building development and any material changes in the use of a building and of land would, henceforth, require planning permission, to be issued by the local planning authority. The legislation established just what would or would not require planning permission. Since 1947 all town planning legislation has provided a definition of 'development'. To understand the workings of the system it is necessary to understand just what falls within the provisions of the definition of development to establish what does and does not require planning permission.

This chapter will examine the principal legislation that defines what does and what does not require the submission of an application for planning permission. Detailed reference will be made to the TCPA 1990, Town and Country (Use Classes Order) 1987 and Town and Country Planning (General Permitted Development) Order 1995. The latter section of the chapter will deal with the enforcement of town planning control, a specialist area of planning legislation that deals with remedial action against the development of land undertaken without the benefit of planning permission. The chapter will be subdivided as follows:

- The definition of development
- Use Classes Order and General Permitted Development Order
- Enforcing town planning control.

The definition of development

Section 55(1) of the 1990 TCPA defined 'development' as:

> the carrying out of building, engineering, mining or other operations in, on, over or under land or the making of any material change in the use of any buildings or other land.

This definition of development provides the very basis for the development control system and introduces a distinction between operations (building, engineering, mining or other) and material change of use (activity). The definition is itself broad in content and must be considered alongside the General Permitted Development Order (GPDO) and Use Classes Order (UCO). Read in isolation it would result in a vast number of operations and uses falling within the definition. The GPDO and UCO create a whole series of exceptions to the need for planning permission, effectively releasing many types of development from the need for planning permission (Grant 2003).

The TCPA 1990 does help clarify some issues that either do or do not fall within the definition. For the avoidance of doubt, the matters that do not amount to development are:

- Any internal works or external works that do not result in a material impact on the appearance of a building. Such external works would depend upon the circumstances of an individual case but include the addition of guttering and downpipes and repointing of mortar between bricks.
- Maintenance/improvement works within the boundary of a road undertaken by a highway authority or the laying out of an access to a highway.
- Inspection/repair/renewal of sewers.
- The use of any building or other land within the curtilage of a dwelling-house for an incidental use for example the use of a garden shed for hobby activities.
- The use of land for agriculture[1] or forestry (agricultural or forestry related buildings may require permission).

However, an operation that specifically does amount to development is the conversion of one dwelling into two (e.g. subdivision of a house into flats).

The Act does not list all matters that may or may not require planning permission beyond these specific groupings. The decision whether or not any other proposal falls within or outside the definition of development will be the subject of interpretation. The following section will now set out some guidelines that will aid such judgements.

Operational development

The principal characteristic of operational development is that it results in some permanent physical change to the appearance of the land concerned. The works may be building, engineering, mining or other operations, and these will be considered in turn.

Building operations

Building operations include the demolition of buildings, rebuilding, structural alterations and extensions, and are works usually undertaken by a builder. Case law dealing with what is and is not a building operation has established three tests of a building operation, namely:

- Does it have size?
- Does it have permanence?
- Is it physically attached?

In practice, if two of the three tests are satisfied, the matter in question will constitute a building operation. For example, we may conclude that the

Table 3.1 Summary of building operations

Definition	Key points to remember	NB
§336(1) and §55(1A) of the TCPA 1990 to **include** demolition, rebuilding, alteration, extension, or addition; to **exclude** any plant or machinery comprised within a building, structure or erection.	3 tests – size – permanence – physical attachment. If any two are decisive then it will usually follow that the proposal constitutes a building operation.	Does not have to look like a building to be a building operation, e.g. Oxford shark or Croydon marlin.

Table 3.2 Summary of engineering operations

Definition	Key points to remember	NB
§336(1) of the TCPA 1990 states it **includes** the formation or laying out of a means of access to a highway.	The limited definition in the Act has been **interpreted** as including any works requiring the skills of an Engineer.	Many engineering operations may be tied in with building operations. It is acceptable to consider them together.

erection of a new warehouse, industrial unit, a block of flats or a dwelling house each constitutes a building operation as they incorporate size, permanence and physical attachment. They all fit the common everyday use of the word 'building' and we should experience little difficulty in establishing that they are operational development. However, it is important to recall that a structure need not look like a normal building to constitute a building operation, so that erection of a radio mast aerial, satellite antenna, and metal security shutters to a shop front all constitute building operations. In 1986 a fibreglass shark sculpture was erected on the roof of a terraced house in Headington, Oxford. In similar vein, a marlin was attached by a homeowner to his roof in Croydon. The works constituted a building operation and required planning permission.

Engineering operations

Engineering operations are taken to include operations normally undertaken by a person carrying on business as an engineer. This has been interpreted in case law as not meaning that an engineer need always be employed but instead that the works in themselves call for the skills of an engineer.

It is sometimes difficult to distinguish between engineering and building operations. For example, in the construction of a new office development an engineer may be called in to survey the subsoil and deal with the foundation details (clearly an engineering operation) and then the office is constructed (clearly a building operation). In such cases it would be acceptable to regard

Table 3.3 Summary of mining operations

Definition	Key points to remember	NB
Not defined in the Act but taken to include surface or underground extraction of minerals.	Coal, iron ore, china clay extraction.	Any extraction of minerals.

Table 3.4 Summary of other operations

Definition	Key points to remember	NB
Works that result in some permanent physical change to land yet do not easily fit within engineering, building or mining operations.	Consider only in exceptional cases, or as a last resort.	Rare. Not a helpful concept for students or practitioners.

this as both an engineering and building operation, thus amounting to development, although only one grant of planning permission (to cover both aspects) will be required. Other examples of engineering operations include the creation of a hard-standing, excavation of soil to form an artificial lake, or the deposit of soil to form a golf course or embankments.

Mining operations

Mining operations, although specifically mentioned within the definition of development, are not defined within the Act. 'Mining' can be taken to include the winning and working of minerals in, on or under land, whether by surface or underground working.[2] 'Minerals' are defined within the Act as including 'all minerals and substances in or under land or a kind ordinarily worked for removal by underground or surface working, except that it does not include peat cut for purposes other than sale'.

Other operations

The inclusion of 'other' within the definition of development is rather unhelpful to both student and practitioner, because of its vague 'catch all' quality. The concept of 'other' defies adequate definition. It may be useful to consider it where works involve some form of physical alteration to land, which appears to constitute an operation yet does not sit easily within the previous definitions of building, engineering or mining operations. For example, it was held in one appeal decision that the tipping of soil onto land for the purpose of raising the level of the land did not, in that case, constitute an engineering operation, but did constitute 'other' operations. The decision as to whether raising of ground level constitutes an 'engineering' or 'other' operation will depend upon the merits of the individual case. However, as a general rule, it would appear that the creation of embankments or larger-scale projects such as golf courses would constitute engineering operations, whereas smaller-scale tipping and raising of ground level would fall within 'other' operations.

Demolition and operational development

Considerable legal debate has prevailed[3] over the question as to whether demolition of buildings falls within the definition of development. Certainly, if we go back to the definition of an operation as something resulting in a change to the physical characteristics of the land, then demolition works would be covered. Demolition may involve the work of a builder or engineer and may be considered to constitute either a building or engineering operation, yet, on examination of the tests of a building operation, demolition would not easily fit within the criteria of size, physical attachment and permanence. Case law has in the past resulted in conflicting findings on this issue. The definitive statement on the subject was made in 1991 by Mr David Widdicombe QC sitting as a High Court Judge in *Cambridge City Council* vs *Secretary of State for the Environment and Another*. It was held that demolition would constitute development where it was an operation that a builder normally carried out. Thus, demolition was found to be a building operation. To avoid a vast additional burden of planning applications on local planning authorities, the government issued a specific direction to clarify the matter. Demolition of the following would not constitute development and therefore would not require submission of a planning application:

- Any listed building or unlisted building in a Conservation area (remember that Listed Building Consent and Conservation Area Consent respectively would be required) so that some measure of control is exercised, but is not achieved by a planning application.[4]
- Any building except a dwellinghouse (includes a flat) or building adjoining a dwellinghouse.
- Any building smaller than 50 m^3 volume
- Any gate, wall, fence or other means of enclosure.[5]

Material change of use

Taking the second limb of the definition of development, it is necessary to consider material changes of use. These have been defined as activities done in, alongside or on land, but do not interfere with the actual physical characteristics of the land. It is therefore important to remember that it is important to understand the concept of a material change in the use of land and that this deals only with activity (uses) and does not deal with physical works on the land, such as building operations. In dealing with material change of use it is important to establish primary uses, ancillary uses and mixed uses and to define the exact area of land affected by the change of use (the 'planning unit').

What is material?

Determining whether or not a material change has occurred will depend upon the merits of the individual case. For a change or shift in use/activity to result in a material change it will be necessary to establish that the change has been substantial or significant, rather than some minor shift in activity.

To determine a material change in use it is necessary to examine the character of the use. For example, is the character retail (sale of goods to the public) or non-retail (services such as banking or food and drink users such as pubs, restaurants). Following this, it is necessary to examine the consequences of the use in terms of planning issues (e.g. noise, smells, hours of operation, traffic or pedestrian generation).

If either the consequences or character has changed to a significant degree, then it can be established that a material change of use has occurred.

In determining a material change, two problems are usually encountered. The first problem relates to the choice of the unit of land to be considered (referred to as the planning unit), which will influence the decision on materiality. For example, if we consider an industrial estate which comprises 10 factory buildings and a small office building and the office is then converted to a warehouse/storage use, the decision as to whether this is material will very much depend on the planning unit considered.

The main principle derived from case law[6] is that the planning unit should be taken to mean the unit of occupation or ownership. However, a separate unit is created if within one unit of occupation two or more physically separate and distinct areas are occupied for unrelated purposes.

Taking the previous example it would follow that, if each industrial unit and the office building are within separate ownership, then the office building forms its own planning unit and a material change of use has occurred, within that unit. If the whole industrial estate was within one ownership, it could be argued that the whole estate is one planning unit and no material change of use has occurred to that unit as a whole, by alteration in the use of such a small component. The second problem relates to the fact that, within any one site, several uses may take place. To help establish a material change of use it will be necessary to establish the primary (main or principal) use of the land. It will often be the case that ancillary (second or incidental) uses may function alongside such a primary use.

Consider the examples in Table 3.5. Provided that the ancillary activities remain functionally related to the primary activity, then no material change will have occurred. If the ancillary activities increase to such an extent that they could no longer be said to be ancillary, then a mixed use has occurred.

Intensification is a widely misunderstood concept within consideration of change of use. The intensification of a use may occur (e.g. increased levels of production output in a factory), which in itself does not result in a change of use. Intensification can be said to result in a change of use only where the intensification itself results in a change in the character and town planning consequences of the land. For example, if a clothes shop sells more clothes, it has intensified its activity, but no material change of use has occurred. It is a better practice to look for a material change in use rather than intensification.

Table 3.5 The relationship between primary and ancillary uses

Primary	Ancillary
(i) Hotel with . . .	Bar, restaurant, laundry, swimming pool, sauna, open to hotel residents.
(ii) Shop unit with . . .	Office at rear dealing with associated administration.
(iii) Retail warehouse or departmental store . . .	Associated café/restaurant
(iv) Office building with . . .	Staff gym.

Summary of material change of use

- To establish a material change of use consider the character of use and consequences of that use.
- Define the area to be considered by establishing the planning unit (unit of occupation in which uses are functionally linked).
- Remember that in dealing with character/consequence of a use the primary use will need to be identified, together with ancillary uses that are secondary to it. If no primary/secondary relationship can be established, then a mixed use is created. If a secondary use grows to such an extent as to create a mixed use, then a material change of use has occurred from primary to mixed.
- Intensification of use is a misleading concept; consider instead the characteristics of a material change of use.

Use Classes Order 1987 (SI 764) (UCO) and General Permitted Development Order 1995 (SI 418)[7]

The GPDO and UCO establish a series of freedoms from the need to apply for planning permission, taking each in turn:

The General Permitted Development Order (GPDO)

The GPDO has two principal benefits for the planning system:

- it covers classes of development considered to be of relatively trivial planning importance and, in most cases, are environmentally acceptable
- it relieves local planning authorities of a vast administrative workload for (generally) acceptable operations.

How does the GPDO function?

Article 3 of the current order (the current order being Statutory Instrument 418, dated 1995) grants planning permission for a variety of the operations and some changes of use identified. In other words, any operations or uses

Table 3.6 Some examples of permitted development within a GPDO[a]

GPDO	Example
Part 1	Dwellinghouse, e.g. • Side or rear extensions to a cubic limit of 50–70 m^3 or 10–15% value of original dwelling (varies between terraced and semi- or detached). • Porch • Garage • Sheds/greenhouses/swimming pool enclosure • Hard-standing • Satellite antenna or dish (within size limits)
Part 2	Minor operations, e.g. • Gate, fence, wall or other means of enclosure • A means of access other than to a trunk or classified road • Painting exterior of building
Part 3	Changes of use, e.g. • A3/A2 to A1 • B2 to B1 • A3 to A2
Part 4	Temporary buildings and uses, e.g. • Structures/plant required in construction • 28 day temporary use in any one year (reduced to 14 if a market, motor rally or clay pigeon shooting)
Part 5	Caravan sites
Part 6	Agricultural buildings and operations
Part 7	Forestry buildings and operations
Part 8	Industrial and warehouse development

[a] Examples to illustrate some freedoms from planning permission established by the GPDO. Refer to the Order for an exact list of the criteria that must be satisfied to constitute permitted development.

that adhere to the criteria laid down in the 33 separate clauses of Schedule 2 constitute development, but permission for that development is automatically granted; that is, it is permitted by the Order without the need to submit a planning application and is therefore known as 'permitted development'.

The most important classes are:

- Part 1: Development within the Curtilage of a Dwellinghouse, e.g. extensions to a dwellinghouse of a certain size and siting are permitted development.
- Part 3: Changes of Use, e.g. to change from A3 (Food and Drink) to A2 (Financial and Professional Services), from A3 or A2 to A1 (Retail), from B2 (General Industry) to B1 (Business) and from B1 or B2 to B8 (Storage and Distribution).
- Part 8: Industrial and Warehouse Development, e.g. small extensions to such buildings.

Where permitted development may not apply

- Residential permitted development does not apply to flats, only to dwellinghouses.
- Residential permitted development rights are reduced on Article 1(5) land, i.e. in National Parks, Areas of Outstanding Natural Beauty, or Conservation Areas.
- Where the local planning authority has served an Article 4 Direction.[8] Such Directions require the direct approval of the Secretary of State. Normally Article 4 Directions withdraw permitted development rights for a particular class of development within a specified area. This is mostly employed in Conservation Areas; it protects the amenity and gives the planners greater control over development, for example, requiring planning permission for such activities as exterior painting or the installation of double glazing.

The local planning authority in granting planning permission for new development may seek to remove future permitted development rights by imposing a condition. However, they must have good reason to do this; for example, in high-density residential developments this will protect the amenities of the neighbouring occupiers.

As we have seen, we must refer to the General Permitted Development Order with operational development, whereas with the vast majority of material changes of use, we refer to the Use Classes Order.

The Use Classes Order

The UCO places certain planning uses into classes, with a total of 16 classes and a variety of subdivisions within each class. To move from one use to another within a class is not development (Grant 1989, Home 1989). Conversely, to move between any of the 16 classes is development and therefore requires planning permission. (The current order is the 1987 Order, Statutory Instrument number 764.)

The twofold purpose of the Order is stated in Circular 13/87,[9] first to reduce the number of use classes while retaining effective control over change of use, which, because of environmental consequences or relationships with other uses, need to be subject to specific planning applications; and, second, to ensure that the scope of each class is wide enough to take in changes of use that generally do not need to be subject to specific control.

The Use Classes Order is not comprehensive. Any use not covered by the Order (and therefore outside the provision of the Order) is considered to be *sui generis* (in a class of its own). Any movement to or from a *sui generis* use is outside the provision of the UCO and would require planning permission.

The relationship between the GPDO and the UCO

Consider, for example, Class A1 (shops) of the UCO. The Order states that Class A1 use is for all or any of the following purposes:

Table 3.7 Summary of examples within the UCO

Use class	Principal examples (not exhaustive)
A1 Retail	Any shop selling retail goods to public ⇒ post office ⇒ travel agent ⇒ off licence ⇒ sale of cold food for consumption off the premises
A2 Financial and professional services	Bank ⇒ building society ⇒ estate agent
A3 Food and drink	Pub ⇒ restaurant ⇒ sale of hot food ⇒ wine bar
B1 Business	(light) industry ⇒ office ⇒ research and development

⇒ Denotes a movement 'within' the use class, which is not development and therefore would not require planning permission.

- the retail sale of goods
- as a post office
- the sale of tickets or as a travel agency
- the sale of sandwiches or other cold food for consumption off the premises
- hairdressing
- the direction of funerals
- the display of goods for sale
- the hiring out of domestic or personal goods or articles
- the reception of goods to be washed, cleaned or repaired, where the sale, display or service is to visiting members of the public.

Therefore, to change from a hairdressing salon to a travel agency is within the A1 class and would not require planning permission. To change from a hairdresser to a use outside A1 would require planning permission. It follows that, in the vast majority of cases, to move between individual classes is a material change of use for which planning permission will be required. In a few cases (see Table 3.6, Part 3: p. 71), such movements, although accepted as constituting a change of use and therefore development, are themselves automatically granted planning permission by Part 3 of the GPDO, so that to move from A3 (Food and drink) use to A1 (Retail) use is development, but it falls within the provision of Part 3 of the GPDO and therefore constitutes permitted development for which no planning application is required. Although it is somewhat confusing to include provisions relating to use in the GPDO, the simplest way to remember these issues is that after establishing that a proposed use results in movement between use classes, cross-reference to Part 3 of the GPDO to ascertain whether this is permitted development. Figure 3.1 illustrates a summary of this.

The overall relationship can be summarized in a flowchart (Fig. 3.2).

Review of the Use Classes Order

In January 2002 the government published for consultation a series of 'possible changes' to the Use Classes Order. Such revisions adhered to one of

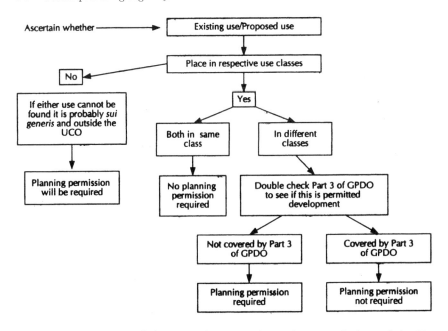

Figure 3.1 A summary of the General Permitted Development Order and the Use Classes Order.

Figure 3.2 A summary of the definition of development.

the principle tenets of the 1987 order, namely that the maximum possible level of deregulation of planning control should be permitted. Such deregulation should be allowed within the boundaries set by planning policy. A new order is anticipated in 2005. The consultation identified a number of key areas for revision:

Table 3.8 Key areas for revision

Proposed changes	Rationale
• Combine classes A1, A2 and A3 to create a 'mixed retail use' class subject to certain floorspace rules. e.g. Mixed retail use (Aa) for retail sale of goods → financial and professional services → food and drink up to 100 sqm gross lettable floorspace.	To reflect market changes comprising the 'super-pub', dramatic increase in food and drink industry (juice bars, coffee shops and sandwich shops) leading to doubts over their use class and new uses like internet cafes.
• Separation of component classes within B1 to give a distinction between office/research and development and production e.g. A separate office/research and development use (Ba) and one for 'clean' production (i.e. acceptable in a residential area) (Bb).	To reflect the difficulties in trying to distinguish between office, research, and development and light industry. *and* a need to promote office use in town centre locations by giving a more focussed definition in the Use Class.
General production (B2) and storage and distribution to remain unaffected (B8).	

Review of the General Permitted Development Order

The Planning Green Paper (2001) signals a review of the General Permitted Development Order. Such a review will not be as wide-ranging as that undertaken for the Use Classes Order. The Green Paper made it clear that the government would not be seeking any wide-ranging relaxation of permitted development rights. Instead, the principal aim of the review would simplify the document to make it easier to understand. Further, the Green Paper explores the idea of introducing locally based GPDOs, compared to the national system as currently exists. The 1995 GPDO allows this local discretion in conservation areas where the local circumstances dictate the detailed nature of a more restrictive withdrawal of permitted development rights. In the future and when revisiting the order, the government may allow councils greater discretion to impose local controls, in other words selective withdrawal of permitted development rights as dictated by local circumstances. An ODPM-commissioned consultants report of September 2003 recommended detailed textual revisions to the criteria used to establish permitted development (ODPM 2003).

Enforcing town planning control

When the development of land is undertaken without the benefit of planning permission, the local planning authority has enforcement powers to seek a remedy to those breaches of control that they consider to be unacceptable.

A breach of town planning control is defined as the carrying out of development without the required planning permission or failure to comply with the terms of any condition attached to a grant of planning permission.[10] Such an unauthorized development does not constitute a criminal offence. It will only become a criminal offence in the event of enforcement action being taken by the LPA that is subsequently ignored or not complied with by the landowner, or if works have been carried out to a listed building. It should also be remembered that carrying out development without planning permission is not automatically followed by enforcement action. The LPA has discretion in deciding whether or not to enforce. Enforcement normally follows in cases where the breach of control results, in the opinion of the LPA, in some form of harm to amenity (which may be contrary to planning policy). If the LPA considers the breach to be acceptable, they may invite the owner to submit a retrospective planning application, so that the matter can be decided through the normal development control procedures. Once such a retrospective application is granted, then the matter becomes regularized.

The Carnwath Report

In 1988 the Secretary of State for the Environment appointed an eminent planning lawyer, Robert Carnwath QC, to undertake a review of enforcement procedures (Carnwath Report 1989).

The findings were published in 1989 with a series of recommendations designed to make enforcement more effective when dealing with unacceptable breaches of control. These recommendations were introduced into the system by the Planning and Compensation Act 1991 (Sections 1 to 11), that added new powers and amended those existing under the TCPA 1990.

The various enforcement powers available to the LPA in the post-1991 system can be summarized as follows:

Planning Contravention Notice (PCN)

Prior to taking formal enforcement action, the LPA needs to determine whether a breach has in fact occurred. This may not always be an easy matter to ascertain. To assist, the LPA may serve a Planning Contravention Notice requiring information from the owner or other people with an interest regarding operations, uses or matters in respect of planning conditions relating to the land.[11] For example, a landowner or operator may start digging a trench on a site or may begin to service/maintain motor vehicles. A PCN can help to ascertain whether the trench is for the construction of a building or that the motor repairs undertaken in a domestic garage are for a commercial purpose and not merely a hobby. From this response, the LPA may initiate formal enforcement action, but the service of the notice will alert the owner to the council's concern, from which further dialogue between both sides may overcome the problem without recourse to any further action. The decision to serve a PCN is an option available to the LPA. They do not have to serve one as a precondition of future action. However, once served, failure to comply with its requirements within 21 days or to give misleading information constitutes a criminal offence.

Enforcement Notice

The enforcement notice constitutes the principal enforcement mechanism at the disposal of the LPA when seeking to remedy a breach of planning control. Prior to the service of an enforcement notice the LPA should normally, as a matter of good practice, undertake a land registry search to ascertain ownership or other interest in the land. They may have previously served a Planning Contravention Notice to gather information, or they may serve a Section 330 Notice, that requires the occupier of the land to provide information of interest in the land or the interest of other persons. The enforcement notice is issued by the LPA and served upon the landowner or any other person with an interest in the land who will be affected by the enforcement action. It will stipulate a course of action (steps to be taken) to remedy the breach and will indicate a time period within which such action must be taken. Reasoning must be provided to support the decision to issue the Notice, which will in most cases allege that the continued implementation of the breach results in some form of planning harm or loss of amenity that may be contrary to policy or other material considerations. A right of appeal exists against the service of an enforcement notice.[12] Any appeal must be submitted within a 28-day period following 'service' of the notice. If an appeal is lodged, then the Notice does not take effect but is held in abeyance and the matter must be determined by the Secretary of State or an appointed Inspector who may quash, uphold or vary the notice in some way. The enforcement notice appeal may be pursued by written representation, informal hearing or public inquiry method. The informal method is unsuitable if there are complex legal considerations. An award of costs is available in all three methods.[13]

Summary: characteristics of an Enforcement Notice

- Deals with remedying unacceptable breaches of planning control.
- Provides for a timescale within which the matter should be rectified.
- Allows for an appeal, in which case the effect of the notice is suspended and the matter is dealt with by the Secretary of State or Inspector. An appeal must be lodged within 28 days of service of the notice, otherwise the notice becomes ineffective.

Stop Notice

The stop notice provides the LPA with its most Draconian enforcement powers. Unlike the enforcement notice, which allows for a reasonable period for compliance, the stop notice requires a halt to activities (uses or operations) within three days of its service upon the landowner or other person with an interest in the land who will be affected by the stop notice. It is therefore served only in cases of serious breaches of planning control.[14] A stop notice can be served only if an enforcement notice of similar content has also been served and before the enforcement notice takes effect. An appeal can only be lodged against the enforcement notice as no right of appeal is available against a stop notice. If on appeal the Secretary of State or Inspector either quashes the enforcement notice or varies it to the extent that the matter 'stopped' no longer constitutes a breach of control, then the LPA is liable to pay financial compensation to the owner for the loss incurred by the imposed cessation of activity.

Summary: characteristics of a Stop Notice

- Deals with remedying unacceptable breaches of control that might require immediate cessation.
- No appeal, however, as a stop notice can only be served alongside or after an enforcement notice (of similar content) then an appeal may be made against the enforcement notice.
- Compensation payable if enforcement notice appeal is successful in authorizing the breach stopped by the notice.

Breach of Condition Notice (BCN)

This procedure permits specific action against failure to comply with a planning condition imposed on a previous grant of permission by service of a Breach of Condition Notice.[15] As with the enforcement notice, the LPA must specify steps to be taken to remedy the matter, together with a period of compliance. Failure to comply with such a notice is a criminal offence. No right of appeal is available against such a notice; therefore, if an onerous condition is imposed on a planning permission, the landowner is well advised to pursue an appeal against the condition rather than await any future breach of condition notice.

Certificates of lawful existing use or development and proposed use or development

Such certificates are considered by LPAs in the same way as applications for planning permission. They allow an owner to have a ruling as to whether an existing operation or use of land, without the previous benefit of planning permission, is lawful or to ascertain that a proposed operation or use would also be lawful and therefore not require the need for a grant of planning permission.[16] This would remove any uncertainty that a matter was outside the realm of planning control, for example it was either permitted development (e.g. a small residential extension), or not development at all (e.g. movement within a use class), or was immune from enforcement action whereby an operational development was substantially completed for at least four years,[17] or, if a change of use, for a minimum period of at least ten years.

Both certificates help to remove any uncertainty an owner may have about the planning status of a site. The LPA can refuse to grant either certificate, which carries a right of appeal to the Secretary of State.

Injunctions

The local planning authority also enjoys powers strengthened by the Planning and Compensation Act 1991[18] to seek an injunction in either the High Court or County Court to halt an actual or anticipated breach of planning control. Such injunctions are generally, but not necessarily, employed by LPAs as a second line of attack, although such a legal mechanism is a very effective way of controlling any contravention of the planning system, because, if an injunction is granted by the courts and if its terms are subsequently ignored by the owner, then the person involved risks possible imprisonment for contempt of court.

Discovering breaches of planning control

The majority of breaches of planning control are discovered by the LPA following the receipt of a complaint from a member of the public, usually a neighbouring occupier. Local planning authorities usually establish a specialist in-house team of enforcement officers who investigate such complaints and advise both owner and complainant on the possibility of action being taken. Decisions to pursue enforcement matters involve legal judgement (establishing facts to determine that a breach has occurred) and planning judgement (to remedy the situation to overcome any loss of amenity that results from the unauthorized use or operation).

For this reason, enforcement activity involves both town planning and legal personnel, and government guidance encourages a strong level of co-operation between such staff to ensure effective implementation of this important planning function.

Conclusions

Town planning legislation creates the procedures by which control may be exercised over the use of land and operations that take place on, over or under that land. Such legislation is applied consistently across England and Wales and it sets out to create a regulatory system, yet it must also establish freedoms or exemptions from the system where 'development' would not result in any harmful environmental impact. Thus, a balance must be struck between necessary environmental protection and unnecessary bureaucratic burden. Such decisions are not easy and are particularly contentious in the realm of residential permitted development, where some homeowners will resent any form of planning control that will restrict their desire to extend, or otherwise alter, a dwelling. The introduction in 1988 of town planning control over external stone cladding to dwellinghouses illustrates the problem, with the government finally being convinced, after many years of debate, that the residents' right to alter their property in this way was eroding the quality of the environment.

Table 3.9 Summary of enforcement powers

Procedure	Objective	Example	Right of appeal
Planning Contravention Notice	To require information regarding the use of or operations within land	To seek information on a use of land to determine if it is a change of use, so LPA can enforce	No
Enforcement Notice	To remedy a breach of control resulting in harm	To remove a scrap metal dealer from a site	Yes
Stop Notice	To almost immediately cease an activity (use or operation) resulting in (serious) harm	To remove a scrap metal dealer and immediately stop any further activity	No
Breach of Condition Notice	To remedy the failure to comply with details of a planning condition	Enforce hours of use imposed on a change of use permission from shop to restaurant	No
Injunction	To halt a breach or anticipated breach of planning permission	Prevent use of land for motorbike scrambling once permitted development has been used up	No Civil legal proceedings
Certificate of Lawful Use/ Development	Establish existing use or development is lawful	Establish immunity under 10 (use) or 4 (operation) year rule	Yes
Certificate of Proposed Lawful Use/ Development	Establish that proposed use or development is lawful	Establish permitted development	Yes

Town planning legislation creates the all important 'ground rules' that provide a structure for the planning system. All participants in the planning process must comply with these 'ground rules', although it is important to remember that legislation is the subject of continual revision by case law in which the courts provide rulings on the interpretation of statutes.

4 Planning appeals

A planning appeal is a challenge to the merits of or lack of a planning decision made by a local planning authority and should be viewed as a decision of last resort.

Most decisions made by local planning authorities carry with them the right of appeal to the Secretary of State for the Environment. Such appeals provide a form of arbitration on the town planning merits of a decision and represent the final stage of the development control process. Any further appeal is a matter of legal submission in which the decision is challenged in the courts on grounds of procedural unreasonableness, namely that matters were taken into account by the decision-maker that should not reasonably have been taken into account or were not taken into account when they should have been, or the decision was so manifestly unreasonable that no reasonable decision-maker could have come to it. Such legal appeals to the High Court, Court of Appeal or House of Lords should not be confused with a planning appeal. A planning appeal deals solely with the technical town planning merits of the case and only involves legal argument where it has some influence upon decision-making regarding technical town planning matters. It is important to draw this distinction from the start.

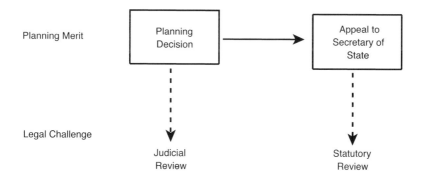

This chapter deals with appeals based *exclusively* on matters of planning merit. Any further reference to case law is employed to assist in the clarification of planning issues only. This emphasis reflects town planning practice, where a grasp of law is employed to throw light on matters of process (how the system works) and matters of substance (the contents of the decision).

So, in starting the chapter it is necessary to draw an important distinction between planning appeals and legal appeals.

Legal appeals are submitted by means of two mechanisms:

- First, there are matters for *Statutory Review* (section 288 of Town and Country Planning Act 1990), in which an appeal decision issued by the Secretary of State (after 2002 the Deputy Prime Minister) or an Inspector is challenged. Such a challenge is most commonly made on the grounds that a decision was taken that was either procedurally unreasonable or fell outside powers established in (town planning) legislation.[1] This mechanism is employed by parties to an appeal decision issued by the Secretary of State or the Planning Inspectorate.

- Second, there are matters for *Judicial Review* (section 31 of the Supreme Court Act 1981), in which any decision issued by a local planning authority is challenged, usually on grounds of being procedurally unreasonable. This mechanism is employed by third parties to challenge a grant of planning permission on the basis that the decision was not valid or legal because procedural matters were not correctly followed by the planning authority. To proceed in judicial review the High Court must grant 'leave to appeal', in other words a judge accepts that an arguable case has been presented and may be submitted before a court for interpretation and determination.

These two matters of legal challenge may therefore be contrasted with the *planning appeal*. The main right of appeal is enshrined in the Town and Country Planning Act 1990 (section 78), which established that 'a right exists against the refusal of a planning permission or the failure to take such decision'. This right is available only to the applicant (the person or body who made the original planning application that is now the subject of an appeal). High-profile pressure groups like Friends of the Earth have called for this right to be extended to third parties, in other words the public can appeal against a council's decision to grant planning permission. Government policy appears to be firmly against such a change. The Green Paper of 2001 re-states this opposition. Evidently government fears that to extend the right of appeal in this way would clog the system with numerous appeals where residents were merely attempting to block acceptable development for non-planning related reasons such as loss of view or reduction in property value.

Appeals are available against a vast array of planning decisions issued by local planning authorities.

The planning appeal system

Historical background

The TCPA 1932 introduced the right of planning appeal, whereby someone could challenge the decision of a local authority to refuse planning permission. The Public Inquiry had been introduced 23 years before in the Housing, Town Planning etc. Act 1909. However, at that time it did not represent a method of planning appeal as it does today, but instead was a means by which the public could voice objection to town planning schemes. The TCPA 1947 introduced a limited system of planning appeal that was tightly controlled by the Minister of Housing and Local Government. All appeals were considered by Public Inquiry. The rules governing the conduct of such inquiries were not publicly available as the relevant government department was unwilling to publish them. Although the ultimate decision either to allow or to dismiss the appeal was published, the reasoning upon which the decision had been based was kept secret. Such a system was not only secretive in its procedures but also largely excluded the public from the area of appeal decision-making.

Such a situation was to change in 1958 (Franks 1957) following the implementation of recommendations made by the Committee on Administrative Tribunals and Inquiries (the Franks Committee) (Layfield 1993) of the previous year. These reforms introduced statutory rules for procedure in Public Inquiries, publication of the Inspector's report, and established the key attributes of openness, fairness and impartiality in all appeal proceedings. These three 'Franks' principles' still apply today and have governed all procedural reforms since 1958. Further changes in the early 1960s and 1980s introduced new appeal methods in the form of the Written Representation and Informal Hearing. In 2000 further reforms were added to both modernize and streamline the process, and the 2001 Green Paper countenanced the introduction of alternative means of settling planning appeals by recourse to mediation. Any formal system of mediation is unlikely to be introduced before 2005 (if at all).

The Planning Appeal is a critical stage within the development process. Unnecessary delay will frustrate both developer and local planning authority. However, it is important that every decision is made in full knowledge of the proposal to enable the appeal system to produce the correct decision and therefore enhance the development control process.

Key characteristics of the Planning Appeal system can be identified: there are many different rights of appeal against LPA decisions, and these rights are exercised by the applicant (person making the planning application) and in enforcement matters the person who occupies or has an interest in the land. The decision to appeal is free of charge and the appeal is considered by the Secretary of State for the Environment or an Inspector. Administration of the appeal is co-ordinated by the Planning Inspectorate (England) or the Welsh Office or Scottish Office. The Secretary of State will issue a decision either to allow (grant) or to dismiss (refuse) the appeal, with the system being paid for by the government at a cost of around £26 million a year.[2]

Four principal purposes may be advanced. First, Planning Appeals provide a form of *arbitration* whereby an aggrieved applicant or owner may seek an independent assessment on a wide variety of decisions made by the local planning authority. Second, they ensure that there is a degree of *consistency* in decision-making across the country. Inspectors will consider each case on its own merit but will take some account of national planning policy in the form of Circulars and PPGs. Third, they provide an opportunity for *public participation* by which third parties can view the decision-making process and make their own representations. Third parties have been defined as 'those other than councils or appellants who, in relation to a particular appeal, think they will be affected by its outcome'. Third parties are therefore members of the public who consider that they may be affected by a development proposal (Keeble 1985: 80). Third parties enjoy no right of appeal. They are consulted about the appeal and may participate. At Informal Hearing and Public Inquiry they appear at the discretion of the Inspector and are usually allowed to ask questions of the appellant. Fourth, they provide a *safeguard* against unreasonable decisions by the local planning authority. Appellants are expected to pay their own costs in all appeal proceedings. An award of costs can be made against either party if unreasonable behaviour is evident. This unreasonable behaviour would cover failure to follow relevant appeal procedures or to provide evidence to support the case.

Who considers the appeal?

All planning appeals are submitted to the Secretary of State for the Environment. In practice, the jurisdiction for considering such appeals is split into either transferred or recovered decisions. Decisions are 'transferred' to a Planning Inspector appointed on behalf of the Secretary of State. This applies to all Written Representations, most Informal Hearings and about 95 per cent of Public Inquiries. The Planning Inspector is an 'arbitrator', with a property-related professional specialism, who is employed by government but is entirely independent in determining appeals. Decisions 'recovered' (i.e. not transferred) are determined by the Deputy Prime Minister. Such appeals are usually heard by Inquiry and involve major proposals and ones that raise significant legal difficulties or public controversy. Although some of these may be personally referred to the Secretary of State for a final decision (as in the case of sensitive appeals like New Settlements), it is usual practice for a senior official within the Office of the Deputy Prime Minister to make the decision upon receiving a recommendation from an Inspector who has been appointed to hold an Inquiry on behalf of the Deputy Prime Minister.

The necessary administration and processing of appeals are undertaken by the Planning Inspectorate, an executive agency of the Department of the Environment, or by the Welsh Office and Scottish Office. The Planning Inspectorate was established in 1909 and became an agency in 1992. Today it employs around 300 Planning Inspectors, with gross running costs of approximately £26m. Its work covers around 200 different types of appeal, with planning appeals comprising the single largest volume at around 60 per cent of its workload. Proposals decided by the Secretary of State tend to be co-ordinated by the relevant regional office of the Office of the Deputy Prime Minister.

The decision will be conveyed in a letter format addressed to the appellant or agent and will set out in summary the case as presented by either side and any third parties, followed by the reasoning of the Deputy Prime Minister or Inspector, dealing with policy matters and other material considerations, and concluding with the decision to allow the appeal (with conditions) or to dismiss the appeal. Any appeal beyond this point is based on a point of law and is made to the High Court.

In the appeal decision letter the Inspector will deal with findings of fact, such as whether the plan is up-to-date, and findings of opinion, such as whether the proposal is in character with the surrounding development. A distinction between the two may not always be easily apparent; for example, whether something was visible may appear as a matter of fact, although it is possible that it could be a matter of opinion. By contrast, a judgement whether some proposed development was visually intrusive would reasonably form a matter of opinion. Nevertheless, in many cases, especially those concerning appeals against the refusal of planning permission, the decision is based on a balance between findings of fact and matters of professional judgement.

Using past appeal decisions

A past planning appeal decision may constitute an important material consideration and may, therefore, be of sufficient value to allow the provisions of the Development Plan to be set aside (i.e. that material considerations should 'indicate otherwise' when considering the duty imposed by section 54A of the Town and Country Planning Act 1990, see Chapter 2). Planning appeal decisions, while important, do not set a 'precedent' that binds the decision-maker; it is necessary to rely on the fact that decision-making should be consistent. However, a distinction has to be drawn between 'precedent' and 'consistency'.

Precedent is undoubtedly a material planning consideration yet it refers to somewhat restrictive circumstances in which a planning authority refuse planning permission because to grant it . . . 'would be likely to lead to a proliferation of applications for similar developments, which the authority would find difficult to refuse'.[3] In other words, to grant permission on a given site may create pressure to develop a wider area. Once this pressure is unleashed the council would be unable to resist it. In practice this claim is difficult to prove as most sites are dealt with on their own individual merits.

The courts have accepted that mere fear of establishing a precedent or some generalized concern is not sufficient and that some evidence must exist before reliance on such grounds may be justified. It follows that the courts have sought to define precedent in a relatively narrow way. The existence of a previous planning appeal decision on a given site would *not* of itself create a precedent. Rather, when using past appeal decisions it is preferable to examine consistency in decision-making.

Consistency refers to circumstances in which detailed examination of the planning history of a development site reveals the existence of past decisions (application or appeal decisions). When reading past planning appeal decisions, their relevance in establishing matters of consistency may not always be immediately obvious. What if you have an interest in a site and you want to examine other appeal decisions, either in the locality or which deal with similar issues? How much weight should you give to a planning appeal decision in such circumstances?

As stated earlier, many planning decisions involve matters of professional judgement where a Planning Inspector will weigh up a series of factors (some legal, some factual and others of development control merit) in arriving at his or her determination. Indeed the whole planning process is built upon such determinations and judgements. When using a past appeal decision you may wish to rely upon it in support of granting a fresh consent on the same or another site. Additionally you may want to use a past favourable appeal decision (i.e. granted) when pursuing a current application or appeal that is deemed contrary to provisions of the Development Plan. The existence of this past appeal, you argue, constitutes a material consideration that 'indicates otherwise', in effect that it outweighs any objection contained in the Plan (if unsure on this legal point go back to Chapter 2, 'The Decision-maker's Duty' in section 54A of the Town and Country Planning Act 1990).

It is necessary to rely on the argument of consistency in decision-making and not precedent. Consistency in decision-making is a matter of importance. This was acknowledged in a decision of the High Court in 1990 when it was established that . . . 'the principle [of consistency in decision-making] is justified by a need to ensure that developers know where they stand'.[4]

Inspectors, in their decision letters, will often deal with matters of general applicability. Examples include:

- An Inspector establishes a general 'rule of thumb', e.g. in respect of separation distances between new and existing dwellings.
- An Inspector gives an interpretation of national planning policy (in PPGs/PPSs) as it should apply locally, i.e. how PPG3 for example may seek higher residential densities in certain locations.

Key guidance in this area is provided by the judgement of Lord Justice Mann in the decision of *North Wiltshire District Council* vs *Secretary of State for the Environment and Glover* (in the Court of Appeal, 12 April 1992).[5] This provides helpful clarification as to when a previous appeal decision may constitute a material consideration. Lionel Read QC, sitting as a Deputy High Court Judge, had previously quashed an appeal decision on the grounds that the Inspector, in *granting* permission, failed to explain why he did not follow a previous appeal decision some seven years earlier in which his Inspectorate colleague had *dismissed* an appeal dealing with an *identical proposal* on a similar, albeit larger, site. The Judge considered that this omission in the decision amounted to inadequate justification and he quashed the planning appeal (by Lionel Read QC). The Secretary of State and appellant sought to reverse this High Court decision by appeal to the Court of Appeal (before Lord Justice Mann). In dismissing this challenge and thus upholding the decision of the High Court, the Court of Appeal established some important features of general applicability to developers and their professional agents when relying on past decisions.

First, in relying on a past decision the merits between past and present cases must be *materially indistinguishable*. The Inspector in writing his decision benefits from a wide-ranging discretion. Yet as Lord Justice Mann observed in the North Wiltshire case . . . 'like cases should be decided in a like manner so that there is consistency in the appellate process'. The fact that every case is determined on its own individual merits must take account of this. The Court of Appeal established in this judgement that for a previous appeal to be 'material' it must be 'indistinguishable' in (at least) critical areas. Such 'indistinguishable' decisions may be 'gold dust' in the pursuit of cases because, although they are no guarantee of victory, they will persuade the Inspector or Planning Officer to look very carefully at the issues you set out to target. Second, the Court of Appeal in the North Wiltshire case stressed that such areas could not be defined . . . 'but they would include interpretation of policies, aesthetic judgements and assessment of need . . .'.

The Court was not saying that consistency must always be applied but rather that a lack of consistency must be explained. Analysis of this case reported in the *Journal of Planning and Environment Law* stated that Lord Justice Mann accepted that . . . 'there is a presumption that there shall be consistency in decision-making but that it cannot always be achieved'. Consistency must therefore be an important objective of the system but this must not lead to excessive rigidity in decision-making. The existence of a previous appeal decision was an important material consideration and may be advanced by developers to support consistency, where this would assist their case. Yet the Inspector enjoys sufficient discretion to disagree with such earlier judgements, but must give reasons. Such reasons can be short, such as 'I disagree,' but this will, depend on the case merits.

Types of appeal

The most common type of planning appeal is against a refusal of planning permission. It is a common misconception that this is the only type of appeal. In fact, many different types of appeal are available under the provisions of town and country planning, listed building and advertisement legislation (Table 4.1).

Submission of appeal

All planning appeals are submitted on standard forms issued by the Deputy Prime Minister and co-ordinated by the Planning Inspectorate or government regional office. Any appeal against refusal of permission, planning conditions or reserved matters must be submitted within three months of the LPA decision. Appeals against enforcement notices must be submitted within a prescribed period (usually 28 days), that is indicated on the notice. The appeal forms require submission of supporting documentation including plans, notices of refusal, correspondence and certificate of ownership. The right of appeal is free of charge, although in some enforcement matters the appellant may be required to pay a fee.

The choice of appeal method is an important decision. It will affect the procedure for deciding the case, the overall time over which a decision will be reached and the costs involved, not in lodging the appeal, as this is free, but in the professional time required to pursue each method. The choice of

Table 4.1 Types of planning appeal

Type of appeal	Example
Refusal of planning permission	Refusal to build on or change the use of land
Against a condition on a grant of permission	Hours of opening condition imposed on a grant of hot food take-away
Against refusal of reserved matters application following grant of outline planning permission	Reserved matters – siting, means of access, external appearance, design and landscape, e.g. refuse submitted landscape details
Against refusal of any details required by a planning condition	A condition may require details of proposed materials to be submitted, which may subsequently be refused
Against failure to determine a planning application (non-determination)	LPA do not issue decision within eight weeks or an extended period as agreed by each party
Against the issuing of an Enforcement Notice requiring some remedy against unauthorized development	Notice to remove a building or structure or cease a use – all undertaken without permission
Against failure to grant a certificate of lawfulness of existing or proposed use or development	LPA refuse applications to establish that a building without planning permission has existed for 4 years minimum or a use has existed for 10 years minimum; any appeal would need to produce evidence to prove otherwise
Against refusal of Listed Building Consent	Refusal of application to extend or alter a Listed Building
Against conditions on a grant of Listed Building Consent	A Listed Building condition may require specific materials or methods of construction to be used to match existing
Against the issuing of a Listed Building Enforcement Notice	Specific grounds similar to a planning notice, e.g. requires removal of extension built without Listed Building Consent
Against failure to grant Conservation Area Consent	LPA refuse consent to demolish an unlisted building in a Conservation Area
Against refusal of permission to display an advertisement	Consent refused as advertisement may be too large or result in highway problems
Against an application to top, lop or fell a tree preserved under a Tree Preservation Order	Permission is refused to alter a preserved tree usually due to the loss of amenity involved and/or good health of existing tree

method is unfettered by the type of case or nature of evidence to be produced, although the agreement of both parties will usually be required. It is conceivable, if rare, that the most minor appeal may go to Public Inquiry. The appellant may exercise a 'right to be heard' by an Inspector, i.e. to convene an Inquiry or Hearing. It is not possible, when submitting an appeal, to insist that an Inquiry be held, while the Planning Inspectorate may impose a Hearing upon the parties if they deem this to be the most appropriate method. It is the common practice of the Inspectorate to consult with the parties before such a decision is made.

The appeal methods

Following the initial decision to pursue an appeal, the most important decision on the appeal forms is the choice of appeal method (Lavers & Webster 1990). The choices available are Public Inquiry, Written Representation or Informal Hearing. Only one method may be chosen. The Planning Inspectorate has always sought to encourage use of the written method, which is quicker and cheaper to implement. Since September 1994 the appeal forms have displayed a clear choice of the three methods.[6]

All three methods are designed to embody the rules of Natural Justice. Such rules state that the decision-maker (Inspector or Secretary of State) is impartial and that, before a decision is taken, individuals should be given a chance to put their points of view. Inquiries and Written Representations and Hearings are all governed by statutory rules of procedure.[7]

These three appeal methods each represent a balance between the need for administrative expediency and for a proper examination of the planning issues of the case. It is widely accepted that the Public Inquiry results in a greater rigour of detailed examination than the written method (McCoubry 1990, Purdue 1991, Moore 1997).[8] However, it also takes longer to process and it costs more to both the Office of the Deputy Prime Minister (in Inspector time) and the appellant (in professional fees). Not all planning appeals involve complex policy or other issues. Therefore, it may be expedient to sacrifice the detailed examination of issues in preference to a quick and less expensive method of appeal. An appraisal of the three Planning Appeal methods is shown in Table 4.2.

Which method to choose?

Determining factors can be identified that will influence the choice of appeal method (Table 4.3). The decision to appeal is a decision of last resort. Around 30–35 per cent of all appeals are allowed, so, crudely speaking, the appellant has a one in three chance of success, although the Inquiry on its own gives slightly better odds at around 40 per cent allowed.[9] If the LPA would give favourable consideration to some form of amended proposal, then this would be a more secure way of realizing development potential. Although some appeal proposals will stand a better chance than others, the appeal pathway will always remain a lottery to the developer, as the Inspector is making an entirely fresh (*de novo*) development control decision.

Table 4.2 An appraisal of Planning Appeal methods

	Advantages	*Disadvantages*
Written Representation	Cheapest method	Evidence is not rigorously tested
	Shortest period to get decision	Written evidence only – little opportunity to clarify issues or allow Inspector to ask questions
Informal Hearing	Informal atmosphere	Role of Inspector is central to proceedings. If an Inspector does not control the discussion then this method loses its advantages
	Some oral discussion – testing of evidence and clarification of issues	
	Hearing avoids time-wasting – usually half-day duration	Discussion basis, is not adversarial and may help to readily identify issues
	Opportunity for costs to be incurred	Costs may also go against
Public Inquiry	Cross-examination allows for a rigorous testing of evidence and clarification of issues	Formal and sometimes excessively adversarial
		Most expensive
	Opportunity for costs	Longest period of time to get a decision. Costs may also go against

Procedures involved in each appeal method

Written representation

> These are rough justice, greater speed of determination being purchased at the cost of less thorough exploration.
>
> (Keeble 1985)

Such criticism has been levelled at the written method on the basis that, in pursuing a relatively quick decision, the procedures inhibit a rigorous exploration of the planning merits of the case (McNamara *et al.* 1985). Such a view must be qualified by the fact that the written method is best employed in minor cases with straightforward planning issues (Case study 4.1). The Planning Inspectorate encourages use of this method, as the appeal forms state 'Do you agree to the written procedure?' Since this method was first introduced in 1965 as an alternative to the Public Inquiry, it has increased its percentage share of all methods from 30–35 per cent to 80–85 per cent of all appeals. The written appeal has many benefits for the Planning Inspectorate in that the cost of each appeal is cheaper, involving generally less adminis-tration or Inspector's time to reach a decision and therefore the combined advantage of offering a cheaper unit cost per appeal[10] to the Treasury and speedier decisions to appellants and local planning authorities. During the 1990s the Secretary of State for the Environment set targets for the handling

Table 4.3 Factors to consider when choosing a method of appeal

Determining factor	Method
(a) Magnitude of case: the size and scale of development proposed	Public Inquiry suitable for major proposals,* Written Representation for minor ones
(b) Complexity of case: the number or depth of policy and material considerations involved	Public Inquiry for complex and Written Representations for straightforward cases
(c) Financial considerations (professional fees) imposed by (a) and (b) above	Public Inquiry will involve greater professional input to prepare evidence and appear at Inquiry
(d) Time available to appellant	Written – 18 weeks† average from submission of appeal to decision notice being received Informal – 26 weeks† Inquiry – 44 weeks†
(e) Possibility of seeking costs for unreasonable behaviour	Costs applications only available at Inquiry and Hearing, not at written method
(f) Level of third-party involvement (number of objections at application stage prior to appeal)	All appeal methods permit the appellant to deal with third party comments; however, if many are expected the Hearing is an unsuitable method within which to deal with many objections; consider either Inquiry or written

* 'Major' is 10+ houses or 10 000 ft^2 floorspace for industrial, commercial or retail.
† Expressed as overall handling time in 80% of cases, see Planning Inspectorate *Annual report* for year-to-year fluctuations.

Case study 4.1

Proposal: The LPA refuses planning permission for a two-storey extension to a dwellinghouse for the reason:

> The proposal by reason of its excessive bulk would result in a loss of light and overshadowing of the neighbouring property, detrimental to the amenities enjoyed by the occupiers of that property.

Appraisal: The planning issue is clearly defined. The case is of little magnitude or complexity. On this basis it would not warrant a great deal of professional input and the owner is keen to have a decision as soon and inexpensively as possible. In this case a Written Representation would be the best method.

---

of written appeals from the submission of forms to the issue of the decision notice.[11] It is therefore in the interests of the Planning Inspectorate to continue to promote the Written Representation appeal with the benefit of a decision period of around 18 weeks to be reflected in the statistical returns issued every year.

Table 4.4 Timetable for the Written Representation appeal process

Time	Procedure
Decision to appeal is made	Appellant submits appeal forms and supporting documents to Inspectorate
Start date	Issued by Inspectorate after checking to ensure appeal is valid and documents correct
Two weeks	LPA return questionnaire and key documents (extracts of policy and correspondence)
Six weeks	LPA submits statement of their case (optional as they may rely on questionnaire only)*
	Appellant submits statement of their case*
	Third parties (objectors) to submit their case*
Nine weeks	Observations on case advanced by other party or any third party must be made*
Close of representations	Date set for site inspection if site cannot be seen from public land. The site inspection permits both sides to show the Inspector various features and not to deal with arguments over the merits or otherwise of the appeal
Site	Decision letter issued either granting (allow) or refusing (dismiss) the appeal

* These time limits are the subject of Statutory provision. Failure to comply may result in them being ignored (if late) or the Inspector proceeding to a decision in their absence.

Since 1987, Written Representation procedures have been governed by statutory rules,[12] which established a timetable to govern the operation of the appeal (Table 4.4).

It is intended that this timetable should establish a set of deadlines to be followed by parties to the appeal. Such time periods are rarely observed, although failure to meet them is usually by a matter of days or weeks, and not months.

The written procedure allows for a single exchange of written statement and the opportunity to comment on that evidence. However, additional written exchanges beyond this point are discouraged. Nothing is gained from having the last word. One frequently expressed criticism of this procedure is the inability of local authorities to adhere to the procedural timetable and the unwillingness of the Planning Inspectorate to enforce it.[13] This criticism perhaps best explains the motivation behind the 2000 reforms and the draconian measure of allowing Inspectors to proceed to a decision in the absence of (late) evidence by one party. It is doubtful that such a penalty will be used on every such occasion for fear of the criticism that it prejudices fairness in decision-making.

In August 2000 a revised timetable was introduced with the intention of improving the system. Nick Raynsford, the (then) Planning Minister, stated in a written reply to a Parliamentary question that 'The changes being introduced will improve the speed and efficiency of the system without

Case study 4.2

Proposal: The LPA refuses planning permission for a change of use of a retail shop (A1 use class) into a restaurant/food and drink use (A3 class). The proposal satisfies local plan policy and was recommended for a grant of planning permission by the case officer. The Committee overturned this recommendation and refused permission.

Appraisal: A straightforward case involving one policy issue. Although A3 uses involve the potential for several material considerations (especially odour emissions, late night activity, traffic generation and non-retail frontages), they are not considered to represent complex cases of great magnitude. Such a proposal could be adequately dealt with by Written Representation. However, there is some evidence of unreasonable behaviour and the possibility of an award of costs being made against the LPA.* In such a case, only Hearings/Inquiry allow either party to pursue such an award. A Hearing provides the better forum for dealing with costs in relatively straightforward or minor cases, whereas the Inquiry is the most suitable method for dealing with costs in the more complex or major cases.

* The award of costs is considered at the end of this chapter. The overturning of the recommendation of the Chief Planning Officer does not of itself constitute unreasonable behaviour, resulting in costs. However, if evidence is not forthcoming at the appeal to support the Committee's action, there is a strong chance costs may be awarded.

impairing the quality, fairness or openness of the process or people's ability to participate'. Also refer to (DETR) Circular 5/00 Planning Appeals: Procedures.

Summary: Written Representations – key characteristics

- suitable for minor cases
- written exchange of evidence
- quickest appeal method
- cheapest appeal (in professional fees)
- preferred by Planning Inspectorate
- procedure (timetable of events) governed by statutory rules
- most used method: 80–85 per cent of appeals.

Informal Hearings

Informal Hearings were first introduced in 1981 as an alternative to the Public Inquiry. During the 1980s they grew in popularity, so that by 1993 in England and Wales more appeals were decided by the Informal Hearing method (1862 appeals) than the inquiry method (1609 appeals).[14]

The Informal Hearing has been described as a 'half-way house' (Morgan & Nott 1988: 310) between the other methods, although it does have its own

Table 4.5 Timetable for the Informal Hearing appeal process

Time	Procedure
	Appellant submits appeal forms.
Start date	Issued by Inspectorate after checking to ensure appeal is valid and documents correct.
Two weeks	LPA return questionnaire and key documents (extracts of policy and correspondence).
Six weeks	• Both LPA and Appellant submit statements of their case and (wherever possible) evidence on which they agree. • Third parties (objectors) submit statements of their case. Nine weeks Observations on case advanced by other party or any third party must be made.*
Twelve weeks (or earlier)	Hearing† (3–4 hours duration), followed by site visit and subsequently a decision letter issued granting (allowing) or refusing (dismissing) the appeal.

* These time limits are the subject of Statutory provision. The Inspector may disregard comments which fail to satisfy the nine week target. First statements (i.e. six week deadlines) are not the subject of this measure.
† If at any time before or during the Hearing one party deems the Hearing Method inappropriate and the Secretary of State/Inspector agrees then it will be suspended and Inquiry held instead.

distinct advantage in that discussion is allowed on the site visit. The procedure involves an exchange of written evidence between the parties prior to the Hearing, and at the Hearing the Inspector leads a discussion between both parties and any third parties who attend.

Legal representation and formal cross-examination is discouraged. The Inspector plays a pivotal role in proceedings, leading the discussion, structuring the debate and intervening when the procedure departs from the code of practice. The Informal Hearing has been described as a 'round table discussion led by the Inspector' (Purdue 1991) or as a 'significant business meeting free from archaic ritual but not by any means an unconstrained social gathering' (McCoubrey 1990). The Inspector does have considerable discretion to structure the discussion, which may result in differing approaches by different Inspectors (Stubbs 1994). Most certainly, the Informal Hearing gives the Inspector greater control over the exact workings of the process compared to either the written method or the Inquiry. The procedure is shown in Table 4.5.

In 1993 the Planning Inspectorate commissioned research into customer perceptions of the Hearing method.[15] The report findings demonstrated a high level of satisfaction with this procedure, with appellants and LPAs citing the benefits of cost (professional fees), efficiency and suitability of a discussion-based forum. One of the key recommendations was that the automatic choice of a Hearing should be available. This was accepted by the Inspectorate. From September 1994 the planning appeal forms contain a clear choice between Written Representation, Informal Hearing and Public Inquiry. The LPA would still be required to agree to a Hearing; however, this amendment clearly established the role of Hearings as a clear alternative to not just Inquiries but also Written Representations. Since 2000 Hearings have been governed by statutory rules, having previously been enshrined in a non-statutory code of conduct. This change gives greater force to the rules that shape this method, while continuing to reinforce the central characteristic that an informal discussion takes place to examine evidence without the more formal employment of cross-examination. The Hearing method was itself the subject of legal scrutiny in a 'landmark' judgement of the Court of Appeal in 1998 in *Dyason* vs *Secretary of State for the Environment and Chiltern District Council*.[16]

In his judgement, Lord Justice Pill established that the absence of an accusatorial procedure, as in the seminar-style hearing, places an inquisitorial burden on an Inspector to ensure that all issues are examined thoroughly. In discharging this burden and in its conclusion that a fair Hearing did not occur in this case, the Court sounded a warning that 'the "more relaxed" atmosphere could lead not to a "full and fair" Hearing but to a less than thorough examination of the issues. A relaxed Hearing is not necessarily a fair Hearing . . .'.

The *Dyason* case examined the way that evidence is tested in the Hearing, namely by virtue of discussion and not cross-examination. Lord Justice Pill established something of a 'benchmark' against which hearings in particular and planning appeals in general may be measured when he stated that

> Planning permission having been refused, conflicting propositions and evidence will often be placed before an Inspector on appeal. Whatever procedure is followed the strengths of a case can be determined only upon an understanding of that case and by testing it with reference to propositions in the opposing case. At a public local inquiry the Inspector, in performing that task, usually has the benefit of cross-examination on behalf of the other party. If cross-examination disappears, the need to examine propositions in that way does not disappear with it. Further, the statutory right to be heard is nullified unless, in some way, the strength of what one party says is not only listened to by the tribunal but is assessed for its own worth and in relation to opposing contentions.

While this case of itself did not result in reform of the Hearing method, the judgement of Lord Justice Pill made Inspectors acutely aware of their inquisitorial duty to examine evidence at the Hearing. After *Dyason* it was more often the case that Inspectors would rather play an active than a passive role in the discussion of planning merits. Research into perception of the Hearing by Stubbs (1999–2000) revealed favourable endorsement of this method by planning consultants and planning officers alike. *Dyason* when set alongside these findings was viewed as an isolated case of bad practice. Stubbs (1999) found that following a survey of planning practitioners they were . . . 'more than content that Hearings can maintain high standards of openness, fairness and impartiality within an informal setting'. Two years after *Dyason* the government revised the guidance covering conduct of the parties at the Hearing.[17] It countenanced the limited introduction of cross-examination at

Hearings, where deemed appropriate by the parties, to test evidence. Apart from such a somewhat odd innovation (which may potentially compromise the informality of the Hearing method) no material revisions were made to the guidance following *Dyason*. It appears reasonable to conclude from this that the government and Inspectorate also viewed *Dyason* as an isolated case of bad practice, with few longer-term ramifications for the overall fairness of this method. Nevertheless, lessons were learnt from this case, especially that Inspectors may need to be inquisitorial in their own questioning and examination of evidence.

Public Inquiry

The Public Inquiry is the most formal, as well as formidable, method of planning appeal. Procedure is governed by a set of statutory rules, which establish that written statements of evidence shall be exchanged by both sides prior to the Inquiry. At the Inquiry, each side will appear with an expert witness or witnesses who will be open to cross-examination by, in most cases, trained advocates (see Case study 4.4 and Table 4.6).

The exact procedure varies between cases decided by Inspectors (transferred cases) and those decided by the Deputy Prime Minister (recovered cases).

Cases determined by the Secretary of State (recovered cases)

In such cases an Inspector will be appointed to hold an Inquiry and to produce a decision letter with a recommendation. The Deputy Prime Minister or a senior official will consider this recommendation and either agree or disagree with the Inspector's findings.[18] Such cases usually involve large-scale proposals, with an Inquiry lasting many weeks. A pre-Inquiry meeting may be held during which practical and procedural issues will be considered, such as establishing a timetable of witness appearances for the duration of the Inquiry. The Deputy Prime Minister will provide a statement of matters on which he wishes to be informed by the parties. This will assist the parties in their preparation for the Inquiry and guide them in identifying certain key areas for the principle focus of their evidence.

Summary: Informal hearings – key characteristics

- written exchange of evidence followed by 'round the table' discussion
- Inspector plays important role in controlling the decision
- increasing popularity from mid-1980s onwards; since 1992/3 more popular than Inquiry
- procedure governed by a code of practice and not statutory rules
- half-way house between Written Representations and Public Inquiry in speed of decision, and professional fees involved
- since 1992, application for an award of costs can be made at Informal Hearing
- accounts for 5–10 per cent of all appeals (dramatic growth to 20% – 2003).

Table 4.6 Timetable for the Public Inquiry (transferred cases)

Time	Procedure
	Appellant submits appeal forms
	Secretary of State (Inspectorate) issues an acknowledgement letter, establishing start date (referred to as relevant notice or RN)
Two weeks	LPA return questionnaire
Six weeks	• Both LPA and Appellant submit statements of their case (full particulars of the case including relevant statute and case law, but not detailed evidence) • Third parties to submit any comments/observations
Nine weeks	Observations on case advanced by other party or any third party must be made
(By) Twelve weeks	Inspectorate may send the parties a list of the matters about which it wishes to be informed
4 weeks BEFORE Inquiry	LPA and Appellant submit proofs of evidence (detailed professional evidence) and statement of any common ground reached between the two sides (agreed factual information)
INQUIRY No later than 20 (Inspector cases) or 22 weeks (Secretary of State cases) from start date/relevant notice	Each witness presents evidence by reading from proofs of evidence (or a summary) which is then open to cross-examination
Site visit	Accompanied site visit, similar to that conducted for the Written Representation site visit
Decision letter issued	No target set (i.e. minimum number of weeks after decision).

Cross-examination

The Inquiry procedure rules are designed to ensure that the Inquiry time is used most effectively in helping the Inspector in arriving at an informed development control decision. Successive reforms of the Inquiry rules have been designed to avoid wasted time, while allowing each party to fully present its case and 'test' the planning evidence presented by the other side. In 1992 the rules were reformed to require a written summary to accompany any proof of evidence exceeding a threshold of 1500 words. Summaries themselves should not exceed 10 per cent of the length of the proof. Brevity in evidence was thus encouraged and if this were not possible then only the summary and not the full proof would be read out at the Inquiry (although all evidence is open to cross-examination). The 2000 rules, in similar vein, required submission of a 'statement of common ground' between LPA and appellant. This would cover matters of fact (site dimensions, planning history) and technical methodologies (such as how design standards or

Case study 4.3

Proposal: The LPA refuses planning permission to build two new houses within a backland site in a Conservation Area. At the application stage, considerable local opposition is voiced against the proposal. The application is refused permission for several reasons:

- The proposal is contrary to the nature and form of development within this Conservation Area.
- The proposal would result in an unacceptable loss of existing trees within the site, which make an important contribution to the appearance of the Conservation Area.
- The proposal is contrary to conservation policies within the local plan.

Appraisal: The magnitude and complexity of the case are greater than in Case study 4.1, yet they are still relatively straightforward, principally the impact on the character and appearance of the Conservation Area. However, the possibility of considerable third-party representation rules out the Informal Hearing, leaving either a Written Representation or Public Inquiry. If the developer is happy to bear the additional cost and time involved, an Inquiry allows the opportunity to deal effectively with any third parties who wish to appear by means of cross-examination.

air-quality standards were arrived at). By therefore identifying matters not in dispute valuable Inquiry time is saved. The most tangible advantage of the Inquiry is the ability to cross-examine witnesses who appear on behalf of the LPA, appellant or third parties (see Case study 4.3). In this respect the Inquiry may take on the appearance of a court, with the adversarial stance taken by either side and the frequent use of barristers or solicitors to present the case for either side. It is not, then, uncommon for the Inquiry to be viewed as a judicial hearing, but this is misleading. A court hearing involves strict rules of evidence that may rule some evidence inadmissible, for example hearsay evidence. A planning Public Inquiry, although governed by statutory rules, deals with a good deal of opinion-based argument, for example the professional judgement of a witness in how to interpret a particular policy, or the relative balance between policy and other material considerations in arriving at a decision, constitute such judgement.

In an Inquiry, cross-examination should not be used to discredit any witnesses but instead to test the validity of facts or assumptions, explore how policy relates to the merits of the case and to identify and narrow the issues in dispute. At the inquiry only the applicant (or appellant), local planning authority and any statutory party (such as English Heritage, who are consulted on specific Listed Buildings/Conservation Area matters) are entitled to cross-examine. The Inspector enjoys the discretion to allow other persons to do so, notably third parties (objectors). In 2002 and for a trial period it was agreed by the Planning Inspectorate and Planning Bar (representing advocates) that barristers would remain seated during cross-examination of witnesses. This change to protocol was introduced to reduce the adversarial nature of Inquiries.[19]

Case study 4.4

Proposal: The LPA refuses planning permission for an office redevelopment within a town centre location for the following reasons:

- The proposal is considered to be contrary to local plan policy that identifies the site as being suitable for retail development.
- Insufficient parking is provided within the site, resulting in congestion on the neighbouring highway.
- Excessive height, and mass, of proposal resulting in a form of development out of scale with surrounding development.
- In the absence of any contribution towards highway improvements on surrounding roads, the LPA considers that the additional traffic generated will result in an unacceptable increase in congestion, detrimental to the free flow of traffic and highway safety.

Appraisal: This appeal raises several complex technical issues (policy, material considerations and possible need for planning obligations) and a proposal of some magnitude. The financial cost of professional representation would be high, involving possibly several different professionals (planning, highway engineering and architectural) to deal with the different reasons. The Public Inquiry presents the best method with which to deal with these issues, with the significant benefit of being able to cross-examine the other side.

Inquiry format

The Inquiry format and various tactical considerations can be considered as in Table 4.7.

The nature of evidence

In all methods of planning appeal 'evidence' may be produced in several ways. In all appeals this evidence may comprise both fact and opinion/ judgement. For example, note the distinctions between facts and opinion in Table 4.8.

Summary: Public Inquiries – key characteristics

- suitable for more complex cases
- written exchange of statements and proofs of evidence followed by Inquiry with formal rules of procedure involving evidence in chief, cross-examination, re-examination and submission
- appeal method of longest duration
- most expensive (in professional fees) for appellant and Inspectorate (in administration and Inspector's time)
- procedures (exchange of evidence and Inquiry conduct) governed by statutory rules
- least used method but tends to deal with the most important cases
- smallest proportion of all appeals: 5–10 per cent

Table 4.7 Planning Inquiry format 'on the day'

Format	Details	Tactics
Inspector opens Inquiry	Statement that Inquiry is to be held and short explanation of procedure. Inspector notes names of advocates, witnesses and any third parties. The Inspector will identify the principal issues to be considered at the Inquiry.	
Local Planning Authority's case		
LPA Evidence in Chief	As below	As below
Appellant may cross-examine		
LPA may re-examine		
Inspector may ask questions of witness		
Appellant's case		
Appellant's Evidence in Chief	Each witness reads proof or summary plus any additional oral explanation.	Deal with reasons for refusal point by point.
LPA may cross-examine each witness	Opportunity to test evidence by oral examination.	Agree common ground + Focus on differences + Test validity of differences.
Appellant may re-examine	Advocate may deal with issues raised in cross-examination.	Must avoid leading witness or introducing fresh evidence.
Inspector may ask the witness questions.		
*Third Party Evidence**		
Closing submissions by LPA, third parties* and appellant	Summary of case as emerged from evidence/cross/re-examination.	An extremely important opportunity to target what has been conceded in cross-examination. The appellant enjoys the last word.
Inspector will close Inquiry, then . . .		No discussion of the merits of the case, while on site.
Site visit		

* At discretion of Inspector. Third Party individuals or groups may be permitted to present their own case and question the appellant.

Table 4.8 Examples of evidence produced in Planning Appeals

Facts	Opinion
Planning policy issues, i.e. the site is or is not covered by policies A, B or C. This is a matter of fact.	Some policies are vague in detail or broad in their application and require opinion to decide on how they should be interpreted.
It is a matter of fact that the site is within a Conservation Area.	Conservation policy states that development must preserve or enhance the character/appearance. It may be a matter of opinion that a proposal satisfies such criteria.
Carparking or amenity space standards, i.e. does the proposal satisfy such standards. This is a matter of fact; e.g. proposal provides five spaces and standards require seven spaces – fails standards by two.	Whether rigid adherence to carparking standards is required is a matter of opinion; e.g. surrounding roads contain plenty of parking on the kerbside, so two additional cars would not result in any harm to the free flow of parking.

Instructing an advocate

The professionals who appear at a Planning Inquiry divide into two distinct kinds: the advocate and the expert witness. The advocate principally presents and leads the case by making speeches and submissions to the Inspector and by examining and cross-examining witnesses. The advocate is 'neutral' with respect to the case merits. He or she does not express a personal view and need not even believe in the merits of the case. While advocates must not knowingly mislead or deceive the Inspector, their main goal is to present their case in its best possible light. The advocate can be a barrister, solicitor, planner or surveyor. Planning Inquiries are not the subject of strict rules of audience, so anyone may appear as an advocate, although a professional grasp of advocacy skills is desirable. With the increased formality or 'judicialization' of planning appeals over the last 40 years, specialist planning barristers have emerged as the most commonly used advocates. Most are members of the Planning and Environment Bar Association (PEBA) and their principal work involves environmental and planning law and advocacy.

Members of a number of property related professional bodies, including the Royal Town Planning Institute, Royal Institution of Chartered Surveyors and Royal Institution of British Architects, may instruct a barrister without reference (as was required in the past) to a solicitor. This 'direct professional access' means that the instructing planner, surveyor or architect must brief the barrister concerned with all relevant papers and is responsible for the payment of fees.

The witness provides an expert view consistent with a professional opinion. This will require the witness to present a distinct body of expertise in a proof of evidence and oral defence of it under cross-examination at the Inquiry. This evidence *must* be consistent with the witness's own professional opinion. The expert planning witness is not a 'hired gun' who will simply say whatever the client or planning committee wish them to say. Such matters of professional conduct or ethics are dealt with by the various professional bodies. The Royal Institution of Chartered Surveyors[20] guidance in such matters is that . . . 'The Surveyor's evidence must be independent, objective and unbiased. In particular, it must not be biased towards the party who is responsible for paying him. The evidence should be the same whoever is paying for it.'

In similar vein the Royal Town Planning Institute's professional code states . . . 'The town planner as a witness at an Inquiry is there to give evidence which must be true evidence . . . if the evidence is . . . given in the form of a professional opinion it must be the planner's own professional opinion if it is to carry weight as expert evidence'.[21]

It may be the case that the planning officer is giving evidence after the planning committee had overturned a recommendation to grant permission. This situation may appear rather odd, in that the planning officer who recommended a grant of permission is now given the onerous task of defending that refusal at appeal. Professional guidance is unambiguous: 'care must be taken to avoid giving the impression that any statement made or views expressed at the Inquiry represent a planner's own view if these are contrary to his or her bona fide professional opinion . . . [the planning officer should be] . . . frank and open about his or her professional opinion.'

This situation is a product of the democratic process in which a planning committee may reject officer recommendation providing that they have sound planning grounds for so doing. It is preferable that a member of a planning committee gives evidence in these circumstances. However, officers are on occasion called upon to represent their council without compromising their own personal and professional views.

The award of costs

In all planning appeal proceedings, each party is expected to pay their own costs. The power to award costs in planning Appeals was first introduced in 1933. Since 1972 the Local Government Act has enabled the Secretary of State or Inspector to require that one party pays the costs of another in planning appeals.[22] Key features of this provision are that:

- it is available in all public Inquiry and Informal Hearing appeals[23]
- it is also available in all enforcement appeals or listed-building enforcement notice appeals submitted by Written Representation
- applications for an award must usually be made within the appeal procedure; at Public Inquiry or Informal Hearing this is usually before the close
- the award covers the costs of attending and preparing for the appeal. It does not deal with the financial costs relating to the purchase of a site, the development of which has been delayed by the fighting of a planning appeal, loss of profit, and so on
- the award is made because of unreasonable conduct by a party, which has caused another party unnecessary expense

- the award does not automatically follow the appeal decision, e.g. if the decision of the Inspector is to allow the appeal it does not infer costs will follow. If an LPA fails to support a reason for refusal with evidence, this can constitute unreasonable behaviour, and costs may be awarded to the developer. However, the merits of the appeal and merits of costs are dealt with entirely separately.
- In an average year the Planning Inspectorate will deal with 14 000 planning appeal decisions of which 3000 involve Inquiries or Hearings from which most applications for reimbursement of costs are made annually. One-sixth of such applications for costs are granted. In a typical year, therefore, around 500 cost awards are made out of a total of 14 000 appeals, an incidence of one award in every 28 appeal decisions.

The award of costs represents a penalty against either party for unreasonable conduct in appeal proceedings. During the 1980s the majority of awards were made against local planning authorities. Research undertaken between 1987 and 1990 indicated that costs had been awarded against an LPA 6.5 times more frequently than against appellants (Blackhall 1990, Association of Metropolitan Authorities 1989). During this period the government was seeking to 'deregulate' the planning system by establishing, in policy guidance, a presumption in favour of granting planning permission. A development boom resulted in the submission of many more planning applications, and planning committees found themselves overturning officer recommendations and refusing planning permission in order to pacify local opposition to this 'tide' of new development. Research (ibid.) indicated that costs were more likely to be awarded in cases where the planning committee had rejected a recommendation by the Chief Planning Officer.

The volume of costs awarded in favour of the appellant or the LPA has fluctuated over the years. Both government planning policy and the level of property development in the economy has influenced these statistics. For example, during the property boom of the 1980s, when policy established a 'presumption in favour of development', appellants were winning around 90 per cent of all cost applications. Local government planners at the time understandably viewed the costs regime as a penalty against them and the Planning Committee. By the 1990s, with boom turning to recession and policy changing to a presumption in favour of the Development Plan, the 90 per cent statistic fell to 60 per cent. During the 1990s and into the 2000s the level of awards granted has stabilized at around two-thirds to appellants and the remainder to LPAs. Consequently the professional perception of costs has changed among LPAs and the current regime is increasingly viewed as a more even handed sanction against unreasonable behaviour.

Costs were only marginally more likely to be granted in favour of the appellant after a planning committee had rejected a recommendation by the Chief Planning Officer. Stubbs (2000 and 2001) concluded after analysis of a sample of 500 costs decisions . . . 'Costs were granted in 35 per cent of all councillor-led decisions, compared to 27 per cent of officer-led ones . . . a straightforward conclusion is that a refusal based upon a reversal of the Chief Planning Officer's recommendation is absolutely no guarantee of success on a costs applications'.

Table 4.9 Examples of the award of costs

Facts		Evidential	
(A) Unreasonable behaviour	(B) Resulting in unnecessary expense	(A) Unreasonable behaviour	(B) Resulting in unnecessary expense
Failure to provide adequate pre-Inquiry statement, i.e. not setting out case or documents to be used. **Both sides.***	Waste of Inquiry time to establish the case produced by one side **or** results in need for adjournment.	Failure to provide evidence to support refusal. **Award against LPA.***	P/app should not have been refused in the first case or LPA have not justified their case so appeal unnecessary.
Failure to provide supporting information or late submission of proof of evidence.	Waste of Inquiry time to establish the case produced by one side **or** results in need for adjournment.	Planning policy† establishes that proposal was in accord with policy and therefore p/app should have been granted. **Against LPA.***	Matter should not have proceeded to appeal in the first place.
Introduce at late stage a new ground of appeal or legal ground in an enforcement appeal. **(Appellant)*** or reason for refusal **(LPA).***	Waste of Inquiry time to establish the case produced by one side **or** results in need for adjournment.	It was apparent from PPG or Circulars that the appeal had no reasonable chance of success (e.g. green belt policy).	Matter should not have proceeded to appeal in the first place.
Unreasonable/late withdrawal once Inquiry/Hearing has been arranged.	One side has wasted time in preparing for Inquiry unnecessarily.	It was apparent from a previous appeal on the site that a resubmission with amendments would be acceptable. **Against LPA.***	LPA should have granted resubmitted proposal, following the material consideration of the previous Inspector's decision.

* Party against whom costs would be awarded if an application for costs was made at the Inquiry/Hearing and the Inspector agreed.
† Some caution is required when considering this case. Most planning policy requires a good deal of interpretation and of course material considerations may 'indicate otherwise', making it difficult to establish unreasonable behaviour against either an appellant who proceeds to appeal on a matter that appears contrary to policy or an LPA that refuses an application that appears in accord with policy.

Evidently during the ten year period after the work by Blackhall (1990) the incidence of cost awards between LPAs and appellants had narrowed. While the chances of regaining costs following planning committee's rejection

---

Case study 4.5: Award of costs

Blackacre Holdings apply for planning permission to erect a block of flats with accommodation in the roofspace at Sylvan Avenue, Melchester. The Planning Officer recommends approval to the Melsham District Council Planning Committee. The Sylvan Avenue Residents Association (SARA) mount a vigorous campaign against the application. At the Committee Meeting the Sylvan Ward Councillor pleads with the committee to refuse permission. The committee decide to defer the application and visit the site to assess the impact of ten proposed dormers in the roofspace. At the next meeting they decide to refuse permission on grounds that 'The design of the roofscape is harmful to the character of the streetscene on Sylvan Avenue, which is predominantly of two-storey detached dwellings without dormer windows.'

Appraisal: The recommendation of the Chief Planning Officer has been over-turned by Planning Committee but this of itself does not mean that costs will follow. If the LPA can bring to an Inquiry/Hearing some evidence of harm they should be able to defend any application for costs by the appellant. The matter for the Inspector in deciding the planning merits is both a professional and subjective assessment of design-related issues. The committee visited the site and thus formed their own view on this matter. This case involves assessment of evidential and not procedural matters, and the extent to which the LPA can put forward a case (such as photographs and plans showing the character of the area and visual impact of the proposal). If they can present such a case then an Inspector will in all probability refuse any application for costs made by the appellant.

---

of officer's recommendation made a decision more vulnerable to an award.[24]

Examples of costs

To gain an award of costs, it is necessary to establish that one party has acted unreasonably, vexatiously or frivolously and that this behaviour has resulted in unnecessary expense for the other side (LPA, appellant or, in rare cases, third party).

In the majority of cases, applications for costs can be divided into those based on procedural issues and those based on evidential issues. Table 4.9 shows a series of examples to illustrate some common features of costs applications; however, they are by no means exhaustive. It is important to remember that criteria as stated under (A) and (B) must be satisfied for an award of costs to be granted in favour of one party. For an application for costs to succeed it may be helpful to consider the notion of a 'threshold'. In procedural matters this threshold is crossed when it can be demonstrated that by failing to follow various rules the other party was put to some tangible waste of time and, importantly, expense. In evidential matters the threshold is crossed where the evidence fails to have substance in its own right (see Case studies 4.5 and 4.6). It is not necessary for the Inspector to be

Case study 4.6: Award of costs

The fast-food chain, Tasty Burger, apply to change the use of an existing retail shop to a restaurant (A3) in the historic town centre of Wykham-in-the-Vale. Wykhamstead District Council, the LPA, refuse permission as 'The proposed ventilation ducting is unacceptably close to neighbouring residential property, resulting in a loss of amenity to those occupiers'.

Tasty Burger appeal. At the Hearing the appellant produces a report commissioned from an acoustic engineer, which concludes that noise trans-mission would be minimal and insufficient to be audible by neighbouring occupiers. The Planning Officer representing Wykhamstead District Council produces no technical report but argues that he has observed ducting at other A3 take-away uses while on his holidays at Compton-on-Sea and concludes that noise levels would be unacceptable.

Appraisal: The LPA have refused consent on a technical ground, dealing with noise levels arising from fume extraction ducting. To defend this at appeal technical acoustic evidence must be produced. The appellants have produced this evidence but the Council have failed to do so and rely on mere observation made by the Planning Officer when on his holidays (thus unrelated to this site).

The LPA have failed to produce any technical evidence and have not crossed the necessary evidential threshold. The appellant was put to unnecessary expense in paying for an acoustic report. If the appellant can demonstrate this then an Inspector will, in all probability, grant an application for reimburse-ment of the costs incurred in producing the acoustic report.

sufficiently persuaded by this evidence to rely upon it when determining the appeal. It is conceivable that an LPA may lose an appeal yet save costs by producing some evidence of demonstrable harm. What matters is that the LPA have produced some evidence, because to do so, even if the Inspector is not swayed by it in his decision, will render the LPA to be immune from any costs application mounted by the other side.

Conclusions

The planning appeal process plays a vital role in the town planning system granting power to challenge the decisions of the LPA. The procedures upon which the system is based are themselves shaped by the needs of natural justice and administrative efficiency. Most appellants seek speedy decision on appeal, but they also seek a system that allows for a full explanation of their case and requires the LPA to account for its decision. All three methods of appeal contain a balance between administrative efficiency and the rules of natural justice. The written method is quickest, with the least rigour in its examination of evidence, and the Inquiry is the longest, with the most rigour in its examination of evidence; the Hearing falls somewhere between the two. Changes to procedures have increasingly sought to improve efficiency by introducing timetables, rules and the award of costs.

It is important to recall the desire for appeal decisions to be made in a cost-effective way (for the Exchequer, which funds the system at an annual cost of around £26 million) and a speedy manner (for the benefit of appellant or LPA) as delay in the appeal system will delay the development process and act as a disincentive to any applicant seeking a review of a development-control decision. The Inspectorate is required to meet a series of performance indicators agreed with the Office of the Deputy Prime Minister and Welsh Office, together with its own internal 'Quality Assurance' standards. In a typical year such targets deal with both speed of decision-making (80 per cent of written representations in 18 weeks, public inquiries in 36 weeks and hearings in 24 weeks) and cost (e.g. cost to Inspectorate of processing a written representation to be around £700). A 'quality' target is also imposed in which 99 per cent of appeal casework is free from justified complaint (i.e. any factual error in a decision letter or inadequate or incorrect reasoning). In 2003 of 18554 decisions by the Inspectorate only 40 justified complaints arose. Such matters are independently vetted by an independent advisory panel on standards.[25]

In past years this drive towards procedural efficiency has resulted in some reforming proposals that have subsequently been dropped by government, following criticism that they would compromise the ability of appeals to deliver natural justice. Such ideas have included dropping the automatic entitlement to a Public Inquiry, issuing policy guidance to the effect that pursuing an Inquiry instead of an alternative method could be grounds for the award of costs, curtailing the opportunity to cross-examine at Inquiry, and widening the power to award costs to Written Representation. None of these ideas have been acted upon[26] and both the Planning Inspectorate and the Deputy Prime Minister have supported the appellant's automatic right to insist on a Public Inquiry. However, critics of the system are concerned that the increasing support of alternatives such as Informal Hearings is only the tip of the iceberg to reduce both the costs of appeal and length of time to reach a decision by ultimately either restricting access to the Public Inquiry method or the ability to cross-examine within that method.[27] This remains to be seen; however, the final push towards such dramatic reforms may ironically be the result of the activities of the property industry.

The key defining feature of the English and Welsh appeal system remains that it is essentially an adversarial system of dispute resolution in which the parties seek to challenge the evidence presented by the other side in a variety of written and oral exchanges, considered by an independent decision-maker (i.e. the Inspector). Further, with the Inspector's decision binding all parties the current planning appeal orthodoxy is best encapsulated as a form of 'independent professional decision-making' in which the Inspector brings an independent, objective and impartial determination of disputed facts or issues to the evidence presented by all sides (Bevan 1992). The Planning Inspectorate perform their duties to a very high standard indeed and Inspectors apply the Franks principles of openness, fairness and impartiality in the conduct of their duties. This high standard was recognized by the House of Commons Environment, Transport and Regional Affairs Select Committee report of 2000, *The Planning Inspectorate and Public Inquiries* (House of Commons 1999). The Committee noted that . . . 'The Planning

Inspectorate performs an extremely important task and we conclude that, in most aspects of its work, it is doing an excellent job'. Any criticisms were not levelled at the conduct of Inspectors but were a call for more transparency in their training, the handling of complaints, recruitment practices, and use of technology (such as the Internet). Such concerns dealt more with a desire to break down a perception by the Committee that the Inspectorate was secretive than to challenge the very high standards it achieves in the discharge of its decision-making functions. By 2005 the Inspectorate will introduce an Internet 'portal' allowing appeals to be submitted electronically and progress monitored.

The establishment of the Franks principles of openness, fairness and impartiality have created valuable quasi-judicial guidelines to establish due process in the conduct of planning appeals. The importance of these principles cannot be understated. Yet, one notable consequence of them has been a trend towards increasing levels of judicial control over planning. It is perhaps arguable that the recovery of costs at Inquiries and Hearings and the introduction of strict timetables for the submission of evidence fit into this trend by imposing greater mechanisms of control over the conduct of a case. Planning appeals are, however, also responsible for the discharge of an administrative/development control function, notably to determine the merits of a case. Hearings may be seen as representing a refreshing diversion from or counter to this trend of progressive judicialization. Michael Howard, when Minister for Planning, said in 1988 of the hearing method: '. . . there are obvious limits to its use but it is a development I welcome which I believe in many ways gets nearer to the original intention of an inquiry than the much more formal way which has developed over the years' (Howard 1989).

It is arguable that Hearings allow for a more direct way of uncovering development control issues than by cross-examination at Inquiry. Part of the concern, as expressed in the *Dyason* case, was that planning issues may not be exposed to sufficient enquiry or testing, the corollary of which is that unfairness may result and the Inspector be unaware of all relevant issues. Further, it may be conceivable that as an appellant may not automatically opt for public inquiry and cross-examination then evidence may not always be subjected to a thorough scrutiny.

Consideration of the *Dyason* case may help us to focus future debate about planning appeals towards certain key areas. 'Informal dispute resolution' has a role to play in the planning system. Set against a post-Franks trend towards greater judicialization of planning appeals, the favourable endorsement of hearings uncovered by research by Stubbs (1999) demonstrates that it is possible to depart from an adversarial and formal testing of evidence and maintain a professional view that the process is fair and that an adequate discovery and testing of development control issues is undertaken. One of the most meaningful lessons to emerge from the work by Stubbs (ibid.) is that informality of method and delivery of fairness are not mutually exclusive. By striking an acceptable balance between them as hearings do facilitates an acceptable uncovering of appeal merits in a manner that obviates the need for judicial techniques such as cross-examinations to test a case or expose an argument.

Future directions

The planning appeal system is the subject of almost constant review and reform. During the 12 year period 1988–2000 three sets of procedural timetables were introduced. External pressures imposed by both government (in targets for decision-making) and by 'users' of the system (in their expectation of efficiency and fairness) result in an almost constant 'drip feed' of new initiatives. In past years such changes have maintained the central foundation of planning appeals, notably the traditional method of dispute resolution previously encapsulated as 'independent professional decision-making'. Since 2000, two new developments may serve to change this traditional landscape of dispute resolution and ramifications arising from their introduction should be closely monitored in the period 2001–5. First, the introduction of the Human Rights Act 1998 (enacted in England and Wales in October 2000) may 'open a can of worms [and] nobody had any idea of the size of the can.'[28] Second, the result of a pilot study of Alternative Dispute Resolution in 2000 may herald future reforms that set out to change the 'traditional' culture that influences the way in which planning appeals are resolved. Both are the subject of greater attention in the following chapter. Their amalgamated influence on the system may result in 'root and branch' reform over the next decade. Whatever happens, any such future reforms will be assessed, in similar fashion to past reforms, against the benchmarks of due process established by the Franks Committee of 1957, namely the discharge of openness, fairness and impartiality in all decision-making.

5 The future for dispute resolution in planning

Two distinct areas will be considered, namely those of Alternative Dispute Resolution (mediation) in planning, and human rights legislation and its consequences. Both challenge current thinking and provide innovative solutions to some existing problems in the appeal system. Over the next few years both planning practitioners and casual spectators of the system are well advised to monitor developments in these two areas.

Introduction to alternative dispute resolution

Alternative Dispute Resolution (ADR) is a convenient, if imprecise, expression by which a whole raft of dispute resolution procedures may be classified. Mediation is one of the best known methods of ADR. The methods covered are considered to fall outside traditional litigation and arbitration (including planning appeals). Brown and Marriot (1993) provided a good definition: 'ADR may be defined as a range of procedures which serve as alternatives to the adjudication procedures of litigation and arbitration for the resolution of disputes'.

Mediation, therefore, represents but one method of resolving dispute within the broader spectrum of ADR. ADR has been viewed as an umbrella term (Bevan, 1992) to cover a variety of dispute resolution systems that share a common aim of seeking to act as alternatives to traditional methods in which disputes are resolved by the imposition of a decision upon the parties. Such traditional methods (i.e. litigation or arbitration, mostly in courts) have been criticized, for the high cost imposed on parties, the delay in getting a case heard and the formality and adversarial nature of the proceedings (Rogers, 1990). ADR mechanisms have been credited with many advantages, perhaps the most frequently cited ones being that they seek a consensual outcome that is acceptable to both parties, in which each party enjoys ownership of the decision (thus increasing the likelihood of improved user satisfaction) and that it is administratively expedient because it may save time and expense to the disputing parties.

The Land and Environment Court of New South Wales introduced town planning mediations in 1991, representing one of the first such innovations to be used in environmental disputes world-wide. This was introduced for a number of reasons. First, there was a recognition of a growing awareness and promotion within Australia of the benefits of ADR in general to solve disputes (Astor and Chinkin, 1992). Second, there was an increasing awareness of the costs involved in litigation and the fact that a major source of costs in local government legal expenditure was accounted for by litigation to defend council planning decisions on appeal to the Land and Environment Court (Parliament of New South Wales, 1991). Finally, there was a desire to make decision-making more open, accessible and less formal (Pearlman, 1995), coupled with the fear that litigation, environmental or otherwise, was becoming increasingly lengthy, complex and prone to delay (Fowler 1992). This lead taken by the Land and Environment Court established an important prototype that has subsequently influenced the system in England and Wales. This section will consider the theory and practice of ADR, to be followed by discussion of how this process may affect planning decision-making.

ADR: establishing a definition

Literature on ADR abounds with many definitions. This material provides a useful starting point by establishing common terms and allowing certain technicalities to be unravelled.

At the most elementary level ADR represents a generic term (Mackie 1997) or convenient label, as claimed by diverse interests, under which a whole series of non-binding dispute resolution techniques may be collected (Heilbron 1994). Such techniques have evolved as a reaction to the formal determination of disputes by means of litigation (Street 1992, Briner 1997). Litigation is viewed as a sovereign remedy of dispute resolution, in which a judicial determination in a court of law will produce a transparent and binding settlement built upon the traditional adversarial principle, where the parties dictate at all stages the form, content and pace of proceedings. Arbitration, by contrast, is based upon the parties to a dispute giving power to an independent third party to make an adjudicatory award which will, in similar terms to litigation, determine the dispute and be binding upon both sides (Miller op. cit.). The UK literature considers arbitration to fall outside ADR and within the traditional system.

It has been argued that it would be more accurate to refer to ADR as 'Complementary' Dispute Resolution (Harrison 1997), 'Appropriate' Dispute Resolution (Acland 1990, Mackie *et al.* 1995) or even 'Additional' Dispute Resolution, in that they reflect more accurately the desire for ADR to provide for a series of subsidiary processes that are often pursued simultaneously with court proceedings, rather than seeking to compete with the established legal system (Astor and Chinkin 1992, Street 1991). Further employment of an approach based upon adjudication and adversarial encounter may be viewed as inappropriate where personal or working relationships need to be preserved between the parties to a dispute (Brown and Marriot 1993, Chapter 2). ADR has a defined role to play in providing appropriate methods of dispute resolution when a settlement is to be based upon consensus, in which relationships are to be maintained between the respective parties. This means that ADR will not replace litigation but would necessarily be employed to make traditional adjudicatory or adversarial systems work more efficiently and effectively.

ADR theory

A whole raft of literature deals with process and mechanism. A series of individual ADR systems has been described and evaluated against ADR theory or against other 'traditional' methods of dispute resolution. The whole machinery of ADR has commonly been viewed as referring to a series of processes such as conciliation, mediation, mini-trial, or neutral evaluation (Mackie 1991, Mackie *et al.* 1995). The outcome of the process is determined by mutual consent of the parties, with varying assistance from a neutral facilitator. In Britain, as many as 13 possible derivatives of ADR have been identified (O'Connor 1992) drawing upon the variations of techniques adopted by specialist ADR organizations and hybrid methods that amalgamate a selection of procedures such as 'med-arb' and 'concilo-arb', mediation/conciliation and arbitration methods (Newman 1996a and b). The subject area can easily become confusing. It is therefore often easier to focus upon a number of shared characteristics, namely that processes are largely informal (Folger and Jones 1994) in content with no prescribed or set method (Beckwith 1987, Kendrick 1995) and that consent will be required from all parties. Such features are key to establishing the fundamentals of ADR. ADR techniques may be classified broadly into those directed towards reaching agreement over an issue or set of issues, and those that seek to develop greater understanding while falling short of actual agreement (Dukes 1996). As a consequence, ADR techniques may produce a settlement outright, or serve to narrow the dispute, combined with greater understanding of the stance taken by the other party.

Mediation is a 'facilitative' process (Brown and Marriot 1993: 99) whereby a neutral third party (mediator) assists the parties to a dispute to reach a self-determined agreement (Dana 1990) based on consensual solutions (MacFarlane 1997). The mediator enjoys no authoritative decision-making power to assist the disputing parties, who must reach their own mutually acceptable settlement (Moore 1996: 14), but strives to create conditions that are conducive to concluding a successful negotiation (Moore 1996).

Definitions of mediation concentrate on how it incorporates techniques that assist parties to explore and/or achieve a voluntary negotiated settlement after consideration of the alternatives. Such settlement may be identified as an 'early stage procedure' to prevent disputes entering the Courts or as a 'settlement conduit' after legal proceedings have been commenced (Roberts 1995). The most straightforward purpose of mediation has been viewed as the creation of an atmosphere favourable to negotiation (Curle 1990). No set procedure is prescribed, and it would be misleading to infer that the term 'mediation' implies one consistent and uniform procedure adopted by all practitioners (Brown and Marriot, op. cit). The mediator will, however, be responsible for helping to establish a number of key features governing the confidentiality of the technique, the way in which joint discussions and negotiations are held, and the holding of private caucus meetings between mediator and individual party (Williams 1990). The neutrality of the mediator ensures that he or she is impartial towards all sides. It does not prohibit the mediator from expressing a view on the merits of the case (i.e. from being evaluative), although this is not a precondition of the mediator's role and he or she may seek to act in a purely facilitative capacity (Dana 1990) by seeking to foster negotiation and settlement between both sides without expressing an opinion. Some commentators view mediation as being exclusively within the realm of facilitative settlement, indeed referring to it as 'facilitated, collaborative problem solving' (Burton 1988).

The distinction between facilitative (or interest-based) mediation and evaluative (or rights-based) mediation does itself establish a division of methodologies in the mediation process, and this is reflected in literature and theory. A spectrum is established in which some commentators hold that a mediator should only facilitate, others that evaluation is the principal means by which settlement can be created and others, a midway position in which both are employed, to varying degrees, in an attempt to move the process forward (Brown and Marriot 1993: 114). The role of the mediator is central to the process, assisting each party to examine and highlight the respective strengths and weaknesses of their case (O'Connor 1992) and to explore options that may lead to a settlement. To achieve this, the mediator must possess different qualities and skills from that of a judge (or planning inspector), principally the ability to act in a facilitative capacity (Robertshaw and Segal 1993). Such facilitation by the mediators is used to build and secure a settlement and is best considered as a three-tier process. This comprises information gathering (to understand priorities), diagnostic tactics (to make predictions about the basis of settlement) and movement tactics (in which the mediator attempts to tackle power relationships between the parties) (Kolb 1983). Such movement tactics involve fostering communication by procedures such as chairing joint and private sessions and by reporting between each side (ibid.).

Many advantages and disadvantages have been attributed to ADR (Heilbron 1994, Newman 1997, Mackie 1995, Shilston 1996). One of the most commonly cited advantages is the saving of time and expense to participating parties (O'Connor 1992, Acland 1995a, b and c, Dukes 1996), usually a benefit claimed without any real evidence in support of it. Again, limited research into this area during the 1980s (Williams 1990), together with the reported findings of specialist mediation centres such as the Centre for Dispute Resolution (CEDR) (Mackie 1997), have reinforced the perception that ADR can produce settlements in more than 70 per cent and sometimes as high as 90 per cent of cases. Furthermore, the suitability of case is determined not by the issues or legal questions involved but by what the parties want to achieve (ADR Group 1993). Alongside such benefits to the participants are the tangible benefits to the courts, as a backlog of cases may be cleared and the general level of litigation reduced (Heilbron 1994). The other body of advantages tend to focus upon how ADR improves the quality of decision-making by seeking an outcome that is based on consensual settlement and not imposed arbitration (Kolb 1983) and in which harmonious relationships may be maintained between the parties.

ADR and justice

A distinctive body of literature identifies a fundamental concern over the procedural fairness of ADR systems. This material also examines the relationship between ADR and the courts, seeking to identify problems in, for example, court-annexed ADR. Such concerns are important and attention needs to be drawn to them at an early stage before considering how this process may be accommodated in the planning system. Justice may itself be perceived as relating both to procedural matters and to the distribution of resources in society. Literature on jurisprudence (the philosophy of law) establishes that procedural justice is heavily dependent upon the individuals' perception of fairness in the rules or procedures that regulate a process or produce a decision. This may require that legislation result in a generally beneficial consequence for at least one party and that most people will obey such rules or guidelines (Harris 1980). Justice is often held to involve adherence to a judicial process and its outcome (ibid.). Justice is not the same as fairness and indeed a number of influential works in the early 1980s dealt with the central criticism that justice was not routinely achieved by litigation (Twining 1993), also that ADR was unlikely to deliver greater access to justice within 'American' society (Abel 1982, Auerbach 1983: 146). Such work may reflect wider inequality in society than just that related to legal mechanisms. Nevertheless, in delivering judicial fairness or a wider access to justice, it is important that public perceptions of the process are taken into account.

Mediation, for example, involves the possibility of a series of private caucus meetings between one party and the mediator, designed to encourage greater candour in establishing the criteria for settlement of a dispute. In addition, the combined informality and confidentiality of mediation/ conciliation may restrict the proper disclosure or discovery of expert evidence (O'Connor 1992). Third parties may appear only at the discretion of the principal parties and the wide discretion given to the mediator may result in considerable inconsistency across the number of cases considered.

It has been reported that the greatest cause of concern among lawyers is a mediator in private caucus with one side, because it is impossible to assess the impact on the mediator in the absence of the right to question or rebut what is said (Elliott 1996). Natural justice concerns are seen to be raised most often in mediations that rely heavily on private caucusing (ibid.). The caucus may greatly assist the mediator to broker a settlement by allowing for the ventilation of grievances/justifications, consideration of respective strengths and weaknesses, and exploration of bargaining or settlement positions. Much of the literature focuses on such attributes, albeit that several commentators dealing with the ethical foundations of mediation acknowledge the sensitivity of the caucus and the problems it raises for delivery of natural justice (because the mediator hears one side in the absence of the other) and public perceptions (a potential misconception that deals are being struck in private).

Associated with these concerns about the inclusion and measurement of fairness of some ADR methods is the view that such criticisms render ADR obsolete as a dispute resolution procedure to be employed within court jurisdiction. Mediation is gradually being used as an adjunct to the court system in England and Wales, following practices established in the US and Australia (Brown and Marriot 1993: 38). Such court-annexed mediation began with family law in County Court jurisdictions in the mid-1980s and

Table 5.1 Basis of principled negotiation

People:	Separate the people from the problem.
Interests:	Focus on interests, not positions.
Options:	Generate a variety of possibilities before deciding what to do.
Criteria:	Insist that the result be based on some objective standard.

From: Fisher and Urry (1997).

has spread into a variety of civil cases and commercial matters. Some lawyers have expressed concern that mediation practices like caucusing run counter to the openness and fairness required by the courts in the maintenance of procedural justice (Street 1992, Naughton 1992). One of the most important and sensitive questions, therefore, is 'who should be responsible for the mediation process?' The exact location of the process is a key factor in shaping people's perception of mediation, such as should it be part of a court or appeal body like the Planning Inspectorate or should it be entirely separate and independent?

ADR in practice

The task of the mediator is to 'oil the wheels of communication' (CEDR 1997). The parties are responsible for solutions and discussion of merits, while the mediator is responsible for the process. What is fundamental to achieving a settlement is that the parties move from what is referred to as 'positional bargaining' to 'principled negotiation'. Fisher and Urry (1997) have written the most important single work in this area. They advanced the view that in most disputes parties adopt an initial position (often an extreme one) and in negotiation reach a mid-way compromise after entrenched positions have been adopted. Such an outcome is often unsatisfactory and arrived at only after much haggling and often anger. Fisher and Urry (ibid.) developed the concept of 'principled negotiation' based upon an understanding of the 'best alternative to a negotiated agreement' (BATNA). The key to unlocking the respective BATNAs of the disputing parties is to grasp their underlying interests so that the ultimate settlement satisfies those interests and is therefore fair in its outcome.

This method of negotiation may be broken down into four key components (set out in Table 5.1) which are designed to ensure that the ultimate settlement is fairer and more durable than one reached by positional bargaining.

The process itself involves a number of key stages (see Figure 5.1) although no rigid or set model is imposed and a more flexible interpretation is a matter for the mediator and the disputing parties. One fundamental principle is that commitment to a mediation is entirely voluntary and that either party may walk away from the negotiations at any time and return to a more traditional model of dispute resolution (i.e. back to court or planning inquiry).

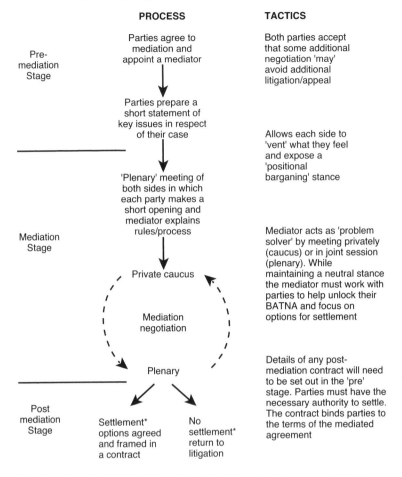

PROCESS   **TACTICS**

Pre-mediation Stage

Parties agree to mediation and appoint a mediator

Both parties accept that some additional negotiation 'may' avoid additional litigation/appeal

Parties prepare a short statement of key issues in respect of their case

Allows each side to 'vent' what they feel and expose a 'positional bargaining' stance

Mediation Stage

'Plenary' meeting of both sides in which each party makes a short opening and mediator explains rules/process

Mediator acts as 'problem solver' by meeting privately (caucus) or in joint session (plenary). While maintaining a neutral stance the mediator must work with parties to help unlock their BATNA and focus on options for settlement

Private caucus

Mediation negotiation

Plenary

Details of any post-mediation contract will need to be set out in the 'pre' stage. Parties must have the necessary authority to settle. The contract binds parties to the terms of the mediated agreement

Post mediation Stage

Settlement* options agreed and framed in a contract

No settlement* return to litigation

* Settlement may be partial or full. In a partial settlement a number of issues may be agreed, thus reducing the areas in dispute that remain.

Figure 5.1 Mediation process (typical model).

Mediation in town planning

Two trends running in parallel may be identified over the period 1995–2000, which have shaped a number of reforms culminating in the potential introduction of planning-based mediation. These trends may be distinguished as 'planning pull' and 'legal push'. Each will be considered.

'Legal push' in favour of ADR/mediation deals with the growing cultural awareness of ADR and in particular, with the emergence of court-annexed ADR over the period 1996–98. The Woolf Report of 1996 *Access to Justice* and subsequent reforms to the civil justice system in England and Wales were influential in promoting greater awareness generally of mediation. ADR/mediation is not without its sceptics in the legal profession, but the profile of civil law mediations is certainly rising. For example, Practice Directions promoting the employment of ADR are in place in the Court of Appeal, High Court and Commercial Court. Such directions thereby oblige lawyers to review cases for their ADR suitability at the commencement of court proceedings. Two pilot mediation programmes ran in the Central London County Court (CLCC) and Patents County Court, in 1996. In July 1999 a family mediation pilot project was instigated whereby solicitors, in certain areas of London, had to advise clients to consider mediation when seeking legal aid for family disputes. The introduction of mediation into such legal jurisdictions has pushed the legal profession into a greater awareness and employment of such an alternative mechanism of dispute resolution. Research work has also influenced awareness among lawyers.

Findings drawn from the Central London County Court pilot were published by Professor Hazel Genn (Genn 1998). These research findings were significant. For example, it was reported that despite rigorous attempts to stimulate demand for the available mediation option, demand for it among disputing parties remained consistent at about 5 per cent of all cases. Take-up was highest among disputes between businesses and lowest in personal injury cases. Where mediation was employed it resulted in settlement and withdrawal of court action in 62 per cent of all cases. Genn (1998) concluded that '. . . mediation appears to offer a process that parties on the whole find satisfying and, handled carefully, can lead to a situation in which a sense of grievance is reduced . . . [and that] . . . there is also strong evidence in this report that mediation at an early stage can reduce the length of cases even when cases do not actually settle at the mediation appointment.' Yet the report was also aware that actual take-up was 'pitifully small', and that greater promotion and a 'cultural shift' by lawyers away from traditional litigation would be required for it to increase in its popularity.

Such a cultural shift was evident even in its early stages, between 1998 and 2000. The Lord Chancellor, Lord Irvine, endorsed the benefits of mediation in civil justice on several occasions and new Civil Procedure Rules implemented in Spring of 1999, on the back of recommendations by Woolf (1996), required judges to promote the use of ADR in civil courts. The pre-eminence of such Law Lords as Woolf and Irvine, and endorsement by researchers like Professor Genn and practitioners like Professor Mackie, have raised a high profile for mediation that far exceeded its numerical impact on civil justice (measured by the number of cases mediated). This has kept a constant spotlight on mediation in legal journals, periodicals and books. While this means that mediation may be 'punching above its weight', the consequences are that this has influenced other disciplines in which disputes are to be settled. A number of government departments have introduced mediation pilots, including the Department of Trade and Industry, the Department of Health and (the then) Department of Environment, Transport and Regions. Town planning has been no exception to this trend.

In 1996, the Chief Planning Inspector promoted a discussion on the merits of planning mediation at the Royal Town Planning Institute National Conference. Later that year, speaking to the North West Branch of the Royal Town Planning Institute,[1] he said of ADR: 'It is a technique which is spreading rapidly. . . . It should be considered as part of the planning process.'

Three years later, also at the National Conference, he hosted a workshop session on a simulated planning mediation. The Chief Planning Inspector's enthusiasm for a debate in this area followed similar lines to the approach of many lawyers as previously addressed, namely that it is an innovation laden with sufficient benefits to render it worthy of further employment.

'Planning pull' deals with the way mediation is drawn or pulled into the planning system by government for the less than utopian desire to reduce the burden of appeals to be determined by the planning inspectorate. By reducing this burden the appeals remaining in the system would be dealt with more efficiently (i.e. quickly) as resources were freed. Government and the planning inspectorate have set out, over many years, to improve the service provided to appellants, third parties and local planning authorities at appeal. An appropriate balance must be struck between delivery of the Franks principles (dealt with in the previous chapter) and efficiency (unit cost of each appeal to government and time taken to reach a decision). Between 1990 and 2000 various measures have been considered in pursuit of the goal of efficiency. Some have been implemented (such as adherence to procedural timetables for the exchange of evidence), while others have not (such as dropping the automatic right to cross-examine at Inquiry). Mediation in planning may be part of this general trend, in which reform of the system is principally designed to promote speed and reduce the cost of decisions. Perhaps not surprisingly, governments have promoted consideration of mediation in planning more in terms of its wider benefits to disputing parties. In May 1998 Richard Caborn, the (then) Planning Minister, in heralding a pilot programme of planning mediation said '. . . This pilot study will consider whether greater use of mediation can help to modernize the planning system'. By placing mediation within the modernizing agenda of government policy, Richard Caborn set out to establish a more utopian vision of mediation than one framed within the more grubby policy of cost-cutting and efficiency savings. The reality may fall somewhere between the two.

The potential for ADR in planning

Evidently the planning system is capable of accommodating some kind of ADR, with mediation being the most probable method. Research in this area presents a case in favour of its introduction but also draws attention to significant problems that must be addressed. The planning system is distinctive in having a democratic base, especially when compared to, say, purely commercial decisions. A planning mediation will decide upon matters that have been the subject of public comment or scrutiny and are usually made by locally elected councillors in a planning committee. In a commercial mediation the two parties may settle the matter, sign a mediation contract and walk away from the negotiating table. In a planning mediation a similar outcome would affect the powers of the planning committee and public perception of the local democratic process. In the 'worst-case' scenario, the planning committee would lose control in determining an application and the local electorate would perceive the mediation as a private deal struck between developer and LPA. Such potential criticisms must be addressed in any model of planning mediation. Indeed, the corollary of this is that planning mediation will need to be a tailor-made version of the commercial or court-annexed mediation to reflect this distinctive democratic constitution.

The potential enjoyed by planning mediation has been explored in two areas of research work by Stubbs (1997) and by Michael Welbank (DETR 2000e). These works examined respectively the potential to 'import' the New South Wales (Australia) model of planning mediations and the findings of a pilot study of 48 planning-based mediations conducted in England and Wales.

The work by Stubbs (1997) was based on examination of 108 town planning appeals. A matter of some significance is that the planning system in New South Wales is comparable to that in the UK (especially England and Wales), with appeals being determined on their development control merits (see Case study 5.1).

These 108 planning mediations represented about 5 per cent of all planning appeals submitted over a four-year period, a figure comparable to the take-up experienced by the Central London County Court in its 1998 pilot study (Genn op. cit.). Similarly, once a mediation was held settlement of the dispute was more than likely to follow, with 70 per cent of cases subject to settlement (compared to 62 per cent in the Central London County Court pilot). A questionnaire survey of practitioners within New South Wales did not reveal opposition to mediation, but the reverse: 'the opinions expressed by planning officers and consultants provided favourable endorsement of mediation of town planning appeals, with a significant amount of agreement on the suggested advantages of this option and some emphasis on the savings in time and money' (Stubbs op. cit.).

The findings of the study suggested that mediation, while demonstrating the benefit of saving time and money to the parties involved (assuming that settlement was reached), also improved the *quality* of dispute resolution by avoiding the adversarial and confrontational nature of the traditional appeal. The low take-up was not a function of unpopularity but rather of the number of cases in which negotiation was possible. In other words, 5 per cent reflected the volume of cases suitable for mediation, i.e. where additional assisted negotiation would yield agreement. This would work only in cases where the dispute was over matters of detail and not principle, such as in design layout, siting, landscaping, and materials. If a policy objection was raised against the very principle of the development, then mediation would be inappropriate. By concentrating upon cases with potential for negotiated settlement it was perhaps a matter of little surprise that agreement was reached. Cases involving objections in principle were siphoned off from this pool of potential mediations. The most popular mediated case, measured by land use category, involved minor residential schemes (less than 10) and domestic extensions. Matters in dispute frequently centred upon amenity-based arguments such as the relationship of a building to neighbouring builds, the shape of a landscaped area, the position of windows, car parking layout, and proposed materials. Negotiated outcomes included the reconfiguration of housing layouts/siting, amendments to materials and reduction of bulk, and deletion of windows in extensions. The mediation itself provided a valuable opportunity to continue negotiations or simply to begin

Case study 5.1: The New South Wales planning system

The planning appeal system in New South Wales

In New South Wales all planning appeals are dealt with by the Land and Environment Court. This specialist court was established in 1980 with jurisdiction over a range of planning, environmental and enforcement matters. The creation of a single court, by the Land and Environment Court Act 1979, was itself a rationalization of a number of appeal tribunals and powers previously exercised by the Supreme Court and District Courts of the State, so that the new court enjoys powers to determine both matters of administrative appeal and of judicial review. In recommending the relevant legislation to the New South Wales Parliament, the Minister for Planning and the Environment stated: 'The proposed new court is a somewhat innovative experiment in dispute resolution mechanisms. It attempts to combine judicial and administrative dispute resolving techniques and it will utilize non-legal experts as technical and conciliation assessors.'

Appeals to the court are heard by both Judges and Assessors. Assessors are professional experts, with relevant qualifications in town planning, engineering, surveying, land valuation, architecture, local government administration, or natural resource management. The principal method of appeal is by a Full Hearing in the Court in which evidence is presented in both written and oral form and is tested by adversarial cross-examination. The Assessor or Judge will decide the appeal, with Assessors determining the vast majority of appeals that deal with the planning merits of the case and Judges ruling on matters of civil and criminal enforcement and cases raising points of law. The decision to allow or dismiss the appeal is binding upon both parties and constitutes a form of independent expert arbitration. The Full Hearing is a lengthy and expensive form of appeal determination, involving many professionals and usually taking several days to hear a case. One council located on the Sydney metropolitan fringes defended 57 planning decisions in the Court in the financial year 1994–95, with a total professional cost comprising legal fees and production of planning evidence amounting to A\$1 144 533.

Mediation was introduced by the Court in 1991, by means of an amendment to the Land and Environment Court Rules. The Rules state that at a 'call over' meeting the Court Registrar may refer proceedings to mediation in accordance with the Court's Practice Direction. A Practice Direction, published in April 1991, stated that mediation would be offered in matters within the jurisdiction of town planning, building and rating appeals. This guidance was incorporated into the Court's Revised Practice Direction of 1993. Under its provisions, optional mediation was available, if both parties requested. The mediation is held before an Officer of the Court (the Registrar to Deputy Registrar) who conducts the mediation as a neutral and independent party to assist negotiations between the principal parties. No record is kept of any content of the discussions, only a record of the outcome, relating to whether the matter was settled, and some data on the type and location of the development proposal.

In 1994, by an amendment to the original 1979 Act, statutory procedures dealing with mediation came into force and, importantly, this process was defined as follows: 'A structured negotiation process in which the mediator, as a neutral and independent party, assists the parties to a dispute to achieve their own resolution of the dispute.' The mediation lasts on average three to four

> hours and is held either in the court or on site. Seven days prior to this each side will exchange a summary of the principal issues, which should be only two to three pages in length. As part of the process the mediator may caucus with each party, meeting with them privately to discuss their side of the case. Such discussions are confidential and designed to assist the mediator by providing the opportunity for frank and open statements to be made on a 'without prejudice' basis, from which options can be explored and ideas for settlement proposed.
>
> The caucus is an important procedural device to be employed in the conduct of a mediation. The fact that mediation within the court results in a Court Officer becoming involved in a private meeting with one side has been subject to the criticism that it devalues the court, in that 'views are expressed in the absence of the other party, [which] is a repudiation of basic principles of fairness and absence of hidden influences that the community rightly expects and demands that the courts observe' (Street 1991). Such criticism has been rebutted by the Chief Justice of the Court.

them for the first time, and to extend them (with the benefit of the mediator's influence) until a successive conclusion was reached.

The work by Michael Welbank (DETR 2000e) reported and analysed the findings of a pilot study of 48 planning mediations co-ordinated by the planning inspectorate and conducted between 1998 and 1999. The mediations were drawn from existing planning appeals and applications following either a direct approach by the research team to LPAs asking them to take part or in response to a mail-shot distributed with planning appeal forms.[2] The format followed the 'facilitative' model in a similar style to that set out in Table 5.1. The outcome (settlement or otherwise) was recorded as a 'memorandum of understanding'. Of the 48 cases, half of the disputes in question dealt with design-related issues and the majority (54 per cent) dealt with householder applications (mostly domestic extensions). In 65 per cent of cases an outcome was recorded (taken to be an agreed solution or action plan for future steps designed to achieve an outcome). Participants views were sought. The overriding majority of participants reported satisfaction with mediation, whatever the outcome. Many endorsed the value of mediation in establishing an effective channel of communication between LPA and appellant. In similar fashion to the experience in New South Wales, detailed development control issues were the most common matters to be resolved and householder applications the most popular case by land-use type. The principal issues for negotiation in these planning mediations dealt with domestic extensions (to side, rear or front), porches, conservatories, garages, sheds, and outbuildings. Beyond this the mediations dealt with a variety of 'house improvements' such as insertion of new windows, addition of dormer windows and replacement of wooden windows by PVC alternatives. In a number of cases it became apparent that certain works as proposed fell within the provisions of the General Permitted Development Order (see Chapter 3) and therefore planning application was not required.

Case study 5.2: Planning mediation

Chris Wren, Architects, submits a planning application to the London Borough of Richville, an outer suburb authority of distinct low-density character. The application seeks consent to replace an existing dwelling and rebuild with some additional accommodation in the roof space. The clients, Geoffrey and Gloria Green-Sward, want the new dwelling to be in accord with 'sustainable and ecological' principles. Chris consults the Richville Unitary Development Plan prior to the submission of the application and draws comfort from a policy which states that 'the Council will support applications that use "green" architecture'. He informs Geoffrey and Gloria that the plan supports their proposal.

The planning case officer, Penny Wise, telephones Chris to inform him that she likes his design and welcomes his use of solar panels and timber frame construction. Chris awaits his permission and informs Geoffrey and Gloria accordingly. They are delighted, as this means construction will be completed before their baby is born in the following summer.

Two weeks later Geoffrey is dismayed to receive a notice of refusal of permission stating that 'the height and bulk of the proposal is considered to be out of scale with its surroundings and detrimental to the amenities of neighbouring occupiers'.

Geoffrey and Gloria consult Chris. He advises them that an appeal will take anything between four and a half and six months to determine, and statistically has only a 30 per cent chance of success. He suggests mediation. At the beginning of the mediation Chris, Geoffrey and Gloria feel a mixture of anger, hurt and bewilderment at the way they have been treated.

Positional bargaining: Each of the parties (Chris, Penny and Geoffrey/Gloria) would begin the mediation from a positional stance. Geoffrey/Gloria are baffled and hurt by the process, Chris is angry with the planning officer for 'misleading' him over the telephone, and Penny feels she has acted within her professional and ethical standards, which allows her to alter her position in this way, albeit that she regrets being quite so enthusiastic to Chris on the telephone. Such positions are revealed in the opening 'venting' stages of the mediation proper. The mediator will need to manage this and set out to channel any anger expressed into more productive dialogue.

Unlocking their BATNAs: As a problem solver the mediator will meet with each party and get them to appraise their own stance. It transpires that Geoffrey/Gloria seek a speedy decision without recourse to appeal, Penny is willing to negotiate on detailed design matters and Chris wants to save face with his client following his embarrassment over the refused consent. If the mediator can get the parties to confront these positions and reveal them to the other party, movement from initial positions to principled negotiation may follow. If all three parties confront their BATNAs, it will become evident that they agree on a revised planning permission as the solution. In such a case the acceptable revisions can be agreed at the mediation, subject to ratification by the LPA planning committee. Where matters of detail (such as in design of materials) and not principle are at stake mediation in town planning is an appropriate mechanism.

Where mediations dealt with the construction of a new dwelling, negotiations centred on a number of amenity considerations such as the relationship to neighbouring properties with regard to the massing, scale and layout of the proposal. In four cases the matter in dispute dealt with replacement dwellings in Green Belt locations and negotiations dealt with the size of the replacement with regard to the existing building.[3] All such matters constitute 'classic' development control negotiations in which the details of a planning application are agreed once the planning officer has accepted the development in principle (by reference to the Development Plan). The research concluded on this matter that 'These are all matters on which a degree of subjective judgment can be exercised and do not normally produce conflicts with key land use policies . . . sitting down with an applicant in the atmosphere of a mediation can allow a more creative mood to be established'.

This research produced six recommendations. The key recommendation (the first) was that 'the use of [planning] mediation on a voluntary basis . . . should be encouraged'. Analysis of the 48 mediations conducted during 1998–99 reported a benefit to householders submitting planning applications (i.e. people who were not represented by professional agents). The mediation process and particularly the conduct and presence of the mediator created a valuable and 'user-friendly' 'communication linkage' (DETR 2000e) between householders and planners. The householders were able to put their case to the planner and benefit from the presentation and unravelling of any technical matters (such as those involving permitted development rights – see Chapter 3). In other areas mediation still had the potential to resolve or reduce planning disputes, but based on the reported results, benefits were much more likely to be felt in small-scale design and detailed development-control matters, like extensions and small-scale residential schemes. This study thereby produced a seminal finding in England and Wales, that mediation in some areas of planning dispute would produce tangible benefits to the system.

A model of planning mediation

The work of Stubbs (1997) and Welbank (DETR 2000e) led to the construction of a hybrid model of (facilitation-based) mediation, designed with particular regard to the democratic nature of the planning process. In this model a number of key features must be accommodated. Six may be distinguished.

(a) Mediation is voluntary

A key principle established by both the 1998–99 pilot programme in England and Wales and mediation option available in the Land and Environment Court of New South Wales is that the process is entirely voluntary. Any party may simply walk away from it at any time. Compulsory mediation would diminish its effectiveness and constrain the parties from engaging in the proper level of discussion.

(b) Mediation is case-dependent

Mediation is unlikely to succeed in cases involving any objection to the very principle of development (established by planning policy). As mediation itself is no more than assisted negotiation, some common ground must exist between appellant and LPA. This common ground is invariably based on matters of detail such as design and layout considerations.

(c) Mediation is confidential

Another key principle of the process. No record is made of the discussion, only the outcome. In New South Wales such an outcome would be expressed in an agreed contract (if successful). In England and Wales the DETR (2000e) pilot programme recorded the result as a 'memorandum of understanding' in which a plan of future action was minuted, if some agreement had been reached.

(d) Mediation is binding

To ensure that planners or applicants use mediation in the first place, they must be confident that what is agreed during the mediation will subsequently be implemented. In New South Wales a frequent problem was that planners lacked sufficient authority to settle, once some agreement had been reached. This proved to be a major obstacle because in such cases, the appellant may consider the process to be a futile waste of time. Yet planning officers are not 'supreme' decision-makers. They are servants of the planning committee, who bear ultimate responsibility in decision-making. The public will also need to be involved, as the outcome may require a fresh round of public consultation. These issues will need to be addressed in any planning mediation. If the mediation were to fail then the excursion into ADR would have served to increase and not diminish time taken to reach a decision, for the appellant would have to revert to the traditional appeal method. Research indicates that this will occur in around one third of all mediations. This constitutes a powerful disincentive, for in such cases the entire mediation will have been a waste of time or at best a 'fishing expedition' (perhaps to explore the merits of the case put forward by the other side but with no real incentive to settle.

(e) Mediation is inclusive

Third parties (the public) will need to be accommodated in any mediation process, if they so desire. It would, however, be inappropriate for third parties to block the achievement of a successful outcome if the appellant and LPA agree. In such circumstances it would be acceptable to note that various individuals dissented from the mediation outcome.

(f) Mediation is a sovereign method of dispute resolution

Planning mediation as a constituent method of ADR is an alternative to the traditional appeal pathway. It follows that the organization of a mediation service should be at 'arms length' from the traditional method to which it provides an alternative. Ideally, this means creating a separate body to co-ordinate the conduct of mediators. The alternative of creating a 'mediation arm' of, say, the planning inspectorate is not in itself unacceptable, but the complete independence of the mediator and mediation process must be preserved. Court-annexed mediation services exist (as in the Land and Environment Court of New South Wales and Central London County Court) in which traditional and ADR mechanisms are located within the same institution. They can only do this if disputing parties perceive and discover each distinct wing of the organization to be wholly independent. As discussed earlier, such court-annexed systems have been criticized for diminishing the authority of the court in the eyes of the public. If, for example, a planning mediation service were to sit within the Inspectorate and LPAs, and appellants or the public perceived this to lack independence, then the system would collapse. The assertion that the Inspectorate only employed mediation to reduce its workload of traditional appeals would be difficult to refute. So, if mediation is to grow in the planning system it must be placed within the control of an independent body. If this is not the case then, in the words of the (DETR) 2000 report, it must be shown to be 'demonstrably independent of other functions [of that organization] . . . with its own distinct image and status'.

The model of planning mediation presented below (Figure 5.2) adapts the facilitation model set out in Figure 5.1 and accommodates a number of the previously discussed key principles. The establishment of mediation within the planning system in England and Wales provides an important and extremely significant 'first step' towards greater employment of ADR. Supporters of mediation often portray its advantages in dramatic language: 'mediation can be magical' (Higgins, 1997); 'Mediation . . . has grown like a silent revolution across the globe' (Mackie, 1997); and 'Mediation is a process which offers commercial disputants meaningful, creative solutions at a fraction of the cost of the litigation system' (Choreneki, 1997).

Statistics to some extent support this enthusiasm, with 73 per cent of cases in the DETR pilot programme resulting in some kind of 'resource saving' to the LPA (i.e. settling or narrowing any future conflict) and Stubbs (1997) reporting that in New South Wales some 736 hours spent in mediation sessions resulted in approximately 405 days saved in court time. On receiving the DETR 2000 report, the (then) Planning Minister, Beverley Hughes, said 'I would like to see further investigation of the use of mediation at other stages in the planning system, for instance, at development plan stage or in resolving particular issues in cases going to inquiry'.[4] In 2001 the (then) Secretary of State, Stephen Byers, further reinforced the government's enthusiasm for this idea by incorporating it in the planning Green Paper. This endorsement in effect ensured that mediation would be introduced to planning during the period 2002–5.

The period 2000–5 will bear witness to an increasing presence of mediation in planning appeals. It is anticipated that it will also permeate into the development plan process, with initial experimentation in this area in 2000–1.[5] Beyond further deployment of mediation in planning it is conceivable that the next few years will see other innovations drawn from the ADR toolbox.

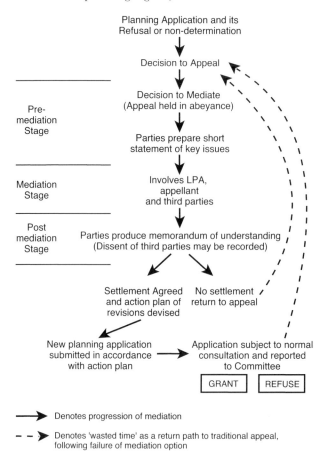

Figure 5.2 Planning mediations.

Pearce (2000) speculates on the intriguing possibility of 'med-arb' (or 'mediappeal'), which combines arbitration with mediation 'where the arbitrator (the Inspector in our case) functions first as a pure mediator, helping the parties to arrive at a mutually acceptable outcome and then, but only if the mediation fails, reverts to her normal role, arbitrating between the parties' cases and argument and issuing a final and binding decision. In effect the parties would first seek to reach agreement through assisted negotiation (mediation) but agree to submit to binding arbitration (i.e. a conventional appeal procedure conducted by an inspector) should they reach impasse.'

Problems exist in such an amalgamation of traditional and alternative processes, notably that parties will be less likely to reveal their underlying needs and concerns (i.e. unlock their BATNAs) in the initial mediation phase for fear that this may 'backfire' and adversely influence the subsequent arbitration phase (should the attempt at a mediated settlement fail).

Pearce (ibid.) demonstrates the value of continued reflection in this area. Alternative Dispute Resolution has arrived in town planning. Its future will

Table 5.2 European Convention on Human Rights

Article or Protocol	Rights Guaranteed
Article 2	To life
Article 3	To freedom from torture
Article 4	To freedom from slavery or servitude
Article 5	To liberty
*Article 6	To a fair and public trial
Article 7	To no punishment without law
*Article 8	To respect for private and family life and home
Article 9	To freedom of thought
Article 10	To freedom of expression
Article 11	To freedom of assembly
Article 12	To marry
Article 14	To prohibit discrimination
*Protocol 1 – Article 1	To peaceful enjoyment of possessions/property
Protocol 1 – Article 3	To free elections
Protocol 2 – Article 2	To access to education Protocol
Protocol 6 – Article 1 & 2	To abolish the death penalty

* Of key relevance to planning system.

be assured when applicants and LPAs experience its benefits, whether they be time and cost savings or improved quality of decision-making achieved by a process based on building consensus and not adversarial exchange.

Town planning and human rights

Introduction

In December 1948 the United Nations agreed a Universal Declaration of Human Rights. Such action came as an essential component of post-war reconstruction, motivated by the powerful desire to protect against a repetition of the many atrocities committed during the Second World War. Two years later (1950), the Council of Europe applied these principles to the Member States of the European Community in the European Convention of Human Rights (ECHR), designed to guarantee some 16 specified civil rights and freedoms as enshrined in the UN Declaration (see Table 5.2). The following year (1951), the Convention was ratified by the UK government, although for a further 47 years (until 1998) the UK government resisted proposals to incorporate the Convention into domestic law (Grant 2000). Instead these various rights were adapted by virtue of 'ministerial discretion', so that, for example, the principles were referred to in planning and environmental policy without specific reference being made to their existence in planning statute. If a UK citizen sought redress against the government or any other public body, prior to 2000, for their failure to comply with the rights and freedoms contained in the ECHR, then this would ultimately require legal challenge in the European Court of Justice.[6]

Over the years the Strasbourg court adapted a number of principles in relation to the ECHR, notably that the detailed language of 1950 be subject to broad interpretation. Indeed, the court has described the Convention as a 'living instrument' that must be interpreted in the light of present-day conditions.[7]

The UK government changed the constitutional position of the ECHR in passing the Human Rights Act 1998 (Royal Assent, September 1998), which came into force on 2 October 2000. The Human Rights Act 1998 (HRA) therefore served to perform a relatively simple structural reform by adopting into domestic law all the rights identified in the Convention, in other words formally 'importing' provision of the ECHR so that it was incorporated into UK law. This reform was subsequently described as 'not exactly a major constitutional resettlement' (Grant 2000), although the longer-term ramifications for planning have been considerable and far-reaching. The Human Rights Act 1998 will influence both the process and substance of planning control and for the first time since the enactment of the Town and Country Planning Act 1947 its implementation heralded a fundamental rethink in the relationship between the powers held by the Executive (government), Judiciary (courts) and individual citizen. The key consequences would be that some planning functions (especially appeals) would become more autonomous of government, while third parties (objectors) would benefit from increased power and representation in the system. Legal opinion differed on the consequences of these reforms, and when the HRA was debated in the House of Lords its impact was viewed both as an opportunity 'to freshen up the principles of common law' and 'a field day for crackpots' (speech by Lord McCluskey).

Running alongside this increased focus on environmental civil rights, the United Nations introduced guidance on freedom of information. The UN Economic Commission for Europe adopted the Aarhus Convention in June 1998, which stipulated that

> In order to contribute to the protection of the right of every person of present and future generation to live in an environment adequate to his or her health and well-being, each Party shall guarantee the rights of access to information, public participation in decision-making and access to justice in environmental matters.[8]

Such a document reflected an awareness of growing public participation in environmental decision-making and reflected principles previously agreed by the UN (its Rio Declaration). Indeed, Article 9 of the Aarhus Convention, in parallel with developments like the ECHR, considered the increased momentum gathering in favour of access to justice in environmental decision-making, by stating that all members of the public should have access to a review procedure (i.e. court of law or independent tribunal) that allows a review of both the substance of and process followed in environmental decision-making.

Human rights: general principles

The ECHR thus 'imports' (or repatriates from European to UK Courts) (Grant 2000a) a number of individual rights that protect the citizen from unacceptable actions by the state (usually the national government). To protect individuals in this way, the HRA places an obligation on the state (including public bodies) to uphold convention rights. After its introduction into UK legislation in 1998 (and operative after 2000) the citizen can assert such individual rights by challenging actions, decisions or indeed omissions by public bodies in the UK and not European courts, thus avoiding the time-consuming complicated and costly excursion to Strasbourg as had previously been required.

The HRA incorporated a number of central provisions that exacted fundamental change in actions of national government and the judiciary. All new legislation passing through Parliament would require scrutiny to ensure compatibility with Convention rights. Ministers will be required to address this directly by making a statement with regard to the compatibility of any proposed legislation to the Convention. All UK public bodies must act in a manner that is compatible with Convention rights and freedoms. Failure to do so can be challenged in UK courts by any person, individual or company. The courts cannot 'strike down' any legislation they consider incompatible but may make a 'declaration of incompatibility' to encourage swift revision of it by Government and Parliament' (Hart 2000).

Three articles in particular addressed the regulation of land use, dealing with procedural guarantees such as Article 6 (fair trial), protection of substance as contained in Article 8 (respect for home life) and Protocol 1 – Article 1 (peaceful enjoyment of property). Their impact was spread over a wide area, as the HRA made it unlawful for any so-defined Public Authority[9] to act in a way considered incompatible with the Convention. Many planning organizations were thus affected. Provisions were both far-reaching and deep-rooted, by affecting the actions of numerous public and semi-public bodies in a fundamental way. The Convention and subsequent HRA set out to protect individual citizen's rights by allowing complaint to the courts. It was, therefore, possible for a person, individual or company (not a group, such as an interest or amenity group) to bring an action against a public body only if that body had violated a Convention right (Purchas and Clayton 2001). That person must constitute a 'victim' in the strict definition within Article 34 of the Convention, which restricts such qualification to someone 'directly affected' by the action or omission at issue (Hart 2000).

If the actions or omissions of a public body are the subject of challenge, the courts[10] are duty-bound to consider the 'proportionality' of that action when addressing the remedy to the situation. In other words, any interference with a Convention right must be both fair and specifically designed to pursue a legitimate aim: 'The underlying idea is that a sledgehammer of interference with rights should not be used to crack a nut of social need' (Hart 2000). It follows that a balance will need to be struck between the rights of the individual and the interests of the community. This means that some infringement of individual civil rights *may* be permissible in justifiable cases, but that this interference must not be excessive (in other words, it must be proportionate). For example, certain rights (freedom of assembly in the case of a public demonstration) might be acceptably limited to prevent criminal damage or riot. Such restrictions must be proportionate; a total ban on all public meetings would be a disproportionate response to the potential threat of, say, a single gathering leading to civil unrest. Such a disproportionate response would, in all probability, be an unacceptable erosion of civil/human rights, whereas by contrast the banning of one meeting (on the basis of evidence of unrest) would be proportionate. In town planning, enforcement proceedings against unauthorized development are a common example of this principle in action (Purchas and Clayton 2001). The question is posed, are the remedies against such breaches of regulation 'proportionate' to the offence? It is possible to appeal against an enforcement notice on grounds that the steps required (to make the matter acceptable) exceed what is necessary to remedy the breach.[11] If, for example, the notice requires total removal of a building without planning permission in a case where the key area of harm relates to an inappropriate roof design (bulky with overlooking windows) then such a requirement could arguably be disproportionate. A more proportionate response would require revisions to the roof.[12] The HRA establishes that a landowner may seek remedy against such matters by virtue of the proportionality principle contained in the ECHR. Judges in matters of judicial review will make decisions that go beyond interpretation of such legislation as existed previously and become embroiled in judgements on the 'value' attached to legislation in its defence of human rights. In dealing with legal challenges on the basis of disproportionate interference with Convention rights, judges will need to decide upon the balance of competing factors and not just mere interpretations of the law.

Human rights: applications to planning

The Human Rights Act and the ECHR have several implications for the operation of the UK planning system. Specific reference is made here to the impact on the system in England and Wales. Grant (2000) reflects upon how the relatively simple 'importation' of the ECHR to domestic law has changed the whole foundation of the planning system. A seemingly straightforward legislative reform has undergone a seismic change. This change has altered the very basis of policy formulation.

The post-war planning system withdrew a landowner's right to develop land and replaced it with the right to submit a planning application, with subsequent appeal should the LPA refuse to grant consent (Grant, ibid.). Applications were then, and still are today, assessed against planning policy and other material considerations. The key powers of regulation over land-use control were given to the executive (government, both national and local). The whole system was constructed on the basis that government ministers assumed key supervisory responsibility. A government department produced statements of national planning policy (in PPGs and Circulars), enjoyed a right of 'call-in' to determine certain major or controversial applications and had the power to 'recover' jurisdiction over certain appeals, similarly for determination by the Secretary of State. The Planning Inspectorate formed a part of the executive as an agency of a government department (the DETR). It was, therefore, not wholly independent of government. A 'settlement' was thus achieved in which the executive assumed an administrative responsibility for control of the system and the courts, through the exercise of judicial review and statutory challenge, protected against abuse of power and sought to respect citizens' rights.

The ECHR fundamentally changed that post-war compromise between executive and judiciary. Article 6(i) of the Convention provided for the most significant reforms, followed by Article 8 and Article 1 of the First Protocol. Each will be considered in turn.

Article 6 deals with process, i.e. the manner in which the system allows for a fair and equitable representation of people's interests. Five key components are identified, such as that individuals enjoy civil rights, the opportunity of a fair and public hearing (by way of an independent impartial tribunal) and a decision within a reasonable time.

Article 8 and the **First Protocol** deal with matters of substance (the right to enjoy property). Fairness, openness and impartiality have been fundamental principles in post-war planning appeals, indeed are described as both the 'mission and hallmark of the Planning Inspectorate' (Grant 2000). Article 6 will further promote this mission and hallmark across the entire system, although it is not so much the impartiality of decision-makers that Article 6 calls into question as their independence.

Article 6(i): Right to a fair trial

> In the determination of his civil rights and obligations or of any criminal charge against him, everyone is entitled to a fair and public hearing within a reasonable time by an independent and impartial tribunal established by law. Judgement shall be pronounced publicly but the press and public may be excluded from all or part of the trial in the interest of morals, public order or national security in a democratic society where the interests of juveniles or the protection of the private life of the parties so require, or to the extent strictly necessary in the opinion of the court in special circumstances where publicity would prejudice the interests of justice.

Article 8: Right to respect for private and family life

> (1) Everyone has the right to respect for his private and family life, his home and his correspondence.

The First Protocol: Article 1: Protection of property

> Every natural or legal person is entitled to the peaceful enjoyment of his possessions. No one shall be deprived of his possessions except in the public interest and subject to the conditions provided for by law and by the general principles of international law.
>
> The preceding provisions shall not, however, in any way impair the right of a State to enforce such laws it deems necessary to control the use of property in accordance with the general interest or to secure the payment of taxes or other contributions or penalties.

In town planning a fair and public hearing by an independent and impartial tribunal (Article 6) affects planning application, plan making, enforcement action, and the appeal process. Article 8 (and the First Protocol) restricts government in how far it may influence private property. This will similarly affect planning decisions, especially on applications. A number of key areas will be considered in respect of planning applications, plan making, planning enforcement, and planning appeals.

As regards *planning applications* the immediate ramifications of the HRA relate to citizen rights in the application process. Private or individual interests have not traditionally been placed 'first' in the priorities of the system (as the ECHR tends to dictate in Article 8). Indeed, government guidance in PPG1 of 1997 states that:

> The planning system does not exist to protect the private interests of one person against the activities of another . . . the basic question is not whether owners and occupiers of neighbouring properties would experience financial or other loss from a particular development but whether the proposal would unacceptably affect amenities . . .'.

By contrast, the Convention puts private interests first and places emphasis on individual rights (including property rights) in respect of planning decisions. Lowes (2000) speculates that as a consequence LPAs will need to show they had taken such convention provisions into account. One manifestation of this is that planning committee reports will be not only longer but much more precise in detailing how matters in respect of Article 8 and the First Protocol have been complied with.

As regards *plan making functions* the LPAs and other relevant bodies (such as county councils and regional planning bodies) will need to pay closer regard to personal circumstances and private interests when producing regional planning guidance and development plan policy. It follows from the Convention that those individuals who deem that their health, property or commercial activities could be affected by the outcome of such plans may seek to rely on Article 6(i) as a means of gaining audience to participate fully in the decision-making process. Article 6 requires reasons to be given (i.e. 'judgement shall be pronounced publicly . . .').

In a local plan inquiry, the Inspector responsible for the inquiry will make recommendations on land-use allocations (such as a green-field site being allocated for housing), after consideration of representations by the LPA and other interested parties. The LPA is not obliged to follow the Inspector's recommendations (i.e. they are not binding). Initial speculation on this process concluded (in 2001) that the development plan process was 'potentially' incompatible with principles established in Article 6(i). An LPA may simply reject the Inspector's recommendation and may have a strong political or financial interest in the outcome of the process. Further, it is possible that the LPA's reasoning for departing from the Inspector's recommendation is 'brief and uncommunicative' (Hart 2000). No independent review process exists by which an individual may challenge the planning merits of the LPA's action, in this regard. Compliance with Article 6(i) may require that this is a necessary post-HRA reform.

In *planning enforcement* the newly established test of 'proportionality' (previously discussed) will affect the nature of enforcement action. LPAs must have regard to this part of the Convention and be prepared to demonstrate that the action taken to remedy a breach of planning control is in proportion to the legitimate aims pursued. Such 'proportionality' must balance the interests of the community against the individual's right to respect for their home (Article 8). This principle equates to 'reasonableness', i.e. whatever a public body may do it must be proportionate (Samuels 2000).

In *planning appeals* Article 6(i) has had the most significant and far-reaching impact. The right to an independent and impartial tribunal is one of the most important features of the Article and has considerable significance in the planning and environmental context (Hart 2000). Grant (2001) considers the key ramifications of this Article on the appeal process. First, prior to HRA the public (third parties) enjoyed only restricted rights of access in appeals. They appeared only at the discretion of the Inspector and enjoyed no right of appeal themselves (against, for example, a grant of planning permission). Such a lack of civil rights . . . 'does not reflect the ideals of a participative democracy of the twenty first century' (Grant, ibid.). Second, the ideal of an independent tribunal is not undermined by virtue of the reserved intervention powers of the Secretary of State and since 2002 Deputy Prime Minister who may himself determine planning applications (call-in) or appeals (recovered jurisdiction). While this may amount to only a small volume of appeals (1 per cent recovered or around 100–150 appeals per year), it deprives the planning inspectorate of the necessary *appearance* of independence. The ideal of independence (as interpreted by the European Court and set out in the Article) is arguably not met by the planning inspectorate, which sits as an agency under the ultimate control of the Deputy Prime Minister. The strict legal position is that the Deputy Prime Minister appoints planning inspectors to assist him in conducting and discharging the appellate decision-making process. The planning inspectorate is thus *not* a sovereign independent body as Article 6 would require. While the inspectorate has an established and widely acknowledged reputation of impartiality in decision-making, this lack of independence provides something of a stumbling block to the complete implementation of the Convention in planning appeals.

The HRA vests in the courts strong powers to 'police' the implementation of the Convention. At its most extreme a UK higher court (such as the House of Lords) may declare domestic legislation incompatible with Convention articles. In other cases it is possible for a court to strike down a piece of subordinate legislation. In town planning such subordinate legislation covers statutory instruments, which set out detailed procedural guidance (in, say, appeals) or detailed policy matters (in, say, requirements of permitted development thresholds in a domestic dwelling). A number of court rulings have already brought valuable judicial guidance to bear on the future functioning of the Convention in town planning. Some legal decisions (as in *Bryan vs UK* – see Case study 5.3) pre-date the HRA 1998, being made in the Strasbourg Court. Others (as in *R vs Secretary of State for Environment, Transport and the Regions, ex parte Holding and Barnes plc*)[13] post-date HRA 1998 and were issued by a UK court (in that case the House of Lords). In both cases they perform the same task in giving valuable interpretation of the Convention with HRA 1998. Such legal determination will be pivotal in shaping the future direction of human rights legislation in planning. In the key decisions made to date it appears that the compatibility of Article 6(i) to planning appeal systems is a matter heavily dependent upon the right of legal challenge (Judicial or Statutory Review) after the planning appeal has been determined. This particular interpretation may not endure; indeed, eminent commentators (Grant 2000) viewed the decision in Bryan (and by implication in Alconbury) as 'unsatisfactory' due to the courts being restricted in what they can do, i.e. they cannot rehearse the planning merits of the case, only consider the grounds of legal challenge. An aggrieved third party cannot use a legal challenge in the courts as a means of re-opening the case merits (i.e. whether planning permission should or should not be granted) but only to achieve a review of the legality of a decision or the process by which it was made. The outcome of the Bryan case appears unlikely to last in the longer term. Indeed, Grant (ibid.) looks towards more structural change, with a number of far-reaching (even tantalizing) reforms. Such ideas countenance broadening the jurisdiction of the courts to hear merit appeals and making the inspectorate wholly independent of government. The findings of a (then) DETR-sponsored research project of 2000 (DETR 2000e) rather opportunely considered the potential to introduce an Environment Court to the UK. Such a court would combine both merit appeals and legal challenges, in similar fashion to other jurisdictions (notably New South Wales). The report itself acknowledged that the HRA 1998 may promote a review of the relationship between planning inspectorate and government and also 'creates an opportunity for the development of a new jurisprudence in relation to environmental rights'. In any event, such structural reform (a new Environment Court or the total splitting off of the inspectorate, to give it complete autonomy) will create a more 'convention-friendly' system than the one that existed when the Human Rights Act 1998 came into force in October 2000.

Case study 5.3: Human rights: case law: Bryan *v* United Kingdom

An enforcement notice was served on Mr Bryan requiring the demolition of two buildings on his land. Mr Bryan appealed to the Secretary of State against the merits of this decision. The appointed Inspector subsequently dismissed the appeal and upheld provisions of the notice. Following this, Mr Bryan mounted a legal challenge in the High Court, also subsequently dismissed. He then took his case to the European Court of Human Rights in Strasbourg. The European Court of Human Rights held that the decision made by a planning inspector was not consistent with Article 6(i) and did *not* constitute an independent and impartial tribunal, since the Secretary of State could at any time revoke the powers of the Inspector and deprive that Inspector of the appearance of independence required by the Convention. Yet the European Court of Human Rights went on to determine that this deficiency was *cured* by the opportunity given to a planning appellant to challenge the decision of a planning inspector in the courts and was content that the grounds on which the court could review the decision of a planning inspector 'were wide enough to provide the necessary safeguards' (Grant 2000b).

Key issues:
That Article 6(i) 'fair tribunal' is satisfied in spite of the planning inspectorate *not* being wholly independent of the Secretary of State *because* of a 'cumulative effect' (Hart 2000) in which the proceedings held before an Inspector may be challenged in the High Court (by judicial review or statutory challenge), which *is* wholly independent but cannot rule on issues of planning merit, only legal irregularity.

Case study 5.4: Human rights organization: An bord Pleanála

An bord Pleanála, the body responsible for determining planning appeals in the Republic of Ireland, has been much praised by UK commentators in respect of Human Rights legislation. Much of this praise has been directed at its independence from government. Established in 1977, An bord Pleanála is currently vested with appellate powers by the (Irish) Planning and Development Act 2000. Individual Planning Inspectors, when determining appeals, offer a recommendation to a Chairman and Board. While responsible to the Minister for the Environment and Local Government, in terms of organization, efficiency and finances, the Chairman and Board or Inspectors are wholly independent in their decision-making responsibilities. Indeed, the Chairman's annual report for 1999 celebrated this fact when stating 'the Board remains at all times acutely conscious of its stated objectives to carry out its work in an independent manner . . . [and] . . . I wish to stress the fact that there is no political or other interference in decisions by the Board in individual cases'.* Under the terms of the Act while the Minister appoints the Chairman and all seven Board members (usually nominated by various prescribed organizations), they enjoy complete autonomy in the decision to allow or dismiss any individual planning appeal that comes before them. The Minister can submit representations on appeals, as indeed can any individual, but the Board enjoys ultimate decision-making authority. This contrasts markedly with the strong, if infrequently used, intervention powers enjoyed by the Secretary of State in the equivalent system in England.

* An bord Pleanála (1999) *Annual Report*, p. 4.

Case study 5.5: Human rights case law: the Alconbury case

The independence of the planning inspectorate was reviewed further in three High Court appeals heard together in the House of Lords in 2001. These three appeals are referred to as the Alconbury judgement* and owing to their importance in respect of human rights they were passed direct to the House of Lords, leapfrogging the Court of Appeal along the way.

As with *Bryan*, the ability of the planning appeal system to deliver the rights enshrined in Article 6(i) was again brought into question. As the judgement of the House of Lords established, no complaint was raised over the independence and impartiality of planning inspectors, or indeed the very fairness of the Inquiry method as measured in, say, the ability to make representations, call or challenge evidence. Instead the central issue related to the potential interventions in decision-making made by the Secretary of State, whose independence and impartiality was compromised by the fact that he lays down national planning policy in Circulars and PPGs: 'all of these are bound to affect the mind of the Secretary of State when he takes decisions on called-in applications or on appeals which he recovers'. Lord Slynn of Hadley quoted from paragraph 24 of judgement in (2001) UKHL 23, or (2002) 1 PLR 58.

This lack of independence in these appeals was further compromised, it was argued, by the fact that the government itself was a landowner in one case (the Alconbury site being owned by the Ministry of Defence) and had promoted a road improvement scheme in another (the Department of Transport having previously promoted a road at the Newbury site). All four Law Lords hearing the appeal were unconvinced by such argument, relying on the provision (as established by *Bryan*) for legal review (by virtue of judicial or statutory review of a planning appeal decision) rendering any decision taken by the Secretary of State as compatible with Article 6. Further, this scope of review power was deemed sufficient to comply with standards set by the European Court of Human Rights. Their Lordships accepted the point put by the Secretary of State's barrister, that the key issue was not the existence of complete independence or impartiality of the Secretary of State but the decision-making process within which such powers were exercised. In other words, the fact that the Secretary of State lacked independence by virtue of being both policy-maker and decision-taker (Holgate and Gilbey 2001) was not the deciding issue. What was material here was not the existence of an independent and impartial tribunal but the existence of sufficient opportunity to scrutinize any decision made by the Secretary of State by way of statutory challenge or judicial review to guarantee an acceptable discharge of rights contained in the Convention. Their Lordships concluded that this level of review was adequate and as a result . . . 'the Secretary of State's powers to intervene in the planning process . . . remain undiminished' (Holgate and Gilbey 2001).

This endorsement of the status quo received a 'mixed press' among planning and legal commentators. Some felt this decision represented an opportunity missed (Grant 2001) to embrace the Environmental Court approach, that it was pragmatic in tone in order to achieve a political solution to the dilemma facing the Secretary of State (Holgate and Gilbey 2001) while others argued that its reasoning was consistent with decisions previously made by the European Court of Human Rights (Elvin and Maurici 2001). Grand (ibid.) perhaps comes to the most robust judgement in arguing that Alconbury was not just a simple endorsement of the status quo. Instead it helped to clarify the future role of the Secretary of State (now Deputy Prime Minister), permitting ministerial involvement in planning appeal decision-making. The Minister is thus able to come to a different view to that of a planning inspector.

* R. *(Alconbury Developments Limited and Others)* vs SSETR, R. *(Holding and Barnes)* vs SSETR and SSETR vs *Legal and General Assurance Society Limited.*
Legal references to the House of Lords Decision are [2001] 2 WLR 1389 and [2001] 2 All ER.

Summary of Possible Revisions

Figure 5.3 Human Rights Act.

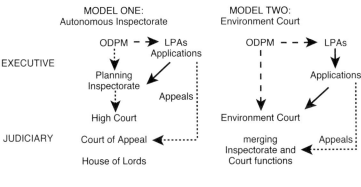

Figure 5.4 Planning decision making.

6 Planning gain and planning obligations

Planning gain is a term familiar to many professionals working in property development. However, it is also a misleading and ill defined term. Since 1991 the government discouraged its use and preferred the term 'planning obligations'. This chapter will seek to define the planning gain and obligations system and will consider the subject in two sections dealing with the legal and philosophical context of the subject.

The study of planning gain/planning obligations exposes the tension that exists between the town planning system and the property development industry. At its most fundamental it involves examination of who should pay for the wider environmental impact of a development proposal, the developer or the local authority. This chapter will examine the workings of the system, dealing separately with the legal or procedural rules that guide the practical implementation of planning obligations, and the broader, more philosophical, debate as to whether such obligations represent a form of development tax or a legitimate development cost. A series of case studies will focus on what is considered to constitute good and bad practice. In 1999–2000 the government-appointed Urban Task Force (Urban Task Force 1999) and subsequent Urban White Paper (DETR 2000b) both countenanced a review of the planning obligation system. The review, conducted between 2000 and 2002, culminated in the government issuing a consultation paper that advocated the introduction of 'tariffs' in place of obligations (DETR 2001a). Future reforms to the system will also be considered.

Background

The many misconceptions surrounding this subject are in part explained by the lack of a single and widely used definition and the use of a variety of titles relating to the practice of planning gain. Research (Healey et al. 1993) discovered the use of 12 terms to describe the same function.[1] The term 'planning gain' provides a convenient umbrella under which benefits in either cash or kind are offered to a local planning authority (LPA) by a developer, following the grant of planning permission and controlled by an agreement between the local planning authority and landowner or by planning condition. This implies a situation in which the local planning authority benefits from something for nothing, that is, by simply granting planning permission the developer will provide 'sweeteners' or 'goodies' (Case Study 6.1). Such a view would be an unsatisfactory start to the topic. At this stage

---

Case study 6.1

Proposal
Residualbuild Developments submits a planning application seeking permission to build 20 detached houses. The chief executive of Residualbuild calculates the profit margins of the development and writes to the LPA, offering them £1 million to spend on community projects within the area or indeed on '**anything they so wish**'.

Tests (see Table 6.1)
Similar to Case Study 6.4, in that the cash payment will not satisfy any facilities necessary for this development to proceed. If some form of community use had previously existed on this site, or the new development would itself require community facilities, then a case could be made for a payment or offer of land to compensate for the loss. However, merely offering a 'blanket' sum unrelated to the requirements of the case is not the correct approach.

Conclusions
Again, an unreasonable pursuit of a planning obligation by a developer. Such an example is used to demonstrate that the generation of unreasonable obligation is not the exclusive privilege of the public sector.

---

we must acknowledge the important procedural role played by the system, which allows both local authority and developer to overcome and control the environmental impact arising from development proposals enabling planning permission to be granted in cases where, without these controls, it may have been refused (Case Study 6.2). Planning obligations thus bring to the system the very powerful benefits of allowing the developer the opportunity to remedy a planning problem (such as inadequate site access or provision of bus facilities in the neighbourhood) or to enhance the quality of a development (such as provision of communal facilities like open space for sports use or schools).

Provision for agreements relating to the development of land have existed in planning legislation since 1909.[2] The current system can effectively be traced back to 1968 when the need for ministerial consent was removed and such agreements were left for straightforward negotiation between the local planning authority and landowner/developer, as exists today.

In 1980 the government commissioned the Property Advisory Group (PAG)[3] to examine the practice of planning gain. Their report (Property Advisory Group 1980) concluded: 'We are unable to accept that, as a matter of general practice, planning gain has any place in our system of planning control.'

However, the DoE did not accept such a finding and in 1983 they issued Circular Guidance on Planning Gain. Paragraph 2 of the Circular provided a definition:

'Planning gain' is a term which has come to be applied whenever in connection with a grant of planning permission, a local planning

Case study 6.2

Proposal
Ecoville Developers acquires a former landfill site within green belt land and propose to build a business park on approximately 30 per cent of the site, a golf course on 20 per cent and parkland on the remaining area. Various highway improvements are required on land adjacent to the site. A planning obligation would allow the use of the park and golf course for access by the public, together with a (single) cash payment towards the cost of adjoining highway improvements to serve the site.

Tests (see Table 6.1)
A business park within the green belt would in normal circumstances be contrary to policy. In this case the use of an obligation allows an area of previously spoiled green belt land to be brought into recreational use. The obligation is needed to allow the development to proceed. Together with the associated highway works, it is clearly both functionally and geographically related to the development.

Conclusions
An acceptable planning obligation, clearly allowing planning benefits to both sides by restoring green belt land and allowing a business park. Green belt policy is strictly applied by LPAs and this example should not be viewed as a means by which planning gain may be employed to permit exceptions to planning policy. However, it does illustrate the role of negotiation, illustrating how an obligation is used to facilitate improvements to spoilt green belt by permitting some development. A planning agreement is required as both sides are involved.

authority seeks to impose on a developer an obligation to carry out works not included in the development for which permission has been sought or to make payment or confer some extraneous right or benefit in return for permitting development to take place.

The Circular set out a series of broad rules or 'tests of reasonableness', to establish what could be considered to be acceptable practice. These tests established that any gains should be reasonable in content, and both geographically and functionally related to the development to be permitted (Case Studies 6.3, 6.4).

Planning gain practice during the 1970s and 1980s was not viewed by many local planning authorities as a quasi-legal function, based upon the application of these Circular tests, essentially to overcome objections to a scheme and allow permission to be granted. Instead, some local planning authorities were employing the system to extract community benefits from developers. This benefit in social or physical infrastructure (building a community centre or a new road) was sometimes either unrelated or shared a tenuous relationship with the development to be permitted.

Case study 6.3

Proposal
Blackacre Developments acquires a church, now redundant, within a high street location. Behind the church is a car park. Blackacre acquires the car park to assemble a site large enough to accommodate a new shopping mall.

The demolition of the church would provide a direct link with the existing high street and the pedestrian flow necessary for the economic viability of the new centre.

Following the sale of the car park to the developer, a planning obligation would permit the developer to offer to build another community use elsewhere within the site to replace the church displayed by the development. The council may seek to maintain some element of public access to the car parking within the new scheme, which is likely to be in a basement underneath the new shopping mall.

Tests (see Table 6.1)
Replacement of 'lost' uses (car parking, church) within these new provisions would satisfy the 'necessity' test, namely the offset loss of amenity. The maintenance of public parking in the area would overcome any objection to the loss of car parking. The obligation would appear to be fairly and reasonably related to the proposal.

Conclusions
An acceptable planning obligation serving a land-use purpose. A planning agreement would be the most appropriate method, with both sides benefiting in some way.

Towards the end of the property boom in the 1980s, a growing suspicion emerged that both local planning authorities and developers had violated the 'tests' in the pursuit of planning consent or wider benefits by the local authority. In 1989 the Royal Town Planning Institute raised doubts over some

---

Case study 6.4

Proposal
Flexible BI Developments proposes an office building within a town centre location. The LPA seeks a financial payment towards a local civic/community festival.

Tests (see Table 6.1)
A cash payment which will not contribute towards satisfying facilities necessary to allow the development to proceed. This example is not fairly and reasonably related to the proposal.

Conclusions
Unreasonable pursuit of a planning obligation by the LPA.

---

activities that were being reported as planning gain:

> Planning gain is a somewhat misleading term. A key element of our statutory land-use planning system in this country is action by local planning authorities to influence developers to come forward with proposals which are in accord with the Authorities' development plans and other policies. This may include essential infrastructure provision of various kinds. This should quite properly be termed planning gain. However, the term has more recently been applied to agreements entered into by local planning authorities and applicants, to ensure that a development when permitted includes wider benefits.
>
> (Byrne 1989)

The Planning and Compensation Act 1991 introduced a series of reforms and a new term: 'planning obligation' (Redman 1991).

Alongside these reforms to the operation of the planning gain system, Circular 22/83 became superseded by Circular 16/91, entitled *Planning obligations* (issued on 8 October 1991). This Circular stated in paragraph B2:

> The term planning gain has no statutory significance and is not found in the Planning Acts. . . . In granting planning permission, or in negotiations with developers and other interests that lead to the grant of planning permission, the local planning authority may seek to secure modifications or improvements to the proposals submitted for their approval. They may grant permission subject to conditions, and where appropriate they may seek to enter into planning obligations with a developer regarding the use or development of the land concerned or other land or buildings. Rightly used, planning obligations may enhance development proposals.

Circular 16/91 was itself replaced in January 1997 by 1/97: *Planning Obligations*. This guidance was more positive in tone than its predecessors, detailing quite restrictively both good and bad practice, and clarifying government planning policy in light of case law. The Circular echoed much that was previously in Circular 16/91 and laid down the broad principle that . . . 'To retain public confidence, such arrangements [for negotiating planning obligations] must be operated in accordance with the fundamental principle that planning permission may not be bought or sold'. In the same year Lord Justice Nolan was to conclude in a report on the planning system that it was a widely held view among the public that obligations amounted to just that, namely the buying and selling of planning permission (Committee on Standards in Public Life 1997).

The legal issues

Planning obligations

Planning obligations are created under Section 106 of the TCPA 1990. A new Section 106 was introduced into the 1990 Act by the Planning and Compensation Act 1991,[4] together with a new Section 106A (powers to modify or discharge an obligation) and Section 106B (appeal against refusal to modify or discharge an obligation). The Section 106 obligation forms the legal contract by which the objectives of the planning obligation are legally honoured and enforced.[5]

In addition, local planning authorities may enter into legal agreements with developers under Section 111 of the Local Government Act 1972.[6] It is common practice for such legal agreements to recite that they are made in compliance with both statutes. It is possible for a planning condition to be used to control various land-use matters instead of a planning obligation. However, a condition may be of limited use because in the majority of cases it may deal only with land-use planning related issues within the application site[7] and, this notwithstanding, many local authorities simply prefer the legal enforceability associated with Section 106 and Section 111. If a proposal involves a financial payment or an off-site matter such as a highway improvement, then a legal agreement will normally be required. With the very limited use of conditions, it follows that Section 106 planning obligations provide the most popular and effective method of control. Section 106 establishes that any obligation used specifically to restrict the development or use of land may require specific operations or activities to be carried out or that a sum of money be paid to the LPA.

The 1991 Reforms to the system were:

* Planning obligations were introduced and came into force on 25 October 1991.[8] The new concept of the planning obligation comprised either a Planning Agreement, whereby the developer/landowner enters into an agreement with the local planning authority, or a unilateral undertaking, whereby the developer/landowner gives an undertaking to the LPA. Such obligations may restrict the development or use of land, require specific operations (works) or activities (uses) to be carried out on land owned by the applicant, which may be within the application site or may be on neighbouring land, require land to be used in a particular way, and

---

Case study 6.5

Proposal
Megabuild Limited proposes a new retail warehouse development on a site identified in the local plan for residential use. The eastern boundary of the site adjoins existing residential development and Megabuild offers additional tree planting on this side and will also pay for double glazing for these properties.

Tests (see Table 6.1)
It is considered that the proposed obligation would be needed to overcome a potential loss of amenity caused by delivery vehicles manoeuvring alongside this boundary. This would satisfy the guidance in 1/97 and would be functionally related. However, the principle of development is unacceptable to the local authority because the retail warehouse use is contrary to local plan policy. The offer of an obligation is rejected and the application is refused because:

(a) it results in a loss of amenity to residents
(b) it is contrary to policy.

Conclusions
If Megabuild goes to appeal, it can offer a unilateral undertaking to 'target' reason (a) and thereby concentrate its case on fighting reason (b).

---

require payments to the local authority periodically or at one time. (This was the first statutory recognition that an obligation may include an undertaking to make a financial payment, although the practice had existed since the 1970s.) There is no specific requirement within the Act that payments relate to the land itself or the development that is the subject of the planning obligation.

- The introduction of powers to modify or discharge a planning obligation. Following a period of five years from the date the obligation is entered into, an application can be made to the local planning authority on the grounds that the planning obligation no longer serves a useful planning purpose or should be modified in some way. The right of appeal to the Deputy Prime Minister is available in the event of the local authority either failing to determine the application or deciding that the planning obligation should not be modified or discharged.[9]

- The reforms were designed to overcome certain procedural inadequacies of the previous system. The unilateral undertaking allowed the developer to act independently of the local authority in offering to enter into an obligation at appeal (see Case Study 6.5). This would be binding upon that developer and any successors in title. Under the old system, an Inspector could consider the matter at Inquiry only if both parties had agreed to its provisions. The unilateral undertaking represents an important tactical benefit to the developer. If an application goes to appeal, then such a unilateral offer can be used to target specific objections to the scheme, such as the improvement to the neighbouring highway to overcome the impact on traffic generation from a proposed development. The introduction of unilateral undertakings will not render the planning agreement redundant, as in some instances the developer will require the local authority to do certain things, for instance, to use the money they provide to undertake certain works. A planning agreement provides a legally enforceable contract in circumstances in which both sides are required to perform certain duties as a consequence of the planning obligation.

Modification or discharge allows the lifting of obsolete obligations. Under the old (pre-1991) system, such a result could be obtained only by application to the Lands Tribunal,[10] who could only consider if the matter was obsolete in legal terms and not on planning grounds. For example, a planning obligation may be agreed that provides for the construction of a community centre within a new residential development, as well as an access road across the site. In future, a new highway could be constructed along the eastern boundary of the site providing a road frontage to the centre. The original access road will no longer be required and its future maintenance will not serve the original planning purpose provided for in the agreement, and the planning obligation should therefore be discharged.

Examples of planning obligations

Government planning policy establishes that if properly used, planning obligations may both enhance the quality of development schemes and permit the granting of planning applications that would otherwise have to be refused. The government was, however, keen to state that acceptable applications should never be refused because an applicant is unwilling to offer benefits, or conversely that simply because benefits are proposed does not render an unacceptable scheme to be automatically acceptable. Instead the relevant circular establishes a number of relevant 'tests' or pre-conditions that must be satisfied. Yet, and somewhat confusingly for the student of planning, failure to satisfy these pre-conditions does not render any subsequent obligation 'unlawful' rather, it effectively invalidates the merits of what is agreed as a material town planning consideration. In practice this means that such an obligation (which will be 'tied' to a planning permission) will carry little weight if LPAs or developers wish to rely upon it in future years to justify a repeat of the principles as established. Circular guidance is broad in its content, but does establish that any obligation must be both 'necessary' and 'fairly and reasonably related' directly in proportion with the requirements of the site in question. Circular 1/97 made it clear that 'Developers should not be expected to pay for facilities which are needed solely in order to resolve existing deficiencies nor should attempts be made to extract excessive contributions to infrastructure costs from developers' [by LPAs]. The government was at pains to ensure that planning obligations did not form some kind of backdoor betterment[11] levy in which community or other benefits are extracted from a development scheme in proportion to the increased value of the land following a grant of planning permission.

Circular guidance establishes something of a broad canvas onto which the planning obligation system may be painted, albeit that government often

Table 6.1 Prerequisites of a planning obligation

1/97	Relevant paragraph	Key points
Obligation is 'needed'	Paragraph B9 of 1/97	• Needed to allow development to go ahead, e.g. access • Needed from a planning point of view, e.g. to deal with replacement of open space and provision of schools.
Obligation is 'fairly and reasonably related'	Paragraph B12 of 1/97	• Developer payment to facilities must be reasonable, e.g. construction of access is paid for by developer or provision of open space restores facilities to an equivalent quality to that existing before development.

views such guidance as restrictive (DETR 2001a). Very little is specifically ruled inside or outside the guidance. Instead much is left to the individual interpretation of planning officers, planning inspectors and developers or their professional representatives. Considerations as to the Circular's prerequisites or 'need' or 'reasonable relationship' allow a wide discretion over what obligations are within or outside government policy. Ultimately negotiation will play a part, which may result in the unsatisfactory situation in which the public consider private deals are being struck. The planning officer (and planning committee) will need to arrive at a professional judgement as to whether an obligation is appropriate and if so the nature of its content. The system is thus based on local discretion within a framework of policy, established by government.

Planning obligations have been classified as land-use/amenity related gains and social/economic related gains (Debenham Tewson Research 1988). Certainly, in the latter category it is harder to satisfy all the tests of reasonableness, and such provision of social and economic infrastructure within planning obligations tends to produce greater controversy and provides critics of the system with an easy target. The starting point should be that an obligation is required only to overcome some legitimate planning objection to a proposal. Yet, the British system in general and the planning obligations system in particular, are based upon negotiation and bargaining. If a developer wishes to offer land or financial payment towards social and economic infrastructure beyond the strict requirement of the consent, then that is the prerogative of the developer. This may be viewed as 'buying planning permission' on one hand or as an acceptance of the need towards betterment in society. Either way, it does not make the obligation illegal within the rules of the system.

The lack of detailed guidance by government will result in difficulty in interpreting the tests. The system has been described as 'fuzzy' (Lichfield

Case study 6.6

Proposal
Barcode Developers proposed to build a new food superstore. The local planning authority required several highway improvements around the application site, including new roundabouts, new traffic signals and upgrading of several roads. These works had been required for many years. Since traffic generation has been steadily rising from an adjoining business park, opened three years before, highway improvements had become a matter of urgency. The local planning authority argued that the new works were necessary because its scheme represented 'the last straw to break the camel's back'. The developer considered this unacceptable, arguing that it was being required to solve problems of traffic generation produced by other sites.

Tests (see Table 6.1)
An unreasonable pursuit of an obligation by the LPA as it is seeking to penalize one developer for traffic generation resulting from other sites. This is not fairly and reasonably related to the development to be permitted. In *Safeway Properties Limited* vs *Secretary of State* (1990),* the Court of Appeal considered such highway improvements in the general locality to be unrelated to the building of a new superstore proposed.

Conclusions
Although some highway improvements may be required to cope with the new superstore, it is unreasonable to request that this scheme shoulders the burden of previous developments. This is an example of land-use gain that is substantially unrelated in functional terms with the development and, as such, unreasonable. If the gain was more directly linked – perhaps one new round-about opposite the application site – then it could be seen as being both reasonable and related. Traffic generation resulting from this scheme constitutes a material planning consideration and the local planning authority could refuse planning permission on this basis. However, it is unreasonable for gain to be sought (dealing with highway matter or otherwise) on the grounds that this would remedy problems (land use or social) not related to the application site.

* For a detailed report see *Journal of Planning and Environment Law*, October 1991, pp. 966–73.

1989). It will continue to be fuzzy as long as the government maintains such policy guidance, which is based upon the application of 'tests' to the vast array of suggested planning obligations that arise from consideration of planning applications.

Stronger criticism has been expressed by two eminent former Chief and Senior Planning Inspectors, respectively Stephen Crow (1997) and John Acton (1998). Crow (ibid.) argues that while developer payments towards infrastructure provision is a legitimate activity, the 'gain' system brings the planning profession into disrepute by promoting a culture in which planning permissions may be bought and sold. Acton (ibid.) goes further, arguing that the system fuels public suspicion and cynicism about the planning process. Some developers and LPAs manipulate the system to either buy (or enhance chances of gaining) their consent or by extracting benefits without good reason. Lord Justice Nolan (Committee on Standards in Public Life 1997) added further authority to such opinion when, set against the background of standards in public life, he found with respect to planning obligations (and gain) that 'The potential problems have little to do with corruption, but have a tremendous impact on public confidence', and that should the post 1991 regime continue, 'planning permissions will continue to be "bought and sold"'.

As with many critics of the system, Nolan was not opposed to the principle of the wider community (via the planning system) imposing a charge against developers for infrastructure. The key issue was the means by which such a charge was levied and public scrutiny of or confidence in that system. Nolan recommended that government should reconsider the wording used in Section 106 of the Town and Country Planning Act 1990 to make more explicit the fact that permissions should not be bought or sold. No such revisions were forthcoming and calls for reform fell on deaf ears in government during the late 1990s. It was not until 2000, in the Urban White Paper, that a fresh review of planning gain was heralded. A consultation paper reviewing the 1991–2000 system of planning obligations was issued in 2001 (DETR 2001a). In large part this was in response to calls for reform made by the Urban Task Force (1999). The Task Force was generally supportive of the notion of planning gain: 'our main conclusion is that the use of planning obligations to secure planning gain is necessary and justified', although they then added . . . 'but that the process is not currently being applied consistently'.

The Task Force reported three principal problems[12] in the system: that Section 106 Agreements were taking too long to process, were not produced to standard formats (in drafting) across the country and often revealed little grasp of commercial reality by planners. The Task Force made three specific recommendations: that national guidance be revised, arbitration be introduced when Section 106 negotiations were not proceeding to a conclusion and standardized impact fees be introduced to extract 'gain' in smaller urban development schemes. Such influential lobbying for reform galvanized government to set in progress a review and subsequently reform. What remains a matter for decision is whether the post 2004–5 planning gain system will continue with the Circular guidance and negotiation of the previous approach, or will it embrace impact fees to create an entirely different approach.

Case law

These examples are used to illustrate important interpretations of Circular advice. A planning obligation is often the result of negotiation between both parties and not an offer made by one side. The application of the tests of reasonableness is an important material consideration in the assessment of any planning obligation. Several judicial pronouncements on this issue provide an important interpretation of planning legislation. In

Newbury District Council vs *Secretary of State for the Environment* (1988),[13] the Court of Appeal said that any planning obligation should serve a planning purpose, related to the development and not be unreasonable (to the extent that no reasonable planning authority could have imposed it). In *Regina* vs *Plymouth City Council and others ex parte Plymouth and South Devon Co-operative Society Limited* (1993),[14] the Court of Appeal, in supporting a previous decision by the High Court, cast doubt on the role of the 'tests' as a legal guideline (which are now replaced by the pre-requisite of an obligation, see Table 6.1 for summary). The legal test was the one stated in Newbury, the tests themselves only represented government policy and not statute. They must always be viewed in this context. The contention that planning obligations amount to the 'sale of a planning permission' was considered in *Regina* vs *South Northamptonshire District Council ex parte Crest Homes* (1994). The LPA was seeking to finance infrastructure provision in the absence of sufficient public funding to achieve this. The Court of Appeal held that, in this case, such a policy *was* lawful. Particular emphasis was laid on the fact that the LPA had identified specific infrastructure projects and sought to distribute the infrastructure cost equitably among a consortium of developers and landowners in the area.

In *Tesco Stores Limited* vs *Secretary of State for the Environment*[15] (11 May 1995), the House of Lords upheld the Secretary of State's decision to grant planning permission to Sainsbury for a site in Witney, Oxfordshire (where Tesco were also promoting a superstore site). In so doing, the Secretary of State had overturned the decision of the Inspector hearing the original appeals, who had recommended in favour of the Tesco proposal, which included the offer of a £6.6 million contribution to highway works for their store. It was held, following an appeal by Tesco, that their proposed planning obligation had been taken into account, quite properly, by the Secretary of State and that it was within his discretion, and not a matter for the courts, to accord it whatever weight he considered appropriate (apparently whether or not it was disproportionate to the development proposed).

This decision may cast further doubt on the value of Circular guidance in interpreting what is, and what is not, a reasonable offer of planning gain. The Court seems to seek to rely on a simpler, yet broader and more vague, test: that the proposed planning obligation constitutes a material consideration, that it is entirely within the decision-making body's discretion to weigh in the overall evaluation of an application. This would throw a very wide net indeed. It is clear that, with such large sums of money involved, litigation in this area of planning law will continue. The outcome of all this litigation, especially the consequences arising from the Tesco case, is that while the LPA and developer should follow the guidance laid down by the Circular, failure to so do does not render the obligation 'illegal', but merely bad practice. What is strictly required is adherence to the terms laid down in Section 106 of the Town and Country Planning Act 1990, i.e. that it involves financial payment to the LPA or details specific restrictions on or requirements to construct buildings or regulate use(s).

We may go on to consider the wider philosophical issues surrounding this system in the knowledge that interpretation of the Circular's rules is a matter left to local planning authorities and developers, and the rules them-selves are by no means clear cut.

Summary: planning obligations – characteristics

- Section 106 of the TCPA 1990 provides legal powers to enter into planning obligations.
- The 1991 reforms to the system introduced the new term 'planning obligation' to cover both agreements between the LPA and the developer/applicant, and unilateral undertakings offered only by the developer/applicant, as well as the power to discharge or modify an obligation.
- Cash payments are detailed as permissible in the 1991 Statute.
- New Circular guidance issued at this time reflected the stance of previous guidance.
- These reforms did not result in a radical restructuring of the system but more an attempt to amend certain procedural tools or mechanisms.
- In 2004–5 the system will be the subject of review to contemplate intro-duction of 'tariff' (see the section below on reforming planning obligations).

The philosophical issues

> For some 'planning gain' was a legitimate contribution from developers to community development but it has been viewed by others as both an unconstitutional tax and a form of negotiated bribery corrupting the planning system.
>
> (Healey *et al.* 1993)

The practice of developers offering a variety of benefits to local authorities has resulted in many emotive, if easy to remember, phrases, such as 'planning blackmail', or 'cheque book planning'. Such a response to the system tends to ignore the more significant issue of whether or not a developer should pay something back to the community after taking profits from a development that will inevitably have some impact on the locality. The question for debate should be whether a developer should pay anything towards alleviating the impact of a development and then in what form should this charge be levied? Although these points are being considered, it should also be remembered that the planning obligation gives the developer a legal mechanism within which planning objections may be overcome, therefore improving the chances of gaining permission.

Historical background

In considering such issues, it is important to recall the historical development of the British planning system. The TCPA of 1947 nationalized the right to develop land. The ability to build or change the use of a building became a decision for society to exercise by means of the decisions of local planning authorities. However, land with planning permission would, in a country

with limited land resources, carry a premium. The planning system introduced a new control mechanism, which means that obtaining planning
permission would both enhance the value of land and increase the value of
adjoining land that benefits from the 'amenity' created by development.
These benefits introduced by the planning system or indeed any other
activities of government are referred to as betterment.

The 1947 Act was based upon the key philosophical position that, alongside the nationalization of the right to develop land, any future increases in
the value of land following the granting of planning permission should be the
property of the state (Ward 1994: 108). The new legislation introduced by the
Labour administration resulted in a 100 per cent tax on betterment (i.e. all of
the increased value of land resulting from gaining planning permission would
be taxed). This has been described as a contradiction at the heart of the Act
(ibid.), because private ownership of land would be maintained, yet any
increases resulting from the speculative grant of planning permission would
be taxed, thereby killing off a good deal of private sector activity by
attacking the profit motive. Not surprisingly, this proposal was unpopular
and the incoming Conservative administration of 1951 soon announced their
intention to end it. The Planning Act of 1953 abolished the development
charge without introducing any alternative tax measure to collect betterment.

A betterment tax was not to return until the late 1960s with the Land
Commission Act 1967. This time a levy of betterment at 40 per cent was
introduced. A new agency, the Land Commission, would oversee the system.
The new 1970 Conservative government abolished the Land Commission
after one year in office. The final betterment tax came with the Development
Land Tax Act 1976, which introduced a new tax on land value increases,
initially set at 80 per cent of betterment, with the intention that it would
eventually rise to 100 per cent. However, this Development Land Tax suffered
from a poor level of implementation hampered by a serious property
recession in the mid-1970s. This, then, represented the third post-war attempt
at betterment and it was itself abolished in 1986.

To assess the role of the planning gain/obligations system properly, we
must view developer contributions as either a modern form of betterment,
or instead as a legitimate development cost.

Betterment tax?

Planning gain/obligation represents indirect betterment tax in that it imposes
a charge on development grounds. The actual cost of developer contributions
will vary dramatically across the country and across development proposals.
The measure of tax will crudely depend upon the size of a development
proposal – the larger the proposal the greater the impact and the greater
proportion of gain required. It is unlikely that planning authorities undertake detailed economic appraisals of development proposals and then 'top
slice' a percentage towards community 'goodies' in the form of obligations.
(This view was voiced by the Urban Task Force 1999 as a criticism of the
system because the lack of economic awareness by planners resulted in
'blanket' calls for gain that ignored the financial realities of certain proposals.)
Most planners lack any professional training in such matters, and little

liaison is made with valuation officers employed within the local authority. It is largely a myth that planning authorities operate in this way, although it would be foolish to state that in large development proposals there is no expectation among planners and planning committees that some cash or contribution in kind will be forthcoming from the developer.

A betterment tax imposes a set of uniform criteria to be applied nationally and consistently. An obligation does not work in this way and the ultimate outcome reflected in cash terms will depend upon the merits of the case and the negotiation and bargaining between the two parties, influenced by government Circular advice. Planning gain/obligation may be viewed as at best a crude form of land taxation. It is not a continuation of betterment as introduced in 1947, 1967 and 1976, but in the absence of any other form of levy or development land tax it becomes associated with this subject.

Development cost?

The idea of developer contribution is based on the view that the planning obligation system represents a legitimate cost to a developer, who must accept that all development has some impact on the environment and that some level of contribution should be made towards either controlling or alleviating this impact. Such an impact may be physical (roads, landscaping, drainage, sewerage measures) or social (provision of social housing, community uses, access to open space or recreation facility). Government Circular advice is more aligned with this view than the betterment concept, in that it establishes guidelines for acceptable practice based upon functionally and geographically related criteria applied to each case.

It seems reasonable that the developer should make some form of contribution to the impact of a development proposal. In some ways the current system, when correctly applied, permits a developer to overcome matters that would otherwise result in refusal of permission. The problem that we return to is that the lack of clear definition and the application of vague government Circular advice means that, although obligations lean towards a development cost, they are a legitimate cost only if they are correctly applied.

To determine fully the extent to which legitimate obligations have been pursued by local authorities or indeed developers, reference should be made to research on this topic. Before the 1968 reforms, little real use was made of such legal agreements. It has been estimated that between 1932 and 1967 only some 500 such agreements were made. A dramatic increase followed over the next few years. A survey of 106 English planning authorities revealed that more than 50 per cent admitted seeking some form of planning gain (Jowell 1977). Research into the use of planning agreements by district councils (MacDonald 1991) revealed that around 70 per cent of all respondents were intending to include planning obligation policies in emerging local plans to strengthen their stance in negotiation with developers. The most comprehensive survey in recent years was published in 1992 (DoE 1992a). The survey findings of a sample of local authorities taken between 1987 and 1990 discovered that on average only 0.5 per cent of all planning applications were accompanied by a planning agreement. This could be projected to an annual total in England and Wales of between 6500 and 8000 agreements and in

Scotland of between 300 and 350. Significantly, the research concluded that local authorities generally adhered to policy guidance set out in government Circular advice and that only 12 per cent of all agreements in the survey contained provisions dealing with financial payments, most notably related to infrastructure provision. Only a small proportion of obligations related to matters that involved the provision of wider benefits not considered to be necessary to the grant of planning permission. One other significant issue raised by the research was the time taken to grant planning permission when an agreement was involved. In 80 per cent of such applications it took around one year to seal the legal agreement.

In 1993, research commissioned by the Joseph Rowntree Foundation (Healey *et al.* 1993) examined a total of 206 legal agreements signed between 1984 and 1991.

The final recommendations stated that 'The challenge for policy-makers concerned with planning agreements is to identify roles which enable market opportunities and transactions to develop efficiently while safeguarding legitimate environmental and community concerns.'

In its general support for the system, it recommended, *inter alia*, that social economic and environmental impacts should be considered as legitimate obligations.

Reforming planning obligations

Two models of future reform may be advanced, notably that of impact fees and tariffs.

Impact fees

The introduction of (US-style) impact fees is not a new idea. Such a system may indeed be something of a panacea for the many problems of planning gain, most often encapsulated as its arbitrary case-by-case approach (*Estates Gazette* 1999). Professor Malcolm Grant, one of the leading advocates of impact fees, argued as long ago as 1993 that . . . 'planning gain can be rationalized, and made more predictable, and impact fees are a step in the right direction'. Indeed Grant (1993) concluded that while impact fees were by no means perfect they performed far better than planning obligations when measured against criteria of transparency, equity, predictability, and efficiency.

A conference organized by the Royal Institution of Chartered Surveyors in 1999 considered both criticism of planning gain and the potential to introduce impact fees in its place. A paper presented by Professor Chris Nelson from the University of Georgia considered the functioning of US-style impact fees.[16] The starting point is that the local government must consider that a need exists for infrastructure. Such need is most commonly associated with growth, in which an urban area is projected to grow over the next 20 to 25 years. Local government planners are thus vested with the responsibility to devise growth plans and related infrastructure requirements. Such infrastructure must be costed and account taken of existing federal (i.e. national), state and local taxation that may (partially) fund such necessary services. The impact fees provide the 'gap' or 'bridge' between identified infrastructure (and its cost) and existing revenue allocated to local government via taxation. As Professor Nelson pointed out, 'The shortfall in revenue becomes the basis for assessing . . . impact fees'. The shortfall is then broken down into a 'impact fee schedule' of necessary works. Each development project, therefore, is responsible for paying a proportionate share towards the identified infrastructure. This system may be summarized as follows:

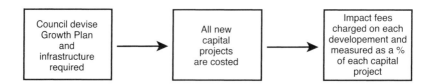

It follows and was noted by Professor Nelson, that . . . 'Impact fees are the last step in a planning process', in that they deliver on strategic infrastructure requirements as set out in the local land-use plan. An example cited is set out in the box below.

> The local land-use plan establishes standards for recreational and open space at 5 acres per 1000 residents. It is projected over the plan period that a town will grow by 10 000 people, creating the need for 50 acres of parkland. As housebuilders come forward they will need to pay a proportion of this cost. The local council will need to identify and implement these parks, acknowledging the source of their funding.

Professor Nelson divided US-style impact fees into four categories of infrastructure: that directly required (such as water supplies); that providing public services (such as schools, roads, parks); or a social function (such as subsidized public housing); and that providing for the maintenance of the whole process (mostly in payment of professional time to devise such schemes). In summary, this system of collecting infrastructure charges against development proposals is vested with several benefits over planning gain. First, impact fees are collected for a specific purpose and may be used only for that prescribed project. Planning gain is less tightly defined and may be used for a vast array of matters providing that council and developer agree. Second, impact fees are based on equality, being applied in a proportionate and fair way. Planning gain is less clear-cut, with the exact proportion falling on the developer dependent upon individual negotiations between developer and council, and varying on a case by case basis. Third, impact fees are simple to calculate and transparent in application. This assists all parties to understand the process and presents a favourable image to the public. By contrast the planning gain process is opaque, sometimes shrouded in private negotiations and the subject of public mistrust (as noted by Lord Justice Nolan). Finally, impact fees are deemed flexible. The calculation of fee is based on the relative proportion of infrastructure required. Planning gain can also be flexible, based as it is on negotiation. Such a benefit of impact fees may also be attributed to gain. Taken overall, however, planning gain appears at a disadvantage compared to the tangible benefits attributed to impact fees. Such benefit may account for the growing popularity associated with impact fees over recent years. The government-appointed Urban Task Force (1999) did not call for planning gain to be abolished but that standardized impact fees be introduced 'for smaller urban development schemes (for example, an end value of less than £1 million)'.

Tariffs

Tariffs represent the other planning mechanism and are most likely to replace planning obligations. Importantly, their employment was significantly endorsed in the 2001 consultation paper *Reforming Planning Obligations.* While this document was issued to invite comment, even debate, among interested individuals and groups, this powerful support is indicative of government thinking and the direction of future reform. Conversely, the consultation paper argued against impact fees because they would remove necessary flexibility.

Tariffs themselves involve a schedule of planning obligations, seeking various works and/or financial contributions. They are given foundation, even authority, by virtue of their integration into the Local/Unitary Development Plan (or Local Development Framework, when this reform is carried forward). Each council would be able to tailor its own tariffs to the prevailing development circumstances that it confronts. If an element of negotiation were to be required in small sites say, then this could be written into the policy to allow a measure of local discretion. National planning policy guidance would be issued (say in a PPG or PPS) in which the government would establish some broad rules regarding the setting of a tariff (i.e. when it would/would not apply) and the monitoring and accounting involved (i.e. by a standard form of legal contract between the parties). Otherwise government would effectively devolve powers to the local planning authority.

This system would arguably involve more clarity, certainty and even transparency than the planning obligation system introduced in 1991. The tariff would be set in local planning policy within a series of broad rules as established nationally. One somewhat prickly issue would be the exact calculation of the tariff. Government themselves implicitly acknowledge this in the 2001 consultation paper by providing four options: (i) cost measured by floorspace; (ii) cost measured by unit (e.g. dwellings); (iii) cost as a proportion of development value; or (iv) a combination of these. The ultimate calculation of the tariff set will be difficult, even controversial. It will obviously influence the nature and pattern of development. Such an approach can be used to encourage sustainable development, itself a necessary attribute of any new system. For example, tariffs could be higher for green-field housing schemes compared to brown-land and equivalents. Nevertheless, potential exists for conflict in a number of areas. First, there are cross-boundary issues, when two councils either side of a local government boundary set wildly differing tariffs. This may greatly encourage commercial, industrial and residential development in one council to the exclusion of the

other. Second, disputes could arise over valuation matters. If the development value of a planning application forms the basis of a tariff calculation
then disagreements may arise as to the assumptions employed in arriving at
those figures. Finally, there could be controversy surrounding how the tariffs
are to be spent. They would need to be carefully formulated to ensure
that any financial contributions collected were used directly towards the
necessary infrastructure works as dictated by the tariff schedule. Any
pooling of tariffs by a group of councils to pay for major infrastructure (such
as a by-pass relief road) would need to be carefully considered to prevent the
accusation by a developer that they were paying a disproportionate amount
of the total tariff.

In summary, tariffs present themselves as the most likely reform. They
enjoy many benefits, especially the clarity and certainty they bring as all
parties know what to expect after reading the schedule set out in policy. Some
of the uncertainty surrounding Circular 1/97 would be gone. What would
replace it, however, would be a system based loosely on betterment taxation
as a standard levy extracted from specified development types of schemes.

Conclusions

The system whereby developers contribute towards social and physical
infrastructures in return for obtaining planning permission has remained
largely unaltered since 1968. In spite of some important procedural changes
introduced in 1991, the system is based on negotiation between developers
and LPAs with, since 1983 and 1997, some broad policy guidance issued by
the government. Nothing is specifically prescribed as either acceptable or
unacceptable, and the application of government guidelines or tests may
result in considerable uncertainty as to what is acceptable. Developers may
feel that they have little choice but to comply with LPA demands for benefits,
as to pursue the matter at appeal has no guarantee of success. Yet, within this
somewhat imperfect system and in the absence of any formal betterment
taxation, it would appear that both sides in the development process have
made the system work in practice. Research in the early 1990s has indicated
that the tests are generally followed by the LPA and in the majority of cases
the obligations were required to facilitate the grant of planning permission.
As long as the system operates on this level, then it is clearly a legal
mechanism by which a developer can rectify the physical and sometimes
social impact of the proposal. In this respect it is clearly a development cost.
The problem occurs when the system is used as a means by which LPAs
can extract *wider* social benefits. Although research in the early 1990s has
demonstrated that this is not the case in the vast majority of proposals, when
it does occur it creates frustration and fuels the misconceptions of 'planning
blackmail'. Further, as the system is currently constructed, there is no
effective braking mechanism that could prevent this occurring in future years.
By taking the matter of appeal (usually against non-determination) to expose
the unreasonable pursuit of an obligation, the developer risks a great deal.

Several alternatives have been proposed: for instance, the American model
of impact fees (Grant 1993, 1995b) or the concept of a community benefit
(Lichfield 1989). In America a standard fee is payable according to the type

and size of a development proposal, which contributes towards a public schedule of a proposed infrastructure. Such a system has an element of openness and certainty within which the developer can clearly calculate the expected contribution before an application is submitted. However, it is difficult to standardize all development types into a shopping list of contributions, as development projects and their impacts are variable and prove difficult to measure uniformly. Such a system inevitably involves greater bureaucracy than currently exists.

A community benefits system would represent a reformulation of the current system, whereby each development application would be subject to a valuation appraisal, agreed by both sides, and a community benefit either on site or off site, but related to the use and development of the land, would be calculated to determine what would be affordable. This would give greater formality to the role of economic appraisal within the system and it attempts to create a refined version of a betterment tax. Its association with betterment makes such a proposal unpalatable to any Conservative government.

The system has been made to work. Indeed, the number of obligations is likely to increase during the decade as local government's own funding becomes increasingly squeezed by fiscal restrictions on public sector expenditure. Such trends are not exclusive to Britain. In Australia, for example, both state and local government bodies have, since the late 1980s, increasingly sought contributions from developers towards both physical and social infrastructures. It may be perceived as representing planning blackmail, but this view is not based on evidence of its operation in practice but instead, in a minority of cases, the perception of perhaps being on the receiving end of bad practice. In the current system, planning obligations represent a means of extracting development contributions to lessen the impact of planning applications. It is not a formalized form of betterment and as such represents a hidden form of taxation. The post-1991 system provides a framework within which the impacts of planning permission can be controlled. The cost is therefore concealed within a planning framework. It may be convenient for governments to keep it concealed, instead of adopting a system such as impact fees, which applies additional and formal taxation to potential developments, instead of the British system, which leaves the matter to local negotiation subject to the merits of the case.

It appears likely that following a review of the system between 2001 and 2004 the planning obligations system (of 1991) will be scrapped. A number of possible scenarios were considered by government. These involved impact fees and tariffs. The idea of keeping the status quo but enforcing more rigorously the tests in the Circular guidance was considered but dismissed. The government exhibited an appetite for wholesale change in preference to minor revision. This change is anticipated by 2004–5. It will require fresh legislation and new national planning policy guidance. Once this new system is up and running, its implementation will feed through into new Local and Unitary Development Plan policy (or Local Development Frameworks). A new system thus born of fresh primary legislation will establish a pipeline out of which new locally produced tariffs will flow. Such a pipeline could take any time between two and five years to achieve national coverage of such policies.

Part Three

Urban planning issues

7   Specialist town planning controls

'Specialist planning controls' provides an umbrella term under which we can examine topics dealing with the preservation of the built and natural environment. In urban areas in particular, listed building and conservation area controls seek to protect historic and architecturally significant buildings and areas, whereas urban design seeks to improve the quality of urban fabric when those areas are developed. In rural locations those considerations also apply, but many additional controls seek to ensure the protection of the natural environment for its beauty (i.e. National Parks, Areas of Outstanding Natural Beauty or National Scenic Areas) for its flora and fauna (i.e. Sites of Special Scientific Interest, Environmentally Sensitive Areas and Nature Reserves) and for its recreational value to Britain's mostly urban-based population (i.e. Country Parks and an objective of National Parks designation). Other environmental controls applicable to both urban and rural locations are Ancient Monuments, Archaeological Areas and Tree Preservation Orders. Green belt designation applies a multi-faceted approach, seeking to influence land-use issues applicable to both urban areas and rural areas located on the urban fringe (see Table 7.8 for a summary of these policies). This chapter will deal with each of these topics and will be organized as follows:

- Listed Buildings
- Conservation Areas
- design control
- green belts
- countryside planning.

Listed Buildings

A building or group of buildings considered of special architectural and historical interest, which are included in a list compiled by the Secretary of State for National Heritage and protected from demolition, alteration or extension without obtaining Listed Building Consent from the local planning authority.[1]

Procedure for listing

The list is compiled by the Secretary of State for National Heritage (or respective Secretaries of State for Scotland or Wales) on the recommendation of:

- His own Inspectors, who will undertake a survey of buildings. They may act upon the recommendations of local authorities or members of the public (a procedure referred to as 'spot listing').[2]
- English Heritage (The Historic Buildings and Monuments Commission), whose recommendation may be accepted with or without modification. English Heritage was created in 1983 to secure the preservation of all listed buildings in England. As a part of their role, they also provide specialist advice, acquire and manage a limited number of buildings and co-ordinate grant aid to secure the preservation of listed buildings, conservation areas and the public's enjoyment of such heritage. English Heritage undertakes periodic surveys to update the lists. A second survey was undertaken in the late 1980s to increase the proportion of Victorian and Edwardian buildings on the list and in the early 1990s to consider the listing of post-war buildings. Since 1970 the work of these re-surveys has increased the number of listed buildings fourfold to an estimated total of 500 000. The equivalent bodies in Scotland (Historic Scotland) and Wales (CADW) make recommendations to the Scottish and Welsh Secretaries, respectively.

The survey of a building, and consideration of its merits for listing, may be undertaken without notice to the occupier or owner, to avoid any demolition prior to listing. In 1980 the Firestone Building, an Art Deco 1930s factory, was demolished during the weekend prior to its listing coming into effect. To avoid further recurrence of this, powers were introduced to allow the service of a Building Preservation Notice to prevent demolition, alteration or an extension of a building without consent for a period of six months while the building is considered for listing. The owner or developer may seek a certificate that a building is not intended to be listed (a Certificate of Immunity) to avoid any uncertainty regarding its future potential for development. This immunity certificate, if granted, lasts for five years, after which the building may be considered afresh for listing. Such a certificate was issued against the former Bankside Power Station on the South Bank of the River Thames in London in 1994. This allowed the owners of the site, Nuclear Electric, to market the building for sale and redevelopment without the possibility of listing until 1999. In 2000 the building re-opened as Tate Modern, housing the Tate's collection of twentieth-century international art and contemporary exhibitions. The building's vast internal spaces and boiler house was well suited to providing gallery space, at a cost of some £80 million, but without the need to obtain Listed Building consent.

What kinds of buildings are listed

Specific groups may be identified in terms of listing:

- All buildings prior to 1700 that survive in anything like their original condition.
- Most buildings erected between 1700 and 1840.
- Buildings erected between 1840 and 1914 of definite quality and character, for example, the principal works of important architects, or those exhibiting particular design quality of workmanship employed in the building's construction and ultimate external or internal appearance.
- Buildings of high quality, erected between 1914 and 1939, for example, Hoover Building, Perivale, London, which has an Art Deco Facade on a 1930s factory, and Battersea Power Station (a unique power station in the middle of London). These buildings represent examples of high-quality design during the inter-war period. However, listing is no guarantee of preservation; Battersea has lain empty and increasingly derelict since the power station use ceased.
- Post-war to present day: only outstanding buildings. This criterion applies to buildings more than 30 years old and if under threat of alteration/demolition, and, in exceptional cases, buildings as recent as 10 years old may be considered for listing. The first building to be listed under the 30-year rule was Bracken House in the City of London (former home of the Financial Times newspaper and designed by Sir Albert Richardson), built 1956–9 and listed in 1991. Other examples include Centre Point in New Oxford Street, London (by Seifert and Partners) built 1961–5 and listed (at the third attempt) in 1995. The listing criteria acknowledged this building's architectural innovation and pre-cast sculptural concrete curtain walling to decorate the external elevation. This tower block of offices, flats and shops was admired as a symbol of 'swinging London' (Harwood 2000). Post-war listing has resulted in many unique and unusual structures being protected, such as a vast concrete sugar silo in Liverpool (Grade II*), a road viaduct near Wakefield (Grade II), a university engineering building in Leicester (Grade II*), and a new court house in Chesterfield (Grade II). The architectural or historic rationale behind these listings may not always be apparent. Arguably it is the case that . . . 'listing has to be one step ahead of fashion' (Harwood ibid.). The consequence is that such buildings are protected ahead of any threat of demolition and that the next generation will appreciate them more than the existing one for their preservation of the past.

Table 7.1 gives further examples.

What is listed?

Once a building is listed, then Listed Building Consent (LBC) is required for any works that would result in its demolition, alteration or extension in any manner likely to affect its character as a building of special architectural or historic interest. The need for planning permission is entirely separate from Listed Building Consent and, in practice, LBC extends far beyond what would require planning permission, because it deals with 'any matter' affecting the character of the listed building. The building itself is protected and this includes both internal and external fabric; for example, a period

Table 7.1 Examples of listed buildings

	Building	Reasons
Prior to 1700	Hampton Court	1515 begun by Cardinal Wolsey and later enlarged by Henry VIII in 1531 using Renaissance architects.
1700–1840	Radcliffe Camera, Oxford. Part of the Bodleian Library, University of Oxford	1739–49 by James Gibbs. A unique building in England with a circular form and strong Italian influence in its design.
1840–1914	Midland Hotel, St Pancras railway station, London	1868–74, Victorian neo-Gothic architecture, by Sir George Gilbert Scott.
1914–1939	Penguin Pool at London Zoo	1934–8 by Berthold Lubetkin with a novel use of moulded reinforced concrete to create curved shapes.
	Red telephone box (Kiosk No 2 or K2)	1925. Design by Sir Giles Gilbert Scott. The wooden prototype is outside Burlington House, Piccadilly, London.
1945+ 30-year rule	Bracken House, City of London	Highly decorative facade. Built 1956–9
10-year rule	Wills Faber office building	Excellent example of a modern office building with external appearance strongly influenced by lighting technology. Built 1975 and listed in April 1991 following proposals to alter the interior to construct a swimming pool within the interior.

plaster ceiling or a particular type of mortar used between brickwork may be considered to be of historic or architectural importance, and works to them will affect the character of the building and therefore require LBC. General cleaning works would not require LBC, whereas painting (in a different colour) probably would require consent. Any object or structure fixed to the building that is either external (e.g. guttering downpipes) or internal (e.g. wall panelling) is also protected, as is any object or structure within the curtilage and forming a part of the land since before 1 July 1948; that is, any outbuilding (garden house, statues, gazebos) will be listed only if it was constructed before 1948.

Grading of buildings

A grading system applies, which does not affect the level of statutory protection but does indicate the importance of the building. Three grades exist, as shown in Table 7.2.[3]

Once it has been determined that a building is listed and that the proposed works affect the character of that building, then it is necessary to apply to the

Table 7.2 Listed Building grades

Grade I	of exceptional interest (around 6000 buildings or, in England, 1.4 per cent).
(Grade II* (referred to as 'two star')	of particular importance more than special interest (around 18 000 buildings or 4.1 per cent in England).
Grade II	of special interest (around 417 000 buildings or 94.5 per cent in England). In Scotland 37 000 buildings are listed within a different classification of A, B and C. In Wales around 14 500 buildings are listed and classified in the same manner as in England.

LPA for Listed Building Consent. Although many churches are themselves included as listed, listed building controls do not apply to works for the demolition, alteration or extension of an ecclesiastical building that is currently used for ecclesiastical purposes. This would cover the place of worship and not any building used by a minister of religion for residence.

The LPA may grant Listed Building Consent, subject to conditions, or refuse it. The LPA must notify English Heritage (or CADW, Historic Scotland) of all applications dealing with Grade I and Grade II* Buildings and whose consent must be obtained before Listed Building Consent can be granted for these buildings. Every year English Heritage processes around 6500 such consultations. If an application involves the partial or complete demolition of a listed building, then the LPA must notify six national amenity societies who each have a specific concern regarding various periods of architecture or historic interest.[4] Refusal or failure to reach a decision within eight weeks carries with it the right of appeal to the Secretary of State.[5] All these listed building matters are considered separately from applications for planning permission. It is a common occurrence that many development proposals involve both listed building and planning proposals, and this will require separate applications and decisions.

Consider the following example. A brewery owns adjoining listed buildings: one is a public house, the other a retail shop. It proposes using the shop as a part of the public house and removing a party wall to connect the two buildings. The change of use requires planning permission and the removal of an internal wall requires Listed Building Consent. Each application would be considered separately with a separate decision issued. It is possible for either one to be granted and the other refused.

Other Listed Building powers

Unauthorized works

It is a criminal offence to carry out unauthorized works to a Listed Building. Therefore, the LPA may prosecute under criminal law, or it can issue an enforcement notice[6] seeking restoration of the building to its former state

Case study 7.1: Repairs notice and compulsory purchase – St Ann's Hotel, Buxton, Derbyshire

The hotel was built at the end of the eighteenth century as a principal attraction in the Duke of Devonshire's attempt to make Buxton a spa town to rival Bath. The hotel's fabric was neglected during the 1970s and 1980s, ending with its forced closure on environmental grounds in 1989.

In 1992 the Secretary of State, in consultation with High Peak District Council and English Heritage, served a repairs notice, followed by the compulsory acquisition of the property and works of repair and restoration. At the time there was some speculation among property professionals that this case heralded a new interventionist stance by the Department of National Heritage, and willingness to serve notices/acquire listed properties that had fallen into neglect and involved repairs that the LPA on its own could not afford to pay. Such speculation was unfounded and, since 1992, the Secretary of State has used these powers in only a handful of other extreme cases. If they were to be more widely used, then the Department for Culture, Media and Sport or English Heritage budget would need to be greatly increased.

or other works as deemed necessary. A Listed Building Enforcement Notice carries a right of appeal.

Buildings falling into disrepair

If a building has been neglected, the LPA may undertake the necessary repair works and recover their costs from the owner, or serve a Repairs Notice, which requires the owner to undertake such remedial works. If this request is ignored, then, after two months, the LPA may acquire the building by compulsory purchase.[7] No right of appeal is available against a repairs notice. These powers are used only rarely. It has been estimated that, between 1984 and 1990, only 300 such notices were served in England, resulting in 40 compulsory acquisitions. Such powers of repairs notice and compulsory purchase are also available to the Secretary of State and were used in 1992 to acquire the Grade I St Ann's Hotel in The Crescent, Buxton, Derbyshire.

Listed Buildings and the development process

When a building is listed, it has consequences for the owner or developer. Listed Building Consent is required for the alteration, extension or demolition, covering both internal and external fabric. This control is in addition to planning permission and may be perceived as either an additional bureaucratic burden or important control over the nation's built heritage. Decisions on Listed Building Control involve detailed architectural and historic appraisals and decision-making on applications takes longer than for most planning applications. Government policy establishes a presumption

Case study 7.2: *Demolition of listed buildings: the Mappin & Webb Site, No. 1 Poultry in the City of London*

The site comprised a group of eight Grade II listed buildings located within the Bank of England Conservation Area in the ancient heart of the City. The buildings were listed between 1970 and 1975, but towards the end of that decade the upper storeys, previously used for small offices, became vacant. Such small office suites were no longer required in the City of London, and the site's owner, Lord Palumbo, sought to redevelop it for modern office floor-space. Lord Palumbo's first proposal, in 1985, involved demolition of all the buildings and their replacement by a 90 m tower designed by the modern architect Mies Van der Rohe. The Planning Authority, the Corporation of London, refused Listed Building Consent, and planning permission and subsequent appeals were dismissed.

In 1986 a second proposal was submitted, by the architect Sir James Stirling. This also incorporated demolition of the existing buildings, but replacement with a modern building of similar bulk. Again, Listed Building Consent and planning permission were refused, but the Secretary of State granted a subsequent appeal. Save Britain's Heritage (SAVE) a heritage pressure group and third party at the appeal challenged the decision in the Courts. The matter was finally considered by the House of Lords* in 1991, five years after the submission of the original planning application. The key legal issue was whether the Secretary of State was entitled to permit demolition, contrary to his own policy in Circular guidance, in which a presumption was established in favour of the preservation of a listed building. The Inspector's decision letter, accepted and supported by the Secretary of State, concluded that the Stirling scheme was an 'architectural masterpiece' and that this was considered sufficient to override that presumption. Their Lordships accepted that the Secretary of State was entitled to take this view on the merits of the case, although this did not establish that in future the demolition of all listed buildings would be permitted in the event of the replacement being considered to be of greater architectural merit.

The presumption remained intact if perhaps a little 'dented' by this outcome. The appeal decision, supported by legal judgement, illustrates the wide discretion in decision-making within the British system to permit the demolition of a listed building in certain cases.

* *Save Britain's Heritage vs No. 1 Poultry Ltd and the Secretary of State* [1991] 1 WLR 153, *The Times* (1 March), *Estates Gazette* (Case Summary 24), *Chartered Surveyor Weekly* (28 March).

that listed buildings should be preserved. It is highly unlikely that Listed Building Consent will be granted for demolition (see Case study 7.2 on the Mappin & Webb site). Development potential can be restricted with greater attention required to design and materials used, resulting in higher costs. Grants are available from English Heritage for restoration and repair. Around £30 million is available in grant aid every financial year. However, no legal duty exists whereby the owner must keep the building in good repair. Repairs

Case study 7.3: The Hoover factory, Perivale, West London

The Hoover Building was built in 1932 and formed part of a complex of several buildings comprising factory, offices, staff club and canteen, commissioned by Hoover for its British headquarters and designed by the architectural practice of Wallace Gilbert and Partners. The frontage building incorporated into the Art Deco style of the 1930s Gilbert's love for Egyptian decoration, to create a spectacular façade. The factory buildings were hidden behind this elaborate façade.

Hoover vacated the building in 1980, and in 1985 the frontage buildings were listed as Grade II* which resulted in the automatic listing of all the factory buildings (either attached to the frontage or within the curtilage and built before 1948). The buildings remained vacant until 1990, when the entire site was acquired by Tesco Stores Limited, with a view to some form of superstore development.

The London Borough of Ealing, in consultation with English Heritage, granted a series of listed building consents and planning permissions, following a change in their own policies that had previously resisted a loss of industrial employment uses on this site. The Tesco scheme involved demolition of rearward factory buildings and construction of a 41 500 ft^2 superstore, together with extensive refurbishment and restoration to the frontage buildings. Work was completed during late 1992.

By permitting the new superstore, this outstanding landmark listed building could be returned to the glory of its original 1930s architectural splendour.

notices and compulsory purchase are available to Secretary of State or LPA, as well as enforcement powers and criminal proceedings against owners who have undertaken unauthorized works. The fact that a building is listed may enhance its value because of the cachet of period features or reduce the value as many institutional investors perceive such buildings as resulting in higher costs and poorer returns compared to unlisted ones. Maintenance work to residential listed buildings is exempt from value added tax (VAT). However, research by the Investment Property Databank has shown that listed commercial buildings have resulted in an investment return comparable to unlisted ones (Scanlon *et al.* 1994). Some institutional investors seek a series of building standards such as special floor loading capacities, which most historic properties cannot satisfy. Research has suggested that the fall in value associated with listing is a one-time cost, normally imposed at the time of listing, and such a fall is highest in small buildings (presumably suitable for conversion to other uses) in areas of high development pressure but outside conservation areas (RICS and English Heritage 1993)

Listed Building control and future directions

By 1970 120 000 buildings were listed. By the mid-1990s the figure had increased to 440 000 listed structures and (by 2001) 368 700 historic buildings in England (about 1 in every 40 of the country's total stock of buildings). It was estimated by English Heritage in January 1992 that 8.3 per cent (36 700) of all the listed buildings in England are 'at risk' (i.e. in very bad or poor condition and unoccupied) and that a further 16.5 per cent (72 850) are 'vulnerable to neglect' (i.e. in a poor condition but occupied); 2400 Grade I or II* buildings were considered to be at risk (including at the time the Grade I Midland Hotel at St Pancras Station in London, which was subsequently externally repaired and refurbished by British Rail). This lamentable situation meant that around 25 per cent of all listed buildings were in an unsatisfactory state of repair at the beginning of the 1990s (English Heritage 1992a).

This sorry state of affairs led English Heritage to monitor the progress of Grade I and II* buildings and Scheduled Ancient Monuments considered to be at risk or vulnerable to becoming so. The 2001 survey recorded 3.8 per cent or 1148 of Grade I and II* buildings to be at risk. This represents a significant reduction on the equivalent figure for 1992 (2400 Grade I/II* found to be at risk), although such a total was derived by estimate while the 2001 statistic was the result of more accurate survey analysis. Nevertheless, this is still a high figure, especially so when it relates to the categories denoted for being of exceptional, and more than special interest, respectively. It means that one in every 25 of the nation's most important heritage buildings are in an unacceptable state of decay. A number of factors may be identified as influential on the future preservation of listed stock and to a reduction in the volume of buildings in an unacceptably poor state of repair or occupation.

Dialogue between public and private sectors

Greater understanding between these two groups will help to break down misplaced perceptions about listed buildings. In 1991 and 1992 a series of joint seminars were held between representatives of RICS and English Heritage.[8] From such meetings it was evident that:

- English Heritage staff should learn about property values, and property professionals should learn about architectural history.
- Work was required to change the negative perceptions of funding institutions towards listed buildings.
- The importance of keeping a building in an appropriate use was viewed as essential to achieve its long-term survival. Some degree of flexibility in listed building control must be exercised to maintain viable economic uses. This can be achieved without compromising the important historic or architectural fabric of a listed building.

Such lessons are of importance currently, especially the need to maintain a building's occupation as an essential pre-requisite of its survival. In 1998 the Department for Culture, Media and Sport (DCMS) announced its intention to streamline control of built heritage, in particular to develop a better strategic approach. English Heritage would be merged with the Royal Commission of Historic Monuments in England in an attempt to exercise more strategic control of heritage, without diminishing government funding to this sector.

In December 2001 the government published its own review of the historic environment. Emphasis was again placed on a review of the role and function of English Heritage. In July 2003 the DCMS issued a wide ranging review of heritage protection policy and legislation. This review involved a wide consultation on a comprehensive overhaul of the system. The proposals countenanced the creation of a unified list of heritage features (buildings, archaeology and conservation areas), greater use of management agreements and the right of appeal against a listing. All listed buildings would require a comprehensive 'Statement of Significance' which details important features justifying the building's protected status. The outcomes of this review, during 2004–5, would enjoy the potential to reshape considerably the policy and legislation governing heritage protection in England.

In recent years English Heritage has enjoyed considerable success in association with the private sector to implement a policy of 'heritage regeneration'. Two policy initiatives during the late 1990s and into 2000 demonstrated success in matching (or exceeding) public-sector funding with private-sector contributions to act as a catalyst for 'long-term sustainable regeneration through conservation and to breathe new life into previously declining communities' (English Heritage 1998 and 1999). In the period 1994–9 English Heritage invested £36 million in 357 Conservation Area Partnership (CAP) programmes, and for the period 1999–2003 has committed a further £18million under the Heritage Economic Regeneration Scheme (for areas that have not previously benefited from other conservation-led regeneration schemes). Such funding is targeted at rescuing historic buildings and conservation areas in an effort to renew the economic prosperity of deprived urban and rural areas. Research has indicated that for every £10,000 invested by English Heritage via the CAP programme an additional £48,000 was matched by the private sector and other public sources (English Heritage 1999). This impressive 'leverage ratio' improved and regenerated commercial floorspace and provided employment. Such a model of public and private partnership has regenerated the conservation areas or historic properties of a host of diverse locations, ranging from inner city areas (Manchester's historic Ancoats district), to coalfield towns (the renovated market place in Bolsover), market towns (restoration of a historic shop in Towcester), mill towns (restoration of a range of town-centre buildings in Wigan), and seaside towns (restoration of a series of small hotels in Scarborough (English Heritage, ibid.).

Availability of grants

Grant aid towards listed-building preservation has traditionally been reactive in that a building has needed to fall into disrepair before it becomes eligible for assistance. The grant aid system operated by English Heritage was criticized by the National Audit Office in 1992.

By 2000/2001 English Heritage was responsible for allocating £68 million on conservation expenditures of which half represented grant aid to a variety of projects. Within this overall sum £5.7 million was allocated to 98 buildings at risk (English Heritage 2001a). To remove all Grade I and Grade II* buildings alone from the register would require a total expenditure of some £400 million. This would by far exceed the total grant aid budget of English Heritage (in the region of £110–120 million given annually by central government) and would consume the organization's entire annual income for nearly three years. Clearly English Heritage is a publicly funded organization and does not enjoy the financial means sufficient to solve this problem. Further, it would be wrong to expect such a body to do so given that, in 20 per cent of cases, the actions of the owner are the primary cause of the building's decay (English Heritage 2001b). What is required is a whole package of measures, including legislative coercion and targeted assistance. The problem is perhaps that English Heritage is committed to other responsibilities (including maintaining its own properties, education, and statutory guidance on certain conservation and listed building applications), so that it can devote only 0.03 per cent of the total income to 'at risk' buildings. This small sum must be used prudently and it is thus inevitable that Grade II buildings 'at risk' will be a lower priority than Grade I and Grade II* . However, the Heritage Lottery Fund (HLF) may also award grants to such buildings if they are in private ownership. Not surprisingly their resources are limited, although up to 2002 the HLF had provided over £300 million annually for projects relating to the historic environment. No standard or set criteria have been established in assessing an English Heritage grant award for a building at risk; however, the awards are intended for those buildings facing the most serious or immediate problems of repair (English Heritage 1995b). Beyond this work, heritage lobby or pressure groups have a vital role to play. Pre-eminent among a number of such groups is Save Britain's Heritage (SAVE), which has catalogued more than 1000 buildings at risk and publishes annual registers in the hope that an individual will take on the burden of the renovation of such properties (SAVE 1999).

Post-war buildings

Since the late 1980s, English Heritage's survey of post-war buildings has sought suitable examples of architecturally or historically important buildings drawn from all major building types built up until 1980. In 1993, 95 school, college and university buildings were recommended to and accepted for listing by the Secretary of State.[9] In March 1995, further recommendations were submitted by English Heritage, dealing with many other uses, including commercial, out-of-town offices, industrial and railway buildings. In addition, some post-war buildings have been listed under the 30-year or 10-year rule. The merits of post-war listing generated fierce debate between developers, heritage groups and members of the public. Most post-war buildings were built for a particular purpose and a limited life-span. Such buildings do not always easily lend themselves to conversion into alternative uses, which results in dereliction when the original use becomes redundant and conversion to another use may destroy the fabric of the original building and with it the very reason for listing.

Critics argue that such listings create an obsolete building, unsuitable for re-use, which remains empty for many years until the LPA, English Heritage or Secretary of State accept that demolition is inevitable to release land for redevelopment. Thus, the listing only serves to delay the agony; but this argument should not be used to resist all post-war listing, otherwise an important period of history would not be recorded in its built form. Instead, it should be used to justify a careful selection in which the viability of economic and acceptable re-use is taken into account in the decision to list. An example of failure to adhere to such principles was evident at Brynmawr in Gwent, South Wales. The 1951 former Dunlop tyre factory, with its dramatic vaulted concrete roof, was listed Grade II* in 1986. For 14 years the building lay empty and became increasingly derelict, with new occupiers discouraged by its vast size and high costs of remedial repair. In 2001, after some bitter rows regarding preservation of the building, the decision was taken to permit its demolition to make way for a purpose-built business park. Ironically the business park was not built and the site is currently cleared but devoid of any replacement scheme. Failure to take into account economic re-use means that post-war additions to the list will serve to increase the number of buildings 'at risk' or 'vulnerable to neglect'. In 1995 the Secretary of State for National Heritage announced that, for the first time, further additions to the list would be the subject of a wide-ranging public consultation of proposals to include professionals, amenity societies, private citizens and owners of the buildings.

Notwithstanding such additional consultation over this matter, the decision to list a post-war building remains a controversial one. Officers at English Heritage have themselves acknowledged that after an initial concentration on the period 1940–57, they have (since the 1990s) turned their attention to an eclectic range of 1960s and 1970s architecture. It seems inevitable that some of these 'little known but exciting buildings' (Harwood 2001), which do not share any single overall style, movement or period, should invite outrage and support in equal measure. Scruton (1996) and Harding-Roots (1997) have argued that a requirement of listing is the need for a measure of flexibility. In other words, the structure, both internally and externally, must be capable of change to accommodate new uses . . . 'to list a building is not merely to endorse its aesthetic or historic merit. It is to express confidence in its versatility. A listed building must be able to change its use, for human uses last on average no more than three decades' (Scruton 1996). It follows that most post-war buildings have been constructed for a specific purpose, such as offices, railway stations, schools, and industrial buildings. Consequentially they are not flexible and do not lend themselves to other uses without higher costs and considerable structural alteration, which itself compromises the rationale behind listing. It is more often the case, therefore, that such buildings will fall into disrepair. Commercial buildings are seen as being more vulnerable to such a problem, being . . . 'frequently constructed of materials with a limited life expectancy. They fulfil a role of providing modern commercial floorspace – nothing more – and they have little in the way of any wider purpose in attracting, for example, recreating or tourist-related activities' (Harding-Roots 1997).

A number of solutions have been proposed, including post-war listing being limited to the exterior only, periodic reviews in which derelict post-war buildings could be removed from the list and a specific category of 'M' to denote a modern listing. While none of these suggestions have become reforms, English Heritage themselves have placed emphasis on the deployment of 'management agreements' to facilitate preservation and economic re-use of such buildings. Such agreements between English Heritage, the relevant LPA and owner of the building provide detailed guidance on matters of particular merit in the building, stipulate various minor works that may be undertaken without Listed Building Consent and detail works where Listed Building Consent will be required and is likely to be forthcoming. Greater certainty is established as the owner is made aware of just what will or will not require consent and the likelihood of Listed Building Consent being granted. One of the best examples is the agreement at the Willis Faber and Dumas building in Ipswich (now Willis Corroon), which stipulated the importance of maintaining a specific type of partitioning and floor coverings in this Grade I office block (built 1972–5) but stating that the basement area 'is of little intrinsic special architectural character' and that partitioning here could be rearranged without requiring Listed Building Consent. The future direction of post-war listing requires greater deployment of such management agreements in pursuit of greater certainty and predictability, so that owners become more engaged in the process (English Heritage 1995b). Further, the decision to list a post-war building must be made with greater regard to issues of future re-use and the avoidance of its potential redundancy. While the decision to list is made on decisions of architectural or historic merit only, it may be necessary in the future to bring to bear an economic criterion to prevent situations as found at Brynmawr from being more commonplace. A government consultation document on listed building control (Department of National Heritage 1996) argued that 'major difficulties' would follow if economic, financial or even personal considerations were allowed to be taken into account in the decision to list. The government expressed a strong endorsement of the existing system of listing based only upon architectural or historic merit: 'the current regime is clear and defensible'. Once a building were listed, however, such matters could be entertained in any decision to alter or extend or even demolish the listed building. Introduction of such criteria at an earlier stage in the decision to list would result in protracted and often inconclusive debate over matter of repair costs, maintenance requirements, and a building's potential for restoration and economic re-use. In light of this definitive view of government it seems unlikely that decisions to list post-war buildings will, in the future, benefit from the added consideration of economic factors. The sensitivities of listing post-war buildings was acknowledged in 2001, when government announced that in the decision to list a post-war building, the Secretary of State would also seek comments from The Commission for Architecture and the Built Environment (CABE).[10]

Table 7.3 Examples of post-war buildings

Category	Building date	Built	Listed	Reasons
Educational	Templewood School, Welwyn Garden City, Hertfordshire; Herts County Architect. Still in educational classroom use.	1949–55	1993	Use of prefabricated building systems – architectural innovation in post-war construction methods.
Commercial, industrial	Centre Point, Charing Cross Road, London WC2	1961–5	1995	1960s office block illustrative of London speculative office development of the period.
30-year rule (Grade II)	Brynmawr Rubber Factory, Gwent. Architects Co-Partnership Grade II*. Derelict since 1980. Demolished 2001.	1952	1986	Roof involves nine spectacular roof domes the largest of their kind in the world. Example of architectural form.
	Keeling House, New Lane, East London – Sir Denys Lasdun Grade II. Vacant and derelict, subject to a dangerous structure notice in 1994. Renovated by a developer.	1955	1993	Post-war council housing tower block. Example of social housing policies in post-war years and early example of high rise tower block architecture.
10-year rule (usually Grade I – exceptional and under threat of alteration)	Alexandra Road Estate, Camden Borough Architects Grade II*. Listed during Council renovation works. Still in residential use.	1978	1993	Medium rise council housing block of 1972. Unique low–medium rise design.
	Wills Faber Domas Building, Ipswich. Norman Foster. Listed Grade I following threat to interior. Still in office use.	1975	1992	Novel use of a curving glass skin on the exterior to create an entirely glazed facade. The glass is not divided by mullions, but by translucent silicone to enhance the effect.

Summary of issues concerning Listed Buildings and future directions

- Grant availability is limited. Repairs notice and CPO will be used only to limited effect because of financial restrictions.
- Improved dialogue between English Heritage and the property industry will result in better understanding of the problems, and should reduce the number of listed buildings in a poor state of repair. However, without increased grant aid, the private sector will be required to fund the majority of maintenance costs.
- Post-war listing requires a balance between the preservation of the nation's heritage and the economic reality that certain post-war buildings are not capable of re-use without extensive alteration, which would dramatically change their character.

Conservation Areas

A Conservation Area is an area of special architectural or historic interest the character or appearance of which it is desirable to preserve or enhance.

'Special' infers being set apart from or excelling others of its kind.[11]

Evolution of conservation policy

Conservation Areas were introduced by the Civic Amenities Act 1967. Local planning authorities were provided with statutory powers to designate such areas, resulting in a stricter regime of planning control over development proposals. The first Conservation Area was in Stamford in Lincolnshire, designated by Kesteven District Council in 1967. Since that date LPAs have been enthusiastic about the additional powers that flow from Conservation Area designation, and every year has seen an additional number of designations. 1975 witnessed the highest number of individual designations, with 602, resulting in a total of 3000 Conservation Areas. By the mid-1990s this figure had risen to 8315 in England (English Heritage 1995) covering an estimated total of 1.3 million buildings (4 per cent of the nation's buildings; Rydin 1993: 108), 550 in Scotland and 350 in Wales.

Types of Conservation Area

No standard specification exists beyond the statutory definition of special architectural or historic interest. It is not always easy to separate the two limbs, and many conservation areas contain a mixture of both components. For example, Shipley Saltaire in Yorkshire is a conservation area designated by Bradford City Council in 1971. The area represents an important piece of both social and town-planning history, created by Titus Salt as a 'Model' Community in the mid-nineteenth century. The architectural layout combined good quality Victorian workers' houses and a park, church, shops and library. The design and location of its buildings reflect (and are a result of) the social ideas of Titus Salt in seeking to create a better environment for his workers. Therefore, both architectural and historic issues are closely linked.

Conservation Areas are designated for a whole range of varied reasons. The one factor common to all designations is that they are based on areas, not individual buildings, whether listed or not. The spaces within Conservation Areas are just as important as the buildings. These spaces may include parks or open land, streetscapes, public squares and village greens, or simply relate to the separation between buildings.

The following examples illustrate the diversity of such areas:

- Oxford City and the University of Oxford, including many ancient and historic buildings of the University and historic streetscapes; designated 1971 and extended 1985.
- Durham: ancient cathedral and university; designated 1968, extended 1980.
- Undercliffe Cemetery, Bradford; Highgate Cemetery, London; Necropolis, Glasgow; examples of Victorian cemeteries; designated 1984.
- Leeds–Liverpool Canal; designated 1988: example of Victorian engineering, not based around buildings.
- Hampstead Garden Suburb, London; designated 1968 and extended 1988: uniformity of architectural design and use of open space. Important post-Howard example of the Garden City planned layout.
- Bloomsbury (Fitzrovia), London: groups of Georgian town houses with square and open spaces; designated 1969 and extended 1985.
- Thame, Oxfordshire: medieval street pattern; designated 1969 and extended 1978.
- Royal Crescent, Bath; designated 1969 and extended 1985: Regency terraced houses with open spaces as an integral part of the layout.
- Finchingfield, Essex or Church Green, Witney, Oxfordshire; designated respectively 1969 and 1968: traditional English village green with buildings around.
- Leicester Square, London; designated 1984 (within Soho conservation area): highly varied architectural, economic and social character.
- Swaledale, North Yorkshire, designated 1989: rural area in Dales National Park with characteristic pattern of Dales barns and walls.

Implications of Conservation Area designation on development control

Conservation Area designation enables many additional development control powers to be exercised and will therefore influence the decision to grant or refuse planning applications.

Schemes of enhancement

The LPA is required to formulate and publish proposals, from time to time, for the preservation and enhancement of Conservation Areas. Such schemes must be submitted to a public meeting for consideration, and regard shall be paid to any views expressed. Proposals may include traffic calming measures to reduce and restrict car access, tree planting schemes, provision of street furniture (litter bins, street lights and seating, bus stops, etc.) or works to improve pavements and road surfacing (e.g. paviours or cobbles) to enhance the appearance of the area. Although many planning powers are viewed as 'negative', in that LPAs refuse permission to develop, these enhancement schemes allow for a 'positive' role in improving environmental quality in the Conservation Area. Unfortunately, financial squeezes on local government funding have restricted such works in recent years and many LPAs have ignored their duty under the Act to bring forward such schemes of enhancement.

Duty when considering planning applications

Conservation Area legislation imposes a duty on the decision-maker (LPA or Secretary of State/Inspector on appeal) when considering development control in Conservation Areas as follows: 'Special attention shall be paid to the desirability of preserving or enhancing the character or appearance of that area.'[12] This section of the legislation enables the LPA to exercise far greater control than would otherwise be possible over matters such as design or materials. 'Appearance' refers to the visual impact of a proposal and 'character' refers to the use or activity within a proposal. The terms 'preserve' or 'enhance' have proved more problematic in their definition, and the period 1988–92 witnessed considerable legal argument regarding the exact meaning of these terms in the exercise of development control and a degree of uncertainty within planning practice as to their exact interpretation (Stubbs & Lavers 1991). The matter was finally clarified in a decision of the House of Lords in *South Lakeland District Council* vs *Secretary of State for the Environment and the Carlisle Diocesan Parsonages Board* [1992].[13] Their Lordships relied upon the meaning of 'preserve' in the *Oxford English Dictionary* – i.e. 'to keep safe from harm or injury' – and therefore, where character and appearance were not harmed, they were preserved. Thus, preservation would imply a neutral impact; positive improvement goes beyond what is necessary to meet that requirement.

The meaning of the term 'enhance' was not considered in the *South Lakeland* judgement. However, following from part of an earlier decision in *Steinberg* vs *Secretary of State for the Environment* [1988],[14] enhancement is taken to produce a positive outcome, so to 'enhance' would imply a positive effect. See Table 7.4 for examples of how such legislative wording is applied to practical examples. For more guidance on development control powers in conservation areas see Suddards and Hargreaves (1996) Chapter 3, and Mynors (1999).

Table 7.4 Examples of how to apply Conservation Area legislation

Planning proposal	Harm (negative)	Preserve (neutral)	Enhance (positive)	Character (use)	Appearance (visual)
Externally refurbish existing hotel in Conservation Area by rebuilding part of structure and repaint, repair elevations.	–	–	Benefit as previously in a poor state of repair	No impact	Benefit to visual and external impact of building.
Conclusion: Enhancement of appearance of Conservation Area (positive)					
Remove ugly metal shop front and replace with wooden painted version in Conservation Area.	–	–	Benefit as previously an eyesore.	No impact	Benefit to external impact.
Conclusion: Enhancement of appearance of Conservation Area (positive)					
Change of use shop to bank in Conservation Area.	–	No difference in impact with similar hours and activity	–	No impact	No impact as shopfront the same.
Conclusion: Preserves existing character of Conservation Area (neutral)					
Change of use shop to pub in Conservation Area.	Late night noise and activity	–	–	Change in character with more activity	No impact.
Conclusion: Harms existing character of Conservation Area (negative or harmful result)					

Overall conclusions: A finding of either no impact or a positive impact to either character or appearance would satisfy the statutory duty imposed by Section 72 of the Planning (Listed Building and Conservation Areas) Act 1990. Any finding of harm (negative impact) fails the duty and planning permission would be refused on grounds of unacceptable harm to the Conservation Area in question.

Summary of Conservation Area powers

Statutory duty

If a proposal results in either neutral or positive impact on the character or appearance of the conservation area, it will pass the duty and should be granted planning permission. If a proposal results in neither a neutral nor positive impact, it will invariably result in *harm* and planning permission should be refused. These decisions are not always easy ones. They require both a thorough examination of the merits of the case and the application of professional judgement.

Conservation Area consent

Substantial or complete demolition of all unlisted buildings within a Conservation Area requires Conservation Area Consent. A few exceptions to this have been established by the government, notably any building smaller than 115 m³, any agricultural building erected since 1914, any industrial building up to 500 m² in area, or gates/walls erected before July 1948. Partial demolition may fall outside these controls. Listed buildings are already protected by Listed Building Consent, so this provision applies only to unlisted buildings. This Conservation Area Consent was introduced in 1974[15] and it allows LPAs to protect buildings that, although not worthy of listed status, do contribute to the character of an area. Government policy advice states that . . . 'consent for demolition should not be given unless there are acceptable and detailed plans for any redevelopment'.[16] The decision to grant Conservation Area Consent is like any other development control decision in a conservation area and is subject to the statutory preserve/enhance duty. The decision-maker will need to consider whether the loss of existing building and the proposed replacement would preserve or enhance the character or appearance of the Conservation Area.

Restrictions on permitted development rights

Freedom from the requirement for planning permission in respect of certain development in a conservation area under the General Permitted Development Order (GPDO) is much more restrictive, especially in terms of the volume tolerances for the enlargement of a dwelling house (reduced to 50 m³ for a side or rear extension to all types of property) and the exclusion of any external cladding (stone, timber, plastic or tiles) as permitted development.

Many LPAs seek to restrict permitted development still further by means of an Article 4 Direction. These Directions under the GPDO take away selected permitted development rights and must be approved by the Secretary of State. Without an Article 4 Direction, permitted development rights, albeit restricted, can dramatically alter the appearance of residential property. Works of maintenance are still permitted in a Conservation Area and can include extensions, re-roofing, double glazing and painting of brickwork.[17] By bringing such work within control and introducing a Direction, many house-owners are angered by the need to obtain planning permission to alter their own property and by the fact that the planners may insist on expensive materials being used in construction, such as handmade bricks or slate roof tiles to match existing period details.

Advertisement control

Advertisement powers may also be severely restricted,[18] to reduce categories of 'deemed consent' (advertisements that would normally be exempt from control). So that most advertisements will require permission. Most LPAs encourage painted shop signs, without internal illumination, within conservation areas.

Control over trees

All trees within a Conservation Area, whether or not they are already protected by a Tree Preservation Order, are given limited protection. Six weeks' notice must be given to the LPA prior to removal or any lopping or topping of such a tree.[19] If the LPA considers that the tree is of amenity value and should remain, they can then serve a Tree Preservation Order to protect it.

Publicity

Any applications that in the opinion of the LPA would affect the character or appearance of a Conservation Area must be advertised in the local press. This will be in addition to any neighbour notification that may also be required.

Conservation Area Advisory Committees

LPAs are encouraged to set up committees of local residents to advise on conservation policy and individual applications. These committees are usually composed of people drawn from local historic amenity or civic societies, as well as resident professional architects, planners or surveyors.

Exploding some myths about Conservation Areas

Do Conservation Areas prevent development?

No: Conservation Area designation only prevents unacceptable development. Although the planning regime is made tougher in a Conservation Area, government advice clearly states that 'Although conservation of their character or appearance must be a major consideration, this cannot realistically take the form of preventing all new development: the emphasis will generally need to be on controlled and positive management of change' (PPG15, *Planning and the historic environment*, para. 4.16).

Conservation Areas are based around Listed Buildings

No: they may often be centred around listed buildings but not always. The reasons for designation do not stipulate that the inclusion of a listed building is required.

Conservation Areas help preserve buildings

Yes: but they also preserve areas; therefore, open spaces and the separation of development are just as important as the buildings within.

Conservation Areas remove all permitted development rights

No: some permitted development rights remain. The only way to remove such rights is for the local planning authority to apply to the Secretary of State for the Environment to issue an Article 4 Direction (see section above).

Character and appearance represent the same thing

No: character tends to relate to use, and appearance tends to be visual (e.g. the buildings' elevations).

Conservation Areas and the abuse of designation

Conservation Areas introduce a restrictive planning regime. An LPA may designate as many conservation areas as it deems necessary. There is no statutory duty to consult anyone prior to designation although the government considers consultations with local groups to be 'highly desirable'. The agreement of the Secretary of State, following notification by the LPA, is only required for an Article 4 Direction, not a Conservation Area. However, the restrictive planning regime that follows designation may make planning permission harder to obtain and, subject to many factors, that will influence development cost by imposing the need for a high quality of design and materials. Conversely, this designation gives effect to valuable protection of the built environment. As conservation area designations have continued to grow over the years, critics have expressed concern that the procedure is now being abused. The early designations gained the support of the public and the development industry, but, more recently, designations have allegedly been made for political reasons, with greater control in areas that do not warrant Conservation Area Status.[20] Research commissioned by the Royal Town Planning Institute (RTPI) stated that:

> In a very small number of cases, new conservation areas appear to be designated for political reasons rather than for the benefit of the historic townscape.

This report recommended that Conservation Areas should be the subject of regular reviews by the local planning authority, which should ensure that policies and designations remain valid and up to date. There is still no legislative duty imposed upon an LPA to undertake such a review, and this recommendation is only an attempt at good practice and not a requirement of town planning legislation. It must also be remembered that many of the early conservation area designations contained boundaries that were narrowly drawn (Suddards and Hargreaves 1996), leading to a desire to extend or add fresh conservation areas around them. Since 1967 local planning authorities have become more adept at appraising areas, enabling them to define more accurately the special architectural or historic qualities on which a designation depends.

Summary: key characteristics of Conservation Areas

• strict planning regime
• development proposals must preserve or enhance the character or appearance
• debate that further designation beyond 8000 is resulting in a potential for abuse of the system.

Design control

Design control within the planning system operates at two levels covering, first, aesthetic control and, second, urban design or townscape. These will be considered in turn.

Aesthetic control

The dictionary definition of 'aesthetic' is an appreciation of beauty. In town planning, the term 'aesthetic' refers to the external design of a building. Many architects would argue that planning authorities should not be permitted to exercise any aesthetic control over development proposals and that such matters should be left to the architect and his client, because of the subjective nature of design. Since 1980[21] government planning policy has sought to limit the exercise of such control where it does not affect and/or is located within, either a Conservation Area, an Area of Outstanding Natural Beauty, a National Park or a Listed Building (either the building or its setting). Planning policy guidance in the early 1990s established that

> Good design should be the aim of all involved in the development process but it is primarily the responsibility of designers and their clients. . . . Planning authorities should reject obviously poor designs that are out of scale and character with their surroundings. But aesthetic judgements are to some extent subjective and authorities should not impose their taste on applicants for planning permission simply because they believe it to be superior.[22]

By the late 1990s this line was softened somewhat with PPG1 (of 1997) stating

> Local planning authorities should reject poor designs particularly where their decisions are supported by clear plan policies or supplementary design guidance which has been subjected to public consultation . . . local planning authorities should not attempt to impose a particular architectural taste or style arbitrarily. It is however proper to seek to promote or reinforce local distinctiveness particularly where this is supported by clear plan policies.

A refusal of planning permission based solely on an aesthetic judgement, such as the design of a window or door, could constitute unreasonable behaviour, sufficient to warrant an award of costs on appeal in favour of the appellant. Nevertheless, during the 1990s it was apparent that design was given greater weight as a material planning consideration, especially so where it was related to local policy.

Design control, therefore, is increasingly contained in local planning policy and in supplementary guidance (more commonly referred to as design guides). Such documents are produced at the most local level and therefore contain guidance that details matters of local architecture distinctiveness or vernacular, covering materials, style, and scale or mass of buildings. Many give guidance on such matters as the need for a pitched roof on a two-storey domestic extension, or the nature of shop advertisements (printed fascia signs, with external spotlights). In past years various design guides made some bold attempts to intervene in aesthetic matters. The most famous of these was the Essex Design Guide of 1973, produced by Essex County Council, which incorporated guidance on details, materials and use of local architectural styles (Essex County Council 1973). Such an approach is no longer in vogue and current design guides tend towards broadly based policies that avoid aesthetics and focus on such considerations as landscaping, height, mass and scale of new residential planning applications. What is essential is that such policies are given 'legitimacy' by virtue of their inclusion in policy that has been the subject of public comment. Providing that this essential pre-condition is satisfied, then government policy is content that design (and aesthetics) may be dealt with in the planning process.

Some of the most stinging and well received (by the public, at any rate!) criticisms of modern urban redevelopment and aesthetic control have been expressed by HRH Prince of Wales (Prince Charles). Some definitions of modern architectural terms are set out in Table 7.5.

The 1980s and 1990s was to witness a period of intense and at times acrimonious debate about the quality of architecture. While some of the subject matter was particularly British in content, much comparison was made with good practice in other countries. This debate was very much international in perspective, although its foundation was primarily in the critique of British architecture.

Study of this topic began in earnest on 30 May 1984 when Prince Charles delivered a speech at the 150th anniversary of the Royal Institute of British

Case study 7.4: Aesthetic control and urban design – Paternoster Square redevelopment, the City of London

The Paternoster area is located to the north of St Paul's Cathedral. The area developed around the original St Paul's which was founded in 604 and rebuilt by the Saxons in the late seventh century. The Paternoster area has been destroyed and rebuilt on two occasions. First, following the Great Fire of London in 1666, which also destroyed the Cathedral, replaced by Wren's masterpiece design, completed in 1710; and, second, by incendiary bomb attack in 1940. In spite of the extensive rebuilding following the Great Fire, Paternoster retained its original medieval street patterns, including principal thoroughfares and a series of tightly packed lanes and squares/courtyards incorporating three- and four-storey buildings used for residential and commercial purposes. The post-war reconstruction ignored this form and layout, with a series of 1960s high-rise buildings constructed on a grid layout. The brutal architectural style, use of concrete and separation of vehicles from pedestrians reflected the prevailing architectural and town planning thinking of the time, but it soon became unpopular among the people who worked in or visited Paternoster.

In 1992, outline planning permission was granted for the redevelopment of 1.7 ha (4.2 acres) of the total 2.8 ha (7 acre) site, which, with its location alongside St Paul's, is perhaps the most sensitive planning site in Britain this decade. The scheme submitted by Paternoster Associates proposed to re-establish the traditional street pattern, employing many urban design techniques to create a diverse and interesting street layout and provide 70 000 m² (750 000 ft²) of offices and 80 shops. The architectural form employed neoclassical aesthetic treatment of keystones, round windows, brickwork, limestone detailing and metal railings, drawing inspiration from the work of many classical architects. This ultimate choice of design has not been without a degree of controversy, illustrating how aesthetic judgement is a matter of personal opinion. The approved scheme has been described as '. . . the most outrageously theatrical classical-style architectural development London has ever seen since the construction of the titanic Ministry of Defence headquarters in Whitehall',* and the Royal Fine Art Commission has compared a part of the scheme to Disneyland. A previous proposal by Arup Associates, incorporating a modern architectural solution, was dropped following strong criticism by HRH Prince Charles in 1987.† Detailed planning permission was granted in early 1995.

The debate surrounding the redevelopment of Paternoster illustrates that the exact choice of a building's external treatment can, especially in sensitive locations, raise heated debate about what are matters of personal taste. Most property professionals and members of the public would agree on what may constitute good urban design, but it would be impossible to gain a consensus of opinion on what constitutes good architecture. Aesthetic decisions are important in conservation areas and when dealing with listed buildings. However, the many views expressed over Paternoster show that aesthetic control is a subjective matter and that local planning authorities should avoid becoming arbiters of taste concerning the external appearance of a building.

The design battle for this prestigious site was finally settled in 1998 when a second planning consent was granted. The scheme by architect Sir William Whitfield was chosen largely due to his close links with the views of Prince Charles. Six office buildings of 88 275 m² and associated retail space will create a new public square and restore views of St Paul's. Aesthetic treatment is modern. Demolition of the 1960s blocks was completed in 2001, with the redevelopment due for completion by 2004.

* The *Independent*, 3 February 1993.
† His Mansion House speech, 1 December 1987.

Table 7.5 A glossary of modern architecture

High tech:	Plentiful employment of glass and steel with exposure of building techniques, e.g. external siting of piping and ducting.
Classical Revival: (or neo vernacular)	Plentiful use of Greek and Roman architectural decoration in treatment of the facade.
Post-modern:	A mixture of historical details/style to create unusual shapes and forms.

Architects (RIBA). The guiding principles of his architectural and aesthetic pronouncements, throughout the 1980s and beyond, were established in this speech. The key points may be identified as community involvement, symbolism and decoration.

On community and public involvement in town planning, Prince Charles said . . .

> For far too long, it seems to me, some planners and architects have consistently ignored the feelings and wishes of the mass of ordinary people in this country . . . a large number of us have developed a feeling that architects tend to design houses for the approval of fellow architects and critics, not for the tenants.

By contrast, he advocated community architecture, wherein architects act more as servants than as masters, helping local communities to redesign their local environments.

On symbolism and ornamentation in design he made his (now famous) jibe at the high-tech extension to the National Gallery (in Trafalgar Square)

> What is proposed is like a monstrous carbuncle on the face of a much-loved and elegant friend.

On scale and decoration in architecture he advocated greater attention to the scale and decoration of new architecture, identifying deficiencies and bemoaning the post-war destruction of the London skyline:

> It would be a tragedy if the character and skyline of our capital city were to be further ruined and St Paul's dwarfed by yet another giant

Table 7.6 Key speeches on architecture by HRH The Prince of Wales

Speech	Key points	NB
26 February 1985	Promoted community architecture and gave examples. Called for architecture to *'lift the spirit'*.	*'Developers are coming to realise that good design produces a sound investment.'*
13 June 1986	That *'good architecture* both *makes money as an investment'* and creates a better environment.	Endorses classical revival architecture in inner city renewal.
27 November 1986	Brown-land to be used for new housing in preference to green fields. Promoted architecture with a *'human scale'*.	Emphasized beauty and harmony of classical Greek architecture.
3 July 1987	Desire for greater partner-ships in urban regeneration between public, private and voluntary sectors.	Professionals to act as enablers/facilitators to promote quality design.
1 December 1987 (Mansion House Speech)	Dire post-war redevelopment in the City of London especially Paternoster Square, especially in the 1960s and 1970s.	Need for a *'sense of vision'* in our system of architecture and planning.

* Source: Jenks (1988).

glass stump, better suited to down-town Chicago than the City of London.

During the period 1984–8 Prince Charles was to make several more speeches on architecture, including the notable Mansion House Speech. His views were the subject of further elaboration. A summary of some key points is set out in Table 7.6.

The Mansion House Speech was arguably the most reported of his many architectural pronouncements during this period. It contained some of the most widely quoted passages and produced the most vociferous backlash from professional groups (notably from architects).

In the space of a mere fifteen years in the 1960s and 70s, and in spite of all sorts of elaborate rules supposedly designed to protect that great view, your predecessors, as the planners, architects and developers of the City, wrecked the London skyline and desecrated the dome of St Paul's.

. . . the Department of the Environment [now Office of the Deputy Prime Minister] does not encourage planning authorities to set firm

Table 7.7 Ten principles of good design

1. The Place	Respect for landscape. All new buildings must respect their setting and avoid visual intrusion into the surrounding landscape.
2. Hierarchy	Size of building to signify its importance.
3. Scale	Relate to human proportions and respect buildings which surround them.
4. Harmony	Respect for the size/setting of a neighbouring building.
5. Enclosure	Enclosed spaces to create a community spirit.
6. Materials	Use of local materials and avoidance of concrete, plastic cladding, aluminium, machine made bricks and reconstituted stone.
7. Decoration	Detailed ornamentation to soften the appearance of buildings and enhance their visual appearance.
8. Art	Public art including sculpture and painting.
9. Signs and lights	Avoid corporate imagery and promote individualistic design notably in shop fronts and signage.
10. Community	Closer consultations by property professionals with the users/occupiers of those buildings.

aesthetic guidelines in development. As things stand, they are only justified in rejecting a proposal if it is absolutely hideous; anything merely ugly must be allowed to get through.

I am sometimes accused by architects of always being negative, so here is my personal vision . . . [build] at a human scale . . . at ground level . . . materials . . . ornament and detail of classical architecture . . . [add] character and charm [and] . . . ennoble commercial buildings . . . reassert a sense of vision and civilized values amidst all the excitement of the city.

In 1988–9 Prince Charles presented his views in a BBC television documentary and book entitled *A Vision of Britain*. At the core of this work he established 10 principles, which he advanced as general guidelines for the town planning system. He sought to stand back from detail and/or bureaucracy and examine the key concepts which will yield 'quality'. His design and aesthetic theories are summarized in Table 7.7 (HRH The Prince of Wales, 1988).

These concepts were put into practice at Poundbury in Dorchester, Dorset over the period 1996–2015. This site involved some 180 hectares of agricultural land owned by the Duchy of Cornwall and located on the western edge of the town. A master plan produced by the architect-planner Leon Krier was designed to create an urban and traditional townscape to the development. Traditional street layouts would incorporate terraced housing, courtyards, alleys, and squares to foster a traditional urban feel or 'grain'. Krier was keen to avoid suburban layouts of the post-war years in which housing was spread out and of a low density. The community theories of Prince Charles were to be realized by a mixture of tenure (housing association/owner occupier) and house type The urban design master plan gave rise to an 'urban style' using local materials and with vernacular detail, combined with a series of public spaces and community uses.

Poundbury presents a model of housing development that accentuates the aesthetic. Its construction has resulted in much comment and debate among planning professionals. While it displays Prince Charles' personal vision, it has influenced much debate on the design and layout of residential environments. In this respect the development of only a small parcel of land in West Dorset has been highly instrumental in shaping an appraisal of how planners and developers may improve the aesthetics of domestic dwellings.

Urban design or townscape

Urban design represents the subject area where town planning and architecture meet, that is, the design and layout of the urban spaces. In the 1960s a distinct urban design subject area emerged as a reaction to the many failures of comprehensive redevelopment during this period and the realization that both the architectural and the planning professionals were ignoring the design of public space (Tugnett 1987) '. . . the void between buildings, the streets and spaces which constitute our everyday experience of urban places' (Hayward & McGlynn 1993).

Works by Nairn (1955), Cullen (1961) and Jacobs (1961) warned against mediocre town planning and architecture, and sought to establish a series of urban design principles. During the past 30 years, various people have added to and refined such principles, including HRH The Prince of Wales (1989). A summary of urban design principles is shown in Table 7.8. Perhaps the most seminal work in this area was undertaken in the mid-1980s, culminating in an influential text that set out to create responsive environments or environments that offered both visual and pedestrian choices to their inhabitants (Bentley *et al.* 1985).

The principles previously promoted by people like Cullen and Jacobs were to be incorporated into an action plan of ideas, in an attempt to make environments more 'responsive'. But what did this term imply? The starting point, in the eyes of the authors, is that the urban environment should . . . 'maximize choice to urban occupiers'. One of the authors has subsequently argued that choice in the urban environment is very heavily influenced by economic power (McGlynn 1993). The fact that public space has been seen to decline in the last 30 years reflects decisions made by property developers (and the ultimate consumers of that property, the occupiers) who determine that, for example, a building should maximize use of the site to the detriment of other wider environmental issues, like design of public space or external appearance of the building. So, while the concept of 'responsiveness' may provide for choice in the built environment, the importance of other economic and social factors must not be ignored. Seven criteria of what it means to be responsive are advanced in Table 7.9. A combination of these will make an environment suitable with respect to choice and mobility of urban dwellers.

Table 7.8 Good and bad urban design

Urban design principles	A reaction to 1960s and 1970s architecture and town planning
Build on a human **scale**, low- or medium-rise development with regard to the nature of the surroundings.	High-rise commercial and residential buildings, with a brutal and intimidating appearance.
Use of traditional and local **materials**, e.g. stone, local brick.	Use of concrete in facing and roofing materials, with a harsh external appearance.
Ensure pedestrian **access** and **priority** within urban areas, e.g. traffic restrictions, and pedestrian only areas.	Dominance of motor car, with only secondary consideration to pedestrians (Ministry of Transport 1963).
Create a **community** with a mix of land uses (shops, residential and employ- ment) and housing ownership (rent or buy), together with community participation in planning decisions.	Subdivision between council rental estates and private housing estates and different uses in different zones in planning policy; local people feel isolated from planning decision- making.
Reflect the importance of the **function** of a building, so a civic building is identifiable by its grand design and decoration.	Similarity of buildings, making it difficult to distinguish the function of each.
Make the urban form **diverse** and **stimulating**, with the use of squares/ piazzas, narrow and winding streets, landscaping and traffic calming.	Urban form dictated by rigid and detailed road layout, creating uniformity of width and building plots, resulting in a boring and monotonous urban form

Table 7.9 Responsive environments

Permeability	'the number of alternative ways through an environment.'
Variety	'variety of uses is . . . a second key quality.'
Legibility	'. . . how easily can people understand its layout.'
Robustness	'. . . places which can be used for many different purposes . . .'
Visual appropriateness	'places as having meaning.'
Richness	'details' such as materials and construction techniques.
Personalization	'people can put their own stamp on their environment.'

After Bentley *et al.* 1985.

The period 1985–2000 witnessed gathering momentum in favour of quality design in urban environments. Assessing the success or failure of design schemes (measured against criteria laid down by, say, Ian Bentley or HRH The Prince of Wales) is not easy. Such decisions are based upon an individual's sensory response to a combination of factors involving an historic attachment to a place (or our 'sense of place'). Ultimately these factors (as identified earlier) combine to give 'meaning' to urban quality. Such judgements may not be easy yet nevertheless we know what urban environments we like and dislike: 'the element of meaning in our surroundings is essential to our psychological well-being. A meaningless environment is the very antithesis of what we need and expect our urban surroundings to be' (Parfect and Power 1997).

Arguably the most significant issue for urban design in the twenty-first century will be the incorporation of urban design principles into the renewal of certain 'cultural quarters' in major cities (such as alongside the Thames Embankment at Bankside in London or the jewellery quarter in Birmingham or Ancoats in central Manchester), and into the redevelopment of both brown-land inner-city sites and green-field urban extensions, as well as in identified major growth poles (such as an East Thames Corridor City between London and north-east Kent/southern Essex) (Smith-Morris 1997).

By the late 1990s and into 2000 government policy caught up with this new mood in favour of quality in urban design. Two documents have been influential: *Places, Streets and Movement: A Companion Guide to Design Bulletin 32* (DETR 1998d) and *By Design – Urban Design in the Planning System* (DETR and CABE 2000). *Places, Streets and Movement* acknowledged the poor-quality residential urban design created by previous adherence to a 'roads first and houses later philosophy' (Prince's Foundation 2000), in which 'The geometry of road design and the highway authority's adoption standards have frequently created places which relate badly to their locality and are indistinguishable one from another'. The document drew upon good practice (with many examples drawn from The Prince of Wales' development at Poundbury) to demonstrate how the technical requirements of radii and visibility could be achieved in a way that protects local context, sense of place and creates a 'high-quality public realm'. In effect and consistent with other policy directions (such as in the Urban Task Force Report) in which an urban renaissance would be created, *Places, Streets and Movement* promoted higher density 'urban'-style housing around public space and discouraged the low-density suburban pattern built around a hierarchy of estate roads, as had predominated in the past. *By Design*, in similar vein, promoted regard for local context and character in the redevelopment of urban areas, with an urban-design emphasis that promotes character in townscape, defined public and private space, quality public-realm accessibility, and pedestrian permeability, a diversity of uses and development that can adapt to social, technological and economic change.

Such reports are statements of 'best practice' and do not carry the same statutory weight as a planning consideration as, say, a local Development Framework policy or a PPG/PPS, although the need for high-quality urban design is itself acknowledged in PPG1 (of 1997). Nevertheless, these reports illustrate the growing importance attributed to urban design by government, on the back of previous work by eminent practitioners like Ian Bentley. As a new urban renaissance takes grip in the period 2000–10, increasing emphasis will be placed on the design of public space and the relationship between buildings as created by quality urban design. Research undertaken for the Commission for Architecture and the Built Environment (CABE 2001) found that 'good urban design brings better value'. Increasingly property developers, funding bodies, occupiers and planners have become aware of the interrelationship between urban environments and economic and social value. This relationship is symbiotic and provides an important foundation upon which an urban renaissance may be built.

Green belts

> A green belt is a special policy defining an area within which only a highly restrictive schedule of changes constituting development under the planning acts will normally be permitted.
>
> (Elson 1986)

Evolution of green belt policy

Green belts were first introduced by Ebenezer Howard in his theory of the Garden City, published in 1898. Howard imposed his own green belt around Letchworth and Welwyn Garden City, by limiting the outward expansion of his developments into the surrounding agricultural land, which was also owned by the Garden City Corporation. It was a self-imposed restriction on future expansion. Such early examples represented isolated cases in which undeveloped land provided a 'buffer' around the Garden Cities, no national or statutory system of green belts was in existence. Movement towards a national statutory system began with Raymond Unwin, who took this green belt concept and applied it to the problems of London's rapid growth during the inter-war years (Oliver *et al.* 1981). Unwin advised the Greater London Regional Plan Committee in 1933 and recommended that an estimated 250 km² of open space were required to restrict urban expansion within the belt of land surrounding London's urban fringe. Patrick Abercrombie echoed these ideas in his Greater London Plan of 1944. In 1947 the modern town planning system was created and, for the first time, a system existed whereby, through the exercise of planning policy, green belt restrictions could be imposed by local authorities.

In 1955 the government introduced planning guidance that established the purposes of green belt policy. In heralding this guidance, the then Minister for Housing and Local Government made a statement in the House of Commons:

> I am convinced that for the well-being of our people and for the preservation of our countryside, we have a clear duty to do all we can to prevent the further unrestricted sprawl of the great cities.

This was the beginning of the current system.

The original objective of preventing unrestricted urban sprawl remains valid today. Fourteen separate green belts are now in force in England, covering a total of 1.8 million ha (4.5 million acres) of land, and five in

Table 7.10 Green belt policy since 1955

Purpose of green belts (1955, 1988 and 1995 policy)	Policy objectives for land use (1955 and onwards)
• Check unrestricted urban growth.	Provide access to open countryside.
• Prevent neighbouring towns from merging.	Promote use of land near urban areas for sport and leisure use.
• Safeguard countryside from encroachment.	Retain attractive landscapes near urban populations.
• Preserve the special character of a town.	Improve derelict land around towns.
• Assist in urban regeneration.	Secure nature conservation and retain agricultural, forestry and related land use.

Scotland covering a total area of 15 000 ha (37 000 acres) of land. No green belts have been designated in Wales. The majority of this land is in agricultural use, although this is not an essential prerequisite of green belt designation. The important issue is that the land enjoys an essentially open character, so that land may be woodland or farmland, or may incorporate some buildings as long as its maintains its open character (Thorne 1994).

Indeed, derelict or waste land without a use, and even unattractive in appearance, may still serve a green belt purpose, although the existence of such land in the green belt serves to weaken the effectiveness of such policy.

In 1989 a study by the London Planning Advisory Committee reported that in nine outer London boroughs some 980 ha of green belt land were derelict. London's green belt has a total area of 485 600 ha,[23] stretching out some 40 km (25 miles) from the urban fringe into the surrounding countryside.

Following an extensive review of green belt policy commissioned by the DoE and reported in 1993 (Elson *et al.* 1993, Elson & Ford 1994), the government published a new policy guidance in 1995,[24] superseding the earlier guidance issues between 1955 and 1988. The 1995 guidance repeated the principal purpose of green belt policy, but for the first time set out objectives for the use of land within green belt designation (Table 7.10).

Green belts: post-1995

The period 1995–2000 witnessed implementation of a new green belt policy agenda. The 1995 guidance heralded this new approach with a greater emphasis towards enhancing the quality of green belt land and making greater use of its recreational potential for use by neighbouring urban dwellers. Since the mid-1950s green belt policy has been very successful in restricting urban sprawl. It has been less successful in protecting the quality of land on the urban fringe, and the proportion of derelict land has increased. Little evidence has been produced to show that if developers cannot build on green belt land, then they consider inner-city sites. It has been estimated that about 61 000 ha (157 000 acres)[25] of derelict land still exist in the urban areas of Britain, and in England the estimated annual loss of rural land to urban uses stands at about 11 000 ha (27 170 acres) (Sinclair 1992). More recent estimates still calculate a considerable area of derelict and/or vacant land, with the Urban Task Force (1999) suggesting some 58 000 ha of brown-land is available for redevelopment.

It therefore appears that developers refused permission on green belt land are more likely to leapfrog the belt and look for sites beyond, instead of redirecting their attention towards the inner city. A report by the Regional Studies Association (1990) argued in favour of 'green areas', that is, green belts covering a far wider area to prevent this leapfrogging and to create a more sustainable regional planning policy. Such ideas have not found favour with the government, which in past years has expressed a desire to maintain green belt policy but not to widen its geographical scope beyond current limits around the major cities. The 1995 Guidance links green belt policy with the promotion of sustainable patterns of development so that LPAs should '. . . consider the consequences for sustainable development (for example in terms of the effects on car travel) of channelling development towards urban areas inside the inner green belt boundary, towards towns and villages inset within the green belt, or towards locations beyond the outer green belt boundary'.[26] The government's desire to prevent 'leapfrogging' and building upon open country beyond the green belt may focus greater attention towards the regeneration of the urban area within the green belt. Yet the availability of grant aid has always been a more effective 'carrot' to facilitate urban regeneration than the 'big stick' of the green belts' restrictive planning regime. Green belt policy may contribute to such sustainable objectives, although in isolation from other strategies it will have little real impact on development patterns beyond its own boundaries.

Green belts or concrete collars?

Green belt policy will continue to operate into the next century. The 1994 review represents a shift in policy, not a fundamental change in direction. Yet such policy will continue to exact a price on the property market. By limiting land supply, green belts will increase land values and house prices. A 1988 survey by Business Strategies Limited estimated that green belt policy increased house prices to the extent that four million households in the area covered by the London green belt had to pay an additional £36 a month on their mortgage repayments. Critics argue that green belt policy strangles urban areas, preventing even limited growth necessary to provide for housing and employment needs and that many local planning authorities draw an excessively tight inner boundary that restricts the release of some land for development on the urban fringe (Evans 1988). At the other extreme, groups such as the Campaign for the Protection of Rural England argue that green belts are not strong enough and should be more rigorously applied to enforce the redevelopment of redundant land in inner cities.

Case study 7.5: The Oxford Green Belt

A green belt around Oxford was first proposed in 1958, although the outer boundary was not confirmed until 1975 and the sensitive inner boundary was not finally agreed upon until the mid-1990s, when the four local planning authorities responsible for its implementation gained approval in their local plans, resulting in a total area of 100 000 acres of land 'washed over' by green belt designation. The consequences of the Oxford Green Belt have been fourfold:

- virtually no outward extension of Oxford during this period
- the limited release of housing land on the city fringe on a sporadic basis to meet certain housing needs
- substantial growth of a number of smaller settlements within the Green Belt or beyond its outer boundary
- promotion by the County Council of a 'county towns' strategy where a series of five market towns beyond the limits of the Oxford Green Belt would accommodate new dwellings to take pressure away from Oxford with its restrictive green belt regime: the market towns of Bicester, Didcot, Witney, Abingdon and Banbury. County Council policy to 2016 maintains this stance.

Decisions regarding the identification and release of the 'white land' (non green belt land on the urban fringe) for future development raise many problems for local authorities, who must draw a clear and defendable line between the green belt and the urban area and yet allow for some release of land for future needs without eroding the future maintenance of the inner green belt boundary.

If green belt policy is to retain its role within the planning system, it will need to address the problems of derelict green belt land and availability of suitable 'white' land, so that the important policy objectives of green belts can be achieved without unacceptably increasing land values and development densities within existing urban areas (see Case study 7.5).

New policy directions

Green belts will be instrumental in fostering the government's schemes for an urban renaissance by 2008. They are an essential ingredient in the mixture of policies necessary to direct development back into cities/urban areas; this much has been accepted over the last 50 years or so. Indeed, green belts have been viewed as a cornerstone of planning policy and a key element of environmental policy (CPRE 1994). Beyond this important 'headline' objective, a number of other policy implications of green belts must be addressed: first, to do with affordable housing and second their relationship with strategic gaps/green wedges.

Green belts impose a necessary restriction on the outward development of settlements. In rural areas 'washed over' by green belt designation, this designation may prevent various local needs (such as provision of low-cost affordable housing) from being properly accommodated and a shortage results. Planning Policy Guidance Note 2, Annex E (of 1995) permits, in exceptional circumstances, the release of small-scale low-cost housing schemes of sites within existing settlements and covered (washed over) by the green belt. Yet research in this area (Elson *et al.* 1996) covering implementation of such rural exceptions concluded that only very few houses had been built in such locations. In the period 1989–96 only 300 new low-cost homes had been built in villages in English green belt locations. The research concluded that among other things, both national and local planning policy needed to be more sympathetic to this problem. For example, Development Plan policy could be clearer in establishing necessary pre-conditions for such affordable housing locations with reference to need, location, scale, design, and maintenance of an affordable component. Further, this could be achieved without compromising green belt objectives or indeed eroding or encroaching upon such protected land (Elson ibid.).

Now to consider the relationship with strategic gaps/green wedges. Such policies share the green belt objective of preventing the coalescence of settlements; they are usually contained in structure/local plans and are not (as with green belts) the subject of national planning policy guidance. Yet such a restrictive land-use designation is a popular planning tool, especially in south and south-east England beyond the existing Metropolitan Green Belt outer boundaries (Elson *et al.* 2000 and DETR 2001b). Indeed, it is argued that such strategic gap/green wedge policies provide a more flexible, even sustainable, way of achieving urban restraint than the alternative of a green belt (with its more rigid adherence to checking unrestricted sprawl). The strategic gap (protecting the setting of a settlement) and green wedge (preserving important open land on the edge of a settlement) allowed for tight controls with a measure of flexibility to permit small-scale and insignificant changes when an appropriate case for development can be advanced. The long-term rigidity of green belt policy may, in the future, lead to a decline in their use as alternative regimes like strategic gaps/green wedges offer better solutions. Finally, this leads conveniently to the review of green belt policy. Nationally green belt policy serves an important purpose, but it must be the subject of continued review and reflection. By 2008, if government policy has failed to deliver 60 per cent of new housing on brown-land or through conversion, then green belts may be viewed as something of a villain, unable to effectively contain urban sprawl and foster an urban renaissance. An interesting study of the Edinburgh Green Belt (Llewelyn Davies 1998) made the point that green belts were 'conceived in an era before sustainable development became the over-riding objective of planning policy' (ibid.). Indeed, citing comments made in the Lothian Structure Plan (1997), the Edinburgh green belt, it was argued, promoted unsustainable development patterns by encouraging new development to 'leapfrog' the green belt in favour of less-sustainable car-reliant outer suburbs. The report itself concludes that green belts are a fundamental component of sustainability but accepts that the existing Edinburgh green belt, largely unchanged since drawn up by Sir Patrick Abercrombie in 1949, is in need of substantial revision. Such revision would be based upon a dramatic increase in width from the existing 4–5 km (and at its narrowest only 1–2 km) to 6–8 km, comparable with cities like York (7 km) and Cambridge (6 km).[27] The conclusion of this study is to call for more and not less green belt but also to acknowledge the need for an association between such policy and sustainability. For instance, a rigorous defence of green belt policy would be coupled with other initiatives to increase urban capacity, to concentrate high-density new development along transport routes and a presumption against car-reliant development.

Such a case study highlights the key issues facing all green belts, notably how to maintain their relevance by contributing to a sustainable agenda. Failure to do this by virtue of careful linkage of green belt restrain to other sustainable areas will result in a steady erosion not of green belt land itself but instead the perceived importance of the policy. Selective erosion of green belt land need not be deemed 'unsustainable'. By way of example, the 'Garden City 21' extension of Stevenage would create a sustainable new community on green belt land to the west of the post-war new town.

Countryside planning powers

> The statutory purposes of National Parks are to conserve and enhance their natural beauty, wildlife and cultural heritage, and to promote opportunities for public understanding and enjoyment of their special qualities.[28]

National Parks are designated by the Countryside Commission, since 1999 the Countryside Agency, in England, and Countryside Council for Wales, under powers contained in the National Parks and Access to the Countryside Act 1949. No national parks have been designated in Scotland.

The first park to be designated was the Peak District in April 1951, followed in the same year by the Lake District, Snowdonia and Dartmoor. The most recent designation was the Norfolk and Suffolk Broads, designated in 1988 and New Forest, designated in 1994,[29] and resulting in a total of eight National Parks in England and three in Wales, which cover an area of 1.4 million ha (9 per cent of the land mass of England and Wales). The largest National Park is the Lake District (2229 km^2) and the smallest the Norfolk and Suffolk Broads (288 km^2) (MacEwen & MacEwen 1987).

National Park authorities

Each park is administered by a National Park Authority (NPA). Reforms in 1972, 1991 and the Environment Act 1995 have resulted in enhanced powers for these bodies, so that they are now responsible for development control, preparation of a National Park management plan and countryside management activities. Each NPA must produce its own local plan and will determine all planning applications submitted within the Park.

Such local plan policies will need to consider the conservation of the high standard of the natural environment and the economic and social needs of the local population. Government planning advice states that major development should not take place in National Parks except in exceptional circumstances.

It is not always easy to strike a balance between the needs of the local economy and environmental protection. Some parks contain traditional mining and mineral extraction industries, which provide valuable local employment yet whose activities can scar or blight the local environment. The restoration of such workings, once they are no longer active, should usually be completed to a high standard so that the landscape is returned to its former beauty.

The Edwards Report (Edwards 1991) advocated stricter planning policies against some categories of development, including certain agricultural and forestry buildings and roads, noisy outdoor recreational pursuits (clay pigeon shooting, war games and motor-cycle scrambling), farm diversification into non-agricultural uses, and installation of satellite dishes. The General Permitted Development Order of 1995 has withdrawn permitted development rights for clay pigeon shooting and war games within Sites of Special Scientific Interest. A recommendation was made that firm planning policies should be continually required to protect the special character of these areas, including the landscape and traditional buildings and structures (such as stone walling). The total annual funding of all National Parks is about £22 million every year, paid directly by government.

In 1997 the Council for National Parks, a charity vested with responsibility to promote public enjoyment of National Parks, set out its own vision for the next 40 years or so (Council for National Parks 1997). National Parks were viewed as being critical to achieve national and international sustainable development objectives, notably in respect of bio-diversity, countryside management and cultural heritage. Yet, future delivery of such objectives was threatened by a number of sustainability trends. Seven such trends were identified: demand for energy (with climate change resulting in soil-vegetation and bio-diversity loss in National Parks); acidification (acid pollution in soils caused by burning fossil fuels); intensive agriculture (and consequential loss of semi-natural habitat); increased demand for aggregates (mostly from the extension of existing quarries, with 116 active surface mineral workings in existing parks); road traffic growth (with consequential pressure to make roads more urban to accommodate such growth); development pressure (mostly to increase housing provision); and finally threats to water quality and supply caused by pollution in groundwater (such as wildlife loss caused by the introduction of phosphates as a by-product of sewage treatment). The report concludes that to maintain and enhance the longer-term protection of National Park areas requires strong support at governmental level, with adequate funding and new designations (such as the New Forest and South Downs). The Environment Act 1995 gave National Park Authorities greater and more unified powers in respect of matters like sustainability. From 1995 (in force from 1997) each Park Authority became a free-standing local government body responsible for drawing up a management plan, a development plan and determining planning applications. By integrating such powers with a sustainable agenda, the report sets out the key objective that national parks become 'models for the whole countryside and pinnacles of environmental achievement not islands of sustainability' (Council for National Parks ibid.).

Areas of Outstanding Natural Beauty (AONBs) or National Scenic Areas (Scotland)

> An AONB is a countryside conservation area of high landscape beauty considered worthy of protection.

AONBs are also designated by the Countryside Commission, since 1999 the Countryside Agency, subject to the confirmation of the Secretary of State for the Environment. The grounds for designation are similar to National Parks in seeking to protect areas of high landscape importance. The key differences from a National Park are that:

*   AONB designation does not include a duty to promote recreational use and public access may be restricted.
*   AONBs tend to cover a much smaller area.
*   AONBs are not governed by a special AONB Authority. All planning controls remain with the local authority. Policies to protect the landscape quality are usually incorporated into development plan policies. A strong presumption exists against any development in these areas, with the promotion of the preservation and enhancement of natural beauty.

Forty-one such AONBs have been designated in England and Wales, covering a total of 2.4 million ha of land (15 per cent of total land area). Examples include the Chiltern Hills in Buckinghamshire and Bodmin Moor in Devon. A total of 55 have been established in England, four in Wales and one shared. Designation of AONB may be undertaken irregardless of the area affected and such protection affects 16 km^2 of the Scilly Isles in the same way as 1738 km^2 of the North Wessex Downs (Garner and Jones 1997).

In recent years, increasing importance has been attached to the co-ordinated management of such areas, and government has encouraged the creation of 'joint advisory committees' to bring together local authorities, amenity groups, farming and other interested parties to agree a common strategy for protection of the landscape while facilitating activity such as agriculture, forestry and public access. During the last 50 or so years since the inception of this policy, AONBs have been the subject of much change. Holdaway and Smart (2001) have categorized such changes as those affecting landscape, tranquillity (unspoilt by urban influences such as traffic noise) and rural communities (provision of shops and services). It must be remembered that the visual quality of many of these areas is affected greatly by agricultural and forestry management matters themselves 'largely beyond the ambit of planning control' (Garner and Jones ibid.). Such activity can dramatically change the quality of landscape; for example it has been estimated that between 1947 and 1983, 95 per cent of lowland grassland and hay meadow in England has disappeared or been affected by agricultural intensification (Evans 1997). Other changes in similar vein have resulted in a loss of hedgerows, lowland heath land, heather moorland, chalk downland and wildlife habitats. As a consequence the visual (as well as social and economic) characteristics of AONBs have changed, 'all too frequently for the worse' (Holdaway and Smart 2001). Long-term monitoring and a possible reappraisal of legislative control over land-use changes in such areas may be required as the solution to this creeping erosion of the environmental quality of these areas.

In Scotland, similar powers are vested in 40 National Scenic Areas, covering much of Scotland's beautiful landscapes, such as extensive parts of the Highlands. Planning controls, as with AONBs, are held by LPAs, although extensive consultation is required with Scottish Natural Heritage before any planning applications may be granted. Some 13 per cent of Scotland's land mass, amounting to just over 1 million ha, is protected by such designation. Scottish National Heritage may also designate National Heritage Areas to manage recreational and conservation needs in other parts of the country. This new power was introduced in 1991.

Sites of Special Scientific Interest (SSSIs)

> SSSIs are areas of special nature conservation interest that are designated to protect habitats and wildlife/plantlife.

SSSIs are designated[30] by English Nature (the nature conservancy body for England), the Countryside Council for Wales or Scottish Natural Heritage, on the basis of detailed scientific criteria. Once a site is so designated, English Nature is obliged to notify the relevant local authority of the flora or fauna or geological or physiographical features of the site, and any operations likely to damage such matters of special interest. Anyone performing such operations in contravention of this is liable to criminal conviction 'carrying a curiously low maximum fine of £2500' (Garner and Jones op. cit.). By 1995 3794 such sites had been designated in England, 892 in Wales and 1377 in Scotland, covering a total of 9750 km^2 (6.5 per cent of the land area). Examples include Oxleas Wood, Greenwich, London, and Loch Sheil in Scotland. This land is not excluded from development pressures. Most reported damage to SSSIs is short-term, from which sites recover. By the mid-1990s this figure was put at 1000 ha damaged annually, a dramatic reduction compared to the position in the late 1980s, when some 89 000 ha was damaged. Such damage was caused by pollution, unauthorized tipping and burning. Longer-term harm resulting in the complete loss of part or all of a site has fluctuated over recent years, resulting in figures of between 1200 and 5800 ha lost annually throughout the 1990s. Such losses are most commonly caused by inappropriate agricultural activities and land management. Such erosional harm, while regrettable, must be placed against a background of growing designation of SSSIs. In 1984, 4000 such sites in Britain were designated (covering some 1.4 million ha). By 1995, this figure had increased to just under 6000 sites covering around 2 million ha, representing an increase of 70 per cent (DoE 1996). It is worthy of note, therefore, that designation does not render a site 'inviable' (Garner and Jones ibid.) but instead establishes what operations would constitute an offence.

Environmentally Sensitive Areas (ESAs)

ESAs are areas of high wildlife importance maintained by non-intensive agriculture.

ESAs are designated by government and administered by the Ministry of Agriculture, Fisheries and Food, following recommendations of the Countryside Commission. Such a designation will need to be considered by local councils in the exercise of development control. Farmers benefit from specific grants to continue to exercise traditional land management techniques to preserve wildlife habitats.

By 1994, 22 such areas were designated in England, six in Wales and 10 in Scotland. Examples include the Norfolk Broads (to continue traditional grazing instead of draining and ploughing land for arable cultivation), the Pennine Dales (to maintain stone walled hay meadows), the Southern Downs (to protect grazing on chalk downland), and the Somerset Levels (to resist draining of grazing marshlands).

Nature Reserves

Nature Reserves are habitats considered to be of national importance.

Nature Reserves are designated by English Nature, Scottish Natural Heritage and the Countryside Council for Wales[31] and may deal with protection of habitats of rare and migratory birds or waterfowl, by the introduction of specialist habitat management policies. Protected wetlands are referred to as 'Ramsar' sites following Britain's signature to the Convention of Wetlands of International Importance, signed in Ramsar, Iran, in 1971. Such nature reserves may be terrestrial (National Nature Reserves) or marine (Marine Nature Reserves); 273 terrestrial and two marine reserves have been designated. Where the nature conservation issues are not deemed to be of national importance, a local authority may so designate its own local nature reserve. To date 519 such local reserves have been designated. Additionally it must be remembered that numerous non-statutory and privately owned reserves exist, for example the 76 reserves managed by the Royal Society for the Protection of Birds (RSPB). For a history of nature conservation in Britain see Sheail (1998). In Britain 75 Ramsar sites have been established. Examples include Lundy Island (marine), the Island of Uist, Shetland (terrestrial) and Bridgwater Bay, Somerset (Ramsar). Additional controls over wildlife are found in Special Protection Areas to protect the habitats of vulnerable or endangered species, in particular bird habitats. In England 45 exist, with eight in Wales and 37 in Scotland.

Country Parks

> Country Parks are areas for countryside recreational use in proximity to urban areas.

Country Parks are designated[32] and managed by the local authority for the recreational benefit of the local population. An example is Aldenham on the borders between northwest London and Hertfordshire. Currently around 220 such parks have been established.

Special Landscape Value

> An area of great landscape value not covered by AONB status.

Areas of Special Landscape Value are designated by means of the planning policy of local planning authorities. As a planning policy, it counts as a material consideration in planning decision-making but does not benefit from the status of AONBs, National Parks or other protected areas, and is something of a poor relation compared to these controls.

Tree Preservation Orders (TPOs)

A TPO constitutes an order imposed under town planning legislation to protect trees or woodland considered to be of amenity value.

- Neither 'amenity' nor 'tree' is defined within town planning legislation. In most cases a TPO will seek to protect a fine or rare specimen, usually mature in growth and exceeding 20 cm in diameter. The decision as to what constitutes 'amenity value' is left entirely to the local planning authority. The LPA must serve a notice on owners/occupiers of the relevant site, stating that they intend to make a TPO. A period of 28 days is then given for any representations or objections to be submitted, after which the LPA may confirm the Order. No right of appeal is available against the service of a TPO.
- Once a TPO is in force, consent is required from the Planning Authority before the tree can be cut down, topped, lopped or uprooted. A right of appeal exists against a refusal of such consent or failure to issue a decision. Unauthorized removal, topping, lopping or uprooting is a criminal offence, usually punishable by a fine. The LPA may also require the planting of replacement trees of the same maturity.
- In a conservation area, six weeks' notice is required to cut, lop, top or uproot *any* tree.
- Under provision of the Environment Act 1995 (section 97) the government introduced legislative reform to provide limited protection of hedgerows. Removal of a hedgerow requires 42 days prior notice to the local planning authority. The authority, within this time period, may duly serve a hedgerow removal notice or hedgerow retention

notice. In the latter case the government have provided guidance on which hedgerows are worthy of protection, with criteria dealing with archaeological features, wildlife importance and landscape interest (see Schedule 1 to Hedgerow Regulations 1997, Statutory Instrument number 1160).

Ancient monuments and archaeological areas

An ancient monument may constitute any building structure or work, including a cave, excavation, or remains, considered to be of public importance.

The Secretary of State for Culture, Media and Sport is responsible for compiling a list[33] of ancient monuments, usually following the recommendation of English Heritage in England or specialist boards established for Scotland and Wales.

The vast majority of the 13 000 scheduled ancient monuments in Britain comprise archaeological sites incorporating ancient structures and buried deposits. However, other examples include various bridges, barns, castles and other fortifications. Scheduled monument consent is required to undertake any works, including repairs to such monuments, and this is permitted only by application to the Secretary of State. No right of appeal exists if consent is refused, although compensation is payable. Unauthorized works are liable to criminal prosecution. Government policy establishes a presumption that such monuments shall be preserved.[34]

In areas of known archaeological remains, developers may be required by the LPA to permit an investigation of the ground before redevelopment and this can be controlled by planning conditions. The designation of an area of archaeological importance by a local authority or Secretary of State delays any construction work, to allow a full site investigation to extract sufficient archaeological information from the site. This status has been conferred upon the historic centres of the five English towns of Canterbury, Chester, Exeter, Hereford, and York. The legislation requires that appropriate notice must be served on the local authority prior to commencing certain building or other operations.

Agricultural land

The Ministry of Agriculture, Fisheries and Food (MAFF) have classified all agricultural land. This does not represent a protective designation or form of special control; however, it may be a material consideration if a local authority wishes to refuse planning permission for a proposal, such as for residential development, that will result in the loss of agricultural land.

The grading of agricultural land is shown in Table 7.11 and reference should also be made to MAFF (1997) dealing with agricultural land classification.

Table 7.11 The grading of agricultural land

Grade		Description
1	Excellent quality	All suitable for current and future agricultural needs.
2	Very good	
3a	Good quality	
3b	Moderate quality	Changes of use to non-farming use will not be restricted on agricultural grounds.
4	Poor quality	
5	Very poor	

The grading assessment is based upon the physical and chemical characteristics of the land, which determines its suitability for long-term food production.

Around 45 per cent of all land in England and Wales is covered by some form of special planning status, 15 per cent is urban and the remainder is in rural use (agriculture, forestry or horticultural). Such special powers give the planners additional controls in pursuing a variety of (sometimes overlapping) planning objectives. The maintenance of these special planning controls will involve a complex balance between the need for environmental safeguards and the need for development to satisfy the economic requirements of a modern industrialized society. Maintenance of these special policies is not sacrosanct and sometimes decisions are made to build on green belt land (such as the Bluewater Park Regional Shopping Centre in Kent) or on SSSIs (e.g. the new road building at Twyford Down near Southampton, Hampshire).

The existence of such special powers has become familiar to many members of the public, and land-use decisions that result in the erosion of these areas are usually met with strong opposition. However, the longer-term retention (into the next century) of these planning policies appears to be assured.

Conclusions

Britain, like many of its continental European neighbours, is a densely populated country in which considerable pressures are placed upon the development of land to accommodate the needs of a modern industrial society. However, the supply of land is finite and, as a consequence of being a relatively small nation in geographical terms, areas of considerable natural beauty and landscape value are often located in close proximity to major sources of population in large urban areas. The creation of the post-war system of planning control has provided the necessary mechanism by which specialist policy areas can be introduced to protect important environments,

Table 7.12 Summary of special first planning control areas

Title	Year control was introduced	Statute today	Town and country planning objectives	Numbers in force and percentage of land or building stock
Green Belt	1955 (limited introduction in 1940s)	No green belt statute – control exercised under Town & Country Planning Act 1990.	Maintain open character around urban areas and prevent sprawl.	15 14% England
Listed Buildings	1947	Planning (Listed Building & Conservation Areas) Act 1990.	Preserve buildings of historic and architectural importance.	440 000 buildings in England, 37 000 in Scotland, 14 500 in Wales
Conservation Areas	1967	As above	Preserve/enhance areas of historic and architectural importance.	7500 Conservation Areas in England. 550 – Scotland, 350 – Wales
National Parks	1949	Environment Act 1995	Conserve natural beauty and allow public access/enjoyment.	10 9% England and Wales
Areas of Outstanding Natural Beauty or National Scenic Areas (Scotland)	1949	As above	Conserve natural beauty.	35 England, 4 Wales 13% – Scotland and 40 established
Sites of Special Scientific Interest	1981	Wildlife & Countryside Act 1981	Nature, conservation of plants, habitats, wildlife.	3794 England, 1377 – Scotland, 892 Wales
Environmentally Sensitive Areas	1986	Agriculture Act 1986	Protect landscape, wildlife and agricultural features.	22 – England, 6 – Wales, 10 – Scotland
Nature Reserves – National (Land) and Marine	1971 & 1981	Wildlife & Countryside Act 1981	Nature conservation of habitats.	National: 150 England, 52 Wales, 71 Scotland Marine: 1 England, 1 Wales

Country Parks	1986	Town & Country Planning Act 1990	Public recreation.	*
Special Landscape Value	1971	Town & Country Planning Act 1990	Development plan policy to keep landscape quality.	*
Tree Preservation Orders	1947	Town & Country Planning Act 1990	Protect trees of amenity value.	*
Ancient Monuments & Archaeological Areas	1913	Ancient Monuments & Archaeological Areas Act 1979	Preserve ancient monuments in the public interest.	20 000 monuments

* Figures/data not available. All figures for Britain unless otherwise stated.

both rural and urban; it sought to reconcile these objectives with the need to permit urban expansion to facilitate economic growth. Since the mid-1940s a whole host of controls have been introduced to deal with urban and rural protection, to maintain and guarantee the future survival of significant natural and built environment, while providing for the agricultural, recreational, cultural and biological needs of a modern industrial society. In this way, the town and country planning system, in protecting many diverse facets of environment and society, seeks to ensure the future enjoyment of features such as buildings of heritage value, or countryside of high landscape value, thereby contributing simultaneously to environmental standards and quality of life.

8 Sustainable development

Sustainable development, sustainability or environmental stewardship are all terms that refer to the relationship between environmental protection and the economic development associated with industrial society. Just as the early public health legislation of the nineteenth century was a reaction against disease associated with slum housing, so in the 1990s the introduction of sustainable development was a reaction to the environmental degradation of the latter half of the twentieth century, which is associated with pollution, depletion of non-renewable resources (fossil fuels, minerals, aggregates), erosion of the ozone layer, pollution and the warming of the Earth's atmosphere because of the production of carbon dioxide (global warming). Consequently the world's climate will change, with profound implications for agricultural production (as some areas become more arid and others more wet) and the ability of cities to support their populations (with limited water or energy supplies). In the UK it has been forecast[1] that by 2020 average temperatures will increase by 1 °C, increasing to 1.5° by 2050. Average global surface temperature has increased by between 0.4° and 0.8 °C since the end of the nineteenth century. Between 1860 (when records began) and 2000, eight of the 10 hottest years on record fell within the 10-year period after 1990 (Department for Environment, Food and Rural Affairs 2002). The evidence for such climate change is compelling. Such rises may appear inconsequential in themselves but the resulting climatic change could produce more erratic weather systems, so that winter storms and flooding in the UK would be more commonplace.

Sustainable development is difficult to define and can mean different things to different people. As a subject area it deals with the relationship between economic growth and environmental protection. In some ways it represents a marriage between these two issues, seeking to ensure that future economic growth and development is achieved without longer-term environmental degradation. As Blowers (1993: 5) suggests:

> Sustainable development requires that we have regard to the Earth's regenerative capacity, the ability of its systems to recuperate and maintain productivity. Thus, the conservation of resources is a strong component of sustainable development.

The following definition, provided by the United Nations World Commission, commonly referred to as the Brundtland Commission after its

Chairperson, Mrs Gro Harlem Brundtland, is the most quoted, and has been adopted by many national governments in their own policies on the matter:

> Sustainable development is development that meets the needs of the present without compromising the ability of future generations to meet their own needs.

(World Commission 1987)

A strategy of sustainable development will therefore deliver economic growth and development without resulting in long-term damage to environmental resources. How does town planning and property development fit into this equation?

In Britain the town planning system has, since 1957, been concerned with decisions relating to land use. Sustainable development has the following implications for British town planning. It will influence the existing nature of land-use decisions so that new developments will be assessed against environmental planning criteria, such as the need to halt processes that lead to global warming or ozone depletion. It will broaden the realm of material town planning considerations so that environmental issues become important in decision-making. It will influence the very nature of that decision-making process, with greater public involvement in the production of local policy and other initiatives. The planning system is ideally placed to engage the public given its long-established practice of public participation in planning applications and policy production. Planning policy will be widened to take such matters into account. The chapter is organized as follows:

- background
- current environmental problems
- conclusions and future directions.

Background

In 1972 a report entitled *The limits to growth* (Meadows 1972) was published by the Club of Rome, a group of industrialists who had commissioned research into the relationship between industrial growth and environmental protection. It argued that economic development associated with a modern industrialized society was resulting in environmental damage. The choice had to be made to continue with economic growth and create further environmental degradation or halt further economic activity and preserve the environment. It was argued that it would not be possible to 'balance' economic needs with environmental protection.

In 1980, a report on World Conservation Strategy identified an increasingly alarming trend towards damage to ecological systems by economic development. However, unlike *The limits to growth*, the report concluded that, instead of a 'no growth' strategy, a balance was required so that economic development could be continued as long as ecological interests were unharmed. A strategy of sustainable development would deliver this 'equilibrium' between the economy and the environment, so that future industrial growth with its associated urban growth could be achieved without a continued erosion of natural resources and environmental quality. In 1987, the United Nations' World Commission on Environment and Development published a report of proceedings entitled *Our common future* (the Brundtland Report: World Commission 1987). Sustainable development was defined in a way that implied that future generations would still be able to use and benefit from environmental resources. Action would be required to arrest environmental problems of global warming, acid rain, pollution, consumption of non-renewable resources and reduction of the ozone layer. As with the 1980s report, further economic growth and development were not viewed as incompatible with such objectives.

In 1992 the UN held a Conference on Environment and Development in Rio de Janeiro.[2] The tangible outcome of the conference was published as *Agenda 21*, in which national governments committed themselves to an 'action plan' of strategies for sustainable development. The document[3] set out policy areas dealing with social and economic issues (combating poverty, protecting and promoting human health and promoting sustainable human settlements), and conservation of resources to allow for future development (meeting agricultural needs without destroying the land, protecting ecosystems, safeguarding the oceans and halting the spread of deserts). A United Nations Commission on Sustainable Development was established to monitor the progress made by countries in implementing *Agenda 21* within their own political systems.

In Britain and in the European Community, *Agenda 21* has found its way into several policy initiatives. The European Community published the fifth Environmental Action Programme (1993–2000) *Towards sustainability* and the fifth Environmental Action Plan. Both documents set out a broad range of policy areas in which sustainability must be considered by member nations, including control of industrial pollution, spatial land-use planning policy, education and training. The British government published discussion documents, notably the government White Paper, *This common inheritance* (DoE 1990a), that set out the broad policy agenda for sustainability in Britain, including tackling global warming and the role of land-use planning decisions. In addition, the government commissioned a series of environmental studies, notably the 1993 joint DoE and Department of Transport study *Reducing emissions through planning* (DoE 1993c) and introduction of new legislation, notably the Environmental Protection Act 1990, which imposed a duty on Her Majesty's Inspectorate of Pollution and Local Authorities to establish registers of data, on potentially polluting processes, which are open to public inspection. A requirement, under Section 143 of the Act, that all local authorities maintain a register of contaminated land (e.g. sewage sites, former industrial sites and completed landfill sites) was never introduced by the government, following opposition from the development industry, especially house-builders. The Environment Act 1995 imposes a duty whereby a local authority must designate sites of serious contamination. The issue of government policy guidance to influence the planning system has been recognized, with several PPGs being revised to accommodate sustainable policy objectives. Finally, the government has published a series of strategy documents to set out its aims for the implementation of sustainable development, following on from its commitment to *Agenda 21* at the Rio Earth Summit. Four documents were published in January 1994, dealing with sustainable development,[4] climate change,[5] biodiversity,[6] and sustainable forestry.[7] Each document takes a long-term view of the various environmental problems to the year 2012 (20 years from the Earth Summit). As with Brundtland, the UK policies have always taken the view that economic development and environmental protection can be achieved together. In many ways the British government went further than Brundtland, when they stated in the *UK strategy*:

Sustainable development does not mean having less economic development: on the contrary, a healthy economy is better able to generate the resources to meet people's needs and new investment and environmental improvement often go hand in hand . . . what it requires is that decisions throughout society are taken with proper regard to their environmental impact.

This is not a universally accepted view. Although the views of the Club of Rome are not given wide support today, many commentators on the subject still argue that sustainability brings with it a *conflict* between economic activity and environmental quality. To improve and protect the environment requires a curb on some economic activities.

A growing awareness of sustainability in the post-Rio Summit world has been translated into local *Agenda 21* strategies, whereby local government has sought to adopt policies on sustainability in many topic areas. In town planning, local government is well placed to develop and codify these local ideas into planning policy. During the 1990s, with increasing momentum in this subject area, it is envisaged that growing numbers of local councils will publish such strategies, either incorporated within an all-embracing local *Agenda 21* document or within planning policy. During the 1990s, with momentum increasing in this subject area, growing numbers of local councils published such strategies, either incorporating Agenda 21[8] concepts or introducing fresh planning policies geared to a sustainable agenda. By the mid-1990s some county councils took a lead on this by reviewing the environmental content of policies in their structure plans. Beyond this more strategic application of sustainable principles, increasingly district/city and unitary councils formulated local sustainability policies in their local or unitary development plans and subsequently Local Development Frameworks.

During the late 1990s and into the new century, government policy became increasingly influenced by the sustainability agenda. The genesis of this policy was influenced in two ways. First, government was reacting to international policy and second it was embracing the findings of many eminent reports and influential 'think-tanks', some themselves government-sponsored.

In 1998 the Kyoto Agreement (Framework Protocol on Climate Change) established a series of international targets to limit the increase in production of carbon dioxide, already running at around 3 billion tonnes of carbon released into the atmosphere annually. The UK government committed itself to reduce national production of such gases by a figure of 12.5 per cent, so that by the period 2008–12 the volume of such emissions would be reduced to 1990 levels. To deliver on this binding commitment, the government would be required to introduce a raft of new policies.

Among the influential reports and findings of respected bodies that raised awareness of sustainability issues, a common theme was evident: that the planning system had a central role to play. The Commission on Sustainable Development (previously, prior to 2000, the British Government Panel on Sustainable Development and UK Round Table on Sustainable Development) constitutes the single most influential body in this area. Being appointed by the Prime Minister and able to discuss a wide array of issues, the Commission's findings enjoy authority and respect. The land use planning system was described by the Commission as 'crucial' in securing sustainable development objectives and importantly, as 'one of the few current mechanisms which clearly links national goals with local ones' (UK Round Table 1999). Indeed, the Commission recommended that planning guidance increasingly reflect the growing sustainability agenda and became much more integrated with other public policy areas, notably economic policy. Such a 'holistic' or cross-disciplinary approach to sustainability was highlighted in 1999. The UK Round Table had argued in favour of stronger powers of implementation for the planning system and greater reliance on 'economic instruments', such as fiscal measures to tax green-field development and fund infrastructure benefits to brown-land alternatives (UK Round Table 1999).

Government policy has become increasingly sympathetic to such an approach. In 2001 the Chancellor of the Exchequer embraced this 'holistic' concept, introducing new taxation measures to encourage restoration of historic buildings,[9] greater conversion of empty space over shops[10] and increased levels of conversion/refurbishment of existing residential stock.[11] This was a start, but much more remains to be done. Indeed, the UK Round Table, prior to their absorption into the Sustainable Development Commission, argued in favour of a more dramatic set of reforms in which the planning system incorporated a set of stronger 'tools' to achieve more effective implementation of the sustainability agenda. Such powers would cover matters of land assembly (for instance, to create suitable redevelopment sites from previous vacant and/or brown-land sites) and decontamination of previously polluted land after previous industrial and/or commercial activity. Historically local planning authorities have enjoyed few significant powers in such areas. In the medium to longer term, therefore, it is important that the planning system moves beyond its traditional land use 'base' if it is to tackle the demands of sustainable development. A more 'pro-active' stance towards site assembly and contamination, which is currently a matter mostly for the property owner/developer, would permit LPAs to promote brown-field sites for redevelopment. The planning system is, however, currently much more 'reactive' to the initiatives of the owner/ developer through its powers to accept or reject a planning application; in future years, a more radical orthodoxy may prevail.

The current system must deliver the new sustainability agenda using the toolkit cast and created in 1949. It may be argued that such a system is inadequate to confront this new agenda. In any event, it is the one currently in place. Furthermore, it is now a policy-led system, so the greatest single influence on future thinking will be by means of planning policy. Since the mid-1990s new thinking has indeed emerged. After 1998, with the publication of a major piece of work in this area (DETR 1998c) and subsequent reporting of the findings of the Urban Task Force (DETR 1999) and Urban White Paper (DETR 2000b), the notion of sustainability in planning policy became commonplace. The impact of such work will be considered later in this chapter and in the following chapter on urban regeneration. Suffice it to say at this stage that these reports have been instrumental in affecting this new thinking towards sustainable development, but that the implementation of this agenda (by virtue of changes in planning policy) will to some extent be constrained by the system in which planners react to the development proposals of developers (planning applications) without recourse to the more 'pro-active' ability to assemble land, engage in its remediation (from contamination) or control taxation benefits in its sustainable promotion.

Sustainability and town planning

In 1998 it was reported that 'The planning system has a vital part to play in promoting some sustainable land-use patterns and use of resources' (DETR 1998). The notion of sustainability is indeed a broad one and is often perceived as a 'process' as much as a 'set of solutions' (UK Round Table 5th Report). The planning system is well-placed to address matters of process by involving many interested groups in the formulation and implementation of planning policy. As for substance (or policy and decisions) the verdict is less certain. Indeed, it may be too early to judge the system on such a matter. Nevertheless, it is appropriate that consideration is given to current environmental problems and the role of town planning in providing a solution. A number of key areas will be considered.

Current environmental problems

Use of urban land

In Britain, post-war development patterns have increasingly been influenced by the rapid growth in private ownership of the motor car. This has resulted in increasing levels of out-of-town development such as retail warehousing or business parks, not easily served by public transport. As a consequence, people and businesses have relocated away from existing urban locations. It has been estimated that by the late 1980s between 60 000 and 110 000 ha of wasteland existed in urban areas of Britain.[12] During the 1990s the calculation of such statistics became more accurate. In 1993 a Derelict Land Survey estimated that there were about 39 600 ha of derelict land in England. Five years later (1998) the government-commissioned Compilation of National Land Use Database (NLUD) statistics reported 28 800 ha of previously derelict land and 16 200 ha of previously developed vacant land, a total of 45 000 ha. While not all of this land would be suitable for redevelopment (in around 10 per cent of these sites it would remain economically unviable to reclaim or remedy) the Urban Task Force (DETR 1999) calculated around one quarter was suitable for housing, yielding just over two million new housing units. This would make a substantial inroad into the oft-quoted headline figure of 3.8 million new units required between 1996 and 2016 as a result of population change. Groups such as the Friends of the Earth and the Campaign for the Protection of Rural England have argued for many years that 'Cities have great capacity to be more resourceful' (Houghton & Hunter 1994: 45). Clearly, sustainable planning policies can contain urban growth (e.g. by green belt policies) and ensure that derelict urban land is developed while existing land is recycled through redevelopment. However, this strategy alone will not accommodate all future land-use needs. It has been estimated by the DoE that between 1981 and 2001 the urban area of England will increase by 105000 ha.[13] When one considers that 40 per cent of all urban expansion in Britain during the 1980s was on previously agricultural land, it becomes apparent that the planning system must balance competing demands for finite land resources and make difficult decisions regarding urban containment or expansion.

In 2000 the government announced a 'step change' in policy designed to deliver new housing on previously developed land or through conversion. By 2008, 60 per cent of all new housing would be required to be built on previously developed land or through conversion. To achieve this would require a new focus on urban redevelopment, in effect an 'urban renaissance'. Densities would need to be higher than previously and a new emphasis would be placed upon making more 'efficient' use of land, whether on urban brownland or on green-fields. To reach a 60 per cent target posed a considerable challenge when it is recalled that between 1995 and 2001 this figure remained static at 57 per cent with little improvement, notwithstanding much effort to do so (*Land Use Change in England Bulletin* No. 16, 2001). Reliance upon a target alone with the absence of other measures like taxation (tax on green-field schemes and tax relief for brown-land equivalents) would render delivery of the 60 per cent figure less likely.

Global warming

The production of carbon dioxide, methane, nitrous oxide and chloro-fluorocarbons creates a heat blanket around the Earth, trapping some of the sun's energy and producing a rise in global temperature. Such increases in temperature have been predicted to be around 0.3 °C every decade, resulting in changes in weather patterns (affecting agricultural production) and rising sea levels, in the range of around 6 cm every 10 years (Houghton *et al.* 1992). During the 1970s, UK emissions of greenhouse gases declined as a result of restrictions on industrial production and domestic heating. However, the dramatic rise in the number of motor vehicles meant that by 1984 any further decline was arrested and that, by the year 2000, projections anticipate an increase in such greenhouse emissions.[14] To achieve its agreed target at Kyoto[15] the UK Government has agreed to cut UK emissions of greenhouse gases by 12.5 per cent relative to the 1990 level over the period 2008–12. This target was achieved by 2002 (DEFRA 2002) leading the government at the time to estimate and project that by 2010 UK greenhouse gas emissions could be reduced to 23 per cent below their levels in 1990. This would exceed the government's own domestic target (which is not legally binding, as Kyoto is) to cut carbon emissions by 20 per cent below 1990 levels (DETR 1999a *A Better Quality of Life*). Climate change is recognized as 'one of the greatest environmental threats facing the world today' (DETR ibid.). Such a conclusion has not been reached without debate, even disagreement among some scientists as to the reality of global warming. Politicians and policy-makers are now acutely aware of the importance of this issue. Indeed, Sir Crispin Tickell, panel convenor for the Sustainable Development Commission, summarized the situation thus: 'When the panel was first established in January 1994 the somewhat slippery concept of sustainable development was peripheral to mainstream thinking and policy on the environment. That is no longer so' (British Government Panel 2000). Research in 2002 concluded that while the policy objectives of sustainability were unavoidable it was unlikely there would ever be one agreed definitive or a standard set of indicators by which it could universally be measured (RICS Foundation 2002).

Depletion of the ozone layer

The ozone layer protects the Earth from excessive levels of ultraviolet radiation. This layer is being reduced by chlorofluorocarbons (CFCs), which are found in chemicals such as halon, used in the manufacture and operation of air-conditioning solvents, refrigeration and aerosols.[16] An international commitment was made in 1987 to reduce such substances.[17] Depletion of the ozone layer is measured by the effective chlorine loading in the atmosphere. UK measurements during the 1990s showed a gradual reduction and predictions based on 1996 data (DoE 1996) appear accurate in their forecast that chlorine loading will decline substantially after 2050.

Deforestation

Trees, woods and forests absorb carbon dioxide, which helps to reduce the effects of global warming. Tropical forests have been destroyed annually for a variety of reasons, including the harvesting of timber. In Britain around 10 per cent of land (2.4 million ha) has tree cover, compared to an average of 25 per cent in the European Community. Nevertheless, this figure represents a dramatic increase on the situation prevailing at the beginning of the century and is largely the result of planting undertaken by the Forestry Commission, which was established by government in 1919.

Biological diversity

Activities such as the burning of forests, draining of wetlands and growth of urban areas and road networks have led to the loss or near extinction of many species of plant or animal life, resulting in the loss of sources of food, medicine and industrial materials. It has been estimated that about 2 per cent of agricultural land is eroded by city growth around western European cities every 10 years (Houghton & Hunter 1994: 7). In Britain the amount of land occupied by urban areas continues to grow. Urban growth is usually accompanied by an increased demand for infrastructure, especially roads, and development pressure on urban fringes becomes intense. Between 1985 and 1990 around 14 000 ha of land were used to build new roads in Britain (DoE 1994c).

Industrial pollution

Industrial pollution is discharged into the air, sea and ground, and includes the dumping of industrial waste at sea. Many industries in the former Soviet Union are responsible for a heavy discharge of pollutants. 'Acid rain' refers to rain, snow, fog or mist that has become contaminated by contact with sulphur and nitrogen dioxide, which are produced by industrial processes. Motor vehicles account for about half of all nitrogen oxide emissions. While such emissions have fallen since 1970 levels (by around one quarter), traffic volumes accounted for an increasing proportion of this figure. Indeed this situation is unlikely to change as statistical projections point to an increase in car ownership, to 30 million by 2025. Levels of sulphur dioxide, produced mostly by power stations (burning fossil fuels) have fallen far more dramatically since 1970 levels (by around three-quarters) as a result of alternative energy supplies, most notably a switch to gas as an energy source. UK sulphur dioxide emissions surpassed UNECE targets for 2000 (50 per cent reduction from 1980 baseline), with future reductions set at 70 per cent (by 2005) and 80 per cent (by 2010).

Depletion of non-renewable resources

All of the Earth's natural resources of fossil fuel, minerals and aggregates (sand, gravel and crushed rock) are in limited supply. The long-term supply of such resources can be maintained by policies that ensure a greater degree of efficiency in the use of such finite materials and substitution of their use by renewable resources, especially in the supply of energy, by using wind power and solar power.

The role of town planning

Following an examination of these various environmental problems, it is necessary to pose the question 'How can the British land-use planning system affect these environmental issues?' Several key areas may be examined (Table 8.1). Each environmental issue will be considered and reference will be made to the influence of town planning.

Greenhouse effect

British governments' adherence to the principles agreed to at Rio (1992) and Kyoto (1998) resulted in ambitious targets being set for reductions in carbon emissions. To deliver on such commitments required both a reversal of the upward trend in emissions of recent years but also real cuts in carbon production. Such a policy agenda was given further emphasis at the World Summit on Sustainable Development in Johannesburg (2002). The 2002

Table 8.1 Town planning and sustainable development

Environmental use	Land-use planning influence
(1) Greenhouse effect/ global warming	• Planning policies to restrict use of the motor car.
(2) Use of urban land	• Green belt policy to contain urban areas. • Urban density policies to ensure urban land is used efficiently. • Strategies such as urban villages and an urban renaissance to reduce car use by ensuring a mixture of employment and housing or shopping land use within close proximity.
(3) Pollution Ozone depletion Deforestation	• Control over industrial emissions when deciding new planning applications. • Use of procedures such as Environmental Impact Assessment to assess the exact potential for pollution and other environmental harm.

summit permitted appraisal of global, nation and local sustainability initiatives in the 10 years since the Rio summit. Johannesburg re-emphasized the pivotal link between the developed and the developing world in the implementation of sustainable development. It is important to remember that implementing sustainability is not solely confined to effective protection of the environment (albeit that this is important) but also extends to matters of social progress, prudent use of natural resources and maintaining high and stable levels of economic growth. A reduction in global inequalities (say in health provision, education and maintenance of a stable economy) will themselves influence how the environment is managed in future years. Sustainability is a holistic subject and it would be folly to consider environmental issues alone, although this chapter is primarily concerned with land-use planning issues. To create a sustainable city requires appraisal of urban planning but also of health, transport, production, agriculture, urban design, and resource management issues. Such interdependencies must not be forgotten when considering land-use matters (Satterthwaite 1999).

In pursuit of the *Agenda 21* strategy agreed at the Rio conference, the UK government pinned great hopes on the implementation of sustainable patterns of future land-use planning, to control and restrict motor vehicle usage and therefore carbon emissions. Reducing global warming has been identified as the environmental imperative to sustainability.

We can also employ the land-use planning system to influence the siting of new shops and offices, where we work, where we go to enjoy ourselves and where we go to shop – these choices are all significant for the use of the car . . . we need to deliver development patterns over the next 20 years that will enable people to continue to choose to walk or cycle or use public transport. We should stand firm against the urban sprawl that would deny those choices.[18]

In 1999 the government published its strategy for the implementation of sustainable development, *A Better Quality of Life* (DETR 1999a). This took forward policy previously established in the *UK Strategy* of five years earlier. The government set out four principal aims for sustainable development: achieving social progress; effective protection of the environment; prudent use of natural resources; and maintenance of high and stable levels of economic growth. Contrary to the conclusions published by the Club of Rome 27 years before, the UK government did not accept the argument that continuing economic growth would be incompatible with environmental protection. These apparently conflicting objectives could be reconciled and economic growth would not be contrary to the implementation of environmental protection. A key priority was established in respect of the built environment, 'improving the larger towns and cities to make them better places to live and work'. The effective implementation of sustainable cities and their resident communities would require action at national, regional (via newly created Regional Development Agencies) and local (via LPAs) level to achieve a 'basket' of sustainable objectives. Such objectives included the need to reduce car travel (in part by siting major developments alongside good public transport) and to improve various land-use and design standards in pursuit of higher-density green-field development. A key factor would be the need to direct 60 per cent of new housing onto brown-land (or converted land) by 2008. Yet delivery of such an apparently easy to measure target would challenge many previous planning practices. Future development patterns would require more concentrated urban areas, with extensive re-use of previously developed land, considerable attention to the maintenance of urban amenity (by, say, provision of green space and through urban design) and giving preference to sustainable urban extensions instead of building isolated new settlements in circumstances where green-field development must be countenanced (by implication this will occur in 40 per cent of all new housing development by 2008). Planning policy would need to promote regeneration and more sustainable patterns of land use, for example by locating high-density development in or near transport corridors and through promotion of mixed-use schemes (such as in urban villages). Further, it would need to promote energy-efficient buildings, and good architectural and urban design.

The 1999 UK strategy committed the government to report annually on progress made in delivering sustainable development. Such appraisal itself requires the establishment of indicators or benchmarks against which sustainability can be measured.

Some policy areas would lend themselves to easy measurement, such as a 60 per cent brown-land target. Others would be less easily appraised, such as the improvement of quality in architecture and urban design, themselves matters of personal opinion. Nevertheless, the government have sought to identify a series of key statistics, notably 15 headline indicators, whereby implementation of sustainable development and quality could be measured in local communities (DoE 1996, DETR 2000). With regard to land use such indicators were restricted to the solitary quantifiable factor of how many new homes were built on previously developed land. Others were drawn from a variety of topics such as economic issues (such as employment or output levels), social issues (education, health, social exclusion) and environmental issues (climate change, air quality, road traffic levels, biodiversity, and land use). Such headline indicators are not the only means by which sustainability can be measured. Research published by the Royal Institution of Chartered Surveyors (RICS Foundation 2002) uncovered a . . . 'bewildering array of approaches which are sometimes in contradiction . . .' to the measurement of sustainability, itself a reflection of the different political, social and economic forces affected by the sustainability agenda. The report additionally concludes with respect to the property and construction industries that for a limited investment such sectors . . . 'can embrace sustainable development, and thereby gain a considerable advantage'. Such an approach emanated from work commissioned by the Secretary of State six years earlier, in which a government interdepartmental working group produced a number of key indicators to monitor sustainability (DoE 1996a). Key land-use indicators included household growth, re-use of brownland and loss of rural land to development. Appraisals based upon more subjective (or opinion-based) assessment, such as the quality of new architecture or urban design, could not be so readily measured and were not included as key indicators of sustainability.[19] Nevertheless, the importance of such policy areas should not be overlooked, even if it is acknowledged that easy measurement is not possible.

Implementation of strategies in such new policy areas would necessitate a cross-cutting or 'cross-cultural' approach. This would require integration across Local Agenda 21 strategies, development plans and regional policy. Land-use decisions, such as raising urban density or promoting mixed use, would need to be linked to other policy areas like transport (such as mixed-use development around transport nodes) and social policy (so that new development brings with it economic opportunity and helps redress social imbalance). The government set the planning system the ambitious target of promoting urban regeneration, social inclusion and the creation of more sustainable patterns of development. Additionally, the system would be vested with the responsibility of engaging the public in the process by virtue of public consultation and participation.

Urban growth

The Earth Summit considered how sustainable development could be applied to patterns of human settlement to create the 'sustainable city'. This urban sustainability deals with the achievement of urban development subject to the condition that natural resources are not depleted so as to threaten their long-term future.

The sustainable city must enjoy a harmonious relationship with its region or subregion, so that its existence and potential for growth are balanced against the long-term maintenance of water supply, air quality, land in agricultural production, and drainage/sanitation. Thus, urban sustainability is directly influenced by land-use controls, which ensure efficient use is made of urban land and which protect non-urban land from urban encroachment (Jenks et al. 1996).

In Britain, some land-use policies have emerged that address such issues. Although they largely pre-date the sustainable development policies of the 1990s, they can be adapted to reinforce the implementation of a sustainable strategy.

GREEN BELT POLICY

Until 1994, Green Belt policy had been principally concerned with checking urban sprawl, so that only a restricted schedule of development activity had been permitted around the major conurbations of Britain. In 1995 the government issues amended policy guidance with a new emphasis on how such policy, by operating at a regional and subregional level, can deliver sustainable patterns of development. Green belt policy, while continuing to resist outward urban expansion, can play a positive role in retaining attractive landscapes, promoting outdoor recreation, improving the quality of spoilt land (subject to tipping or extraction) and encouraging development within the existing urban envelope, whether by development of derelict land or redevelopment of existing sites within towns and cities. One problem is that such areas of restraint are 'leapfrogged' by developers.

CONSERVATION OF BUILT ENVIRONMENT

Both listed building and conservation area controls deal with the preservation of the built environment. Such special policy régimes would satisfy the Brundtland definition in that they seek to maintain the nation's built heritage for the benefit of future generations. Such policies also focus attention on matters such as the sympathetic re-use of listed buildings or the enhancement of conservation areas.

> The UK strategy on sustainable development supports the need to maintain and protect the built environment, stating that 'Failure to do so would result in irreversible loss of the nation's heritage'.
>
> (DoE 1994c: 88)

CONSERVATION OF NATURAL ENVIRONMENTS

Several policies deal with the relationship between development activity and conservation of natural resources to protect biological diversity:

- Sites of Special Scientific Interest and landscape quality, introduced by the Wildlife and Countryside Act 1981.
- Controls introduced by the European Community Habitats Directive[20] or Birds Directive,[21] which establishes a European system of Special Areas of Conservation to protect wildlife and where development will only be permitted if there is no alternative solution and there are 'imperative reasons of overriding public interest' (which includes economic and social considerations).[22]

- Control over trees, either by Tree Preservation Orders or by conservation area legislation (temporary protection for six weeks).
- National Nature Reserves
- National Parks
- Areas of Outstanding Natural Beauty
- Biosphere reserves
- Environmentally sensitive areas.

EFFICIENT LAND USE

Some planning policy initiatives dealing with new housing provision have championed the cause of sustainability and sought to be associated with this new policy agenda, including both urban villages and new settlements, providing for a mixture of residential, commercial, industrial and leisure-related activities. Urban villages promote the idea of medium- to high-density (not high-rise) mixed-use redevelopment. Such proposals offer redevelopment within existing urban areas and seem to minimize commuting by providing for both employment and housing within an area of approximately 40 ha (100 acres), with most parts of the urban village within a walking time of around 10 minutes. The consequence is that urban land can be 'recycled', providing for industrial and residential needs without eroding land outside the city. The new settlement can create a more self-sustained community, less reliant on the motor car, as homes and workplaces can be provided side by side (DoE 1993b). Clearly our urban areas have the potential to be more sustainable. The urban village presents this vision in a cogent way, namely provision of a high-density, mixed-use 'quality' environment in which residents enjoy both employment opportunity and local amenity. Consistent with the findings of research commissioned by DETR (1998) and Lord Rogers (Urban Task Force 1999), such development could be used to 'retrofit' or repair existing urban fabric damaged or blighted by either dereliction and vacancy or by past planning of either low-density, single-use suburbia or by high-rise housing without access to local amenities. Work commissioned by DETR (1998c), entitled *Planning for Sustainable Development: Towards Better Practice*, addressed this policy area and argued that 'the approach to increasing sustainability in urban areas essentially involves improving accessibility, raising densities and achieving a mix of uses in selected locations' (DETR ibid.). A key threshold was established in which an area or district was determined by a radius of 800 metres from a 'node' such as a bus stop, shop or local park, or other focal point. This rather simple concept was somewhat revolutionary in determining the shape of cities and residential areas.

It is itself constructed on a number of assumptions. First, it requires a flexible application of many planning standards in respect of parking, density (i.e. habitable dwellings per hectare) and overlooking/separation of development. In past years a criticism of the system has been that planners adhere too rigidly to standards which prevent innovation in density or design. Second, it requires that density standards are themselves raised due to the simple economic truth that 'as densities rise, it becomes increasingly viable to provide facilities, such as shops, health services and public transport, within walking distance of the population necessary to support them' (DETR 1998c). Yet density itself is no guarantee of achieving sustainability and requires that increased provision of public transport is linked with such developments.

Research work undertaken by the DoE in 1997 examined the relationship between housing density and area of land used. This work made fascinating reading in a subject that is somewhat dry and technical. It concluded that as density increases the amount of land saved is not commensurate; in other words, the proportionate savings in land diminish once a certain point is reached. The research found that the best savings were achieved by increasing density from 10 to a minimum of 20 dwellings per hectare, for provision of 400 dwellings (a land saving of 50 per cent). Yet as the density standards were increased the amount of land saved diminished. So it followed that the greatest or at any rate the optimum savings on density would require only a modest increase from low to medium, that is to say by reaching a minimum threshold of 40 dwellings per hectare. Subsequently (in 2000) a new PPG3 (DETR 2000a) would advocate raising housing density to between 30 and 50 dwellings per hectare. Therefore, to achieve a noticeably more efficient use of land would not require a dramatic shift in density policy. Third and finally, it requires that if development is to be acceptably accommodated outside existing urban areas, which government policy accepts in 40 per cent of all housing by 2008, then this must replicate key principles of sustainability in land use. Such principles encompass development around nodes (such as transport corridors well served by rail and bus modes).

This concept of 'sustainable urban extension' is not new. It has previously been promoted in British planning as both Garden Cities on the model designed by Ebenezer Howard in 1898 (Ward 1994) and by private companies like Eagle Star in their sponsoring of a new settlement at Micheldever in Hampshire. The noticeable departure of sustainable urban extensions from these previous models, apart from their linkage or proximity to existing urban areas, is their emphasis on efficient land use with a much higher density profile at 30–50 houses per hectare than, say, that advocated by Howard himself at 37 houses per hectare (Hall 1992). More efficient land use is thus achieved by raising density around key nodal points, greater integration between land use and public transport networks, and ensuring that if green-field development is to take place it adheres to such principles while also linking to existing urban centres. The promotion of numerous new settlements undertaken during the 1990s, in which free-standing and self-contained towns were promoted on green-field and some previously used land (mostly disused airfields) is unlikely to be repeated in future. Instead, far greater energy than previously will be devoted to 'retrofitting' higher-density schemes into existing urban areas and into sustainable urban extensions. Developers, especially housebuilders, have embraced such thinking, and centrally located and brown-land sites are increasingly being developed for medium-density and mixed-use schemes. Considerable opportunity exists here, especially in the so-called 'Golden Belt' area of predicted higher rates of change to urban areas stretching from south-western England to East Anglia via Wiltshire, Oxfordshire and Northamptonshire (Hall 1988 and DoE 1995).

GOVERNMENT PLANNING POLICY

The culmination of influential reports like *Planning for Sustainable Development: Towards Better Practice* (DETR 1998c) and *Towards Urban Renaissance* (Urban Task Force 1999) helped to shape the future direction of a sustainable planning policy agenda, as established in statements of national planning policy (PPGNs).

Such works were also supplemented by a series of research findings and best-practice reports that contributed empirical findings and promoted good practice. Several cascaded onto the desks of practitioners during the period from the late 1990s and into the new century. Work on the relationship between density and efficient land use has been previously cited (DoE 1997). Additionally, work by Llewelyn-Davies examined practical ways in which density could be raised (DETR 1998b). Parking policies were scrutinized in a comprehensive study of standards completed in 1998, also by Llewelyn-Davies, consultants for the DETR and Government Office for the South East (DETR 1998b). The report, while accepting that . . . 'it is . . . unreasonable to rely solely on parking standards to bring about . . . sustainability', promoted a more structured approach to the application of standards. While parking requirements would in future be based on maximum (i.e. ceilings) as opposed to minimum standards, the key recommendation was that parking policy should be more closely integrated to location in preference to the mere blanket application of standards as had previously been the case. A locational matrix was proposed in which development plans geographically divide areas into zones, with differing maximum standards. Such an approach was subsequently implemented in Edinburgh in 1999, whereby the zone covering the urban centre or other high-density areas well served by public transport (such as a district centre) could entertain car-free or dramatically reduced provision. In fringe or rural areas then a maximum standard of one space per dwelling is set. Parking policy is, as a result, more flexible and able to respond to a sustainable agenda in which car-free/reduced development can be acceptably accommodated in central nodes or other areas well served by public transport.

Alongside such research findings additional best-practice documentation set out to improve standards in urban design (DETR 2000d) and the relationship between development layout and car parking/highway considerations (DETR 1998). Sustainability was promoted by the concern to improve urban spaces and to ensure that in future parking provision and layout did not encroach upon the importance of creating a high-quality public realm.[23]

By 2000 such a body of work had gathered considerable momentum among policy makers in the (then) DETR. Planning Policy Guidance Notes (PPGs) issued from this point on would step-up the national implementation and the new focus. It should be remembered, however, that sustainable inputs to PPGs go back to the mid-1990s. In 1996, PPG6 was issued, establishing a sequential test in assessment of retail development, clearly favouring town-centre retail and discouraging out-of-town developments (as much favoured during the 1980s). Town centres, with their traditional focus of bus and rail interchanges. are less likely to rely on car-based shoppers than an out-of-town equivalent. Similarly the (now cancelled) PPG13 of 1994 sought to discourage out-of-town business parks or leisure/retail complex, with their almost total reliance upon car-based transport modes, in preference to existing centres where people are more likely to arrive by a variety of modes. So a sustainable agenda is not of itself a new concept. What significantly changed during the late 1990s and after 2000 was the depth and breadth of this agenda. PPG12 (DETR 1999b) produced guidance on the content of development plans, stating that the content of development plan policy (in paragraph 4.1) should 'implement the land use planning aspects of sustainable development and must be capable of being addressed through the land use system'.

To add some clarity on this matter the PPG gave a series of prescribed areas where environmental considerations should be taken into account in such planning policy. These included matters pertinent to energy conservation (such as reducing the need to travel and energy-efficient buildings), improving air quality and conservation of habitats and landscapes (such as biological diversity and countryside areas), improvements in the built environment (by means of urban design, provision of open space and protection of urban functions such as shopping), protection of heritage (such as listed buildings and archaeological sites) and protection of the environment (from contamination, waste disposal and mineral extraction). PPG12 (DETR 1999b) accepted the government's key premise that continued economic development and growth is not incompatible with implementation of sustainability. In preparing development plans all local authorities are expected to audit such policies by means of an environmental appraisal that includes attention to sustainable objectives and has regard to other relevant national and regional policies.

From 2000 all PPGs sought to herald greater urgency in the need to produce sustainable land use patterns and extend further the work of PPG12. A new PPG13 (DETR 2001c) took a more rigorous approach than previously to parking standards by advocating the employment of maximum parking standards and abolition of minimum standards, which when combined with other measures (such as park and ride, traffic management and public transport) served to 'promote sustainable transport choices' (Paragraph 52). By limiting parking provision to maximum ceilings, say one space maximum provision per 30 m² B1 (Business) space, additional benefits would be derived, notably a reduced land-take for development and consequently greater ease in accommodating schemes in central urban locations. Concentration of more amenities and uses in central locations promotes multi-purpose visits, in which people are less likely to use their cars as the cost and convenience benefits of public transport take effect.

PPG3 (2000) emerged as the strongest statement to date on this new direction. As government policy it took on board much that had been recommended by the Urban Task Force and the government's own White Paper *Planning for Communities of the Future* (House of Commons 1999). The House of Commons Environment, Transport and Regional Affairs Committee when commenting on the (draft) PPG said 'we welcome the draft PPG3 as an important step in promoting urban regeneration, encouraging housing development in appropriate locations and protecting the countryside' (ibid.) and in respect of re-using urban land and buildings went on to say that 'The government should set national and regional targets for the percentage of dwellings to be built on brownfield land in urban areas'.

The 60 per cent target discussed earlier in this chapter emerged in the finalized PPG3, Paragraph 23. A 'step change' in appraisal of residential schemes followed incorporation of a sequential approach to housing, with preference in favour of re-use of previously developed land within urban areas, followed by urban extensions and finally new development at nodal points in areas of good public transport. Each LPA will be charged with the responsibility of producing urban housing capacity studies to provide an appropriate assessment of housing needs and calculation of how much green-field development is necessary once the capacity of the urban area has been exhausted, while density thresholds were also to be raised. The objective of the guidance was to set a density 'window' of between 30 and 50 dwellings per hectare to make more efficient use of land and to avoid the low densities of around 15 dwellings per hectare so prevalent in past years, which it says are 'less likely to sustain local services or public transport, ultimately adding to social exclusion' (Paragraph 57).

Given past development practice, such a reform has been a long time coming. Land use change statistics issued by the (then) DETR (taken from DETR 1998a) in the period 1989–95 show that 54 per cent of all land taken for residential development was built at a density of less than 20 dwellings per hectare. In effect, around one quarter of all housing units built over this six-year period occupied just over half of all residential land. Such grotesque inefficiencies in land use could not be countenanced in the future. PPG3 of 2000 represented a fresh start. It went beyond density guidelines by promoting the need for more mixed-use and urban-village redevelopment of brown-land. By say 2005, five years after its introduction, it will be interesting to assess the extent to which the new policy regime heralded by this guidance will have raised densities and produced more efficient mixed-use and less car-reliant patterns of local use that could be said to be truly sustainable.

PROTECTION OF THE OZONE LAYER CONSERVING RESOURCES AND
FORESTS AND REDUCING POLLUTION

Conservation of resources such as minerals, aggregates and reduction of industrial emissions, with consequences for the ozone layer, fall within the realms of planning consideration.[24] Since the introduction of the modern system of planning controls in 1947, LPAs have enjoyed considerable planning powers to control industrial pollution. However, until recent years, with the introduction of a new 'sustainable' agenda, these powers were largely unused, because of inadequate training for planners in this subject, lack of effective government guidance, attempts by council environmental health departments to deal with such issues, and the fear that such planning restrictions would result in job losses. Sustainability has provided the much-needed incentive to 'kick start' many planners into a reconsideration of their role in the area. Such a new awareness of pollution issues within town planning has been accompanied by a wider range of controls over the regulation of industrial pollution. The Environment Act 1995 introduced new procedural systems for the regulation of industrial and water pollution, establishing a new Environment Agency to co-ordinate implementation of such powers. New Planning Policy Guidance as well as case law[25] accepts that potential pollution from a proposed development is a material consideration to be taken into account when deciding to grant or refuse planning permission. In particular, the planning system should consider matters such as location, impact upon amenity, impact upon other land, nuisance, impact on road or other transport networks, and feasibility of land restoration in the longer term, when considering potential pollution issues.

The increased employment of environmental impact assessment in large-scale development proposals allows for an examination of potential pollution emissions from industrial development. However, an LPA enjoys power to refuse planning permission for any type of development proposal, with or without an environmental impact assessment, which may result in unacceptable pollution (DoE 1994d). The Earth Summit identified the contribution of industrial activity to causing airborne pollution, which is harmful to human health as well as damaging to forests and trees, creating acid rain and resulting in depletion of the ozone layer. PPG 12 (1999) heralded a much more pro-active approach in this area by including matters such as energy conservation, global climate change and reduction in greenhouse gases squarely within the purview of planning policy. Coupled with this PPG13 (2001) and PPG22 (1993 with a revised version in 2004) respectively set out to reduce car travel and promote the use of renewable energy sources (such as wind, geothermal or plant materials), both objectives being designed to limit greenhouse gas emissions, principally carbon dioxide. By the mid-1990s some English county councils began to adopt structure planning policies that included language dealing with such issues as ozone layer depletion, fuel emissions, longer-term maintenance of non-renewable resources and industrial pollution (Barnard 1993). Between 1995 and 2000 this initial trickle of 'sustainable' policy became a flow of new ideas and initiatives. From 2000 to say 2004, it is anticipated that all development plans and frameworks will contain an amalgam of sustainable policies designed to address global warming by means of land use planning decisions. It is also inevitable that planning permissions will be refused for such environmental reasons and, when these decisions are the subject of a challenge at appeal, then the Secretary of State or an Inspector will be required to arbitrate on the outcome. At such a time, the government's resolve will be tested in the degree towards which it supports local councils who seek to use planning policy to protect the ozone layer or the finite supply of fossil fuels and the means by which they deal with attempts to calculate the environmental impact of schemes, for example, due to carbon emissions (Pearce 1994). Such an issue was dealt with in a decision of the High Court in 1994 regarding the construction of a new regional shopping centre at Trafford Park (also called Dumplington), in Manchester. Mr Justice Schiemann stated:

> The evidential problem of establishing the amount of CO_2 to be generated by the Trafford Centre and establishing how much of this would have been generated by shopping trips that would no longer take place if shoppers went to the Trafford Centre instead of their habitual shops is

manifestly enormous. The results would inevitably have to include a vast range of error. Such a result if it turned out to show that there would be a net increase in such gases, would then need to be balanced against the undeniable benefits of the proposal.[26]

Conclusions

In 1991, legislative reforms[27] introduced a presumption in favour of the development, which superseded the 'presumption in favour of development' that had reigned throughout the 1980s property boom. LPAs have, since the 1990s, been encouraged to adopt sustainable strategies within new planning policy, and the DoE, DETR and now Office of the Deputy Prime Minister produced increasing volumes of guidance, with a strong emphasis on sustainability, especially in using planning policy to discourage use of the motor car. The 1994 *UK strategy* (DoE 1994c), as a response to the Earth Summit's *Agenda 21*, represented a further move in the direction of this 'greening' of the planning system, whereby environmental considerations are given considerably more weight in the decision-making process than would have been the case in the 1980s. Yet the *UK strategy* contained few detailed targets or timetables to establish guidelines by which government policy can be assessed. The climate change document (HMSO 1994a) set out a programme for curbing carbon emissions up to the year 2000 and the *UK strategy* identifies the important role town planning can play in helping to change land-use patterns and reduce car dependency. Since the late 1990s and the publication in 1999 of *A Better Quality of Life. A Strategy for Sustainable Development* (DETR 1999a) and the revised PPG12 of the same year, the direction of sustainable planning policy has been consolidated. This direction has increasingly pointed towards mixed-use, higher-density, well-connected urban environments. More efficient use of land that is focused, by means of the sequential test, towards urban land use that helps sustain local communities by ensuring proximity to shops, services and transport networks.

The objectives of such policy, as laid down in *Planning for Sustainable Development* (DETR 1998) and *Towards an Urban Renaissance* (Urban Task Force 1999), are two-fold. First, they seek to reduce the need to travel, or at least the need to travel by car, and thus contribute to agreed reductions in greenhouse-gas emissions (as required by the Kyoto Protocol). Second, they contribute to a new 'urban orthodoxy', in which the planning system redirects development not simply back to urban areas but into an urban renaissance of our towns and cities.

Critics have argued that government pronouncements merely serve to 'shoehorn' previous planning policies into a sustainable setting, that the strategy delivers nothing new and instead just 'repackages' existing commitments to the environment so that they *appear* to be pro-sustainability. Such a view may have held sway in the 1990s, when sustainable policy was in a somewhat embryonic state. Since 2000 that view has diminished as sustainable planning land use has become the 'norm' and not the 'exception' for development plan policy matters.

The implementation of sustainable land-use town planning is not an unattainable vision. Town planning has an important role to play by ensuring

Table 8.2 Summary of key statistics

Issue	Statistics	Source
Derelict urban land land	28 800 ha derelict land	*National Land Use Database* (1998)
Urban growth	Projected change of urban area of England from 10% land use (1981) to 12% by 2016. Between 1991 and 2016, 169 000 ha will change from rural to urban uses.	*Indicators of Sustainable Development* (1996) and *Urbanization in England Projections* (1995)
Agricultural land	77% land area (Britain) 1985–90 of all urban increase, around 40% was previously in agricultural use.	DoE land-use change statistics
Forestry	2.4 million ha (Britain).	*UK strategy*
Road building	12 000 ha land used for road building in the period 1985–90 (66% on rural land).	*Indicators of Sustainable Development* (1996)
Reclamation of derelict land	95 000 ha derelict land reclaimed in the period 1988–93.	*Indicators of Sustainable Development* (1996)
Re-use of urban land	Around 7000 ha per year recycled 1985–90 and necessary to increase this figure by 2008.	DoE Statistical Bulletin: *Land Use Change in England* (1995)
Household projections	Household formation in England and Wales expected to grow to 2.5 million by 2006 and over the period 1991–2016 the total increase in households is projected to be 23%	DoE *Projections of Households in England to 2016* (1995)
Global warming		
All greenhouse gases (methane, nitrous oxide & carbon dioxide)	Government target: all emissions to be at 1990 levels by 2000	Climate change document
Carbon dioxide emissions	1990 calculated at 160 million tonnes carbon. By 2000 between 157–179 million tonnes carbon	*UK strategy*
Car/vehicle ownership	20 million 1990 30 million 2025	*UK strategy*
Pollution	Sulphur dioxide/black smoke fallen by 70% 1970–93. Nitrogen dioxide risen by 70% 1980–93	Climate change document
Climate change	Estimate 0.3 °C increase in temperature and 6 cm rise in sea level every 10 years at 1990 rates	Climate change document and Houghton *et al.* (1992)
Changes in land-use patterns 1982–92	Out-of-town retail – 4.1 million m² and 3.4 million in town (Compare: 1960–81 – 1 million out-of-town and 6 million in town)	*UK strategy*

that urban or greenfield development incorporates a mix of uses integrated with a range of public transport systems. The wider issue is whether planning can make any real impact on such issues as global warming and vehicular emissions. Any planning strategy must be linked to other areas of public policy if such objectives are to be realized. Reducing the use of the private car will require a combination of planning policy with financial policy (subsidy to public transport) and a coherent transport strategy (reduce new road building) before the real growth in car ownership can be arrested, as people will opt for other modes of transport that provide greater accessibility at lower cost. The planning system operating in isolation of these other areas will not make any significant impact on such environmental issues as global warming. The Royal Commission on Environmental Pollution (1994: 159) concluded that 'In isolation, land-use planning is a relatively blunt instrument for changing travel behaviour, critical though it may be in the long term. . . . The problems of traffic growth and congestion must, in the first instance, be tackled by more direct means.' In considering the role of the land-use planning system, the report acknowledged the interaction between land use and transport issues, but emphasized the role of a coherent transport policy framework alongside purely planning-based strategies.

Planning authorities are being encouraged to adopt sustainable policies in their local structure or unitary development plans. Between 2000 and 2005 it is evident that such policies will be widely applied throughout the system. Sustainable development has been, and will continue to be, a 'buzzword' in town planning. Land-use decision-making is an important arena within which a balance may be struck between economic development and environmental protection; therefore, town planning plays a vital role. Although it alone cannot deliver sustainable development, it enjoys considerable potential to direct key areas towards these goals. The key test for the future will be the political will of national government to support such a role for the town planning system.

The term 'sustainable development' is not subject to one universally agreed definition. This may be of little surprise when one considers the broad subject area encompassed by the term 'sustainability', namely that of the relationship between economic development and global environmental conservation. This chapter has focused upon the role of land-use planning in delivering sustainable development. That in itself is a broad subject area. Nevertheless, the British government has sought to initiate some debate, as well as action, on the role of the planning system. It is too early to judge whether such policy has been a success or failure. Nevertheless, the threat of environmental degradation posed by global warming necessitates that the implementation of such policy cannot come too soon.

9   Urban renaissance and urban regeneration

Background

On 16 November 2000 the Deputy Prime Minister launched a new Urban White Paper entitled *Our Towns and Cities: The Future* (DETR 2000b). This document laid down a vast array of policy initiatives dealing with the social, economic and environmental dimensions of urban life. It was billed as presenting a new 'joined-up' and long-term approach to the co-ordination of financial–fiscal measures, policy agendas (including planning), and the functioning of various government and non-governmental agencies, all seeking to promote urban 'renewal' and arrest long-term decline and under-investment. Such a document, the first White Paper to address exclusively urban policy issues for some 23 years, was constructed upon other works, notably the findings of the Urban Task Force (chaired by Lord Rogers) (Urban Task Force 1999), and research reports into *The State of English Cities* and *Living in Urban England: Attitudes and Aspirations* (DETR 2000c). The White Paper set itself a number of ambitious targets, with detailed monitoring by a newly formed cabinet committee and Urban Summit in 2002.

The creation of environmental sustainability, local participation and mixed communities in urban area renewal represented key themes that reverberated throughout the White Paper and warrant closer inspection. In 20 years time, it seems reasonable to conclude, commentators will look back to 16 November 2000 either as a day when new thinking emerged to shape the fundamental approach to urban renewal, or when yet another raft of regeneration initiatives was launched that failed to understand the complex interrelationship between economics, planning and society. This chapter will focus primarily on the implications of these new initiatives for physical planning, although other (social and economic) policy areas will be dealt with where appropriate.

The context of urban change

Demographic change over the last 100 or so years has resulted in a population movement from rural to urban areas. At the start of the twentieth century around 10 per cent of the world's population lived in towns and cities. A century later this figure exceeds 50 per cent. This urban population accounts for almost all pollution (Urban Task Force 1999), while England's urban areas (in which 90 per cent or 47 million live) accounts for 91 per cent of total economic output and 89 per cent of all employment (Urban Task Force 1999).

Urban areas predominate in the economic and social life of the nation. While Britain is highly urbanized, land-use patterns are increasingly viewed as 'inefficient'. For example, while London and its hinterland constitute the second most densely populated region in Europe, prevailing post-war density standards in Britain have produced housing layouts as low as 5–20 dwellings per hectare. A clear link is drawn between density and car usage, in which 'land-grabbing' low-density housing encourages car use (as shops and services are beyond an acceptable threshold of five minutes/500 metres distance) and discourages public transport (it is uneconomic for a bus route to serve sprawling low-density areas). In post-war Britain the planning system has encouraged this low-density suburbanization around many small- to medium-density towns, while at the same time restricting the outward expansion of the major conurbations (where 40 per cent of the population live) by imposition of green belts.

It may come as little surprise, therefore, that these development patterns (coupled with peripherally located business and leisure uses) have promoted car dependency. Between 1980 and 1996, Britain's roads experienced a 63 per cent increase in motor vehicle traffic (almost entirely composed of car use) and between 1992 and 2021 car ownership is projected to increase from 24.5 million to 30 million. The planning system and house building industry has hitherto operated on a model of regulation dominated by conformity to prescribed road layout, density and parking standards, and separation of development (typically 21 metres rear-to-rear elevation). This has produced some uninspiring layouts in which a low-density, low-rise suburbia predominates.

Demographic change and its implications for land use have brought into sharp focus the problems created by continuing to replicate this model. The government's prediction in 1996, that over the following 25 years 3.8 million new households will be required (a product of increasing numbers of single-person households, coupled with a population drift away from urban areas of around 90 000 net outward migrants every year, has resulted in a reassessment of priorities. The spectre emerges of satisfying the call for 3.8 million new dwellings on a density model of less than 20 dwellings per acre and creating over the next 15–20 years an additional urban area the size of the West Midlands conurbation (Urban Task Force 1999). Alongside this statistic it should be remembered that (as at 2000–1) 700 000 homes were empty, 250 000 of which had been so for in excess of one year. This reassessment of past town planning values has led to calls for an 'urban renaissance'. It is this renaissance that must be given detailed attention.

The task is by no means an easy one. Past drift away from urban areas (especially among more affluent social groups) must be reversed, standards of urban development and design must be improved, and the private sector must be encouraged (and supported) to recycle urban land that may be derelict, vacant and even contaminated. By 2021 the student of urbanism (that is to say, town planning, architecture and management, or urban design) may become the student of urban renaissance. Here, consideration will be given to a number of important policy documents that have established an agenda for change and to several case studies. Specific attention is given to matters of urban density, urban design, local democracy, sustainability. and mixed-use/mixed-tenure projects, principally presented as case studies.

Agenda for change

The Urban White Paper *Our Towns and Cities: The Future*, constitutes the key policy document, itself being influenced by the findings of the Urban Task Force chaired by Lord Richard Rogers, a 'think tank' created by the Deputy Prime Minister in April 1998. Further, it has been shaped by (the then) DETR-sponsored reports into the state of urban life (DETR 2000b) and a review of the way housing has been allocated by the planning system (in PPG3). The Urban Task Force (UTF) made some far reaching criticisms and called for a radical rethink of many urban planning policies. The UTF report, *The State of English Cities* and the Urban White Paper will all now be considered. PPG3 (2000) is considered in greater depth later, in Chapter 18 on residential development.

The Urban Task Force Report (1999)

The UTF findings were critical of several failings in the planning system, although not all blame was laid at the door of LPAs as the overall direction of the system (created by government) was also responsible. The Report championed the status and importance of the city in supporting key cultural, educational and welfare institutions 'to perform a unifying civic function' (UTF 1999). The future of the city will be influenced by technical innovation (such as in information technology), ecological threat (i.e. sustainability) and social transformation (as life patterns change and the level of one-person households increases). The Task Force identified a number of threats to the future of cities, notably the economic decline of many (northern English) cities, their weakening manufacturing base, and disproportionate percentage of poorer social groups and less-productive manufacturing capacity. Such structural weaknesses combine to create a vicious spiral, which generates a poor public image and unfavourable perceptions of city life, whether justified or not by the facts. These influences on future success are set out in Table 9.1.

Table 9.1 Future success of urban area (from Urban Task Force Report 1999)

1 Quality	&longrightarrow;	In design and the promotion of compact urban form.
2 Economy	&longrightarrow;	To achieve sustained investment to target economic decline and social exclusion.
3 Environmental responsibility	⟶ ⟶	Use resources more efficiently; energy efficient buildings: awareness of biodiversity and housing on recycled land.
4 Governance	&longrightarrow;	Promote participatory democracy through urban government.
5 Society	&longrightarrow;	Give priority to social well-being to ensure neighbourhoods have a balance of tenure and income groups.

The Report confronted the problem of accommodating an additional 3.8 million households in England by 2021. Cities (and urban areas) contain vast swathes of derelict and vacant land, with estimates ranging between 17 000 and 39 000 ha derelict and 16 000 ha of vacant land (58 000 ha of brown land is available for redevelopment). Public opposition to green-field development is increasing and a significant proportion of housing demand is from one-person households. The UTF, in a highly creative strategy, identify the potential to satisfy this demand on urban land in such a way as to repair 'current tears in our urban fabric' and create a renaissance in both the physical fabric of and attitudes to our urban areas.

Such repair is to be achieved by the creation of mixed, diverse and well-connected urban areas in ways that regenerate or 'retrofit' existing environments. A strong commitment is attributed to design in this report: 'successful urban regeneration is design-led'.

The Task Force gave a great deal of attention to the physical ways in which the planning system may 'repair' the city. The way forward is set out in a number of key recommendations. First, they judge that past reliance on rigid planning standards has stifled creativity. For example, adherence to highway standards (such as road widths, radii and visibility at junctions)[1] has dominated urban layouts by establishing a 'roads first, houses later' priority. The ease of car movement predominates over pedestrian or cycle priority. By contrast, they recommend that streets should be seen as places and not transport corridors.

Second, to foster both sustainability and urban quality, the Task Force promoted the notion of a compact city. Sustainability would be achieved by linking urban density to a hierarchy of urban centres/local hubs providing shops and services within well-connected public transport and walking routes. The Report declared that 'there is a proven link between urban densities and energy consumption'. An appropriate integration of density and the 'connected compact city' would reduce the reliance on the motor car. Urban quality would be achieved by improved urban design, that is to say the design of public space and proper acknowledgement that quality public space provides vital 'glue' between buildings, creating integrated city spaces. The

Table 9.2 Density comparables (from Urban Task Force Report 1999)

Barcelona	400 dwellings per hectare
London (Islington/Bloomsbury)	100–200 dwellings per hectare
Most of UK	5–10 dwellings per hectare
Post-war 'norm'	20–30 dwellings per hectare

report laments a recent demise in the quality of city space (i.e. the public realm between buildings) that demonstrates the loss of a rich urban tradition evident in medieval and Georgian civic planning in cities such as York and Bath.

Third, and related to the compact city, they recommend that the previous adherence to density standards must be dropped: 'density is not an indicator or urban quality'. The report sets out to destroy the previous orthodoxy that density dictates an acceptable urban form. Indeed, it argues that higher densities (and not necessarily high-rise developments) contribute to both urban sustainability and supports a greater number of public amenities and transport facilities. Previously, half of all land used in England for new housing has been at prevailing densities of 20 or fewer dwellings per hectare, equating to 54 per cent of all land used providing just one quarter of all housing units completed. Not only is this form of housing highly inefficient but it is no longer a viable means of providing housing when confronted with the dual priorities of providing 3.8 million units while people continue to leave urban areas. In raising density levels, quality need not be diminished. Indeed, the Urban Task Force makes reference to the density of a city like Barcelona, compared to Britain's post-war norm, as summarized in Table 9.2.

New government policy on housing (PPG3 of 2000) attempted to lift density standards, albeit modestly, to above 30 dwellings per hectare. The Report recommended imposition of a planning presumption against excessively low-density urban development.

Finally, regard is given to the utilization of urban design to facilitate mixed-use/mixed-tenure development to foster sustainability (by living and working in close proximity) and allowing people to change tenure type to meet changing circumstances while remaining in the same locality. The Report raised the status of design in urban regeneration as a pre-eminent consideration. Good urban design should encourage people to live near to the services they require on a regular basis. Key principles to be employed include consideration of the context/density/sustainability of the site and the promotion of mixed tenure/mixed activity development built in an environmentally responsible way (see Case Studies 9.1 and 9.3).

The Task Force set out to deliver this new vision by a combination of measures dealing with taxation, planning policy and design. Such integration across physical and economic policy, and the establishment of government agencies may not be new. The Report, reflecting its overall emphasis on design, promoted the spatial masterplan as an 'engine' of change set within a national urban design framework. This masterplan would promote a three-dimensional model for urban regeneration, prepared by a local authority

Case study 9.1: Urban renaissance: good practice in urban design

To promote excellence in urban design, between 1999 and 2003 the government sponsored a series of Millennium Communities or Villages (development projects following design competitions) and Urban Regeneration Companies (government-sponsored agencies to target investment in deprived cities and link public with private action).

The Greenwich Millennium Village was one such project, located on London's Greenwich peninsula and involving a 'high-profile international competition' (Urban Task Force 1999) to create a mixed-tenure community comprising high-density, energy-efficient development integrated with a variety of public spaces (streets, square, open spaces, and communal gardens).

The nature of the resulting development was commended by the Urban Task Force as a model of design-led regeneration that harnessed a competitive process to produce innovation in design and sustainability (energy efficiency).

Between 2000 and 2003, 15 Urban Regeneration Companies (URCs) were established, following the successful pilot of 'Liverpool Vision'. This URC was funded by three public agencies and the private sector, and established a 'Strategic Regeneration Framework' to stimulate sustained long-term investment in the city. A co-ordinated strategy recommended action in a wide variety of areas, including urban design projects, cultural projects (seeking nomination as European City of Culture) and public participation to engage local people in the new strategies. Such an approach established a new agenda in which physical and economic regeneration was no longer viewed as the exclusive preserve of the public sector. Instead a partnership was formed between public and private sectors, in close liaison with the views of local people.

or other regeneration agency and designed to focus on the integration of buildings and spaces. This methodology is viewed as more dynamic and design-led than the traditional two-dimensional approach, in which plans were produced that dealt with 'zoning' of use, density and access, and largely ignored the shape of the consequent urban form/public space, building design and integration between pedestrian, vehicular and public transport routes.

Urban Task Force – the way forward

The Urban Task Force Report was highly design-orientated and viewed quality urban design and urban form as an essential engine of change in bringing about urban regeneration. While not ignoring other considerations (economic policy, fiscal incentives and matters of governance), the Report places design at the centre of all issues. The Report's promotion of the compact city is not new (Jenks *et al.* 1996, DETR 1998c and Coupland 1997) but is part of a dynamic attempt to change the low-density suburban and 'non-place' orthodoxy of much post-war British residential town planning (see Case study 9.2). Perhaps the most exciting recommendation to emerge from this work centres on the deployment of the 3.8 million new homes to be built by 2021 to repair the existing residential fabric, utilizing this to connect and thus integrate existing environments to create higher-density well-planned places.

Considering the fact, as the Report establishes, that more than 90 per cent of our urban fabric will still exist in 30 years time, then such a 'retrofitting' approach, while a significant policy change, will only bring about a limited spatial change, measured in hectares affected. The Report issued a series of qualified warnings that the government's target for 60 per cent new housing by 2021 on previously developed sites is unlikely to be met, concluding instead that 'from our models we have estimated that based on current policies and trends just under 2.1 million dwellings will be developed' on such land. But given that, in 1996 for example, only 40 per cent of urban housing was provided on such sites, a 'step change' is required in planning policy and other areas (taxation and subsidy) to prevent the current (2000) achievement of around 50–55 per cent built on recycled land falling back to the 40–45 per cent equivalent of less than a decade before. (For details of how new housing land is allocated, see Chapter 18.)

Urban Task Force – conclusions

The Urban Task Force Report gave fresh momentum to an urban renaissance in our towns and cities. It accepted that a cultural change would be required, in which people perceived urban living more positively than previously, but argued that a new focus on the urban fabric (by means of better urban design) will assist greatly in bringing about this change in attitudes. The planning system needs to be less concerned with rigid adherence to set standards on density, parking or layout of development. Instead LPAs should adopt a more three-dimensional and flexible approach to policy standards, should promote mixed uses and refuse permission for low-density schemes. The overall strategy for accommodating new housing projections in the system needs to be more flexible and the Report endorsed the government's decision (of 1998) to adopt a more flexible stance on housing allocations and their delivery over the plan period.

The Report made 105 detailed recommendations for change, with a summary of key ones set out at the end of this chapter. While it contended that the 60 per cent brown-land target was unlikely to be met (although it may be possible upon implementation of the Report's recommendations) it was ultimately optimistic that an urban renaissance could be delivered and could effect lasting change in the planning of urban space in England.

The state of English cities (1999)

This Report addressed the change in intellectual orthodoxy over the last 20 years in the nature of urban policy. For the period from the mid 1970s to the 1990s, the predominant thinking at government level involved targeting of resources specifically at the poorest areas, in pursuit of redistribution of wealth. A new agenda, evident towards the end of the 1990s, attempted a more connected (or 'joined-up', to quote from the Urban White Paper)

Case study 9.2: Urban renaissance: urban extensions

In 2000 The Prince's Foundation published a report *Sustainable Urban Extensions: Planned Through Design*, which advocated an alternative model of community involvement deemed preferable to past public participation, in which local people merely commented on a completed scheme instead of getting involved with its formulation. The Foundation's own mission was to promote . . . 'a return of human values to architecture, urban design and regeneration' and their report took a critical view of much in the design of past residential environments, railing against the piecemeal low-density outward expansion of towns and cities. Private-sector housing estates offered little choice of house type and was predominant in creating 'placeless' low density suburbs. The rigid enforcement of highway rules (seeking vehicular visibility) prevented innovative urban design because of creating cul-de-sacs, visibility splays and radii in a low-density suburban style. This 'roads first, houses later' approach and the consequent inefficient low-density suburban form, is unable to justify bus services and so increases car dependency.

The Report argued that a consensus was emerging among planners and the public that greater priority needs to be given to urban design, environmental sustainability and public involvement. New green-field development will continue (40 per cent is accepted by government in its housing projections) so a new approach is needed. The Foundation holds 'Enquiry by design' community workshops in which landowners, council officials and public and other interested groups assemble to devise new-build residential layouts on an anti-sprawl and sustainable agenda. Workshop facilitators help the 'stake-holders' to debate, discuss, enquire, and design collaboratively, usually focused on the key criterion that housing is organized into walkable neighbourhoods of a five minute/500 metre radius from public transport or community facilities.

The approach was employed in two English case studies, Basildon and Northampton. Two urban extensions into green-field sites designed on the model of a traditional low-density volume householder were redesigned to create significantly greater housing yields and more sustainable layouts. In Basildon a 35 hectare site would yield 1120 houses (preserving 7 ha open space) at 40 dwellings per hectare, compared to 875 units of traditional low-density detached houses. In Northampton 6400 houses were located on a site of some 250 hectares, compared to 3700 on the traditional model. This 70 per cent increase in the yield of dwelling units was achieved not by compromising the amenities enjoyed by future occupiers but the very reverse, in which quality urban design (based on urban and not suburban principles) allows for higher density with integration of public spaces and transport networks. Such an 'Enquiry by Design' approach creates better, more sustainable and more democratic environments. It is unsurprising, therefore, that this approach should be strongly endorsed by the Urban Task Force when the direction of government policy (as expressed in PPG3) accepts that urban extensions will occur in the future. Taking this on board, such an approach will need to be brought to bear on the future development of the many green fields that will need to be ploughed up for housing by 2021, in order to render that development more sustainable and more efficient in its use of land.

This focus on the importance of urban design has been reinforced by research published by The Commission for Architecture and the Built Environment (CABE 2001). Following detailed examination of the literature in this area and appraisal of six recently completed developments, the CABE research concluded that good urban design not only added economic value* but also social and environmental value. Further, the cost of such urban design need not be high. One of the case studies dealt with Standard Court in Nottingham, a 2.6 hectare mixed-use office, retail, leisure, and residential redevelopment of a former hospital site in the city centre. A public space is created (the public arena), defined by both new and refurbished buildings (mostly listed). The researchers considered the scheme to be 'a disconnected place', poorly integrated into the neighbouring historic environment of Nottingham Castle and with the main entrances of the office buildings not facing onto the arena. The result is an unused, desolate space that does not benefit from passing trade, with detrimental effects on the retail/catering premises in the scheme. Office rents have been below the best Nottingham levels, indicative of a satisfactory but not excellent economic performance for Standard Court. Compare this with Barbirolli Square in central Manchester, another case study in the research. This involved a 1-hectare redevelopment of former railway land to create a concert hall, two office blocks and a cafe/bar. Again a public space is created, linking and opening up a former canal basin. The site was considered to be reasonably well-connected and creates 'a new landmark gateway to Manchester'. The offices have commanded high rents and an economic/social ripple effect is evident, in which five new restaurants have subsequently opened up in the surrounding area.

Such case studies demonstrate that the design, configuration and use of urban space can either hinder or enhance the economic, social and environmental prosperity of the surrounding area. Good architecture, while important, is not the sole factor in creating success. Design of buildings must be linked to design of space, so that redevelopment schemes connect with their surroundings and link to the neighbouring morphology (the shape and features of the urban space), such as that found in historic areas. The importance of urban design is thus critical in fostering successful and sustainable urban renaissance.

* Economic value in this context means higher profits for owners and investors, by virtue of higher capital values and rents. Social value refers to job creation, while environmental value refers to the urban realm and its infrastructure.

relationship between social and economic life. Alongside this, more weight than previously was given to matters of 'space and place' or urban design.

The Report established an 'urban asset base' of factors that have influenced the success or failure of cities, including location, age, economic structure, company characteristics (growth potential), skills and innovation, communications, environmental quality, and nature of local governance. It reports that cities have endured: 'whilst there is some evidence of the continuing relative economic weakness of British cities, there are also signs of a renaissance in their roles as centres of economic strength'. The Report appraises the economic and social dimensions of cities. Economically they exert a powerful 'propulsive' or wealth-generating impact upon their regional hinterlands. This impact goes beyond just employment opportunities to include provision of learning, education and a better regional image. Economics and demography (population change) are interlinked. The annually accelerating population losses from urban centres of the 1980s slowed in the 1990s and became population growth by the late 1990s. It is worthy of note, however, that 'in most conurbations, rates of net out-migration are highest for the better-off . . . this has implications for house prices and development pressures in adjacent areas and it reinforces social-spatial segregation'.

Socially it is apparent that cities perform badly when measured against indices of socio-economic deprivation: 'unemployment, educational levels, health, crime, and poverty tend to be worst in the big cities'. Evidence cited on poverty and social exclusion shows beyond doubt that there is a widening gap between 'comfortable' Britain and the poorest, as factors like child poverty and above-average mortality (in poor areas) increased at the end of the 1990s. The Report called for some hard thinking if child poverty is to be ended in the next generation. Tackling social exclusion (from employment opportunities) is a priority. A cyclical problem emerges, in which low levels of educational achievement and related social/life skills are a major source of social exclusion. This cycle is reinforced by the inability of poorer families to relocate to the catchment of schools with good social infrastructure. Conversely, those who can move away from the catchment of schools with poor educational records, entrenching the problem. In the Report, emphasis is placed on the importance of neighbourhood or community-led action to engage residents in the implementation of projects to tackle local problems. One important area of city regeneration is the way the various agencies operate. In reflecting on many past policies, the Report established that a number of key features may be identified. For example, appraisal of City Challenge[2] (1992–8) and the Single Regeneration Budget[3] (SRB) Challenge Fund (from 1994) identified key benefits in their partnership of public, private and community groups. Further, these groups adopted a cross-disciplinary approach, linking across several agencies and/or professions to target resources at key problems. Greater partnership across the work of all regeneration agencies, combined with a regional focus, were identified as key features, leading the Report to state that . . . 'At the end of the 1990s the key principles of regeneration policy were partnership, spatial targeting, integration, competition and a commitment to combined economic, social and environmental regeneration'.

The Report called for greater clarity in the role of the Regional Development Agencies (RDAs) and financial resources available to them. The eight RDAs were established in 1999 to provide a regional dimension to regeneration strategies, although little fresh money was made available because their resources were largely transferred from SRB and English Partnership funding. The principal focus of RDA strategy was to be delivered by local partnerships (reflecting many lessons learnt from City Challenge and SRB projects), but in their early years they lacked the 'joined-up' dimension so sought-after by government, and suffered from an ill-defined relationship with the other big regional agencies for regeneration, the government regional offices.

A comparative study of regeneration strategies in other European countries endorsed the model of targeted and local spatial initiatives, based upon partnership. Further, it confirmed that policy solutions to the problems of regeneration are not easy: 'achieving the goal of regeneration is proving as great a challenge to (other European countries) as it is for the British'.

The Report concluded by explicitly stating the key principles of regeneration, given the experience of the last 20 years. Four key principles were identified: integration of policy approach across agencies and areas; the establishment of public–private–community partnerships; a pivotal role to be taken by local government; and policy initiatives to be carefully linked to both regional and local implementation strategies. Qualified endorsement was given to the 12 Urban Regeneration Companies, with their cross-disciplinary and city-wide focus. A key feature of successful integration policy is that all agencies integrate their work. Failure to adopt this holistic view can have far-reaching (if not always readily apparent) consequences. For example, government decisions on the brown-land/green-field targets 'can have profound effects on the likelihood of urban regeneration', as in northern cities demand is less buoyant for new housing, resulting in less incentive to develop recycled urban land.

The Report provides a valuable appraisal of past and current urban programmes. The need to maintain partnerships, local governance and for a wider grasp of socio-economic factors (especially social exclusion) are fundamental. All regenerative agencies must work together, at neighbourhood, city and regional levels to create the conditions for local partnership considered necessary for effective implementation of renewal policies. Figure 9.1 provides a summary.

The Urban White Paper: Our Towns and Cities (2000)

This White Paper married a number of existing policies with a variety of current or forthcoming policy reviews. The document, therefore, presented itself as a vast amalgamation of policy areas and action plans. Key themes emerged, most notably its attempt to promote an integrated approach to urban policy by linking planning, sustainability, transport, economics, and social exclusion policies into one holistic framework. This ambitious remit may account for its sometimes confusing stream of initiatives and policies.

A key feature is that local leaderships and partnerships are seen as fundamental to achieving an enduring change in urban renewal projects. In response to the House of Commons Environment Committee's observations on the (then proposed) Urban White Paper,[4] the government accepted the need for an urban renaissance to create sustainable mixed neighbourhoods and economically powerful cities by emphasizing that alongside physical regeneration, 'strong and effective local leadership and close partnership working both locally and between tiers' are required. When considering the future direction of urban policy, regard must be paid to the government's emphasis on local political structures and the co-ordination of initiatives. The need for local democratic processes reverberates across the many policy areas in the White Paper. An element of 'self-help' is often an underlying theme behind an array of policies, and the White Paper declares that 'a clear

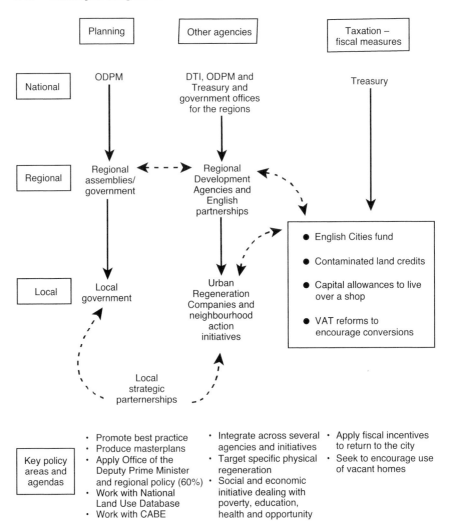

Figure 9.1 Key agencies in the urban renaissance.

message from the regeneration initiatives of the last 30 years is that real sustainable change will not be achieved unless local people are in the driving seat'. Emphasis is placed on reforms of local government democracy within the provisions of the Local Government Act 2000 (such as appointment of directly elected mayors or cabinets) and for greater deployment of Local Strategic Partnerships (linking community and voluntary groups to tackle social, economic and environmental issues).

The White Paper incorporates many of the conclusions of the Urban Task Force, although it is less hard-hitting in certain areas. As with the Urban Task Force, a clear relationship is established between density in urban areas

---

Case study 9.3: Urban renaissance: best practice in urban design

The Urban Task Force placed considerable emphasis on improving urban design standards, calling for greater promotion of good practice and innovation by bodies such as the Commission for Architecture and the Built Environment (CABE). Contemporaneous with such recommendations the DETR promoted 'best practice' in two Reports, *Places, Streets and Movement* (DETR 1998d) and *By Design* (DETR 2000d). Both demonstrated a fresh awareness of the urban realm and the importance of creating a sense of place in urban development that reflected the local historic context and traditions.

Places, Streets and Movement is a companion guide to *Design Bulletin 32* (DoE 1992), with the stated mission 'to ensure that DB32 is used more imaginatively than has previously been the case'. The 'roads first, houses later' approach (see the critique by the Prince's Foundation in Case study 9.2) has not only contributed to car dependency but also to the design of layouts that give priority to the car. Matters of vehicular visibility and passing capacity (road widths and radii) have promoted low-density and predominantly suburban housing models. The local (urban) historic context and sense of place have been destroyed by the proliferation of these suburban layouts. A series of technical solutions are put forward (see Table 9.4 below) to create 'a network of spaces rather than a hierarchy of roads'. Many examples in the Report are drawn from Poundbury (HRH The Prince of Wales' Urban Village in West Dorset) and Coldharbour Farm* (a mixed-use satellite urban village in Aylesbury, providing 1500 houses).

By Design (DETR 2000c) drew much inspiration from work such as *Responsive Environments* (Bentley *et al.* 1985), which argued for greater attention to 'form' (the physical fabric of the city). To be 'responsive' an environment would need to offer appropriate choice to its citizens. *By Design*, in similar fashion to the Urban Task Force, views urban design as providing 'a key to creating sustainable developments [and] lively places with distinctive character . . . that inspire because of the imagination and sensitivity of their designers'. Successful urban design and its employment in masterplans (see also the Urban Task Force findings) must be employed at an early stage in the planning process and not as an afterthought. The Report proposed seven principal objectives of urban design (see Table 9.4 below) and describes them as 'prompts to thinking', in which they influence good practice without necessarily constituting 'rigid formulae to be followed slavishly'. The Report drew attention to how the planning process can be shaped by the inclusion of urban design policies in development plans, development briefs and masterplans, and in urban design frameworks (detailed urban guidance for areas undergoing change).

* Also referred to as Fairford Leys.

---

and consumption of energy (petrol), and in similar fashion a strong conclusion is drawn that past development patterns must be changed to secure sustainable cities and halt the continued exodus of the urban population. The White Paper somewhat sidesteps the worrying and central conclusion of the Urban Task Force, notably that the 60 per cent brown-field target may not be reached, instead seeking to rely on the establishment of a

Table 9.3 Best practice in urban design

Places, streets and movement		By design	
Technical innovations	• Variation in road width between 4.1 and 5.5 metres. • Use of tracking, i.e. changing carriageway width. • Junction design with an urban form, e.g. tight angles with 'raised tables' (bumps) to calm traffic. • Use of traffic calming by employment of street parking, chicanes, raised junctions and tables.	Objectives of urban design	• Character: *promote townscape* • Enclosure: *continuity of street frontage* • Quality urban realm: *accessible public space* • Ease of movement: promote pedestrian movement. • Legibility: recognizable landmarks and easy to understand environment. • Adaptability: can respond to changing social, technological and economic conditions.
Overall emphasis	• Parking in rear courtyards and squares. • Look for the place and not the car. • Look for local context, e.g. density, layout of buildings and spaces, scale, mass, and local materials. • Give priority in movement to foot, bicycle and car.		• Diversity: mixed uses and diversity of environment.
		Applied to planning system	• Development briefs • Urban design frameworks. • Development plan policy

vision for the repopulation of the urban core (based on greater physical attractiveness and enhanced economic opportunity) and greater flexibility in housing allocations (by scrapping the 1990s 'predict and provide' approach in favour of 'plan, monitor and manage').[5] This 'vision' is encapsulated, for example, in the championing of the recovery of Manchester's urban core in recent years and resulting population increase from 300 to 6,000 in the two years between 1998 and 2000, in part a consequence of conversions of existing stock and mixed-use schemes devised by innovative developers such as Urban Splash. No real strategy is presented to address the anxieties of the Urban Task Force in respect of recycled urban land, notably the historically poor take-up of such land for housing and associated problems of long-term dereliction. Instead the White Paper adopts a four-fold strategy to meet the projected 3.8 million new homes target.

First, government planning policy will implement a 'step change' in the way we plan for housing. PPG3 (2000) will raise density standards and adopt a sequential test[6] in Paragraph 30, in accord with the Urban Task Force. The Deputy Prime Minister will reserve the power to 'call-in' and himself decide on any green-field housing applications in excess of five hectares or 150 dwellings that the LPA seeks to grant. Alongside such new policy directions the establishment of a National Land Use Database will permit more accurate monitoring of the amount of brown land available for development.

Second, the dissemination of best-practice guidance (on urban design) will promote better design and management of urban space without recourse to policy. Third, a greater role for masterplanning (as sought by the Urban Task Force) coupled with more resources allocated to the Commission for Architecture and the Built Environment to promote design training and establish 12 regional centres of excellence. Finally, there is a combination of financial and fiscal measures, including an exemption from stamp duty for disadvantaged communities (covering property transactions), tax credits for cleaning up contaminated land, capital allowance for creating flats over shops, and a reduced VAT tax burden on residential conversions.

Alongside this the government encourages public–private partnerships (English Cities Fund) to fund mixed-use development projects in certain priority areas. The government's intention is that this should provide a framework, so it is simply impossible to assess whether this will meet the 60 per cent target (which includes conversions). The document lacks the radical and reforming edge of the Urban Task Force. The national taxation measures were reported as amounting to a £1 billion package in the 2001 budget, but the government avoided more contentious measures, such as a property tax on green-field development or vacant land.

Review and reform of relevant agencies responsible for delivering an urban renaissance is an essential component of the comprehensive framework for action promised by the White Paper. At the strategic level a new Cabinet Committee on Urban Affairs was established to support the implementation of the White Paper, while an Urban Summit was convened in 2002 to review progress. Many other agencies responsible for renaissance/regeneration have been the subject of review. Such review has manifested itself in a modernization of existing organizations (democratic processes and best value in local government), the promotion of new thinking in regeneration (continued in government guidance and promotion of good practice) and establishment of new ones (such as Regional Development Agencies to co-ordinate initiatives across several local government areas).

The government vision for urban areas, namely provision of a high quality of life and opportunity for all, is ambitious and is readily acknowledged as such in the White Paper. The biggest caveat in the document is at the end, where the success of this vision is qualified by the statement that while government will lead the way forward,

> action will ultimately depend on everyone contributing to change whether as individuals in their own street and neighbourhood, as investors and businesses in shaping the economy of their city, or as local representatives creating the vision for their city.

Table 9.4 Key recommendations of the Urban Task Force

Number	Policy areas	Subsequent action
3	Density – avoiding low-density schemes	PPG 3 (2000) established new thresholds of 30–50 dwellings per hectare (paragraph 58)
5	Spatial masterplans – basis of all area regeneration schemes and linked to public funding	Approach endorsed in the Urban White Paper, Chapter 4
6	Significant area regeneration projects to be the subject of a design competition	Approach endorsed in the Urban White Paper, Recommendation 8
7	Develop a national Urban Design Framework to promote good practice	PPG1 revisions to place greater emphasis on urban design
8	Promote design-led regeneration	Approach endorsed in the Urban White Paper, Chapter 4
11	Establish legal status for Homezone environmental areas	The Urban White Paper supports pilot studies of the operation of Homezones (car-free or reduced) and clear zones (low-emission zones) in town centres
19	Establish maximum parking (i.e. ceiling) standard of one space per dwelling	PPG3 (2000) encourages no greater than 1.5 spaces per dwelling
31	Creation of urban priority areas to facilitate neighbourhood renewal	Little government reform to support this, with reliance upon local participation and action at neighbourhood level
41	Production of detailed planning policy guidance to support urban renaissance	PPG3 (2000) and PPG1 revisions to support
42	Increase regional planning guidance (RPGs) to foster brownfield (recycled) development	New Regional Guidance published from 2000
44	Achieve comprehensive development-plan coverage in England by end 2002	PPG12 (1999) attempts to speed production of such plans
45	Encourage speed and efficiency in decision-making on planning applications	Best value regime introduced 2000 (see Chapter 4 of this book)
49–51	Revise planning obligations/gain system to seek a more streamlined system with a standardized system of impact fees	Considered in policy reviews 2001–3 with new guidance emerging
54	Support a new 'plan, monitor and manage' approach to housing demand	PPG3 (2000) creation of urban capacity studies and 60% brownland targets

Number	Policy areas	Subsequent action
56	Support a sequential approach to used housing land release (i.e. green fields only after inner and edge urban capacity is exhausted)	PPG3 (2000) and new emphasis on LPAs conducting studies of that urban capacity (as above)
64	Prepare a scheme for taxing vacant land to deter vexatious delay of its development	None (with respect to tax) because the government questioned effectiveness of this method
75	Establish a national framework to deal with remediation of contaminated land	The Urban White Paper supports the existing assessment regime. A new database on condition of such land was established (2001) and tax relief granted (2001)
81	Measures to encourage restoration/re-use of historic buildings	Reduced VAT for listed places of worship (2001) and a review by English Heritage (2001–2)
84	Encourage property conversions by tax and VAT inducements	Reduced VAT (on conversions) and zero rating (on renovations after 10 years and empty) (2001)
100	Give Regional Development Agencies (RDAs) more freedom to establish funding programmes	Greater budgetary flexibility introduced from 2001

Arguably, this sets the White Paper apart from the views of the Urban Task Force. While the Urban Task Force accepts that a cultural change in attitudes to urban life is required, it contends that this will be brought about by improved physical and economic circumstances. The White Paper, while accepting that cultural and physical/economic factors are linked, sees the relationship as more symbiotic. In other words, individuals have as much (or even more) responsibility than the government to affect change. Should the many initiatives enshrined in the White Paper be deemed to have failed to reverse the decline of our cities, incorporated as a general strategy in *Sustainable Communities: Building for the Future* (ODPM 2003), then government may revert to this warning in order to absolve itself of blame.

Part IV

The real estate development process

10 The property development process

The property development industry is both complex and diverse: complex, in that there are many agencies, public and private, large and small, undertaking development in a variety of organizational forms and legal entities; diverse, in that it involves a vast number of businesses across a wide range of sectors, having different aims, objectives and modes of operation.

The property development industry is also risky, cyclical, highly regulated and lengthy in production. In addition, it comprises three major groups: consumers, producers, and providers of public infrastructure. This seeming imbroglio thus requires close consideration and understanding, so that the process of property development can be managed in a way that optimizes the benefit to all concerned. The point has been made more eruditely by one of the leading thinkers in the field of real estate development, as follows:

> Unlike many mass production industries, each real estate project is unique and the development process is so much a creature of the political process that society has a new opportunity with each major project to negotiate, debate and reconsider the basic issues of an enterprise economy, i.e. who pays, who benefits, who risks, and who has standing to participate in the decision process. Thus, the development process remains a high silhouette topic for an articulate and sophisticated society. The best risk management device for the producer group, which is usually the lead group in the initiation of a project, is thorough research so that the development product fits as closely as possible the needs of the tenant or purchaser, the values of the politically active collective consumers, and the land-use ethic of the society.
>
> (Graaskamp 1981)

The growing intricacy and sophistication of the property development industry has led to the need for a deeper understanding of public policy, physical planning, municipal regulation, market research, the legal framework, site appraisal, economic evaluation, financial arrangements, contractual procedures, building design, construction techniques and marketing strategy dimensions of a development scheme, together with a much more professional approach towards the management of projects in terms of time, quality, cost and asset value.

To facilitate the study and understanding of property development, several models of the development process have been devised since the mid-1950s.

These have been grouped as follows (Healey 1991):

(i) **Equilibrium Models**, which assume that development activity is structured by economic signals about effective demand, as reflected in rents, yields, etc. These derive directly from the neo-classic tradition in economics.

(ii) **Event Sequence Models**, which focus on the management of stages in the development process. These derive primarily from an estate management preoccupation with managing the development process.

(iii) **Agency Models**, which focus on actors in the development process and their relationships. These have been developed primarily by academics seeking to describe the development process from a behavioural or institutional point of view.

(iv) **Structure Models**, which focus on the forces which organize the relationships of the development process and which drive its dynamics. These are grounded in urban political economy.

For the sake of clarity, and in order to respect the principal aims of the text, this chapter essentially adopts an 'event sequence' approach. Nevertheless, mention is made of the various agencies involved in the property development process, the respective members of the professional team responsible for development projects and those other parties concerned with or affected by development decisions. Furthermore, the point is made that the development of real estate may be seen as a set of interrelated processes and not merely a single sequential process. Indeed, it is important to recognize that, although it is helpful to distinguish a series of steps or stages in the property development process, such as in an apparently consecutive flow-chart approach, it by no means reflects the concurrent nature of most, if not all of those stages. A successful developer must maintain a perspective overview of the whole process all the time and be prepared to undertake almost constant repositioning of the constituent elements of the development scheme, as well as continually negotiating agreements with the other participants in the process.

It should also be appreciated that there are any number of ways in which the development process can be described as a sequence of events or series of stages from the start to the finish of the project. There might be slight variations, but by and large the stages identified are similar and they embrace the same range of activities. By way of example, one relatively simple approach divides the development process into four phases (Cadman and Topping 1995):

1   Evaluation
2   Preparation
3   Implementation
4   Disposal.

Another more detailed model of real estate development distinguishes eight stages (Miles *et al.* 1991):

1 Inception of an idea
2 Refinement of the idea
3 Feasibility
4 Contract negotiation
5 Formal commitment
6 Construction
7 Completion and formal opening
8 Asset and property management.

To explore the process of development and those professional disciplines participating in it, this chapter is divided into two main parts:

* property development: a five-phase process
* participants in the development process

Property development: a five-phase process

For the purpose of this text the following five phases in the property development process have been identified:

1 Concept and initial consideration
2 Site appraisal and feasibility study
3 Detailed design and evaluation
4 Contract and construction
5 Marketing, management and disposal.

Concept and initial consideration

Establishing objectives for the development organization and generating ideas to meet them

In the private sector of the property industry the overriding objective is unashamedly one of profit maximization. However, potential return must be weighed against potential risk and the degree of uncertainty. Operational objectives are paramount in the public sector, although strict budgetary constraints might be imposed. Image may also be an important factor in decision-making. In terms of the generation of ideas to meet established objectives, however, property development is at root about imagination, opportunity and venture. Successful developers are invariably those who arrive at different conclusions from others against similar sets of information. So too, it should be said, are unsuccessful developers.

Determine a basic strategy for the development organization

Strategy determination will normally entail a consideration of several related factors:

* the very purpose of development activity, whether it is for owner occupation or for speculation
* the size of a potential project in respect of financial commitment

- acceptable locations in terms of function and project management
- specialist knowledge related to selective sectors of the property market
- portfolio 'fit', taking into account existing investments and other development proposals so as to maintain an appropriate balance
- a surfeit of capital resources leading to pressures to invest
- the need to sustain an active and credible development programme
- the capacity of the development organization to undertake the scheme
- and, perhaps above all, how auspicious is the timing.

Time, for example, might outweigh all other considerations, and the planning approval position may be of paramount importance, or acquisition itself could be a problem. Conversely, quality of design, construction and finish might be the overriding consideration, or cost the critical factor. Where the client is an industrial or business concern intending to occupy the completed property, great attention must obviously be paid to operational needs and balanced against the continued marketability of the building. In satisfying the requirement of the development organization, once established, different forms of management structure will be most suited to particular projects according to such variable factors as size, complexity, time, sophistication, economy, degree of innovation and extent of external forces. It will also be necessary to identify the key decision points in the process of development, such as when planning permission is granted, acquisition completed, building contract completed, or sale or letting agreements entered into, and to determine the consequences that flow from such events, dependencies that arise, involvements that occur and costs that are incurred. A critical path through the development will also usually be constructed at this stage to assist planning control in the decision-making process.

Undertake market research and find a suitable site

The significance of sound market research cannot be stressed too strongly. Indeed, market research and marketing underpin every stage of the property development process. Market research is fundamentally concerned with demand and supply. Demand, be it proven, perceived or latent, being the most difficult element to investigate with confidence. Although market research is commonly considered to be formal, focused and systematic, it has been pointed out that market research for generating ideas for development has a very large informal component made up of experience, observation, reading, conversation, networking and analysis. Both formal and informal approaches are necessary, as recognized elsewhere:

> The generation of ideas, marketing and market research have both intuitive and rational elements. Successful developers are able to maximize both the intuitive and the rational. Formal knowledge of marketing principles and market research enhances the use of both facilities.
>
> (Miles *et al.* 1991)

Finding a suitable site involves establishing a set of criteria by which alternative locations can be identified and assessed. These would broadly relate to market, physical, legal and administrative conditions and constraints. Once a shortlist of, say, three or four options has been drawn up, a preliminary appraisal will be conducted in order to determine the most suitable choice. This is the proverbial 'back of the envelope' analysis, which combines an objective assessment of likely cost against value with a more subjective judgement based upon experience and feel for the market. Ideally, of course, the right site looking for the right use meets the right use looking for the right site. But there is no magic formula.

Site appraisal and feasibility study

*Undertake a more refined appraisal of the viability of the
proposed project, taking into account market trends and physical
constraints*

Decide to what extent will further enquiries, searches, surveys and tests have to be conducted, by whom and at what cost, so that there is sufficient information available in order to analyse the financial feasibility of a development proposal. This will normally entail a more detailed assessment of market demand and supply; a close examination of the changing character of the sector; projections of rents, values and yields; and estimations of costs and time. An initial consideration of the structural engineering design foundations and subsoil will also be undertaken. Having assembled all the data, a check should be conducted to ensure that the basic concept achieves the optimum use of the site or buildings and maximizes the amount of letting or operational space.

*Consult with the planning authority and other statutory agencies with
regard to the proposed development*

Apart from making sure that all the initial inquiries are made in respect of preparing and submitting applications for planning approval and building regulation consent, it is also essential for the developer to create a positive climate within which the development can progress. This means that the right people in all the various authorities and agencies concerned with accrediting the proposal must be carefully identified, and approaches to them properly planned and presented. It is vital for the developer to galvanize the professional team in such a way that everyone involved generates an enthusiasm for the scheme and conveys that interest to those responsible for assessing it. First impressions are always important, and simple precautions can be taken, such as consulting with all the contributors to the project to compile all the preliminary inquiries together, to avoid duplications and despatching them to the authorities and agencies in sufficient time to allow proper consideration and formulation of response. Among the principal factors the developer will seek to establish are the prospects of being expected to provide elements of planning gain by way of legal agreements and the likelihood of obtaining a consent, the possibility of having to go to appeal, the chances of success, and the consequent probable timescales and costs resulting.

Identify the likely response from other interested parties to the proposed development

The developer needs to have a heightened understanding of how a particular scheme of development will be received by those likely to be affected by it, or have a voice in how, and if, it proceeds. This implies a knowledge of the wider consequences of development and a comprehension of, say, urban renewal policy. They must, therefore, be able to predict who will oppose, why, how they might organize their opposition, what influence they exert, and how best to negotiate with them and reduce potential conflict.

Establish the availability of finance and the terms on which it might be provided

Because the parameters set by a fund can influence and even determine the design and construction of a building, great care must be taken in selecting a suitable source of finance and in tailoring the terms to meet the aims of both parties to the agreement. This will involve an evaluation of alternative arrangements for financing the project in question, including an assessment of the financial, legal and managerial consequences of different ways of structuring the deal. In doing so, it will be necessary to determine very closely the absolute limits of financial manoeuvrability within the framework of the development plan and programme, for, during the heat of negotiation, points may be conceded or matters overlooked, which could ultimately prejudice the success of the scheme. Different sources of finance will dictate different forms of control by the fund. The major financial institutions, for example, increasingly insist that some kind of development monitoring be undertaken by project management professionals on their behalf, whereas a construction firm might provide finance for development but demand more influence in the management of the building operation. The developer must be wary. Presentation of a case for funding is also a task deserving special attention, and any message should be designed to provoke a positive response. Subsequent to a loan being agreed in principle, it will be necessary for the developer, in conjunction with their lawyer and other relevant members of the professional team, to agree the various drawings and specification documents to be included in the finance agreement. These will normally comprise drawings showing floor layouts and cross sections of the entire project, together with drainage, site and floor-related levels, and outline heating and air conditioning proposals, as well as a performance specification clearly setting out the design, construction and services standards to be met. The financial dimension to project management is critical, for a comparatively small change in the agreed take-out yield can completely outweigh a relatively large change in the building cost.

Detailed design and evaluation

Decide the appointment of the professional team and determine the basis of appointment

It is essential that the developer, or an appointed overall project manager, has a good grasp of building technology and construction methods, together with an appreciation of their effect upon the development process. To this must be added a perception of the decisions that have to be taken and an ability to devise appropriate management structures necessary to carry them out. In deciding such questions as whether to appoint a small or large firm, appoint on the basis of an individual or a firm, select professionals for the various disciplines from the same or from different firms, choose professionals who have worked together previously or who are new to each other, or opt for existing project teams or assemble one especially for the job in hand – the respective advantages and disadvantages must be explored and weighed most carefully. The chemistry is all important, but the opportunity to take such a deliberate approach towards the assembly and integration of the professional team is one of the great advantages of property project management. In this context, however, it is essential that the contractor is seen to be a central member of the team, playing a full part in the design process and now somehow placed in a competitive position. Increasingly, moreover, a choice has to be made between different methods of producing building services, such as package deal, design and build, selective competitive tender, two-stage tender, serial tender, negotiated tender, management fee contract or separate trades contract. However, a true project management approach might be said to be superior to all other methods. The members of the team, once appointed, will usually be required to enter into collateral warranties as to their professional obligations and be prepared to produce reasonable evidence of the adequacy of their professional indemnity insurance. It may also be that the fund as well as the developer will expect similar undertakings and will insist that the conditions of engagement reflect this part of the financial agreement.

Prepare a brief that outlines the basic proposals for design, budgeting,
taxation, planning, marketing and disposal and sets out all the
management and technical functions, together with the various
boundaries of responsibility

The preparation and agreement of an initial client's brief is an indispensable stage in the project management process. Misunderstandings are common without a clearly identified set of client's objectives being established. In this, the traditional responsibility of the architect as client's representative or leader of the professional team has been found seriously wanting. Therefore, it is very important to define the separate functions and management activities of individual members of the professional team, as well as those of any project manager, and how they all relate to one another. Equally, it is necessary to ensure that everyone understands the brief. Sometimes a very formal agreement at the outset allows for greater flexibility thereafter. Furthermore, time expended at this stage can often save much wasted energy and ire later. Likewise, fee negotiations must be conducted and terms agreed at this stage, including a clear understanding and record of any departures from standard professional terms of appointment. Frequently, it is beneficial to seek outside advice on certain matters such as town planning, taxation and space planning, so that the organization of the project and functional use of the building can be optimized, even if it is expensive and provided by specialists who will not be involved in the development itself.

Arrange for the design team to prepare and submit preliminary detailed drawings for the planning approvals and budget forecasting

The most important aspect at this stage is to make sure that strong and effective liaison takes place between the architect, the quantity surveyor, the agent and the fund.

Submit the planning application and negotiate with the local authority, statutory undertakers and other interested parties

An enormous amount of time and effort can be spent on fruitless discussions unless the right relationships are established with the right people. The presentation of the submission can have a considerable effect, especially for significant schemes of a sensitive nature. In such negotiations, steps should be taken to preserve as much flexibility for future action as possible.

Make any necessary changes to the scheme, adjusting the various programmes and obtaining final approvals from all concerned

It should be appreciated that changes may have to be made and incorporated within the plans for the project at almost any time, which emphasizes the need to maintain flexibility. For example, changes may have to be made in respect of occupancy, division of space, time of completion, technology used, design, layout, materials, finishes, contractor, costs, services, and even use.

Contact and construction

Establish the preferred procedure for selecting a contractor, arrange the appointment and approve the various contract documents

There is now much wider acceptance of the benefits to be derived from selecting and involving the contractor at the earliest possible point in the design process. Alternative methods of building procurement will demand different procedures for appointing a contractor, and it is ultimately for the developer to recommend or decide how best to proceed, reconciling the two often countervailing factors of competitive cost and quality of work. A combination of tender and negotiation is, therefore, frequently the preferred approach. Performance bonds of around 10–15 per cent of contract value will also have to be negotiated with the selected con-tractor and any nominated subcontractors, and any specialists or suppliers offering a design service will normally be required to provide a design warranty.

*Establish a management structure to take account of the communication
between the parties and the responsibilities borne by all those involved,
paying particular attention to administration, accounting, purchasing,
approvals reports and meetings*

Traditional relationships established during the construction process are not
always the most suitable means of communication and collaboration
between the various parties engaged in a particular project. However,
although it has been suggested that the quality of work is best, and the
efficiency in production greatest, where discretion over detailed design is
highest, it is often the case that the setting up of a very formal structure with
a strict routine of meetings and reports to begin with, but allowing for
subsequent and deliberate relaxation or amendment as matters progress,
works best.

*Set up an appraisal system to monitor the viability of the project
throughout the building period*

It is the fundamental responsibility of the project manager on behalf of the
developer to ensure that the project brief is being satisfied. Because of the
task of constantly relating the requirements of the brief to the programme of
development and the constraints of the budget, it is necessary for the project
manager to prepare some kind of master programme. The monitoring of this
programme will mean that they must make certain that the members of the
professional team are producing all the required information at the right time
and in the proper form. It will also be necessary to liaise with other parties,
such as the fund and the various statutory bodies, to reassure them that
the building and its construction is in accordance with the requirements of
the various consents and agreements. Careful control will also have to be
exercised over interim and stage payments to those claiming them.

*Ensure that on completion of the development, arrangements are made to
check all plant, equipment and buildings before they are commissioned*

It will normally be the duty of the project manager to accept the building on
behalf of the client, sometimes their duty to prepare it for acceptance by the
client or their advisers or the funding agency, and sometimes a mixture of
both. In certain circumstances, it may be appropriate to make provision for a
phased completion and handover. Generally, a minimum maintenance period
of 12 months will be required of those responsible for supplying and
installing building services and equipment.

*Generally supervise all contractual affairs in order to anticipate and
solve problems as quickly as possible*

At the beginning of the construction process the development project
manager should consider the desirability of appointing a nominated expert
to settle any building disputes that may arise between the parties. Occasionally the project manager will assume a greater responsibility than normal for

arbitrating between contributors to the building operation. In any event, part of the project management function will always be the sensitive oversight and control of the building and associated contracts on behalf of the developer. Very simply, the risks of the development vary in proportion to the degree of detail and commitment to the project produced by the members of the professional team, and to the level of successful orchestration achieved by the project manager.

Marketing, management and disposal

Determine the point at which a marketing campaign is best started, how it should be conducted and by whom

All too often, concern for marketing is too little and too late. However, the prime aim of any private sector development scheme is to produce a marketable building, even if that market is a client who is already identified. Right from the start, therefore, it is the job of the developer to focus the attention of all the contributors to the professional team upon the marketing dimension of the project. Many of those concerned with design and construction have, in the past, tended to neglect the demands of the market. However, now that clients are better informed they are, arguably, more demanding than hitherto. Couple this with the common requirement to achieve a pre-let to secure funding and it becomes apparent that market issues are at the top of everyone's agenda. It is imperative for the developer or his project manager to forge a close link between the selected architect and the instructed agent. Where the project is speculative, the keynote must be flexibility – in both physical and tenurial terms. In selecting an agent, the developer will be faced with almost the same set of questions as when choosing any other member of the team, such as, national or local, small or large, firm or individual, regularly retained or new, generalist or specialist, and sole or joint instruction. Decisions must also be made between the developer and those engaged in the actual marketing of the development about the size of the marketing and promotions budget and the pattern of expenditure during the selling or letting period. As part of the process of planning the marketing campaign, it will be necessary to determine what specialist services such as market research, public relations and advertising might usefully be retained and on what basis they will work.

Decide on the form of lease or sale contract, so as to preserve an optimum return on the investment

Given the changing conditions of the market, this decision will involve the developer considering very carefully such matters as how many tenancies can be accommodated, what lengths of leases might be accepted, on what terms in respect of rent review and repairing and insuring obligations might leases be agreed, what incentives might effectively be offered, and whether there are any tax advantages to be gained from conducting sale or letting arrangements in a particular way. In respect of a forward sale agreement transacted with a financial institution, it is important to ensure that the conditions are reasonable so far as the client is concerned. Too sanguine a view of the programme for development, and the prospects for letting can often lead to the acceptance of a contractual straitjacket. It should also be appreciated by those acting in a project management capacity on behalf of clients undertaking speculative commercial development that, with most funds, the issuing of an architect's certificate no longer automatically triggers the machinery to release development profit and the start of a lease. Normally it takes a separate document issued collectively by the architect and project manager, together with the fund's professional representative, to release payment.

Establish a management and maintenance programme and, where the development is to be retained or a prospective occupier agrees, recruiting and training the necessary personnel to provide a smooth handover

Besides making sure that the necessary operating manuals have been prepared, and the drawings, plans and approvals are collected together for transmission to the client's or purchaser's management organization, the project manager might often now have to set in train and supervise recruitment and training programmes for continuing management staff. This has been the case for some while in the development of planned shopping centres and certain forms of leisure development. It is now spreading to other commercial sectors, such as multi-occupied office schemes, and industrial and business estate developments. Even in the residential sector, large-scale housing projects will require the establishment of selling, management and maintenance operations. Certain apparently minor, but in practice very important, tasks must be commissioned and checked. These include such matters as the provision of a fire insurance valuation, the effectuation of a defects rectification programme with appropriate liabilities and the verification of other insurance and maintenance policies.

Maintain the security and safety of the building at all times

It is essential to ensure that the site is both secure and safe during the construction period. In particular, the Construction (Design and Management) Regulations 1994 (CDM) were designed to encourage greater site safety in the industry by co-ordinating health and safety across disparate contracting organizations, employees and agency workers. It is also increasingly important to produce a building that throughout its economic life complies easily and inexpensively with ever more stringent regulations regarding health and safety at work. One example is that by the end of 2004 the Disabilities Discrimination Act will require all buildings to be made accessible to disabled people. Moreover, with the advent of more advanced systems of information technology and the movement towards multiple occupancy of commercial premises, there is a growing need to create accommodation capable of installing and operating business security systems. The project manager must take this into account at all stages of development.

Monitor the performance of the retained agents

Given that marketing is a critical ingredient in the project management process, close contact must be maintained with the agent. Regular meetings must be held, detailed reports prepared, and explanations provided for disappointing or unexpected results. The developer or project manager should also be consulted about advertising material and its placement. The image of the project and the way it is presented can be significant. Commitment and care on the part of the agent must be watched, and the developer or project manager must not be reluctant to take alternative or novel advice regarding the sales potential and marketing of a building. It is also important that, once identified, the prospective tenant or purchaser is fully involved in decisions taken during the completion of the development.

Reorganize the financial arrangements where necessary

Depending upon the progress of the development programme, the state of the market and the success of the marketing campaign, there may or may not be a need to renegotiate the terms of the funding agreement, seek additional financial support or restructure the cashflow projections and budget allocations. Aspiring tenants or purchasers might have occupational requirements that dictate a reordering of the financial arrangements. Alternatively, the original funding agreement might have certain stipulations in the way of rental guarantees or priority yield, for instance, which are either incompatible with, or detract from, potential disposal terms. Furthermore, for a variety of reasons it may be beneficial to rejig the financial agreement because of the taxation position of the parties.

Participants in the development process

The property development process involves the constant interaction of various agencies, groups and individuals. Given the all-pervasive nature of property in the lives of everyone, few, if any, are exempt from participating in the development process in one way or another.

A celebrated model of the real estate process collects the participants into three major groups:

• **The Space Consumer Group** – which includes 'individual space users' attempting to rent or buy real estate space to house their specific needs; collective users generally pursuing their interests in real estate activity through the political systems that purchase open space, provide for public infrastructures, or regulate space production with pooled funds from taxation; and 'future users' who are typically represented by proxy, either by developers who anticipate the need to change the use of a building in the future, or by the judiciary or special interest groups, who perceive some trusteeship of the land for future generations. Provision for future users being a hidden charge to present consumers . . .

- **The Space Production Group** – which includes all forms of expertise necessary to convert from space–time requirements to money–time. The system includes those who assemble the capital and those who prepare materials as well as those who contribute to the assembly of these on-site . . .
- **The Public Infrastructure Group** – which comprises all those enterprises that provide a network of tangible and intangible off-site systems for the individual space user, including physical networks of roads, sewers and other utilities, services such as education, police and fire and operational systems for land registration, government regulation, adjudication and all forms of economic activity with efficiencies of scale that suggest off-site action . . . (Graaskamp 1981).

In a more prosaic manner this text divides the participants in the property development process into 'development agencies' and the 'members of the development team'.

Development agencies

The generic term 'developer' embraces a wide heterogeneous breed of agencies, from central government at the one extreme to the small local housebuilder at the other. The aims and objectives of different property-developing organizations also varies enormously, as does their relative efficiency. Many indulge in property development as an ancillary function of a larger prime operation, such as the major retail chains and the principal banking houses, whereas others concentrate their efforts solely on the activity of land dealing and property development. Even within the mainstream of the property development industry, considerable specialization in respect of region, sector and size is experienced and a general description is difficult to manufacture. Nevertheless, the following classification serves to identify the principal agencies involved in property development.

Property development companies

As already stated, a great range in the type and size of property development companies can be discerned. There are large companies with extensive development programmes capable of undertaking complex major projects and small companies content to operate on a more modest and selective basis. Many large companies are publicly quoted on the Stock Exchange and portray a higher profile, as well as arguably bearing greater accountability for their actions than the bulk of others not so placed or exposed. Some specialize in particular sectors of the market such as office, shop, industrial or residential, where others spread their attentions and apply their skills across the market. There are also those who have established a niche market in such areas as church conversions, waterside developments, sheltered housing and historic buildings refurbishment. Some development companies concentrate upon projects in or around a particular town or city; others operate regionally, nationally or even internationally. There are also companies that trade predominantly in completed developments, whereas others are more concerned with building up a sound and balanced investment portfolio. In terms of organization and structure, it is hard to characterize the typical company, for some, even the very largest, run extremely lean operations, preferring to employ outside professional expertise for virtually the whole range of development activities, whereas others maintain substantial in-house teams. It is true to say, however, that most property development companies were originally founded as the result of one man's initiative, and the importance of the individual remains paramount in the private sector property development industry. They all, moreover, share a common goal: that of profit maximization.

Financial institutions

Since the mid-1950s many insurance companies and pension funds have involved themselves to varying degrees in direct development on their own behalf. The role of developer has often willingly been sought by the more venturesome funds, seeking to secure the full measure of equity return from development projects, but has also frequently been the result of having to take over the affairs of defaulting property companies to whom they advanced loans or purchased a significant interest. The extent to which such financial institutions become active developers in their own right is largely a function of the prevailing general investment climate and the particular performance of the property market. By the mid-1990s, it is a far more attractive proposition to acquire ready-made developments at a discount than indulge in the lengthy and speculative process of building from scratch. Conversely in a buoyant or rising market, or in anticipation of one, there is much to be gained by financial institutions participating directly in development schemes.

The predominant characteristics of the financial institutions as developers are that they take a longer view of, and adopt a more cautious attitude towards, development proposals than would most private property companies, being concerned with future income and capital growth over a prolonged period of time. An inherent advantage enjoyed by institutions acting in a development capacity is, of course, the financial confidence with which, of course, they can proceed, given the underlying capital strength they command. They also seem to attract a higher degree of respectability than their property company counterparts, because, no doubt, of their policy-holder, rather than personalized, ownership. Partnership schemes with local authorities and prospective owner-occupiers, as well as with property companies and construction firms, have also proved popular development vehicles for financial institutions where risks can be shared, attractive covenants gained and expertise acquired. Perhaps the major drawback that can be levelled at the insurance company or pension fund as a direct developer is that, although they possess all the attributes of a large corporate organization, they also suffer from some of the associated disadvantages in lacking a certain amount of flexibility, flair and enterprise. They tend to be extremely conventional in their approach towards location, design, covenant, tenure and management.

Construction firms

Traditionally, building contractors have always been closely connected with the positive promotion of speculative development. Of recent years, most major construction firms have all been active in the development field. Construction is a high-risk undercapitalized operation with very sensitive margins, and many contracting firms have built up property portfolios of respectable size in order to ensure greater continuity of income and a more substantial and secure asset base. The most obvious advantages derived from the horizontal integration of building and development is that it can internalize the risk of obtaining contracts, facilitate the borrowing of funds, and sustain the employment of a skilled workforce. Joint ventures have often been established between contracting firms and other property development companies on an equity-sharing basis. Likewise, with financial institutions, one of the benefits gained by the builder as developer is that profitability can be viewed across both development and construction activities, providing a competitive edge in the bidding process for land.

Public sector agencies

The direct development activity undertaken by public sector agencies varies enormously according to their nature and function. Local authorities provide by far the most diverse range of development experience, with some councils pursuing an extremely adventurous approach towards commercial schemes, particularly in the light industrial sector, in locations where small nursery factories have not been provided by the private sector. Others have attempted to engage in central area shop and office schemes, but with very mixed results. Residential development has, quite naturally, played a traditional role in municipal development, but has substantially diminished in significance after the introduction of the right-to-buy scheme for public-sector tenants and the transfer of a significant proportion of public-sector housing to housing associations and the private sector. In general terms, the degree of involvement in different forms of development naturally varies between authorities according to their geographical location, persisting problems, potential opportunities, landownership, financial resources and political complexion. Probably the main differences between public and private sector development are the degree of accountability that attaches to the former and the extent to which community consultation and participation takes place. Local authorities must demonstrate the highest levels of probity and disclosure in all that they do. They also have differing objectives in that such aims as the provision of shelter, the generation of employment, environmental protection and the supply of services outweigh the overriding profit-maximizing goal of the private sector.

The positive part performed by central government in direct development is strictly limited, as opposed to the determination of a strategic framework and the promotion and control of the property industry by way of fiscal incentives and statutory regulation. Most state development, in fact, is confined to the provision of accommodation for their own purposes and, to this end, the Office of Government Holdings acts in the capacity of agent on the government's behalf. Regional development agencies such as the North West Development Agency (NWDA) and the Scottish Executive Development Department have been established, but with the main task of attracting business investment and stimulating employment rather than the direct construction of commercial premises. In fact the NWDA is proposing to outsource the management of its existing property holdings in order to concentrate on its 'core' business. Public services such as health, prisons and education are looking to the private sector to meet their property development needs through the Private Finance Initiative (PFI), introduced by the Conservative government in 1992 and now embraced by the current Labour government as the preferred means of financing major public capital projects. Slightly different in kind are those public or quasi-public bodies who have a surplus of land for their own operational requirements, or who are able to combine their functions with other commercial endeavours on the same site and become energetic development agencies in their own right. Deserving of special mention in the context of public sector development agencies, albeit in a somewhat historic perspective, are the New and Expanded Towns, for, since their inception as part of post-war construction and interregional planning policy, they have played an ambitious and successful entrepreneurial role in providing civic, residential and commercial accommodation. In a similar vein, there have been the Urban Development Corporations and a host of other public and quasi-public agencies set up to tackle the task of regeneration in declining inner-city areas.

Large landowners

By dint of circumstance, many large landowners almost inevitably become property developers. Some of the most notable, such as the Grosvenor, Portland and Duchy of Cornwall estates, are long established and have set high standards in terms of building design and management. The Crown itself is, of course, a leading landlord and a major participant in the property market. Despite the recession of the past few years the Crown Commissioners have restructured their portfolio to great effect, although this has entailed a concentration upon investment in completed developments rather than active development on their own account. Conversely, the Church of England, another major landowner and property manager, has indulged in the development market with dire results. Oxford and Cambridge colleges have also been involved in property development over many years on land endowed to them.

Business concerns

Where there is a need for a highly specialized building, or a non-traditional location is proposed, and there is likely to be little or no general market value attached to the completed development, then it falls to the prospective occupiers to provide their own premises. This can prove a hazardous affair, and professional expertise of the highest order is required. However, it should be stated that many businesses have opted to develop their own property; often in conjunction with a property development company, and using some form of sale and leaseback arrangement. In fact, there has been an appreciable growth in the involvement of various business concerns in direct property development since the mid-1970s. Many major retail shopping chains have initiated, funded and managed the development of their own schemes. Other business organizations, such as breweries, have undertaken commercial projects on their own otherwise redundant property, an activity normally seen as outside their province. One developing area is that of total property outsourcing (sometimes known as corporate PFI) whereby companies outsource both their property and facilities management to an external organization (or consortium) in order to concentrate on the 'core' business. This could have a major impact on private-sector property requirements.

Many of the activities that were traditionally part of the public sector, such as the privatized utilities – gas, water, electricity, and telecoms – and the rail-operating companies are now part of the private sector. British Rail, in particular, implemented an ambitious development programme from the mid-1970s until privatization. Following privatization Railtrack continued this programme, although to a lesser degree.

The development team

It almost goes without saying that the quality of a development, and the level of efficiency by which it is produced, is dependent upon the ability and application of those involved in the process from inception to completion. Even where the individual contributions from the various disciplines are capable of producing work of the highest standard, it is imperative that their separate skills be co-ordinated in a manner that eliminates delay and harmonizes effort. Although the scale and complexity of particular projects will vary, and thus the professional demands will differ, the following catalogue of disciplines describes both the principal participants who would normally be involved in a major scheme of development and their respective terms of reference.

The developer

Developers vary enormously in the degree of expertise they bring to the development team. Their backgrounds may be in building, estate agency, engineering, finance, law, architecture or business management. They also differ in the extent to which they are involved in the actual process of development. Some assume total responsibility for the management of every stage of a project from start to finish, whereas others are content to delegate a substantial amount of responsibility to a project manager, retaining a more strategic policy role.

Above all, however, a developer is an entrepreneur: someone who can identify the need for a particular property product and is willing to take the risk to produce it for a profit. In stating this, a sharp distinction should be drawn between the private developer to whom this entrepreneurial tag truly belongs and the salary-earning corporate professional in either the public or private sector who really acts as more of a project manager. Thus, the developer is seen to play many roles.

- promoter and negotiator with regulatory and approved authorities as well as other parties with an interest in the proposed development
- market analyst and marketing agent regarding potential tenants or purchasers
- securer of financial resources from the capital markets; employer and overall manager of the professional team engaged on the project.

The job description of the developer has been said to include:

> . . . shifting roles as creator, promoter, negotiator, manager, leader, risk manager and investor, adding up to a much more complex vision of an entrepreneur than a person who merely buys low to sell high. They are more innovators – people who realize an idea in the marketplace – than traders skilled at arbitrage.
>
> (Miles *et al.* 1991)

With regard to general matters of concern in relation to the development function, one leading developer has identified the following requirements (Jennings 1984):

- *Motivation and leadership.* Probably the most important attribute of all, without which roles and objectives become confused and confidence eroded.
- *Selection of development team.* Another most important function as a considerable amount of collaborative work is required at all stages and mutual confidence is essential if misunderstandings and wasted effort are to be avoided.
- *Funding policy.* This will inevitably be a mix of market conditions and the developer's aspirations, but it must be kept constantly in mind and the relevant members of the professional team involved as appropriate.
- *Pre-letting objectives.* Since these can often have a material effect on various aspects of design and funding, they are bound to be at the front of items for close consideration.
- *Quality requirements.* These are not always easy to lay down in detail at an early stage and can tend to be rather subjective. Nevertheless, they are important to the team and can often best be defined by comparison with other existing buildings.
- *Who does what.* Although this should not be difficult, it is important to recognize that at the creative stage of a project the crossing of traditional disciplinary lines may often be beneficial.
- *Programme.* Although form and content will change frequently, it is imperative that at all times any activity should know where it stands both as to time and as to sequence.

From all this, it can be seen that developers spend a large part of their time on a project managing the input of others. However, an alternative is the appointment of a project manager to whom the developer, as client, devolves significant managerial responsibility.

Project manager

Project management has been defined as:

> The overall planning, control and co-ordination of the project from inception to completion aimed at meeting a client's requirements in order that the project will be completed on time within authorized cost and to the required quality standards.
>
> (CIoB 1992)

Likewise, the duty of the project manager acting on behalf of the client has been stated to be:

> Providing a cost effective and independent service correlating, integrating and managing different disciplines and expertise to satisfy the objectives and provisions of the project brief from inception to completion. The service provided must be to the Client's satisfaction, safeguard his interests at all times and, where possible, give consideration to the needs of the eventual user of the facility.
>
> (CIoB 1992)

The function of project management and the role of the project manager have become increasingly important in the property development process since the mid-1980s. In practice, the project manager could be an in-house executive of the client development company or an external consultant specifically appointed to the project. It is also the case that each project is unique and the means by which the task of project management is fulfilled are subject to variation.

Construction manager

A distinction is drawn in this text between project management – where the span of control normally stretches from involvement in the initial development decision, right through to the eventual disposition of the completed building, covering every aspect of development in between – and construction management, where responsibility is restricted to the building-related stages of the development process. The appointment of a construction manager is most common where the developer acts in the capacity of total project manager and, for reasons of either managerial efficiency or lack of technical expertise, or both, prefers to delegate responsibility for overseeing all the construction activity to another.

The construction manager might be an architect, a builder, an engineer, a building surveyor or a quantity surveyor, and extensive practical experience in the type of project being built is essential. The prime task is similar to that of the project manager, seeing that the building comes in to time, to cost and to specification. In doing so, the construction manager is often called upon to

Table 10.1 Architects' services: the work stages

Inception	This stage is primarily concerned with an initial analysis of the client's brief and the provision of advice regarding the appointment of other consultants and specialist contractors.
Feasibility	Based on site surveys and consultations with the various regulatory authorities a set of broad alternative options are prepared and a review of the design and construction implications undertaken in the light of the client's aims.
Outline proposals	From the agreed concept, option outline proposals and approximate construction costs are prepared for the client's approval.
Scheme design	The design is developed according to agreed spatial arrangements, materials and appearance, coupled with a cost estimate. An indication of possible building contract start and completion dates. Application for planning permission is also made at this stage.
Detailed design	In conjunction with other relevant consultants and specialist contractors, a detailed design scheme is developed. Quotations are also obtained, cost checks conducted and building regulation approval sought. At this stage the architect is also required to obtain the client's approval regarding the type of construction, quality of materials and standard of workmanship.
Production information	This involves the preparation of such information as drawings, schedules and specifications of materials and workmanship. It also includes preliminary tendering procedures and the engagement of nominated subcontractors and suppliers.
Bills of quantities	These are prepared with sufficiently detailed information so as to enable the contractor to prepare a realistic tender. Site inspectors are also appointed and any necessary corrections made to the drawings.
Tender	The architect provides advice on the list of tenders and obtains the client's approval for those selected. Tenders are then invited, meetings held, contractors' questions handled, tenders received and advice again proffered prior to a decision being made. Alternatively, a negotiated contract might be arranged.
Project planning	A final decision as to the successful contractors is made, and respective responsibilities of the client, architect and contractor apportioned under the terms of the building contract. Product information as required by the building contract is also prepared. Site supervisory staff are appointed and briefed.
Operations on site	The architect is responsible for administering the building contract; making general site inspections; commissioning and testing; providing, with other consultants, periodic financial reports to the client; and preparing a maintenance manual.
Completion	This stage involves administering the building contract in relation to completion of the works, as well as giving general guidance on maintenance, including the production of a Building Maintenance Manual with all the necessary drawings. The architect is then responsible for pre-handover inspection, outstanding works and defects, and finally handover.

reconcile conflicts between other professional members of the team involved in the building process.

The architect

The role played by the architect is critical to the development process. Invariably the design team leader, except where a project is essentially an engineering problem, the architect translates the developer's concept into a workable and attractive solution. Probably the best way of describing the various functions performed by the architect during the development process is to list the 'architect's services', as laid down by the Royal Institute of British Architects, which are divided into the work stages summarized in Table 10.1 (Parnell 1991).

It can, therefore, be seen that the architect is fully concerned with several major elements in the development process: the acquisition of planning approval, the design of the building and the control of the building contract.

Engineers

Several engineering disciplines are involved in the construction process of a development project. Working closely with the architect, they combine to ensure that the plans are structurally sound and that the mechanical systems will service the building adequately.

STRUCTURAL ENGINEER

The role of the structural engineer is to provide the skills necessary to create structures that will resist all imposed forces over the life-span of the structure with an adequate margin of safety. The relationship between the structural engineer and the architect is inevitably a close one. A decision as to the choice of structural frame – reinforced concrete, precast concrete or steel – has to be made early in the design process, as does the form of foundation adopted and the measure of resulting loads and stresses. Such decisions have consequential effects upon the basic design, construction and use of the building. It is also important to provide sufficient flexibility in the initial design to permit changes during construction and even after completion. With the growing sophistication of modern commercial buildings, flexibility in routing services through floors, ceilings and vertical ducts is another prime consideration at the structural design stage. Throughout the process, of course, attention must also be paid to building cost, and the structural engineer, together with the architect and other engineering consultants, needs to liaise with the quantity surveyor.

GEOTECHNICAL ENGINEER

Usually responsible to the structural engineer, the geotechnical engineer is retained to perform initial tests of the bearing capacity of the soil, evaluate drainage conditions and generally assist in planning to fit the proposed project onto the site in an optimum manner, balancing physical effectiveness with building costs.

MECHANICAL AND ELECTRICAL ENGINEER OR BUILDING SERVICES
ENGINEER

Together, these engineering disciplines supply the life-blood of a building. It is estimated that around 60 per cent of total building cost these days can be attributed to the provision of building services in commercial development projects. Such facilities as heating, water supply, lighting, air conditioning, communications, fire precautions and lift services must be carefully planned and co-ordinated. Alternative systems must be assessed in respect of capital and running costs, energy conservation, main plant location and size, duct sizes and routes, partitioning flexibility, special computing requirements, control mechanisms and the facility to add on services or increase capacity. It should be noted that, given the singular service they provide and problems they can cause, the specialist lift engineer is an important member of the professional team.

The climate change levy is already adding about 15 per cent to energy costs (Battle 2003). Part L of the Building Regulations has been introduced to reduce energy consumption and therefore reduce the country's carbon emissions. In order to comply with these stringent guidelines fenestration, lighting, building plan form, building slenderness and building services systems need to be considered together. This suggests that significance of the role of the M&E engineer will increase in the coming years.

ENVIRONMENTAL ENGINEER

The environmental engineer is playing an increasingly important role on the design team. At one time, environmental engineering was relatively straight-forward, usually dealing with water and soil run-off onto surrounding property. Following the discovery that asbestos in existing buildings posed a serious health hazard, and with the advent of 'sick building syndrome', there are now a new set of environmental problems related to toxic waste and a much wider range of concerns requiring environmental impact analysis and control.

The quantity surveyor

The quantity surveyor is basically charged with the task of cost analysis and cost control. It is advisable for the quantity surveyor (or building economist) to be included in the initial design deliberations and financial appraisal, particularly as the question of construction cost has become so critical over recent years. The original function of the quantity surveyor was mainly restricted to the preparation of bills of quantities and the variations of accounts. However, they have progressively become more involved in providing cost advice throughout the development process, but they remain principally concerned with supplying cost information through the feasibility, outline and detailed design stages, culminating in an agreed cost plan linked to an acceptable preparatory design. This is followed by a process of cost checking; assistance on tendering procedures and contractual arrangements; the production of specifications for the main contract and nominated subcontractors; examination and report on submitted tenders and negotiations; approval of variation orders, interim certificates and final accounts. However, it is worth emphasizing that the concept of cost-effectiveness is of greater consequence than ever before, and the application of associated techniques such as cost-in-use, life-cycle costing and value engineering have been in the ascendant.

The builder

The builder is not normally included as a full member of the professional team at the outset of the development process, but rather is viewed as a contracted agent at the procurement stage. However, some more enlightened property developers have found that early, prompt and sympathetic advice on the building aspects of construction and design, particularly such aspects as labour, site management and materials, can be extremely useful in respect of savings in both time and cost. The builder's function in the development process can best be described as follows (Somers 1984):

- *Feasibility.* Understanding the developer's overall timescale; preparing an outline network so that discussions relating to key dates can be meaningful at all principals' meetings; and providing general assistance to the whole team on matters relating to site conditions and construction.
- *Outline proposal.* Participate in site investigations and any surveys and schedules of dilapidations; produce initial method statements; liaise with the quantity surveyor on a range of cost information; supply examples of contracts and subcontracts; provide material samples; draw up alternative construction programmes; and develop the project network and report progress.
- *Scheme design.* Advise on design matters relating to trade sequencing and degree of difficulty; help in advising on the design details relating to weather proofing, which must be guaranteed; consider long-term delivery aspects; continue with cost information advice; interview specialist subcontractors; and update the project network to include the detailed design stage and report progress.
- *Detailed design.* Prepare temporary support work designs; establish all special conditions to be included in subcontract documentation; prepare and agree the total budget for construction; detail all quality control and instruction procedures; update the project network to include construction activity and report progress; order long-term delivery items; advise local authorities, neighbours, local residents and unions of intentions; define the extent of all remaining details to be provided by the consultant teams and complete project network accordingly; and agree all work packages.
- *Construction period.* Follow the basic tenets of building safety, within budget, on time and to specification; update the project network

to include show areas, letting procedures and key dates together with handover arrangements and maintenance period work; and be in a position to report time and financial progress accurately at all times.

*   *Post-contract*. Monitor the users' acceptance and allocate a senior member of staff to be responsible for final certification and to act as a long-term contact for the client, consultants and users.

The agent

It should be appreciated that the agent might be but one contributor to the overall process of marketing, albeit an important one. Nevertheless, the agent is an integral member of the development team, whose principal functions are fully described and discussed in Chapter 14.

The valuer

Many development agencies supply valuation expertise from within their own organization. Where this is not the case, it is common for the estate agency firm retained also to provide valuation advice. Sometimes a separate consultant is employed. In essence, the valuer might be asked to estimate the likely value of land identified for a development project, the possible level of profit that might be derived from undertaking the scheme, or the capital value of the completed project. Again, the various components of the residual valuation, and the methods of conducting development valuation, are fully explored in Chapter 12.

There may be separate valuations that have to be conducted for such purposes as land assembly, compensation, taxation, funding, letting, sale and asset valuation. The initial valuation will almost certainly have to be revised and updated during the development process, as the picture of probable income and actual expenditure becomes clearer.

The solicitor

The services of a solicitor are unavoidable in the property development process, right from acquisition through the various stages of planning approval, contracts for construction, to eventual sale or leasing. How much legal work is involved in any particular project will naturally depend upon the complexity of the scheme and the number of parties concerned. It is also possible that specialist advice might have to be sought on certain matters. In simple terms, it has been said that the solicitor is well suited to undertake several roles: of advisor, especially in the complex area of planning law and construction contract law; negotiator, to explain, to persuade, to reach agreement and to discover for and between the various parties; advocate at meetings, representations of all kinds and inquiries; co-ordinator, between all parties to the project and all those who can regulate or otherwise have an influence upon it; and draftsman, of all the relevant formal documentation (Hawkins 1990).

Other specialist team members

According to the nature of the proposed development project and the problems encountered, a need to bring in specialist consultants will often arise. The most common of these can be listed as follows:

*   *Accountant.* Who might be called in to advise on certain tax issues, funding agreements, and disposal arrangements, as well as how the development relates to the overall position of the company.
*   *Town planning consultant.* Employed in circumstances where the planning position is more complicated than a matter of pure design and layout, especially if the approval is likely to be difficult to obtain and there is a possibility of the proposal going to appeal. Sometimes an actual environmental impact statement or its equivalent is required.
*   *Planning supervisor.* Ensures health and safety on site through compliance with the CDM regulations.
*   *Landscape architect.* High-quality landscaping is increasing in popularity and importance, and a good landscape architect can promote the marketability of a project and enhance the value. When necessary, it can also cover up defects in design!
*   *Interior design.* The internal appearance of offices, houses and especially shopping centres is of utmost importance, and an interior designer might be called in to assist the architect in beautifying the building, especially the common parts, display units, reception areas and shopping malls.
*   *Facilities manager.* The management of an organization's facilities, its built environment and its infrastructure must take into account the nature of the activities that take place within the building and which the facilities are serving. For an office building where the eventual occupant is known, the introduction of a facilities manager into the team is becoming increasingly common. Even where the occupant is not known, such advice is beneficial. The equivalent in the retail sector is the early inclusion of shopping centre management expertise into the development plan.
*   *Others.* Might include political consultant, accessibility co-ordinator, insurance, archaeology, party walls, traffic engineering and public relations consultants.

Conclusion

Although a description of the property development process and those professions participating within it can be relatively simple, the activity itself grows more and more complex. Increasingly, development requires more knowledge than ever before about prospective markets and marketing, patterns of urban growth, property legislation, local planning regulation, building procurement and disposal, elements of building design, site development and construction techniques, financing, controlling risk and managing time, the project and the people concerned. Greater complexity in property development has also resulted in more specialization, and as more affiliated professionals have become involved, the size of the development team has grown and the role of some of the professional disciplines changed.

Development in real estate in the 2000s is different from that in the 1990s and is likely to be different from that in the 2010s. Although developers may not continually address societal trends and changes in the short-term, over the longer-term trends and changes have a tremendous effect on what developers build, where they build it, for whom and on what basis.

11 Development site appraisal

Once a potential site has been identified, or a number of sites put up for selection, it is necessary to analyse the respective merits or otherwise of each before a formal valuation can be conducted. In many ways, this stage of appraisal is one of the most important in the development process and, given the ever tighter margins within which development takes place, deserves more attention than it has sometimes received. Several well reported cases of professional negligence highlight the need to undertake critical surveys and investigations with care and consideration. The project size, capital resource commitment and degree of community concern evoked determines the level of analytical detail required. This chapter does not cover in depth the extensive detailed analysis that would normally underlie summary calculations and recommendations undertaken for major development projects. Rather, the intent is to indicate the basic nature of the comprehensive methodology that should be employed in the appraisal of development sites.

The first step is to consider the developers' goals and objectives regarding the project. These must be clearly established and agreed before specific uses for the site are studied. This will require consideration of the developers' motivations, business capacities and financial situation. Increasingly complex objectives underlie the goals of development agencies. It is a fair assumption, however, that the private developer is motivated by financial considerations as opposed to the social or community characteristics of the project, although the latter should be of supreme concern to government agencies because of the public responsibility they bear. Even though developers are motivated primarily by financial considerations, their objectives may still vary substantially. Developers may have nothing more than an idea that a certain type of project may profitably be developed. They may or may not have a particular site in mind. Alternatively, they may have a site and be searching for the most profitable use. Some development agencies, such as local housing authorities or municipal development departments, may be socially motivated and concerned primarily with weighing social costs against social benefits within a given budget (Barrett & Blair 1982). In any event, once the developer's goals and objectives have been established, site appraisal may commence. For convenience, the principal factors that have to be studied at appraisal have been grouped as follows:

- planning policy and practice
- economic climate for development
- site survey and analysis.

Planning policy and practice

It may seem an all too obvious starting point to state that a clear understanding of prevailing planning policies as they relate to the site or sites in question should be gained, but in one of the leading cases of professional negligence, involving a very substantial green-field development site, it was not possible to prove that the surveyor responsible had spoken to the local planning authority, even over the telephone. It is vital to recognize, therefore, that planning policy provides the frame within which development takes place.

The formal procedures and practice of planning and development are examined elsewhere in this text (see Part II). What the following section seeks to do is to explore some of the less formal aspects of planning policy as they affect the appraisal of sites for development.

Non-statutory documents

In addition to the statutory planning process, land planning policy is also expressed by way of a variety of non-statutory plans, briefs and guides. Planning documents treating individual subjects such as housing, transport and employment have been produced regularly by local planning authorities (LPAs). Furthermore, site-specific planning and development briefs, as well as more generalized design guides, have been produced.

A planning brief is compiled by an authority when it does not own the site in question and has no intention of doing so. It is a non-statutory written statement and site plan, sometimes accompanied by supporting maps and illustrations indicating a local authority's policy and aspirations towards a specific site or group or related sites, which possess development or redevelopment potential. The brief is intended to bring together the requirements for a particular development, hoping to form a basis of agreement between interested parties before planning permission is granted.

A development brief, on the other hand, is prepared by an authority, or other landowner, where it owns a site or intends to acquire interests in the land. It usually contains similar 'core' information regarding the site and relevant planning guidance, as does the planning brief, but it also includes details concerning how interests in the land are to be disposed. It should be appreciated that development briefs can be prepared by landowners other than local authorities. Nevertheless, where they are produced by a local authority, several enquiries regarding their production are worth pursuing. Where, for example, they have been approved by resolution of council they are much more authoritative and reliable than otherwise. Those briefs that have been the subject of consultation with all the relevant departments within the authority, with other statutory authorities and undertakers outside and with the public and their representatives, tend to be a great deal more dependable than those where they have not.

Despite the degree of detail and level of commitment given by the authority producing a planning or development brief, it is important to stress that they only represent the author's standpoint. According to the relative needs and bargaining strengths of the parties concerned, they should be seen as negotiable instruments, but at least they simplify appraisal by bringing together many different policy objectives in a single document.

Another type of non-statutory planning document occasionally encountered is the design guide. This is prepared by some planning authorities for development control purposes as an advisory document, backed, where applicable, by standards and statutory requirements. It describes preferred forms of development, giving advice on design techniques and materials to be used across an entire planning area. Less important at appraisal stage than other documents, it might influence market research and the choice of architect. One good example of such a design guide is held to be that produced by North Norfolk District Council, which seeks to conserve the local vernacular and to inspire good new architecture using sensitive materials. An attempt has been made to extend the concept to an entire district area in East Anglia where areas are identified and different sets of design policies applied to them relating to design density, form, style, materials and landscape requirements. Another approach aimed at providing 'development briefing' has been looked at by the Housing Research Foundation. Here, the intention is to supply supplementary guidance to ensure that developers of residential areas know what is expected of them by using a system of 'housing plus' elements. These would define and cover social housing, additional open space and extra facilities, and quality of design, and they would be applied to specific sites prior to schemes being submitted, using agreed checklists in an 'open process' – a trifle too interventionist and deterministic for most developers, especially as the idea is to fund such elements out of the development land value. Nevertheless, a more structured approach towards design issues might be welcome and might also reflect the requirements of policy planning guidance consideration. Some authorities produce a regularly updated statement of planning policy, whereas many others prepare proposals maps showing all known proposals on a district-wide basis. Land availability schedules and maps are also frequently published, especially for industrial and residential development.

The weight that should be attached to informal plans and other non-statutory documents will depend upon their purpose, the date when prepared, and whether or not they have been approved by full council or by the planning committee exercising a delegated power.

The government also produces a number of public-funded research documents, such as the DoE's *Quality of Urban Design* in 1996 and White Papers for consultation, such as the DETR's *Our Towns and Cities: The Future* in 2000, which give positive guidance about current government thinking on key planning and development issues.

Planning matters can be addressed in unexpected ways. Planning Minister Richard Caborn was criticized in 1999 for changing national planning guidance through the mechanism of written parliamentary answer when he sought to 'clarify' national planning guidance in PPG6 but, in fact, signalled a significant change of policy.

The planning application

An examination of the past performance of a given planning authority can usually give a pretty reliable indication of the likely reception a particular development proposal will receive and the approximate length of time it might take to obtain a decision. The starting point for this examination is the Planning Register, which records applications and decisions for all current and past applications, refusals and permissions. From this can be gained an overall impression of the authority's attitude towards development: the type of conditions they are inclined to attach to planning permissions, especially where they are unusual or generous; the refusals to approve applications and the general tenor of the reasons given; and the number of applications that have been called in by the Secretary of State and appeals made to him, together with the decision letters and inspectors' reports resulting from them.

Relevant ministerial Circulars and planning policy guidance should be consulted and the manner in which these are interpreted by the local authority considered. It may transpire that the local planning authority pursues a particular policy towards certain forms of development that is not in accord with central or strategic planning policy, and are not perturbed by their failure rate at appeal. In these cases it may be apparent that an appeal is inevitable, and protracted negotiation futile except to judge the strength of the authority's argument, so that the procedural wheels are best set in motion early.

Less pejoratively perhaps, the planning history for the site in question should be studied, with note taken of past applications, previous decisions, outstanding consents and current proposals. The same exercise should be conducted for neighbouring properties in order to identify any intended development schemes that could affect the site concerned. A more comprehensive approach might benefit all parties on the one hand, whereas possible overdevelopment might detract from the viability of the proposed project on the other. Anyway, it could make a difference to the timing and presentation of an application.

One of the most difficult aspects of appraisal to describe in comparatively objective terms is the effect that personalities and politics have upon planning decisions. They can, however, be crucial. Many an application has foundered, or progressed less easily than it should, on the lack of awareness on the part of the developers or his advisers of certain individual or political sensitivities existing within the authority, its officers and its representatives. Where a developer is faced with an unfamiliar locality, it is often worthwhile compiling a scrapbook of cuttings from the local newspaper stretching back a year or so that deal with planning and development matters. The front page and the letters column are most productive. These extracts can help paint a most revealing picture, spotlighting issues and individuals in the forefront of local planning affairs. Slightly harder is the task of identifying those within the council who are most influential with regard to planning decisions. Time taken with finding informal contacts is rarely wasted. If the developer does not have those informal contacts, there are now professional organizations that will investigate the political scene in a particular locality and provide a report on local politics and the movers and shakers in the planning and other committees. In politically sensitive situations it pays to check the date of local elections and the likelihood of political change – either way.

These days the authority and influence of various interest groups can play an important part in the planning process, and some consideration of their presence and power at appraisal stage is expedient. Apart from those local amenity groups formed to promote and protest about particular causes, there are established national bodies concerned with specific facets of our urban heritage. These include the Georgian Society, the Victorian Society, the Society for the Protection of Ancient Buildings, the Royal Fine Arts Commission and the Town and Country Planning Association. A sympathetic attitude towards the views of such interests at an early point in the development process can often prevent unnecessary conflict and smooth the path to approval.

An absolute must in all appraisals of any significance is the holding of informal discussions with officers, and occasionally members, of the local planning authority. The main purpose of these enquiries is to elicit information and details that may not have been forthcoming from published documents, and to clarify the background to previous decisions and published statements so as to avoid confusion. Apart from those matters already mentioned, these discussions might usefully cover any relevant policy work in progress, the timetable for the production of any new plant or policies, suitable land-use survey information that could be made available, the relationship and need to consult the county council and other bodies, the dates of the appropriate committee meetings and agenda deadlines, the immediate reaction of the authority to the particular development proposal, and any special information that should be provided by the applicant. It is suggested that, at the conclusion of the meeting, the local authority be asked if there are any other matters to which the authority would like to make reference, and recommended that following the meeting the subjects discussed are confirmed in writing. It is a well known axiom in planning and development circles that the quality or usefulness of an answer obtained from planning officers is only as good as that of the question posed; it is also only as good as the person answering, and their standing. Commonly, it has been found that developers are often concerned about the quality of advice they have received at pre-application inquiry. They frequently find that junior staff are used to deal with enquiries and that their views are over-ridden by more senior staff at later meetings, or when a planning application is submitted. As a result, they feel misled when committees do not support officers' recommendations. In particular, frustration is felt when proposals are amended before planning applications are submitted, in response to advice received from planning officers, and officers later recommend refusal of something that they appeared to support earlier (Taussik 1992). It has further been stated that officers are often unprepared, overly cautious and preoccupied with detail. Conversely, developers have been accused of being too vague in their proposals, over-expectant of the off-the-cuff on-the-spot responses, and tending to hear what they want to hear. Nevertheless, proper preparation prior to a meeting, an appointment with the appropriate officer, a careful agenda drawn up, sufficient information provided (preferably in advance), objectives identified, notes taken and written confirmation of the discussion made after the meeting – should help make pre-application inquiries fruitful.

These days, communication is of the essence, and it has been stated that information or development proposals should be concise and frank, with a clear style of presentation that makes them easy to understand (Boys 1983). An increasingly common practice among developers and their consultants, once they are serious about a proposal, is to produce a single package of information for the authority and other involved parties. Typically, this would provide an introduction to the company's affairs, give a history and summation of the development proposal, discuss the commercial back-ground to the company's plans, explain the development proposals in relation to various topics, and provide annexes in support of earlier parts of the statement together with any supplementary information. Later in the process this might be followed with a public exhibition, using additional aids such as enlarged plans, models and audiovisual programmes.

Consultations with other bodies

Most development projects of any size will involve consultations with at least two or three bodies in addition to any consultations with the LPA. If the proposal is thought to have strategic implications, it may be necessary to discuss it with the relevant county council planning department or, in the case of London, the Mayor must give his approval for large-scale develop-ment and development that may affect strategic policies. Similarly, where development has traffic consequences, then having discussed the matter at first instance with the district or borough council, it may be advisable to check certain points with the county council in their capacity as highway authority. This may relate to possible changes in public transport routing, any required improvements or alterations to the road system, adoption and maintenance of new roads and appropriate parking and servicing standards.

In respect of large development schemes generating a substantial amount of public transport travel, it will be necessary to consult the local passenger transport services if any rescheduling, re-routing or stopping provisions are required. Further, it is always worth checking with those services, or where appropriate with the relevant rail network operator, that local services are likely to be maintained at their present level of provision, especially where those travelling to the development for business, shopping, work, leisure or housing are dependent upon public transport.

In addition to detailed investigations regarding the supply of services to the site, it is incumbent upon the developer to approach statutory under-takers, such as the water authority and the gas and electricity companies, to ascertain if there are any capital programmes or proposals that they may have formulated and which could have a bearing on the project. Sometimes certain other bodies such as the Environmental Health Officer, the Health and Safety at Work Executive, the National Coal Board or the British Airports Authority might have to be consulted if the circumstances of the scheme dictate.

With regard to infrastructure requirements, most statutory undertakers are governed by statutes that enable them to assist developers either by re-routing existing services or linking-in with existing services up to the site boundary. However, the provision of major off-site infrastructure can bring major problems, financial and legal, so it needs to be assessed very carefully. For example, it is not unknown for an authority opposed to a development proposal on planning, or even political, grounds to find the most surprising highways, drainage or other service reasons for refusal. Conversely, a co-operative authority can be very helpful, even to the extent of being prepared to use their powers to assist a developer in acquiring any necessary land. The likely reaction of a local authority must, therefore, be carefully assessed.

Planning obligations and planning gain

Probably the most controversial issue surrounding planning and development since the mid-1970s has been that of 'planning gain'. Sometimes known as planning agreements (or S106 agreements), and now described as planning obligations, the extraction of community benefits from a development project through the exercise of the planning approval mechanism has been the subject of continuing legislation, litigation and debate. (This section should be read in conjunction with Chapter 5.)

Several competing rationales justifying the imposition of planning agreements upon developers in return for the grant of planning permission have cogently been set out in a 1993 report (Healey *et al.* 1993). The first rationale is concerned with the implementation of planned development. Within such a framework, agreements may be used to address management problems with respect to development, or developers may be encouraged to contribute to the provision of planned infrastructure to enable their development schemes to proceed. The second rationale focuses on the adverse impacts of the development and the subsequent need to alleviate or compensate for the social costs of that impact. Unlike the first rationale, it is not so much concerned with making the development work on its own terms as with accommodating the development over a wider area. It is suggested that this rationale can be used to justify a wide range of community benefits. Under a third rationale, the developer is seen as having a duty to return some of the profit from the development to the community – a form of local development charge. In both the first and second rationales, reasons can be established for refusing the proposal on the grounds that, without the planning gain or obligation agreement, the development would be unacceptable in planning terms, in the former by making the proposed development project fit with an already envisaged scheme, and in the latter by amelioration of the impact of the project. The third rationale, however, is founded solely on the perceived need to impose some form of local tax on the developer (Edwards & Martin 1993). One example of this is in the Draft London Plan (DLP), which proposes a requirement of 50 per cent affordable housing in new residential developments across London.

The Government has for long been concerned over the extent to which local planning authorities seek to extract planning gain from developers and the means by which they go about it. The position is now largely governed by the provisions of the TCPA 1990 as significantly amended by the Planning and Compensation Act 1991, together with Department of Environment Circulars 16/91, 28/92 and 1/97, as well as the Town and Country Planning (Modification and Discharge of Planning Obligations) Regulations 1992. There has also been a DoE research report, *The use of planning agreements* (1992). One of the main changes introduced by the 1991 Act, amending the TCPA 1990 Act, was a section allowing for the possibility of unilateral undertakings. It also provides a statutory regime for modifying and discharging such unilateral undertakings and other planning obligations. A system of appeal to the Secretary of State was introduced and Crown land was brought into the ambit of unilateral undertakings and planning obligations. Furthermore, certain new formal requirements were introduced. For a planning obligation to have statutory force, it must be made by deed; it must state that it is a planning obligation for the purposes of the 1990 Act; it must identify the land to which it relates; it must identify the person entering into the obligation and their interest in the land; and it must identify the local planning authority by whom it is to be enforceable (Martin 1993).

It is now provided expressly that a planning obligation may be conditional or unconditional, and be either indefinite or limited in time. A planning obligation requires registration as a local land charge, but, controversially, it is not capable of being recorded in the public planning register. As long as the formal requirements are met, then a planning obligation is enforceable against the person entering into it and those subsequently deriving title, unless otherwise specified.

Planning obligations can be positive or negative: positive, in that they might relate to the provision of services or facilities such as highways, sewerage, low-cost housing, open space, landscaping or other physical community benefits; negative, in respect of controls over the use and occupancy of the land or building. They can also require sums of money to be paid to the local planning authority, both one-off and periodic payments. DoE Circular 1/97 provides the current policy guidance to local planning authorities on the use to be made of planning obligations. Properly used, planning obligations may enhance the quality of development and enable proposals to go ahead that might otherwise be refused. They should, however, be relevant to planning and directly related to the proposed development if they are to influence a decision on a planning application. In addition, they should only be sought where they are necessary to make a proposal acceptable in land-use planning terms. When used in this way, they can be key elements in the implementation of planning policies in an area. For example, planning obligations may involve transport-related matters (such as pedestrianization, street furniture and lighting, pavement and road surface design and materials, and cycle ways). Planning obligations may relate to matters other than those covered by planning permission, provided that there is a direct relationship between the planning obligation and the planning permission. But they should not be sought where this connection does not exist or is considered too remote. The tests to apply for their use are that they should be necessary, relevant to planning, directly related to the proposed development, fairly and reasonably related in scale and kind to the proposed development, and reasonable in all other respects (Circular 1/97, Planning Obligations, Annex B). The likelihood is that there will be a continued growth in the use of planning obligations, and possible refinement of their application by government. It is imperative, therefore, from the viewpoint of the developer at appraisal, that they identify the general policy and practice of a particular local authority towards planning obligations, and their success in implementing them.

Economic climate for development

A study of the market to estimate the range of specific land uses, and the rate of physical development that can be supported within the constraints imposed by demand and supply conditions, is perhaps the most important stage in the development process. However, it is one of the most difficult to undertake.

Market appraisal is used not only to inform prospective developers and to assist them in reaching a decision, but also to gain support from local planning authorities, leading financial institutions and potential tenants and purchasers. It must be conducted in a manner that is systematic, rigorous, logical, defensible and reasonably detailed. However, the degree of objectivity required is not always a trait most immediately associated with the natural optimism or bullish behaviour of the developer. Thus, the services of a more dispassionate consultant analyst are often felt advisable. Nevertheless, problems persist, most notably the basic lack of relevant date; the dated and non-comparable nature of such data as does exist; a frequent reluctance on the part of public authorities and their officials readily to co-operate; a similar, though natural, recalcitrance by competing developers, estate agents, property managers and occupiers or owners to share market knowledge; and the fact that there is often no direct precedence to act as a guidepost. In similar vein, the developer invariably wishes to act at this stage with a high degree of confidentiality, if not downright secrecy. An independent consultant acting as analyst also often faces the problems of an inadequate budget for undertaking a thoroughgoing market appraisal, and sometimes a developer with a preconceived notion as to the preferred outcome of any analysis. Moreover, there is the somewhat invidious pressure placed upon the consultants themselves to produce positive results that may lead to further work on the project.

It should be appreciated that a market appraisal may be undertaken for one of two basic reasons: where the use is known, but the site has to be determined, or where the site is known but the use has to be determined. Many of the factors to be studied remain the same, but the processes of analysis are somewhat different.

General market condition

Overall economic climate

All development decisions are inevitably affected by the overall economic climate prevailing in the city, region and country concerned. Increasingly, moreover, international markets are exercising a considerable influence over national and local ones. A market appraisal should, therefore, start with an examination of global as well as national conditions and projected long-term trends, then narrow the focus upon the characteristics of the region, locality, neighbourhood and ultimately the site.

Business cycles

Within national economies, and even within regional and local economies, there are distinct business cycles that affect investment and development decisions in the property market. The reverse is also the case, because it should be borne in mind that there is also a situation of 'simultaneous causation', whereby events in the property market can impact upon other sectors of the economy as well as vice versa. In this context, four types of economic fluctuation bearing upon property investment and development decision-making have been identified (Barrett & Blair 1982). These are random fluctuations, which are short-term irregular changes in business activity; seasonal fluctuations, which are regular and reasonably predictable; business cycles, which are fluctuations affecting the total economy having expansion, recession, contraction and revival phases; and secular trends, which represent the underlying economic conditions that might influence generations. Construction and property cycles do not normally match the average cycle for the economy as a whole, tending to peak before the total economy peaks, and bottoming out before the rest of the economy. This is mainly attributable to investor and consumer confidence, the fact that property is usually one of the first sectors to be adversely affected by rising interest rates and that a slowdown in construction and development activity itself depresses other parts of the economy. The important issue so far as analysing the economic climate for development is to make sure that the timing of the development is related to the turns of the business cycles.

Urban structure theories

In searching for a site, or deciding the highest and best form of economic assessment, developers are advised to reflect upon certain basic economic theories of urban structure and change. Some regard should be paid to the traditional concepts of concentric zone theory, axial theory, sector theory and multiple nuclei theory. Concentric zone theory states that, assuming no variations in topography, transport or land supply, land uses are sorted out according to their ability to benefit from, and therefore pay for, the position of greatest accessibility. Axial theory accounts for development along transport corridors, with accessibility considered in time-cost terms so that changes in transportation lead to changes in land use and land value. Sector theory also recognizes the importance of limited transportation in urban areas, but suggests that specialization of land use takes place according to direction rather than just distance from the position of greatest accessibility. And multiple nuclei theory observes that urban areas may have more than one focal point, each of which influences the location of certain land uses. One cautionary note. Schiller (2001) suggests that:

Since the early days of the twentieth century, the movement from heavy to light industry has reached the point where this model [location based on the idea of cost minimisation, in particular proximity to markets and raw materials] is of little relevance. Improvements in transport and the globalisation of the markets for raw materials means that these costs vary little between different locations in Britain.

Economic needs

There are also a set of urban economic models or concepts that provide a less descriptive and more analytical approach towards the examination of growth and change. These include economic base analysis, shift and share analysis, input–output analysis, econometric models, simulation, time-series and other hybrid models. Between them, these macroeconomic tools allow a perspective of general economic forces to be gained and translated into the demand and supply of urban land and property resources. The range of forecasting techniques is large, and the choice lies with the user, and with a sound understanding of the strengths and weaknesses of each approach, as well as an equally sound understanding of the particular forecasting or analytical problem facing the developer's consultant. Only through the exercise of informed judgement based on a knowledge of local conditions, the problem to be studied, and the techniques available for studying the problem and the area concerned, is it possible to construct and present usable studies of urban economic systems.

Local markets

Most property development markets, however, are essentially local markets. Local developers will have a good understanding of their own area – the policy of the local planning authority towards property development; prevailing rents, values and costs; other projects in process or contemplated; and the potential for future expansion from contact with tenants, purchasers, financiers and the construction industry. Newcomers will obviously have to find out. Nevertheless, a broad understanding of the property market and an intuitive grasp of the particular situations should enable a prospective developer in unfamiliar surroundings to feel at the outset if they like the town, like the location and like the site. This personal judgement is not to be despised, for as in most lines of business, confidence in the final product is essential. Even without sophisticated analyses of the local market it should be possible to tell if, for example, a town is under-shopped, lacks sufficient housing, has a buoyant industrial base, is well placed for distribution services, or lends itself to office relocation.

Market delineation

It is important to define exactly what is the relevant local and non-local market area for the proposed project as a specific site. The local market might be contiguous, such as that for retailing, or diffuse, such as that for housing. Office and industrial development can be both. Apart from recognizing a geographical identity, it is also necessary to study market-area dynamics taking account of the compatibility of the proposed use with surrounding land uses and in the light of neighbourhood growth trends, the location of competitive sites and the degree of spatial monopoly (Miles *et al.* 1991).

Demand and supply

Any market study must focus on the determinants of demand and supply. It should be appreciated, however, that in doing so there is an inherent difficulty in differentiating the many economic factors influencing the property development industry between demand and supply. There are large areas of overlapping influence where certain factors can be said to affect both demand and supply. Nevertheless, there are certain basic forces that clearly affect one side of the demand and supply equation more than the other. These have been stated as follows (Barrett & Blair 1982):

- Demand = (population, income, employment, relative prices, taxes, interest rate, down-payment requirements and future expectations).
- Supply = (expectations of demand, planned supply, competitive environment, availability, and cost of land, labour and capital).

Demand for development

The demand for property is both derived from and driven by the market: market-derived in that many occupiers locate in a given market area in order to provide goods or services for that area, or be accessible to resources and customers, and others, to secure employment within a reasonable commuting distance; market-driven in that the local economy must remain competitive to support sustained demand for accommodation, so that spatial arrangements within an area become important in influencing firms' profitability and local residents' wellbeing. A typical market study of demand for property development would analyse a number of basic factors, of which the following may be considered to be of notable importance.

Catchment area

For most forms of commercial property development the demand for space is a function of the catchment area or hinterland commanded by the site or the activity proposed on it. The exact nature of the centripetal forces at play will vary according to the size, use, location and accessibility of the planning developments. The prime concern at appraisal is to establish whether or not those forces external to the scheme that affect the extent of the hinterland are likely to change. Rail and road closures, diversions and by-passes, motorway extensions and ringways, parking provision or restriction and traffic management schemes of all kinds can have a major impact upon development viability.

Population

The population factor would include an examination of past trends and current estimates regarding population size, birth and death rates, age structure, migration, family size, and spatial distribution. In terms of forecasting, natural births and deaths are relatively easy to gauge, but migration is more difficult. It is also hard but necessary to categorize the population properly into consuming units, especially for retail and housing studies.

Income

Again, income data is mainly required for retail and housing studies, and include a study of past trends and current estimates of personal income, socio-economic distribution, household formation and change over time. In the housing market it is important to distinguish between 'need' (the desire for a property) with 'effective demand' (the intention to occupy backed by the ability to pay) in respect of affordability. In the retail market it is necessary to estimate actual consumer expenditure between sectors, and forecast likely future disposable income on consumer durable and convenience goods.

Employment

This would include an examination of past trends and current estimates of employment among different sectors and occupations, so as to give an overall picture for a given community. This study is especially important in smaller communities, where dependence upon certain major employers can be high, and also in larger urban areas where there is an agglomeration of businesses in the same field of service or production activity. Comparatively small or selective changes can have a significant and multiplier effect upon total employment. Predictions of location and relocation of actual or potential employers, inwards and outwards, can have a dramatic impact upon forecasts of effective demand.

Labour supply

In the context of employment, several different surveys have shown the importance of labour supply to those intending to occupy completed developments, mainly in the industrial sector. In one the calibre of staff required was placed second, just after transport considerations, as the reason for selecting a particular location, while in another it was put top, so some recognition of the effect of labour supply upon property demand at appraisal is required.

Rents and values

The most reliable indicators of demand for space are rental values for commercial schemes and capital values for development land and housing. In analysing values for property it is the general direction of rents and prices for the area over a period of time that is important, and the broad pattern of their incidence across the market, not individually quoted deals struck in isolation from the rest, which might result from pressures to purchase unconnected with the prevailing conditions of the property market. Moreover, care must be taken to ensure that only achieved rentals are used in appraisal, and not asking-rents, which may differ considerably. Any incentives to either party, such as rent-free periods or premiums, should be taken into account. In the same way, where seemingly comparable transactions are being analysed, adjustments must be made to take account of variations in location, size, use and date. As with most preliminary appraisal it is sometimes sufficient to employ a break-even rental figure as a rule of thumb to find out if it is worth pursuing investigation further.

Vacancy rate

Another useful guide to effective demand is the vacancy rate persisting in a chosen locality. Some degree of care must be exercised, however, in reacting too immediately to a forest of estate agents' signs on high street frontages. It may just be that old leases have fallen in at the same time. Nevertheless, where a surplus of existing property development has been overhanging the market for some time, it is obviously a warning sign not to be ignored.

Informal enquiries

Discussions with those actively involved in local property markets can give a good picture of the current scene. Existing tenants in competing projects, estate agents acting on behalf of buyers and sellers, property managers concerned with occupiers' requirements, investors involved with financial performance, and contractors providing building services can all provide informed and informative views of present conditions and prospects. However, it should be remembered that the picture they paint can be highly coloured.

Other factors

There are many other factors affecting the demand for development, including taxation, special incentives, interest rates, local amenities, leisure facilities and environment. All must carefully be considered.

Supply of development

An appraisal of actual and likely future supply of property is generally agreed to be easier than an appraisal of demand. It is conducted so as to compare resultant supply figures with those of demand so as to gauge the amount, if any, of excess demand and the prospects for development. Many factors need to be considered in any assessment of the demand for development, as follows.

Anticipated supply

Put simply, anticipated supply (AS) is:

> AS = existing stock + (space under construction, expected starts, planned new projects and conversions of space) − (demolitions, removals of stock and abandoned projects).

Existing and planned supply

This involves an examination of past trends, current estimates and future forecasts of stock for the particular types of property under scrutiny. Data on existing stock are relatively easy to gather, but predictions of future supply beyond a three- to five-year time horizon are difficult to make reliably. Some important assumptions regarding market behaviour, and central and local government responses to any significant market changes, need to be made. It is also important to recognize that longer-term supply is sensitive to fluctuations in the business and construction cycles.

Competition

It is essential in appraising supply to study most assiduously actual and possible competition. In general terms, this necessitates an assessment of projects under construction, their size, number of units, quality, location, special features, management and stage of development. Competitors themselves must be studied, their number, activities, aspirations, capacity, confidence, contacts, image and performance.

Land availability

It is imperative to ascertain the amount of land allocated in the development plans for the area under study, and the total amount of development that might result if taken up. Possible changes to land release, zoning policy and density control must be considered. Furthermore, the potential for conversion of existing buildings to a new use, and the refurbishment of older premises to provide competition to fresh development schemes, must be assessed.

A survey of cleared sites and other evident development opportunities should be undertaken, for latent supply can be just as telling on market conditions over time as that possessing formal recognition. Floorspace targets, land allocation and infrastructure programmes established by the local authority must be studied, so that a full picture of the potential supply of development land can be presented. In linking land release with permitted levels of commercial floorspace, a certain amount of circumspection is often advised about land owned by local authorities and the final resolution regarding the preferred location of commercial development.

The Planning Register

As already mentioned, one of the main sources of information is the Planning Register, which will show the number of outstanding planning permissions for various forms of development within the planning area. From this, a rough calculation of the probable proportionate increase in the existing stock of buildings and supply of floorspace can be performed. If possible, an attempt should be made to ascertain who is the likely developer and, even more pertinently, whether or not the scheme is designed with a prospective occupier in mind. Where the development is intended for a known owner-occupier, or has already been pre-let, it can be argued that there will be less impact upon the overall supply base. Conversely, the search of the Register might reveal one or more directly competing schemes, which, upon further inquiry, might prompt a complete reconsideration of the planned development. In any case, the prospect of the take-up of these competing schemes and their likely timing should be considered, for it might be possible to pre-empt them by swift action in progressing the planning approval and making an early start on site. However, care should be taken in scrutinizing the Register because several applications and approvals might relate to the same piece of land. Some official surveys have been distorted by adopting crude aggregates of potential floorspace with planning permission and neglecting to sift-out duplicate consents. A check should be run on permissions previously granted to ensure that they are still valid. Outline consents expire after three years and full approvals last for five, unless extensions are sought and approved.

Neighbouring markets

It is not always sufficient to restrict the appraisal of the supply of development to a particular authority area or presumed hinterland. Extensive land release and a profusion of planning consents in adjoining towns and areas can exert a very considerable influence upon property markets. This can apply across the board, but is especially significant in the retail development sector, where shopping patterns are notoriously vulnerable to changes in supply.

Local construction industry

One aspect of market conditions that is sometimes overlooked when it comes to appraising the supply of development properties is the capacity of the local building industry, and its ability to cater for the level of construction required by the proposed development programme. This check should extend to the availability of materials as well as labour. The effect of swings in the business cycle can be profound on the construction industry, but major problems emerge for the developer, of course, during boom periods where skilled labour and experienced supervisory staff are short and delays in delivery materials long.

Absorption and capture rates

The rates at which supply soaks up demand (absorption rate) and the proposed project penetrates the market (capture rate) are of great consequence to the developer. There are three levels to such absorption or capture rates: the overall market for the type of property concerned, the relevant market segments, and the subject property – the intention being to ascertain what surplus or unfulfilled demand exists and the extent to which the project in question can attract that demand. Thorough market research should provide a good basis for appraisal, but it has been stressed that the capture rate of the project and its eventual profitability will actually depend on how well the developers understand demand and what the competition is doing, beyond cursory market studies (Miles *et al.* 1991).

Informal enquiries

As with the appraisal of demand, it pays an aspiring developer to talk to a range of parties who might be able to give insights into the supply side of the market. In the public domain, elected representatives, community associations and interest groups will give an indication of what might be favoured and what opposed. In the private sector, property owners, occupiers and managers can give an idea of what is preferred, where, when, why and how.

Other factors

Other factors also tend to affect the supply side of the development equation, including infrastructure costs, land assembly problems, land-holding issues and capital investment programmes, and the availability of grants and subsidies for development, urban regeneration and economic development projects.

   With the appraisal of both demand and supply for property development, it is important to recognize the inherent risks that exist. Sources of information can be suspect, long-term forecasts are notoriously unreliable, policies towards land release and planning consent can change quickly, market studies do not necessarily determine the highest and best use for a site or the best site for a given use, and the attitudes and behaviour of owners and occupiers can be volatile. Some form of risk analysis or simulation to test the sensitivity of project proposals to change is well advised.

Site survey and analysis

Having considered the planning position, and explored the likely level of potential demand and the overall prospects for supply persisting within a particular town or given locality, a developer must assure himself about the capabilities or a selected site to meet his development objectives. For convenience the various surveys and analyses that are necessary to achieve this can be grouped into those of a legal, physical and functional character.

Legal considerations

Ownership

To begin with, it is clearly essential to establish the ownership of all the various interests that may subsist in the land and property. If the site is offered as a freehold, it is necessary to ensure that full vacant possession can be obtained. It is possible that, in disposing of the freehold interest, the vendor might seek to impose legal requirements placing the developer until some form of obligation to fulfil certain conditions relating to the nature and performance of the development scheme. If the vendor is a public authority, for example, it might seek to retain certain rights to approve the layout or design of the development or to compel the developer to complete the project within a stipulated period of time. The developer will wish to be satisfied that such conditions are acceptable, that they are expressed in reasonable terms and that they allow enough flexibility for the proper execution of the scheme. If there are leasehold interests to be taken into account, then the developer will need to ascertain the period of any lease, the amount of rent payable, the review pattern, the main provisions of the lease, the position with regard to security of tenure, and the respective responsibilities on reversion. A check should also be made about any licences that might have been issued, and the terms on which they were granted. Unauthorized entry and occupation by squatters might have been effected, and both time and money could be expended in obtaining possession. Appearances of vacancy or dereliction can sometimes be deceptive. The land registry is developing a system called Land Registry Direct, a service that will allow instant access over the Internet to 18 million registers of title, including title plans, using a personal computer. With the government pushing e-conveyancing, the National Land and Property Gazetteer and the National Land Information Service, this could transform the way that we negotiate the red tape of property sales.

Land assembly

The process of land assembly in the private sector can be a somewhat secretive affair. The skill and guile of the developer, or more usually his agent, is employed to piece together a site in such a way as to acquire the various interests at the lowest possible price. Sometimes a developer who has identified a site containing many different interests will instruct more than one agent to act independently on separate plots in order to maintain anonymity and suppress expectations. One of the major problems faced by the private sector in the piecing together of a mosaic of plots is the creation of what have been called 'ransom' sites. These occur where a developer has been unable to secure all the land necessary for a scheme, and one or two key sites remain, such as those required for access or essential services, with the owner holding out for an extravagant price, only too aware of the 'blackmail' or 'marriage' value of his interest. Colourful stories can be related about commercial schemes developed above and around recalcitrant owners, but the lesson in terms of expeditious and economic assembly is that such key sites should be pinpointed and purchased at the earliest possible opportunity.

Option to purchase

Many private purchases can be highly speculative in nature and be undertaken well in advance of likely planning permission. A common device in such transactions is the taking of an 'option to purchase', normally enforceable upon the grant of planning consent. The purchase of an option postpones the need to incur heavy capital investment in successful circumstances and it safeguards the developer where the scheme proves abortive. Care must be taken, however, to ensure that the figures determined in the option agreement are realistic, and do not unduly reflect the uncertainties of inflationary growth.

Boundaries and obligations

One of the earliest tasks to be performed in the survey of a site is the precise identification of the boundaries and the way in which they are defined. Although this may seem a somewhat obvious precaution, it is surprising how often in practice discrepancies are found with boundary alignments, and how relatively small, but frequently critical, parcels of land have been either omitted or wrongly included in the disposition.

Some very costly renegotiations have been witnessed. At the same time as identifying the boundaries of the site, the responsibilities for repair and maintenance should be determined. Furthermore, in some development situations, particularly those in congested highly developed parts of major towns and cities, it is necessary to consider rights of support that might have to be afforded to adjoining properties both during and after development. Highway agreements might also exist. In more rural locations, wayleaves, such as those to accommodate overhead cables or underground public trunk mains can cause problems. Party walls should be considered with an awareness that an award might have to be negotiated. It is essential, therefore, to obtain from the existing owners a copy of a plan showing their legal title, and to compare this with an updated Ordnance Survey sheet by walking the boundaries with the plans in hand. This may well show up anomalies between the title plan and the physical boundaries of the site. These anomalies must be checked out very carefully, for even Land Registry plans can be in error.

The Party Wall Act 1996 and the Access to Neighbouring Land Act 1992 lay down specific procedures for dealing with party wall, boundary and access issues. If a developer fails to recognize his obligations there could be significant financial and legal consequences. One developer in Manchester redeveloping two sites that shared supporting walls with a public house purchased the public house specifically to avoid party wall problems (and used it as the site office).

Covenants

Covenants running with the land that restrict its free use must be investigated and, where necessary, early steps should be taken to refer such matters to the Lands Tribunal to have them removed or modified. Rights of light, rights of way and rights of entry are the most common forms of easements encountered in a legal search for development land, and it may sometimes be possible to reach a satisfactory accommodation with those entitled to the enjoyment of the rights without recourse to the uncertainties and expense of the legal system. Again, it is important to carry out a careful inspection of the site for evidence of easements that might have been acquired by prescription and will not necessarily be disclosed on title, such as gates, doors in boundaries, or drains crossing the site. With restrictive covenants, however, they are always expressed and never implied (save only those rights of indemnity implied by the Law of Property Acts). Nevertheless, there are some very complex rules governing whether or not restrictive covenants are still binding on the land. As a rule of thumb, the best approach at initial appraisal is to assume they are still effective and to try to gauge either the likelihood of getting them amended or discharged, or the cost of taking out an indemnity policy with an insurance company. The Land Registration Act 2002 aims to make easements more obvious on the register. Many types of easement that first arose after October 2002 must be entered on the register in order to bind the buyer.

Planning permission

It may be that the site being appraised has the benefit of an existing planning permission. Even if an alternative planning permission is to be sought, it is necessary to scrutinize the current consent and any conditions that are attached. Obviously, if the site is to be bought on the strength of a particular planning approval, a thorough perusal is essential – of the permission, the planning application and accompanying drawings, and all the subsequent correspondence leading up to the decision. Special considerations might have to be given to any planning conditions, and an assessment made of the need to have certain conditions struck out or modified, together with the chances of being able to do this. There may also be the question of an outstanding planning agreement or obligation that could constrain development, and that might outlast the expiry of any existing planning permission.

Planning and preservation

Since the introduction of 'conservation areas' in the Civic Amenities Act 1967, more than 7500 'areas of special architectural or historic interest, the character or appearance of which it is desirable to preserve or enhance' have been designated. Individual buildings can also be listed for protection. The current legislation being the Planning (Listed Buildings and Conservation Areas) Act 1990. Although it is clear that conservation areas can embrace acceptable change, and should not be regarded as 'preservation' areas, close attention must be paid by a prospective developer when considering a site within a conservation area, or where a conservation area impinges upon a site. Even more care must be taken where any buildings on the site are listed as being of special architectural interest, for they may well constrain development. A developer must obtain Listed Building Consent before carrying out any demolition or renovation work that could affect the character of a building. The development of land within a Conservation Area entailing any demolition work will also usually require the express consent of the local planning authority. Further, any tree on the site that is protected by a Tree Preservation Order, or any trees within a Conservation Area, must not be cut or damaged without special permission from the authority. Even if consents are eventually forthcoming for protected trees or buildings, there is often an effect on the development programme or a compromise with the proposed scheme.

Nevertheless, planning new development in a conservation area, or on a site containing protected buildings or trees, can be a particularly challenging and rewarding experience. Outstanding and profitable results can often be achieved, but this requires a sensitive and constructive attitude from both the planning authority and the private developer.

Environmental protection

Awareness of environmental issues has increased dramatically since the mid-1970s. For some major development proposals the European Community Directive 85/337, as reflected in the subsequent Town and Country Planning (Assessment of Environment Effects) Regulations 1988 for the UK demands the preparation of an environmental assessment (EA). This mandatory requirement relates to very special types of development having obvious environmental consequences such as crude oil refineries, thermal power stations, chemical installations, radioactive waste stores, major roads and the like. There is, however, a discretionary power under the Regulations where an EA may be required that includes such proposed uses as energy production, processing of metals, manufacture of glass, chemicals, rubber textiles, the food industry, infrastructure schemes and miscellaneous 'other projects'. This is more significant for the conventional developer since it can include industrial estate development projects, certain urban developments, yacht marinas, holiday villages and hotel complexes. Evidence to date suggests that the majority of EAs have been concerned with waste disposal sites and the extractive industries. Nevertheless, there is a distinct possibility that the application of the regulations could be extended and, further, that many development proposals already have to submit a form of EA or environmental impact statement in support of a planning application. There is also more and more attention being paid to such ecological issues as water quality and resource management, air quality management, wildlife management, solid waste disposal control and noise control. Developers must increasingly be able to anticipate these problems and proffer acceptable solutions.

Physical considerations

Site measurement

The first physical survey to be carried out should be an actual measurement of the site and its boundaries in order to determine the exact area. Too much reliance should not be placed on third-hand reports, estate agents' details, or figures arrived at from measurements taken off Ordnance Survey maps. An accurate assessment of the area of the site is essential in arriving at the permissible density of the development in accordance with development control standards and any agreements made with the local planning authority. It is also vital where a financial offer based upon a design scheme is to be prepared, as will usually be the case.

Ground conditions

It is necessary to discover the character and stability of the land and subsoil. There are three basic deposits beneath a site: artificial ground created by man; drift deposits such as sand, clay, gravel, silt and peat; and rock such as mudstone, sandstone, siltstone and granite. If there is a shallow water table, this should be identified, especially when the site in question is located on the floodplain of a river. Particular attention should also be paid to the presence of any underground rivers, ponds or springs. The existence of any of these features will have implications for the kind of foundations that would need to be laid to support the development. For the same reason, the type of soil or soils covering the site should be classified and the degree of permeability investigated to check how easily water will drain from the site. Any contamination of the soil by a previous use (e.g. gasworks or chemical works) should be recorded and investigated, especially if the proposed development is to be residential. The load-bearing nature of the subsoil should be ascertained, particularly where the site is composed of made-up ground, or has recently had trees removed.

It is sometimes also necessary to find out if any part of the site could be liable to subsidence because of the underlying geological formation or as a result of previous mining operations. Air shafts and walls of underground activities must also be located. The appraisal of one major development site revealed the existence of a forgotten railway tunnel, another was found to mark the scene of a notorious mining disaster, and yet a further site, unbeknown to the prospective developer, concealed a vast lake not that far beneath the surface. In most circumstances, therefore, it pays to sink a few trial boreholes, or at the very least to do a little hand-auguring or probing at first instance to see what subsoil conditions are like, although more sophisticated techniques might have to be employed by geotechnical engineers at a later stage in exceptionally difficult or uncertain conditions. Ground investigations are often given too low a priority, especially in highly competitive situations where time is of the essence. Even a simple desk study, plus site visit by a specialist firm, is rarely undertaken, although the costs of a full site investigation should not exceed 2 per cent of building costs.

Topography

The topography of a site can occasionally be a significant factor in appraisal. Certainly, extreme gradients can cause problems and, although some interesting design solutions might be produced by the architects, cost penalties can be high. Where widely varying and irregular levels exist on a site, it is essential to commission a proper land survey from which the constraints on building layout and design can be gauged and implications for both development cost and value assessed. In this context, physical site appraisal might also include a consideration of the aspect and climate relating to the land in question. Views to and from the site can again affect building design and development value, especially in housing schemes, and south-facing developments benefit very generally in terms of sunlight and rainfall evaporation. There may even be odd instances when local climatic conditions are worthy of appraisal, since, in the event of severe weather the development programme might be affected, and in singularly exposed positions marketing might be difficult and viability subject to modification. On the other hand, certain existing landscape features might enhance the site, and their careful retention and exploitation be reflected in the value of the development, either directly by an uplift in rents or prices or indirectly by easier letting or sale.

Of particular note in recent years is the issue of flood risk. For years, experts engaged in understanding UK rivers have been warning that progressive changes in river morphology and land management, together with increasing flood-plain development, will lead to problems. This prediction came true in 2000 with widespread demonstrations that rivers in flood are usually an unstoppable force. The need for preventive action has resulted in PPG25 imposing a duty on LPAs to identify areas that are liable to flooding and to assess the likely extent and effect of that flooding. It also identifies developers' contributions for the provision of flood defence and mitigation work (Reeves 2001).

Archaeological remains

Since the mid-1970s it has become increasingly important to make sure if a selected development site contains archaeological or historic remains. Almost by definition, the interests of the developer and the archaeologist are diametrically opposed, but responsible developers have normally allowed reasonable access for excavation and provided funding for it. Ever since the introduction of the Ancient Monuments and Archaeological Areas Act 1979 there have been statutory powers enabling access and postponing the start of development to allow excavation. There are also designated Areas of Archaeological Importance such as the old town cores of Canterbury, Chester, Exeter, Hereford and York. In addition, the British Property Federation and the Standing Committee of Archaeological Unit Managers have drawn up a code of practice that appears to be effective, and there is a British Archaeologists and Developers Liaison Group to further co-operation between the respective parties. Even the best codes of conduct and collaborative agreements can go awry and give cause for conflict. Because of this, a few basic rules have been suggested for developers who might face the problem of archaeological remains (Thame 1992). First, make sure a full site evaluation is undertaken. This includes trial excavations, remote radar sensing, bore holes and documentary research, so that, even if there are remains, any final archaeological agreement regarding access, an agreed timetable and financing is based on adequate knowledge of what is likely to exist below the surface. Second, organize an exploratory dig (Gregory 1989). There is not always a need to demolish a building for this, and the excavation of exploratory trenches in basements is standard practice in cities such as York. In any event, new government planning rules in the form of PPG16 mean that local authorities are very likely to insist on some modest evaluation work in propitious situations, and archaeological remains are now a material consideration in the planning process. Advice taken early usually pays off. Third, retain experienced consultant architects and engineers who can produce sensitive and economic design solutions. And fourth, be prepared to contribute, sometimes significantly, to the costs of excavation. The Rose ('Shakespeare') Theatre 'debacle' is a salutary tale that led to the introduction of PPG16, which makes archaeology a 'material consideration' in the determination of planning applications.

Building surveys

Most of the above searches and investigations are equally relevant where some form of refurbishment or rehabilitation of existing buildings is contemplated. In addition, of course, it will be necessary to conduct a physical survey ('referencing', as it is known) of the existing buildings. In brief, this will cover the following matters. An appraisal report on the buildings themselves will describe their design and construction, probable age, existing use, current occupation, present access, available services, provision of amenities and any special installations. Measurements of gross external, gross internal and net internal areas, as well as cubic capacity, will be calculated for different purposes, and particular attention paid to existing eaves heights, clear heights and column spacing. Performance standards will be assessed in respect of the general repair and condition of the building, together with specialist requirements relating to health and safety, fire, heating and ventilation, insulation and floor loading. A special eye will be kept open for defects such as the presence of high alumina cement, blue asbestos, woodwool roof slabs and other deleterious materials, as well as evidence of subsidence or flooding. The extent to which these investigations are pursued will depend upon the degree of redevelopment envisaged. The mere retention of a facade or external walls will call for a more restricted but highly specific survey, and the simple renovation of the existing structure will demand a comprehensive and thorough survey of the entire building. A record of existing and established uses for planning purposes might also be required. Even where existing buildings are to be demolished, there is a need to carry out a careful survey of the structure of the premises, along with any plant and machinery contained therein, to find out how much demolition will cost, how long it will take, what safety and security problems arise and whether or not much can be salvaged.

Functional conditions

Transportation

Transportation linkages to a project must be reviewed carefully at the preliminary stages of site appraisal. Proximity and access to motorways, connecting streets and the availability of public transport are all important to the competitive posture of the project. Time and distance to major sources of employment, commercial activities, schools, and health and recreational facilities should be plotted and compared to existing and planned competitive projects. In some cases, consideration will have to be given to the alteration of existing road configurations to accommodate the additional burdens imposed on the road network by the new development. As part of this appraisal process, a traffic survey studying the traffic records of the local authority, traffic counts and patterns, delay analysis and noise levels. The provision of alternative means of transport other than the private car is becoming increasingly important to the success of development proposals. PPG 6 (relating to retail development) and PPG 13 (transport) demonstrate the government's commitment to reducing the public's reliance on the automobile.

Mains services

Availability of mains services is crucial to development, and from the developer's point of view is likely to become more so, as utility companies are ever more alert to the possibility of extracting the costs of off-site infrastructure directly associated with the scheme from the developer. With gas supplies it should be established whether the local mains are high or low pressure and if governors will be required. With electricity, the probable loading capacity must be estimated and, when the scale or nature of the scheme dictate, the construction of a substation may be needed and a decision reached as to where and how it can be located. The only normal problem experienced with water supply, unless the scheme is particularly large or there are special industrial requirements, is with existing pressure. However, sewerage capacity can often be difficult, but at appraisal it should be ascertained whether the existing system is a joint drainage system, or a split foul and surface water system; if the size of sewer is sufficient to cope with the additional flow; and if the present configuration of the sewers is suitable for the proposed development. Alterations and improvements can be extremely expensive. It is, therefore, important to determine the need to stop up, divert or replace any such services and whether the utility companies will insist upon undertaking the work themselves. Where large distribution mains are involved, it is also common for the utility companies to insist on the work being carried out at a certain time of year; hence the need to co-ordinate this into the development programme. Where new mains services are being installed, utility companies sometimes demand that new mains are sized in excess of those required solely by the development in question, and financial contributions can be negotiated accordingly.

Other facilities

The proper and prompt provision of some facilities and services is often overlooked in development appraisal. Among these are telephone and data communication, refuse disposal and treatment, and postal deliveries and development nomenclature, and the availability of certain social amenities such as schools, shops, restaurants and banks. Leisure and medical services should also be taken into account. It may also be necessary to identify and measure the major sources of noise within the vicinity of the development.

Problems and pitfalls

Although the preparation of site appraisals and analyses has become more professional and reliable since the mid-1980s, there are still problems, short-comings and pitfalls that have been identified (Eldred & Zerbst 1985). These can be summarized as follows:

- an over-optimistic developer unduly influencing the consultant's analysis
- an unclear set of objectives established by the developer, leading to resultant studies being incomplete, inconsistent and misleading
- consultants too concerned with producing a positive recommendation, which might lead to further fees from the project
- fragmented development planning where the full survey and analysis process has not properly been followed
- inadequate analysis of indirect forces affecting the feasibility of the project, such as changing planning policies, consumer behaviour or community reaction
- misrepresentation of data, either deliberately to enhance the prospects of the project, or inadvertently where key data may not be sufficiently substantiated by market fact
- mis-specification of supply and demand by the indiscriminate use of aggregate data, such as population, employment, income, values and vacancy rates, coupled with a failure to correlate supply and demand factors
- inattention to economic indicators regarding likely future conditions through the business cycle
- underestimation of infrastructure costs
- inadequate techniques of analysis
- too much statistical data and not enough analysis or judgement
- lack of primary data and overreliance on secondary sources
- lack of consumer surveys exploring preferences and attitudes
- lack of sensitivity analysis testing the effect of potential changes to the constituent factors determining the feasibility of a project
- overvaluation of land caused by too sanguine an approach towards income flows
- faulty financial analysis and inadequate methods of computation
- avoidance of responsibility on the part of consultants.

As a cautionary note to conclude the subject of development appraisal, it is recommended that anyone concerned with the valuation of development land should read, or re-read, the decision in Singer & Friedlander, which is reported in full elsewhere (Singer & Friedlander 1977). The procedures and pitfalls are well described. Finally, it should be recognized that, although there is no unvarying approach towards appraisal, there is a necessary attitude of mind, which has been succinctly summarized by the American Institute of Real Estate Appraisers as follows:

> Making an appraisal is solving a problem. The solution requires interpretation, in terms of money, of the influences of economic, sociological and political forces on a specific real property. Characteristics of real property differ widely. This does not mean, however, that there is wide variation in the orderly procedure for solving appraisal problems. The best experience in the appraisal field has crystallized into the appraisal process.
>
> This process is an orderly programme by which the problem is defined, the work necessary to solve the problem is planned, and the data involved are acquired, classified, analysed, and interpreted into an estimate of value. It is a dependable method of making a thorough, accurate appraisal in an efficient manner. It can also serve as an outline of the appraisal report.

(AIREA 1977)

Development valuation[1]

It has been said that property possesses development potential whenever an element of latent value can be released by the expenditure of capital upon it (Baum & Mackmin 1989). Generally, this may arise through the development of a bare site where planning permission has been, or is likely to be, obtained; by redevelopment through the demolition and replacement of existing buildings following the grant of planning consent; by renovation through the upgrading of existing building, with or without planning approval for a change of use; or by a combination of new development, redevelopment or renovation.

There is nothing especially complex about the basic theory of development valuation, or indeed the traditional techniques employed. In fact, its very simplicity often attracts the disfavour of those seeking the mystical qualities of more advanced techniques of financial appraisal. In essence, development valuation merely involves the calculation of what can be achieved for a development once completed and let, less what it costs to create. It is, therefore, the most explicit and straightforward of valuation tasks, but can, at the same time, be the most prone to error and most responsive to individual supposition. Consequently, it depends above all upon sound professional judgement and a thorough investigation of all the circumstances prevailing in individual cases.

One fundamental factor, however, is that the reliability of any development valuation depends entirely upon the quality of the appraisal information described in the previous chapter.

The purposes

A development valuation or viability study can basically be undertaken for various different purposes, which include:

- calculating the likely value of land for development or redevelopment where acceptable profit margins and development costs can be estimated
- assessing the probable level of profit that may result from development where the costs of land and construction are known
- estimating the required level of rental income needed to justify the development decision
- establishing a cost ceiling for construction where minimum acceptable profit and land value are known.

A combination of the calculations can be conducted to explore alternative levels of acceptable costs and returns, but all valuations for development purposes require an agreed or anticipated level of income or capital value with which to work.

Several methods of assessing viability can be employed, with the appropriate choice of technique largely resting upon the individual circumstances and objectives of the developer concerned. The principal method used is that of capital profit, by which total development costs are deducted from gross development value and a residual profit is established. An alternative approach is the estimation of the yield or return produced by a development scheme. This can be a simple comparison of the anticipated initial income expressed as a percentage of the likely development costs; or it can be a more refined relationship between estimated income allowing for rental growth and the attainment of a specified *yield* by a selected target date. A further method, more commonly employed abroad, is that of *loan requirement* whereby the period it takes to repay a fixed interest loan is used as a comparative test of viability between alternative projects.

Component variables

To conduct a development valuation, there are variable components about which quantitative data is normally required. These are explored in more detail later in the chapter, but typically can be listed as follows:

- rental income or sale price
- investment yield for capitalization
- gross building size
- net lettable area
- construction costs
- fees
- cost of finance
- land cost (if known)
- required profit (if not the purpose)
- development period
- construction period
- acquisition and disposal costs
- contingency sum
- void period.

In examining the valuation of development properties, this chapter is organized into three subsequent sections:

- the residual method
- discounted cashflow analysis
- risk and uncertainty.

The residual method

The technique most frequently employed in the financial analysis of development projects is generally known as the residual valuation method. In essence, the residual method of valuation simply calculates what you can get for a development scheme once completed and let, less what it costs to create. Put another way, the conventional approach to a residual valuation is based upon the simple equation:

gross development value − (costs + profit) = residual value

The following two examples describe in bare outline ('back-of-the-envelope') residual valuations to find land value and development profit figures respectively. All figures are for illustrative purposes only.

Example 1: to find land value

A prospective developer finds it necessary to ascertain how much he can afford to offer for a small prime provincial site, which has planning permission for 2000 m² of offices producing 1600 m² of lettable floorspace. The projected development period is expected to be 24 months and the building contract period 12 months. Six months have been allowed before building works start to take account of detailed design, estimation and tendering. Six months following practical completion have been allowed for any possible letting voids that may occur. Finance can be arranged at 1.2 per cent per month, comparable schemes have recently yielded 6 per cent rents, of around £185 per m² net of all outgoings have currently been achieved on similar properties, and a developer's profit of 15 per cent on capital value is required. Construction costs have been estimated at £800 per m². A development valuation to assess the residual value of land can be conducted as in Table 12.1

Example 2: to find development profit

A vacant and partially derelict deconsecrated church building in the centre of a large provincial town is being offered for sale at £2.5 million. A local property development company is interested in converting the building into a small speciality shopping centre on two floors. The reconstructed building will be approximately 3000 m² gross in size providing about 2000 m² of net lettable floorspace divided into 18 units of between 50 m² and 250 m². Rental income is predicted to average out at around £300 per m². An investment return of 7.5 per cent is sought. Building costs are estimated at £550 per m². Bridging finance is available at 1.4 per cent per month and the development will probably take 21 months to complete and let. The development company is anxious to know what will be the likely level of profit (Table 12.2).

Component variables

Probably the most important part of the development valuation process is the analysis of all the determining factors that underlie and condition the various component variables.

Table 12.1 Valuation to assess land value

Valuation	£	£
A. Capital value after development		
Anticipated net rental income	296 000	
YP in perpetuity at 6%	16.67	
Estimated gross development value		4 934 320
B. Development costs		
(i) Building costs		
2000 m² gross floor area at £800 per m²	1 600 000	
(ii) Building finance		
Interest on building costs 1.2%		
for 18 months × ½	191 606	
(iii) Professional fees		
12.5% on building costs	200 000	
(iv) Interest on fees		
1.2% for 18 months × ⅔	31 934	
(v) Promotion and marketing		
Estimated budget (including interest)	50 000	
(vi) Contingency		
5% on costs (including interest)	103 677	
(vii) Agents' fees		
Letting at 10% on initial rent	29 600	
Sale at 3% on capital value	148 030	
(viii) Developer's profit		
15% on capital value	740 148	
(ix) Total development costs		3 094 995
C. Residual land value		
(i) Building costs		
(i) Sum available for land, acquisition and interest		1 839 325
(ii) Let x = land value = 1.00 x		
(iii) Finance on land		
(iv) 1.2% for 24 months = 0.33/x		
(v) Acquisition costs		
(vi) 0.04 at 1.2% for 24 months = 0.053 x		
1.384 x = £1 839 325		
∴ x = residual land value now		1 328 992
	Say	£1 330 000

Density of development

Having investigated the general climate for development and the broad planning policies in an area, it is a necessary first step in any residual valuation to establish the optimum amount of achievable gross floorspace or units of development. Assuming that no improvements can be made by further land assembly, a consideration of the relevant density controls must take place. For residential development this will usually be expressed in habitable rooms, dwellings or bed spaces per hectare. Habitable rooms are more popularly applied as a measure in concentrated urban areas; dwellings persist as the

Table 12.2 Valuation to assess likely level of profit

Valuation	£	£
A. *Gross development value*		
(i) Estimated rental income at £300		
(ii) per m² on 2000 m	600 000	
(iii) YP in perpetuity at 7.5%	13.33	
Gross development value		7 998 000
B. *Development costs*		
(i) Building costs at £550 per m² on 3000 m	1 650 000	
(ii) Professional fees at 15%	247 500	
(iii) Contingencies at 5% on (i) and (ii)	94 875	
(iv) Promotion, say	50 000	
(v) Finance on (i) to (iv) at 1.4% pm		
for 18 months × 0.65	377 486	
(vi) Letting fees at 10% of rent	60 000	
(vii) Sale fee at 3% of GDV	239 940	
(viii) Land cost	2 500 000	
(ix) Acquisition at 4%	100 000	
(x) Finance on land and acquisition at 1.4%		
for 21 months	881 532	
(xi) Total development costs		6 201 333
C. *Development profit*		
(i) Residual value in 21 months		1 796 667
(ii) PV of £1 in 21 months at 1.4% pm		0.747
Value now		£1 342 110

(iii) Profit on cost in 21 months

$$\frac{1\,796\,667 \times 100}{6\,201\,333} = 28.97\%$$

Profit on cost now

$$\frac{1\,342\,110 \times 100}{6\,201\,333} = 21.64\%$$

(iv) Profit on value in 21 months

$$\frac{1\,796\,667 \times 100}{7\,998\,000} = 22.46\%$$

Profit on value now

$$\frac{1\,342\,110 \times 100}{6\,201\,333} = 16.78\%$$

Investment return on cost

$$\frac{600\,000 \times 100}{6\,201\,333} = 9.68\%$$

most familiar form of density control in private residential estate development; and bed spaces are normally found as a governing factor in public housing schemes. With regard to the commercial development of offices, and to some extent shops, the two major instruments of density control are floor space index and plot ratio. The former is based upon the total area of gross floorspace measured externally and expressed as a proportion of the site, plus half the width of surrounding roads up to a usual maximum of 6.1 m (20 ft), whichever is the less. The latter is similar but excludes the half width of surrounding roads. Variations occur between authorities in respect of whether or not certain elements such as basements, vaults, carparking, plant rooms, fuel stores and other kinds of special storage are included or excluded from the calculation. It is also fair to say that many local authorities now place greater emphasis upon design and other environmental considerations than they do on arithmetical formulae. With industrial development, the conventional way of assessing density is by site cover. Most modern industrial estates are developed to meet an eventual coverage of 45–55 per cent. Some inner urban projects, particularly those creating small nursery units, can produce as high as 65 per cent site cover, and at the other end of the spectrum the new business and science park concept with high-technology operations is often designed to provide around 15–25 per cent cover.

Again, it should be stressed that there are many other planning, and design considerations that determine the permissible volume, bulk and massing of new buildings. Among these are such matters as carparking, access, height, landscaping and light. There might also be the question of conservation, and the existence of listed buildings or protected trees and views, either on or around the site, can exercise a stringent control over the density of development. On the other hand, it is sometimes the case that local planning authorities will be prepared to approve schemes of development that are in excess of normal density levels as a result of a planning obligation, and exceptional design or the peculiar nature of the site.

Where the development project involves the refurbishing of existing premises, either in whole or in part, a detailed survey should be undertaken to establish gross and net areas so that existing use rights can be appraised. By rearranging the internal layout of the building, making more efficient use of common space, redesigning stair and light wells and exploiting basement and roof-space, considerable gains in lettable floorspace can be made from these existing use rights.

Economic design

In the context of property development it has been written that 'The economic design is not necessarily the cheapest; it is the one that gives the best value for money'. Costs in the development equation used to be taken at too crude an average and with little recognition of real design and construction implications. All parties involved in the process of property development are becoming increasingly aware of the need to create an economic design. The developer is concerned with the costs that must be borne to obtain the best return on capital seeking to maximize lettable floor area from a given gross area. The investor is more interested in the relationship between annual expenditure and the capital tied up in the project, looking for a building that is lettable and saleable and an asset that promises good rental growth with a sound economic and physical life. The occupier is concerned with the total costs of operating the building and the value it affords in terms of comfort, convenience and appearance, and the consequent effects upon business. There has been a 'flight to quality' in recent years. A paper, *Quality of Urban Design*, funded jointly by the RICS and the (then) DoE in 1996 as part of the 'Quality in Town and Country' initiative, was an early attempt to define what was meant by quality in design.

In attempting to minimize non-lettable floorspace it is possible to make a few generalizations about the 'efficiency ratio' of different kinds of commercial development, that is, the relationship between gross external and net internal floorspace. With new offices the target is to achieve around 80 per cent, but in refurbishment schemes this figure can drop to between 60 per cent and 70 per cent. Shopping development varies considerably, but somewhere between 65 per cent and 75 per cent is normally sought. In industrial and warehouse development it is possible to achieve 90 per cent and more. Naturally, there are various factors that influence the efficiency ratio and design economics of a building, and without going into too many details it is worth recording some of them.

To begin with, the plan shape of a building has a significant effect on cost. It is, therefore, necessary to have regard to the 'enclosing ratio' in order to compare the economics of various plan shapes, for the lower the ratio between the perimeter of the building and the floor area, the lower the unit cost. Heat losses can also vary according to layout, and change in shape may have an effect on the provision and cost of external works such as paved areas and drainage systems. Although the shape of a building is determined by a combination of factors, it has been ascertained that overall costs increase as the perimeter wall length increases in relation to floor area, and, further, that this becomes more marked when the building is increased in height by adding extra floors without altering the total floor area.

Because certain fixed costs connected with demolition, transportation and erection do not appreciate proportionately with increases in the size of a building, unit costs are usually reduced as a building becomes larger. More-over, wall-to-floor ratios are again reduced with larger projects, and in some high-rise buildings there may be a cost advantage where certain services, such as a lift installation, serve a larger floor area and reduce overall costs. In certain forms of construction the grouping of buildings can affect cost. If, for example, buildings are arranged together rather than erected separately, there can be some cost saving by the combined use of separating walls between the two structures. This is particularly important when the facing walls are expensively clad.

A good economic design for a building will seek to reduce circulation and core space to a minimum. Entrance halls, corridors, stairs, plant rooms, lift wells and passages are all examples of dead space that cannot be used for any profitable purpose, yet all these areas have to be enclosed, heated, decorated or maintained in some way. Of course, cost is not the only criterion, because the value of the completed development will depend upon the appeal of the property to prospective tenants. Nevertheless, it is desirable to avoid unnecessary core provision and limit circulation space to an effective minimum.

Another factor is the height of buildings and, in very general terms, as storey height increases over about three or four storeys, upper floors become more expensive to provide. This is largely because of increased costs of scaffolding, the hoisting of materials and equipment, the extended provision of services and the need for formwork and additional reinforcements. Moreover, the demand for circulation space tends to increase slightly with height, and structural components are inclined to occupy a larger area. Wind is an important factor in high-rise buildings, which is not always considered as fully as it might be. Prevailing winds against the structure can cause eddies and whirlwinds affecting pedestrian flow at ground level, require the installation of plate glass windows at extra cost and dictate the incorporation of an air conditioning system. In addition, maintenance costs will usually be greater on high-rise buildings, but, on the other hand, heating costs can fall with the reduction in roof area, and economies can be experienced by repetition in the construction of successive floors through standardization and familiarity of work.

Therefore, it can be seen that the most economic design solution for a building is that which gives the best value for money, having regard to the need to contain initial, periodic and user costs, but taking into account the rental and capital values created. Depending upon the stage in the development process at which the residual valuation is being made, all the above design factors must be considered to varying degrees of detail in order to explore the cost–value implications.

Estimation of rental value

Possibly the most critical factor in the development equation is that of rental income, and yet all too frequently the chosen figure must rest upon hunch and intuition. Estimates of rent are usually based upon comparison with transactions conducted on similar properties in the locality, but, as already stated in the previous chapter, true comparables are sometimes difficult to discover. Adjustments will often have to be made to allow for differences in size, location, age, condition, occupancy and lease terms. It may seem obvious, but care should be taken to ensure that quoted figures used for comparison are achieved-rents and not asking-rents, and that any premiums, discounts, rent-free periods or special lease terms are allowed for in analysis. Another problem is that, although some valuers are tempted to employ subtle zoning or apportionment techniques when comparing rental values for development proposals, this is not how the majority of commercial occupiers look at rent. In fact, it is increasingly common to find that prospective tenants tend to have greater regard to the full annual cost of occupying space, which on top of rent will include rates, maintenance and repair, insurance, cleaning, security, lighting and heating. For the purpose of valuation it is assumed that the tenant is normally responsible for all outgoings such as repairs, maintenance and insurance, or that a separate service charge would be levied to cover management costs.

Conventionally, rents are assessed on current rental values, but in practice the majority of developers also conduct valuations to take account of any likely rental growth up to completion. The argument for this is that, if rental values, which are a significant and sensitive component in valuation, were not projected in some way, then a developer would invariably be outbid at auction or when a sealed tender offer was made. The percentage to be taken for growth would depend on the local market where the scheme was situated, and a demand assessment study would be required (Marshall & Kennedy 1993).

In the absence of comparables, or in certain other special circumstances, rent may be calculated as a proportion of profit. The most notable situation where this occurs is in the use of turnover rents in planned shopping developments. These fix the rent at a percentage of current rental value plus a proportion of takings according to use. Nevertheless, in the valuation of a development scheme where such rents are proposed, many valuers will ignore the turnover element but adjust the year's purchase to reflect additional security and potential growth, others will adopt two different rates in capitalizing the rental income, one rate for the relatively secure base income and a higher rate for the riskier turnover income.

A further method of assessing rental value is by taking a percentage on cost, following the logic that rent is a return for investment risk. Very much a method of last resort, it is used occasionally in checking the viability of development projects.

The most certain conditions for establishing rental value are, of course, where a pre-letting of the development has been agreed. In this instance, it is likely that the tenant would have negotiated a preferential rent up to first review at a level something below full rental value at the date of occupation. Equally, however, it would be reasonable in any valuation to adjust the yield downwards so as to reflect the increased security conferred by a pre-let. Thus, there is a compensating effect.

Selection of capitalization rate

Most residual valuations rely upon the conventional 'all-risks' yield to determine the rate at which estimated rental income should be capitalized. Also known as the initial or investment yield, it is market-derived and, one can argue, price-dominated. As already intimated, the main complication arising from the use of yields produced by analysing allegedly similar market transactions is that prices often reflect special circumstances. Initial yields deduced from the analysis of existing investments in a current market should not be employed indiscriminately in the selection of capitalization rates for assessing the viability of development schemes. However, they do have to reflect factors including probable future rental growth, security of income, flexibility of use, ease of letting, likely economic life of the building, acceptability of design and layout and responsibility for management.

Although most projects are highly sensitive to small changes in yield, especially at time when prime commercial yields are running at very low levels, it is the component of the residual valuation over which the developer has least control. With all other factors such as costs, rents, fees, time, and even finance, much more scope exists for improving project performance by skilful negotiation or management. Invariably the yield, and thus the capitalization rate, are determined within very narrow margins by the funding institutions. Even so, it is always worth presenting a scheme to a variety of funds in the hope that the special nature of it, in terms of situation, size, tenure, covenant and use will exactly meet certain outstanding requirements of their portfolio, in which case they may be prepared to accept a slightly lower yield. As it is usually the asset value upon completion, and through time, that is the overriding objective to an investing institution, they will often take a longer-term view than the developing agency. It is not uncommon for funds to put together a package deal with a chosen developer that includes a forward sale commitment and demands a slightly higher return. In such circumstances it is vital to agree a specified yield rate at the take-out date.

For whichever party to a development proposal the valuation is being prepared, it is important to explore the possible range of yields that might be adopted by all other interested parties and to study the effects on value and profit levels. A vendor will wish to examine the likely spread of bids and a potential purchaser will want to identify the manoeuvrability of any competition.

In order to achieve a desired yield, a purchaser of the development as an investment would need to meet the costs of legal fees, agents' fees, stamp duty and other disbursements. With recent increases in stamp duty these could amount to anything from 2.5 to 4.75 per cent of gross development value (GDV) and would need to be deducted from the GDV to arrive at the required net yield. However, it is sometimes assumed, as in the examples described in this chapter, that the yield is analysed net of purchasers' costs and so it would be double counting to deduct the costs again. In practice, especially where a developer has entered into a commitment to sell the project on completion to a fund, these costs would almost always be deducted.

Building costs

The precision with which building costs are gauged will differ according to circumstances, becoming more refined and exact as the valuation is worked up. At the outset it is likely that very indicative figures will be employed, drawn from roughly similar schemes on an overall basis. If the result is encouraging, then an outline scheme will normally be prepared by the architect, and slightly more detailed figures calculated against a general specification will be used. Several more stages of sophistication will follow if the auguries are propitious.

Again, a few very general factors merit attention. To begin with, demolition can be a very expensive item, particularly where heavy fixed plant has been installed, special foundations or superstructure provided, or the site is tightly positioned in a busy urban area. Likewise, in older central locations where existing and redundant underground services are present, or in fresh situations where the ground lacks stability or access to infrastructure, site preparation costs can be high.

Probably the largest single element in terms of the costs of development and the potential economic life of a building is the provision of mechanical and electrical services, and in the past too little consideration has been given to the environmental engineering aspects of a development too late in the design process. It has been suggested that over 60 per cent of building costs can be attributed to these services, and it has been argued that more problems arise around matters of power, lighting, lifts, air conditioning, heating, water supply, drainage and communications, than with any other aspect of development. The heating and ventilation system of a building, for example, should be designed in sympathy with the structure for which it is intended, and considered in respect of both initial capital costs of installation and future annual running costs.

One of the greatest irritants to occupancy is the lift system and, as a broad guideline, buildings exceeding three storeys usually have a passenger lift and those taller than six storeys require a second. In addition, where a substantial flow of goods takes place within a building, a separate goods lift will have to be provided, even at two storeys. The two most commonly used types of lift installation are electrical traction drive and oildraulic drive. From a development valuation point of view, the cost of installing an oildraulic lift can be approximately twice that of a conventional electrically driven lift. Running costs are about the same for both, but, because the oildraulic system has no large driving motor, maintenance costs during its working life are negligible, and it is a very much more flexible system to install in refurbishment schemes, tending to optimize lettable floorspace. Lifts can be of varying speeds, but faster lifts require the use of either two-speed or voltage motors to provide smoother acceleration and deceleration, thereby increasing capital, maintenance and running costs. On the other hand, the extra cost of high-speed lifts is usually justified by the saving of valuable floor area.

With regard to other services, the amount of artificial lighting will depend upon the use of the property and vary according to the depth of the building, its orientation and the type of windows incorporated. The onset of advanced technology has meant that the accommodation of communications equipment has assumed more importance, and presently the ability to bring power, telephone, audiovisual, computer and other cabling to desk, check-counter or operating position is a basic design consideration with both cost and value implications. Another fundamental factor is the supply of plumbing and waste disposal facilities, and any hot and cold water system, together with their related utilities, will be more economic the more compactly they are planned and the shorter the pipe runs that result.

To aid the accurate spread of building costs throughout the construction period, most experienced developers have drawn up cost profiles for the various sectors of the property development industry, but these are only used in an indicative way in the residual method of valuation, as opposed to DCF analyses where they can be employed more positively. Techniques for appraising total building costs, which have gained in popularity within the quantity surveying profession, are costs-in-use analysis, life-cycle costing and value engineering, whereby the initial construction costs and annual user costs of a building can be reduced to a common measure. Initial and future expenditures for selected alternative designs are discounted to their present worth and compared in the knowledge that small changes in design can often have significant effects upon running costs as well as capital costs.

Striking a note of caution in respect of building costs, it can be argued that they have been held down over the past few years by competing contractors absorbing a substantial proportion of increasing costs in order to win contracts, but significant escalation is likely to take place within the next year or so. In practice, a majority of developers allow for an inflation in building costs in the same way as rental projections are made until practical completion.

Professional fees

Many developers prefer all fees to be expressed as a percentage of the total costs of construction. The traditional allowance is around 12.5–14.5 per cent, but may fall to 10 per cent or even lower for straightforward and repetitive work such as that in certain industrial and residential estate development, and rise as high as 15–17 per cent on unusually complex schemes or projects of refurbishment.

In very broad terms these fees may be broken down among the various contributing professionals as follows. The architect usually receives about 6 per cent on construction cost, excluding disbursements, but this figure can easily rise to 10 per cent on refurbishment schemes, and there is an entitlement to stage payments. Quantity surveyors' fees vary but are normally in the range of 2 per cent to 3 per cent inclusive on cost, depending upon the value of the work, being a lower percentage the higher the value. It is traditional for consulting engineers to relate their fees to the cost of the relevant engineering works with which they are concerned, not to total construction costs, at a rate of around 6.5 per cent exclusive of disbursements, but pressure is applied by some developers to have engineering fees expressed as a proportion of the whole. Where this is done, structural engineering fees work out at approximately 2.25 per cent of total construction cost and other engineering fees at a further 2.25 per cent to 2.75 per cent. Project management fees are around 2 per cent.

The majority of commercial agents would seek a letting fee of around 10 per cent of the initial rent, unless a specially reduced rent has been agreed with the incoming tenant. Fees on sale are likely to be about 1.5 per cent of the sale price. All fees are to some extent negotiable, and where developers use regularly retained agents they will sometimes look to secure a discount. It should be noted in most circumstances that, on sale, the tenant will pay the legal costs of the landlord. In some development projects it will be necessary to call upon specialist advice relating to such matters as planning, tax and party walls, in which case the fees are normally charged at an appropriate hourly or daily rate by the consultant concerned.

Apart from the agent's letting fee, the finance on fees tends to be somewhat front-heavy. Architects, for example, are entitled, in theory at least, to three-quarters of their fees before building work begins.

Finance for development

Chapter 13 is devoted to this topic in some detail. For the purposes of conducting a basic residual valuation it is pertinent to make a few comments regarding how the cost of finance is accounted for in an initial feasibility study. More complex calculations would follow.

In allowing for finance charges on construction costs in the residual valuation, adjustments are made to reflect that funds are borrowed only as they are required, cashflow being critical. Three basic alternative methods are variously employed, all being nothing more than rough estimates. Either half the rate of interest is applied for the full building period, or the full rate is applied for half the building period, or the full rate is applied for the whole period and half the result is taken as the finance charge. All three give different figures, the last quoted producing the highest. In calculating the finance on other components, similar proportions are adopted. For example, the accumulated debt charge on fees is often taken at two-thirds to three-quarters of the interest rate. In fact, a variable percentage, such as 60 per cent or 65 per cent, can be applied to building cost finance to take a rough account of higher charges resulting from such items as costly demolition or site preparation at the beginning of development, or void periods at the end. In practice, the most popular calculation is 50 per cent of total costs for the building period.

Unless special arrangements have been agreed with the vendor, the finance charges on the cost of land and land acquisition are invariably compounded at the full rate of interest over the entire development period and, as stated above, it should be remembered that, if there are any void periods following completion, the total outstanding amount should be rolled-up at the full rate to account for interest on interest, not simply deferred.

The actual rate of interest by which the costs will be rolled-up depends upon the source of finance available to the developer. Conventionally, however, where these are not known or have yet to be agreed, a rate of interest some few percentage points above the base rate (such as London Inter-Bank Offered Rate, LIBOR) will be employed. Even where a substantially lower rate of borrowing has been negotiated or internal funds are to be employed, it is correct at earlier stages of valuation to adopt a full opportunity cost of finance approach so as to identify other possible bids and a minimum open market value for the land. Again, refinements will follow.

Promotion and marketing

The amount of the budget allowed for promotion and marketing in the development valuation varies considerably and depends largely upon the nature and location of the project concerned. Many schemes are either wholly or substantially pre-let and will require little or no additional funding during the development period. However, it should not be forgotten that an extensive marketing campaign may have been involved prior to construction, and the financing of those costs will have to be carried throughout the gestation period of the scheme.

Because marketing needs will vary so widely between projects, it is unwise to adopt an easy proportion or percentage of some other figure. Rather, a figure related to the probable costs of promoting the individual development must be estimated, and the early advice of agents is desirable.

Likewise, although it is often true that the larger the development, the larger the budget, there is no direct relationship with the size of the project, and some of the largest may be relatively easy to let. Nevertheless, it is possible to identify certain fixed costs, and even the very smallest development will rarely require less than £50 000 as a promotions budget.

Contingency

There is a certain amount of disagreement within the ranks of development surveyors whether or not a contingency sum should be included within a residual valuation, and if so, how much it should be. It is argued that a contingency should be set aside in the calculation to allow for any unforeseen and financially onerous occurrences that would take place during the development period and affect viability. This might cover such circumstances as the need to provide for unforeseen service requirements, overcome undiscovered physical problems on the land or supply special facilities for a particularly attractive tenant. On the other hand, some would argue that all the other components in the residual should be properly estimated, and that effective project management should ensure that a project or development comes in within total budget. On the whole, however, it is sensible to make provision for a contingency sum. The exact amount will vary, but a commonly accepted margin is around 5 per cent on construction cost or alternatively 3 per cent on gross development value. With schemes of refurbishment it is usual to allow much more. The amount of the contingency item can vary according to the date of the valuation. Prior to the preparation of plans or cost estimates it can be as much as 8 per cent of building cost, after the preparation of sketch plans and cost estimates it is more appropriately put at 5 per cent, and after the award of the building contract it can be reduced to as low as 3 per cent of building cost (Jolly 1979). As an alternative to allowing for a separate item in respect of contingencies, it is common practice to add a further margin to the developer's profit. In Example 1, for instance, a developer's profit of around 17 per cent instead of 15 per cent on gross development value would suffice. In any event, the actual figure should be determined by the degree of detailed research and survey work undertaken both before and during appraisal.

Land acquisition

The very purpose of many residual valuations is to identify the likely price that may be paid or received in respect of an opportunity to develop land. On the other hand, sometimes the cost of land is ignored, sometimes it is known, and sometimes it is assumed. This is either because no change of ownership is contemplated, or because disposition has already occurred at an agreed sum, or because the calculation is being performed against an asking or offer price. In all circumstances, however, it should be remembered that the value of land is a residual, even if it resides from another or previous computation.

As stated above, in the majority of cases the cost of acquiring land is charged at the full rate of discount throughout the entire period of develop- ment. However, there may be instances when an arrangement is made between the vendor and the purchaser to phase acquisition or postpone payment. Conversely, an option to buy the land may have been taken out some time prior to purchase and must itself be charged in the calculation. In similar vein, special arrangements regarding the timing or phasing of payment might be agreed between the parties, and adjustments may have to be made to land acquisition costs as a result, depending upon the precise nature of the agreement. Refinements in the purchase agreement leading to delayed, reduced or staged payments should not be ignored, as their effect upon viability can often be quite dramatic.

Theoretically, a formula-based approach incorporating the notional costs and the consequential finance charges should be employed, although in practice some valuers simply apply a discount factor to the sum available for land acquisition at the end of the development period.

Developers' profit

A figure to take account of the reward expected by a developer for taking the risks associated with a scheme of development and applying his management expertise to the project is either included within the residual valuation or is the result of it. Sometimes, indeed, it may be a combination of both, where the calculation is being conducted to ascertain a surplus.

There are two conventional methods by which a developer's profit is included in a residual valuation, the choice depending upon whether or not the cost of land is known. Where land acquisition costs cannot be ascertained and are likely to be the result of the valuation, then a proportion of gross development value is taken, usually 10–20 per cent. Where land costs are known, and can be included as part of total costs, then a proportion of that total cost is adopted, normally 15–25 per cent. Research has shown that a figure of 15–17 per cent is the minimum return on cost accepted by most developers (Marshall & Kennedy 1993).

If the purpose of the valuation is to identify probable levels of developers' profit, then the same proportions of gross development value and total construction cost can be used as measures. In addition, profit may be expressed as a proportion of the yield relationship between anticipated rental income and gross development value. Put another way, a developer will look for a percentage margin above the initial investment yield, normally between 1.5 per cent and 3 per cent, so that if the funding institution requires a 6 per cent return on the project at disposition, the developer will be seeking something between 7.5 and 9 per cent yield in total. Some smaller, more speculative developers might merely look for achieving a simple capital gain and not assess minimum acceptable profit as a percentage of cost or value. In other circumstances, certain development agencies may adopt different attitudes towards development profit. Financial institutions, building firms and major retailers are known at times to operate lower margins of profit, being respectively interested in creating new investment, ensuring continuity of construction work, and obtaining fresh outlets for retailing. In practice, it is also becoming increasingly common to see developers adopting a basic project management fee approach towards their first slice of profit and sharing additional equity in a predetermined manner with a funding institution.

Example 2 shows that the developer's profit on both cost and value can be calculated as being receivable either upon completion or as a discounted sum now. In practice, the former future figure is often used to judge acceptable levels of profit, whereas in theory, the latter discounted figure is more suitable for comparing alternative development schemes having varying periods until completion. In fact, most developers examine profitability from all angles before making a land bid.

The impact of time

In periods of high interest rates, inflation and erratic changes in both costs and rents, the impact of time upon development valuation can be quite startling. In this respect, the residual method is arguably less sensitive to changes through time than the discounted cashflow analysis approach. The most important starting point is to ensure that the appropriate discount rate is employed to defer future income and expenditure. Whereas the initial investment yield is the proper rate to capitalize rental income once the scheme is completed and let, the correct rate at which to discount the residual sum during the development period, whether it represents land value or development profit, is the opportunity cost of capital for internal funding or the cost of borrowed finance for external funding. Any other rate should be based upon explicit policy assumptions made or approved by the client.

In conducting an appraisal it should be appreciated that, whereas rental growth during the development period will have the effect of inflating the value of the completed scheme by the whole amount of the increase, the total costs of construction will only increase by about half the rate of growth. This is because only a proportion of the debt charge is outstanding. This inherent gearing builds in a margin of enhanced profitability and explains why some developers undertake projects that on the face of it appear highly suspect.

Although risk and uncertainty can be incorporated much more easily into residual valuations by courtesy of microcomputers, it must be stressed that more, if not all, appraisals should be subjected to a simple sensitivity analysis by varying the component factors of rent, cost, yield, finance charges and time in order to explore the effects of change and the different attitudes that might be taken by the market. At its very simplest a basic optimistic–realistic–pessimistic set of appraisals should be conducted to establish the range of values.

Taxation and allowances

Allowance for taxation is rarely made in residual valuation. The discounted cashflow technique described below, however, can be used to incorporate the effects of individual tax liabilities, as well as tax relief against interest charges and tax allowances for the installation of plant and machinery, and for construction in assisted areas. In most other circumstances it has been held that the effects of tax on the residual valuation are ignored so that rents, costs and values are calculated on a before-tax basis. So far as the capitalization of rent is concerned, this is a well established principle in any open market valuation where it is likely that potential purchasers will pay tax at the standard rate of corporation or income tax. Tax relief against interest charges and tax allowances for the provision of plant and machinery are again not usually taken into account in an open market valuation, because they are dependent upon the circumstances of the particular developer (Jolly 1979). Likewise, value added tax is usually ignored in residual valuation, but there is evidence that, where appropriate, a majority of developers are allowing for VAT in any cashflow analysis (Marshall & Kennedy 1993).

Criticisms of the residual method

Most notable, and often quoted, among the critics of the residual method of valuation have been the Lands Tribunal, which has demonstrated a reluctance to accept the technique as a primary method of valuation within the aegis of their jurisdiction. Although it has employed the approach on a few very exceptional occasions, either in whole or in part, the Tribunal has stated that residual valuations are far from being a certain guide to values, because minor adjustments to constituent figures can have a major effect on the resultant variation. Further, they have argued that 'once valuers are let loose upon residual valuations, however honest the valuers and however reasonable their arguments, they can prove almost anything (*First Garden City Ltd* vs *Letchworth Garden City* 1966). A close examination of some of the cases placed before the Tribunal would seem to support a measure of criticism and, in the notable case quoted above, the continuous revision of figures between disputing parties caused the Tribunal to comment that their process of residual valuation 'continued like a seemingly endless game of battledore and shuttlecock, until even such a veteran player as the District Valuer was showing signs of exhaustion'. The criticisms made by the Lands Tribunal become even more understandable when one appreciates that the parties before them are not actually intending to use their quoted figures for purposes of disposition for actual development. As the Tribunal itself has stated in another case, the valuations they see are immune from 'the purifying fires of open market dealings' and 'with captive parties there can be no acid test'.

Setting aside the strictures of the Land Tribunal, the residual method was brought into greatest practical disrepute during the worst excesses of the property boom in the early 1970s. A phenomenon aptly described as '130 per cent valuation' was witnessed, whereby negligent, unnerved, and occasionally nefarious valuers sought to establish hyperbolic levels of value in order to secure for clients full funding from banks who would normally advance around two-thirds of the valuation figure. Bullish views of anticipated rents were combined with a bearish attitude towards costs, and compounded by a dismissive approach regarding potential planning problems. Unprofessional practices experienced at that time in the area of development valuation, only some of which have been exposed in the courts, have tended to cast a shadow over the residual method, and while it is true that in many respects it lacks degrees of precision, is often insensitive to changes of cost and value through time and many of the component factors are either crude averages or very approximate guesses, there is another side to the argument. When performed properly with carefully considered assumptions, well researched figures regarding costs and rents, an informed view of the development programme and a justified set of decisions in respect of marketing, management and disposal, it becomes a comparatively overt and reliable means of appraising the viability of, and constructing a valuation for a prospective development scheme relating to, a specific site, a known developer and established conditions for finance, design and building. In any event, it is an appropriate valuation technique where no readily comparable transactions are available or where the scale of the scheme could itself distort the local market. The Lands Tribunal did concede that:

> it is a striking and unusual feature of a residual valuation that the validity of a site value arrived at by this method is dependeant not so much on the accurate estimation of completed value and development costs, as on the achievement of a right balancing difference between these two. The achievement of this balance calls for delicate judgement, but in open market conditions the fact that the residual method is (on the evidence) the one commonly, or even usually, used for the valuation of development sites, shows that it is potentially a precision valuation instrument.
>
> (*Clinker & Ash Ltd* vs *Southern Gas Board* (1967) 203 EG 735)

There are really only two alternative ways to the residual method for valuing development properties: by direct comparable evidence and by discounted cashflow analysis. Even so, it should be recognized that the first is a derivation of the residual and the second an extension to it.

When employing comparable evidence, it is important to appreciate that the resultant figures are derived from prices achieved in the market and that the sum agreed by an individual vendor and a particular purchaser is likely to be unique, reflecting their personal predilections, tax liabilities and non-property interests. In this way, there is rarely such a thing as a true comparable, and it can be argued that the various adjustments to value or profit that might have to be made to take account of such matters as location, size, date of transaction and proposed use are every bit as contrived and prone to error as the manipulation that takes place in attuning the residual. Furthermore, many of the transactions selected for comparable analysis will, in all probability, have been based upon a residual approach in the first place, and it is surely more credible to construct an explicit and specially prepared residual for the property in question than to rely on the end results of other unknown computations. Markets are notoriously aberrant in both space and time.

Discounted cashflow analysis

The main criticism of the residual method of valuation is that it is not precise enough in the way it reflects the incidence of time and money payments during the period of development. In practice, expenditure upon construction is incurred at regular stages throughout the building contract period, with payments to the contractor usually being made on a monthly basis and assessed on the cumulative value of the work carried out and certified by the quantity surveyor. A typical pattern of payments on a commercial development project has been described as follows:

> During the first few weeks of the building period the valuation will be for relatively small amounts because the contractor is engaged in erecting site offices, taking levels, preparing the site and forming excavations. The rate of expenditure will then start to accelerate as the foundations are put in. If heavy plant, such as a tower crane, is necessary this may be brought in at a fairly early stage and the hire costs will start to be certified by the quantity surveyor after a month or two. Scaffolding costs and structure erection will follow, and the monthly payments will then build up to a fairly consistent level until the first specialist subcontract work begins, such as the installation of lifts and boiler, when there will be a surge in expenditure. After these first large items of equipment have been paid for, there is sometimes a slight fall in the size of the monthly payments until the expensive finishing and fitting out work such as specialist joinery, light fittings, carpeting, panelling and marble work starts. After practical completion, some expenditure may still be outstanding on items such as landscape and planting. There will be an average time lag of approximately five weeks between the date on which the contractor carries out the work on site and the date on which the developer will pay him.
>
> (Jolly 1979)

Other items such as professional fees and promotions budget will also display an irregular pattern of expenditure. As a consequence of this variable spending profile, the finance charges will accrue at a similarly fluctuating rate. Furthermore, in many development schemes, particularly those in the residential and industrial sectors, it will be possible to let or sell completed parts of the project as they become available. In this way, rental income or capital sums will be realized during the development period, which can be set-off against expenditure elsewhere.

Because the residual method only 'guesstimates' the time value of money, making some heroic assumptions about finance costs, it is at best really a rapid screening device employed in selecting among several alternative projects. What is needed is an approach that examines much more closely the cashflows of expenditure and income throughout the process of development, and apportions them to the appropriate time-periods showing the real cost of finance.

Some advantages have been suggested in using a discounted cashflow analysis (Newell 1989).

- In phased, multi-use developments, the cashflow associated with each phase of the scheme can be spelt out and summed into a monthly or quarterly cashflow framework.
- The timing of both expenditures (notably building costs, which may be allocated manually or by use of built-in S-curves) and receipts can accurately be allocated to each month or quarter. This will increase the reliability of the interest rate calculation.
- Interest rates may be allowed to vary during the period of the project, allowing greater flexibility and accuracy.
- The developer obtains an accurate picture of potential cash exposure and will be able to identify points of greatest cashflow risk.
- Additional investment criteria including net present value (NPV) and internal rate of return (IRR) may be obtained as a supplement to the traditional 'return on cost' measure.

There are different methods by which cashflows during the development period can be valued. These include the:

- phased residual valuation
- residual cashflow valuation
- net present value discounted cashflow analysis
- internal rate of return discounted cashflow analysis.

Phased residual valuation

The following example shows how the basic residual method can be modified to take account of phased development projects.

Example 3

Consider the freehold interest in a cleared site that has planning approval for the construction of 90 detached houses. It is thought probable that any prospective purchaser would develop the site in three phases, each of 30 houses. The total development period is estimated at three years, with separate contract periods of 12 months for each of the three phases. The sale price of the houses is set at £150 000 each. Construction costs are estimated at £85 000 per house plot. Finance is available at 1.5 per cent per month and a developer's profit of 10 per cent on gross development value is considered likely to be sought.

A phased residual valuation can be conducted as in Table 12.3

It can be seen that the value of each phase is in the order of £386 000 if development on all three phases started immediately. However, allowance has been made for the cost to the developer of holding phase 2 for a further 12 months and phase 3 for a further 24 months. Even if the three phases were sold separately to different developers, it is assumed that the local demand for new housing would not hold up sufficiently to permit consecutive development of all 90 houses within the first year. An alternative calculation with adjusted selling prices to reflect increased supply could with advantage be performed.

Table 12.3 Phased residual valuation

Valuation	£	£
Phase 1		
A. Sale price of house		150 000
B. Development cost		
Building costs	85 000	
Site works and services	8 000	
Professional fees at 10%	9 300	
Advertising, say	2 000	
Finance on £104 300 at 1.5% for 12 months × ½	10 201	
Disposal fees at 3% of sale price	4 500	
Developer's profit at 10% of sale price	15 000	
Total development costs		134 001
Balance per plot		15 999
C. Site value of phase 1		
Number of plots		30
		479 970
Amount available in 12 months		
Let site value =	1.000x	
Acquisition costs =	0.040x	
Finance at 1.5% on 1.04x for 1 yr =	0.203x	
	1.243x	
1.243x = 479 970		
∴ x = 386 138		
Site value of phase 1, say		386 000
D. Site value of phase 2		
Site value phase 1	386 000	
PV of £1 in 12 months at 1.5%	0.836	
		322 696
E. Site value of phase 3		
Site value phase 1	386 000	
PV of £1 in 24 months at 1.5%	0.700	
		270 200
F. Value of entire site	Say	978 896
		£980 000

Although the method suggested above is an improvement to a global residual, it still gives only a broad indication of value. A detailed discounted cashflow analysis would provide a much better approximation of value.

Residual cashflow valuation

The example below demonstrates that the phased residual valuation can be taken a stage further, so as to produce a residual cashflow valuation.

Example 4

Consider a 10 ha site on a motorway location, which has planning permission for 'high technology' B1 industrial development with a site coverage of around 30 per cent. Rents of £120 per m² are forecast and a major financial institution has shown interest in buying the scheme once completed if it can show an initial yield of 7 per cent. The total development period will be about three years, but it is considered possible to develop and let the equivalent of 1 ha every three months, starting in month nine. Construction costs are estimated at £500 per m² and short-term finance can be arranged at 16 per cent. The site is on offer for £12 million. A residual cashflow valuation, to take account of the effects of expenditure and revenue during the development period and show the likely level of profit, can be performed as follows (Tables 12.4 and 12.5):

Preliminaries
- 10 ha = 100 000 m².
- Site coverage at 30% = 30 000 m² gross.
- Less 5% = 28 500 m² net lettable floorspace.
- Building costs of £15 000 000 averaged at £1 250 000 a quarter.
- Promotion costs of £300 000 spread over the first 2.5 years at an average of £30 000 a quarter.
- Professional fees taken at 10% of building costs and paid at an average rate of £125 000 a quarter.
- Letting fees taken at 10% of initial annual rents and paid as quarterly rents are received.
- Sale fee of £1 466 154 being 3% of gross development value payable upon completion and sale.
- Rental income at 10% of the total quarterly rent roll to commence in month 9 and grow by a further 10% each quarter until month 36 when the full quarterly rent roll of £320 625 is reached.
- Gross development value of £48 871 800 calculated by capitalizing rental income of £3 420 000 a year by 14.29 YP and received in three years' time.
- Annual interest of 16% to be taken at 3.78% a quarter.
- All cashflow figures rounded to the nearest thousand.

Discounted cashflow analysis (NPV and IRR)

This example compares the conventional residual method of valuation with a discounted cashflow analysis, using both net present value (NPV) and internal rate of return (IRR) approaches, in order to demonstrate the need to be more conscious of the effects of time and the incidence of costs and revenue in the valuation of development of properties.

Example 5

A local property development company have been offered a prime corner site on the high street of a prosperous provincial town for £1.5 million and is anxious to establish the probable viability for development with a view to

Table 12.4 Conventional residual valuation

	£	£	£
A. Gross development value			48 872 000
B. Land and construction costs			
Land	12 480 000		
Building	15 000 000		
Promotion	300 000		
Fees	3 306 000		
Interest	10 490 000		
Total		41 576 000	
Less:			
Revenue during development		4 700 000	
C. Total development costs			36 876 000
D. Development profit			
(i) Development profit in 3 years			11 996 000
(ii) PV of £1 in 3 years at 16%			0.641
Development profit now			7 689 436
(iii) Profit on cost in 3 years =			

$$\frac{11\,996\,000 \times 100}{36\,876\,000} = 32.53\%$$

Profit on cost now

$$\frac{7\,689\,436 \times 100}{36\,876\,000} = 20.85\%$$

(iv) Profit on value in 3 years =

$$\frac{1\,996\,000 \times 100}{48\,872\,000} = 24.55\%$$

Profit on value now

$$\frac{7\,689\,436 \times 100}{48\,872\,000} = 15.73\%$$

Return on cost

$$\frac{3\,420\,000 \times 100}{36\,876\,000} = 9.27\%$$

disposing of it to an institution once fully completed and occupied. The site is currently used as a builder's yard with some vacant and near-derelict shops and has a high street frontage of 120 m and a depth of 45 m. It lies within an area allocated for shops and offices with an overall plot ratio of 1.5:1 and a general height restriction of three storeys. Preliminary discussions indicate that the usual parking standards of one space to every 200 m^2 of office floorspace and five to every 100 m^2 retail floorspace could be relaxed if 30 spaces are provided on-site and a Section 106 obligation under the TCPA 1990 is entered into, whereby a further 50 spaces are funded by the developer in a nearby local authority carpark to be constructed in one or two years time. A condition limiting a substantial proportion of any office floorspace to local firms will almost certainly be imposed on a planning permission. All ground-floor development must be retail and rear access to shops is considered essential. A small supermarket of approximately 100 m² is thought likely to attract support and, because the local planning authority are concerned that some form of suitable development takes place as soon as possible, negotiations should be relatively straightforward, with permission probably granted in three months.

The quantity surveyor retained by the company has supplied the following information:

- A 6 m grid to be used throughout with 5 m ceiling heights for retail space and 3 m ceiling height for offices.
- Building costs for shops to be taken at £400 per m², excluding fitting out and shop fronts and equally phased over nine months. Standard shop units to be 6 m × 24 m.
- Building costs for offices to be taken at £800 per m² for letting, including lifts and central heating and equally phased over 15 months.
- Demolition and site preparation to be allowed for at £20 per m² across the entire site.
- External works, including landscaping, will cost £200 000.
- All payments to be made three months in arrears.

The property development company's knowledge of the area indicates rental levels of £150 per m² per annum for supermarket space, an average of £29 000 per annum or approximately £200 per m² per annum for a standard shop unit and £100 per m² per annum for offices. Given three months to obtain planning permission and prepare the site and nine months to construct the shops, it is envisaged that a further three months should be time enough to allow for a successful letting campaign and to complete the superstructure of the building, so that the shops could be let at the end of 15 months. In view of the probable local user condition, the letting climate of the offices is slightly more uncertain, and it is considered appropriate to allow a full six months following completion before they are fully let and disposition to an institution can be effected. Professional fees to the architect and quantity surveyor have been negotiated so that £60 000 is paid as a lump-sum following planning permission, and the remainder calculated subsequently at 10 per cent of building cost on a three-monthly basis. Short-term finance has been arranged with a merchant bank at 15 per cent (3.56 per cent per quarter).

It is well reported that institutions are interested in schemes of this nature, scale and location, but seek yields of between 7 and 8 per cent. It is therefore necessary to establish whether a yield can be accomplished that provides for this and also allows for the developer's risk.

Notes on Tables 12.6–12.9

- The present value of the profit indicated by the residual is £1 575 118. This may be compared with an appraisal by discounted cashflow. It is

Table 12.5 Residual cashflow analysis ('000s)

Timescale		Cash outflows				Cash inflows		Cumulative cashflow	Interest at 3.78% pq
Year	Month	Land	Building	Promotion	Fees	Rent	Sale		
0	0	(12 480)		(30)				(12 510)	(479)
0	3		(1250)	(30)	(125)	85		(13 915)	(544)
0	6		(1250)	(30)	(125)	171		(15 793)	(618)
0	9		(1250)	(30)	(159)	256		(17 691)	(692)
1	0		(1250)	(30)	(159)	342		(19 577)	(766)
1	3		(1250)	(30)	(159)	427		(21 452)	(840)
1	6		(1250)	(30)	(159)	513		(23 315)	(913)
1	9		(1250)	(30)	(159)	598		(25 167)	(986)
2	0		(1250)	(30)	(159)	684		(27 006)	(1058)
2	3		(1250)	(30)	(159)	769		(28 833)	(1130)
2	6		(1250)		(159)	855		(30 616)	(1200)
2	9		(1250)		(159)			(32 386)	(1270)
3	0		(1250)		(159)			(34 140)	
					(1466)		48 872	11 996	
Total		(12 480)		(300)	(3306)	4700	48 872	11 996	(10 490)

commonly thought that a discounted cashflow analysis produces a more accurate result (in this case £1 572 170, virtually the same as the profit produced by the residual method).

- The principal advantage of using cashflows is that there is considerably more flexibility in the timing of payments and receipts. Generally, the same information (costs and values) are used initially in residuals and cashflows such that inaccuracies in these inputs will lead to errors whichever method is adopted. For investment and development appraisal, two discounted cashflow approaches are used commonly.
- The net present value approach involves the discounting of all inflows and outflows. The sum of the discounted inflows and outflows produces the net present value of the developer's profit. Individual developers have their own 'target' discount rates, but for initial appraisals it is logical to use the short-term finance rate. A positive NPV indicates that, potentially, the scheme is profitable, and a negative NPV that a loss is likely.
- Table 12.7 shows how the present value of developer's profit may be calculated. All the costs used are as in the residual, but an attempt has been made to indicate how these costs might be spread throughout the scheme.
- If the finance rate is used for discounting, the difference between the discounted residual profit and the NPV derived from the discounted cashflow results entirely from the treatment of construction finance in the residual and the inclusion of income in the discounted cashflow before the scheme is sold. An alternative discounted cashflow approach enables the calculation of the internal rate of return (IRR) of the scheme. The IRR may be defined as the discount rate that when applied to inflows and outflows, produces a net present value of £0.
- The necessary calculations are shown in Table 12.8, which involve discounting the net cashflows at two trial rates, hopefully producing one negative and one positive NPV.
- The IRR is then found by interpolation, in this case 31.5 per cent pa, confirming that the return exceeds the finance rate of 15 per cent per annum (3.56 per cent per quarter). A full discussion of discounted cash-flow theory is beyond the scope of this chapter, but it is felt necessary to repeat that measures of returns produced are not automatically more accurate than those given by the residual.
- Table 12.9 shows a cashflow analysis. With this method an accounting process is undertaken; that is, interest is added to expenditure on a period-by-period basis. The interest in each period is calculated at 3.56 per cent on the cumulative cost in the previous period. This analysis produces a developer's profit of £2 077 658 comparable approximately with the residual profit of £2 083 490. (Once again, the difference between these figures is attributable to finance charges and inflows of rent before the development is completed.)
- Cashflows are useful in that they enable a developer (or the provider of finance) to assess the likely financial commitment throughout the scheme (i.e. in quarter 4, total spending amounts to £7 365 516). This facility is not available with residual or discounted cashflow methods. As a check,

Table 12.6 Conventional residual valuation

Preliminaries			m²
(a) Site			
Site area = 5400 m²			
Plot ratio = 1.5:1			
Therefore, gross permitted commercial floorspace		=	8100
(b) Shops			
Supermarket 30 × 36 m		=	1080
Standard units 90 × 24 m less 2 ground-floor			
offices entrances 3 × 12 m		=	2088
Total gross retail floorspace		=	3168
(c) Offices			
(Gross permitted commercial floorspace −			
gross retail floorspace) 8100 − 3168 m²		=	4932
Taking account of 6 m grid constraint:			
2-storey above shops 120 × 18 m		=	4320
Single-storey extension above supermarket			
18 × 24 m		=	432
Add − 2 ground-floor entrances 3 × 12 m		=	72
Total gross office floorspace		=	4824

(d) Gross areas to net			
Gross	*Deduction*	*Net m²*	
Supermarket 1080 m²	10%	972	
Standard units 2088 m²	15%	1775	
Offices 4824 m²	20%	3859	

(e) Income		*£pa*
Supermarket − 972 m² at £150 per m² pa	=	145 800
Standard units − 1775 m² at £200 per m² pa	=	355 000
Offices − 3859 m² at £100 per m² pa	=	385 900
		£886 700

the discounted cashflow method should produce the present value of the cashflow profit (subject to rounding).

NPV or IRR?

One of the main advantages of IRR is that it avoids the arbitrary or subjective selection of a discount rate. It is said that the IRR method produces a true yield that obviates the need to anticipate alternative costs of funding. Otherwise, where a net present value approach is adopted, finance charges must be estimated as part of the calculation. Thus, where a project already comprises a mass of complex information regarding cost, rent and time, and the cost of capital is uncertain, it allows the developer to make, accept or reject decisions apart from, or against, the opportunity cost of capital.

On the other hand, it is possible to show that the IRR method is not always reliable in ranking alternative projects in order of their attractiveness. Using a discount rate of 10 per cent to ascertain the net present value of the two projects in Table 12.10, it can be seen that conflicting answers can result.

Conventional/residual	£	£
A. *Capital value after development*		
(i) Estimated net rental income	886 700	11 819 711
(ii) YP in perpetuity at 7.5%	13.33	
(iii) Gross development value		
B. *Development costs*		
(i) Building costs	1 267 200	
Shops – 3168 m² at £400 per m²	3 859 200	
Offices – 4824 m² at £800 per m²	108 000	
Site preparation	200 000	
External works	5 434 000	
Total		
(ii) Professional fees		
Architect and QS by negotiation	603 440	
(iii) Contingencies		
5% on (i)	271 720	
(iv) Finance on building		
3.56% pq for 7 quarters × ½ on (i) + (ii) + (iii)	875 297	
(v) Agents' fees		
Letting fees 15% on initial rent	133 005	
Sale fees at 3% on GDV	354 591	
(iv) Land costs		
Land	1 500 000	
Acquisition	60 000	
Finance at 3.56% for 8 quarters	503 768	
(vii) Total development costs		9 736 221
C. *Residual capital value*		
(i) Capital value in 24 months' time	2 083 490	
(ii) PV of £1 in 2 yrs at 15%	0.756	
(iii) Net present value (developer's profit)	£1 575 118	
D. *Profit*		

(i) Profit on GDV $\frac{1\,575\,118 \times 100}{11\,819\,711} = 13.33\%$

(ii) Profit on cost $\frac{1\,575\,118 \times 100}{9\,736\,221} = 16.18\%$

(iii) Development yield $\frac{186\,700 \times 100}{9\,736\,221} = 9.11\%$

Similarly, the method poses problems where projects have unconventional cashflows, such as large negative payments following a series of positive payments. Moreover, it sometimes produces multiple yields; for example, the cashflow series −2000, +5000, −3150 has no internal rate of return at all. The technique is further affected by the volume of capital expended and the time-period for investment, and is also said to present certain reinvestment problems regarding positive cashflows.

Most of the criticisms levelled at the IRR method, however, apply to cashflows unfamiliar in property development. Comparisons are frequently made

Table 12.7 Discounted cashflow analysis (NPV)

Item/quarter	0	1	2	3	4	5	6	7	8
Land cost	(1 500 000)								
Acquisition costs	(60 000)								
Site preparation		(108 000)							
Building costs:									
shops		(422 400)	(422 400)	(422 400)					
offices		(771 840)	(771 840)	(771 840)	(771 840)	(771 840)			
other			(25 000)	(25 000)	(25 000)	(150 000)			
Architecture and QS fees		(190 224)	(119 424)	(121 924)	(79 684)	(92 184)			
Contingency		(65 112)	(59 712)	(60 962)	(39 842)	(46 092)			
Agency and legal fees						(75 120)			(412 476)
Shop income						125 200	125 200	125 200	
Sale proceeds									11 819 711
Cashflow	(1 560 000)	(1 557 576)	(1 373 376)	(1 402 126)	(916 366)	(1 010 036)	125 200	125 200	11 407 235
PV of £1 at 3.56%	1	0.966	0.932	0.900	0.869	0.840	0.811	0.783	0.756
NPV	(1 560 000)	(1 504 618)	(1 279 986)	(1 261 913)	(796 322)	(848 430)	101 537	98 032	862 870
Cumulative NPV	(1 560 000)	(3 064 618)	(4 344 604)	(5 606 517)	(6 402 839)	(7 251 269)	(7 149 732)	(7 051 700)	1 572 170

Table 12.8 Internal rate of return

Quarter	0	1	2	3	4	5	6	7	8
Cashflow	(1 560 000)	(1 557 576)	(1 373 376)	(1 402 126)	(916 366)	(1 010 036)	125 200	125 200	11 407 235
PV at 6% per qtr	1	0.943	0.890	0.840	0.792	0.747	0.705	0.665	0.627
NPV	(1 560 000)	(1 468 794)	(1 222 305)	(1 177 786)	(725 762)	(754 497)	88 266	83 258	7 152 336
Total NPV									414 716

Quarter	0	1	2	3	4	5	6	7	8
Cashflow	(1 560 000)	(1 557 576)	(1 373 376)	(1 402 126)	(916 366)	(1 010 036)	125 200	125 200	11 407 235
PV at 8% per qtr	1	0.926	0.857	0.794	0.735	0.681	0.630	0.583	0.540
NPV	(1 560 000)	(1 442 315)	(1 176 983)	(1 113 288)	(673 529)	(687 835)	78 876	72 992	6 159 907
Total NPV									(342 175)

Table 12.9 Cashflow analysis. The cashflow is taken from Table 12.7

Item/quarter	0	1	2	3	4	5	6	7	8
Cashflow	(1 560 000)	(1 557 576)	(1 373 376)	(1 402 126)	(916 366)	(1 010 036)	125 200	125 200	11 407 235
Cumulative costs	(1 560 000)	(3 117 576)	(4 546 488)	(6 061 577)	(7 143 819)	(8 375 552)	(8 512 564)	(8 694 868)	2 398 373
Quarterly interest		(55 536)	(112 963)	(165 876)	(221 697)	(262 212)	(307 504)	(313 994)	(320 715)
Cumulative cost at end each quarter	(1 560 000)	(3 173 112)	(4 659 451)	(6 227 453)	(7 365 516)	(8 637 764)	(8 820 068)	(9 008 862)	2 077 658

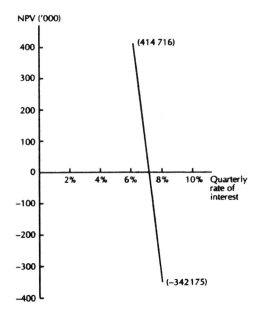

NPV ('000)

Figure 12.1 Graphical estimation of internal rate of return (see Table 12.8).

Formula calculation of IRR

$$IRR = 6\% + 2\% \frac{414\,716}{414\,716 + 342\,175} \text{ per quarter}$$

$$= 6\% + 2\% \frac{414\,716}{756\,891} \text{ per quarter}$$

$$= 6\% + 1.096\% \text{ per quarter}$$
$$= 7.096\%, \text{ say } 7.1\% \text{ per quarter}$$
Effective annual IRR $= (1.071)4 - 1$
$$= 0.316$$
i.e. 31.6% per annum.

between the internal rate of return and the net present value methods of appraisal, and conclusions are drawn as to which approach is best. However, such comparisons are largely invidious, as the two methods can be used to serve quite separate functions.

Currently, the IRR method remains principally a tool of analysis for comparing one project with another or for judging the viability of a project against the opportunity cost of capital where future cashflows are either known or can be anticipated. It is used mainly by development companies, owned by life insurance companies, and by some of the larger and more sophisticated developers. The conventional NPV method is a market-based tool of valuation relying upon a given discount rate, which can be used to determine the capital value of a project as well as explore its feasibility. However, it is fair to say that most appraisals conducted in the development

Table 12.10 Ascertaining net present values using
discount rate of 10 per cent

	Project A (£)	Project B (£)
Outlay	−90 000	−90 000
Proceeds		
Year 1	+30 000	+60 000
Year 2	+50 000	+40 000
Year 3	+60 000	+30 000
Net present value	+23 670	+20 140
Internal rate of return	22.5%	24%

field employ an NPV approach and thereby the market is conditioned by the resultant values and yields.

Risk and uncertainty

So far, all the valuations of development properties used as examples have assumed constant factors in terms of such components as rent, yield, cost, finance and time. In practice, of course, all these are a matter of judgement and are subject to change during the development period. Risk is the very business of property development, and uncertainty the prevailing climate within which development takes place. Over the two or three years gestation period that sees many a development project progress from conception to completion, anticipated rental income at the outset may be adjusted several times in response to changing conditions in the demand for and supply of the kind of premises in question; initial yields in the property investment market may fluctuate according to the general state of the economy or the special circumstances of that particular sector; building costs could increase, either as the result of an overall rise of prices across the construction industry, or because of localized difficulties in the provision of labour or materials; the time taken to execute the building works and let or sell the finished development may be longer than originally expected, because of any one of several reasons relating to planning, design, construction or marketing programmes; and finance charges on borrowed money will be affected by any changes in costs or time, and any agreed alterations to the rate of interest that occur during the development period as a result of external forces. In any event, inflation can wreak havoc upon the best-laid of development plans. Therefore, whereas in more stable times the view could be taken that any changes in development costs would be roughly offset by similar changes in development revenues, that sanguine attitude has been shown to be both misleading and dangerous in what has been a volatile market over the last 20 years.

The traditional method for accommodating the risk of uncertainty in the assessment of the feasibility of projects has been to select a required level of developer's profit that would cover any likely adverse movements in rental income of investment yield, building cost, finance charges or completion time. Typically, high-risk projects would require higher profit levels. Another way of allowing for risk in the construction process is to include an allowance for 'contingencies' expressed as a percentage of building cost.

Over recent years a family of techniques drawn largely from the general field of investment analysis have been adopted and adapted for property development appraisal. The main techniques are sensitivity analysis and probability distribution, but there are a variety of related techniques that explore risk and uncertainty and assist in decision-making in development. Moreover, as a result of the increased use of computers and the greater availability of relevant software packages, the use of these techniques is gaining in popularity.

Sensitivity analysis

It is seldom that a development project can be evaluated adequately on the basis of a single set of figures reflecting but a single set of assumptions. For most projects there are degrees of risk and uncertainty surrounding such assumptions as rent, yield, cost and time. Small changes in any one of these prime variables can often exert a disproportionate effect on the residual solution. This uncertainty as to accurate estimation and sensitivity to change is compounded by the fact that the evaluation or feasibility study must take account of likely changes during the development period. A widely used method of dealing with the inherent risk from such uncertainty is sensitivity analysis. The concept is a simple yet effective one, whereby each of the key variables (rent, yield, cost, time) is altered in turn in an informal and realistic way, so that the developer can test how sensitive the profitability of his project or proposed land bid is to possible changes in those variables. The developer is thereby able to identify the critical variables and take suitable action. If it is rent, for example, a pre-let might be sought; if cost, then close attention is paid to the design brief and building contract; if yield, an assiduous search through the investment market is undertaken for a more competitive buy-out arrangement; if time, then a 'fast track' programme is devised. In any event, the management capability of the developer is enhanced.

Example 6

This study shows how it is possible to explore the effects of changing levels of performance during the development period among such factors as yield, cost, rent, finance and time. To begin with, a simple sensitivity analysis known as a mini–max evaluation is demonstrated, then the sensitivity of a scheme is tested by the extinguishment of profit method and finally the individual components are measured by the percentage change method.

Consider the position of a developer who has paid £500 000 for a plot of land that has planning permission to build a discount cash and carry warehouse of 4000 m² gross. Rents of around £85 per m² overall have been quoted in the vicinity. Initial yields in the region of 8.5 per cent are reported for similar properties. Construction costs are estimated at £500 per m².

Finance can be arranged at about 1.2 per cent per month and the development is considered to take approximately 18 months to complete and let.

It can, therefore, be seen that changes to the various components of rent, yield, cost, finance and time can have profound effects upon the profitability of a scheme when acting in concert.

EXTINGUISHMENT OF PROFIT

Another way of testing the sensitivity of individual components is to gauge the degree to which one factor changing independently can extinguish development profit. This is sometimes known as 'breakdown analysis'. Given the same circumstances as those above rough calculations show that the various components have to change as follows:

- rent from £85 per m² to £67 per m² = nil profit = 21.2% change
- yield from 8.5% to 10.8% = nil profit = 13.3% change
- building costs from £500 per m² to £615 per m² = nil profit = 18.7%
- finance from 1.2% pm to 2.6% pm = nil profit = 220%.

Thus, the scheme can be seen to be relatively sensitive to changes in yield and slightly less so to building cost and rent. However, it is hardly sensitive at all to independent changes in the rate of interest charged on development finance. In reality, of course, these changes would not necessarily take place independently. More likely would be a combination of adjustments, possibly in different directions.

PERCENTAGE CHANGE

Yet a third approach to testing sensitivity is by subjecting the individual components to a percentage and assessing the extent to which the level of profit is affected.

- Rent   10% increase = 32.3% profit on cost
                 10% decrease = 11.7% profit on cost
- Yield   10% increase = 12.7% profit on cost
                 10% decrease = 33.5% profit on cost
- Building costs 10% increase = 14.5%
                 10% decrease = 30.7%
- Finance   10% increase = 20.7%
                 10% decrease = 23.3%

(original profit on cost 22%).

Naturally, the same sensitivities emerge, but at the very least a prospective developer is directed towards those aspects of the scheme that merit the closest attention in respect of optimizing profit. Although the way in which these tests are presented here might appear somewhat simplistic, the advent of computer programs permitting detailed and different adjustments to be made to all the various components enables a development analyst to explore a wide range of possible outcomes according to the information available in

Table 12.11 Minimum–maximum evaluation

I. Median or realistic valuation	£	£
A. Gross development value		
(i) Rental income at £85 per m² on 4000 m²	340 000	
B. (ii) YP in perpetuity at 8.5%	11.76	3 998 401
(iii) Gross development value	2 000 000	3 142 002
(i) Development costs	200 000	
(ii) Building costs at £500 per m² on 4000 m²	263 458	
(iii) Professional fees at 10% of (i)	34 000	
(iv) Finance at 1.2% pm for 18 months × ½	500 000	
(v) Letting at 10% of rent	20 000	
(iv) Land	124 544	
(vii) Acquisition at 4%		
(viii) Finance at 1.2% pm for 18 months		
Total development costs		
C. Development profit		
(i) Sum available in 18 months		856 398
(ii) PV of £1 in 18 months at 1.2% pm		0.807
Profit now		691 113

(iii) Profit on cost $\dfrac{691\,113 \times 100}{3\,142\,002} = 22\%$

(iv) Return on cost $\dfrac{340\,000 \times 100}{3\,142\,002} = 10.8\%$

II. Maximum or optimistic valuation	£	£

Rents predicted at £100 per m²
Initial yield taken at 8%
Building costs estimated at £450 per m²
Finance at 1.0% per month
Development period and letting 15 months

	£	£
A. Gross development value		
B. (i) Rental income at £100 per m²	400 000	5 000 000
(ii) YP in perpetuity at 8%	12.5	2 783 063
(iii) Gross development value	1 800 000	
(i) Development costs	180 000	
(ii) Building costs at £450 per m²	159 359	
(iii) Professional fees at 10%	40 000	
(iv) Finance at 1.0% pm for 15 months × ½	500 000	
(v) Letting at 10% of rent	20 000	
(vi) Land	83 704	
(vii) Acquisition		
(viii) Finance at 1.0% for 15 months		
Total development costs		
C. Development profit		
(i) Sum available in 18 months		2 216 937
(ii) PV of £1 in 18 months at 1.2% pm		0.861
Profit		1 908 783

(iii) Profit on cost $\dfrac{1\,908\,783 \times 100}{2\,783\,063} = 22\%$

(iv) Return on cost $\dfrac{400\,000 \times 100}{2\,783\,063} = 14.4\%$

III. *Minimum or pessimistic valuation*	£	£
Rents predicted at £70 per m²		
Initial yield taken at 9%		
Building costs estimated at £550 per m²		
Finance at 1.4% per month		
Development period and letting 21 months		
A. Gross development value		
B. (i) Rental income at £70 per m²	280 000	
(ii) YP in perpetuity at 9%	11.11	
(iii) Gross development value		3 110 800
(i) Development costs		
(ii) Building costs at £550 per m²	2 200 000	
(iii) Professional fees at 10%	220 000	
(iv) Finance at 1.4% pm for 12 months × ½	410 251	
(v) Letting at 10% of rent	28 000	
(vi) Land	500 000	
(vii) Acquisition	20 000	
(viii) Finance at 1.4% pm for 21 months	176 306	
Total development costs		3 554 557
C. Development profit		
A loss of		(443 757)

a comparatively short time and at little additional cost. This has become known as 'scenario analysis', which, at its simplest, is shown by the optimistic–realistic–pessimistic approach set out in Figure 12.2.

Probability distribution

Where there are significant uncertainties associated with the result of a development project evaluation, it is sometimes useful to list the range of results thought to be likely and to attach to each result an estimate of its probability of happening. The probability of a result may be expressed in terms of frequency of occurrence, that is, as the proportionate number of times the result would be expected to occur in many trial events. In scientific fields, probabilities are estimated either from the statistical records of past events or by conducting experiments using a sampling procedure. This is scarcely possible in the property development industry. Nevertheless, it is possible to present the estimates as a probability distribution that reflects the subjective views formed by the development analyst, or group of analysts, as a result of their knowledge and experience. If, for example, there is a general expectation in the residential development of a rise in the price of new houses over the next year, but observers are uncertain as to the monthly rate at which they might rise, a survey of informed parties could show the following:

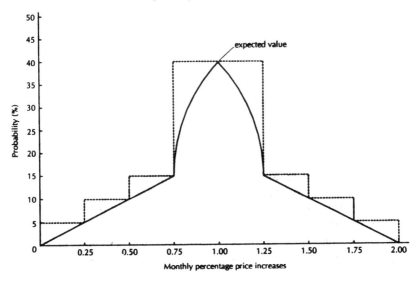

Figure 12.2 Probability distribution.

Monthly rate of price rise	Probability of occurrence
0.25%	5%
0.50%	10%
0.75%	15%
1.00%	40%
1.25%	15%
1.50%	10%
1.75%	5%

The example below shows how results from probability analysis can be used in a residual cashflow valuation where probable changes in costs and values are forecast.

Example 7

Consider the conversion of a terrace of eight Victorian houses, which are vacant and somewhat dilapidated, into a block of 24 luxury flats. The houses are situated in a desirable part of north London and similar flats to those planned are selling for around £100 000 each, but demand is such that prices are confidently expected to rise by about 1 per cent per month over the next year (12.68% pa). Building costs to effect the conversion are estimated at £25 000 a flat but are considered likely to increase by 1.25 per cent per month for the next year (16.08% pa). Building costs are to be evenly spread over a twelve-month development period. It is intended that six flats will be sold in months nine to twelve inclusive. Professional fees are assessed at 10 per cent of building costs, and will be paid by equal instalments of 2.5 per cent a quarter. Agents' and solicitors' fees will be charged at 2 per cent of the sale price of each flat. A development profit of 25 per cent of the sale price is sought and bridging finance is available at 1 per cent a month (12.68% pa).

A prospective developer wishes to know how much he might have to pay for the eight houses now.

Preliminaries

Receipts: six flats sold per month at £100 000 each

Month 9: × 1.0937 + £656 220
Month 10: × 1.1046 + £662 760
Month 11: × 1.1157 + £669 420
Month 12: × 1.1268 + £676 080

Building costs + fees + profits

Total costs are 24 flats at £25 000 = £600 000
Average of £50 000 a month
Increase by 1.25% per month

£

1. 50 625
2. 51 258
3. 351 899 + 10% fees
4. 52 548
5. 53 205
6. 53 870 + 10% fees
7. 54 543
8. 55 225
9. 55 915 + 10% fees + 2% fees + 25% profit
10. 56 614 + 2% fees + 25% profit
11. 57 322 + 2% fees + 25% profit
12. 58 038 + 10% fees + 2% fees + 25% profit

It is assumed that surpluses in the latter few months will be reinvested at the same rate of interest. The resulting residual represents an absolute maximum bid.

The developer might offer £1 million for the eight houses:

Month	Receipts	Costs	Net cashflow	Capital outstanding	Interest
1		(50 625)	(50 625)	(50 625)	(506)
2	656 220	(51 258)	(51 258)	(102 389)	(1024)
3	662 760	(67 277)	(67 277)	(170 690)	(1707)
4	669 420	(52 548)	(52 548)	(224 945)	(2249)
5	676 080	(53 205)	(53 205)	(280 399)	(2804)
6		(69 832)	(69 832)	(353 035)	(3530)
7		(54 543)	(54 543)	(411 108)	(4111)
8		(55 225)	(55 221)	(470 444)	(4704)
9		(249 662)	406 558	(68 509)	(686)
10		(235 559)	427 201	357 925	3579
11		(238 065)	431 355	792 859	7929
12		(257 777)	418 303	1 219 091	

➡

Sum available in 12 months =   £1 219 091

$$\text{Let the value of the houses} = 1.0000\,x$$
$$\text{Acquisition costs at } 4\% = 0.0400\,x$$
$$\text{Finance at } 12.68\% \text{ on } 1.04\,x = 0.1319\,x$$
$$\therefore 1.1719\,x = 1219.091$$
$$\therefore x = 1\,040\,269$$

Simulation

Simulation is a development of the probability distribution using a computer to pick up the variables at random, but within a range according to the probability ascribed to them, and carry out a valuation any number of times (100, 1000, 10 000, . . .). The result is normally a graphical probability distribution.

Summary

Although traditional evaluations of development projects have proved effective and simple to use at the initial stages of appraisal, the vagaries of the market and the availability of useful and inexpensive computer software packages have combined to encourage the widespread adoption of cashflow models of one kind or another. It has been found that this wider use of cashflow techniques has prompted greater examination of not only cost but also the likelihood of incurring liabilities on ancillary costs such as planning fees, party-wall awards, rights of light and other elements that might previously have been ignored or included in a general fee or contingency. It is also more generally accepted that property is not an isolated investment, but one that has to be compared constantly and closely with other investments, resulting in cashflow techniques and risk and uncertainty analyses being more commonly used for evaluating alternative investment opportunities, including property. However, developers still regard some of the more theoretical probability and decision theory techniques as being too 'academic'.

13 Property development finance

It is a truism to state that finance is a critical resource in the process of property development. Nevertheless, when compared to the other resources that combine to produce a development scheme, there often appears to be a disturbing lack of proper understanding about the sources and types of finance for construction and property development, and the arrangements and procedures that accompany them. This is of growing importance, for not only are the margins between revenue and expenditure finer than ever before, but those responsible for providing the bulk of finance to the industry are much more closely concerned, and a great deal better informed, about the management of construction and development projects than they have been in the past. Consequently, they expect and demand development agencies, and those involved in managing their projects for them, to be equally well versed in the evaluation and control of the financial structure and progress of a scheme of development.

A variety of ways exist in which finance for property development can be obtained from a wide array of agencies. The choice normally rests upon the status of the developer and the degree of risk attached to the proposed project. It can almost be stated that every deal dictates its own terms, but for convenience, and to facilitate description, several general areas have been identified below in order to consider the more conventional relationships established between borrowing developers and lending financiers.

In order to explore the increasingly complex subject of property development finance, the chapter is organized as follows:

- sources of development finance
- types of finance
- criteria of funding
- choice of fund
- the financial agreement
- trends and prospects.

Sources of development finance

Most developers will have access to existing sources of finance. Larger companies will usually have multiple funding arrangements with a variety of financial agencies. Nevertheless, the field is becoming so complex and competitive that effective project management is increasingly concerned with the way in which control over a particular scheme will be influenced by the origin and nature of the development finance.

The following selection of possible sources of development finance has no pretensions to be exclusive or exhaustive. However, it does provide an indication of the principal sources that are currently available to the aspiring developer.

Insurance companies and pension funds

Insurance companies and pension funds enjoy a relatively high degree of stability in the availability of funds for investment in development projects, but take a longer-term and more cautious view than most other lenders.

The most popular form of finance provided by the insurance companies and pension funds is the 'forward sale', often coupled with short-term bridging finance at preferential rates. Some funds are also prepared to enter into 'sale and leaseback' arrangements, mortgage advances or an overall borrowing facility.

The lending policies of those financial institutions are characterized by their 'project-based' nature. This means that they tend to exercise extremely tight control over the entire project, including the land acquisition, design, construction and sale or letting programmes. Financial arrangements themselves are almost pre-ordained in terms of yield, interim fixed-rate loans, pre-letting and forward sale. Because of these constraints, a developer might experience problems in maintaining authority, especially once a purchaser or tenant has been found. This situation is further exacerbated where the fund appoints a consultant to monitor development, as happens increasingly.

Another feature is that, because institutions are such big investors in new development, they will usually look for fairly substantial schemes in which to invest. And, not surprisingly, the larger the fund, the larger the average size of scheme financed. But, by far the greatest hurdle a proposed development project must clear before it attracts institutional finance from either an insurance company or a pension fund is that it must be competitive when compared to other forms of investment such as equities, gilts and other forms of property.

Banks

Traditionally, banks are more concerned with the 'asset' base of those to whom they lend rather than the project in hand. The emphasis, therefore, will be more upon monitoring the balance sheet and security cover offered by the borrower. For a developer, this provides a more open and flexible climate in which to work, where such factors as time, cost and quality can be traded off against the clients' ability to generate funds or produce additional collateral. Bank finance, therefore, must be carefully tailored to fit the purpose to which it is applied, and a well designed package must be prepared to meet overdraft, term or equity financial requirements. Sometimes the additional flexibility afforded by more expensive arrangements is worthwhile.

Some clearing or retail banks became over-committed to the property development industry during boom years and found themselves slightly embarrassed by the experience. This encouraged them to step aside for a period. Nevertheless, they show a propensity to return quite quickly to the market once a resurgence is evident, and a similar trait to retreat at the first signs of a slump. Although their policies vary widely, not merely between different houses, but within individual banks, they are generally a great deal more flexible and adventurous than the insurance companies and pension funds, being willing to consider, for example, the refurbishment and redevelopment of older buildings and the development of less conventional commercial properties. One principal reason for this is that a clearing bank is as interested in the business as it is in the property, if not more so. This applies whether the business is the intending occupier or a property development company.

Merchant banks have a reputation for having an even more enterprising approach towards development finance. Being concerned primarily with supplying short- and medium-term money to the development industry, they have evolved packages for linking their short-term lending with other investors' longer-term aspirations. Most leading merchant banks have established their own specialist property investment departments capable of tailoring bespoke financial arrangements to suit the individual needs of a particular developer. In this way, it is by far the most sophisticated sector of the institutional finance market. The more refined yet venturesome stance of the merchant banks is reflected in the high cost of borrowing from them, and their relative opportunism in respect of equity participation.

One of the more lucrative activities recently undertaken by merchant banks is arranging funding packages or syndications, which are then participated out to other banks. Indeed, it has been reported that in this way some banks can make up to half their income from fees.

Trusts and bonds

Within the category of trusts and bonds can be included real estate investment trusts, investment unit trusts, property unit trusts and property bonds. The structure and purposes of these different media for investment is not explained in detail, because from the standpoint of the developer their policies and practices are much the same and largely resemble those of the insurance companies and pension funds. However, their performance has been extremely variable, and their role in the development field is as yet not great.

Internal finance

Even though it is often alleged that the first rule of the developer is 'never use your own money', quite commonly property development agencies either deploy their own surpluses and reserves to support current projects or seek an expansion of their capital base.

Almost by definition, virtually all development undertaken by the major financial institutions, directly or by way of joint venture, can be categorized as internally financed. Similarly, many construction firms acting as developers use their own financial resources to fund projects, as do certain leading business and retail organizations. Funding by prospective owner-occupiers in all sectors of the commercial property market is quite popular. For as long as the capital is available, the risk acceptable and the opportunity cost satisfactory, internal finance has the great attraction of ensuring full recoupment of future rental growth.

A property development company can extend its capital base by increasing its share capital or its loan capital. In simple terms, the holders of the share capital (equity) own the company itself, and the holders of loan capital are creditors of the company. Thus, the holders of share capital are not creditors and have no security, and the holders of loan capital have no rights in the company beyond the receipt of interest and the repayment of the loan in accordance with the terms on which they were issued. The amount a company may borrow by way of loan capital is laid down in the articles of association of the company. There are two principal types of loan capital: debenture and loan stocks. Debentures and debenture stocks are roughly similar to mortgages and are secured either on certain specific assets of the company or as a floating charge over all the company's assets. Secured debts of this kind rank for repayment before unsecured debt in the event of the company being wound up. Unsecured loan stocks, the other form of loan capital, are debts, as their name implies, which are not charged on the company's assets. If the company falls into liquidation, they rank after secured loans along with other general creditors but before the holders of share capital. One kind of unsecured loan stock carries with it the right to convert into share capital on pre-arranged terms and within a limited period: this is known as convertible unsecured loan stock and it comes with a variety of conversion rights. A final form of fixed income company finance is preference shares, which do not form part of the loan capital, and on a winding-up do not rank for repayment until all creditors have been paid in full. Again, there are various types of preference shares, such as 'cumulative', where the right to a dividend can be carried forward from one year to another; 'non-cumulative', where once a dividend is passed for one year the right to receive it is lost; and 'participating' preference shares, where there are rights to share in profits above the fixed dividend.

The share capital held as ordinary shares is usually referred to as the equity. Equity in this sense means that which remains after rights of creditors and mortgagees are cleared and, although different forms of share capital exist, most public property companies do not have very complex share capital structures. The risk-bearing nature of equities is reflected in the 'gearing' of a company, that is the ratio of loan or fixed income capital to share or equity capital. In a period of growth and profitability, in a highly geared company, where loan capital is proportionately greater than share capital, holders of ordinary shares gain commensurately. In bad times, the reverse is true, and profits can easily be wiped out.

A detailed examination of how capital can be raised on the stock market is beyond the scope of this text. Suffice it to say that there are two types of new issue by which this can be achieved. First, the bringing to the market of companies that have not previously been quoted. Second, the raising of additional capital by companies already quoted. The former will normally be effected by an 'offer for sale', whereby an institution such as a merchant bank buys a block of shares from the existing shareholders and offers them to the general public at a fixed price; by a 'placing', where an institution may buy the stock or shares and arrange for the placing of the issue with various funds or companies known to be interested; an 'introduction' when a company already has many individual shareholdings and Stock Exchange quotation simply provides a public market for shares that previously could only be dealt in privately; or a 'tender', which is exactly the same as an offer for sale except that the price of the shares is not fixed in advance. One way in which companies already quoted can raise additional internal funds without increasing their debt charge is the issue of further equity capital. This is normally done by way of a 'rights issue', that is, the issue of shares to existing shareholders at a concession.

The performance of the stock market in the early years of the twenty-first century has prompted some property companies to 'de-list', i.e. buy back their shares and withdraw from the stock market, because their view is that the value of their property assets is not effectively reflected in the value of the company's shares.

As with most financial matters, the question of timing is important, not merely in respect of the general climate for borrowing but also the class of capital to be selected. In times of depressed equity prices, a rights issue is normally to be avoided and, if interest rates are at a reasonable level, a prior charge to increase loan capital is usually preferable. Conversely, when equity prices are high, leading property companies might be best advised to make a rights issue rather than increase their loan capital. However, it must be remembered that, although substantial sums can be raised from the market, the costs involved may be considerable, comprising not only the legal and valuation fees but also the costs of underwriting the issue, producing a prospectus, advertising and stockbrokers' charges.

It is in the field of internal or corporate finance that most innovation has been shown by property development companies over recent years. The range of devices, instruments and techniques has appeared endless, with many American mainstream corporate financing practices being adapted and adopted in global financial markets. The amount of 'commercial paper' issued by property development companies since the late 1980s has been enormous, largely because of its low cost, high flexibility and simplicity to the borrower, and its competitive yield, liquidity and range of maturities to the lender. However, the inherent dangers of such promissory activity were apparent in a period of worldwide recession during the first half of the 1990s.

The construction industry

Development finance is commonly supplied by the major building firms, either directly from their own cash reserves or through sources with whom they have a funding facility. From a pure funding point of view, this form of finance can be very attractive, because the loan will normally be 100 per cent, to include the cost of land acquisitions, all building costs and fees. Speculative work will also be considered, and the debt rolled up at a small mark-up on the cost of finance to the construction company. From the stance of the developer, however, it is very important to be assured that the right contractor, on the right building contract, is appointed to work to the right price. There is always the danger that the authority of the developer and his project manager is diminished where the contractor is also the funder.

Conversely, this familiarity with the property development industry can often be an advantage and help limit risk. Such collaboration is often the result of a limited loan, say 70 per cent of cost, on the part of a bank, and the need by the developer to fund the shortfall through the good offices of an established construction company. Increasingly, this form of finance takes the form of a joint venture between the two parties. On the other hand, the degree of accountability on the part of the contractor during the construction stage and upon completion is likely to be heightened, and the extent of financial control throughout the building period much tighter than normally experienced. A construction company, however, will normally need to see a clearly identifiable exit in the form of a long-term take-out by a financial institution.

Property companies

A less familiar means of obtaining short-term finance is through one of the larger property investment and development companies. This can be by direct loan or by guarantee, and the principal motive is usually a desire to participate in the equity of the project. Apart from an erosion of profit, another disadvantage is that, as far as the developer is concerned, his funds are coming from a source thoroughly conversant with all aspects of the development process, who is likely to exercise an unusual degree of scrutiny.

Government

In a period of continuing worldwide public sector spending constraint, governments find themselves with little enough money for their own national and municipal development projects, let alone to be in a position to fund the private sector. Nevertheless, grants and loans are made available in certain circumstances, and projects are supported in other ways.

The Private Finance Initiative (PFI) is a long-term concession used by the UK government to capture private capital to fund public projects. Instead of following the usual practice of borrowing money, the government commissions services, not buildings or other works, and the contractor (usually a consortium) carries on providing that service for a pre-defined period of time (frequently more than 20 years). Thus public projects are paid for out of annual revenue rather than capital budgets.

Most straightforward is the direct provision of total development finance, which is usually undertaken to promote ventures that would not otherwise attract commercial funds. Government can also provide financial assistance to new or established businesses through loans for land and buildings. A method employed in many industrial development projects has been the 'headleasing' arrangement, whereby a government agency takes a lease from the developer to guarantee rental income and then sublets the floorspace to occupiers.

It may be that a government agency acts as a conduit to other funds. Many cities in various countries now offer incentives to encourage firms to invest in designated areas to promote economic and physical regeneration. This includes guaranteeing long-term loans for the conversion, improvement, modification or extension of existing buildings. Some local government authorities have also set up their own enterprise boards to stimulate economic activity. This often includes an extensive programme of property development and refurbishment projects, either independently or more usually in partnership with the private sector.

Another way in which a local government authority can participate in the overall funding of a scheme, without committing actual cash resources, is by providing land already in their ownership. Similarly, although there is a cost to the authority, the supply of certain kinds of directly associated site infrastructure may often be seen as a financial contribution to a development scheme, and treated accordingly in any negotiations surrounding the apportionment of profit.

There is really no limit to the potential sources available to borrow money for property development. Trading companies, financial services firms, charities, churches and wealthy individuals, either alone or in consortia with others, are but a few. Given sufficient time, therefore, a developer could unearth many sources of finance. Indeed, considerable time and effort can often be wasted by directing attention towards inappropriate sources, and it is surprising what an imperfect market the development industry is in respect of central pool and comprehensive understanding of sources of finance.

Types of finance

Traditionally, the different types of development finance have been examined within the classification of short, medium and long term. Although this remains a perfectly acceptable approach, it tends to oversimplify what has become a more sophisticated and complex market. Indeed, so refined are some funding arrangements that it is increasingly difficult to place them in any particular category, except their own. However, the following description attempts to outline the main methods currently employed in the financing of development.

Development finance

Development finance is also known as building, bridging or construction finance and is used to describe the short-term interest-bearing loans made for periods of anything up to about three to four years, covering all or part of the costs of development. These costs will include land, acquisition, building works, professional fees, marketing, finance itself and any contingencies involved in the development process. Customarily, there have been two main sources for such funds, the commercial banks and the merchant banks, but over recent years other sources have been tapped and other methods of funding employed.

The banks, however, have two basic requirements. First, that the developer must show that they will be able to meet the interest charges, which will usually be 'rolled-up' or 'warehoused' until the development is completed. Second, they must show that they will be able to repay, on time, the principal sum borrowed. This latter requirement implies in most cases the availability of long-term investment funds, out of which the short-term finance may be repaid. The linking of short- and long-term finance must normally be firmly established to the satisfaction of the lender before the development finance is approved. In some circumstances, it is possible that the lending bank might be prepared to assume that long-term financing will be forthcoming before the development is completed, or that the scheme will be sold outright on completion for investment or occupation, and advance the construction finance unencumbered by a forward sale commitment.

As previously intimated, the commercial and merchant banks tend to have slightly different attitudes towards development financing. The former frequently require security over and above that derived from the project in question; they exact a rate of interest 2–4 per cent above base lending rate, depending upon the standing of the borrower; they do not usually demand an equity share; and they provide a procedure that is a relatively simple and standard format, so that the loan is issued quite quickly and with comparative ease. The latter, the merchant banks, in most instances only require the development presented to them as security, but invariably charge a higher rate of interest at about 4–6 per cent above base rate or, more usually, seek to share in the equity of the scheme. In return for the additional cost of the finance, however, the developer will probably find a merchant bank more enterprising than a commercial bank in bearing risk and structuring a loan.

Increasingly, short-term development finance in the institutional market is being provided as part of a complete funding package. A fund will normally acquire a site once planning permission has been obtained and will advance development costs throughout the construction period against architects' certificates and other relevant invoices. Interim finance, as it has become known, is rolled up on the various advances and is payable at an agreed rate that invariably lies mid-way between the prevailing short-term borrowing rate and the ultimate investment yield. Both parties can be seen to gain from such an arrangement. The developer enjoys cheaper finance and the purchaser is afforded more control over the design and progress of development.

Mortgages

For many years up until the early 1960s, the fixed interest mortgage was the predominant form of long-term development finance. Rapid and prolonged inflation then drove lenders away from mortgages towards methods of investment that allowed them some level of inflation proofing through participation in rental growth. From the early 1970s onwards, high interest rates discouraged borrowers from pressing for long-term mortgage advances on fixed rates. The late 1980s and early 1990s witnessed the return of long-term fixed interest mortgage finance to the property development market. Since then, with inflation continuing to run at relatively low levels and interest rates at their lowest point for 40 years, fixed interest mortgage finance is likely to remain readily available, at least for the time being.

The loan term will usually run between 10 and 25 years depending upon the needs of the borrower and the nature of the development project, and the maximum level of advance invariably will be limited to two-thirds of the agreed value of the project acting as security. For other than prime schemes it will often be less, and here lies the biggest drawback in mortgage finance, for a developer will often have to find substantial funds from his own resources if the project in question does not meet certain standard criteria in respect of design and letting.

Unless there are immediate and reliable prospects of an uplift in rents, say within a year of the draw-down of the mortgage facility, then the lending institution will wish to be assured that the initial income produced by the development is sufficient to cover the loan servicing costs. The rate of interest attaching to a loan is usually determined at the date of release of funds by reference to a margin of 1.75–2.25 per cent over the prevailing gross redemption yield on a comparable gilt-edged security on completion. Interest is mostly payable quarterly or half-yearly in arrears.

With most mortgages there will be a choice between interest-only and interest plus capital repayments. Generally, it is only the shorter mortgages of around 10 years that are on an interest-only basis; the longer-term loans of 15–25 years normally require at least 25 or 50 per cent of the capital to be repaid during the term, although they may often begin with a five-year moratorium to allow for rental growth to take place, thereby making the debt easier to service. It is commonly accepted that the annuity-certain method of repaying or reducing a mortgage is probably the fairest and least expensive, both in real terms and as far as cashflow is concerned, as it involves an effective sinking fund under which the benefit of a compound interest rate equal to the mortgage rate is received. Moreover, some companies operate a variable rate system. Although this might seemingly be a more volatile and potentially expensive way to pay off a loan, it will usually be operated on an 'even spread' basis, whereby the capital repayments are calculated at a median that, if market interest rates are lower for most of the term, means the loan will be repaid early, and vice versa.

Although mortgages are commonly considered to be medium- to long-term funding arrangements, it is sometimes possible to obtain interim finance against a limited number of architects' certificates as building works progress, in which case adjustments might have to be made to allow for fluctuating interest rates during construction. In any event, this kind of facility would only be countenanced with a pre-let to a good covenant on acceptable terms.

On the question of whether or not a developer should take up long-term fixed interest moneys, one leading specialist in arranging property finance has summarized the situation as follows:

> Our advice to borrowers has always been never to rely on one particular type of finance or one particular lender. A mix of different types of finance is essential to the well-balanced portfolio and a combination of part variable-rate and part fixed-rate mortgage monies will enable the borrower to take advantage of any further fall in interest rates while protecting against an increase. What can be said with reasonable

confidence is that the present interest scenario presents an excellent opportunity for borrowers to switch a significant part of their present funding to, or to organize new acquisitions on, a fixed interest rate basis.

(Burgess 1982)

As with all other forms of funding, however, mortgage finance has become increasingly sophisticated. For example, repayment patterns can be straight-term, amortized, partially amortized, graduated, renegotiable, shared appreciation or reverse annuity. Interest rate provisions can be straight rate, straight rate with escalator, or variable rate. And the types of security given might relate to what are known as deeds of trust, purchase money mortgages, open-end mortgages, participating mortgages, junior mortgages, and package or blanket mortgages. It has also been reported that financial institutions have started to provide funding in the form of debenture issues as opposed to straight mortgages. A mortgage debenture issue is a method of raising corporate finance whereby the institution makes a loan as a debenture secured against the developer's entire property portfolio. The return from the debenture may be fixed, or yield a 'stepped coupon' linked to the rental value of the property. At the end of the loan period the capital is repayable as a lump sum. This type of loan is known in banking circles as a 'bullet' loan. A variation upon this theme is the 'balloon' mortgage, where the coupon, incorporating both capital and interest repayments, increases and then decreases throughout the duration of the loan.

Two recently popular hybrid varieties of mortgage designed to match the requirements of lenders to the needs of borrowers are the 'convertible' mortgage and the 'participating' mortgage. These are employed where a borrowing developer is seeking to improve the conditions relating to the loan to value ratio, or the rate of interest, by surrendering a portion of equity or profit. Both the convertible and the participating mortgages are debts secured by way of a full charge over the property concerned and a share in the equity of the scheme at some predetermined point in the future. The convertible mortgage will continue to have an interest in the equity of the development following repayment of the principal and any interest secured under the mortgage. This interest will continue to exist until the agreed profit share is received by the lender at some future time. The participating mortgage is similar, in that the lender has an interest in the equity, but the sharing must be made by a certain point in time. The value of the 'equity charge' is usually predetermined, either by amount or by formula, and, whether or not the profits have been realized, the lender's share becomes due. These two instruments are said to be particularly useful in a development scenario where the lender can share in the profits for a higher level of risk (Shayle 1992).

Sale and leaseback

Over the years, the sale and leaseback has been a familiar form of long-term financing in the prime development market. Particularly popular in the 1960s and early 1970s, it returned to favour in the late 1980s and early 1990s. In essence, it involves a developer selling the freehold interest in the completed development to an investor while taking back a long lease at a rent that equates to the initial yield reflected in the selling price. The developer then aims to sublet the property, preferably at a rent in excess of that paid to the investor, thereby creating an immediate profit rent. Sometimes the freehold is owned by a third party, often a local authority, in which case a similar transaction known as a 'lease and leaseback' can be conducted, with the investor buying a long lease of, say, 125 years and the developer taking back a sublease of a slightly shorter term.

An alternative approach frequently adopted when the developer is hoping to trade the scheme (that is, to complete let and sell it), is the 'leaseback guarantee'. By this arrangement, if the development is not let within, say, six months of practical completion, the developer receives a balancing payment from the fund, representing his profit in return for providing a leaseback guarantee at an agreed base rent. This base rent is usually the same as the rental income estimated at the outset of the scheme, and provision is made for the guarantee to be extinguished once a letting to an occupational tenant has been achieved. If a rent in excess of the base rent is eventually obtained, the agreement will normally provide for that extra rent, often known as 'overage', to be capitalized at a more favourable yield to the fund, usually at half the year's purchase applied to the base rent. In this way, the fund is able to share in the growth of rents between commencement and ultimate letting.

Returning to the conventional sale and leaseback, in which the developer is retaining an interest in the project, the most important part of the negotiation between the developer and the fund is the apportionment of rental growth at review. Few funding agreements are now concluded on the basis that the developer receives only an exposed 'top slice' income once the fund has taken a guaranteed 'bottom slice' return. Most arrangements these days involve some kind of 'side-by-side' or 'vertical' leaseback, whereby the two parties share the equity in predetermined proportions at, say, three- or five-year review. They also usually include a device in the contract known as a 'participation clause', which, like the overage adjustment mentioned above, allows the parties to share in any increase in rental income that is achieved at letting over and above the original estimate of likely rents. The possible permutations by which the returns from property development may be divided between the developer and the fund are many and varied. Different slices of income can be treated in different ways at different times. Inevitably, the eventual contract will be the result of negotiation and compromise, with the outcome depending upon the financial leverage and bargaining powers of the respective parties to the transaction. Who needs whom most is the real key.

One disadvantage of the straightforward sale and leaseback is that the developer is often left with an interest that is difficult to dispose of or refinance except at a value determined by a low capitalization factor. One way of overcoming this disability is to enter into a 'reverse leaseback', in which the developer retains a freehold interest at a peppercorn rent and grants a long lease to the fund under which a reviewable ground rent eventually becomes payable on full letting, but one that is subject to a prior charge in favour of the fund in respect of their share. The legal interest held by the developer is thereby made more marketable.

The principal advantage usually claimed for the lessee or vendor is that it frees up capital at a lower cost and for a longer period than would otherwise be available; it can provide 100 per cent financing for a project; the funds released can be used to better advantage or at a higher return; problems of refinancing can be avoided; there can be an appreciation of the leasehold value; it might be possible to pass on certain management responsibilities; retention of use or occupancy can be achieved; and there might be certain tax advantages. In the same way, the main advantages to the lessor or purchaser are said to be that the term of investment is long and thereby early repayment exposure is reduced; it provides an opportunity to invest in large amounts, which reduces management costs; most arrangements, by definition, provide a good covenant; the rate of return after amortization of the principal of the investment is normally relatively high; control over the management of the asset is much higher than with a conventional mortgage; and there may be a substantial remainder of value after the expiry of the lease. There may also be tax advantages to one or both parties.

Forward sale

As mentioned above, most short-term financiers will look for a guarantee that there is an arrangement with a long-term investor or a prospective owner-occupier to 'take out' their interest when the project is completed and often occupied. Contractual details regarding the precise sale date, effect of delays in building work, void lettings and rental growth during development will naturally be the subject of negotiation between the various parties. An outright forward sale along these lines takes place, of course, where a developer is trading and not investing. In such circumstances, the main concern of the long-term investor is to secure a guarantee of rent upon completion, and two principal methods are commonly adopted: the 'profit erosion' method and the 'priority yield' method.

Profit erosion

Also known as the 'profit dissipation' method of funding, profit erosion is a form of rental guarantee arrangement whereby the developer wishes to trade-on a scheme. Instead of taking up a leaseback or entering into a lease-back guarantee if the building is not let within, say, six months of practical completion, the developer stakes his profit, no more, against rent and other outgoings. The developer's profit as a balancing payment is placed on a joint deposit account, with interest accruing to the developer, and the fund draws down the base rent and other outgoings at quarterly intervals.

Once this balancing payment has run out, the developer ceases to have an interest and the fund assumes responsibility for letting the scheme. However, if letting takes place at more than the agreed base rent, the overage provision mentioned before generally applies for a limited period as an incentive to the developer.

Profit erosion schemes are held to be particularly useful where a scheme is large and the developer is either of insufficient strength to offer a satisfactory rental guarantee or, more likely, is of sufficient strength but unwilling to enter into a full leaseback agreement. The objectives of both the fund and the developer can be met in this way so long as sufficient rental cover is provided. Two years is generally thought to be an absolute minimum, and in a difficult letting market four might be more appropriate. In any event, given the greater risk borne by the fund, a slightly higher yield of say 0.25 per cent for prime properties is frequently required.

Priority yield

Priority yield is another variant on the financial sharing theme in trading situations where a fund is looking for a given yield on a development of say 6 per cent and is not prepared to share in anything below that level. If the developer produces a completed development showing an initial return of 7 per cent, then the fund will capitalize this extra point as an additional profit to the developer. Over 7 per cent, and some form of participation would be agreed, usually on an equal share basis.

Priority yield fundings are especially popular when a project of development is difficult to plan in respect of time and cost for one reason or another. It brings the developer and the fund into a close partnership where each party accepts a degree of risk against the potential profit inherent in a speculative development. There is also a considerable incentive for the developer to keep costs down and to complete and let the project as quickly as possible.

Project management fee

Another method of funding relationship becoming increasingly popular is the 'project management fee' basis. This is used primarily as a method of funding for major development schemes where the size, impact on the market and time taken to complete and let the premises are such that neither party would wish for anything less than that the funding institution to bear the full risk. In most circumstances the developer would have identified the potential for development and investigated the planning and market conditions. They may even have taken out options on the land and obtained outline planning permission. Upon successful introduction to a fund, a separate fee will usually be agreed. Subsequently, the developer simply receives a fee for project managing the development, which can either be calculated as a fixed percentage of construction cost or geared to the eventual profit of the scheme. Most project management fee arrangements tend to combine both elements, so that a basic minimum fee is agreed as a fixed sum and a proportion of profit over a certain level is offered as a kind of performance incentive.

General funding facility

'General funding facility' refers to an arrangement whereby an overall financial facility is provided to a development company and is not specifically related to any one project. It is secured across the company assets and it enables the developer to carry out a series of projects working within a pre-set lending limit. The loan is normally repayable over a period of up to 40 years, thereby keeping repayments during the early years, when yields may be very low, to a minimum. A comparatively new kind of development finance is the 'drop lock loan', which is also a form of general funding facility. In general it allows a developer to have access to predetermined amounts of money over a given period of time. The loans may be for terms of anything between 10 and 35 years, and the period during which a developer may exercise his option to use them between three and seven years. The special feature of a drop lock loan is that, if prevailing interest rates fall below a predetermined base rate during the option period, then the option can be exercised in reverse against the developer who is obliged to take up an agreed tranche or all of the loan at that rate, which is then 'locked' for the entire term. If the developer chooses to take up the loan before the predetermined interest rate is reached, he will pay a variable rate linked to that base rate until it falls to the predetermined level, when it is converted into a fixed rate for the rest of the term.

Of increasing popularity in recent years has been the unsecured multiple option financing facility, whereby large loans are made available to property development companies on a broad basis for fixed, but usually extendable, periods of time. One bank will normally act as arranger and facility agent, with anything from between six and 30 other institutions supplying or guaranteeing the loan as managers or co-managers. Multi-option financing facilities encompass a variety of alternative financing methods within one package. Short-, medium- and long-term lending can be related in a versatile manner. Syndicated loans, multi-currency arrangements, commercial paper loans and bankers' guaranteed loans can all be selected and mixed, together with choices of swaps, fixed or floating interest rates, bonds with warrants and the like (Pugh 1992). In this way the borrower can choose the best financing package to meet his individual requirements. The loan size is usually large, from around £60 million to £400 million, with £150 million being the average. And maturities normally range from two to 10 years, with seven years being most popular (Savills 1990).

Term loans

Term loans provide a development company with the facility to borrow a certain amount from a bank or syndicate of banks, which may be drawn upon immediately or in stated amounts throughout the life of the loan. The loans are always made at rates of interest in line with prevailing market rates during the period of the loan. Such loans will specify the date or dates and manner by which the amount advanced by the banks is to be repaid.

Term loans can also carry the option to convert into a limited recourse loan, where the funds are for a project that will produce income soon after completion. In some cases, the interest rates charged on the loan will fall to a pre-specified level when the property under development has been pre-let. Term loans cannot be called in for repayment before the agreed date, which gives them a distinct advantage over overdrafts. Within the property development sector, most term loans are for amounts of less than £100 million, although loans of up to £350 million are not uncommon.

Maturities range from one to seven years, with the two to five-year range being the most popular (Savills 1990).

Overdrafts

In familiar terms, an overdraft occurs when a customer of a bank draws on an account to the extent that he falls into a negative balance. Company overdrafts may be for any size, provided the bank is satisfied by the asset backing and credit standing of the company concerned. Interest on overdrafts is charged at a pre-agreed rate or at the bank's currently published lending rate. Pre-arrangements regarding the interest rate are normally possible only for large corporate customers.

The main disadvantage of overdraft facilities is that repayment may be called for at any time and without notice, and could, therefore, come at a bad time when the company's liquid resources are low. Conversely, the principal advantage of an overdraft facility is that the borrower can repay the whole or part of the debit balance on his account at any time, also without giving notice. This contrasts with a term loan of a fixed amount, where the bank is not obliged to accept repayment before the agreed date, or may charge a penalty for so doing.

In the property development field, overdraft facilities are normally used only as supplementary funds to a principal loan, for exploratory work at the appraisal stage, for financing options to purchase land or for contingency payments.

Standby commitments

Standby commitments arise where a developer needs a temporary loan while seeking a permanent commitment for development finance from another lender. Unlike a take-out commitment in the form of a forward sale, neither the borrower nor lender expects the standby facility to become binding. The developer generally hopes in due course to borrow on more favourable terms elsewhere, but wants to begin development as soon as possible. Often, standby commitments are never concluded and funds never deployed; rather, the facility is used to enhance the confidence of a potential permanent lender in a proposed project. It has been stated, however, that few permanent lenders of development finance are willing to make loans against a standby commitment alone, unless there are very special circumstances (Bruggeman & Stone 1981).

Syndicated loans

The early 1990s witnessed the emergence of the 'syndicated' loan, sometimes known as 'project' or 'consortia' funding. Often arranged by way of tender panels and normally only appropriate for very large schemes, the essential requirement will usually be a blue chip covenant of considerable means, reflected in a substantial asset base, profitability and turnover. This may not be found in the developer client, but with prospective occupiers prepared to lend their covenant to the scheme. The number of parties involved, with their separate interests, can therefore pose problems of authority and control for the developer, as well as time and expense.

Nevertheless, the concept of the syndicated loan has come into prominence because it offers greater flexibility with regard to currencies and interest rates. Other advantages have been said to include flexible maturity, amortization schedules and credit structures, with less rigid documentation requirements than for a securities issue (Savills 1990).

Securitization and unitization

Loan syndication has been supplemented by the securitization of debt, whereby the more conventional loans made by financial institutions are replaced by smaller monetary instruments that can be traded in the investment market. At the time of writing there has been several years of debate about the potential for 'unitization', which is very much the same thing as securitization. The idea is to provide a financial vehicle that facilitates the funding of large single development projects, increases liquidity in the market, enables the smaller investor to participate in the market, increases the flow of capital to the property industry, achieves homogeneity of the market by divisibility, permits wider ownership of property, and increases market information and public awareness. Various issues emerge from the debate concerning such matters as valuation, the size and membership of the market, potential conflicts of interest, the management of the property, liquidity, marketability and taxation. Only time will tell how successful will be the notion of unitization.

One of the principal problems with securitized (and unitized) property vehicles has been that of double taxation: the management company pays tax on the rental income from the property and then the shareholder also pays tax on the dividend income from their investment. This means that if dividends are paid out of rental income it is effectively taxed twice. Real Estate Investment Trusts (REITS) are tax-efficient investment vehicles from the US; there is limited tax payable if the majority of the income and gains are distributed. Such trusts have been investing heavily in UK property. However, at the time of writing, the UK government has no plans to allow similar vehicles to be available on the UK investment market.

Non-recourse and limited recourse loans

Non-recourse and limited recourse loans seek to restrict the lending institution to recovering any unpaid debt from the property in question rather than the borrowing developer. From the developer's point of view it obviously limits the risk, minimizing exposure while maximizing profit, and allows him to structure the transaction so that it is 'off balance sheet' through a joint venture company. From the lender's viewpoint he can expect higher fees and wider margins. Nevertheless, in reality, no loans are truly non-recourse as such, for the bank will impose conditions relating to the front-end injection of equity finance into the project by the developer as well as seeking guarantees against cost overruns and completion date. These facilities are only made to property companies with a proven track record in the management of development projects. The average size of non-recourse or limited recourse loans is in the region of £100 million, with a maturity of between two and seven years.

Joint ventures and partnership

Property companies without an adequate financial base to enable them to fund and carry out their own developments often have recourse to joint venture or partnership schemes. Likewise, public and private landowners lacking construction finance and development expertise have frequently entered into similar arrangements.

The advantages of joint ventures are generally obvious and do not need much explanation. However, they can be summarized as follows:

* to spread risk among participating parties
* to enable the development of large projects
* to attract market knowledge and development expertise
* to secure sufficient development finance.

In like manner, the main disadvantages are:

* control over the development project is dissipated
* disposal of a particular interest in a partnership scheme is more difficult
* the value of a part interest is invariably less than the proportionate share in the whole
* there may be double taxation.

Before embarking on a joint venture, the participants will need to identify the most appropriate form of structure to be used. This will normally depend upon the following:

* the number of participants
* the nature of the proposed scheme and the relative risks inherent in development
* the timescale involved, and the policy towards disposal or retention
* how the venture is to be financed, and the desired mix of debt and equity
* responsibility for losses and limitation on liability
* the tax position of the respective parties
* the way in which profits are to be distributed
* any relevant statutory legislation
* the ability and ease of disposing of interests by the parties involved
* any special balance sheet requirements.

There are various legal vehicles by which a joint venture can be effected. These include a trust for sale, a partnership agreement, a limited partnership, a joint venture company and a property unit trust. There are also potential investors looking to collaborate with reputable property development companies. These include local government authorities with land and planning powers but no money; statutory undertakers with surplus land;

trading companies and business enterprises looking to participate in the development of property, either for their own occupation or as an investment with shared risk; overseas investors on a learning curve for a particular market or location; life companies and pension funds with money but little expertise; and high net worth individuals. It has been stated that all of the above tend to be looking for the 'perfect development property', well let, high yielding and with potential growth. Most of them wish to enter into a 50:50 deal as equal partners, with each party putting up approximately 15 per cent of the equity and the joint venture vehicle borrowing the rest over a five-year term (Bramson 1992).

Venture capital

A phenomenon that has emerged since the mid-1980s is that of 'venture capital'. This can mean different things to different people, but is usually employed to describe those sources of finance willing to invest in higher-risk proposals in return for equity participation and a say in project control. The venture capitalist delves much more deeply into a proposition than does a lending banker, and will often seek a close involvement in the management of a project. Venture capital is also expensive, both in arrangement and through profit sharing. The 'hands-on' approach can constrain a developer, and it is preferable to try to obtain a 'layered' financial package commencing with bank finance, followed by any other loans or grants available and topped off with the venture capital tranche.

Mezzanine finance

With mezzanine finance, a developer seeks the assistance of a second, 'mezzanine', financier. Some prime debt lenders may consider providing a limited facility in excess of 70 per cent of value in consideration of a higher interest rate, or a single fee being taken out of the sale proceeds. It is more likely, however, that the top slice of funds will come from a separate specialist lender. These mezzanine financiers have in the past lent up to 100 per cent of the balance of funds required, but now they more usually look for an input from the borrower, in the form of either cash or collateral security. Nonetheless, they are still able to achieve effective gearing of around 85–90 per cent. There are also occasions when the prime debt financier is not prepared to provide as much as 70 per cent of value and the mezzanine financier may again top up the hardcore facility. This form of arrangement is also sometimes known as 'wrap-around', 'junior' or 'subordinate' financing.

Because there are obviously greater risks involved in providing this top slice loan, the mezzanine financier will seek a return that reflects a share in the anticipated profit from the development. Some lenders will insist on taking shares in the development company, whereas others prefer to take a second charge on the project, although the collateral security will rank behind the prime debt financier. The amount of profit share required will naturally depend upon the individual circumstances of the project concerned. The mezzanine financier tends to become more involved with both the developer and the project, often employing a team of property professionals, which can give considerable comfort to the prime debt financier, because in looking after its own interests it will also protect theirs (Berkley 1991).

Commercial mortgage indemnity policies

The use of commercial mortgage indemnity policies (CMIPs) has increased significantly since the late 1980s. Originally used in the residential market, these policies provide a lender with indemnity cover for sums advanced between their normal gearing limits of 70 per cent up to a level of 85 per cent and sometimes even higher. When used properly these policies provide an invaluable tool to lenders, allowing them to bridge the gap between income and interest rates on investments such as development projects, which are not initially self-funding.

It is generally agreed, however, that these CMIPs were greatly abused, and some insurers are now facing considerable claims on development loans. The problem being that these insurers failed to differentiate between the risks involved in indemnifying a comparatively secure investment loan and the risks involved in taking a top slice position on a development proposal. The returns to the insurer were simply pitched too low. Nevertheless, the lessons have been learned and, although CMIPs are more difficult to come by on development schemes, where they are available they are managed in a much more professional and risk-conscious way.

Deep discount and zero coupon bonds

A deep discount bond (DDB) is a debt instrument issued at significantly less than its par value and which is repayable in full on its redemption. It may also carry a low rate of interest, with the lender being compensated by the high capital repayment at the maturity date. A zero coupon bond (ZCB) is similar, but no interest is ever paid during the loan period. The discount is, therefore, like the rolling-up of interest at a full rate until the redemption date. There is also the stepped coupon bond (SCB) whereby the coupon, or interest rate, rises at fixed intervals over the period of the loan by specified amounts. These different versions of the bond may be combined to form variations on the same theme.

The general terms for the issue of such bonds can be summarized as follows:

- maturity between five and 10 years
- an interest rate margin of 2–4 per cent over base lending rate for development projects
- fees for arrangement, underwriting and participation totalling around 2 per cent of the loan
- security normally in the range of 70–75 per cent of loan to value, using the full redemption value of the bond
- income cover of at least one times, and preferably one and a half
- a good covenant
- borrower responsible for all associated costs
- early redemption penalties.

Although comparatively rare instruments in the property development finance fields, DDBs, ZCBs and SCBs offer attractive rewards in terms of cashflow, running yield and redemption value, as well as certain tax advantages. It has also been suggested that the use of DDBs and their derivatives could have a role in assisting the development of a securitized property investment market (Shayle 1992).

Hedging techniques

Hedging techniques are used by a borrower to 'insure' against adverse interest rate and currency trends. There are a variety of such techniques, the most common of which are:

- 'Swaps', where a borrower is allowed to raise capital in one market, and can swap either one interest rate structure for another, or swap the liability for the maturity value and interest from one currency to another. In other words, the simultaneous exchange between two parties of one security or currency for another where there is mutual benefit to both.
- 'Caps' and 'floors', which are derived from the options and futures market, and guarantee that during the loan period the interest rate paid by the borrower will not rise above (cap) or fall below (floor) a set limit.
- 'Collars', where an agreement is reached combining a cap and a floor putting both a maximum and a minimum level on the interest rate paid by the borrower. A premium is normally paid by the borrower for a cap and by the lender for a floor.
- 'Droplocks', as already mentioned, this facility enables the borrower to change the loan from a variable to a fixed rate of interest for the remainder of the loan period once long-term interest rates reach a predetermined level.
- 'Forward rate agreements', where a borrower can sell the currency in which he has obtained a loan forward by say 12 months in order to lock into a more favourable exchange rate.

Criteria for funding

In most circumstances developers will have well established relationships with the funds from whom they seek development finance. Where it is the first time, a developer approaches a particular source of finance, understandably close scrutiny will be given to the property company as well as the proposal. For new developers setting out to undertake a first project, it is virtually an impossible task to attract financial support from conventional sources, unless on an individual basis they have successfully managed similar schemes for someone else.

In examining the criteria by which development propositions are judged, the following section is based on an established developer making the first approach to a fresh source of funds from a major financial institution.

Past performance

The starting point is bound to be the track record of the developer who is making an application for funding. However subjective the appraisal may be, the financier will probably form a fairly immediate opinion about the developers; in particular, if they were active during the downturn of a previous property cycle, it will reveal quite a lot about their judgement. Increasingly, it is expected that developers should themselves exhibit an expertise in the actual process of development, and the demonstration of true project management skills within the development company is now almost a prerequisite. Moreover, it is not sufficient for those skills merely to exist within the company. It must clearly be shown that they will be fully applied to the scheme in question, for even the most able of project managers can be expected to be responsible for only three or at most four major projects at any one time.

The necessary skills sought are not confined to the physical production of the property. A thoroughgoing competence in all aspects relating to the financial performance of the scheme is of paramount importance, because, when all is said and done, every facet of the development programme has a pecuniary effect. For this reason, it may occasionally be the case that proven financial expertise in another field of business aside from property could be considered as relevant in assessing a request for development funds.

Consideration will also be given to the supporting professional team selected by the developer. Some architects are best suited to particular types of development and certain projects demand the injection of specialist building, engineering, service, surveying and agency skills. The previous record of all the contributing disciplines and their likely corporate chemistry will, therefore, be taken into account.

It should almost go without saying that, even at first blush, the selection of the project by the developer should appear sound and attractive to the fund, for it is well accepted that where a developer sees opportunity a financier sees risk.

Company accounts

The accounts of a property company should tell their own story and will always constitute an essential part of an initial application for development finance. In appraising the assets of the company, the fund will look to see properties of a good physical quality occupied by tenants of repute on beneficial terms with regular upward reviews of rent. They will take note of the portfolio mix of properties owned, with special regard to geographic and sectoral spread. The development programme currently in hand should not appear to be too large for the financial and management resources of the company, and not all the assets of the company should be pledged.

On the other side of the coin, in examining the accounts of the company, an intending financier will be reassured to find a healthy proportion of equity to balance the liabilities. The total term debt borne by the company should ideally have a good balance of fixed rate loans with any variable loans they have taken on. In addition, it is important to ensure that in their financial planning the property company have managed to avoid the bunching of repayments on existing loans and not placed undue reliance on short-term borrowing, both of which could lead to unfortunate pressure to refinance in a manner that might have repercussions upon the security sought by the fund. Where a property company have an overseas position, it is also necessary to establish that their foreign currency liabilities are generally matched by their overseas assets and sources of income.

Overall, therefore, the profit and loss account should demonstrate that the quality and amount of present income should not only be adequate to meet current outgoings, but should also be sufficient to meet any future rises in interest rates and cover any unforeseen exigencies that might occur. In this respect, cashflow is difficult to fudge, but some company accounts are otherwise less than revealing. This is especially true when it comes to the policy adopted towards the revaluation of existing property assets, and most funds pay close attention to how often the property portfolio is revalued, on what basis, and by whom. A careful watch will also be kept for the possibility of any off-balance sheet items, such as guarantees, being in existence and affecting the financial credibility of the company.

The project

From the fund's standpoint, the proposed project must not only meet the portfolio objectives of the developer; more importantly, it must meet their own. Broadly speaking, the project should be of a suitable size in terms of value, with no single investment property forming more than about 5–10 per cent total portfolio. It should be in accord with the sectoral balance of the property portfolio, which might be distributed along the lines of 35 per cent to 40 per cent offices, 35 per cent to 40 per cent shops, 10 per cent to 15 per cent industrial and 5 per cent to 10 per cent other forms of land and property investment. Locationally, it should meet the geographical spread adopted by the fund and critically it must be within easy reach of the developer to make certain of proper project management control.

More specifically, the fund will probably wish to assure itself of detailed property considerations, particularly if the developer is not a previous borrower. This might include conducting its own investigations relating to such matters as precise siting, local demand for space, flexibility of use, and market comparables. Design factors and performance standards loom large in meeting the criteria set-up for funding approval by financial institutions, and are dealt with elsewhere according to their special requirements, sector by sector. Furthermore, virtually all funding agreements will reserve to the fund the right to approve tenants for the scheme and, although in practice this condition rarely proves a stumbling block, it is viewed as being a vital power of control over the project and the developer.

Amount to be borrowed

Most financiers will lend only a proportion of the total amount required to fund a development, normally on the strength of a first legal charge over the development, but although with mortgage finance this is usually limited to

70–75 per cent of cost, banks will usually advance anything up to 80–85 per cent for a quality development with a top-class covenant already agreed, and long-term leaseback or forward sale loans from the institutions covering the interim funding during development can often provide 90 per cent or more of total development cost. However, above 70–75 per cent, borrowings will often be considered as equity and deserving of a higher pricing. Almost as a matter of principle, it is felt right that the developer should make a contribution, however small, towards the financing of the project. As a rule of thumb, however, 25–30 per cent is frequently sought.

Sometimes developers will seek a loan geared to the value of the completed development as opposed to the cost. This may be countenanced by the lender, but usually a lower level of advance is made to compensate and ensure security of the loan. Obviously, different lenders in different markets will view funding applications in different lights and adopt differing criteria in relation to acceptable percentages of cost or value accordingly.

Loan periods

Few banks currently wish to consider commitments of longer than five years, but in exceptional circumstances will consider up to 10 years. The insurance companies and pension funds will consider periods of up to 30 years, and often set 10 years as a minimum term.

Interest rates

For straightforward loans, interest rates are pitched at varying points above an agreed base rate. For example, institutional lenders might look for a margin of 1.5–2.25 per cent over government gilt edged rates. Banks might seek 1.5–2.5 per cent above the prevailing inter-bank lending rate, or even fix the rate for say five years by charging a similar margin over a five-year swap rate.

As already explained, some funding agreements adopt a fixed rate through-out the term, some a floating rate linked to the base rate, and some adopt a mechanism that combines fixed and floating rates. Increasingly, however, the rate of interest applied to a loan is traded against equity participation.

The timing of interest payments is also important, and methods of calculation vary from lender to lender. For example, a few lenders still calculate interest on the balance outstanding at the beginning of each year. If a loan of say £50 million is fully amortized over a period of 20 years at a fixed rate of 12 per cent, it can be shown that this could result in an additional payment of £8 million compared with a calculation on a day-to-day balance.

Yield

The factor by which income, anticipated or actual, derived from a development is capitalized will depend upon the relative degree of risk involved, and the relevant investment yield will be adjusted accordingly.

Where a fund was providing long-term finance for a scheme already completed and let, the appropriate yield might be, say, 5 per cent. If the finance was agreed on a forward commitment only once the scheme was completed and let, with no interim funding, then the yield might be 5.5 per cent. Where a forward commitment also provided interim development finance but a pre-let was concluded on full and acceptable rental guarantees supplied, then the yield could move to 5.75 per cent. If there was no pre-let and rents were only guaranteed for a limited period of, say, two years following practical completion, then a forward commitment with interim funding would require a yield of around 6 per cent. In the highest risk situation, where the fund was working on a priority yield, project management or profit erosion basis, then it would almost certainly look for a yield of about 6.5 per cent.

Rental cover

Very much as a rule of thumb, both fund and developer will be seeking sufficient rental cover in the margin allowed for developer's profit, and held as a balancing payment, to allow the completed building to stand empty for a period of around two and a half to three years. Exactly how long the contingency period should be will rest on the strength of the market at the time. The stronger the market, the less the cover necessary, and vice versa.

Another way in which rental cover is used as a measure of ascertaining the degree of security is the ratio of initial estimated rental income against interest repayments. A ratio of 1.1 or 1.2 to 1.0 is normally sought.

General funding facility

As already indicated, where a developer has generated a high degree of confidence with a fund, it may often prove beneficial to both parties to agree that a general funding facility should be made available to the property company. These are usually provided by the merchant banking sector. The terms and conditions upon which such loans are made will vary, but they will commonly refer to such matters as the total amount available, the take-up rate, the level and compounding of interest charges, proportion of facility devoted to any individual project, maximum percentage of development cost allowed for any particular scheme, restrictions as to planning consent and land assembly position, right to approve individual projects, obligation to offer certain other development projects over a given period, revaluation rights, buy-out provisions for schemes slow in starting, equity sharing arrangements, institutional long-term take-out requirements upon completion, repayment, and reporting and review procedures. Funding facilities of this kind can either be of a fixed term for, say, five or seven years, or 'revolving' subject to review at pre-ordained intervals. Security for the loan may also be attributable to particular assets of the company or arranged as a floating charge across all the company's assets.

More open-ended arrangements

The greater the degree of flexibility and discretion sought by a developer in a funding arrangement, the more a lending institution will look for further security to cover their risk. If the proposed project is anything less than conventional in respect of size, location, design, occupancy or letting terms, then a fund might be persuaded to relax its standard criteria on one or more of the following grounds. The land might already be owned by the developer, the company might be providing a substantial equity injection into the development, cast-iron collateral providing complete cover might be offered from elsewhere within the company's holdings, another financially strong partner such as a major construction firm might put up security alongside the developer, or bank guarantees may be supplied. Although they might not mean much in financial respects, personal guarantees undertaken by principals within the property company are thought to concentrate the mind wonderfully upon the successful outcome of development projects.

Sensitivity

These days it would be unusual for a lending institution not to conduct its own analysis of the sensitivity of a development scheme presented to it to changes in such component parts as rental income, initial yield, construction cost, finance charges and period to complete and let the development. Indeed, they would normally expect to see such an exercise performed for them by the prospective borrower in presenting the development for approval.

Tax

Although tax considerations are rarely the most significant issues in determining whether or not a scheme should be funded, they can affect the way in which a financial package is arranged. For example, because in some countries certain financial institutions are either wholly or partially exempt from tax, it is important to structure the funding agreement so that any concessions such as industrial building allowances or capital allowances relating to plant and machinery pass to the developer so that he can write them off against construction costs and improve his net profits position after tax. Further, it is sometimes the case that, whereas capital repayments do not attract tax relief, interest payments do, and in such circumstances borrowers are well advised to ensure that so far as is possible all fees and charges associated with funding the development are expressed in the formal finance agreement, so that they too become eligible for relief.

Costs

Apart from the obvious cost of interest on the loan and any equity share forgone, it should be recognized that the financing of a development can be an expensive business. There are arrangement fees of between 0.25 and 1 per cent, payable to the fund or to intermediaries for effecting an introduction and putting a funding package together; commitment fees, which are usually about 1 per cent of the loan amount upon acceptance of a formal offer, and are repayable on completion of the advance but forfeitable if the borrower does not proceed; legal costs, which on the loan can amount to about 1.0 per cent of the advance, although it might be lower if it is a very large loan and higher if the deal is especially complex; valuation fees, which on average can cost up to a further 0.5 per cent of the advance; revaluation fees, during the currency of the loan; penalty fees, if by any chance the developer seeks early repayment of a mortgage advance; tail-end or exit fees; and the costs incurred in making the presentation itself.

Choice of fund

So far, attention has been focused upon the necessary attributes of the developer in the eyes of the fund. However, it is just as important that developers should carefully select their source of borrowing.

General considerations

In the same way that developers' underlying resources would be examined, it is for them to be assured about the financial strength of the fund, although this requirement is not as imperative as it was 35 years ago when there sprung up a crop of suspect secondary banks specializing in property investment. Of greater concern to the developer these days is the speed of response made by funds to a request for finance. Associated with this is the extent to which delegated authority is conferred upon the fund manager or executive director. The very location of the finance house can be a consideration in selecting a likely lender, for some funds can have a special regard for, or relationship with, certain towns or regions. It usually helps if the fund has developed an interest and expertise in property matters, particularly at the development end of the market. If so, it will often pay to make a few inquiries of other borrowers as to their experience of dealing with that fund.

The general attitude of the fund towards an approach for development finance will usually give a fair indication of what kind of business relationship is possible and how it is likely to evolve. As with most transactions, the level of success depends upon mutual trust and confidence, and even within the largest of organizations this often comes down to individual personalities on both sides. In this context, stability of management within both the property development company and the financial institution can only assist in forging close and effective links between the two agencies, but large organizations are notorious for moving people about. With this in mind, therefore, and for several other reasons, it is not always a good idea for a developer to rely too heavily upon a single source of money for funding their development programme. People and policies can change.

Given that most major development schemes in the prime part of the property market are funded either by insurance companies and pension funds in the 'institutional' sector, or by clearing, merchant or overseas banks in the 'banking' sector, it is worth considering the different characteristics of these alternative sources from the developer's viewpoint.

Institutional lending

By and large, the lending policies of the major insurance companies and pension funds are characterized by their 'project'-based nature. This means that they tend to exercise extremely tight control over the entire project, including the design, construction and letting programmes. But although institutions are very risk averse and maintain strict standards of building design and performance, many will lend up to 100 per cent of development finance to favoured borrowers.

What is required of the developer is a good knowledge of the institutional funding market. This includes an understanding of the locational and sectoral preferences of different funds, their recent transactions, investment objectives, portfolio balance and the amount of money currently available for particular projects. Some will tend to specialize in certain forms of financial arrangement: short-term bridging loan, medium-term mortgage, long-term leaseback or forward sale. Some will not consider a project costing less than £5 million to them, others concentrate on smaller schemes of, say, £1–3 million, and will have a ceiling figure beyond which they cannot lend. Particular funds will also either favour certain types of development – small industrial workshops, provincial shops or city offices, for instance – or be seeking to acquire them in order to balance their portfolios. A shrewd developer will always shop around. Consequently, contact has to be maintained with a range of fund managers and the agents who act on their behalf, so that by knowing who acts for whom, and which funds prefer a direct approach, careful targeting to selected institutions, rather than a shot-gun blast across the market, can be accomplished.

In the same way, the basis of agreement for obtaining finance can vary among funds and between projects. Some funds, for example, are less keen upon sale and leaseback arrangements than others. Similarly, with regard to the desire for a degree of partnership with a developer, some funds prefer the borrower to bear a reasonable proportion of risk, whereas others are less favourably inclined towards side-by-side arrangements, taking the view that too large a share to the developer gives him a disproportionate involvement in overall responsibility. The reverse can also be the case. It may be that the developer in question has no choice and, having to trade on, must opt for a forward sale. The manner in which such matters as bridging finance, rental projection and additional tranches of loans are agreed also varies across the market, and is often a question of careful negotiation.

A critical factor is the need to establish the extent to which potential profits are placed at risk. In this context, some form of equity-sharing leaseback arrangement tends to be less contentious than a straight taking of a capital profit through a forward sale, because both parties share a common interest. Nevertheless, whether the arrangement provides for rental guarantee, profit erosion or priority yield commitments from the developer, he must be aware of the respective consequences from each kind of agreement. In particular, attention should be paid to the length of the agreed letting period, and thus the amount of rental cover provided.

Pre-letting will also frequently be an important consideration. In fact, it will often be a condition of funding. However, despite what might be seen as the security and certainty afforded by a pre-let, for the developer there can be drawbacks that affect time, cost and quality. Not only might the demands of the tenant be in contradiction to the stipulations of the fund, but the added involvement of the tenant and his professional advisers in the construction process and upon completion can cause extra problems. Furthermore, it can affect the overall planning and phasing of the development programme, especially in respect of common parts and facilities. Nevertheless, the securing of a pre-let can attract a premium and avoid contingency payments, void rental periods and heavy marketing costs.

One area of increasing sophistication is that of funding documentation. In the thrill of the moment of approval, or during the cut and thrust of negotiations, certain matters can be overlooked or onerous undertakings entered into too lightly. Thus, the aim of the developer should be for an agreement that is not too tight and not too loose, but, above all, that the offer letter is binding and operable. Care must be taken about conditions relating to every aspect of the project – design, construction, funding and letting – and the result is usually a compromise between strict compliance with institutional criteria and cost minimization to optimize profit. It is more and more common for an institution to appoint their own consultant firm to monitor development, an arrangement that if not properly formulated can be very irksome to the developer and his project manager. Another important aspect of this kind of funding agreement is to ensure that the client's potential liabilities to the fund are matched by those of the contractor to him, and likewise between the developer, the project manager and the other members of the professional team.

Bank lending

Banks are traditionally more concerned with the 'asset' base of those to whom they lend rather than upon the particular project in hand. The emphasis, therefore, will be more upon monitoring and controlling the balance sheet and security cover offered by the borrower. For the developer this can provide a more open and flexible climate in which to work, where such factors as time, cost and quality can be traded off against the client's ability to generate funds or produce additional collateral. However, bank finance is founded on profitable lending rather than by direct investment in a scheme, and, because banks normally neither provide risk capital under conventional arrangements nor seek to participate in equity profits, it is common for only a proportion of development finance (typically around 70%) to be loaned. It is, therefore, imperative for the developer responsible for securing finance to have an understanding of the policies, practices and procedures that determine bank lending. This is of greater moment here, for although institutional negotiations are invariably conducted between surveyors, bank lending is more usually transacted with a banker. Furthermore, the lending market is far from homogeneous. The banking sector broadly comprises major stock banks, the merchant banks, finance houses and overseas banks. All are different, and all are competitive, so bank finance must be carefully tailored to fit the purpose for which it is applied, and a well designed package prepared to meet overdraft, term or equity financial requirements. And, as interest rates in the market tend to move closely together, so the aim of the developer is to seek the best deal in respect of such matters as quality of service, fees, costs and repayments. Indeed, sometimes the additional flexibility afforded by more expensive arrangements can be worthwhile. For example, the objectives with a smaller project might be for a quick decision, flexibility in execution and an ability to revise arrangements without excessive penalties. With a larger scheme, detailed arrangements regarding the term of the loan, interest rate options and adjustable repayment schedules might be of more concern.

Term loans, which impose a contractual obligation on the bank to provide finance for an agreed period, have become a popular way of funding development projects. Banks are increasingly experienced in tailoring proposals that give flexibility of approach on the one hand but are matched by covenants on the other, which can have considerable effect on the running of the borrower's business in the future. For instance, financial ratios are a valuable tool of control, the breach of which puts the lender in a strong position to call for initial or added security or for changes in the terms of the loan, with such options as accelerating the loan or cancelling any unused part of the facility. There are other alternatives of varying efficacy: the negative pledge, sharing-round clauses and contractual right of set-off. Additionally, where the loan is unsecured, which now is sometimes the case, the bank might also consider various forms of direct involvement in the borrower's company, ranging from the appointment of a nominee director, to a working capital maintenance agreement, with shareholders undertaking to ensure the maintenance of the borrower's capital to satisfy covenanted ratios. Thus, in general, term-lending can afford a flexibility that, depending upon the circumstances, can be preferable to long-term mortgages, sale and leaseback arrangements or debenture borrowing.

A feature of bank lending is that there has been a tendency for the borrower to rely upon the lender to propose the basis and structure of the lending facility. This occurs often through ignorance, and sometimes through a misplaced desire to please. Such a lack of initiative or awareness in negotiations on the part of the developer can all too easily lead to a costly and mismatched facility being accepted.

Customer relationships are a critical factor in bank lending policy. The early training of young bankers dwells on the 'canons of lending' – character, ability, means, purpose, amount, repayment and income (for which the acronym CAMPARI serves as a handy reminder). It is perhaps significant that there is not 'S' for security, for banking theory holds that a perfect loan arrangement should be unsecured. Practice, however, dictates otherwise. In many cases the prospective borrower will have developed a relationship with his bank through ordinary business and overdraft lending, and it is a golden rule in the clearing banks that the current account forms the basis of mutual confidence between banker and developer. Where there is no previous relationship, then it will be necessary to establish the financial status of the borrower and the viability of the proposed scheme with great care.

Several other factors warrant attention on the part of the developer when negotiating bank lending. These are:

- The extent to which standby facilities might be required, and the terms that might be attached to them.
- The type of charge secured over the assets of the borrower: making sure that they are neither overcharged, which can reduce the ability to obtain

further loans, nor unduly restricted, so that, for example, disposal is limited.

- Ensuring that a proper presentation is made of the man, the market, the margins, the management information systems and the money requirement concerned with a particular project.
- Confirming the 'facility letter' from the bank to the borrower setting out the terms on which the loan has been agreed. Apart from specifying the amount, rate of interest, repayment terms and brief details of the security, if any, it will also normally include specific terms and conditions in the form of negative or positive covenants relating to such matters as default, other borrowings, supply of information and provision of warranties.

Whatever detailed arrangements are finally made, the project management objective must be to seek elasticity. Full allowance for the possible effects of inflation, time and cost overruns should be built in. Even the location of the bank and its officials, together with their speed of response, can be of importance. And these days, the very stability of the financial source is equally significant.

Problems in funding

Apart from the basic thesis that lack of knowledge and understanding of the principal sources of finance for property development and their respective policies, practices and procedures presents a major problem for aspiring developers, there are other issues that condition the climate for lending. A few of these are described, in brief, below.

Location

Within and among funding institutions a preferential treatment exists towards certain situations in, around and between selected cities and facilities. Some of this has the smack of hindsight about it, but much has to do with perceptions regarding environment, accessibility and communications. From the point of view of a developer approaching a potential source of funds, therefore, it is helpful to know the attitude and commitment of individual fund managers to particular towns, areas and regions.

Presentation

It is astonishing how little attention is paid to the professional presentation of proposed development schemes. Although not always the declared reason for turning a proposition down, poor presentation probably accounts for many funding refusals. At the very least, the following are required: a detailed appraisal of planning and market conditions, a cashflow analysis and a reasonable set of drawings, together with an explicit statement of the financial position of the intending borrower, contained in a well illustrated, succinct and coherent document.

Personality can also play a part. Character assessment is always a matter of personal judgement, but it is nonetheless important to ensure that any presentation is made in an open, confident, informed and enthusiastic manner.

Speculation

It is almost a cliché to say that one man's profit is another man's risk. Nevertheless, it is probably true to say that developers as a breed are eternally optimistic, whereas bankers, and those of their ilk, are notoriously cautious in their approach towards new developments. Moreover, it is often harder for the small developer to borrow money than for the large established property company, for if one project goes wrong for the former, it will have a more profound effect upon overall security and performance than for the latter.

From the standpoint of the developer or project manager, it is always worth considering the way in which potential profits are placed at risk by the manner whereby funds adjust their yield parameters according to the financial arrangements agreed. For example, as indicated earlier, an office scheme might variously be finely tuned as follows:

5%	completed and let
5.25%	pre-let, interim finance and forward commitment
5.5%	leaseback or lease guarantee
5.75%	profit erosion basis
6%	priority yield basis.

Collateral

A frequent explanation for funding agencies turning down applications to support proposed development projects is the inadequacy of existing collateral guarantees and proffered future equity participation. In fact, research indicates that this is probably the single most common reason for rejection.

Valuation

Lenders will invariably seek their own valuation of a proposed development project. This may often be at odds with the value perceived by the prospective borrower. In stagnant or recessionary markets, for example, the emphasis by the lender and his valuation advisers will normally be placed upon secure cashflow rather than anticipated capital value allowing for potential growth, which can lead to a wide divergence in estimating current open market value.

Thus, although regard is still paid to the loan to value ratio, the ability of the transaction to service the debt becomes of paramount importance. Pre-letting to a high-quality covenant on beneficial terms is, therefore, a vital factor in obtaining full financing in a falling or static market. In such markets it is always advisable to check that the lender's chosen valuer is prepared to confirm an approximate value, albeit verbal, prior to paying commitment fees, solicitors' costs and, of course, the valuer's full fees for a written report (Berkley 1991). Nevertheless, there are always the twin dangers of initial valuation or appraisal of a proposed development scheme being either too conservative or overoptimistic. Great care must be taken to explore the constituent components of rent, yield, building cost, finance, land cost, profit and time.

Currency

Given the global nature of property development finance, foreign currency loans have become increasingly popular. Interest rates can be lower, capital sums higher and terms easier. Foreign currency markets, however, are prone to constant fluctuations, and, in order to take advantage of such borrowing arrangements, developers should ensure access to any one of a number of different currencies, and be able to switch with ease. There are now versatile 'multi-currency' banking facilities available from leading international banks.

Refinancing

In many markets the issue of refinancing is extremely topical. Proper handling of this can often mean the difference between a property company's survival or its insolvency. Refinancing development property presents a particularly formidable challenge in depressed markets, as uncompleted and unlet projects lack the two basic attributes required to reassure a financier: cashflow and marketability.

Developments are most likely to be refinanced as part of an overall corporate refinancing exercise. Alternatively, where the scheme is in an area of strong demand or very prime, a development may be refinanced by the injection of fresh capital by a new equity investor, either as a joint venture partner or as a long-term investor. The unpredictability of development projects is not often compatible with the fine tuning of debt-oriented refinancing packages. A new financier's willingness to provide additional finance will primarily depend upon the quality of the security offered, although the company's past record will also play an important role. An existing financier will look especially at the feasibility of the company's corporate plan in comparison with other realization options, although it has been pointed out that the ultimate decision will invariably turn on the strength of the relationship between the parties involved (Clarke 1991).

Loan workouts

In a period of widespread overbuilding, sluggish leasing activity and other demand-side problems, many development projects are faced with a situation where schemes seem unlikely to service their debt charges upon completion. In these circumstances a lender may agree to what is known as a 'loan workout', which provides the developer with sufficient time and support to achieve a turn round in their project.

Essentially, a workout is the debt restructuring for a single project or many projects or properties normally requiring assiduous management, new money and additional collateral.

A developer should seek a workout as soon as a problem is identified and should try to persuade the lender to participate (not always an easy task). At a minimum, a financial workout will allow the developer to make the best of his current position. Ideally, it will enable him to satisfy his obligations while maintaining equity in the property. Thus, a workout provides better odds that the developer will emerge from the crisis with his business intact.

What a developer basically wants from a workout is temporary relief from all or part of the required debt service payment; an extension of a maturing loan without large extra fees; minimal additional encumbrances on the property or further dissipation of equity; personal liability relief; debt reduction, or even forgiveness; minimization of potential tax consequences; and co-operation to sell existing holdings. The incentives to the lender are a belief that with temporary concessions the problem can be solved; minimization of the risk of foreclosure; reduction or elimination of negative media attention; lessening of the impact on the lender's loan portfolio and income recognition; and the avoidance of protracted litigation. It has been stated that the keys to a successful loan workout are the development and implementation of a financial plan that addresses the maximization of return to creditors, and the long-term survival of the debtor as a going concern, together with the smooth interaction of various functions, including legal, accounting, information systems, asset marketing and management, and business operation. A workout can be a very sobering process to even the most sanguine of developers.

From above, it can be appreciated that it is essential to establish the correct financial base for the project, and for the developer to balance their aims with the aspirations of the lending agency, whose risk/reward criteria will determine the scope for negotiation between the parties. It can, therefore, be suggested that three basic elements of funding have to be assessed in any scheme:

- availability – in terms of knowing the range of possible sources of finance, methods of approaching them and their current position
- economy – in respect of interest rates and how they might fluctuate, as well as equity participation, incentives and penalties, and any hidden costs of borrowing
- practicality – which integrates the elements of availability and economy into a feasible arrangement that might otherwise detract from the viability of the project or invalidate it completely.

Financial adaptability on the part of the developer at a time when the investment character of property is changing is now a must.

The financial agreement

Inevitably, perhaps, the aims of the funder and the developer will often conflict. It is increasingly important, therefore, that the respective responsibilities for control during the development period are clearly apportioned and understood, and that the financial agreement is properly documented. Although a developer or project manager will doubtless have recourse to competent legal advice, the cut and thrust of negotiation is often such that certain matters may be misinterpreted or overlooked in the false hope that, once building has begun, the financial agreement will be forgotten or set aside. However, the opposite is more often the case, for it is at those moments of crisis during development that the parties are more likely to spring to the small print and come to realize the true consequences of their earlier bargaining. A better understanding of the objectives and procedures of financial control and documentation on the part of the developer will normally enable him to negotiate with greater confidence and to deploy his professional team more effectively.

Objectives

In structuring the financial arrangement the **funder** will aim to control certain aspects of the proposed scheme, including the:

* criteria by which tenants are selected and leasehold terms agreed
* negotiations conducted and agreements concluded with third parties
* entry by the developer into any special legal agreements with the local government, authority, and the consequent liability if the developer defaults
* nature and level of indemnity policies and collateral warranties held or offered by the developer, his professional team, the contractor and the subcontractors, so that in the event of failure the developer can be dismissed and the fund can assume full authority for the completion of development
* taxation implications of the project
* the purchase price of the completed project, so that unnecessary premiums and over-rentalization are avoided.

In contrast, the **developer**, whilst wishing to retain long-term goodwill with an interested fund, will seek to ensure that the terms ultimately accepted in the finance agreement provide:

* a smooth flow of funds
* speedy responses by the funder
* minimum interference by the funder's professional consultants
* smooth letting arrangements without undue constraint by the funder.

The 'offer' letter

One of the most important stages of the documentation relating to the finance of development arises well before the formal issue of arrangements. This is the initial 'offer letter' by the funding agency or its professional representatives. In effect, it will set out the basic terms of the deal and outline the intentions and expectations of the funder. Such a letter will have particular significance if the developer has to commit himself to the purchase of land prior to the full finance agreement being formalized. Any condition precedent in the correspondence must, therefore, be carefully appraised as to its implications.

There is no such thing as a standard offer letter, but the following list represents the more usual draft proposed heads of agreement:

- description of the parties concerned
- intention to purchase and basis of acquisition
- type and amount of loan; rate of interest and method of repayment
- identification of site and ownerships
- description of the proposed development
- planning position and local authority interests
- estimate of construction costs
- prospective letting agreements
- initial yield and resultant purchase price
- staged payments of costs and fees
- sharing of surplus rental income
- rental guarantees by developer
- approval building contract
- insurances and warranties.

The contractual agreement

The financial agreement will put into final contractual form the exact degree of control over the scheme the funder will expect to have. It is important for the developer, therefore, to ensure that the conditions imposed are not so onerous as to prejudice the proper management of the project or jeopardize the profitability through no fault of their own.

Apart from confirming the contents of the original offer letter, renegotiated or otherwise, the financial agreement, which is made under seal, will normally start by defining all the terms, procedures, parties and dates involved in the transaction. Of special concern to the funder will be the terms and conditions relating to any actual or proposed building agreements, or agreements for a lease. If the developer defaults, or if some other specified event takes place, the funder will wish to protect its position in respect of the determination of those agreements. The three main remedies normally incorporated into the financial agreement are:

- the power for the funder to assign the benefits under the agreement to another developer
- the power by the funder to complete the development and sell the created investment without any continuing liability
- an agreement whereby if a third-party freeholder exercises their right to re-enter for any reason under another contract, then the funder receives a payment relating to the improved value of the property achieved by the works to date undertaken by the developer.

Practical problems

It is impossible to cover all the matters that may be included in a financial agreement, and ultimately it is up to the developer whether or not the various terms and conditions are acceptable. Nevertheless, there are issues that recur, and they merit close attention on the part of the developer. In no particular order, these are:

- Design documentation attached to the agreement should clearly set out the objectives of the scheme and, as a general rule, the more details provided by the developer the better, so that subsequently the funder's surveyor cannot alter the initial specification.
- A developer is well advised to attempt to restrict the number of outside consultants the funder may appoint to act on their behalf in relation to the project. A single firm of surveyors should suffice.
- The necessity to obtain written approval for the appointment of subcontractors should be avoided by agreeing a list of nominated sub-contractors, although difficulties might arise in the case of a management contract involving many subcontracts, all of which may not initially be known.
- A clear understanding of the definition of the date of practical completion should be established and, wherever possible, the views and visits of the developer's architect and the fund's surveyor should be harmonized.
- The date on which capitalization and transfer of purchase price takes place should be explicit, and not dependent upon the actions of third parties.
- Access to the site by the funder's surveyors and facilities to inspect and test materials and workmanship should be kept within reasonable bounds. Notice of any defects should also be notified at the time of discovery.
- A procedure for arbitration should be agreed.
- It may be necessary for the developer to consider the inclusion of a 'walk-about' clause, so that he can approach other sources of finance if a top-up of funds over and above the funder's maximum commitment is required.
- There should be some mitigation in respect of those delays that push the completion date beyond the agreed date, especially where such delays are outside the control of the developer.

Little has been published in the professional press about funding agreements, although a specialist breed of solicitors have grown up who seem to be developing ever more complex documentation, usually for funding-clients. The aspiring developer, therefore, must be increasingly aware of the many pitfalls ahead.

Trends and prospects

This chapter concludes where it started, by stating that finance is a vital dimension of property development, and a principal concern of project management for the real estate industry.

- The globalization of property finance markets will continue.
- Developers and financiers alike will have to become even more aware of occupational demands by property users, and willing to accept greater innovation in the design, construction and management of commercial premises.
- Construction companies are already an attractive source of short-term development finance, not only providing interim funds but also acting as security for a long-term take-out, and entering into a fixed-price contract in return for an equal share of the eventual profit, and it is probable that, with difficulties in the institutional finance market and continuing uncertainty in the construction industry, the number of joint venture schemes between contractors and developers will grow.
- A specialized market in high-risk development schemes will emerge, depending upon more sophisticated market research, superior management skills and the spreading of risk over a well balanced mix of investments and among enterprising investors. Active risk management through various methods of syndication has already had considerable success in America.
- Joint venture and partnership agreements between public and private sector agencies will gain in popularity.
- The consortia approach towards investment in all forms of property development will become increasingly common: small private, as well as public, investors being grouped together to finance relatively small schemes, and large institutional investors collaborating in funding the major development projects.
- Refined funding techniques, which can reduce dependence upon cash-flow in the early years after the completion of a development project, will be introduced on a wider scale than hitherto, as will funding schemes that allow for the future consolidation of debt charges into equity interest, such as convertible mortgages, which permit the translation of fixed interest loans into equity shares once an agreed rate of inflation is reached.
- Among new arrangements structured specifically to attract additional funds for property development will be special multi-layered agreements in which each tranche of investment funding is designed to meet the tax needs and positions of the various parties to the deal, so as to take maximum advantage of tax allowances and relief.
- Some experimentation will undoubtedly take place in the property investment market with certain of the new techniques that have been developed in other investment markets, such as indexed mortgages, equity-linked bond issues, shelf registration issues and deep-discounted stock issues.
- A new funding ethic needs to be formulated towards the regeneration of older building stock in inner-city areas.
- Occupiers will be more directly active as developers, since they hold the key to financing.
- Environmental aspects of property development will play a larger part in the appraisal equation.

- Higher standards of professionalism will be demanded at every level.
- Worldwide, there is likely to be a contagious reappraisal of the concept of value.

Over the last few years more innovative approaches have, again, started to appear in the UK property market. Debt and asset-backed securitization have become more common, the traditional long UK institutional lease is under pressure and, with the expansion of the serviced office sector, new rent arrangement have been the topic of much discussion.

The search is on for liquid, tax-efficient funding vehicles. In the US, securitization of real estate assets has developed rapidly, and it is estimated that commercial mortgage-backed securities totalling $50 billion were issued in 2000, compared to around $10 billion in Europe. Market capitalization or REITs has grown from $2 billion in 1972 to $139 billion in 2000 (Lizieri *et al.* 2002). These changes in the US have been much influenced by tax changes and state intervention, and the growth of the REIT market resulted from a series of favourable tax changes.

The changing UK environment and innovations in the US are calling into question conventional attitudes to low-risk property development opportunities. Times they are a-changing!

14 Marketing for development

The days of certain markets, easy lettings and malleable tenants have gone, and, for the foreseeable future they are unlikely to return. Property as a product has become more difficult to sell, and those responsible for selling it perforce required to bring a higher degree of professionalism to the market. Users' needs have to be more closely identified and more carefully matched with product design. As with other property services the agency function to date has been performed against a background that has rested heavily upon the historic monopoly enjoyed by established firms and a traditionally constant attitude towards transactions in land and property by owners and occupiers. This is changing.

This chapter is organized as follows:

- the marketing role
- marketing functions
- market segmentation
- selling techniques
- developer's viewpoint.

The marketing role

A useful definition of marketing is one provided by the Institute of Marketing, which runs:

> Marketing is the management function which organizes and directs all those business activities involved in assessing and converting customer purchasing power into effective demand for a specific production or service to the final customer or user so as to achieve the profit target or other objective set by the company.

More simply perhaps, marketing is the skill of matching the needs of a buyer with the product of a seller, for a profit. It is probably true to say that development property used to be a soft-sell product. An estate agent would erect a board, place an advertisement and wait. Nowadays, however, those marketing property developments are faced increasingly with a highly competitive and discerning market, and one that demands better information and more active attention to the selling process.

The agency function

The appointment of an estate agent is the usual means by which the commercial sector of the property development industry disposes of completed projects, whereas in the residential sector most major developers perform their own agency functions with or without the help of agents. There has also been a slight tendency on the part of some developers and local authorities to undertake agency on their own behalf. Nevertheless, despite criticism over recent years about the quality of their work, it should nearly always be possible to gain a wider access to the market by retaining an agent. Depending upon the nature of the development and the circumstances prevailing in the market at the time, an agent might be called upon to perform some of all of the following tasks:

* find suitable sites or properties for development, redevelopment or refurbishment on behalf of clients
* receive instructions and liaise with the developer at an early stage in the project to consider the overall concept of the proposed scheme and, in particular, to advise on those features of design and layout that could add to or detract from the marketability of the completed property
* provide general economic advice and investigate rental levels and capital values in respect of the viability of the project
* comment on the planning implications and assist in discussions with local authority officers
* advise on potential occupiers and tenant mix
* advise on the possible need for special building and occupiers' services, as well as considering the general operation of future management services
* advise regularly throughout the period of development on prevailing market conditions
* advise, arrange and implement a marketing strategy
* monitor responses and handle prospective occupiers' inquiries
* conduct negotiations with interested parties and investigate the credentials of potential purchasers or tenants
* advise on and assist with the provision of development finance
* negotiate and conclude the final sales or lettings.

With regard to payment for the various activities described above, it is usual for an agent to negotiate a separate fee for professional services rendered in connection with acquisition, development appraisal, funding, development consultancy, project management, letting and management. An interesting change that has taken place over recent years in respect of offering estate agency services and attracting instructions, is the increasingly liberal attitudes taken by professional institutions towards advertising. Under current regulations and notes for guidance of the RICS, for example, members are actually encouraged to give interviews to the press and media, and the rules are stated to be designed to give the profession 'maximum freedom in accordance with current thinking'. This has allowed commercial agents quite a broad scope in marketing their own services as well as their clients' property.

There are said to be certain fundamental prerequisites to effective agency, based on the adage 'if you have no information, you have no product sell' (Development Systems Corporation 1983). More specifically, the necessary market intelligence can be broken down into the following areas:

- *Knowing the owners.* Thorough market knowledge involves knowing who owns the buildings and the land in the locality. Ideally, a good agent should generate ownership data on every potential development or redevelopment site, for sale or not for sale, within his bailiwick.
- *Knowing the tenants.* An able agent will gather as much information as possible on tenants, large and small, operating within the market area, particular attention being paid to existing major tenants or high potential tenants. Tenant intelligence should go beyond knowing names to knowing why a tenant is there. Why did a tenant sign a lease on one building and not on another? What is the critical location and site criterion for the tenant? Does the tenant rely heavily on street patterns, demographics, signage, skilled labour?
- *Knowing the deals.* The astute agent will know about all important deals transacted in their territory. Such deals define the economic character of the market, determining the level and pattern of leasing and selling values. The information on current and recent deals is not always easy to uncover, being a matter of confidentiality between the parties involved, but a good relationship is imperative between fellow agents and existing or prospective tenants and purchasers.
- *Knowing the property.* Understanding the physical land and property inventory of an area is the cornerstone of an agent's practice. Knowledge of the types of property in a given area, the amount of each type, the special features of particular properties and the plans for new projects is essential.
- *Knowing the competition.* From the viewpoint of the agent, as well as the client developer, it is important that he is aware of who else is in the market, and what size share of that market they are likely to absorb. Besides market share, it is always wise to know how the competition is operating, its strengths, its weaknesses and its marketing strategies (Development Systems Corporation 1983).

Types of agency

There are four essential bases upon which an estate agent may be instructed to sell a development. These are:

- *Sole agency.* A sole agency arrangement is one in which a single firm is instructed to dispose of a property. Preferred by agents because, if they are successful in selling the development scheme, then they receive the full measure of commission. A normal fee would be 10 per cent of full annual rental value for a letting between 1.5 and 3 per cent of agreed price for a sale.
- *Joint agency.* Where two agents are instructed by a developer to collaborate in the letting or disposal of a property, a joint agency is established.

This arrangement is most commonly used in the sale of provincial property where national and local coverage is required, or in a scheme of mixed development where specialist marketing of particular components is thought desirable. It is also adopted where a property is considered especially difficult to sell and an element of competition is felt advisable, or where one agent has introduced a development to a client on the understanding that they will at least share in the agency, but the developer requires the marketing skills of another firm. Although fees are negotiable, it is probable that the developer will have to pay up to around one and a half times the normal fee, divided by the two agents by agreement.

- *Sub-agency.* It is always open for an agent, unless instructed otherwise, to appoint another firm as subagent to assist in the marketing of a particular property. The main difference between sub-agency and joint agency is that the responsibility to the client rests with the principal firm in the former case and commissions tend to be higher in the latter.
- *Multiple agency.* When several agents are individually instructed to dispose of a property and commission is only payable to the agent who achieves the sale, a multiple agency is formed. Resort to such form of agency is not normally taken in the marketing of a development project, because it invariably leads to a confused marketing campaign, abortive costs and a suspicion on the part of potential purchasers that for some reason the property is difficult to sell.

As already mentioned, some development organizations sometimes opt to perform the agency function themselves. In such circumstances, an 'in-house' team will assume responsibility for the promotion and disposal of a scheme. However, it should be recognized that established firms of estate agents are bound to be more informed about, and have wider access to, both property and business requirements and opportunities. Only very rarely does it benefit an individual developer to market a project entirely on their own.

The role of the provincial agent has also taken on a greater importance over the past few years in the field of development. Although the major national firms of estate agents based in London can offer unrivalled services in respect of the potential national and international occupancy market, and can also supply certain specialized support services such as research, planning and funding, local firms situated in major regional centres also supply invaluable expertise. The provincial agent tends to have a deeper knowledge of local markets, better information regarding the availability of suitable sites, a heightened awareness of the true state of prevailing planning policy and practice, and a favoured insight into the performance and intentions of local businesses and landowners. Furthermore, they will often have a superior understanding of local values and returns, being privileged with the precise details underlying local sales conducted by private treaty. At the letting stage they will also benefit from the accumulated experience of enquiries received across a whole range of properties over time, giving them a good idea of the vagaries of the market. Their ready availability to react to enquiries and respond informatively to questions regarding local services and conditions is an obvious advantage.

Rules and responsibilities

The year 1991 to 1992 proved something of a watershed for estate agency practice. After a decade or more of threats and promises the profession witnessed the introduction of The Estate Agents (Undesirable Practices) Order 1991, The Estate Agents (Provision of Information) Regulations 1991, both introduced under powers conferred by the Estate Agents Act 1979, and the Property Misdescriptions Act 1991.

The procedures dictated by the former two statutory instruments are wide ranging. But in so far as they touch on agents dealing with clients, they essentially fall into two areas: the course of action to take as soon as a client–agent association begins, and the conduct required as that relationship progresses. The regulations, for example, are explicit about the information that must be furnished to the client and, importantly, the moment at which those details must be provided. A client–agent agreement must be established 'before the client is committed to any liability towards the estate agent'. An agreement will cover all aspects of agency: the length of instruction, fees and when they become payable, marketing budgets, circumstances in which other payments are due and definitions of 'sole agency', 'joint sole agency' and the like. Few problems, hopefully, face the experienced developer and worthy agent.

The Property Misdescriptions Act 1991, which became operable from April 1993, presents estate agents, and developers who market their properties directly, with a new form of criminal liability for mis-statements. The kernel of the Act lies in Section 1(1) which provides:

> Where a false or misleading statement about a prescribed matter is made in the course of an estate agency business or a property development business, otherwise than in providing conveyancing services, the person by whom the business is carried on shall be guilty of an offence under this section.

As one leading authority in the field explains, agents and developers now face a criminal offence of strict liability (i.e. one in which the prosecution need prove neither intent to deceive nor even negligence), subject only to the possibility of avoiding conviction where the defendant can prove that all reasonable steps and due diligence have been taken (Murdoch 1993). Nevertheless, the Act does not require any particular information to be given about property that is being marketed. What it does require is that any information given should be accurate, or at least not false or misleading. The detailed degree of care that must be taken over such marketing tools as photographs, models, artists' impressions or demonstration units is not as yet clear, but considerable caution will have to be exercised with sales aids of this kind, and regular updating undertaken. The measurement of floor areas and rooms, whether relating to commercial or residential properties, requires particular care, and resort will inevitably be made to the ubiquitous caveat 'approximately'. With regard to disclaimers, however, the Department of Trade and Industry advises that they must be applied in as bold, precise and compelling a way as the statement to which they relate. Again, developers and agents of good standing will have nothing to fear from the legislation, but the more responsible representatives of the property industry still call for the implementation of Section 22 of the 1979 Estate Agents Act laying down minimum standards of competence and experience, with many preferring a full system of licensing or registration.

Above all else, successful marketing in the property world depends upon confidence and credibility. It is distressing to record the lasting gratitude that both journalists and politicians afford to estate agents for keeping them from occupying the lowest position in repeated professional popularity polls. Nevertheless, in the commercial real estate marketing field, the winning and retaining of trust and confidence by client organizations, whether vendors or purchasers, is critical.

Marketing functions

Current pressures on estate agents to let or sell their clients' buildings is leading to a much higher degree of sophistication in the way development properties are marketed. In addition, as more and more commercial floor-space comes on stream and disposal becomes ever harder to effect, so the realization that getting the product right in the first place grows even stronger. Consequently, however faddish it might seem, the property world must gain a better understanding of the procedures and functions of marketing, and at the same time learn from the array of marketing principles and practices that have been developed in other sales markets. In stating this, however, it should be appreciated that the marketing of planned new developments ahead of construction breaks many basic marketing rules, in that a potential customer cannot test and experience the qualities of a product prior to purchase. The reputation of the developer and the climate of goodwill created between those involved in a potential sale or letting becomes a crucial factor in the marketing campaign.

Marketing tools

A useful classification of the four key tools of the marketing man has been provided as follows:

- *Market research and information.* It is suggested that for the purpose of the estates profession these two functions should be distinguished, because the term 'research' is used by most major firms of estate agents simply to describe the collection of largely retrospective statistics that show trends and can be used for producing forecasts, whereas market research in the true sense is described as an 'action-oriented procedure' aimed at informing the developer of a marketing or advertising plan.
- *Advertising.* This is the process of spreading information by preparing and placing paid-for material such as space in newspapers and journals or time in the broadcasting media. Advertisements are always identifiable with their sponsor or originator, which is not always the case with other forms of promotion or publicity.

- *Promotion.* Covers those marketing activities, other than personal selling, advertising and publicity, that stimulate consumers' purchasing and agents' effectiveness, such as displays, shows, exhibitions, and various non-recurrent selling efforts not in the ordinary routine.
- *Public relations.* The role of public relations is to establish and maintain understanding and goodwill for the development organization's product and services, activities and operating policies. In this, it is not only concerned with communicating for marketing purposes, but also for the broader purpose of creating a favourable atmosphere within which the organization may operate successfully.

Marketing research

The whole process of development essentially starts with market research, the goal of which is to project the rate of absorption for a particular property product based on the supply and demand for similar properties in a specified market area. Conducted at the outset of the development process, the developer seeks to identify an unfulfilled market need that might feasibly be met on a specific site. If the signs are promising, a formal market study might be commissioned and a marketing plan of campaign prepared.

The starting point of any marketing plan of campaign is the identification of the target groups of possible purchasers. Research is, therefore, essential, and it is really only in recent years that some of the leading firms of estate agents and a few of the major property development companies have committed themselves to the serious analysis of the markets in which they operate and consideration of the buildings they produce and sell.

It must be said, however, that certain pieces of published research are in fact just so much window dressing. The compilation of crude vacancy rates for particular sectors, for example, says very little about market performance or prospects except at the most superficial level. Broad indications of rental value across wide geographical areas might be useful promotional material for the firms concerned, but cannot be held to contribute greatly to a better understanding of the property market. Effective marketing increasingly will depend upon more rigorous research into the underlying conditions and determinants of demand and supply in the property market.

In practice, marketing research is usually concentrated on a few recurrent problems, often on a continuous basis, which may be grouped as follows:

Up-to-date market knowledge

- The size of the regional and local markets for particular kinds of property, normally measured in floorspace for commercial sectors and dwelling units or habitable rooms for housing.
- Past patterns of demand and underlying economic, social, political, legal and technological factors that are likely to affect future levels of demand, together with an indication of the timescale involved and any cyclical variations.

- Buying or renting habits of consumers, along with an appraisal of the possible changes in attitude and behaviour by both customers and funding institutions that might take place.
- Actual and potential market share commanded by the development organization, and a breakdown of the market shares of major competitors.
- General appreciation of past and possible future trends in broad socio-economic terms covering such matters as population change, national income and expenditure, sales and output, availability of finance, construction industry performance and legislative or political change.

Overall policy and tactics

- An examination of competitive pricing structures and practices, looking at where, how and at what cost competitors promote and advertise their properties.
- A consideration of how marketing costs compare with other costs and with competitive costs, and what effect any change or differential in policy would make.
- An assessment of how sales and lettings differ by dint of location or type of use, and why.
- An evaluation of the probable effects of any radical change in the pricing structure of the developers' or competitors' property.
- An appraisal of the effect of promotional activity, looking at the effectiveness of advertising copy and placement and the result of incentive schemes to both agents and purchasers.

The product

- What is the company reputation or image for producing quality buildings and providing a good service to purchasers?
- How are previous developments thought of and used, and what features are found to be most important by occupiers?
- Should any changes be made to current or proposed development projects in respect of design, layout, materials or services?
- What property management, legal or planning restrictions might inhibit the ready sales or letting of a development?
- What are the strengths and weaknesses of previous development schemes constructed by the company and its competitors?

Primary and secondary data

- The data collection phase of marketing research draws on two main sources of information, which are distinguished as primary and secondary sources, or alternatively desk and field research.
- Secondary sources are those that already exist, but consist of data collected for purposes peripheral to the main line of research inquiry in hand, so care must be taken to ensure that the information is relevant, can be adjusted to the present problem and is reliable.

- There are internal and external secondary sources. Internally, agents and developers will have a mass of marketing information available from their own records, and although it is not always collected systematically or in the most appropriate form, modern computerized data-processing systems are making the access to and extrapolation of suitable information easier and faster. Externally, there is a growing wealth of published information from other agents, consultants, professional bodies, trade associations, research organizations and government departments. Secondary sources should be consulted before primary or original research is undertaken.
- Primary or field research will usually cover the potential market demand, occupiers' preferences, the precise characteristics of the actual or proposed development, the terms of sale or letting, and the methods of advertising. Original data of this sort may be collected by observation, experimentation or survey. Observation depends heavily upon the skill and objectivity of the observer. Experimentation is rarely appropriate to the property market. And survey can be time-consuming and expensive.

Marketing research process

Although research projects in the property development market are not susceptible to a single and inflexible sequence of steps, the following procedure is a useful guide (Giles 1978):

- Definition of the problems, a step of the greatest importance, and one treated in a cursory way too often.
- Specification of the information required.
- Design of the research project, taking into account the means of obtaining the information, the availability and skills of staff, the methods to be used and the time and cost involved.
- Construction and testing of any surveys, questionnaires or interviews.
- Execution of the project, with arrangements for a check on the reliability of data collected.
- Analysis of data.
- Preparation of report and formulation of recommendations.

However, it should be recognized that marketing research neither provides a panacea nor guarantees success, but it does assist in improving the quality and confidence of decision-making.

Marketing strategy

Over the past few years there has been a significant shift towards the devising of more formally structured and deeply considered marketing plans for proposed development projects. The advantages of a more rigorous planning process are that diverse marketing activities can be better co-ordinated, crisis management can either be avoided or reduced to a minimum, measurements of performance are easier to conduct against known standards, corrective measures can be applied in sufficient time when required, and participation by all those involved can be encouraged with improved commitment and motivation (Giles 1978).

It has been stated that a marketing plan for property should be much the same as for any other kind of product, in that it needs to

> . . . strive to create the tangible from the intangible and present a concept that will stimulate the imagination of the potential client . . . This simple need becomes more and more difficult to achieve as the weight of communication channels and the material sent to them increases each year.
>
> (Watts 1982)

Accepting that the alliteration is a gross over-simplification, a favourite way of remembering the key variables that form the basis of marketing strategy and mix is known as 'the four Ps', namely:

- product
- price
- place
- promotion.

A preferred means of describing the most important steps in preparing a marketing plan to take account of the key variables involved in marketing operations can be more fully stated as follows.

Select the right team

In identifying, anticipating and satisfying customer requirements, profitability – the very nub of marketing – it is essential that all those involved in the entire process of development, from inception to completion and through to management afterwards, are selected with a view to optimizing the collective effort of the professional team. The chemistry between those directly concerned with design and construction and those specifically responsible for the actual marketing campaign must be right. It is not productive, for example, to have an architect who is either oblivious or unsympathetic to the advice of the agent, or to have an agent who is uncomprehending or hostile to those designing and building the project. In the past, the formulation of a marketing strategy has all too often been left to the agent acting alone, and invariably too late in the development process.

Identify the target groups

Properly conducted marketing research as outlined in previous sections should have identified the general categories of occupier that might be interested in the scheme in question, and hopefully the actual manufacturing, trading or business organizations who are either actively looking for new or additional accommodation or who might conceivably be enticed into taking or moving premises. Often the most difficult task is to identify and reach the person within the organization responsible for taking the decision.

Agree the message strategy

This involves deciding on how best to present the special sales characteristics of the building, its situation and wider environs. In the rather 'whiz-word' riddled world of marketing, this is known as creating the 'unique selling proposition' or 'USP', and is concerned with striving to convey a concept that will stimulate the imagination of the potential occupier or purchaser. The overriding aim in designing general and specific 'USPs' should be to see the whole strategy in terms of how it might benefit the eventual client. This might seem a trifle obvious, but somehow agency practice in the UK has been extremely slow in breaking away from a fairly standard and somewhat impersonal property-oriented approach towards a more original and individually directed user-based approach.

Write a communication plan

Having established the broad 'message' about the property that needs to be conveyed, the next step is to plan how best it is communicated. Any 'communications plan' will usually combine a variety of direct and indirect selling techniques, called the 'marketing mix', all of which require careful orchestration. Direct methods such as the use of brochure, personalized mail shots, targeted circulation lists, exhibitions and agents' receptions will need to be synchronized with indirect methods involving national and local media, side advertising and contact networks within the property industry. Again, these techniques may seem patent and familiar, but the early and co-ordinated planning is often missing. There is also a positive wealth of face-to-face selling expertise accumulated in other fields of marketing that has lain largely untapped by the property profession, and might with advantage be explored and exploited.

Ensure follow-up activity

There are two distinct aspects to following through on the communication plan. First, there are those endeavours that have to be made to stimulate only very mild expressions of interest. And second, there are those efforts to make in converting strong interest into an actual sale and subsequently keep the purchaser content. With the former, an agent marketing a development should be aware that there are several kinds of barriers that may block their ability to communicate and must be overcome, or at least lowered. These are personal barriers, arising from the fact that individuals differ, and that different people have to be approached in different ways: organizational barriers, thrown up by administrative structures and hierarchies, so that finding the right person and presenting the case in a corporately acceptable manner becomes even more vital; and mechanical barriers, which exist because some organizations lack the proper points of contact and channels of communication. With the latter, translating a positive response into a trouble-free transaction, it should simply be a matter of competence and professionalism, keeping the customer informed about progress and handling all inquiries and negotiations promptly, efficiently and pleasantly.

Agree a budget

Ascertaining an accurate figure for the total cost of marketing for development is an extremely difficult task. In the first place, however, there is need for a plan in order to determine a budget. From this plan can be extracted the various marketing activities that are proposed. It has been suggested that the following process be adopted (Miles *et al.* 1991):

- A plan is formulated to promote the product to the target market by the developers and their agents as early as possible in the development process.
- The plan typically begins with a description of the product and the target market, based on earlier market research including statements about how the product will be attractive to the target market and how those responsible for marketing will reach that market.
- As more detail emerges, an extensive checklist of possible activities within each category of the marketing plan is prepared excluding no reasonable ideas.
- A realistic cost estimate for each marketing activity on the checklist is compiled, sparing no expense at this stage.
- The initial total cost estimate is then scrutinized and pared down by examining closely and squeezing tightly every item. Each activity must justify itself, deleting rigorously those that do not, so that, although the net is case widely, only the best of what is caught is kept.
- Some of the items in this process might be one-time investments, such as fitting out a show unit, and might last the life of the marketing campaign, whereas others, such as brochures, might have to be replaced periodically. Still others will recur continually, such as media charges, which could keep mounting as the campaign intensifies.
- The grand total is estimated, having predicted how long a presence is required in the market and taking account of likely absorption rates.

Another approach, which can be used as a check on the above, is to pose the question of how many new contacts will have to be made and cultivated in order to generate sufficient positive responses to achieve the predicted absorption rate? The cost of making these contacts can then be gauged. Commercial property marketing relies heavily on this 'prospecting' approach, whereas residential sales rely more upon general advertising (Miles *et al.* 1991).

Yet a further budgeting procedure has been described, termed the 'task method' and based upon a four-stage process:

- Market (what is it? where is it?)
- Message (for that market)

- Media (most effect and most direct)
- Measurement (cost effectiveness and results) (Cleavely 1984).

This task method requires objectives to be set as part of the marketing strategy, which can be monitored and plans adjusted according to the degree of success achieved.

In practice, however, it has to be stated that marketing budgets for property development proposals are generally based upon the experience and judgement of the developer and marketing consultants involved. Moreover, it is important that a high degree of flexibility is afforded to allow for the unexpected in the market.

Methods of selling

An agent's prime objective is to sell or let property for the highest price or rent available in the market, not to pursue his own subjective assessment of value. To achieve this, the property must be freely exposed to the market in an orderly manner. The most appropriate method of selling a particular property largely depends upon the nature of the premises concerned and the prevailing market conditions. Four basic methods of property disposal can be distinguished.

Private treaty

Straightaway, it should be stated that the vast majority of all sales and lettings in the overall property market are normally conducted by private treaty. There have been periods when extreme conditions in the market have encouraged such practices as rental tendering, and formal and informal tenders and public auctions are always popular for certain sectors of the market. It has also been known for various kinds of informal tender to be used in order to resolve difficult and competing negotiations, but such recourse is rare. Private treaty is, therefore, the most prevalent method of selling property across all sectors of the development market. It simply involves the setting of an asking price or rent and negotiating to achieve it. As floorspace in most conventional development schemes, either proposed or completed, is bought and sold between property professionals, the basis of assessing a reasonable level of capital or rental value is likely to be very broadly the same. Therefore, so long as the developer and his agent have set the asking price properly, not so high as to stifle offers and not so low as to cause embarrassment and bad feeling by continued negotiation well above that opening price, all should be well. However, there are two main exceptions in the development world where sale by private treaty is not normally the best means of disposal: first, with the sale of land or buildings possessing development potential, but prior to development taking place, where offers will be determined by many variable and unpredictable factors; and, second, where the market is especially uncertain or volatile. One renowned residential development on the riverside in London was quickly taken off the market when, much to everyone's surprise, offers massively exceeded the asking prices.

Public auction

This method should, in theory, ensure an orderly market, for, if the property has been properly advertised, it should attract everyone with a serious interest and force them to reach a decision in a competitive atmosphere and with no opportunity to withdraw. The preparation of particulars is critically important with this method of sale, for they must be detailed and accurate, yet enticing. The overwhelming drawback in selling agreed or completed developments at auction is that the major financial institutions are rarely interested in buying at auction. Moreover, they are normally unwilling to provide a firm commitment to a developer wishing to buy potential development properties at auction, unless perhaps the value of the site or the existing buildings is less than, say, £1 million, and only then if most of the uncertainties about the proposed scheme, particularly in respect of planning permission, have already been resolved.

Formal tender

The formal tender, whereby prospective purchasers are invited to submit sealed bids on or by a particular date, is similar to the auction in that all the bids constitute contractual offers that, if accepted, are binding. As with the auction, it is essential to reduce uncertainties to a minimum, and preferably to obtain planning consent beforehand. This not only takes time, but however assiduous the vendor and his agent, there can be no guarantee that the consent obtained is the most valuable possible, and prospective purchasers will bid for what has been approved and not what they think they get. The great advantage of the formal tender is that the highest possible bid for the property should be attracted, whereas at auction even an especially keen or special purchaser only has to exceed the second highest offer. As has been stated:

> Formal tenders are particularly attractive for undeveloped land where the planning situation is quite straightforward. Most housebuilders have adequate finance and are well geared up to acquire residential building land at tender, but bidders for industrial and commercial sites normally require funding from institutions and, quite reasonably, institutions are reluctant to enter into funding commitments until the site is secure.
>
> (Armon-Jones 1984)

Informal tenders

The informal tender method involves the selling agent inviting single and highest bids, subject to contract, from prospective purchasers attracted by an initial marketing campaign. Because there is an interval between the acceptance of an offer and exchange of contracts, the method is said to be vulnerable to the successful bidder trying to renegotiate the offer once other tenders have been disappointed and possibly withdrawn. Nevertheless, it is argued that in spite of this weakness the informal tender is often the best form of sale for the disposal of development sites. So long as the procedures are clearly established and abided by, full and consistent information given to all potential purchasers, confidentiality maintained between the parties regarding the various schemes proposed prior to tender, satisfactory financial assurances obtained and a package of relevant legal documents circulated to all serious bidders shortly before the closing date, most of the problems can be reduced or eliminated (Armon-Jones 1984). However, the method does depend upon a high degree of trust and respect on both sides.

Market segmentation

It should almost go without saying that the property market is highly diverse. Not only does this apply to the rich variety of occupational markets it seeks to supply, but also to the varying requirements within those markets, the different sales techniques appropriate to different sectors, the inconsistent attitude of differing client bodies and the divergent approaches taken towards marketing adopted by individual estate agency practices. A brief mention about some of the most notable characteristics of the main sectors of the market, therefore, is appropriate.

Shops

In the context of property development, the marketing of shops normally involves the letting of retail space to tenants and often the sale of the entire scheme to a funding institution. Thus, when an agent is selling shops, he is selling to:

- the investing institutions
- the retail industry
- the shopping public.

Inevitably, any financial institution contemplating the funding of a shopping development will want to be assured about the quality of income and the prospects of rental growth in the future. In large planned shopping centres, it will be necessary to show the actual or probable pre-letting of the major anchor units to one of the leading larger national multiples such as Sainsburys, Boots or W. H. Smith. Smaller schemes would need to be presented to an institution, with commensurate letting agreements involving national multiples and regional superstore chains. A clear indication of the likely overall market penetration for the scheme based upon an assessment of the population catchment area, the accessibility to the development and the existing and possible future competition for trade would have to be shown. And a fund would also be interested in the proposed tenant mix, the leasing structure and the proposals for continuing management services. Pre-letting of a significant proportion of space is often a prerequisite.

In marketing shop premises to retailers, regard should obviously be paid to the general design and layout of the scheme, with special emphasis upon such considerations as access, pedestrian flow, transport and parking facilities, and individual traders' market share. They will also want to know who else might be taking space in the scheme, so that they can evaluate the attraction factor of any anchor tenants and assess the probable degrees of competition and complementarity generated by surrounding units. Naturally, an acceptable level of rent and a lease without excessively onerous conditions will carry most weight in persuading a retailer to take space in a scheme. In addition, they will wish to be convinced by the developer's commitment and ability to promote and market the entire development so as to enhance public awareness of it and to provide reliable and effective management to it.

As far as the public are concerned, a shopping development must show itself to be conveniently accessible, offer a wide range and alternative choice of goods and services, and provide or be close to carparking if possible. With larger planned shopping centres it is also important to create a pleasant atmosphere, make available certain facilities such as restaurants and toilets, and increasingly guarantee a safe, clean and secure environment. It also helps if all or most of the space can be let before opening, and vacant units avoided, or at least attractively maintained.

Offices

In the present competitive climate it is becoming ever more incumbent upon the estate agency profession to possess a thorough-going knowledge and understanding of office users' requirements. Both in terms of crude locational space requirements and the required level of functional performance. An agent seeking to market an office development will, therefore, seek to ascertain if he can identify firms within international, national, regional or local markets who:

- might find advantages from 'hiving-off' certain activities or departments to a new location
- would benefit from consolidating already dispersed operations under a single roof or by bringing them in closer proximity to one another
- could effect substantial savings by moving their entire operation to a new location or new building
- are contemplating expansion
- have already made a decision to search for new or additional premises.

These days, it is essential for an agent marketing an office property to know in a fair amount of detail its relative suitability in respect of different kinds of business operation. Such factors as face-to-face contact within and outside an organization; technological communication, like facilities for satellite, telephone, facsimile, intranet and internet connectivity; internal environment, including temperature range and control, natural light and outside views and type and quality of working space; and corporate image, covering such matters as aspect, setting, entrances, reception area, services and other facilities. A prospective occupier will then primarily be interested in cost. Increasingly, office accommodation is considered by commercial organizations in relation to its 'all-in cost'. An agent must, therefore, be prepared to quote figures for rates, service charges, cleaning, security, heating, lighting, insurance and other maintenance and repair obligations, in addition to rent.

Industrial property

In addition to many of the considerations described above in respect of the shop and office sectors relating to questions of rent, lease conditions, design, layout and management, there are a few aspects of industrial property marketing that merit special mention. Generally, a potential occupier of industrial premises is more concerned about the performance factors of a building, such as quality of construction, eaves-heights, floor loadings, column spacing, loading and delivery facilities, and access and egress to and from the site and building.

Location is of course paramount, and an agent must have an intimate knowledge of the special labour, market, materials and component needs in terms of accessibility that are demanded by different trades and industries. In the same way, an understanding of the distributional hinterlands and networks commanded by various commodity markets is essential in the sale or letting of warehouse developments.

As with other forms of commercial property development, flexibility is fast becoming the keynote of successful letting. The particular problem encountered in the industrial sector, however, is that flexibility not only applies to the ease with which it is possible to effect physical or functional changes within a building, but also to the freedom allowed an occupier to change the proportion of space given over to a particular use. This is often a matter of planning consent, and too constrained a permission can inhibit the marketability of a scheme. It must be recognized, in addition, that pre-lets are harder to achieve in the industrial sector.

Two other factors are beginning to characterize successful industrial sales and lettings. First, environmental quality both inside and outside factory premises is becoming more important to prospective occupiers. And, second, the availability of certain specialist services, whether on an industrial estate, or in close proximity to a particular development, plays a significant part in the decisions taken by industrial space users.

Residential property

At the outset it should be appreciated that residential development of any scale differs in one major respect from commercial property development in that almost all volume housebuilders tend to employ their own sales teams, and have recourse to estate agents as a second line of support, if at all. Because of this, advertising assumes an even more important role in the marketing of housing estates, for there is no network of agents as with the commercial sector, and not the same degree of high street representation as with the second-hand house market.

Prior to development, whoever is responsible for marketing, having established the basic demand for accommodation in the locality, the suitability of the locality, the amenities of the area and the extent of likely competition, is well advised to study former residential sales records in an attempt to find out why any cancellations took place. Non-buying attitudes are critical in the residential sector. Advertising studies, conversely, can show what features and what kind of presentation is most effective in generating interest in a particular development.

The usual method of marketing employed nowadays by the major house-builders is to fit out and furnish one of the completed properties in a scheme as a show house. This will then be staffed up to six and a half or even seven days a week, remembering that the majority of sales are introduced over the weekend. The advantage to the housebuilder is that the rest of the development can be monitored by their own agent, any damage can be made good immediately, access and response to inquirers is almost instant, all the energies of the sales force can be devoted to the one scheme and, in the case of phased development projects, information on reactions and probable market trends can be fed back to the design team. With show houses, it is always worthwhile laying out the garden to a high standard and making sure that the water and heating systems work efficiently.

In the residential sector, the role of aggressive promotion and marketing is probably most telling at either end of the market. Luxury housing is a volatile and predictable product. Well targeted, skilfully presented and extensively placed advertising can reap enormous dividends, for it is really a matter of reaching and attracting individual purchasers to whom marginal amounts of money at or around the asking price are of little consequence once they have decided that they want the house or flat in question. High-quality design and finishes, combined with an elegantly furnished and fitted show unit, are also an essential ingredient in successful luxury developments.

At the other end of the market, competition rages to attract the first-time buyer. A key element of marketing strategy for the first-time buyer of housing is the availability of mortgages. Virtually all the major housebuilders have agreements with one or more of the main building societies, giving ready access for potential purchasers to mortgage finance. These block allocations are a particularly valuable marketing tool when high demand causes mortgage queues and lending restrictions make it especially hard for first-time buyers. Other inducements offered as part of a marketing package often include one or more of the following:

- payment by the developer of legal fees, survey fees and stamp duty
- payment of a mortgage protection policy for, say, two to three years to ease the burden of worry; this has been extended by at least one volume housebuilder to the taking out, on behalf of the purchaser, of a personal protection policy against possible redundancy
- provision of items of household furniture and equipment such as cooker, washing machine, refrigerator, fully fitted units and carpets; in some small starter units this can even reach to chairs, tables and beds
- removal expenses
- subsidized mortgage repayments for up to one year
- repurchase at guaranteed levels of value

- purchase of buyer's existing property
- payment of 5 per cent mortgage deposit.

All these concessions both help the developer's cashflow and give momentum to the sales drive. In a mixed development, moreover, the early sale of the smaller units may prove a useful catalyst in stimulating interest in the remainder of higher-priced units in the scheme.

Selling techniques

It has been stated that there are no new methods of marketing property; all that exists are refinements of long-established techniques (Butler 1982). As with any business venture where management skills count every bit as much as the product, perhaps even more so with the marketing of property developments, for given similar buildings, in roughly the same location and identical promotion budgets, apart from the unexplained foibles of the market; it can only be the personal qualities of those managing the marketing campaign that make the difference. Nevertheless, a basic understanding of the techniques brought to bear by estate agents in selling floorspace is an essential part of the overall management of development projects.

Public relations

Public relations is a form of untargeted promotion aimed at the public at large. The best generator of good public relations is ultimately the quality of the development itself. Nevertheless, it is important to recognize that property development is rarely a popular activity to those in proximity of a proposed project. They often view development schemes as being physically intrusive, socially damaging and a threat to property values. Therefore, the sensitivity with which property development proposals are handled can greatly affect the acceptability and hence the feasibility of a project.

The very way in which the developers present themselves, the company and the retained consultants to the political representatives, professional officers, the press, interested parties and the general public can all contribute to fostering a favourable impression. Supplying full information and readily responding to criticism in a sympathetic and constructive manner further assists in creating an open and positive climate of opinion. Some developers establish an information office on the site or near the project, hold exhibitions, make presentations, conduct their own consultation exercises and produce a regular newsletter regarding project progress. In fact, every aspect of the selling process described below should be seen as part of a broad public relations campaign aimed at merchandising the development group.

Brochures and particulars

Naturally, both brochures and more simplified forms of property particulars must describe the intended or completed development and convey all the details that a potential occupier might require. Normally this will include some or all of the following:

- a geographical description of the general area, which identifies the precise location of the site or building
- communications facilities such as road, rail, air and water transport to and around the scheme
- for some kinds of development a brief social and economic profile of the area is advisable, covering such matters as shopping, housing, education and recreational facilities, as well as the presence in the vicinity of leading commercial organizations
- property particulars describing the accommodation, giving areas, heights and specification
- a description of the services supplied to the building, such as gas, water, cabling and electricity
- the nature of the interest being marketed, together with a broad explanation of the lease terms and a declaration about the existence of any restrictions to tenure
- an indication of the price or rent being sought
- who to contact, how and where for more information, assistance or appointment to view
- a saving clause to protect the agent and developer, which might be along the following lines:

> The agents, for themselves and for the vendors or lessors of this property whose agents they are give notice that plans and drawings are for identification purposes only and do not form part of any contract. Measurements and areas are approximate and although believed to be accurate an intending lessee or purchaser must satisfy himself as to their accuracy. No responsibility is taken for any error, omission or misstatement in this brochure which does not constitute or form any part of an offer or contract. No representation or warranty whatever is made or given in this brochure or during any negotiations consequent thereon.

Vogues and styles in brochures have changed over the years, from the crude letting brochures of the 1960s, through to some of the extravagant productions of the 1970s and 1980s, to the full colour, expertly designed and professionally laid-out publications of today. Even these are being edged out or supplemented by audiovisual cassettes and tapes. Nevertheless, the brochure is likely to remain an important marketing aid, and great care is now given to the presentation of information, so that prospective purchasers or tenants can assimilate the relevant facts quickly. There has also been an increasing emphasis over recent years on the use of good graphic designers, artists' impressions for new development, and specialist photography.

As with direct mailing (discussed below) it is vital that the brochure falls into the right hands. It may be necessary to produce more than one brochure during the course of marketing a development scheme. It also pays to attach a reply-paid card simply requiring interested parties to tick a box if they would like to receive further details.

Press advertising

Press advertising obviously is arranged at reaching the potential occupier or his professional advisers. They will, however, usually have different reading habits. The property professional is fairly predictable, and Saturday's scrutiny of the *Estates Gazette* is something of a time-honoured ritual for the commercial agent. The potential occupier is more difficult to divine, and the agent must attempt to gauge which professions, businesses or trades might be interested in a particular property or unit. Thus, if the space is clearly located and signed to be attractive to architects, then an advertisement in the *RIBA Journal* or in *Building* might evoke a positive response. Similarly, for computing firms, *Computing* or *Informatics* would be appropriate publications and, for advertising agencies, *Campaign* or *Marketing Week*. National press coverage may also catch the attention of the managing director or decision-taker, and do so in a captive situation or reflective mood, as might more specialist publications such as airline club magazines. Again, agents often prefer to design their press advertising to facilitate a direct response by incorporating a reply form to be filled out and returned.

Commonly, agents have recourse to specialist advertising agencies, although some of the very largest firms have established their own in-house advertising departments. A director of one of the country's leading advertising agencies has commented on the best and worst of the output of property advertising copy where internally or externally prepared (Stewart Hunter 1983). The better advertisements were said to stand out from the crowd and break through the 'noise' of competing claims on the readers' attention; be characterized by beautiful photography or illustration; have striking or unexpected headlines; and feature the building attractively or, in advertising language, make the product the 'hero' of the advertisement. The worst press advertisements were characterized, almost by definition, by having nothing striking about them, and likely to put off readers by virtue of the clutter, poorly laid out detail and unimaginative headlines and illustrations. Generally, moreover, property advertising was criticized as featuring the identity of the agents too prominently and yet also lacking a consistency in establishing a corporate identity.

It is generally recognized that the market has become increasingly sophisticated and developers far more aware of the power of the advertisement, in particular that potential tenants and targeted agents are different markets requiring different techniques. Some further comments by leading advertising agencies make telling, and sometimes contradictory, points about the advertising culture:

- Good design and clever ideas are not enough to sell a product – you've got to understand what is important to the audience.
- The biggest mistake is to go for too complex an image. It needs to be simple to survive what is a very noisy environment.
- You must not be afraid to be bold. The property press has been flooded with run-of-the-mill building adverts with square footages, agents' logos and piles of shopping bags. Your advert has got to be different.

- Any advertisement should be jazzy to look at, but it should be full of information.
- Humour has proved a particularly rich source of inspiration for corporate communication via advertising.
- A good picture highlights both the building itself and its chief asset, its location.
- Because we are always overestimating the importance of product, accepting that the product can take second place to concept allows to take about something other than the air-conditioning or lighting (Hall 1993).

One of the frustrations facing the advertising industry, however, is that the relative success of different approaches is difficult to quantify and largely remains a matter of speculation. Alongside press advertising is editorial coverage. It often pays to keep journalists informed of market developments, especially for major or unusual schemes. This is best done in the form of a press release accompanied by a good monochrome photograph with a caption and forwarded personally to the appropriate journalist.

Direct mailing

The use of carefully targeted mail shots has become an extremely popular form of marketing communication. The main advantages are that: it enables direct contact to be made with individuals in the target occupational group; it is highly selective and it avoids unnecessary circulation; it does not compete at the same time with other advertising messages; it is flexible in terms of geographical area, frequency and design; and it is relatively quick and cheap to produce and distribute.

Mail shots are normally used to support a wider marketing campaign, and should be released to coincide with other advertising ploys, but they may sometimes be the sole method of promotion. It must be remembered, however, that the bulk of direct mail letters end up in the waste-paper basket. They must, therefore, be simply but compellingly written, preferably well illustrated and addressed to a named managing director or finance director marked 'personal' to circumvent over-protective secretaries. It is quite common practice for a local mail shot to precede a more widely directed regional or national mailing using one of the better direct mail houses properly briefed.

Despite the deterioration of e-mail, notably via the proliferation of viral and permission marketing and text messaging campaigns, it seems that the mail shot remains a firm favourite of the property sector (*Estates Gazette* 2002).

The Institute of Direct Marketing offers the following checklist for direct marketing planning:

- Set your objectives
- Set your budget
- Outline your campaign activity
- Check on the competition

- Identify your target audience
- Access your target audience
- Develop your creative approach
- Design your mailing package
- Draw up your production schedule
- Brief internal personnel and external agencies
- Analyse and evaluate your results.

A recent report by Susanna K. Hutcheson (ibid.) listed 10 mistakes in direct mail:

- Not knowing your target market
- Mailing to the wrong list
- Not having a clear goal in your writing
- Price before offer
- Price before benefits
- Wrong price
- Inadequate testing
- Wrong objective
- Wrong headline
- Not telling your readers exactly what you want them to do.

A innovation on the mail shot is the 'freemium', the inclusion of some sort of free item, such as a magnet, mouse mat, torch, CD. It is hoped that the recipient receiving the gift then feels obliged to respond.

Despite the widespread use of the word-processor and the increased facility to 'personalize' letters, however, it is quite possible that the effectiveness of the traditional direct mail shot will diminish. Nevertheless, good clear and precise covering letters accompanying other mailed particulars will always be an important marketing tool.

Siteboards and hoardings

Perhaps the most familiar marketing aid is the agent's board, providing on-the-spot advertising of the availability of property. There is a tendency, however, for development sites during the construction period to be weighed down with a welter of different boards – architects, building contractors, engineers and quantity surveyors, as well as developers and agents. In marketing terms they achieve little or nothing, even when sensibly grouped as a single display, unless considerable thought is given to their function and treatment. Moreover, there is often the lingering suspicion in the mind of the client developer that the board on a completed building does more to promote the image of the agent than it does the identity of the development.

However, the contribution made by sale or letting boards to the overall marketing campaign should not be underrated. On a new development such boards can be used not only to state the details of a proposed building or buildings under construction, but be employed as a linking display describing the programme of work and the progress to date. Casual visitors to the site may well be potential occupiers, and be converted into actual tenants by the continuing advertisement.

Over the past few years it is obvious that much greater care has been expended upon the design and location of siteboards by some leading property development companies. Dignified artists' impressions and stylishly presented wording can only help to enhance both the perceived quality of the building and the corporate image of the developer. Nevertheless, it is important to ensure that boards are regularly inspected and maintained, otherwise the opposite reactions might be engendered.

The development in photographic processing, going by the proprietary name of Scanachrome, offers much more scope for creativity and impact in the use of siteboards, letting boards and posters. Large pictorial boards can be produced as massive enlargements of photographic transparencies or prints at relatively little cost and can have a physical outdoor life of up to 18 months.

Siteboards and hoardings are now popular vehicles for developers who have become increasingly enterprising in their use of the medium. For about £10 000 a first-class hoarding can be commissioned for a fairly large development. A site can be made safer and the incidence of graffiti and vandalism reduced. The local community and emerging young artists can also be involved in the content and design of such hoardings. There is now even an annual competition held by the *Estates Gazette* for the best hoarding of the year.

It should be remembered that if a board is larger than 2–3 m^2 it requires advertising consent under town planning controls. Some local authorities apply even stricter controls in what are considered to be sensitive environmental areas. The suggestion has also been made that the creative effort expended in the design and positioning of boards may ultimately be thwarted by the planners, who are increasingly resistant to their use (Wilks & Brown 1980). This notion is reinforced by the activity of a growing number of residents' associations and amenity groups who oppose what they see as a proliferation of estate agent boards, which results in 'visual pollution'. Hopefully, however, innovation and imagination in siteboard and hoarding design might temper any overreaction to what remains an effective promotion and selling technique.

Demonstration

The residential sector has long relied upon the tangible demonstration of its wares to sell property. No estate development of any size is complete and properly ready for marketing until a furnished and fitted show house or flat is made available for inspection. Over recent years this approach has spread to the office and industrial sectors. Show suites of offices, fully furnished and equipped, are now a common feature of marketing. Some shrewd consultants have even been able to persuade office furniture and equipment suppliers to fit out such show space at no cost. Reception areas are also invariably completed, decorated and 'landscaped' to high standards well before final building works are finished. Good housekeeping is important, with windows washed, rubbish cleared and common parts cleaned.

Many major commercial property developers have adopted the principle set by the volume housebuilders and have put their own people on site so that a constant and knowledgeable marketing presence is maintained. This is the kind of service that prospective tenants are coming to expect in the current letting market.

A modern surrogate for on-site demonstration is, of course, the videotape. In producing these, as well as with actual tours of inspection, it is worth recognizing that there is a best way to show someone over the property. Preferred routes should, therefore, be mapped out in advance, and so arranged as to make the first and last impressions of the development the most favourable (Butler 1982).

For major schemes, or ones of an especially sensitive nature, an exhibition might be necessary. Apart from displays put on as part of the process of obtaining a planning consent, the majority of exhibits of development projects are prepared as part of corporate promotions in both the public and private sector. It should be appreciated, however, that the mounting of exhibitions or, for that matter, the participation in exhibitions organized by others, is a costly and time-consuming affair.

Television and radio

The use of commercial television to advertise property is still the exception rather than the rule. The principal reason for this is cost, in terms of both preparation and presentation of material. Despite the expense, television is said to offer wide coverage, to be an intrusive medium that is well suited to demonstrating a building to its best advantage, and to be capable of targeting regional audiences with some precision. View data services such as Prestel, Ceefax and Oracle, however, have not proved as successful as was hoped in the marketing of property.

Local radio is beginning to be used fairly extensively for the advertising of property. Opinions vary as to how effective it is. On the one hand, it is reasonably cheap, offers relatively wide coverage and can lend itself to the creative and striking communication of information. On the other, although it might do wonders for the agent's image, it can be argued that the transitory nature of the message is unlikely to sell property. The right people rarely listen, except at the wrong time.

The internet

A survey carried out by the *Estates Gazette* in October 2001 found that people have become more aware of the power of marketing, particularly using the massive power of the internet. There are no limits to the amount of information, including multiple plans, pictures and spreadsheets, that can be provided at a fraction of the cost of traditional printing and brochure distribution (*Estates Gazette* 2001).

Many firms have established specific websites for prestige buildings, providing all the usual particulars plus virtual walk-throughs, detailed floor plans, etc. One early example was www.201deansgate.com (the site is no longer available), a major hi-tec office building in Manchester city centre.

There are also a number of property listing services: www.rightmove.co.uk offers residential property listings, www.retailpropertymarket.com provides searchable retail property listings. These 'portal' sites are becoming the first port of call for clients wishing to browse a wide variety of properties offered by a range of agents.

Kim Tasso (Tasso 2001) found that users want to get in, get information without lots of drilling, and then get out. The site should therefore be as easy to navigate as possible. John Kelsey of Berwin Leighton Paisner (ibid.) says that agents could at least look at incorporating standard lease information and a synopsis of the title with particulars.

Many brochure sites fail on two counts: poor user interaction, and a failure to encourage visitors to stay longer and return. Web-based marketing is best suited to certain types of property when marketing is more interactive.

Monitoring the effectiveness of a firm's website is crucial to further development. Without strong statistics on the results of web marketing, more investment is impossible to justify.

Many of the techniques to web marketing are equally applicable to other areas. They include:

- Know your objectives
- Know your target audiences
- Integrate your web strategy with the main marketing plan
- Ensure the content is high quality, up-to-date and will promote interaction and repeat visits
- Develop online communities for targeted email campaigns
- Consider how an extranet could be used to reduce costs and enhance service delivery
- Consider how you could do things differently, rather than just put existing material online
- Ensure you can measure the effectiveness, revenue and savings from the site
- Ensure that live contact with people remains on the agenda.

Incentives

Apart from the traditional agents' lunch, and more recently agents' breakfasts and coffee mornings, more and more incentives seem to be on offer in the market. Luxury cars, holidays abroad and additional cash bonuses are all dangled before those who can introduce a successful letting. At the same time, in a difficult market, there is a continuing pressure to offer ever more attractive inducements to prospective occupiers. Rent-free periods, low starting rentals, fitting-out subsidies, reverse premiums and options to break are all employed at the moment, as incentives during negotiations to secure a letting. They should, however, be introduced with care. For it has been pointed out that if a property has been correctly marketed and stands in rental terms on an equal footing with competition, then to use these factors prematurely can often erode the base for negotiation. In addition, it is argued that very seldom is a businessman lured into the market-place purely by marginal short-term financial inducements. If the property is right, and the terms comparatively competitive, the deal should be struck notwithstanding the trappings. Conversely, because they are known to exist in the market, they become expected. In any event they should be properly costed at the outset of the scheme, as should the reception held on completion to launch the building onto the market, whether it has been pre-let or not. This has now become an important part of the promotion campaign, for the agent and funder as well as the developer, and it deserves careful attention. If, for example, it is a pure letting reception, the individual public relations of those concerned with the development should not be allowed to detract from the essential marketing thrust.

Other approaches

More and more firms of estate agents as well as developers and financial institutions are using the service of public relations advisers. With their consumer-based approach, the range and variety of promotional activities are bound to increase. Marketing plans will be more professionally drawn up and more persistently pursued. Special events and novel programmes will become a more common feature of property promotion and marketing.

The use of display models of a development; special naming of a building or the grant of naming rights; the design of a compelling logo and graphics for a project; ground-breaking, topping-out and opening ceremonies with attendant publicity; the use of holograms in demonstration units; special treatment of entrances and common parts; cold calling of possible purchasers; and the despatch or presentation of novelties are all well tried selling techniques. More recently the possibility of using 'interactive' or 'virtual reality' techniques has been explored by some property developers to market their buildings, so that at the press of a button you can move around the premises and experience different forms of finish, enclosure and fitting out. However, it is costly.

Again, whatever combination of selling techniques is employed, the importance of effective follow-up activity cannot be stressed enough. Few sales are closed quickly, and patience and perseverance are invariably required. Follow-up should not stop once an agreement has been made or a deal struck. It should continue between signing and moving in, and beyond into occupancy. The good name of the developer and the reputation of the agent are themselves integral aspects of present and future promotion, marketing and sales.

Developers' viewpoint

It should be the overriding objective of all developers operating in the private sector to ensure that the buildings they produce are marketable. They must, therefore, concentrate the minds of all the members of the professional team, whether they be architects, engineers, quantity surveyors, builders or whatever, upon the marketing aspects of the project. Thus, from the developers' viewpoint there are several general factors that should be taken into account in planning the marketing campaign for almost any scheme of development.

The choice of agent

The question of marketing and the selection of those who will be responsible for the choice of agent should be made at the earliest possible stage in the development process. It may well be that a potential development site has been introduced by a particular agent. Alternatively, a firm might have been instructed by the developer, or by a prospective occupier, to find a suitable development site because of their special knowledge of the land market in a given locality. In both circumstances the agent concerned might wish to remain associated with the project and undertake the sale or letting. Indeed, it would be surprising if they did not, and in the case of an introduction to a site it is difficult to arrange otherwise. However, they may not be the best firm for the job. In selecting the right agent several questions can be posed:

- *National or local?* A national firm of estate agents will have a broad coverage of markets and a wide range of business and property contacts, but on smaller or more difficult developments they may not be quite so hungry for success. A local firm might be eager to perform, conveniently available and familiar with the local market, but they may lack the necessary knowledge and network of commercial contacts and be unable to supply certain support services. Often a combination of the two is the best solution.
- *Large or small?* Much the same arguments as above apply to the size of estate agency firm retained. It is remarkable, however, how many major developers are increasingly willing to entrust the marketing of very large schemes to very small practices. Again, the answer is often a joint instruction.
- *Firm or individual?* It is important to select and instruct agents with care to ensure that it is not just the right firm, but also the right person within that firm who is fully responsible for selling the property.
- *Regular or infrequent?* Although there are often compelling reasons for sticking with an agent who has performed well in the past and has become accustomed to the individual ways of a given developer, it can sometimes be beneficial to try out someone different. Even in professional circles, familiarity occasionally can breed contempt, and it is always interesting to compare alternative approaches.
- *Generalist or specialist?* Certain estate agents gain a particular reputation for marketing expertise in special fields, either by sector or by geographical area. Even within such broad categories as shops, offices or industrial premises, performance can vary. With very special types of property, such as leisure or hotel projects, it is a brave developer, or perhaps a foolish one, who does not avail himself of special marketing advice.

To get the best out of an agent it is not only necessary to appoint them at the inception of a project, but equally essential to make sure that they are involved at every stage of the development process. In this way, marketing factors are built into the original design and the agent gains a deeper understanding of the nature of the property. Although this close collaboration throughout the period of development is bound to be to the benefit of all concerned, it is nonetheless imperative that there should be clearly defined terms of reference and established levels of responsibility for marketing. This is especially true where two or more agents are instructed.

The marketing campaign

It is a cardinal priority for both the developer and the agent to satisfy themselves that the marketing campaign is properly planned and evenly spaced. As has been contended:

> One of the worst offences is the momentous first push, heavy over-exposure and comparative inactivity thereafter. Plan it so that you have a series of nudges rather than one forgettable blast.
>
> (Butler 1982)

Another common failing among development companies is the parsimonious allowance made for marketing at appraisal and project planning stages. It is astonishing that, with the enormous capital sums involved and the difficult market conditions that prevail, how little money is made available for marketing. The developer and agent should, therefore, agree on a reasonable budget for promotion and marketing, remembering that smaller, less prominent, buildings will often require a proportionately higher sum spent on selling them than do their larger, more splendid, counterparts.

As already mentioned, the contribution of the public relations firm to the promotion and marketing of property development schemes has grown over the past decade or so. Although the cost of retaining the services of a good firm of public relations consultants is additional to the usual agency commissions incurred, it is worth the developer of any special kind of development, particularly those dependent upon public custom, considering the use of such expertise. However, experience shows that it is advisable to negotiate a fixed fee rather than work to their preferred quantum merit basis. It is also important to make sure that a good working relationship and clearly defined terms of reference are established between the estate agent and the public relations firm, otherwise an element of suspicion can erode the effectiveness of both.

Naturally, a developer will also wish to approve the proposed selling techniques. Without re-examining the relative merits or otherwise of such methods of selling as brochures, videos, press advertising, direct mailing, siteboards, demonstration units, television or radio, a developer should have a basic understanding of the techniques used by estate agents in selling commercial floorspace. At the very least it is necessary to select the right agent in the first place. At best, it promotes a healthy climate of confidence between the agent and developer.

In any event, it is worth restating that there are really no new methods of marketing property, merely refinements of long-established techniques. But with any business venture where management skills count every bit as much as the product, so with the marketing of property developments. For given similar buildings, in roughly the same location and with identical promotion budgets, apart from the foibles of the market, it can only be the personal qualities of those managing the marketing campaign that make the difference.

With potential occupiers becoming increasingly aware of their space requirements, it is important not to present marketing material is too naïve, or even insulting, a manner. Moreover, if sufficient thought is given early enough in the development programme as to what exactly is involved, and where time and money is best expended, it may transpire that some of the traditional avenues or marketing are not necessary.

Monitoring marketing

Once an agent has been instructed and a marketing campaign agreed, it is essential that the developer retains continuing contact with the agent to monitor progress. Regular meetings, at say, monthly intervals, should be held, preferably on site. Moreover, the client developer should always insist that a written report on the previous month's activity is submitted to him at least two days before the meeting. This would itemize all the inquiries that had been made about the property, the names and positions of those inquiring and whether or not any visit to view had been arranged or taken place, and with what result.

Where appropriate, an explanation of why enquirers had not pursued their interest should be included, together with a reasoned argument examining how lettings have taken place in what are seen as directly competing properties. This discipline is not popular with agents, and there might indeed be occasions when excessive adherence to the routine becomes a contrivance. However, formality is easy to relax, but difficult to reassert. The reporting process must, therefore, be seen as a genuine evaluation of progress and not a mere ritual.

The developer will also normally wish to be consulted regarding the presentation and placement of advertising. Although the agent will be more familiar with the various vehicles for promoting the property to best advantage, it is as well to check that it is the development that has pride of place in an advert, and not the agent's corporate image. Another avenue worth exploring with the agent is the possibility of trailing editorial comment throughout the course of the campaign. It is hard to assess the true value of editorial exposure, but it is free.

There are several other matters worth mentioning regarding the relationship of the developer and the agent during the marketing process. These can be summarized as follows:

* Resist the natural urge to tinker with such matters as the design and format of the brochure or the structure and content of any covering letter. If dissatisfied, reject them; do not compromise.
* Do not be tempted to cut out the agent if an approach is made direct by a potential purchaser/lessee. Always refer such offers to the agent, for there is little purpose served in retaining an agent and conducting negotiations personally. In this way, a secondary negotiating position is reserved.

- Do not change agents midway through marketing unless there are very good reasons for so doing. Continuity is one of the more important ingredients of a marketing campaign. If the service from the agent is thought to be unsatisfactory, it is often better to give them two months' notice to quit or ask them to re-tender for the instructions against a major competitor. It is remarkable how rejuvenating this particular process can be. If, however, the dissatisfaction is deep-seated, then it is better to cut losses and change agents forthwith.
- Decide the degree to which the property will be finished, and what help might be made available to any incoming tenants for fitting out. There is a growing tendency in the office and industrial development sectors, as there always has been in retailing, to complete buildings only to a shell stage. Tenants are then encouraged to select wall, floor and ceiling materials and finishes, with the developer covering the cost up to a predetermined amount. Some developers are even providing free space-planning advice.
- Consider what kind and level of continuing services could be provided by the client and on what basis. It can be argued that, both to generate initial profitability and maintain income flow, the management of commercial property generally needs to be much more aggressive. To some extent, therefore, development does not end once a building is physically completed, but includes the establishment of a property management system.
- Furthermore, in terms of marketing and management, more flexible leases as well as more flexible buildings are being demanded by tenants, particularly by those in the new technology industries and specialized professional services. Tenants are increasingly looking for shorter leases with one-sided break clauses and a range of supporting business and personal services. Thus, good marketing, which has regard to good management, will play an ever more important part in assuring the success of development projects.
- Pay fees promptly, and once agreed do not attempt to renegotiate. There is almost a paradox in the property world whereby an agent achieving a good quick sale or letting is somehow not felt to have earned their fee, whereas the long and costly campaign is in a strange way thought to have shown value for money.
- Consider within the overall context of marketing the corporate image of the client. In these days of greater accountability and ever-growing public awareness, the image a property development company portrays to the public at large is fast becoming one of its more valuable assets. 'Public' in this sense refers to the whole professional and commercial milieu in which the company operates. Thus, it includes clients, competitors, local authorities, the news media, financial institutions, construction firms, professional practitioners and prospective purchasers.

In a business that, rightly or wrongly, is not exactly renowned for its high ethical or aesthetic standards, there is good reason for property development companies to ask themselves a few telling questions regarding their corporate image. It has been suggested that these should include the following:

> How do we think we are perceived by the public?
> How are we actually viewed by them?
> How would we wish to be thought of?
> What image is most likely to assist us in achieving our objectives?
>   (Charlesworth-Jones 1983)

Unless, in the unlikely event of all the answers to these questions coinciding, the next proposition should be, 'How do we go about designing and implementing a desirable corporate image?' This may involve a change in attitude by members of the company, an advertising campaign, public relations exercises, or even a change of name. In any event, the very act of self-assessment can be both salutary and rewarding.

Conclusion

Innovation in the process of promotion and marketing is bound to happen. What confronts the agency business is the extent to which property professionals can retain command over the sales team. Already we see leading firms of public relations consultants, with their skilful manipulation of the media and their flair for promotional activities, beginning to make incursions into the agency field. As mentioned earlier, specialist firms of property marketing consultants importing American selling techniques are starting to spring up. Advanced systems of information technology with wider and cheaper accessibility, together with new methods of conducting business, all point to changes in the way we buy and sell development and other properties. Education for marketing, both for existing members in practice and for new entrants to the estates profession, will become ever more essential.

Nevertheless, there are no magic formulae to the art of marketing. It is simply a logical stage-by-stage approach that employs a range of techniques and disciplines, and it is the firm that uses all the appropriate techniques and skills that will create the synergy that sells.

Part V

Real estate development sectors

15 Retail development

For the 30-odd years following the end of the Second World War, retailing was repeatedly heralded as the most innovative and changeable sector of the property market. New types of shop development emerged one after another: department stores, variety shops, supermarkets, covered shopping precincts, hypermarkets, superstores, district centres, discount warehouses, and city-centre 'metro' stores. Preferred locations shifted away from the high street, to adjacent central-area sites, out-of-town to greenfield sites, back to town-centre and edge-of-town locations and even 'sideways' onto industrial estates. Modern forms of merchandising have altered the shape, size and layout of shops of all kinds, and advances in the methods of distribution have affected the design and position of retail outlets. Nevertheless, there remains considerable volatility in the shop market and a continuing dynamic in the field of retail development.

This chapter is divided into five sections, as follows:

- the context for retail development
- types of retail development
- planning and retailing
- design and layout
- shopping centre management.

The context for retail development

As consumers have become increasingly discerning, affluent and mobile, so retailers have had to respond to changing market conditions and opportunities. In forecasting future trends in shopping and shop development it is worth recording briefly some of the more significant factors that have brought about the process of change in retailing over recent years. These can be summarized as follows:

- Food retailing on any scale has almost disappeared from many traditional town centres as superstore operators have relocated to locations on the edge of or out of town, where they can find sites capable of providing 4645–5574 m^2 (50/60 000 ft^2) or more of space with extensive carparking facilities.

- The fashion industry has extended its market to embrace every sector of society, whereas only a generation or so ago it was the preserve of the better-off.
- Likewise, eating-out was something of an occasional treat for most people, but over the past couple of decades a revolution has taken place in the catering industry, with a consequent impact upon all forms of retail property development.
- The majority of the population have more money to spend than at any time in the past. They are also more likely to own a car and gain from greater mobility.
- Retailers have become more inventive and competitive in their promotional, marketing and merchandising policies.
- Low inflation and rising shop rents created a favourable climate for retail development in both in- and out-of-town locations during the late 1980s.
- The government adopted a much more laissez-faire attitude to out-of-town retailing during the 1980s than had previously been the case. However, current attitudes now favour town centres.
- For most of the past 20 years, the growth of capital investment in UK retailing has outstripped comparable growth rates in almost all other sectors. Investment in shop development has, therefore, enjoyed continued and expanding support from financial institutions and retail operators alike.
- During the last 30 years retailers and developers increasingly detected a consumer need to provide 'one-stop shopping' combining comparison shopping, leisure and catering facilities within an easily accessible, traffic-free and preferably enclosed environment.
- Speciality trading emerged during the 1980s as a powerful force in the retail sector, usually at the expense of the department store.
- As a result of re-targeting and redesigning by retailers, floorspace requirements have constantly been changing. Moreover, unit sizes have been affected by new ways of distributing and storing stock.

Decentralization of shopping, in its many forms, has, and continues to be, the central issue in the planning and development of retail space. The tide of trade flowing away from the high street can neatly be described as occurring in three waves. The first outward wave was that by the food-based superstores to edge- or out-of-town sites. The second wave, now well established, gained momentum towards the end of the 1970s, included retailers selling bulk items such as DIY, furniture and electrical goods. The third wave is represented by the creation of regional and subregional shopping centres, and also includes the drift out of town of groups of major durable goods traders. There is now a determined attempt to reverse this trend back towards the town centre so as to create a fourth wave.

Forecasting and trends

In the context of retailing it has been said that forecasting is much easier than is generally realized, because what the rich do today creates the appetites of the masses in the future (Schiller 1982, McCollum 1985). Moreover, the USA acts as a kind of window into how people will want to work, live and shop in times ahead. There are, however, a few basic ingredients that help determine the likely future nature and mix of retailing, which are described below.

Population changes

Changes in the size, social and age structure of the population have a considerable influence upon property markets. Birthrate, which has been running at less than replacement level since the early 1970s, seems set to remain at a low level. Life expectancy, on the other hand, has increased by two years over the past decade and is steadily rising. Household size appears likely to reduce even further, so that by the year 2010 almost 60 per cent of all households will consist of only one or two people. This all probably means that, with an ageing population and more households, more people will have more time to spend shopping.

Spatial distribution

Although the overall size of the UK population has changed little over the past 20 years and looks fairly stable, if ageing, for the next 10 or so, the spatial distribution is much more variable. Broadly speaking, the only parts of the country where more than 10 per cent population growth is forecast before the end of the decade are 13 counties stretching in a band from Lincolnshire, Cambridgeshire and Suffolk in the east, southwestwards through Northamptonshire, Oxfordshire, Buckinghamshire and Berkshire to Wiltshire, Shropshire, Hampshire, Somerset, Dorset and Cornwall in the south and west. These are the areas where more retail floorspace will be required.

Consumer expenditure

Despite the recession of the early 1990s, the shopping public in general is becoming more affluent. With interest rates at their lowest level for nearly 40 years, historically low levels of inflation and rising residential property values, growth in retail expenditure over the last decade has been significant. Some of this growing affluence has naturally gone into improved housing, additional leisure and better health and education services, but even the terrible events of 11 September 2001 and conflict in Iraq have so far failed to significantly affect levels of consumer spending in the UK.

Mobility and accessibility

Car ownership and its effect upon shopping behaviour is probably even more important than is commonly supposed. The number of cars on British roads is increasing by 2–3 per cent annually. Car ownership doubled between 1960 and 1980, and is likely to double again by the early years of the next century. Among all households with children, 72 per cent have a car.

Work and leisure

The average working week in all industries has fallen from around 42 hours in 1973 to about 40 hours in 1985 and is thought, although conflicting figures are produced, to have decreased to under 37 hours today. In the salaried business sector this is probably lower. Nevertheless, more women will probably work, and 'moonlighting' will increase. Not only will people have more time to go shopping, and more money to do it with, but shopping will itself become more of a leisure activity.

Information technology

Improvements in information and communication technology have revolutionized the comparison, selection and ordering of certain goods. E-retailing in the UK has grown from less than 1 per cent of UK shopping in 1999 to an estimate of 3 per cent in 2003 and 10 per cent by 2009 (Verdict (2000, 2001, 2002); Gibson (1999)). Business to business (B2B) and 'just-in-time' systems have radically changed the stocking, distribution and control of merchandise. Some shopping centre owners even use information systems to record the turnover for each unit in the centre to establish the level of turnover rents that should be charged (where the rent paid by the retailer represents a proportion of sales turnover of their unit) but, as one might expect, retailers are jealously protective of this commercially sensitive information.

Consumer demands

Perhaps above all there has been the realization among retailers and developers that it is the customer that calls the tune. The shopping public constantly have to be wooed. They increasingly demand accessible, convenient, secure and enjoyable shopping environments with adequate parking, a wide and comparative range of goods at reasonable prices and the availability of attractive and useful facilities such as food, child care and leisure.

Basic research procedures

As the retail industry has matured, so shopping centre developers have become more and more aware of the need for reliable market research and analysis. Indeed, such retail studies are of benefit to all concerned. To the developers they confirm the degree of potential opportunity, provide a basis for planning application, set design and site layout constraints, furnish basic data for marketing and funding, and provide information vital to the future sale of the property. To the local community they contribute to the development planning and control processes: identifying existing and future shopping needs, allocating land for retail development, examining and catering for infrastructure consequences, assessing the impact of development proposals upon existing shopping facilities, and determining the outcome of applications for shopping schemes. And to prospective retailers they measure the opportunity for new units, sales potential and floor space, as well as assessing the competitive situation (McCollum 1985).

It should be appreciated that market research is not an exact science, for the analyst is essentially presenting a subjective evaluation of a project's potential based upon available data and drawing upon personal experience and judgement. In fact one leading consultant has gone so far as to state that 'traditional catchment analysis is a thing of the past' (Maynard 1990). Nevertheless, the basic procedure for conducting a retail market analysis is typically an economic area analysis, a trade area analysis and an appraisal of optimum size and mix for the proposed project (McCollum 1985).

Economic area analysis

Economic area analysis is conducted to determine whether a particular market can support additional retail development and it includes an investigation of:

- *Employment trends.* These are critical as the form and level of employment naturally determine the overall purchasing power of the market area.
- *Population forecasts.* Such an analysis would lean heavily upon information compiled and used by the planning authority for the area.
- *Income levels.* Extracting per capita and family income levels and estimating likely increases is a vital preliminary step in estimating retail expenditures for the area in question.
- *Retail sales data.* This study depicts which retail categories have achieved rapid sales growth, which are declining, and how they relate to population and income growth. They are usually divided into comparison or durable goods sales and convenience goods sales.

The prime objective of the economic area analysis, therefore is to reveal the strength and nature of the employment base, the geographical centres of population and potential for population growth, the strongest retail categories, and the sales potential projected for the area. The analysts will then use these data when delineating a trade area and assessing sales potential for a proposed centre.

Trade area analysis

Assuming the economic base study has shown potential growth for the area, a market analysis of the trade area is undertaken to assess the potential of a given site for a shopping centre development. A trade area is the geographic sector for which the sustaining patronage for steady support of a shopping centre is obtained. Also known as the catchment area or hinterland. The boundaries are determined by various factors, including:

- the size and nature of the site itself, as well as character of the surrounding locality
- present and proposed accessibility to the site
- any physical or artificial barriers limiting the site

• the location of competing facilities
• the limitations of travel time and distance.

The total trade area is normally divided into three or more zones as a means to illustrate and assess variations in the impact of the proposed centre by use of established capture or penetration rates. By reference to population, income and capture estimates, total expenditure can be gauged.

Shopping centre sales potential

The principal aim of the market research is to assess the proposed centre's retail sales potential. This demonstrates ultimate profitability and optimum size and mix. There are two basic approaches to estimating sales potential:

• *Share of the market.* This approach essentially assumes that the shopping centre will gain a certain percentage of the total trade area sales potential. Experience, and the analysis of comparable developments in similar situations elsewhere, will indicate the probable proportion of the population falling within the trade area that will be prepared to travel to the proposed centre. An evaluation of the population employment and income data will show how much they might spend and on what.
• *Residual analysis.* The potential trade for a new centre can also be calculated by employing what is variously described as the 'vacuum', 'residual', or 'remainder' method, whereby the total consumer expenditure going to other centres in the vicinity is assessed at first instance. The procedure briefly includes determining the prospective catchment area, gauging the total population by census district, calculating retail expenditure by goods and socio-economic groups, allocating expenditure to more accessible and convenient centres, allowing for local traders' share and estimating the potential trade remaining, for, where positive, the turnover will be available to the new centre, where negative, the area is already overshopped.

Project size and mix

Once total sales potential has been predicted, the need arises to translate this demand into a physical context, in terms of how much floorspace, in how many shops or what type, to determine the size and mix of the centre. This is achieved by use of conversion factors, which simply express turnover per square metre of gross floorspace. These factors display a variation according to broad region and specific locality. Other changing aspects of shopping also play a part in the steady rise of conversion factors: longer shopping hours, the reduction of non-productive space, and improved merchandising.

In the context of retail market research and analysis, it should be stated that over the years there has been a rapid advance in the development of sophisticated techniques that aim to assist in the assessment of the retail hinterland, the measurement of market penetration, and provide some explanation for retail land-use location. These techniques are grouped together as shopping models. They seek to represent a real world situation in terms simple enough to permit examination of past and present shopping patterns and the prediction of future trends.

These models tend to be employed more by planning authorities and major retail organizations than they do by shopping centre developers. Some members of the property profession remain sceptical about the use of advanced techniques of analysis. But more than ever, given the increasingly complex nature of the retail market, the sector needs to be served by good research, not just in the form of quantitative studies, but in respect of customer behaviour and personnel requirements.

Types of retail development

A useful, but less than traditional, classification of shopping centres has been advanced along the following lines:

- Those centres that are free-standing and suburban in location providing for the general-purpose shopping needs of households. They may be neighbourhood, community or regional in terms of catchment, so that the small strip centre and the large super-regional centre are really subtypes of the same category.
- General-purpose centres located in shopping districts, and are sometimes known as renewal or redevelopment centres. Again there are several subtypes according to size and location, as well as their relationship to the shopping district in which they are positioned.
- Multi-use centres, where shopping is only one of several uses within the overall development. Once more there are several kinds of centre within this category. They are a concept developed in the US that has gained popularity in the UK in recent years.
- Those centres where retailing is ancillary to other commercial activities, and is provided to complement the dominant function of the building complex. The so-called subtypes here would be differentiated according to the dominant activity, whether it be hotel, office or transport interchange.
- Speciality centres (such as those specializing in high-class fashion) and focused centres (for example designer outlet villages) that concentrate upon a particular theme or tenant mix, sometimes purpose-built and sometimes housed in a renovated building.

No classification completely satisfies the market, but at least the one outlined above helps distinguish between the different processes of development, methods of funding and styles of operation, as well as forms of retailing. It has also been pointed out that different types of centre will succeed in different ways and must, therefore, be assessed accordingly.

In considering the shopping opportunities that have been taken across the various types of retail operation over the past few years, and exploring those that exist to be exploited in the immediate future, attention is paid primarily to the development side of the market rather than to the investment or business prospects of retailing.

The high street

As planning policy seeks to curb out-of-town development, large retailers and leisure operators are beginning to refocus on the town centre. The food retailers in particular have sought to exploit the growing 'metro' market by providing convenience stores in town centres, petrol stations, etc., often to the detriment of small shops occupied by local traders. The growth in cafes and bars is another facet of this urban renaissance. Some of the leading multiples in certain durable goods markets are also looking more closely at good secondary positions rather than their previous prime pitches, bringing with them a new injection of consumer interest and possible redevelopment potential. Moreover, while there appears to be an inevitable decline in the total number of standard units, it is sometimes surprising to discover the high turnover achieved by individual traders in specialized fields. Locally based development companies are also showing more interest in purchasing, refurbishing and reletting single smaller units. Such developers are inclined to be more sensitive to occupiers' needs. Thus, leases are showing some signs of becoming shorter, review periods more regular and user conditions less onerous. In this way, the rate at which the trading mix of high streets changes is likely to quicken.

Other avenues for possible development in the high street can be summarized as follows:

- The acquisition and exploitation of land to the rear of high street shops to allow for the creation of stores with large floorspace and high street access, but where wide high street frontage for display is not a principal requirement.
- The assembly of several deep standard units, with or without additional rear land, in order to create small malls or precincts branching off the high street.
- The refurbishment of existing units to provide more suitable retal space for the changing needs of multiple traders.
- The incremental upgrading of side streets to the high street to establish a kind of 'Latin Quarter' atmosphere, with a grouping of complementary service trades.
- Capitalizing upon the pedestrianization of high streets or adjoining thoroughfares to refurbish or redevelop otherwise redundant or deteriorating premises.
- The renovation and conversion of historic buildings, or buildings of special architectural merit, to produce a type of speciality centre, probably incorporating some form of catering and leisure facility.
- Some braver developers have contemplated the creation of multi-level trading through the conversion of existing high street stores, normally in absolutely prime positions.

Uncertainty engendered by recession heightened the debate on the future of the high street, one element of which is the role that the major retailers play. The increased concentration of ownership and occupation of the high streets in the UK has been said to have brought both benefits and drawbacks (Bernard Thorpe & OIRM 1990). On the plus side, it has seen an immeasurable improvement in the internal and external appearance of shops, the product ranges on offer and the general ambience of shopping. On the minus side, the further decline of independent shops and a wider assortment of multiple retailers has led to a loss of variety and the 'higgledy-piggledy' character of older, traditional high streets. In the last decade we have seen significant improvements in town centre management addressing issues such as environment, security, investment, accessibility, marketing, and promotion. There is also an increasing presence of pan-European and international multiples on the high street, particularly in the fashion sector. A wider variety of multiple trading names have appeared, encouraging high standards of shop design and quality of merchandise. In the larger cities the renaissance in urban living and enhanced leisure provision have breathed new life into some inner urban areas and this trend is expected to continue.

It cannot be denied, however, that the town centre in general and the high street in particular continue to face a challenge from accessible, convenient and secure out-of-town centres. Nevertheless, as has been maintained, the disappearance of food retailing from the town centre has been more than compensated for by the opportunity for extra retail floorspace for those traders specializing in comparison and durable goods. Moreover, major retailers and investors have enormous capital values and commitments locked into town centres and thereby have a strong vested interest in protecting and preserving their assets for the future. This challenge can be met, but it requires more local authorities to address the problems of their town centres on a comprehensive basis. The lessons learned and experience gained from the private sector management of planned shopping centres could be more widely applied to existing traditional town centres.

Speciality centres

Perhaps one of the most interesting areas of retail development that has engaged the property industry over the last decade has been the growth of speciality centres. These centres characteristically are close to prime locations, have no particular anchor tenant, tend to concentrate upon providing a carefully selected mix of retailers, have a high proportion of small units, and place the accent upon high-class merchandise. In addition, great attention is paid to layout, design and finishes in order to give a more friendly and comfortable atmosphere than that experienced in most forms of planned centre.

Most speciality centres aim to attract the better-off shopper willing to spend their income on goods they believe they 'want' to buy rather than 'need' to buy. Much of floorspace is normally given over to various forms of catering, often around 40 per cent, and the design and environment of the centre usually directed towards a particular theme intended to generate a 'shopping experience'. The tenant mix tends to favour the small independent retailer, often holding on short-term leases or even inclusive licences. New and expanding traders can, therefore, secure representation in or near town centres away from the competition of the high street and the multiple traders.

Intensive management is essential to the success of a speciality centre. It must be imaginative, flexible and highly involved in the trader's business. One of the problems in this respect is that service charges in speciality centres are inclined to be high, and developers state that they can sometimes experience difficulties in demonstrating to tenants the validity of these costs. Such centres also need to be promoted continuously by both advertising campaigns and the staging of live entertainment.

The need for strong and committed management combined with a relative lack of comparable schemes to analyse and appraise has led to a certain degree of institutional caution in terms of investment, and funding is not always easy to obtain. Nevertheless, as standing investments they currently trade at somewhere above more traditional shopping centre yields, although there is evidence that as the market becomes more familiar with them as investment propositions, and witnesses a pattern of good rental growth, these yields are falling. It is probable, therefore, that the speciality centre will play a leading part in helping to retain shopper loyalty to traditional town centres.

One form of speciality shopping that has emerged is 'festival' shopping. This has been described as a completely new type of shopping, because people do not go to festival schemes exclusively for shopping, but for the pleasure of visiting. At least 60 per cent of visitors to such projects give the major reason for their trips as 'browsing', and only 10–15 per cent go primarily to shop. Familiar in the USA since the beginning of the 1970s, and with Covent Garden an early example in the UK, other schemes such as the Albert Dock, Ocean Village, Cutlers Wharf and Quayside have followed. These schemes are said to accept not only the challenges of a new form of retailing and of a flagship role in urban regeneration, but also of an entirely new approach to retail property development and management (Brown 1990).

Another form of specialized retail development spreading across the USA, and beginning to appear in the UK, is what is known as the 'category killer' 1858 to 2787 m² (20 000–30 000 ft²) stores concentrating on such single-product areas as sports, office products and books.

Planned central area schemes

The glamorous end of retail development is unquestionably the planned central area scheme, and it is here that opinions as to future opportunities vary widely. On the one hand, there are those who point to the long and uncertain gestation period, front heavy infrastructure and holding costs, complicated site assembly, political sensitivity and high operating costs attached to such projects. On the other, it has been estimated that about 25 per cent of towns up and down the country remain to be 'done'. Moreover, many towns that built centres in the 1960s and early 1970s are now ready to embark upon further phases, and many of these centres are already in the course of refurbishment.

What does seem certain is that, where planned shopping centres are developed, they will be smaller, more sensitively handled and afford greater energy efficiency. Many will incorporate elements of renewal and conservation in their basic design, others may concentrate upon the complete redevelopment and upgrading of existing older but outdated planned centres.

A few trends can be discerned. There will be less food shopping, apart from catering, which will increase, and the accent will be placed more upon creating a shopping 'experience' with a greater selection and better quality of goods. Centres will depend less and less upon department or variety stores as anchors in the way that they have previously done. More attention will be paid to good management and a satisfactory tenant mix. Turnover rents will become more popular and local traders made more welcome. Leisure and recreation facilities will also figure more prominently.

Since the early 1990s we have witnessed a tremendous improvement in the general ambience of shopping centres, with vastly better detailed design and good use of natural and artificial lighting. They are friendlier, safer and more security conscious places for the shopper. Great advances have been made in improving the external appearances of the buildings. The difficulty is that the main planned town centre schemes form possibly the largest buildings that will ever be constructed in many towns and are prone to appear monolithic.

In assessing the potential performance of a planned shopping centre, there are factors that have been called the 'seven secrets of success' (Ringer 1989). Most of these are dealt with a little later in the chapter, but can usefully be listed here:

- *Location.* Shoppers must be able to get in and out of shopping centres with ease, and therefore access for both car and public transport is vital.
- *Planning.* This relates to the movement of people around the shopping centre, optimizing the flow of pedestrians and maximizing the total potential of all units.
- *Design.* The shopping centre must understand its target audience and then address them through design solutions that create a unique image and communicate the identity of the centre to the public.
- *Amenities.* This really includes everything from well lit and safe carparks, through to toilet, crèche, and facilities for disabled persons, so that customers feel good about being within the centre, stay longer and spend more.
- *Mix.* The tenant mix should be focused on the target audience, with the developer thinking like a retailer and planning the centre layout as one big department store.
- *Programming.* Shopping centre owners, in conjunction with the tenants, should ensure a promotion events programme throughout the year.
- *Management.* The centre must be kept clean and safe, with a sense of common purpose shared by the management and the tenants.

The point has been well made that the coming years will undoubtedly reveal increasingly discriminating consumer tastes, which will need to be assessed by research into community needs and implemented by centre management teams ready to run shopping centres as dynamic businesses (Ringer 1989). Developers and landlords who ignore this approach do so as their peril.

District centres

Perhaps the least contentious retail development is the district centre, apparently popular with planners, developers, shoppers, traders and financiers alike. Serving a catchment area of anything between 20 000 and 120 000 population, but usually around 50 000, it normally provides about 9290 to 18 580 m² (100 000 to 200 000 ft²) of retail floorspace comprising anything from 20 to 40 standard units built around a superstore and invariably a few civic facilities such as a library, health centre or sports hall. Occasionally, the term 'district centre' is something of a euphemism, being coined by a super-store operator to gain a more favourable response from a planning authority. But despite their seeming acceptance by planning authorities, it could be argued that they pose a greater threat to the traditional high street than do single free-standing superstores.

Increasing restrictions on out-of-town and edge-of-town developments have encouraged developers to focus on the development of district centres in declining inner-city areas, which are then used as a catalyst to help regenerate the local economy. The idea is that the land is made available by the local authority and a consortium of retail operators underwrite the scheme via their covenants, with the smaller traders anchored and supported by a major superstore.

Superstores

Once anathema to planners, the superstore or hypermarket became firmly established in the 1980s and 1990s. However, tightening of planning controls in the mid to late 1990s is expected to lead to a decline in superstore development in the new millennium, although as yet there is little hard evidence of a significant decline due to the lead-time for many of these projects. One example of this changing trend cited by Jones and Hillier (2000) is that Tesco opened only four out-of-town food stores in 1998/1999 compared with 10 stores in the preceding three years. Nevertheless 45 per cent of the UK's grocery shopping takes place in stores of over 2500 square metres (Bell 1999).

The ideal state-of-the-art superstore has been described as fulfilling the following criteria (Hawking 1992):

- catchment population: minimum of 20 000 people
- competition: provision of floorspace and potential trade must be in balance
- location: strategic, preferably stand-alone, positioned on arterial roads
- site acreage: six to eight acres of flat land (maximum slope 1:50)
- carparking: minimum of one space per 9 m² (100 ft²) gross
- store size: between 4180–6040 m² (45 000 to 65 000 ft²) gross area
- access: 'comfortable driving'; roundabout or traffic-light junction, clearly signed and visible
- servicing: separate and secure servicing capable of easy access and manoeuvring; able to accommodate three articulated vehicles
- petrol filling station: located on the main exit.

The superstore has become more and more accepted as a part of everyday life, and arguably many of the initial fears voiced by planning authorities about the effect of such stores on existing town centres have not really

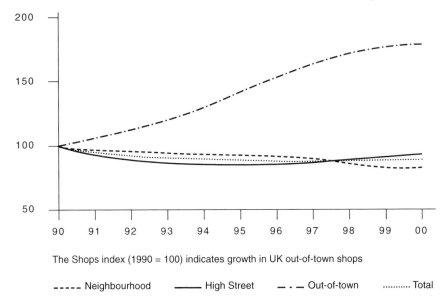

The Shops index (1990 = 100) indicates growth in UK out-of-town shops

- - - - - Neighbourhood   ——— High Street   — . — Out-of-town   .... Total

Figure 15.1 More shops or fewer?
Source: National Statistics/Verdict; Dixon T. (2003).

materialized. Indeed, some positive advantages have been experienced in terms of taking the pressure of excessive traffic off many older town centres. Car-borne customers also demand the convenience, quality and service they provide.

The pace of expansion of superstores scarcely slackened over the last decade, and rental growth and institutional investment interest, where available, has remained buoyant. One reason for this high level of activity is that leading superstore operators frequently act as their own developers, and are not dependent on the vagaries of the financial markets, raising substantial sums through internal cashflow. It has been pointed out, however, that the continuing proliferation of new stores is not just being undertaken for the fun of it. The retailers are not only planning to satisfy what they still see as an expanding market, but there is also an element of 'spoiling', whereby they seek to deny rivals access to promising new market areas, to secure sites that are not immediately profitable, and to push up market share by invading territory occupied by competitors (Cole 1993).

Concerns were expressed in the 1990s that the spread of the discount retail warehouse and the warehouse club could challenge the pre-eminence of the superstore in the shopping hierarchy. These concerns have so far proved unfounded.

Retail warehouses

To some extent, superstores have been replaced as the 'bête-noir' of planning authorities by retail warehouses. These can best be defined as single-level self-contained retail stores, selling non-food goods, often specializing in a particular trade, with at least 929 m² (10 000 ft²) of floorspace occupying a warehouse or industrial-type building and supported by a carpark. Usually they are around 2322–4645 m² (25 000 to 50 000 ft²) in size, and demand a large catchment area of about 100 000 population within a 30 minute drive time. Because they concentrate on bulky goods, such as furniture and electrical appliances, out-of-centre locations are required.

The original concept of retail warehousing has seen significant change during its short evolution. Initially, such developments consisted of scattered units, often trading with planning battles unresolved, tucked away on industrial estates, invariably with inadequate parking. They have quickly developed to such an extent that most recent arrivals can be found on new out-of-town retail parks, which provide purpose-built units allowing the warehouse retailers to congregate together. They also permit enough space for retailers to shop-fit the frontage to their own design and fit-out the interiors, which are now used predominantly for retailing as opposed to storage. The whole development is normally surrounded by numbers of carparking spaces undreamed of in the early 1970s. As experience of warehouse development grows, so characteristic features emerge in terms of their specification and design. These can be summarized as follows:

• Location is the single most important factor, with an optimum balance between accessibility, hinterland and visibility. A catchment population of 70 000 within a minimum drive time of 20 minutes is seen as a minimum.
• Some traders prefer a cluster of complementary retail outlets, and others are perfectly happy with a single free-standing unit.
• Many retailers avoid high-standard specifications and adhere to a 'keep-it-simple' approach towards their stores' interiors. However, corporate image is considered important by all.
• As a general rule, pitched roofs tend to be unpopular, because they are difficult to 'sign'.
• Direct access and exposure to surface carparking is essential, and an ideal ratio is one space to 10 m² (200 ft²), which can be lower in a large retail park where parking facilities can be shared.
• Attention to the internal layout, configuration and subdivision of buildings at design stage is critical. In a park scheme, the design must be flexible enough to allow for a range of unit sizes from, say 464 to 4645 m² (5000 to 50 000 ft²), with a frontage to depth ratio of at least 1:2.
• An increasing number of retailers are incorporating some kind of catering facilities.
• Service vehicles should be separated from customer carparking.
• Pedestrian movement must be facilitated.
• Retail warehouse park layouts have progressed from the initial simple 'parade' of units, to a more efficient use of site area by utilizing shared parking between the different units forming two parallel blocks or occasionally an 'L' or 'U' shaped plan form.
• With regard to tenant mix an ideal size for a retail warehouse park has been suggested at around 11 613 m² (125 000 ft²) typically comprising (Fletcher King 1989):

DIY and garden centre	$3250 \text{ m}^2 +$ $(35\,000 \text{ ft}^2)$
Carpets	$930–2300 \text{ m}^2$ $(10–25\,000 \text{ ft}^2)$
Furniture	$2800–3700 \text{ m}^2$ $(30–40\,000 \text{ ft}^2)$
Auto	1400 m^2 $(15\,000 \text{ ft}^2)$
Electrical	$650–930 \text{ m}^2$ $(7–10\,000 \text{ ft}^2)$

This produces a well balanced park with a variety of users and building size.

- The environment, in terms of landscaping, around retail warehouse parks, is beginning to be improved and some older parks are now being upgraded. As the trend for integrating leisure and retail facilities continues, however, the environmental factor will become increasingly important.
- Building specification has advanced and corporate image has become increasingly significant to retailers who have developed readily identifiable logos, colours and house styles. This is due to both mature traders entering the market and institutional investors setting high standards of building design.
- Pro-active management, earlier neglected in the sector's rapid expansion, is now more and more common.
- Specialist themed retail warehouse parks around a particular use might be the next phase of development.
- The discount food sector seems set to expand, with additional retailers operating simple shop fit, low capital, low storage cost, high-intensity and minimal staff expense outlets.
- The discount warehouse and warehouse club sector, a concept imported from the US and not legally within the strict definition of retailing, was expected to grow significantly in the late 1990s and concern was expressed that these stores would take trade away from traditional retail outlets. However, even the best-known operator Costco has only opened 15 outlets in the UK since its arrival in 1993.

The 1990s have been christened the 'discount decade', and overall the amount of floorspace developed for retail warehousing of one kind or another seems destined to grow.

Department stores

The difficulties facing department stores are generally well known and virtually all major operators have experienced serious trading problems since the mid-1980s, mainly as a result of the costly nature of this type of retailing operation. However, these retailing difficulties give rise to some unusual and exciting redevelopment opportunities. The growth in the use of concessions and franchising, promoting the concept of a store within a store, is not a development activity in the true property sense, but a business reorganization along these lines often forms part of a larger redevelopment programme. It also provides more flexibility for achieving an optimum tenant mix within a single large store than within a planned shopping centre comprising many separate shop units. Management services are also easier to co-ordinate.

Many stores came onto the market as a result of the rationalization of the major chains of department store operators. This released development potential, and some interesting schemes have been undertaken. One of the main problems in effecting a redevelopment of department stores is the preponderance of upper floorspace, but a mixed development of offices above retail space on the ground floor is the conventional solution, although the office space so created is often far less than ideal.

In the cyclical way of things, the department store has enjoyed something of a revival. The major reasons for this were identified by Hall (1993):

- A long-standing appeal remains based upon familiarity and confidence.
- Many specialist traders have performed poorly by comparison.
- They did not embark on highly expansionist programmes prior to the recession.
- Many held property on a freehold basis in good locations.
- Their targeted customer base tends to be older and less financially affected by the recession.
- The massive expansion in shopping centre development during the 1980s benefited many stores, with developers eager to lure them into projects at concessionary rates to secure funding and specialist traders.
- Most stores reorganized themselves, often along North American lines, with the removal of certain product lines, including food, once considered fundamental to the traditional department store, and replacing them with a wider range of clothing, footwear, accessories and homeware. Reliance upon concessions was greatly reduced. Thus, many have become large-space speciality retailers appealing to the mass market for mid-price family and home fashions.
- They offer good staffing levels, delivery and after sales service, and also provide such amenities as toilets.

Generally, the changing demographic pattern of an increasingly ageing population is favourable to the future of the revamped department store.

Arcades

Since the mid-1980s, the shopping arcade has been resurrected. Built originally on narrow strips of land, usually connecting two main streets, by developers anxious to optimize the use of land or owners seeking to prevent incursion or misuse of their property, they often now occupy prime positions and command high pedestrian flows. Probably the best known of all is the Burlington Arcade connecting Piccadilly with Burlington Gardens, but other notable ones that have been refurbished include the nearby Royal Arcade, the Great Western Shopping Arcade in Birmingham, and the Barton Arcade in Manchester. Units tend to be small, with as little as 11.6 m^2 (125 ft^2) on the ground floor, and frequently have a basement and two upper floors. However, rents can be high.

Leases are frequently shorter than usual, at around 15 years, and landlords have come to accept that, as they attract specialist traders and not multiples, there can be more problems, and greater understanding must be afforded. Arcades also need very careful and positive management, but where this has been provided there are definite signs of it paying off.

Regional shopping centres

In many countries the decentralization of comparison shopping has been accommodated in regional shopping centres. Until the mid-1980s, with the notable exception of Brent Cross in north London, attempts to develop regional shopping centres were thwarted, largely on planning grounds due to their presumed impact upon established town centres. However, the outlook for such centres changed dramatically from about 1985.

New regional shopping centres, strategically located close to the national motorway network and intended to serve an extensive catchment population, became an important feature of retailing in the early 1990s. Such centres comprise 100 000 m² (1 million ft² or above) or more of purpose-built retail floor area on a site of 40–60 ha (100 to 150 acres) with a minimum of 5000, and more usually 10 000 to 13 000 carparking spaces at surface level. It has been argued, moreover, that regional shopping centres must be worthy contenders and an alternative to existing town and city centres. Brent Cross (London), the Metro Centre (Gateshead) and the Trafford Centre (Manchester) have all shown that tradition can eventually be created where none previously existed. The tenant mix, therefore, must be a response to consumer requirements and not just a reflection of the development team's aspirations. It should blend the results of research and experience, from which there has been a welcome and understandable desire to break away from look-alike centres occupied almost exclusively by well known multiples who are controlled by a handful of companies (Hammond 1989).

Leisure has also figured large in the design of regional shopping centres. A good example of this can be seen in the Lakeside scheme at Thurrock in Essex, developed by Capital and Counties. Here, a children's ice rink and landscaped area with a water feature forms the focal emphasis of the central mall. The rink can also be used for promotional events. There is also an Enchanted Forest where smaller children can be left under supervision, a Water World for older children, a multi-screen cinema and a range of theme restaurants and small cafés. Because leisure and catering facilities encourage customers to stay longer, there are as many as 13 000 parking spaces. Great care is also taken to locate carparking, model the slope of the land, and design entrances and walkways so as to maximize pedestrian flow equally around the two levels of the centre. The developers recognize that shopping is becoming a leisure activity, and the potential uniformity of shopping malls underlines the need for each of them to be presented as a stylish and individual package.

Although an examination of the potential for regional shopping centre development has suggested that there is capacity for around 35 to 40 full-size schemes in Great Britain, with a third of these in London and the outer Metropolitan area, the number of regional centres opening in the next decade is likely to be severely limited because government planning guidelines towards such out-of-town shopping have become extremely restrictive (Roger Tym 1993).

Planning and retailing

Straightaway, it is tempting to suggest that planners should be more agnostic in their attitudes towards shopping, less afraid of innovation and change, and more prepared to accept the positive part that retail development can play in sustaining the urban economy. Developers, conversely should be more sympathetic to the environmental impact of their projects and sensitive to the needs of the less mobile members of the community. All too often there has been a lack of understanding between local planning authorities and retail developers. The former are seen as prepossessed with protecting and reinforcing the existing shopping hierarchy, whereas the latter are viewed as being narrowly occupied with exploiting a particular trading position for their own gain. There are, of course, merits in both cases, and it is probably fair to say that, of late, much more common ground between the parties has been found.

Development plans

Shopping, as a sector, is prone to sudden and dramatic changes in location, layout, design and operation. Planning authorities, therefore, need to display a fast response towards shifts in retail fashion, facilitating desirable new modes of shopping in line with consumer preference, and controlling the worst excesses of an unfettered competitive market. Some of the major problem areas where planning and development agencies collide can be summarized as follows:

- the development of superstores, retail warehouse parks and regional shopping centres
- the location of retail outlets outside established shopping districts
- the development of large non-food stores
- the loss of local shops and rural shops
- maintenance of a hierarchy of shopping districts
- regeneration of inner-city areas
- urban conservation
- traffic management within established shopping districts
- maintenance of viable shopping districts
- shopping provision on industrial estates.

From the viewpoint of the development industry, those development plans that reflect a traditional shopping hierarchy based upon selective and tightly controlled strategic centres should be re-examined in the face of changing consumer mobility and fluctuations in the economics of shopping development and retail trading. Specialist advice of a kind rarely sought, operational not merely analytical, should be incorporated at plan preparation stage and referred to at regular intervals during implementation. One of the sorrier aspects of retailing in development planning is said to be the conflict that occurs between strategic and local planning authorities. Dissonance of this kind is said not only to produce market uncertainty but also to discredit the machinery of planning and lower the credibility of the authorities involved. Lord Falconer, in a speech to the British Council for Shopping Centres annual conference in 2001, indicated that regional planning bodies will have a greater say over the location of strategic retail schemes in the future.

From a planning perspective, however, the government has produced guidance reflecting a plan-led approach towards development and reaffirming its belief that town centres should remain the anchor of the retailing system. This guidance is set down in revised PPG6 (PPG6), which was published in June 1996, and has subsequently been 'clarified' through ministerial comment. The main objectives are:

- To sustain and enhance the vitality and viability of town centres
- To focus development, especially retail development, in locations where the proximity of business facilitates competition from which all consumers are able to benefit and maximizes the opportunity to use means of transport other than the car
- To maintain an efficient, competitive and innovative retail sector
- To ensure the availability of a wide range of shops, employment, services and facilities to which people have access by a choice of means of transport.

This guidance is consistent with PPG13 published in 1994, which focuses on the inter-relationship between transport and land use and seeks to 'reduce growth in the length and number motorized journeys, to encourage alternative means of transport which have less environmental impact and hence reduce reliance on the private car' (Jones and Hillier 1999).

The revised PPG6 introduced a new 'sequential' approach to site selection for retail development, which requires planning authorities and developers to look first at town centre sites where buildings are available for redevelopment and conversion, then at edge-of-town sites and only then, if these are not available and suitable, at out-of-town sites that are accessible by a variety of means of transport.

In March 1999 Richard Caborn, the then Planning Minister stated in a written parliamentary answer that the need for retail or leisure development is to be taken into account at the planning application stage as well as when the local authority is allocating sites in its development plan. PPG6 only specifies consideration of need in the preparation of the plan. In the RICS response to this statement (RICS 1999) they noted that 'edge-of-town and out-of-centre proposals which are not in accordance with an up-to-date development plan strategy will now be required to demonstrate both the need for the additional facilities and that a sequential approach has been applied when selecting the location'.

Probably the most uncertain and potentially contentious issues relate to the interpretation of the terms 'vitality' and 'viability' in assessing the impact of large-scale development proposals on existing town centres. This, in turn, has raised the whole question of the use of retail impact assessment techniques. Shopping models, of both the manual and gravity variety, extensively employed in the 1960s and 1970s to forecast the effect of super-stores, have been disinterred and employed to predict the consequences of 'mega-centre' proposals on existing shopping patterns. A strictly quantitative approach can lead to problems where even small variations in assumptions about trends in turnover, population, expenditure and the efficiency of use of existing floorspace can lead to a wide range of forecasts. Impact assessment has thus been described as an inexact science coloured by the subjectivity of its users, a better practice being to afford greater weight to a qualitative analysis centre-based survey approach that is simple, robust and pragmatic. This is explained elsewhere and involves the construction of an 'index of vitality' based upon a comparative study of certain main indicators such as:

a   Relative rental levels in centres;
b   Vacancy and occupancy rates;
c   Relative branch performance of major retailers;
d   Level of retailer representation and retail mix;
e   Presence of covered malls, speciality centres and new shopping centre proposals;
f   Presence of pedestrianization schemes;
g   Relative access to the centres for both public and private transport;
h   Level of carparking in the centres relative to their net retail floorspace;
i   Health of secondary shopping areas;
j   Presence of town centre management and promotion schemes;
k   Presence of other unique attractions such as tourism, conference venues, cinemas, theatres; and
l   The size of the local town or town centre employment base.

(Norris & Jones 1993, URBED 1994)

This is argued to provide a more detailed insight into the local property market, which should make a significant contribution to the decision-making process at appeal.

Future planning policy for shopping centres

The House of Commons Environment Committee published a report on shopping centres in November 1994, encouraging the government in its objective to preserve town centres and to restrict out-of-town retail developments, which has substantially informed subsequent retail planning policy.

A report compiled by CB Hillier Parker in January 2000 (CB Hillier Parker 2000), jointly commissioned by the National Retail Planning Forum, the British Council for Shopping Centres and the Department of the Environment, Transport and the Regions, evaluated the impact of the sequential approach to retail development. The results can be summarized as follows.

•   Local Plan policies have changed substantially to incorporate the sequential approach. However, Local Plans vary in the way in which they incorporate the sequential approach and the closeness of their adherence to it.

- Local authorities were not well supported by planning inspectors and the Secretary of State in Planning Inquiry decisions in their long-espoused pro-town centre policies until the current version of PPG6 was introduced.
- Retailers have expressed concern that local authorities are applying the sequential approach in a prescriptive way as a 'test' that has to be passed rather than a process which needs to be followed. There is a widespread perception in the private sector that the sequential approach is being used as moratorium on all out-of-town retail developments, but this is not fully supported by the evidence.
- The 'need' for a proposed development and the availability of town-centre or edge-of-town sites are inextricably linked. Need is generally interpreted by local authorities to be the need for that particular design of development (the built-form interpretation). However the report argues that the need for retail floor space to sell the particular goods that the development proposes to sell (the class-of-goods interpretation) would more accurately reflect the spirit of PPG6 – that retailers should be flexible in their trading formats. The interpretation applied by local authorities could significantly influence the size and type of alternative town-centre sites that should be considered by the developer. The built-form argument would be focussed on larger sites of a particular type. The class-of-goods argument would need to consider any sites that could accommodate new retail development, not necessarily in the form proposed by the developer.
- There is inconsistency as to how sites should be assessed for suitability and availability, and PPG6 provides limited guidance on this issue. This creates significant uncertainty for developers.
- There is substantial confusion about the definition of an edge-of-town development. PPG6 uses the guide of 200 metres to 300 metres from the primary shopping area but there appears to be a lack of understanding by the planning authorities as to how edge-of-town developments would, in practice, relate to existing town centres in functional terms.
- Retailers and developers have not been participating in the Local Plan process because it is seen as too time-consuming and because they wish their proposals to remain confidential. Many local authorities appointed retail consultants to advise on retail capacity and the commercial suitability of potential sites. More recently town-centre partnerships, comprising local-authority and private-sector interests in the town centre, are working up development proposals, including strategies, action plans and the identification of support for proposed town centre developments.
- There is some evidence of retailers changing their formats in recent years, particularly food retailers developing new smaller stores including town centre formats. Others, such as DIY and large furniture stores, consider that, despite the sequential approach, their bulky goods trading format is virtually exempt. Some retailers believe that they cannot trade at all in or on the edge of town centres because the costs of doing so would be much higher and they would be unable to compete with established out-of-town competitors.

Other planning considerations

An important, although at times forgotten, feature of retail development relates to the level of employment generated by new shopping centres. Even a small superstore of around 3787 m² (40 000 ft²) can provide up to 150 full-time equivalent jobs and a hypermarket of 4645 m² (50 000 ft²) as many as 220. Larger superstores can create work for anything from 300 to 700 people and even most of the new DIY stores employ about 20 to 30 people for every 929 m² (10 000 ft²). Even more attractive in employment terms is the fact that these jobs are largely aimed at the young, the unskilled and those seeking part-time work. Furthermore, the development of an individual shopping project will usually have multiplier effects in the locality, generating demand for local goods and services and attracting other employers and business to the area. Case studies of two of the earliest hypermarket developments in the UK tend to support this view, although it is pointed out that any losses in employment are often geographically dispersed and therefore not so noticeable.

Not only is the retail sector of the commercial property development market the one in which local planning authorities have become most involved; it is also the one where most opportunity now exists for the extraction of planning gain from individual private development projects or the provision of community benefits in partnership schemes. Leisure and recreation facilities have been a popular addition to many new town centre schemes, and superstore operators have probably shown themselves to be among the most generous and flexible providers of planning gains. Such negotiations need to be carefully prepared and conducted.

Shopping patterns are particularly sensitive to significant changes in road networks and parking provisions. The requirement to refer planning applications for shop developments bordering major roads to highway authorities has often proved to be a rich source of frustrating and expensive delay. Major superstore operators are especially wary about traffic problems when prospecting for sites, and will usually be willing to make the necessary contributions to upgrade a local road network and create a good access. Nevertheless, some local planning authorities tend to over-react to such retail development proposals with regard to traffic generation, for superstore traffic has an uncanny propensity to adjust to peak hour flows.

Most planning authorities operate some form of retail frontage policy for shopping parades. Within primary parades the policy is normally to seek to maintain a level of around 70 per cent of those retail uses falling within Class A1 of the Use Classes Order, but secondary parades are usually treated much more flexibly. Even so, it has been recognized that some strictly non-retail uses can prove an attractive draw and sometimes generate a greater pedestrian flow than conventional retail uses (Unit for Retail Planning Information 1980).

Several other issues are worth mentioning. First, it has been suggested that even the Use Classes Order 1987 remains an ineffective and redundant instrument of development control in terms of retailing and should be scrapped or drastically amended. Second, the question of pedestrian flow needs greater comprehension on the part of certain planning authorities, in particular the effects of pedestrianization and carparking. Third, a more flexible attitude towards the change of use of accommodation over existing but dated high street shops should be adopted, so as to facilitate redevelopment and refurbishment.

On a more positive note, it is clear that town centres are facing a challenge from out-of-town centres – a challenge of increased accessibility, convenience, environment and security. The argument runs that this challenge can be met provided local authorities look at the problems of their centres on a comprehensive basis. Many planned shopping centres exhibit high-quality management, so there is no reason why local authorities should not examine ways of managing a whole town centre to ensure that it provides the best possible facilities and convenience to the shopping public. This is starting to happen.

Design and layout

It has been said that demographic changes, urban congestion and growing concern for the environment will precipitate a radical reappraisal of the purpose of shopping centres, their appeal, how they function and how their returns can be optimized (Walker 1990). An ageing population placing an emphasis on quality, convenience, high standards of service, leisure and lifestyle will dictate a different pattern of consumer behaviour. The design and layout of shopping centres will play an important part in providing a suitable environment to meet these changing expectations.

Whereas inflation fuelled the surge in retailers' sales volumes during the 1970s and 1980s, they are now having to find real sales growth in a highly competitive market, and are turning to design to achieve it. Retailers increasingly see design as more than a mere extension of architecture or shelf engineering, and rather a mainspring of the marketing drive, so that developers in the UK now continually monitor what is happening to the shops and shopping malls in the USA in order to review their approach here. This accent upon good design is underlined by the statement made by one leading retail designer:

> At its best shopping is an important experience that triggers off all the senses – visual, tactile, oral, audible and smell.

Planned shopping centres

The practical requirements in shopping are space, servicing, parking and accessibility, but increasingly these have to be matched with creative design, visual interest, character and feel. Thus, enormous opportunities exist for both the developer and the architect, and, although there can be no magic formula for success, a few basic principles underlying shopping centre design can be described as follows.

Size and shape

Generally speaking, new centres are becoming smaller and better integrated into the towns they serve. Even within the centres, many major retailers are themselves looking for somewhat smaller premises than they did a few years ago. Elevations are also being designed to a smaller scale. However, there is a recognition that the traditional strict rectangular shape is not essential to successful performance. Knowing retailers' requirements and being flexible enough to accommodate them is the important factor. At the Ashley Centre, Epsom, for example, where Bredero developed a 26 016 m² (280 000 ft²) centre Marks & Spencer increased in size by 25 per cent, Waitrose reduced planned space by 10 per cent and the House of Fraser store was cut by 30 per cent to 4181 m² (45 000 ft²). With regard to the size of standard units within a centre, the favoured size of the majority of retailers is around 279 m² (3000 ft²) with a frontage of 7.3 m (24 ft) and adequate storage and ancillary space either at basement or first-floor level. The choice of size of structural grid is important to efficiency and flexibility, and, although there is no recognized norm, a grid of 11 m (35 ft) allows for a wide variety of unit sizes (Northen 1977).

Enclosure

Opinions vary as to the future of the fully enclosed environmentally controlled shopping centre. Suffice it to say that reports of its imminent demise a few years ago proved to be greatly exaggerated. In fact, many previously open centres have been enclosed. Nevertheless, that fast tempo of centre development during the late 1980s and early 1990s has slackened in recent years. However, where it takes place one major keynote of enclosure is buildability, because problems of cracking, movement, inadequate drainage and water leaks have been relatively common with older shopping centres. Roofs, for example, are frequently a cause for concern, especially with the fashion towards the introduction of atria, and the advice of a specialist roofing contractor early in the design process is imperative.

Cladding

The perimeter of a shopping centre is a massive area, and while light-coloured tiles might be attractive, they can be costly to clean. For this, and for other reasons of taste, there has been a marked return to the use of brick cladding. Whatever material is selected, the important thing is to pay careful attention to the finer detailing, so as to avoid costly difficulties if there is a component failure in the panels of brickwork.

Climate

Where a fully controlled environmental system is provided, the optimum climate is said to be somewhere between an office temperature and the outside temperature. Energy conservation is extremely important, and space heating, lighting and air-conditioning facilities must all be appraised for cost-effectiveness in terms of running costs as well as installation. Nevertheless, architects have become much more skilful at designing centres with a high proportion of natural lighting, but avoiding the excessive heat loss and gain mentioned above.

Environment

Experience drawn from the USA shows that it is crucial for a shopping centre to establish a distinct identity and create a pleasing environment. For too long the temptation has been to mimic successful schemes elsewhere, and, in a sense, one Arndale centre tended to look very much like another. The pressure now is for creativity and innovation, or as one leading American shopping centre developer has described it – 'a touch of the ethnic', arguing further that what people want is a return to the feeling of the Middle East bazaar or the market town of the middle ages, not the faceless could-be-anywhere shopping centre that has dominated the scene for so long. Greater use of domestic architecture and materials could be made, and much more tasteful use of colour and texture introduced. Extensive planting along the malls, with more trees, and not just low level shrubs, together with a wider variety of water features such as fountains, waterfalls and streams, should be encouraged, despite cries of high management costs. The use of carpets on stairs and ramps has also proved popular. Generally, therefore, the movement should be more towards the 'street scene' approach as opposed to the 'grand manner' of so many 1970s centres. As part of this approach, the design of signposting and facades should be sympathetic to the overall theme running through the architecture and landscaping of the centre.

Security

Apart from electrical surveillance equipment and management staff on patrol, the security aspects of a centre should be taken into account during the design stage of the development process. As regards safety, sprinkler systems and fire shutters can sometimes be a headache, and specialist advice is essential. In respect of vandalism and hooliganism, the number and siting of entrances, the clear run of malls, the location of security doors and the existence of blank spots and corners must all be considered.

Mixed use

Large mixed-use development schemes located in central city areas seem to be the order of the day in North America. It has been suggested that the pace of retailing activity fell in shopping centres during the 1970s and 1980s except where such projects were combined with hotels and entertainment facilities. Today, almost every centre across Europe is being re-invented as a leisure 'destination'. Cinemas, food courts, amusement arcades, and fitness centres are common as shopping has itself become a leisure activity. Lawson (2003) identifies the following advantages of the incorporation of leisure activities in a shopping development:

- Leisure can draw in extra visitors
- It can give an edge over competing centres by creating excitement
- It can provide massive extra turnover for hybrid leisure/retail operators such as fast-food operators, which feeds through in higher rents

- It may future-proof a shopping centre against changes in shopping patterns.

Amenities

Most successful shopping centres provide, so far as possible, a wide range of amenities to cater for customers' needs. The most common of these are catering, lavatories, crèches, telephones and play sculptures. The provision of catering is a controversial area, and solutions range from somewhere to sit down for a drink and a light meal to a full-blown food court. It has been found that, although food courts generally increase pedestrian flow into shopping centres, they do not necessarily increase retail sales, because well over half of the food court users do not visit other shops. Food courts are also expensive to furnish, maintain and refurbish. However, the food court concept has proved extremely successful in many centres, with location, circulation, visibility, light, height overhead, good service and variety being important factors. Lavatories are now almost essential, sometimes together with a baby-care room, and should be away from major shopping frontages but clearly signed. A crèche tends to be an expensive luxury, but some developers have partially solved the problem of cost by having properly supervised paying playgroups in their centres.

Parking

It is normally uneconomic to provide surface parking for town centre development schemes, but usually essential to provide such a facility in a suburban or edge-of-town location. Carparking, whether it be multi-storey or surface, can be provided specifically for the centre or as part of a wider community facility. Some retail developers, wherever possible, insist upon control over their own parking areas. The ideal provision is about four to six spaces for every 93 m^2 (1000 ft^2) of retail floorspace, and in town centres this can fall to under three, but the total amount of land for carparking works out to around 32.5 m^2 (350 ft^2) per space to allow for access and manoeuvring room. In respect of carparking provision there are design issues to be addressed, including:

- the attractiveness of the interface of the carpark and the shopping centre
- visible access and egress points with adequate queuing areas
- the suitability of external screening and the sufficiency of cross-ventilation
- effective control systems and efficient operation
- well placed pick-up points and trolley parks
- good standard finishes and services
- a reasonable standard of lighting.

Servicing

A great deal of space is often wasted in overproviding for servicing, resulting in vast open areas. It is now recognized that only about 25 per cent of lorries using service yards are 15 m long (49 ft) or more and not every unit in the centre is visited. Most modern town centre schemes now have centralized unloading and servicing bays with localized trolley distribution. Among the questions that arise in the design and layout of service areas are the degree of security afforded; the extent of separation of service and customer traffic; hours of access; level of ground, bays and ramps (not exceeding 1:10); adequate drainage; provision for waste disposal; sufficient turning room; and proper access for fire-fighting vehicles.

Malls

Shopping centre malls are becoming more varied in all respects: length, width, roof height, layout, frontage and decoration. There is really no such thing as an ideal length to a mall; interest and convenience to shoppers are by far the most important factors. Likewise, with mall widths, although there has been a tendency to design narrower double fronted malls of between 5 m and 8 m (16–26 ft) to encourage shoppers to cross over and shop both sides of the mall. Increasingly, moreover, malls are broken up by squares and courts of varying sizes to create an even more attractive environment. With regard to the shopping frontage, popular treatments over recent years have been the cranked line of shop fronts and the repeated bay-window style along a splayed frontage to a court. Apart from visually breaking up a flat surface, cranked or splayed frontages also give tenants two-sided representation. A further refinement is to distinguish separate malls by differing tenant mix. Mall heights are another design consideration. A low ceiling breaks up the perspective of a long mall, reduces building costs and minimizes energy consumption. A high ceiling can allow for unusual architectural treatments, and may be unavoidable in multi-level centres. Some interesting effects can also be achieved by combining a high roof with low eaves heights. Wherever possible, however, the tendency is for lower ceilings, on cost rather than aesthetic grounds. Other considerations to be taken into account in mall design include the sympathetic use of natural light; attractive entrances; rest areas with seating and plants; focal points for displays and promotions; fixed and free standing litter bins; special features, such as water, sculpture or lighting effects; and public information points.

Levels

Traditionally it has been thought daring for a developer in the UK to provide shopping on two levels, let alone more, and always provident to encourage horizontal rather than vertical movement around a centre. However, eight-storey shopping centres in Singapore and Hong Kong manage to break all the rules and succeed. American shopping developments seem to be able to make two-, three- and even four-storey shopping work well. Underground servicing avoids pedestrian and vehicular conflict and permits efficient exploitation of constrained town centre sites. However, it is relatively costly to construct and sometimes it creates difficulties in access.

Maintenance

It is important to design for low maintenance costs. Maintenance-free and vandal-proof materials and finishes should be selected wherever possible. Structural components should be designed for ease of cleaning, and services installed to facilitate access for inspection and repair. Circulation areas should be laid out with the need to use cleaning machines on a daily basis in mind.

Pedestrian flow

Shopping centres are all about pedestrian flow: the total amount drawn to the centre and the maximizing of circulation around it. The location of magnet stores, careful siting of entrances, skilful arrangement of malls and subtle manipulation of circulation space to create areas of interest all convention-ally contribute to an optimum flow and high trading volume. Some simple guidelines can be laid down from the experience of pedestrian behaviour in various centres developed over the years:

Entrances

The first function of a centre is to attract customers to it. Two basic approaches can be identified to the location and design of shopping centre entrances. First, the strikingly obvious entrance that heralds access to the centre and does not depend overly upon the surrounding area. Featured entrances of this kind are of particular importance to free-standing and wholly enclosed shopping centres as a relief to the otherwise monolithic appearance and as an environmental control barrier; and, second, the psychologically more subtle entrance that entices shoppers into the centre. All entrances should be inviting and should not present the shopper with a choice. The use of tenants having interesting displays at the entrance is effective, and striking signing on the exterior of the shopping centre is critical. For out-of-town centres, the customer will already have decided to visit the centre, but helpful signage for parking and shopping must be provided. In major centres it is essential to indicate clearly the various entrances to different sectors.

Magnets and anchors

There are certain tenants and retail uses whose presence in a shopping centre are held to be critical to the success of a scheme of development. Known as the 'magnet' or 'anchor' tenants, they traditionally comprise department stores, variety stores, superstores and certain other major multiple traders. A magnet not only draws shoppers into a centre, or from one end to another, but as a pre-letting for a new development it is also the bait with which to catch acceptable tenants for other individual shop units. Variations in layout to generate pedestrian flow by the different siting of magnets have been tried over the years. Sometimes a magnet has been placed at each end of a single mall; sometimes several magnet traders have been placed at extreme ends or at intersections of malls; and, with smaller centres where there is only one obvious major space using anchor, it will normally be placed as far away from the entrance as can be arranged. It is also common practice with stores to try to keep them away from prime frontage positions along the mall, because such kinds of retailer are able to trade from what might be thought inferior pitches because of the immense consumer loyalty they command, whereas the standard unit type of tenant depends upon a high degree of comparison and impulse buying, triggered by prominent window displays. However, times are changing with regard to magnets. Department stores are still opening new outlets, but they are also closing down others, and no longer can a developer rely upon attracting such tenants as John Lewis, Debenhams or Selfridges to a scheme. The superstores are an obvious alternative, and the likes of Waitrose, Tesco and Presto are all prepared to consider town centre locations, but prefer predominantly single-storey space and look for generous parking provision. Supermarkets are only effective as true magnets in conjunction with leading non-food stores in schemes of any significance, and, on their own, they tend to give the centre a convenience-good flavour. More recently, the concept of the food court as an anchor to a planned shopping centre has been adopted from North America. One example of this focus on food is the Trafford Centre in Manchester where a substantial two-storey section of the centre is given over to dining. A large range of fast-food outlets are available on the ground floor and more traditional restaurants and bars are situated on the first floor. The variety of outlets concentrated in a themed environment, together with access to a multi-screen cinema, keeps the centre buzzing long after the shops have closed.

Vertical circulation

Many planned centres include two, and sometimes more, levels of shopping with varying access. Sloping sites have helped some, such as Brent Cross and the St George's Centre in Preston, where it has been possible to avoid making either level especially dominant. Elsewhere, by skilful design, shoppers must be persuaded to ascend (or preferably to descend, which they are more inclined to do) to secondary floors. This requires the inclusion of strong visual links between floors, usually by means of open balconies, prominent staircases or alluring escalators, assisted by good signposting and seductive advertising. Themed floors are another possibility, for, in one way or another, a prime objective in the design and management of future shopping centres will be to get shoppers to use more than just the ground floor. However, it must be appreciated that multi-level centres create problems of fire control and smoke as well as heavy reliance on artificial lighting and ventilation.

Refurbishment

Most of the major planned shopping centres built a decade or more ago are now obsolescent and in need of substantial refurbishment. Many of them have problems with open malls or central areas, poor natural light, inadequate services and facilities, and outdated circulation patterns. In addition, many existing centres do not fully comply with stricter fire regulations and they possess certain other inherent design faults. Whereas high streets experience a constant rejuvenation, and leading department stores and superstores under a single ownership have been revitalized in response to economic pressure, shopping centres often have not. With diminishing market share and growing competition, refurbishment is now the name of the game.

Any decision to refurbish on a large scale must obviously be preceded by a careful study to ensure that expenditure is justified. In this, several common problems can be identified:

- The multiplicity of ownership, where there is often a financial institution, a developer, a local authority and sometimes a multiple store holding long-term interests in the property, and it is often necessary to renegotiate the lease structure or buy-in the freehold.
- Retailers are keen to improve their trading prospects, but less willing to pay for the improvements, or suffer the disruption while building works are carried out.
- The formula for viability is extremely difficult to calculate, depending as it does upon renegotiated rents at review related to comparative turnover and profitability.

In the context of the above problems, it has been pointed out that the financial sharing formulae provided in development agreements were often generously loaded in favour of the ground landlord, both in terms of initial rent and sharing provisions. Few imagined that such profound changes at such a high cost would have to be undertaken so soon to sustain the market share and investment worth of centres. The problem is frequently compounded by what is known as 'adverse' gearing, which has been described succinctly as follows:

> Take a centre which originally cost £10 million to build with the developer achieving a notional return of 7.5 per cent on this amount. The fixed element of the ground rent was, say, £275 000 and the original occupational rents amounted to, say £1.3 million with the provision to review the rents to 50 per cent of the occupational rents after allowance for the developer's notional return on his investment. If the occupation rents have now increased to say £4.2 million on such a formula, the local authority's share of the income will have increased from 21 per cent of occupational rents at the outset to 42 per cent within a 15 year time-span. The curve is exponential and the situation continuously gets worse at the expense of the management owners.

Thus, the cost versus income equation to the party responsible for necessary comprehensive refurbishment is often a difficult one to balance with different areas performing differently in different years. A report produced by the British Council of Shopping Centres in 1994 concluded that most refurbishments, stemming from a 'defensive' justification, take place at a later point in the economic cycle of the shopping centre than the optimum period, and that by tracking more closely the shopping centre life-cycle investment decisions can be made earlier to reduce time-lag between the deterioration of a centre's performance and the completion of the refurbishment. The report further suggests various evaluation techniques that can be applied to ensure that the timing of refurbishment is undertaken in such a way as to maximize cashflow, taking into account risk, project running costs and the consequence of not refurbishing.

In general, however, if major retail investments are to be protected they must at least hold on to, and preferably increase, their market share. However, the extent to which reconstruction and reorganization takes place will vary according to individual circumstances. But, inevitably, opportunities will be presented to buy-out leases and re-let premises; to create extra letting space in useless voids or by extending the building or narrowing the malls; to enclose open areas; to install new plant and building servicing facilities; to adjust the tenant-mix and add missing traders; and generally upgrade the environment and decor of the centre. If the work is successful, turnover will increase and higher rents will be achieved on review to produce an acceptable return to the investor.

Shopping centre management

Of all the commercial sectors of the property market, shop developments have traditionally depended upon good management, and arguably have much to teach the office, leisure and industrial sectors.

Much also remains constantly to be learned from good practice at home and abroad, especially from North America. Looking towards the year 2000, shopping centre developers and owners are acutely aware of the continuing set of challenges that face them. It is well recognized that the shift to out-of-town locations, the emergence of new retail concepts, a squeeze on retailers' profit margins and low expectation of growth in consumer spending make it even more important to ensure that a centre has the ability to gain market share from its competitors, for the benefit of its retailers, and ultimately the developer and owner. Location, accessibility, local dominance and tenant mix all play a part in this, but it has been stated that of equal importance is the style in which the centre is managed (Saggess 1993).

Tenant mix

The aim of any shopping development should be to attract tenants who will maximize turnover and profitability, so that rental income can also be negotiated to the highest possible level. For a long time, developers in the UK, having conceived a retail scheme, would place the units on the market and allow market forces to determine the ultimate shopping mix.

In some instances this remains true, especially in difficult letting markets where any tenant willing to pay a reasonable rent is likely to be welcome. However, creating and maintaining a productive tenant mix is essential to the economic performance of any centre, although implementation sometimes calls for a steady nerve. In achieving this there are several criteria to be examined:

- cumulative attraction: produced by the clustering of different but related shops, together in a manner that generates the same magnet effect as that of a major user
- competition and comparison: where several similar shops offering the same kinds of goods are grouped together so that shoppers are attracted to a centre knowing that they will be able to compare and contrast goods and prices
- compatibility: some shops are positively prejudicial to one another in respect of lighting, noise, marketing, smell and crowding, so special care must be taken in both the selection of certain trades and their positioning in a centre.

A useful definition of tenant mix can be provided as follows:

> Tenant mix is a continuous policy of maximizing public patronage of a shopping centre by optimizing the number of traders, the size of their premises, their styles and goods sold or services rendered.

In achieving the above, the objective is to secure a range of retailers who will appeal to the largest possible proportion of the catchment population commanded by the centre. The right mix will, therefore, be determined by the size, composition and quality of the catchment area. Large but low-income group hinterlands would justify an emphasis upon a variety rather than a department store and might encourage a developer to include a market in the centre. A smaller, but more affluent local population would suggest a greater concentration upon high fashion and jewellery shops and less accent upon general convenience shopping. The younger the population, the more fashion, children's wear and electrical goods shops, and an extensive and varied catchment area could support a specialist retailer such as a book shop or healthfood shop. Some of the other considerations to be taken into account regarding tenant mix can be summarized as below:

- What proportions of convenience and durable goods shops to include?
- How many, if any, service shops, such as banks, betting shops, gas and electricity showrooms, launderettes and public houses to permit?
- Whether to try to attract small local traders as well as national multiples?
- Is a 'themed' floor approach focusing on such topics as 'the home' or 'women' or 'leisure' worth developing?
- What steps must be taken to avoid or overcome the creation of 'dead spots'?
- Are fast food outlets to be encouraged and is a gourmet food hall a potential component?
- What is the appropriate ratio between floorspace given over to major 'anchors' and to other units (usually about 40:60)?

A survey of retailers showed that tenant mix is the single most important factor in selecting a suitable trading location, and also a major source of occupier dissatisfaction. The same survey also revealed that the role of anchor stores should be re-examined both in terms of the type of store involved and the amount of space allocated (a little less, and more accent on convenience goods); that the independent retail sector should be allocated twice as much space as at present; however, the argument for incorporating considerable leisure facilities within shopping centres has not yet been made (Watt & Valente 1991). It concludes by stressing that a successful tenant mix does not occur naturally, but requires careful consideration of both consumer needs and those of retailers themselves. However, above all it calls for a positive approach to be adopted, that treats the scheme in its entirety and places due emphasis on both primary and secondary space.

Initial research must be coupled with continuous monitoring of the catchment area in order to change the balance of traders as both supply and demand evolve in a particular location. It can still be argued that this pre-supposes a degree of management flexibility, which does not sit entirely comfortably alongside the current landlord–tenant relationship (ibid.).

Leases

For some time there has been considerable debate about the legal relationship between shopping centre owners and retail tenants. The combination of over-supply, recession and national economic policy during the early 1990s has allowed many occupiers to rewrite lease terms, but major issues still persist. These include:

- *Privity of contract*. Many retail tenants have found to their cost that if an assignee goes bust, then the responsibility for lease and the payment of rent returns to the original leaseholder. Some landlords refuse a re-let, or accept a lower rent, looking to the head leaseholder for the difference, because of the covenant position. However, the Landlord and Tenant (Covenants) Act 1995 has changed the ground-rules, so that for new tenancies the tenant will cease to be liable on assignment; a tenant may be required to guarantee his immediate successor; a landlord can apply to be released from liability after assignment; the landlord can pre-define terms upon which the tenant will be allowed to assign commercial leases; and all covenants are enforceable by and against assignees. For new and existing leases, a former tenant cannot be liable for variations to the lease and has the right to an overriding lease upon paying the arrears.
- *Length of lease*. Pension funds and insurance companies, the major owners of shopping centres in the UK, have traditionally demanded a multiplicity of blue chip tenants contracted on 25-year leases before property investments become acceptable. Turnover rents and short leases, which arguably are needed if a centre is to be run as a business, are treated at valuation as insecure income. There is now a tendency towards shorter leases, prompted by economic circumstance, but also in recognition of the need to concentrate upon quality of income rather than length.
- *Upwards-only rent reviews*. Another chief target of retail tenants is the upwards-only rent review, and support for this view is found from those close to government who see such a practice as profoundly inflationary.

However, institutional investors funding retail development argue that the whole basis of their equity financing of property requires a relatively low return on the basis that rent will grow. Anything less would represent an unfair balance between return and risk.

Further changes towards a more flexible structure in the leasehold relationship between landlords and tenants in the retail sector seem possible. However, it has to be recorded that it all depends on the state of the economy, and on where you stand, as to the benefits or otherwise of particular terms and conditions at any given time.

Turnover rents

Turnover rents first originated in the USA during the 1930s, and now few units in shopping centres there are ever let on any other terms. However, they remain the exception rather than the norm in the UK. Nevertheless, having been pioneered by Capital and Counties in the early 1970s, the use of turnover rents is now more familiar among shopping centres.

Typically, a turnover rent in the UK comprises two elements. First, a base rent, which is usually expressed as a proportion of agreed open market rental, and commonly set at about 75–80 per cent. Second, a percentage of the annual sales turnover of the tenant, which can be as low as 1.5 per cent and as high as 15 per cent, but normally range from around 7–12 per cent according to trade. The basic formula is subject to any number of refinements. The basic rent may refer to an average of past years' rents; turnover provisions may be delayed until, say, the third year of opening; large stores may claim an exempt first slice of turnover; it may be calculated gross or net of tax; or the percentage figure may change according to different levels of sales. Typically, however, the following provide the example in Table 15.1 (Northen 1987).

The advantages of employing turnover rents are that:

- landlord and tenant share an objective to maximize income
- the landlord has an incentive to promote the centre and provide a high standard of management
- the landlord receives an annual share of rental growth
- rent review problems and negotiations are minimized
- it can be a useful device in an inflationary period as far as the landlord is concerned
- it can be helpful in circumstances where the trading potential of a new development is uncertain
- more attention is paid by the landlord to establishing the correct tenant mix.

On the other hand, there are various difficulties associated with turnover rents. These include:

- some trades, such as television hire, building societies and banks, are not suitable for turnover rents

Table 15.1 Turnover rent percentages

	Trade	%
1	Jeweller	10–11
2	Ladies fashion	8–10
3	Men's fashion	8–9
4	Radio and electrical	7
5	Catering	7
6	Shoes (fashion)	9–10
7	Shoes (family)	8–9
8	Records	9
9	Sports goods	9
10	Greengrocer	6
11	Butcher	4–5
12	Baker	5

- new traders might not have a track record and cannot easily be assessed
- the system really works best when traders can quickly and simply be moved around the centre, or poorly performing traders substituted by potential high-turnover ones, as occurs in the USA
- landlord and tenant legislation in the UK is not designed for turnover rents, for apart from the security of tenure provisions there are some doubts about the status of such arrangements
- problems may arise in controlling assignments, and landlords must take care not to disturb the tenant mix
- some traders are reluctant to disclose turnover figures, and the monitoring of accounts can be difficult and costly, but externally audited certificates are normally provided
- unknown levels of rental income are said to deter financial institutions from funding developments let on a turnover basis, but this criticism is probably exaggerated
- Similarly, it is suggested that valuation is a problematic exercise, but again growing familiarity is showing such fears to be groundless
- Many larger centres now have their own websites providing details of retailers in the centre, facilities, location, forthcoming events, and employment opportunities.

In managed centres, overall, the use of turnover rents should forge the relationship between all the parties ever closer and contribute towards mutual success.

Promotion and public relations

A shopping centre will need active promotion before, during and after development. The aim being to increase public awareness and thereby increase pedestrian flow and turnover. To foster or retain goodwill on the part of both shoppers and retailers, there is also a need to ensure a high and constant level of public relations.

The promotion of shopping centres has become almost an industry in itself. Extensive promotional campaigns will normally be mounted at the launch of a new centre, where there are still a substantial number of units vacant or when sales are static, declining or threatened. It is not possible to detail all the techniques of promotion or aspects of public relations that have evolved or emerged over recent years, but some of the most effective policies can be summarized as follows:

- The centre should have a clear identity, reinforced by a memorable name and a striking logo.
- Likewise, a friendly and co-operative stance should be adopted towards local community groupings, such as Chambers of Trade and Commerce, Rotary, Lions Club, Round Table, schools, clubs, women's organizations and the local council.
- Special events of a community nature such as a Christmas carol service, a wine festival or a gymnastics display could be held to draw attention to the centre and make shopping interesting.
- A programme of tenant oriented promotions should be prepared in collaboration with the retailers and might include events such as fashion shows, craft displays or exhibitions.
- Regular press releases should be prepared and carefully placed.
- A survey of shoppers' views about the centre, its competition, travel and parking behaviour, the shopping mix, facilities provided, spending habits and desired changes or additional trades or service should be conducted from time to time.
- Many larger centres now have their own websites providing details of retailers in the centre, facilities, location, forthcoming events, and employment opportunities.

Most important of all, however, is to ensure that all public relations and promotional activities take place against a deliberate and agreed overall policy, otherwise the image portrayed will be at best commonplace, and at worst counterproductive.

Centre management

The primary functions of a shopping centre management have succinctly been described as (Martin 1982):

- paperwork: the administration of head leases and leases, accounting for rent and service costs and secretarial, insurance and legal services
- people: human relations comprising public relations, publicity, promotion and security
- premises: maintenance, primarily of common areas in respect of both buildings and plant.

In a shopping centre of any size there will be a shopping centre manager, representing the interests of the developer or owner. Since the late 1980s there has been a tremendous elevation in the status of the shopping centre manager and a consequent rise in the skills and standards of performance expected of them. A good manager can make the difference between a successful centre and mediocre one. Among the many duties falling upon the centre manager will be the following.

Maintenance of common area

Including routine housekeeping, such as cleaning, polishing, rubbish and litter collection, plant watering and changing of light bulbs and air filters; regular maintenance, such as repainting, turning of carpets and overhaul of plant and machinery; repairs, such as cracked floors, chipped walls and broken elements; and occasional replacement of such components as escalators, lights, carpets, toilets, boilers, mall seating and entrance doors.

Security

Depending upon the size and nature of the centre, its location and setting, the kind of traders represented and the availability of regular fire, police and other services, different levels of security will have to be provided. Aspects of security to be considered will include hooliganism, vandalism, shoplifting, lost children, health and safety at work, protection during building work, fire precaution, emergency lighting, illness or accident procedures and employment of suitable staff. Good security has been defined as:

> A state of benevolent vigilance at all times towards the public, tenants, staff and contractors by way of well thought out and constantly reassessed routines and resources.
>
> (Martin 1982)

Service charge

Being the levy by the landlord upon the tenant for all the operational, maintenance, repair and security charges provided at the centre. Although such charges used to be based upon an agreed sum, the common practice now is for full recovery of all the costs of specified services to take place. Although there are a variety of ways of apportioning charges, in a large enclosed centre this can work out at about £54 per m^2 (£5.00 per ft^2) a year. A proportion of the service charge should also be set aside as a sinking fund for the replacement of major items of plant.

Insurance

The main aspects of insurance with which a shopping centre manager will be concerned are the preservation of income, the reinstatement of property, those liabilities incurred under the terms of the head lease, and any legal liabilities arising out of statute or common law. Rightly, however, it has been stated that insurance is not a substitute for vigilance and good management (Martin 1982).

Traders' associations

There appears to be a notable lack of interest by both landlords and tenants in the formation and running of traders' or merchants' associations in the UK. This is beginning to change as each party recognizes the benefits to be gained. Indeed, most modern leases insist that tenants join an association if one exists. It is really then for the centre manager to ensure that there is an appreciation of the role of the association as being to promote the interests of the centre as a whole.

Town centre management

Many of the principles and practices relating to the effective management of planned shopping centres can equally be applied to town centres themselves. Over recent years the high street has become a fashionable policy focus, which has been formalized with the emergence of Town Centre Management (TCM) initiatives aimed at addressing the issue of enhancing the vitality and viability of town centres. Town centre management has generally been defined by the Association of Town Centre Management as follows:

> Town Centre Management is the effective co-ordination of the private and public sectors, including local authority professionals, to create, in partnership, a successful town centre – building on full consultation.

In particular, TCM is said to provide (Parker 1994):

* a means to co-ordinate the more effective use of public resources
* a new policy/resource priority and focus
* a conduit for establishing private and public sector partnerships
* a lever to secure further private sector investment in the high street
* a co-operative vehicle for community participation and mobilization
* a riposte to out-of-town competitive retail pressures.

Since its inception in 1986, TCM has been adopted by over 80 towns. It has been widely endorsed and actively promoted by government, leading retailers, local community ventures and property-owning institutions, but remains largely a local authority initiative. The origin of TCM lies in the threat posed by out-of-town retail facilities and a growing concern over the health of the high street. It is founded on the property management practices employed by the leading shopping centre owners, but without the legal powers available to them through tenure.

A key element in successful TCM is the appointment of an effective town centre manager whose main functions have been described as follows (Court & Southwell 1994):

- to promote an area rather than a function-based focus to the management of town centres
- to represent the opinions and priorities of all interested public and private sector groups
- to co-ordinate private and public sector roles and policies to achieve a common aim (i.e. the improvement of the town centre)
- to manage effectively town centre initiatives/developments
- to liaise between local authority functions and private sector requirements
- to promote the town-centre and TCM concept.

Research and experience shows that the application of TCM, to date, varies very substantially in organization, finance, power and purpose. Being primarily local-authority based, it is also largely dependent upon public funding, with notable but limited private sector contributions.

A report produced in 1994 found little to suggest that TCM was not considered to be an effective approach to an urgent and obvious problem. Nevertheless, it suggested that private–public sector co-operation was an integral part of successful TCM, which could be encouraged by:

- real participation
- a town centre manager
- aims beyond the janitorial
- an absence of 'political' debate
- effective decision-making
- rational 'business' planning projects rather than politically oriented TCMs
- initiatives backed by authority.

Conversely, it has been argued that it is important to acknowledge that the high street is a market place and not a homogeneous community of common interests. The application of public resources to one priority over another is also seen as a conflict faced by many elected members, requiring political as opposed to 'technical' resolution. In its role as a conduit for public and private sector partnership, moreover, a wider public sector consensus that the high street is worthy of care and that the different cultural approaches to the issues confronted need to be appreciated. Likewise, the argument runs that, for the private sector, whereas the high street is the traditional economic focus of the commercial activities that sustain the urban fabric, it must at the same time be recognized that the high street is also the social and cultural stage for the wider urban community (Parker 1994).

One approach to town-centre regeneration that has been used to great effect in urban regeneration in North America are Business Improvement Districts (BIDs). In essence, BIDs are a technique that property owners and businesses can use to organize and finance improvements to retail, commercial and industrial areas. In the US and Canada, tax is collected by the relevant government agency and then returned to the BID from which they were collected to be used for such items as:

- Improving the appearance, convenience, and day- and night-time appeal of the district for employees, residents, shoppers, and visitors
- Enhance commercial property values
- Increase business profitability.

A hybrid of this type of scheme is just emerging in the UK in response to the powerful Town Centre Management movement.

Conclusion

The face of shopping continues to change. Large stores, having gained a place out-of-town, are now to be subject to much more selective planning control. There is an increasing awareness of the vital need to improve and promote traditional town centres, and a conscious attempt by many councils to adopt a management approach towards the issue. Category killers in such areas as electronics, office goods, household linens and sporting goods are arriving, and bound to grow. Likewise with warehouse clubs and factory outlets. Conventional leasehold terms and conditions are already under attack, and will surely change to produce a much more flexible system. Considerable imagination is also being brought to bear upon the retail sector as witnessed by the refurbishment of many old inner-city buildings to form new shopping centres and arcades. Similarly, dated existing planned shopping centres are being revitalized. Nevertheless, in respect of shopping centre management, we still have much to learn from the active and intensive management practices of US centres.

Despite the dot.com crash, online shopping is growing in the UK with sales having reached £3.3 billion in 2001 (Verdict 2002). This represents only 2 per cent of all retail sales but the proportion is expected to rise by up to 10 per cent by 2009 (Verdict 2002). According to Doige and Higgins (2000) Electronic retailing (e-tailing) is concentrated in the following areas (in order of significance):

- Books
- CDs, tapes, videos
- Groceries
- Software, hardware
- Clothing, footwear
- Gifts.

Dennis *et al.* (2002) suggest that if, as forecast, 'bricks' shopping is set to lose substantial business to internet shopping, retailers might take the following action:

- Multi-channel retailing (internet plus high street)
- The internet shopping centre
- Emphasis on leisure, eating and drinking, which are services the e-shopper cannot consume on the web.

In any event, the assembly and distribution of goods is an expensive operation, and it is the shopper who bears the hidden costs of this at present.

Shop investors, developers and owners should not, however, be too complacent. The likely over-supply of shopping facilities reminds those involved that their shop property can no longer be conceived in purely architectural or geographical terms. Successful centres of the future must be consumer-led and innovative to attract and retain their shopping populations.

16 Office development

The world economy is changing, and with it the nature and function of cities, and the way in which work is perceived and performed. One of the most intractable tasks for urban planning and development in the light of such change is the proper provision for all concerned of office and business space. Not only is there a shift of economic growth from the old economies of Europe and North America to the new economies of the Far East and the Pacific Rim, but there is the potentially explosive impact of the full flowering of information technology (IT) and the question as to whether that impact will be evolutionary or revolutionary in character.

In Europe, the advent of modern management systems and the corporate drive for cost effectiveness has been stated to affect the nature of cities in at least four ways:

1   the historic migration of high volume, low value added – so called back office – activity out of the city;
2   the subsequent, and sometimes simultaneous migration of this type of activity to other lower cost countries;
3   the higher value added, lower volume activity remaining within the urban area but now dispersing from the centre;
4   the reverse of these dispersal trends in the new magnetism of the concentration of specialist, relatively low volume, but high value added, activity into the core of the city especially for those activities which require a great deal of co-operation among people.

(Chapman 1995)

The continuing search for increased business efficiency, especially by the 40 000 or so transnational companies identified in the global economy, has led to the optimization of real estate assets in terms of location, quantity, specification and tenure, as well as the emergence of such corporate restructuring buzzwords as down-sizing, right-sizing, outsourcing, telecommuting, hot-desking and core business concentration. Cities themselves are finding the need to compete as businesses with an awareness of their inherent strengths and weaknesses; an evaluation of the necessary management, skill, resource and marketing abilities required to maintain and enhance the city economy; and the desirability and direction of specialization, excellence and expertise. In this context, it has been argued that effective, properly resourced partnerships of central and local government and the business community, with coherent reliable strategies to underpin the existing economies in order to attract more firms, will be essential for the long-run demand for offices (ibid.).

In the UK the 1980s could fairly be described as having been the era of the office. More was researched and written about modern office needs during that decade than was ever compiled and published over the previous 50 years. This quest continues. However, warnings of the need for change were first signalled during the mid-1970s when, for example, it was stated:

> When planning our buildings we cannot afford to stand still, year by year standards are improving; the office building that was built in the early post-war years began to look a little dated by the 1960s and now in the 1970s that same building will probably require extensive modernization and adaptation to bring it into line with modern requirements. It is reasonable to assume that the rate of change in office standards is accelerating.
>
> (CALUS 1974)

Nothing could have been more true. The advent and application of information technology has brought about the need for changing office design and location even more rapidly than most professional observers anticipated. An awareness and understanding of the requirements of information technology can rightly be said to have been the keynotes of successful space management in the 1980s. Office activities and structures need to adjust so quickly and so often in response to new business demands and services that, however much of a cliché it has become, the watchword in office development is flexibility. This is exemplified in the sales literature produced by one leading property development company, which identifies and prioritizes certain advantages to a particular development as follows:

> The first is flexibility. Tenants can make their offices fit the logic of the organization. The floor size gives great freedom of layout. The modular grid places the minimum constraint on partitioning. The raised floor allows cabling to run to any position.[1]

In addition, it has been argued that the workplace has changed for several other reasons (Steelcast Strafor 1990). Information technology has altered the social composition of the office, producing a more equal, demanding and discriminating workforce who expect to enjoy choice at work. There is greater freedom, moreover, in the use of time and the location of the office. And the economics of office space use has changed so that far more money is now spent on relatively short-life interiors and proportionately less on the shell and exterior elements of office buildings.

Many of the great issues concerning office development that have emerged in Europe over the last decade were originally identified by Dr Frank Duffy as:

- harmonization of environmental and product standards throughout the European Community;

- increasing awareness of what can be learned from the best international initiatives – North American, Japanese, Scandinavian, German;
- the increasing importance of 'green' issues in the workplace; avoiding deleterious products, concerning energy in component manufacturing and building use, sustainability in materials usage;
- rethinking the costs of commuter transportation, given the potential of information technology;
- the increasing power of better educated, more scientific facilities managers;
- the opening up of the design process to end users; and,
- much more inventive use of the increasingly expensive resources of time and space.

(Steelcast Strafor 1990)

It has also been observed that there is a continuing managerial revolution that will eventually change the whole world of work. New managerial ideas, the fruit of the information technology revolution that began in the 1980s, are dissolving all the boundaries and constraints that shaped the conventional office of the twentieth century. This, in turn, is breeding a new culture towards work, the main features of which have been described as:

- much greater attention to the fluid and urgent use of time, e.g. taking the competitive advantage to be delivered from designing serial processes; taking advantage of the redundancies in space use endemic in conventional office design;
- impatience with conventional organizational hierarchies;
- little love of hierarchies;
- a tendency towards smaller more transient organizational units, stripping the organization back to the core, out-stripping redundant and non-central;
- the spatial context and focus for intense, complex open-ended team-work;
- the obsolescence of clerks and clerical ways;
- total confidence in the intelligent and creative use of information technology;
- a wider range of types of work, settings for work, support for work, places for work.

(Duffy 1994)

Over the last 10 years we have witnessed profound changes in the office function that have required of developers a greater appreciation of not only the tenants' operational needs but also of the staff who are employed in the buildings constructed to house those operations. Nothing can be taken for granted for very long in the office world of work.

In examining trends and prospects for the planning and development of offices, this chapter is divided into the following sections:

- location and provision
- planning and office development

- design and layout
- services and facilities
- business and office parks
- facilities management.

Location and provision

Hunch and intuition are no longer sufficient attributes in the analysis of office markets to determine planning policies and development opportunities. Office forecasting has become a more specialized task. For example, trend extrapolation might be a useful starting point in examining market conditions, but as an accurate indicator of future demand it is a poor device. Likewise, vacancy rates give a very broad guide to the imbalance between demand and supply in the market, but conceal the effect of a multitude of determining factors.

What seems clear from a succession of major surveys is that location remains the single most important factor to occupiers out of the four major determinants of location, building design, cost of occupation and lease terms. One commentator recently summarized the pressures on office location as follows:

> Although some demand has been diverted away from city centres to business parks and the communication revolution has allowed such activities as home working and hot desking, the prospects for the city-centre office are still good. First, the concept of the office is remarkably durable. People do not need to work in offices but they choose to do so because of the human need for social interaction. Second, governments and pressure groups throughout the world are pressing for a sustainable use of resources. This implies a long-term reduction in car use, the regeneration and repopulation of city centres, and the development of improved and more modern public transport systems. All of this suggests yet more use for and demand for city-centre offices.
>
> (Havard 2002)

Moreover, the traditional notions of office and business location in respect of towns and cities and town and city centres are being transformed. Advanced tools of communication such as video conferencing, PC video phone, telepresence and remote diagnostics enable business people to be in contact with customers, colleagues, collaborators and support services from almost anywhere to anywhere (Chapman 1995).

In terms of provision, the pre-eminence of London is striking. For the purposes of investment decision-making in the development process, an hierarchical classification of UK office markets can be made as follows (Damesick 1994):

1 Central London
2 London suburbs and M25 location
3 metropolitan regional centres such as Birmingham, Bristol, Manchester, Leeds, Edinburgh and Glasgow

4   major second-tier centres such as Leicester, Nottingham, Newcastle, Sheffield and Cardiff

5   minor second-tier centres such as Brighton, Peterborough and Oxford.

Demand

Demand for office accommodation can be said to arise from one of three causes: growth, replacement or relocation. Growth can be the emergence of new businesses or the expansion of existing ones, resulting from general growth within the economy or specific growth within individual sectors. Replacement implies the need for more modern premises and demand for this can often be gauged from a physical analysis of the existing stock. It sometimes leads to the older properties being re-let and the stemming of rental growth. Relocation can be sponsored by reorganization, rationalization, or again by growth.

There are several basic sources from which the demand for office accommodation can stem: central government, local government, quasi-government agencies, private sector service industry and private business firms and corporations. The sources of demand in the opening decade of the new millennium are extremely varied. Private-sector commercial organizations will be the principal catalyst for office development. However, the growth in public-sector projects procured through the private finance initiative route is likely to continue and therefore the influence of the public sector will not be insubstantial. Generally speaking, the total amount of new floorspace requirements emanating from these various sources is likely to rise, but probably at a slower rate than has been experienced over the past 25 years. What will change more radically is the average size, location and type of office accommodation demanded. The demand by major commercial organizations, for instance, is not usually for more space, but for better space. In the same way, the rash of national and multinational takeovers frequently leads to a fall in the overall demand for office accommodation, but can produce a fresh requirement for new space more appropriately designed and positioned. Nevertheless, in such circumstances it is common to find that the headquarters function is significantly reduced and the requirement for decentralized office space enhanced. Although there might be less aggregate demand for accommodation from some of the very largest corporations already established in the UK, there is a constant call for space from other multinational organizations moving into the UK, and a healthy demand from successful small and medium-size companies looking for new offices to accommodate their growth.

Analysing the market demand for office development is perhaps the most difficult and least accurate of all land uses. Statistics on business use of office space are difficult to come by and are frequently outdated. There is considerable flexibility in terms of the intensity of office occupation. A firm can effectively delay the need to move premises by increasing the concentration of workstations in the existing space. This suggests a demand elasticity not evident in other sectors. Wide swings in overbuilding and underbuilding distort market perceptions. The 'image' of particular locations or individual buildings or the quality of continuing property management can all conspire to make it hard to forecast market demand. Moreover, office buildings do not have a catchment or trade area in the same way as shopping centres or even housing projects. Nevertheless, there are any number of factors that affect the demand for office space. These can be summarized as follows:

- national, regional and local economic performance
- service sector employment growth
- trends within different categories
- communications
- local planning and amenity
- floor space to worker ratios
- level of rents and values
- costs of occupation
- lease terms
- building services and facilities
- complementarity of neighbouring occupiers.

In stressing that the modern occupier of office accommodation is becoming much more selective than his predecessor, it is clear that:

- Conventional concepts of location in the office market are rendered redundant by improvements to communications, and although activities such as insurance, shipping and commodities are likely to remain grouped in traditional areas, other kinds of business are now much freer in their approach and inclined to be more supply oriented.
- In recent years tenants have been seeking shorter leases with one-sided break options, or a series of renewal options, downward as well as upward rent review clauses, and will tend to rely increasingly on their statutory rights. Although this will cause landlords to look more closely at the flexibility of their buildings, and be happier to accept multi-occupation, it is quite likely that rents eventually will rise in compensation for the diminished certainty of income.
- Facilities managers now play a large part in determining the suitability of premises, and the critical factors will be floor sizes and loading, air conditioning, power supply facilities, self-adjustable working environment, underfloor and vertical communication space, servicing costs, and cost-effective divisibility.
- Security is a prime consideration, not only in terms of the physical access to and from buildings, but also access to data and external communications systems.

In addition, various research studies have provided strong evidence that 'teleworking' is expected to become an important factor in the future of office work. Not just individuals working at home, but corporate, executive and contract teleworkings, using satellite offices, shared access telecentres, telecottages or production centres. It has been suggested, therefore, that the increased use of teleworking, and the need for telecentres, will create a market in suitable commercial properties (Todd 1993).

Lowe (1995) suggested that there have been 'repeated forecasts that we are "on the verge" of a profound technological revolution, whereby there will be less commuting and a great deal more working from home using computers, faxes and modems which will transform the way that we live, work and move around'.

Yet probably less than 1 per cent of the workforce is currently employed as home-based teleworkers and these tend to be highly skilled, self-employed or freelance workers based in metropolitan areas.

In assessing the broad measures of demand for offices, it should not be forgotten that, as with other sectors of the property development industry, there is an element of 'fashion' to take into account. Certain towns and cities can suddenly be in vogue. In the 1970s around London and the West, for example, Reading, Bristol, Swindon, Watford and Luton were enormously popular. The early 1980s saw the likes of Aylesbury, Chelmsford and Newbury come to the fore and since the late 1980s we have witnessed a re-emergence of regional centres such as Birmingham, Glasgow, Manchester, and Leeds. Moreover, given that 95 per cent of all office-based organizations employ less than 50 people, the creation of smaller office buildings, and the construction of buildings capable of multiple occupation, will be a major area of future development.

Corporate image will even override marginal financial considerations. Many so-called 'blue chip' companies either relocating from Central London or moving into the UK from Europe and America are looking for buildings in well landscaped settings in a pleasant locality. The increasingly sophisticated nature of the work undertaken by such companies, and the higher executive status of the staff accommodated there, means that developers can no longer be content with providing standard specification buildings. Special space and performance requirements, coupled with a desire to avoid excessive increases in rent at review, are pushing many potential occupiers towards building their own offices.

The changing nature of work itself will obviously exercise a considerable effect upon the demand for office space. As will be discussed below, the information explosion and the increased need for support services by decision-makers will continue to dictate different space requirements. For a variety of reasons, including more room to accommodate the paraphernalia of information technology and the aspirations of employees to work in a more conducive environment, floor space to worker ratios will inevitably rise. In this context, the following trends and factors have been recorded:

- Evidence suggests that floor space to worker ratios have already been increasing since the 1970s. This is explained by the increase in administrative and professional over clerical occupations, the predominance of larger office organizations, which tend to be more generous with space provision, and the scale of office mechanization brought about largely through major advances in information and communications technology.
- Wide variations in individual floor space to worker ratios can occur, often as a result of different gross to net usable floor area ratios between buildings, but also because of differing sizes and types

of office activity between businesses and their stage of commercial development.
- Typical London office workers occupy only about two-thirds of the space occupied by their counterparts in Europe.

Therefore, although it seems possible that worker densities will fall, the extent to which this happens will vary according to the design and age of the building concerned and the business activity, workforce, structure, equipment employed and life-cycle stage. Other factors, such as the extension of flexi-time and job-sharing, the continuous use of certain office premises, the sharing of space between firms, the increasing use of serviced offices, hot-desking and flexible working practices and the movement towards a shorter working week, will all combine to influence demand in respect of office location and design decisions.

Supply

It is important to remember that the office sector of the property development industry suffers from a strong counter-cyclical pattern of performance. In other words, responses to increased demand tend to take so long to put into effect that, by the time supply is increased to meet it, the market has changed so that supply greatly exceeds demand. Likewise, as supply is curtailed, so the market recovers and demand picks up again, overtaking declining supply. This counter-cyclical effect in the late 1970s and again in the late 1980s saw a shortage of office property, a rise in rental levels and a fall in investment yields – all of which combined to produce higher capital values in the office market. Not unnaturally, these symptoms encouraged developers to institute new projects. On both occasions, the country moved into severe recession, just as these projects began to come on stream. An extreme example of this phenomenon was seen in the City of London office development market when in the year August 1989/90 more office space was constructed, $47\,806$ m^2 ($514\,600$ ft^2), than had been built over the previous decade, $47\,639$ m^2 ($512\,800$ ft^2).

As with most other sectors of the property market, supply is much easier to assess than demand. The principal factors underlying the supply of office accommodation are:

- government and local authority policy
- existing approvals (as a proportion of stock)
- projects under construction (likewise)
- projects proposed but not yet approved (likewise)
- vacancy rates (likewise)
- rental and yield trends
- availability of utilities and services
- construction cost trends
- availability and terms of finance.

Once data on demand and supply have been assembled, an analysis can take place to assess the relationship between the two, for the developer is not so much concerned with demand and supply as such, but rather the difference between them, which is known as the 'absorption rate'. Since it takes two to three years to bring an office building onto the market, the developer is principally concerned with the likely future absorption rate for office space in a given locality, rather than present rate. Simple quantitative market models have been proposed but are rarely employed in practice (Detoy & Rabin 1985).

Decentralization and relocation

Perhaps the most hotly debated issue in respect of office location is that of decentralization and relocation, and, linked with it, the future of the main office centres, especially London. However, conflicting views are advanced regarding the pace, degree and direction of decentralized office development.

During the 1980s one of the most powerful engines of the property boom was the growing number of companies that decided to relocate their business premises. The number of jobs that relocated from Central London, for example, doubled from an annual total of 5675 in 1986 to 11 380 in 1990 (Rawson-Gardiner 1993). With the erosion of the property cost differential between London and the regions, one key incentive for companies to relocate office employment to provincial cities became much more reduced. While rapid rental inflation in Central London in the late 1980s helped trigger a record volume of decentralization in the years 1990–2, this tailed off very sharply in 1993–4. Some increase in out-movement is said to occur in the short term, but longer-distance moves beyond the South East became less popular in currently planned relocations (Damesick 1994).

Research has found the following features in the relocation decisions made by companies (Rawson-Gardiner 1993):

- Relocation will continue, but the forces energizing these moves will be different from those in the late 1980s.
- Relocation decisions made since the recession really took grip were driven more by operational and business factors than by purely property cost considerations.
- The restructuring or reorganization of a company often prompted a move, or conversely, the relocation was used as a catalyst to implement cultural corporate changes.
- A significant proportion of the 500 largest companies in the UK feel that scope remains for further reducing property costs through the rationalization of space requirements.
- Although property costs will continue to play an important role in some relocation decisions over the next few years, relocations will be more likely to take place to achieve savings through the reorganization of the property portfolio and/or a desire to downsize, rather than as a means to escape from exorbitant rents.
- The major problems regarding location related to staff matters, especially with long-distance moves, and the use of relocation consultants specializing in human resources was prevalent.

- Relocation overall is an effective tool for achieving both cost control and corporate change.

Looking at the future of London as a main office centre, it is clear that the process of decentralization has been taking place over a long period of time, and is not a sudden phenomenon. In fact, it is unlikely that the scale and type of decentralization that has happened since the mid-1960s will recur. Nevertheless, it is possible to advance the case that in forthcoming years only those activities that absolutely have to be centred in London will remain. Increasingly, operations that depend upon a high level of close business contact, such as finance, property, advertising and the law, will predominate, together with a concentration of top management in the headquarters offices of major national and international companies. Moreover, the influx of foreign business, especially banks, continues apace, and, initially at least, London is viewed as being the only acceptable location. As a consequence of this constant drift towards the provision or retention of higher-level jobs, the overwhelming demand will be for offices supplying superior space standards.

One very noticeable trend throughout the 1980s and early 1990s had been in London itself. Central area development overspilled into several centres around the City and West End, as well as to various suburban locations, for many national and multinational corporations are willing to make only marginal moves. However, it should be appreciated that this process of intra-city relocation is not confined to London, but is also experienced in cities such as Bristol, Birmingham and Manchester.

London continues to attract a certain kind of commercial activity. The recent appointment of a mayor for London and moves towards a London-wide co-ordinated policy for planning, transport and infrastructure development have helped to minimize the flow of businesses away from the capital. However, major increases in house prices in recent years have brought recruitment challenges as workers for key public-sector positions (such as teachers and nurses) find themselves unable to afford housing in the capital. There is already a tendency on the part of large business organizations to situate their corporate headquarters in locations well away from major centres. Even some international banking corporations have opted for decentralized locations and many other traditional central area operations are looking very seriously at the balance of advantages that might lead them to decant a significant part of their business, or to decamp altogether, to more provincial or Home County locations. What could well happen is that office functions and structures might be polarized between very high-order activities occupying top-quality expensive office premises in central-area positions, and all other operations being conducted in low-rise, low-density and relatively inexpensive locations out of town. In this way, it appears almost certain that the South East region outside London is bound to expand. Already, considerable pressure has been placed upon towns along the various motorway corridors; the infrastructure investment in areas such as south Hampshire and Buckinghamshire is proving irresistible; and the completion of the M25 inevitably is exercising a magnetic influence upon commercial property developments.

One of the consequences of a desire to decentralize, the increase in personal transport and improvements in communication technology, is the demand for accommodation situated in office parks. These campus-style developments are characteristically located on the edge of towns and comprise a mix of low-rise, low-density buildings with extensive car parking, a wide range of business and sometimes leisure facilities, set in an attractive environment close to motorways, good schools and high-grade housing. Frequently, they are not restricted purely to office buildings but are composed of various business activities, including research and light engineering as well as conventional clerical and administrative functions. (These forms of development are discussed more fully on p. 486.)

Planning and office development

Many of the basic aspects of planning policy and practice affecting office development are beyond the scope of this text. Nevertheless, some comment on specific planning considerations is called for because office development proposals are so frequently singled out for special treatment by local authorities, especially in London and the South East. There has often, in fact, been a heavy bias against office development in certain areas, sometimes politically inspired and sometimes resulting from pressures exerted by vested interest. Somehow, offices attract a degree of vituperation not directed towards other forms of development such as industry and housing. The fact that office-based activities provide a major source of employment is seemingly overlooked by some councils and the lobbies that influence them. Strangely, vacant new industrial estates attract sympathy, whereas vacant recently completed office premises attract opprobrium. A certain underlying rationale can be divined, in that office developers are typically cast in the mould of persons who display a general indifference to the social ramifications of their proposed schemes and have a particular tendency to ignore the public costs of private development. To some extent the recession of the early 1990s tempered this reaction. Large-scale town-centre office development is in the doldrums. As an example, the RICS recently reported that London office rents dropped by 20–30 per cent in 2002 and vacancy rates have risen to 10 per cent in Central London and the City. This trend is expected to continue. However, out of town the concept of a new generation of business parks faces probable conflict with local authorities in the light of the government's refocus on city-centre regeneration (RICS 2002).

The general principles that govern the framing of most planning policies as they relate to office development can usefully be summarized as follows:

- to control the scale, standards of design and layout of individual buildings according to established planning objectives
- to control the location of office development, in accordance with the objectives of land use or spatial planning
- to control the overall level of office development activity with respect to the objectives of economic development policy.

These policies are abstracted from the late Greater London Council's published approach towards office development control and they epitomize the somewhat negative approach often taken towards offices. There has always appeared to be a basic ambivalence by planning authorities at a strategic level regarding a decision as to whether support should be given towards central area development along with better housing and public transport facilities, or whether suburban decentralization with improved road and traffic management schemes should be encouraged. In any event, policies towards offices have proved difficult to formulate, because of what appears to be an inherent inability to examine and interpret true office needs, which is made worse by the lack of a proper database relating to business occupation.

Strategic planning for office development[2]

The Draft London Plan (DLP) sets out a strategy for accommodating major growth in London in a sustainable way. The plan envisages a 30 per cent increase in the total office floor space in London by 2016 and a pronounced eastward shift in the pattern of office development to serve regeneration objectives (Damesick 2003).

The Mayor of London, Ken Livingstone, has acknowledged that the office development policy in the DLP will work only if the transport infrastructure (especially Thameslink 2000, the East London Line extension and the Crossrail link) is in place.

The DLP also imposes substantial obligations on office developers, in particular in respect of contributions to infrastructure costs.

The DLP uses the predictions of Volterra, a firm of independent consultants, who have estimated that growth in financial and business services (FBS) will generate an additional 460 000 jobs by 2016 creating a demand for 87 million square feet (8.1 million square metres) of office floor space assuming a 7–8 per cent vacancy rate.

However, since 2000 London has experienced a sharp downturn in FBS employment, with large-scale job-shedding and prospects of a sluggish recovery in activity (Damesick 2003).

It has been argued that reshaping the geography of office development in London is essential to achieving the objectives of regeneration. However, many areas of East London are likely to be relatively low-value locations in commercial property terms, and this suggests difficulties in maximizing developer contributions through planning obligations.

This is the challenging environment in which office developers in Central London will have to operate in the coming decade.

In the rest of the South East the strategic context is provided by Regional Planning Guidance introduced in the mid-1990s. This includes a general objective of sustaining the attractions of the region for inward investment and the location of corporate headquarters and facilitating new developments for industry and commerce, but bearing in mind that environmental constraints will limit scope for further growth west and south of London. It acknowledges the extent of vacant space and the very substantial scale of existing planning permissions in all parts of the region. Structure plans provide the existing vehicle for augmenting these regional statements for the main office centres, reflecting local circumstances. However, structure planning, and particularly its function in establishing the basic demand and supply parameters, is under threat from impending local government reorganization and the government's desire to extend unitary government and plan-making for smaller areas.

The new Planning and Compulsory Purchase Bill, which the RICS has described as 'short on detail and in some cases little more than a skeleton, posing as many questions as it answers', provides for a regional spatial strategy (RSS) in every region of England except London. These will replace existing regional planning guidance. The Secretary of State will be able to recognize a body as the Regional Planning Body (RPB) who will, *inter alia*, keep the RSS under review, report on its implementation and prepare draft revisions. The resulting framework will enjoy development plan status (Edwards and Martin 2003).

Many local authorities traditionally opposed to significant office development proposals are beginning to recognize the importance of the office sector in securing overall employment objectives. In this, the attraction of major corporations moving to the country or relocating from Central London has been seen to play an important role. However, it has been pointed out that at the current time there are probably more towns seeking large single-space users than there are potential occupiers for this type of accommodation. Planners and developers alike, it is argued, would do well to pay attention to the regional and subregional role played by a town, which might in future have a greater effect on the office absorption rate, than continued attempts to entice outsiders from the fast-shrinking pool of large mobile companies. There is also a tendency for many towns to resist office development on the edge of the urban area, and in a few less restrictive towns a dual market has emerged between greenfield and town-centre locations.

Planning policy can be highly successful in battening down office development, but it is much less effective in encouraging it. Nevertheless, several principal factors outlined below exercise a considerable effect upon the outcome of office development proposals.

Floorspace

The popular way by which the total amount of planned floor space for a local authority is calculated is to establish a relationship between predicted population levels, proportion of office employees and consequent office space used. Each of these factors is highly susceptible to error, and this is compounded when they are combined. Employment generation assessed by worker density standards, therefore, is extremely difficult to compute and virtually impossible to enforce. From this it can be argued that floor space as an indicator or regulator of office development is a very crude instrument. A more discretionary approach is adopted by many planning authorities, although some are peculiarly reluctant to release additional approvals in order to reduce obvious scarcities and deflate excessively high levels of rent, which discourage business activity and employment. A certain amount of discrimination is also required to ensure the sensitive release of sufficient land and planning consents in the right locations, so as to capture internationally footloose companies. One further aspect of floor space is the means of controlling the intensity of development on individual sites. The nature and operation of plot ratio and floor space index controls is explained elsewhere, but it is important to recognize that different authorities attach varying degrees of adherence to the precise designation of particular areas and density levels. Some are open to negotiation around an established figure, some are not. In general, however, it is fair to say that most authorities are less rigid and less definitive than previously.

Transport and parking

Problems of communication and traffic beset all forms of property development, but despite planning arguments to the contrary, it is possible to put forward the case that in many ways offices cause the least amount of disruption to the transportation system. To a great extent, most office developments are creatures of communications networks, and have a strong capacity to adjust to them. The real question that confronts planning authorities is how, in the aggregate, to preserve a balance between, on the one hand, ensuring that there is a sufficient minimum level of service provision to permit proper access to a proposed development and, on the other, preventing an overload of the existing system. Because of this, sites immediately adjacent to transport termini or interchanges are often favoured. In appraising a potential development, or in making an application for planning permission in respect of offices, there are various factors that should be taken into account. These can be summarized as follows:

- the number of employees who will be working within the building
- the likely number of visitors attracted to the development, and their probable mode of travel
- the amount of delivery and service traffic generated by the prospective users
- the extent to which loading and unloading operations might take place, the noise that could be created, and the time when the building will be used and the various operations occur
- where access is to be provided.

Parking is an important consideration. Standards and regulations vary throughout the country, depending normally upon the proximity to the town or city centre and the degree of congestion enjoyed at the place in question. Some local authorities preclude parking facilities altogether, apart from an absolute bare minimum of spaces. Others insist upon levels as high as one space for every 32.5 m² (350 ft²) of floor space. Outside Central London, however, a commonly sought level of provision for in-town sites separates operational and non-operational requirements, setting standards for the former at around a maximum of one space for every 80 m² (750 ft²) of gross floorspace. For out-of-town office parks the standard is around one space to every 23 m² (250 ft²), and sometimes as one to every 14 m² (150 ft²).

With non-operational parking provision it is not unusual for local planning authorities to try to insist that the carparking spaces should be made available for public use, and also sometimes to look for a commutation of the cost of provision towards the construction of general public carparks. In certain circumstances, where no such commutation takes place, councils will seek to enter into agreements with developers for the transfer of private off-street parks to public use on Saturdays.

The Departments of the Environment and Transport collaborated to produce PPG13 *A guide to better practice* in late 1995, aimed at reducing the need to travel, through land-use and transport planning. The guide provides a practical user's manual for implementing PPG13, which should help local authority planners and councillors in drawing up or revising their development plans and in considering individual planning applications. It should also benefit developers and individuals who wish to see how the concepts in PPG13 can be translated into practice.

Restricted user

As part of a policy of restraint, some local planning authorities attempt to limit or control the use or occupancy of office buildings by means of:

- local user conditions, restricting occupancy to businesses already established and operating in the area
- named user conditions, where specified firms alone are allowed to occupy the premises
- small suite provision, where all or part of the development must be let in small office units of, say, not more than 464 m² (5000 ft²).

Recent years have seen some relaxation of these policies, and a greater record of success against their imposition at appeal.

A radical change in the restriction of use was introduced by the Town and Country Planning (Use Classes) Order 1987. This lists 16 classes, which are placed in four general use categories:

A   shopping area
B   other business and industrial
C   residential
D   social and community uses.

With regard to office development, the Class B1 (Business) brings together offices, so long as they do not provide a service for visiting members of the public, and light industry. For certain projects, therefore, developers might seek a wider range of uses than hitherto had been possible. Nevertheless, local planning authorities still retain their power of development control and can look to restrict the freedom to change uses to a narrower range than the order permits. However, Circular 13/87 makes it plain that the Secretary of State will regard the imposition of such restrictions as unreasonable unless there is clear evidence that the uses excluded would have a serious impact on the environment or on amenity, not susceptible to other control. In practice, the business use class has provided considerable opportunities for the owners of multi-storey industrial buildings to refurbish their properties to meet the demands of a growing studio market.

Planning gain

The subject of extracting community benefits in return for planning consents comes most sharply into focus when considering proposed office developments. Offices are invariably – and often erroneously – taken to be the most profitable form of property development and the essential ingredient in many mixed-use schemes. Local authorities have come to accept, however, that there are often occasions when a certain amount of commercial office space must be included to make some residential or leisure developments viable. It is not uncommon to find phrases along the lines of 'office accommodation to be kept to a minimum level required for the successful implementation of the development package' (Kingston Borough[3]) in local plans and planning briefs prepared for areas and sites otherwise deemed undesirable for offices. Given the present state of the market, the assumption that office construction usually produces the most profitable form of development is fallacious. Traditionally, shopping schemes produce high returns, and in many prime locations luxury housing can be the most profitable use. On some sites in Central London, in fact, permission has been sought to change existing planning approvals from office to residential use.

Nevertheless, it is important to establish the prevailing attitude of planning authorities towards the issue of planning gain obligations and agreements at the earliest stage in the process of redevelopment.

Urban design

Although beauty is said to lie in the eye of the beholder, it is true to say that over recent years the design and siting of offices has become a very much more critical consideration than hitherto. Many local authorities are willing to extend a greater degree of sympathy towards well designed, sensitively proportioned office buildings, or countenance higher levels of density than would otherwise be the norm if a proposed scheme is attractive and harmonizes with its surroundings. In 1994, for example, the City of London abandoned a strict adherence to the use of plot ratio as an instrument of development control in favour of a more discretionary approach towards building design.

The relative popularity of renovation as opposed to redevelopment is becoming general across all sectors of the commercial property market, but the preference towards refurbishment on the part of planning authorities is particularly marked in the case of office development projects. More than this, there appears to be a growing awareness and understanding of the economics of conservation, so that there is no longer quite the antipathy in some quarters towards the change of use of buildings of architectural or historic interest to offices, where otherwise they might have continued to deteriorate. In most instances, conversion to offices is infinitely preferable to redevelopment or radical refurbishment for shops.

Regeneration

Although this section on planning and office development opened on a negative note as to how office projects are seen by planning authorities, it ends with a more positive theme: the role that planned office schemes can play in the regeneration of local economies. Increasingly, it is recognized that many older cities with serious problems of social deprivation, high unemployment, environmental degradation and general decline have large sites, which are otherwise well located, that have potential for the development of business parks or office campuses. An excellent example of this is the Newcastle Business Park, which is one of the Tyne & Wear Development Corporation's flagship developments. Here a vacant, derelict and contaminated 24 ha (60 acre) site has been transformed through the expenditure of around £140 million in partnership with the private sector into a major business park, providing around 4000 jobs when fully let. Although such initiatives do not always directly benefit the local population with long-term employment, they do generate short-term job opportunities and act as a general catalyst for economic growth within the urban area.

Design and layout

For almost 30 years following the end of the Second World War, the design of office buildings was uniformly dull and unimaginative. Architects were all too frequently nervous about the mystical design and performance standards laid down by the major financial institutions and their professional advisers, and as a result tended to allow the control of design to pass out of their hands. In matters of new office development it almost appeared as if the accountant had gained ascendancy over the architect, and the approach to commercial development seemed to be the provision of functionally clad and serviced floorspace. The 1980s can be said to have witnessed a constant improvement in the standard of design of office developments. Nevertheless, the trend in low-rise blocks back to brick as a facing material, prompted by demands from property and planning interests alike, gave rise to a certain amount of fresh criticism. This resulted from the rash of three- and four-storey brick-built developments, topped with lead or copper mansard roofs and adorned by dinky dormer windows, some of which were reasonably well done, some decidedly were not.

Above all, however, the 1980s have been generally recognized as a decade that witnessed a quantum leap in the design of office buildings. Until the early 1980s, the process of designing office buildings had been one of steady evolution and refinement, with the product being supply led. But then the more astute developers began to question the conventional wisdom of office design and started to identify and examine some of the changing occupational trends brought about by the increasing impact of information technology and new organizational structures.

Broad principles

The main principles by which office design and layout might be judged have been set down as follows:

1 relationship of the building to its surroundings in terms of appearance, height and size, and response to outside factors such as railway lines and noisy streets;
2 pedestrian and traffic access, and the position of entrances and service points;
3 structural grid and facility in meeting subdivision requirements;
4 natural light penetration;
5 floor to floor heights;
6 size and shape of floors in relation to likely tenant demand and flexibility in dividing floors or letting separate floors singly;
7 position and design of service cores;
8 efficiency of building, i.e. relationship between gross area and net lettable accommodation;
9 carparking content and location;
10 extent and suitability of any landscaped or other amenity areas.

(Marber 1985)

In terms of the shell, scenery and settings, it has been pointed out that buildings take a long time to build, are difficult to change, and once built are there to last (Worthington & Kenya 1988). Firms, on the other hand, are continuously in a state of flux, as the economy, technology and market changes around them.

Because of this, building design decisions reflect different timescales where:

• building shells have a life-span of around 75 years and may have many owners
• services have a life-span of around 15 years and adjust one shell to specific functions
• scenery may change every five–seven years as organizations grow and change
• on a daily, weekly or monthly basis, scenery may be moved to reflect specific activities.

In very general terms, a typical specification for a modern office building has been summarized as providing (Jones Lang Wootton 1990):

Structure
• 4 m (13 ft) slab to slab height
• 3 m (9 ft 9 in) clear floor to ceiling height
• 15 cm (6 in) accessible raised floor height
• 6 m by 9 m (19 ft 8 in by 29 ft 6 in) structural grid
• 36 kg (80 lb) per ft^2 live floor loading + 9 kg (20 lb) ft^2 for partitions.

External fabric
- high-quality curtain walling of aluminium and granite or stone
- double glazing.

Building services
- variable air volume air-conditioning
- integral lighting with suspended ceiling – 500 lux lighting level
- small power supply of 3 watts per ft^2
- air-conditioning cooling load of 3 watts per ft^2 (small power)
- additional cooling capacity for specialist areas
- emergency standby generator
- facility for tenant's generator
- building management system
- sprinkler installation
- passenger lift providing a waiting interval of 30 seconds
- separate goods lift and loading bay.

Internal finishes
- Use of high-quality materials (granite, marble, timber, etc.) in entrance halls, lifts, atria and lavatory accommodation.

On the subject of specification, however, the era of speculatively driven development in a landlords' market evidenced in the 1980s has passed to a trend of occupier-driven developments in a tenants' market. Many occupiers are now calling for less elaborately specified space that still meets their needs. Huge power and heat-removal capabilities; structural loading provisions twice the British Standard with no credible justification; overestimation of electrical loadings and associated air-conditioning capacity; fitting-out tenant space rather than letting a basic shell; and costly bespoke design of the components – all have led to waste and expense, which with the growing unpopularity of air-conditioning; dropping power consumption needs for information technology; and better building-services control mechanisms, means that the new generation of office buildings could be substantially cheaper than those built during the late 1980s with no loss of effectiveness, and possible gains in occupant wellbeing (Saxon 1993). Stanhope Properties undertook research in this field following its experience with Stockley Park and Broadgate with the results shown in Table 16.1 (Low 1994).

Stanhope also concluded that diversity in a building's occupancy must be addressed in order to design efficiently. Good design will also address how upgrading can be achieved economically, for it is more economic in the long term to adapt regular office space than it is to custom-design specialist areas in the base building.

With regard to office building specification, the British Council for Offices (BCO) has produced a document *BCO Guide 2000: Best Practice in the Specification of Offices*, which supplies a reference source for those needing, providing or investing in offices (BCO 2000). This document aims to achieve consensus towards the approach to office building specification, reviewed as necessary in the light of new technology. It also aims to standardize, wherever possible, the design approach, the choice of materials and of components as

Table 16.1 Impact on development – building specification

Feature	Industry norm	Stanhope recommended
Small power	25 W per m^2	15 W per m^2
Floor loadings	5 kN per m^2	2.5 kN per m^2
Lighting	500 lux per m^2	400 lux per m^2
Air conditioning	21–22 °C	24 °C (max)
Occupation density	1.9 m^2	1:14/1:16 m^2

they relate to the issues of specification, so that the practice of 're-inventing the wheel' is eliminated.

Over recent years a recognition has emerged that, in addition to purely economic considerations, there is a need to adopt a more environmentally friendly approach towards office development. To this end, the Building Research Establishment (BRE) has linked with professionals to devise criteria for measuring buildings from an environmental standpoint and has introduced the Building Research Establishment Environmental Assessment Model (BREEAM) together with related certification (Prior 1993).

It is now possible to suggest, therefore, that we stand at something of a threshold in respect of office design, where all concerned with development are being asked to match space utilization to occupiers' requirements, building cost and premises layout. In exploring new dimensions in design it can be stated that four themes increasingly will dominate the creation of good office space:

- attractive external appearance
- low energy cost
- acceptance of new office technology
- adaptability for organization and acceptability to people.

Size and shape

Naturally there will be a continuing demand for new office developments of all sizes from 232 m^2 (2500 ft^2) to 23 225 m^2 (250 000 ft^2), all that it is possible to do is to point to several trends that are likely to be most apparent in the market. Two particular features that will probably typify the sector in respect of the size of offices are worthy of mention. First, it seems almost certain that smaller individual units of office accommodation will be in demand, with the accent being on the provision of buildings in the 929–1858 m^2 (10 000–20 000 ft^2) range for single occupancy. Second, and related, will be the shift to multiple occupation among business users, and the development of office buildings that have the facility to be divided conveniently into discrete units of anything from 93 m^2 (1000 ft^2) upwards. As a direct corollary of these trends, it would seem reasonable to conclude that the number of large speculative buildings in excess of 9290 m^2 (100 000 ft^2) will decline significantly.

It is equally difficult to generalize about the likely future shape of office buildings, except again to identify the principal direction in which the market is moving. The probable polarization of the office market between central city area and suburban or greenfield site locations has already been promulgated. Suffice it to say that the former will be inclined to retain a concentration upon multi-storey development, whereas the latter will focus more upon two- and three-storey construction. However, the most significant feature in respect of building shape is the optimum width of offices. The era of the shallow rectangular block is over, and so too for that matter is the very deep-plan office design. Few offices in future will be constructed to a width of much less than 12–14 m (40–45 ft), and much more than 15–17 m (50–55 ft). On large sites and for bigger buildings, therefore, a popular form of development shape will be a roughly square building surrounding a central atrium or courtyard. This trend will be reinforced by the increasing desire on the part of the occupiers to have cellular offices with outside views, which, on average, take up about 60 per cent of usable space. Within sensible limits, however, atria should be designed so that a proportion, if not all, can be infilled at a later date.

The BRE suggests that a plan depth of 15–18 m (50–60 ft) is ideal and permits space planning layout in three zones. Dimensions below 15 m (50 ft) preclude this, but flexible space can still be provided down to 13.5 m (45 ft). Below this, efficient space planning becomes difficult. It is important to remember, however, that some deep space in a building, no more than 25 per cent of net lettable area, is necessary to allow efficient space planning for common areas.

Structural arrangement

It has been argued that the importance of structural design is seldom fully recognized, let alone properly appreciated, for it carries with it the genetic code for a building, comprising (Anderson 1985):

*   the method of construction
*   the speed of construction
*   the cost of the structure and related elements
*   the internal planning of the building
*   fire resistance
*   acoustic performance
*   structural stability
*   life-span of the building
*   elevations of the building
*   the articulation of mechanical and electrical services
*   the response of the heating and cooling systems
*   the ability to change.

All structural design elements are to some extent significant, but several deserve special mention from the developer's standpoint: the structural frame, the service core and the floor arrangements.

Structural frame

At the outset of the design process, careful consideration should be given to the position, size and number of columns constituting the vertical dimension of the structural frame, the basic rule being that a building should be as column-free as possible and the main constraint being one of cost. Ideally, columns should form a structural grid more than 8 m apart and preferably situated on a floor edge in order to allow the provision of unobstructed office space. However, structural grids of less than this are quite common. Where columns are placed within the internal area, account must be taken of future division, if desired, and possible corridor construction, if adopted. In the same way, perimeter wall details will need to be able to accept partitioning at many different points. In addition to the structural grid, which dictates the frequency of columns, and both determines, and is determined by, the distance between external walls, there is also the planning grid and the construction grid. The planning grid, of interest to the space planner, is defined by the same items as those of the structural grid, but is further affected by the distances between windows and the frequency of the mullions. The construction, or product grid is the module to which standard building products are made. The successful design is the one in which all these grids are integrated into a harmonious whole (Salata 1990).

The BCO Guide 2000 recommends a 1.5 metre planning grid and a column grid of 7.5–9 metres although requirements for longer spans are becoming more common. The 1.5 metre grid is considered ideal for sizing rooms and the provision of corridors. Clearly, the structural or column grids chosen must be a multiple of the planning grid. It is not considered advantageous to try to create column-free space in excess of 9 m width, however, because of the effect on structural depths and therefore building height, and also because buildings are rarely fitted out in a way that column space would gain any visual or space-planning advantage. In choosing the column grid it is necessary to avoid excessive column size, and perimeter and core columns should be integral with or about the perimeter or internal walls. With creative thought, the base can be put to various uses such as circulation, café or exhibition space, but requires additional life safety systems if it is to be used for general office area. In the life of the larger buildings it may well be an advantage to be able to create a large area of deep-plan space on at least one floor.

In terms of the materials to be used for the structural frame, steel or reinforced concrete are equally acceptable. Concrete solutions incorporating pre-stressing, post-tensioning or pre-stressed concrete floor slabs are less flexible and inhibit the user in altering the building to suit varying needs. However, where these design solutions could confer real benefits, they should be considered.

Service core

The service core of an office building consists of lifts, stairs, toilets, service ducts and ancillary accommodation, such as special storage, cleaners' cupboards and machine bays. An optimum placement is a balance between space maximization and construction cost, taking into account such factors as entrances, circulation routes within the building, vertical interdepartmental communications, natural lighting and means of escape. There are advantages and disadvantages to central, peripheral and offset or external core provision, depending upon individual circumstances. The internal finishes to core spaces should generally be simple, hard-wearing, maintenance-free and attractive.

Floor arrangements

It is usually advisable to avoid the use of power-floated *in situ* slabs as a floor finish. If they are employed, it is important to consider the problems that arise in the eventual distribution of electricity and other services to central areas, particularly if no partitions are planned. With regard to live floor loading for the general area, which normally accounts for about 95 per cent of the total space, the British Standard Code of Practice has a minimum threshold of 2.5 kN per m^2 over approximately 5 per cent of the total area. Where there is a dead load, an extra allowance of 1 kN per m^2 should be made for such items as demountable partitions, raised floors, ceilings and building-service equipment.

Another factor that has emerged in the structural design of some modern office developments, principally those located on out-of-town business parks, is that provision should be made for the creation of several potential entrance points, as opposed to a single front door and reception area.

Internal layout

A positive revolution is taking place in the internal layout of office space. The strictly cellular office blocks of the 1940s, 1950s and early 1960s gave over to the deep open-plan offices of the late 1960s and 1970s. Open-plan offices with liberal indoor landscaping, pioneered in Germany as the 'burolandschaft', claimed savings of 20 per cent in space and in cost, but overall increases in business efficiency have been seriously contested. In short, what we have arrived at is a combination of space uses comprising a mix of cellular, group and open-plan office space, together with suitable integrated space provision for support services. The physical design and layout of buildings is beginning to respond to the demands of effective business organization and preferred commercial practice. Thus, there has been a breakdown in the rigid compartmentalization of activities throughout commerce and industry, be they industrial, research, distributive, storage, administration, executive, clerical, marketing and the like.

With a modern office building it is likely that up to 50 per cent of space will be given over to what conventionally have always been considered to be ancillary uses, such as meetings, conferences, presentations, training, libraries, relaxation and machine rooms. The advent of advanced technology has obviously quickened the pace of change, but this has been put into proper perspective as follows:

> Face to face meetings are likely to remain crucial, with formal technology-based communication channels highlighting rather than detracting from the importance of informal, unofficial and non-routine communication.
>
> (DEGW 1983)

An overriding criterion in the layout of offices is an ability to change the physical environment. Divisibility, therefore, is important, both in terms of facilitating different working arrangements within a single organization as well as allowing for simple subletting of parts of the premises. It is also necessary to create convivial space for small teams working within large organizations. As has already been stated, most people desire their individual work spaces to have an external view if at all possible, and, to this end, nearly all ancillary operations can be situated towards the central core of the building.

Less uniformity throughout an office complex along the lines described requires that the keynote must again be flexibility. This used to mean the basic ability to alter internal partitioning. It now means a facility to change the proportion of cellular offices, open-plan offices, support space and service equipment, together with an ability to respond to changing occupancy and methods of work. Much of this flexibility can be achieved by differentiating the building shell from the relocatable elements in the office scenery. Moreover, the use of certain space-defining components, such as fin walls, can give some backbone to office planning and layout, and can even assist in office management.

From the developer's point of view it is essential to optimize the amount of lettable floorspace, and, as has been mentioned elsewhere in the text, a net to gross relationship of about 80 per cent is the normal target in new buildings. It is sometimes possible to accomplish slightly more, and occasionally acceptable to supply a little less, all depending upon the individual circumstances of the scheme. Small suite provision, for example, will normally be lower than single occupancy design. In this context, entrance halls should be as spacious as possible, with a very high standard of finish and separation from certain service functions.

On the subject of space utilization, a note about worker space or occupational density is pertinent. It is commonly accepted at the design stage that an overall figure of one worker to every 9 m^2 (100 ft^2) of net floor space may be assumed as a minimum requirement. The legal minimum is expressed as one worker to every 11 m^3 (388 ft^3) on the basis of, say, 5 m^2 (50 ft^2) floor space and 2.44 m (8 ft) ceiling height, but this is extremely low. Open-plan offices are credited with easily achieving a space of 12.5 m^2 (135 ft^2) per person as against 14 m^2 (150 ft^2), which would be needed in an equivalent conventional corridor and cellular layout. Combination layouts are also very economic because they concentrate upon function rather than a crude average. People do not occupy their workstations continuously, for example, and conference space can achieve high worker to space ratios. This having been stated, it should be appreciated that the nature of many people's work is changing. Skills are increasing. There is less clerical activity and more managerial, executive and professional. Consequently, there is a growing demand for better quality of space, and this usually means more. This is portrayed by the figures for the old Greater London Council area, where in 1961 the ratio of administration to clerical work was 1:2.2, which had fallen to 1:1.7 in 1971 and to about 1:1.1 by 1986.

One interior designer observed that: 'Unfortunately, the determining factor in 75 per cent of today's design and planning work is not increasing productivity or enhancing interaction, but saving real-estate costs and, ideally, creating more flexibility in the work environment and reducing the cost of churn and change' (Battle 2003).

Glazing

With regard to the provision and design of windows in new office developments, it is becoming increasingly critical to pay attention to insulation and energy-saving standards. Many of the extensively glazed buildings of the late 1960s and 1970s proved costly to run and uncomfortable to work in. More recent developments, therefore, either employ a much more advanced system of glazing or have reverted to a lower proportion of external fenestration set within opaque cladding, or even more commonly, traditional brickwork. However, unless they are well designed, many buildings with restricted window areas can look extremely austere.

Problems of solar glare can often be overcome by the use of tinted glass or blinds, with or without the complement of air-conditioning. Some of the specially coated glasses can greatly increase the thermal value of the building envelope. With many, if not most, major new office development schemes, the incorporation of an atrium in the basic design enhances the provision of natural lighting.

Although every individual office design must be judged on its merits, it can generally be said that the necessary balance of daylight and energy consumption usually results in a proportion of 25–30 per cent glazing of the external surface. More than one-third of the outside area being given over to single glazing prevents proper thermal insulation. Double glazing only normally being installed to combat particular noise problems, rather than enhance environmental conditions, for thicker plate glass will often suffice in that respect. Turning again to design, it has been found that tall thin windows extending from floor to ceiling give the best daylight penetration. Experience has also shown that a certain proportion of a building's windows should be capable of opening, even by way of a caretaker's key, not merely as a fire precaution but in case the air-conditioning system fails. One problem that has recently arisen, which was not anticipated by developers or their architects, is the nuisance caused to neighbouring buildings by strong solar reflections from extensively glazed buildings.

Office refurbishment

Very crudely, in examining the market for office refurbishment a simple division can be made between the renovation of period buildings and the upgrading of post-war offices.

With period office buildings, the cost of refurbishment can be very difficult to assess, for the main structure can suffer from extensive dry rot to timbers or severe rust to steel frames, which might be uncovered only after work has begun. Planning requirements or aesthetic considerations may dictate or favour the restoration of a period building's existing facade, rather than recladding. And the opportunity to create additional office space by constructing extra mezzanine or gallery floors, or by bringing basement space into more effective use. Local authorities are also now empowered to relax certain statutory regulations where refurbishment would enable an historic building or group of buildings to be given a new lease of life.

Many, if not most, post-war office buildings constructed before the early 1970s are now outdated and are in desperate need of refurbishment. The popular 16.5 m width, with a 1.5 m wide central corridor, and 6 m deep cellular offices leading off it, is normally too inflexible to cater for modern office users' demands. An owner or developer will, therefore, need to ascertain if there are design possibilities of re-arranging the internal layout of such a building to remove the rigidly determined central corridor and utilize the space provided, possibly by introducing a mixture of cellular and open-plan areas. The removal of non-loadbearing walls might also provide opportunities to utilize 'dead' areas in the building. Although it will normally prove to be too costly, it can sometimes be worth replacing the central service core with an external core, which creates considerable extra lettable space. In any event, some reduction in the size of the existing core will usually be feasible. A typical refurbishment will also include recladding the building, renewing all the heating and plumbing systems, providing false ceilings and/or raised floors to accommodate new service ducts, as well as upgrading all common parts and renewing windows and window frames.

Services and facilities

The most important change to have taken place in the design and development of offices over recent years concerns building services and facilities. Providing an acceptable level of modern business services within a high-quality working environment has become much more important to the creation of successful office premises than the mere production of a serviced concrete and brick shell it once was. As a consequence, those involved in the process of commercial property development have had to become better acquainted with the range of services available and the level or provision required by occupiers.

In considering the relative importance of different aspects of office design and the provision of services and facilities, a survey of tenants was conducted by Healey & Baker, in which they were asked to rank 10 factors in order of importance (Healey & Baker 1989). The results were as follows:

1 internal environmental control and heating system
2 quality of internal finishes
3 external appearance of building
4 carparking
5 provision for cable trunking
6 entrance hall

7   toilet facilities
8   security
9   lift performance reliability
10   arrangement for kitchen catering facilities.

Provision and distribution

To begin with, the modern office building demands an integrated approach towards building fabric and building services. The previous tendency was for services to be planned following the basic design of the building fabric. Unfortunately, with notable exceptions, current designs still attempt to adjust traditional building types to new service demands.

Design should provide for the possible and easy incorporation of additional facilities at a later date. This may involve the trimming of floor slabs in such a way that shafts can readily be added in the future. Some schemes have been drawn up so as to allow extra lift shafts to be inserted if they become necessary. Surplus vertical ducts are also fast being considered as essential in preserving the economic life of a building. One modern office complex, for example, has elevations that include a series of turrets that not only give a pleasing visual effect but also supply internal voids that could accommodate a variety of additional services, if and when required. The space needed for vertical ducting is roughly 2 per cent of the gross floor area and should be distributed among several risers rather than be concentrated at a single core.

The prime difficulties that arise in the provision and distribution of services usually relate to machine rooms, cabling and localized heat concentrations. The first and last are essentially questions of heating and ventilation, dealt with below. With regard to cabling, however, it is not everyone who likes cable drops from a suspended ceiling, and although it is possible to employ wall mounted cabling systems if there is no alternative, the best solution is commonly considered to be the construction of a raised floor, usually of about 150 mm. This is because it is accessible and it lends itself to workstation cabling and local environmental control. Another method is to provide three-channel floor ducts at, say, about 1.5 m centres, but this approach can actually prove to be less flexible and more expensive. In considering the provision of power, it is worth noting that if a standby generator is not installed at the outset then provision should be made for connecting one to the power supply at a suitable point.

As already mentioned, however, the 1980s witnessed something of an over-specification in the provision services of office buildings, largely as a result of the advances in information technology. Flexibility considerations seemed to dictate that it was necessary for every part of a building to be able to carry any load. With the advent of smaller, portable and distributed computer systems this notion is now seriously in question.

Core and shell

The differing space and facility requirements of different office users has led to a 'core and shell' approach on the part of many developers. It was becoming absurd for a tenant to move into a newly completed building only to have to set about changing and removing many of the finishes and fittings so recently installed. Tailoring floor space areas to the special needs of a particular tenant often involves a great deal of modification in terms of partitioning, lighting and mechanical and electrical distribution.

Core and shell, therefore, aims to provide a development where all common areas are fully furnished and the lettable areas are left for tenants to fit out themselves, or for the tenants' particular requirements to be incorporated before fitting-out work is finalized. Cost and time savings accrue to both parties, and the tenant has 'customized' accommodation.

Opinions vary as to how much fitting-out work is done by the developer. Generally, all vertical distribution of services would be installed, with the duct work, for instance, blanked off where it enters the shell. Fire protection requirements will apply to the whole building and will usually mean the installation of a full sprinkler system. For finishes to shell areas, some developers do not install any floor, wall or ceiling finishes. Others may install a false floor because it improves the appearance and permits immediate partitioning. The entrance hall, staircases, common parts, toilets and core would be fully finished. The key as far as the developer is concerned is being able to predict which elements tenants are likely to remove, adapt or change when they take up occupancy and therefore leave them out. Flexibility again enhances lettability. The developer naturally retains the right to approve any deviation from a standard specification, and differences in cost may either be borne by the tenant as a lump sum, or rentalized.

Interestingly, in the Healey & Baker survey of tenants referred to above only 9 per cent of respondents preferred fully fitted offices, and the rest were equally divided between bespoke accommodation and shell and core, although shell and core, with a developer's contribution towards fitting out, was much more popular in the London area than in the provinces.

Internal environmental control

The nature, form and degree of internal environmental control provided within modern office developments depends primarily upon the design, location and use of the buildings, together with the economics of the market and the requirements of the occupier. From the point of view of both developer and occupier, however, the reduction of fuel costs, allied with the maintenance of a comfortable environment, is a principal objective. Broadly speaking, this is best attained by providing a daylight building of energy-efficient design. Put very crudely, a highly glazed daylit all-electric and fully air-conditioned building is roughly twice as expensive as a deep-planned air-conditioned building with gas heating, and three times the cost to run as an energy-efficient daylit and naturally ventilated building.

On 1 April 2002 Part L of the Building Regulations came into force, requiring building services and offices to be designed to minimize energy consumption and contribute to the UK's stated aim of reducing carbon emissions by 60 per cent over the next 50 years.

In looking to adopt a low-energy design for an office building, it has been stated that it is possible to aim for a target of about 150 kWh per m² gross per annum, which is about half the usual target rate of consumption. This can be done by designing the building fabric to modify the climate, reduce air conditioning, lower the lighting load, recover heat in winter, allow for flexibility in fuel usage and manage energy consumption efficiently (Henney 1983).

Air conditioning is a problematic issue in a country where the climate does not really justify the expenditure of installing sophisticated systems. Again, to a great extent it all depends upon the location of the proposed office development and the state of the property market whether or not it is necessary to install artificial air-conditioning equipment. Although it is often seen as a sign of a 'prestige' building for marketing purposes, tenants are not always impressed by the existence of the service, and are often concerned at the costs of running and maintaining an air-conditioning system. Sometimes, therefore, it is installed quite unnecessarily. External noise rather than excessive heat being a more popular reason for having such a facility. Nevertheless, where it has not been incorporated initially, provision for future installation should be allowed by ensuring that the basic building design has sufficient floor-to-ceiling heights and that the roof, walls and floors have knock-out panels to permit ready ducting. It has, however, been suggested that, where a developer wishes to include facilities for air conditioning, they should be installed in combination with heating radiators, together with variable volume units, so that the tenant may control the environment in separate parts of the building (Salata 1990). Moreover, it is increasingly advisable to consider the provision of separate floor systems and, even further, to make individual controls available in positions that allow sensible partitioning and maintain the proper balance of the system. Although the installation of an overall system is initially very costly, it is often best to design for the full potential and then add or subtract as required.

Several other factors regarding the provision of heating and ventilation systems are worthy of mention:

- Information technology has posed certain environmental problems, because desk-mounted equipment produces local hot spots and requires the introduction of local cooling facilities in selected 20–30 m^2 zones (215–323 ft^2).
- Appropriate systems include variable air volume, fan coils, displacement ventilation and chilled ceiling or beams according to circumstances.
- Space should be provided at the busy interconnecting junctions of vertical and horizontal ducts.
- Where the structure is massive, it may not cool down too much overnight, otherwise if economically possible it is normally best to maintain some background heating at all times.
- Most users prefer to have some proportion of natural ventilation, and a minimum of about 15 per cent of windows should be capable of opening.
- Packaged ventilating or heating units can often be placed on roofs and terraces to give greater flexibility.
- Water is usually preferred as a heating or cooling transfer medium rather than air, because of its compactness.

- Heat recovery systems are becoming very attractive propositions.
- One very useful and efficient development in the field of heating and ventilation is the heat pump, which is basically a refrigeration machine that generates heat in its cooling.

Lighting

Good lighting is extremely important in modern offices. The 1970s saw a general increase in the levels of lighting, but this was found to be both wasteful and uncomfortable. It was not only the level of illumination that caused discomfort and distraction but also the glare caused by the form of lighting employed; since then the tendency has been to lower internal lighting levels from around 1000 lux to 750 lux and even to 400–500 lux in many instances. Some areas of an office building might be dimmer still, and it is more and more common to install adjustable lighting so that tenants can arrange their own requirements as needs change. With the advent of new office technology, lighting systems have to be capable of special adjustment in order to cope with different levels of light emission from visual display units. Providing lighting that is suitable for the mix of different office tasks in a modern business organization is a much more demanding design exercise than it has been in the past. The trend is towards the combination of background and 'task' lighting, with the developer providing the background fixtures and a sufficiently flexible network of power points for occupiers to install task lighting of their own choosing and at their own expense. Over the past few years there has been greater use of 'uplighters' with sodium lamps. These are usually free-standing, which gives a high degree of flexibility and a clean finish to walls and ceilings. They also make the reorganization of partitioned offices much easier, reduce the costs of electricity for lighting by about half, and lower the developers' initial costs of construction. Moreover, soft uplighters are best for users of screen equipment.

Communications

The adoption of ever more sophisticated office machinery and the increasing reliance in business operations of all kinds upon advanced information systems means that modern office building must be designed to house a variety of communications equipment and facilitate flexible usage of it. The need to intercommunicate a range of devices within a building has led to the concept of a local area communications network.

According to a report by Jones Lang LaSalle (2000), the increasing need for corporate agility requires 'e-ready' business space for which a broadband connection is a prerequisite. However, integrating new technology with real estate should not merely be viewed as a defensive strategy. Focusing upon the requirements of an e-ready business world enables investors to strengthen and extend relationships with occupiers, their customers, and thereby open up many new revenue-generating platforms.

The guiding principle for making decisions should be the three Rs – rooms (for the installation of telecoms equipment both centrally and locally), routes (for cable trays or trunking, giving easy access for addition and movement of cables) and risers (making sure that these are accessible from common areas that are not another tenant's domain).

Cabling for both data and voice connections is relatively straightforward as each service provider no longer requires a bespoke cabling system. Many building occupiers now 'flood wire' their buildings – cables that can be used for almost any IT purpose are run throughout the occupied parts of the building on a regular grid for maximum flexibility.

Office machinery

Office machinery includes the possible provision of telephones, faxes, printing, photocopying, scanning, e-mail, internet access, document management, and mobile computing through wireless networks. Many modern offices still require a local equipment room to house communications equipment and servers but these are much smaller than even 10 years ago. The accent here is on flexibility and data security rather than a controlled environment.

One of the consequences of introducing new forms of office machinery is the need to provide more power sources and accommodate heavy-duty cables in the office environment. Humidity levels also have to be regulated, and something within the range of 30–50 per cent is desirable, whereas 20–60 per cent might just be acceptable for most machines.

The creation of workstations is probably the most distinctive feature of the modern office. These combine a degree of personal privacy with varying levels of information technology. There are now a wide range of proprietary packages available on the market. In many, worktops, filing drawers, cupboards and the like are hung from tracks fitted to modular partitions or walls. This permits many variations to be introduced and ensures that there is little waste to floorspace. In this way, workstation systems liberate space, make more efficient use of internal areas, and improve occupancy rates.

Lifts

The planning and development of any substantial office building is inextricably bound up with the matter of lift production. In the past it was a common failure in design to neglect proper consideration of the size, number, type, speed and location of lifts until too late in the process. It is not too much of an exaggeration to state, as has one leading manufacturer, that a successful office scheme of any size and quality has, to a very large extent, to be built around its lifts from the beginning. It is not possible merely to insert them at a later stage in standard-size holes, which have been left in the concrete. The lift manufacturer should, therefore, be brought in at the earliest possible stage of design, preferably in the capacity of a nominated subcontractor.

One of the main considerations in the provision of lifts is the future nature of occupancy that is envisaged. Single tenant or owner-occupation usually calls for a different lift layout and produces a different pattern of lift traffic to multiple occupancy. On the other hand, it is normally advisable to ensure that the flexible letting potential of the building is not circumscribed by an inappropriate lift provision. Lift installation must therefore be capable of satisfying the needs of different users as well as a single occupant. Modern microtechnology now enables lift services to be reprogrammed in accordance with changing occupiers' needs. As a guideline, lift provision of one person per 14 m^2 of net lettable area is considered to be good practice.

In order to maximize the amount of lettable floorspace and facilitate the internal organization of business activity, a popular recourse has been to design the lift and stairwell services as a separate external unit adjacent to the office building shell. Alternatively, 'wall climber' lifts are beginning to be fashionable for office as well as shopping developments.

With regard to lift lobbies, up to three lifts may conveniently be planned in a row, and a row of four is an absolute limit for efficient use, with two facing two preferred. Where the number of lifts exceeds four, three in a row should be the limit in cul-de-sac lobbies. For tall buildings up to 60 levels, conventional lifts can be used, with some form of interchange at, say, every 25–30 floors (Battle 2003) which will usually mesh with mechanical/plant zones. For very tall buildings (more than 150 levels) a less conventional solution may be required. The technology exists to allow cars to travel horizontally from one shaft to another (Otis' Odyssey system is an example) but there have not been the commercial opportunities to use it yet.

A local authority may insist that one or more of the lifts in a building is designated for manual operation by visiting firemen, usually at the principal exit floor. Moreover, large office buildings will normally be provided with a goods lift whose main function is the distribution of heavy items of furniture, stationery, equipment, food and other stores. Escalators are still not common in office buildings, but their ability to handle continuous interfloor traffic makes them attractive in owner-occupied buildings (Case 1985).

Problems with lifts are frequently the major cause of complaint from tenants and need constant care. Therefore, the treatment of lifts as an important part of the overall design is attracting more attention as developers become increasingly aware of the need to create a more attractive and harmonious environment.

Other services and facilities

Among the other services and facilities that might have to be considered in the design and development of a modern office block are the following:

- *Fire protection system.* With attention paid to hose and reel location, dry and wet risers, alarms, sprinklers, gas suppression systems and external access and areas for fire appliances.
- *Emergency lighting.* Should be installed in staircases, lavatories and other common parts.
- *Escape routes.* Designed in consultation with the fire brigade and with the cost effectiveness of office layout firmly in mind.
- *Lavatories.* For both sexes on each floor, with the potential for additional facilities and finishes and fittings to a high quality as well as good ventilation.

- *Ventilated cleaners' cupboards.* On each floor, with power, water supply and drainage.
- *Drinking water.* Supply on each floor.
- *Tea-making facilities.* On each floor, depending upon the size of building.
- *Waste disposal.* Areas should be provided for the storage of waste material as well as the usual waste disposal facilities.
- *Security.* It is increasingly important to provide a full and integrated manned and electronic intrusion system, which can range all the way from access control through to closed-circuit television and movement monitors detecting body heat.
- *Healthy building control.* More and more attention needs to be paid to designing buildings and providing monitoring systems to counteract the 'sick building syndrome'.
- The Disability Discrimination Act 1995 imposes important obligations on building owners and occupiers with respect to accessibility that require careful consideration at both the design and fitting-out stages.

Serviced offices

There is a growing demand for the provision of serviced offices in the UK, by development, refurbishment and reorganization. Services offices have been defined as small office units between 15 m² (161 ft²) and 50 m² (538 ft²) available to let on short lease or licence terms for periods of one month upwards, but outside the security of the tenure provisions of the 1954 Landlord and Tenant Act. They normally provide a combination of secretarial support, photocopying facilities and post handling, telecommunications facilities, catering and dining room facilities, board room facilities, interview rooms, staffed reception area and electricity, lighting and heating. Payment of rent is on an inclusive basis and covers rents, rates, property insurance, a service charge, and include the use of many of the facilities described.

Serviced offices is a sector that, in early 2003, is much in vogue, offering flexibility in occupation and the ability to set up an office without the usual infrastructure costs. A survey carried out by Jones Lang LaSalle in 1999 identified this need for flexibility as the primary reason for using serviced offices, with cost, security and image seen as less important. The most likely period for occupation was less than two years. Banking, business services, electronics and the media have been some of the major serviced office users.

Business and office parks

The late 1980s witnessed the emergence of the business park as a major new force in the UK property market. Without doubt, the growth in development of business parks was fuelled by the introduction of the B1 Use Class in 1987, but the more perceptive developers had already recognized the need for flexible 'office look-alike' space out of town, and had closely researched the American experience (Healey & Nabarro 1988, *Estates Gazette* 1990). Business parks have experienced mixed fortunes over the last two decades.

Declining popularity in the early 1990s was succeeded by revival in the late 1990s, with enormous growth in 2000 and 2001 only to slip back in 2002 and 2003. The principal difference between the downturn in the early 1990s and today is the shift in the market from speculative to pre-let (*Property Week* 2002), suggesting a much softer landing. Much of the space coming onto the market is from the telecoms sector (39 per cent of all lettings in the first half of 2001), which has seen a huge fall in activity.

The term business park tends to mean different things to different people, usually according to the particular circumstances pertaining and the position in which they stand. To some, the concept lies somewhere between high-tech and traditional industrial sheds, with elements of both in many schemes. To others the mix is much richer, to include not only business and office users but also retail, leisure and even residential developments. Moreover, the most recent arrival on the scene has been the corporate office park, which is predominantly office-based, with selected support facilities and normally aimed at substantial organizations often within the financial services or marketing sectors or the economy looking for international, national or regional headquarters buildings located in a parkland setting. For the purposes of this section a fairly catholic interpretation is taken towards the general classification of business and office parks, but one that excludes research, science and technology, described as (Holden 1986):

- a good business location, including easy access to road, rail and air transport
- high-quality, low-density development, well landscaped and with good carparking provision
- an actively managed, well serviced development, including power, security and communications facilities, as well as recreational and business community provision.

Looking more closely at the corporate office or commerce park, the following common characteristics are revealed:

- Most buildings are on two, or possibly three storeys in order to limit the amount of vertical movements.
- Entrances and reception areas should be impressive and spacious, so as to allow tenants to promote a strong corporate image.
- Tenants seem to prefer relatively conventional layout and design specifications, such as an office width of around 14 m (45 ft), at least 40 per cent of partitionable space to create individual rooms and an occupation density of about one employee to 14 m^2 (150 ft^2).
- A carparking norm of around one space per 20 m^2 (215 ft^2) gross being no more than one per 25 m^2 and sometimes as low as one per 15 m^2 all at ground level, appropriately divided, easy to manoeuvre round, well lit and suitably screened.
- A good image for the park as a whole, as well as for particular buildings, necessitating an attractive approach providing a sense of arrival, clear signposting, carefully selected tenant mix and the setting and grouping of individual buildings to create a feeling of dignity and importance.

- A low density of development with a site coverage or 'footprint' of around 15 per cent producing about 929–1161 m^2 (10 000–12 500 ft^2) of lettable floorspace per acre with a two- to three-storey development.
- High standards of landscape to include such features as streams, sculpture and seating.
- A significant element of brick and tile as opposed to curtain walling seems most popular with tenants, together with tiled sloping roofs on timber trusses and rafters allowing the elimination of internal columns.
- The facility in terms of design for tenants to install their own air-conditioning.
- A raised floor to accommodate complex cabling.
- High quality of management.

Although it is already generally accepted that a true business or office park should stand on at least 40 ha (100 acres), the second generation of business parks across Europe have included larger park developments of 162–202 ha (400–500 acres) and more resembling mini new towns. These will be based on a masterplan, which would provide a planned and controlled environment within which companies can retain and express their individual and corporate image, give a clear and functional infrastructure of roads and attractive landscapes, provide a variety of flexible plot sizes that enable occupants to expand and adapt their space to accommodate their own growth, develop a phasing policy to ensure that the development appears complete at each stage while minimizing disruption to existing occupants during construction, and sustain the quality of the original concept through design development guidelines for each plot (Michalik 1990). The attitude of some ambitious developers and their consultants is to create:

> . . . an alternative town centre with a wide range of facilities and amenities provided or close by including shopping, leisure, recreation, childcare and catering with high-quality design building and services standards served by good public as well as private transport facilities so as to recruit and retain key staff. One major obstacle to this is government policy aimed at preserving the status of the town centre and creating a climate of sustainable development. The future of business park development, therefore, has succinctly been stated to be about 'the integration of flexible buildings with a quality landscape – within the community'.
>
> (Auckett, quoted in MacRae 1993)

Government trends in sustainability, regeneration of town centres and reduction in use of the private car suggest that the days of development of the larger business park are numbered.

Facilities management

No examination of office development would be complete without some mention of the emergence of the discipline of facilities management. Until relatively recently the property industry regarded management as very much the unglamorous end of the business – a mixture of rent collection and caretaking. However, property or premises management is changing from being the industry's Cinderella to playing a central role in all sectors of commercial development. Shopping centre management led the way back in the late 1970s and throughout the 1980s. Facilities management for offices is more a creature of the late 1980s and 1990s.

In both private business and public service sectors of society, profound changes are taking place, with a fast-growing emphasis upon the twin related forces of enterprise and quality. Central to this metamorphosis has been the rapid spread of new ideas, technologies and practices resulting from advanced international communications and a much more highly competitive global economy. A major consequence has been the recognition by organizations of all kinds regarding the importance of property – its location, design and use – as a prime asset in the operational effectiveness of commercial and civic undertakings, as well as a principal factor in the equation of capital worth. Simple premises management has, thereby, evolved into the somewhat more complex and sophisticated discipline of facilities management. This is especially true of large corporations and utilities.

It is not surprising, therefore, that facilities management is a sector of property asset appraisal that has evoked increasing interest worldwide from both the design and the real estate professions over the past decade. It is still viewed with uncertainty, however, and remains an ill-defined field. Nevertheless, as organizations strive to cope with constantly changing economic conditions, they are obliged to seek ever increasingly efficient and productive work environments.

Information technology

As already intimated, the workplace is swiftly being transformed, largely because of the introduction of an unprecedented scale of new information technologies in organizations. Work processes, physical environments and the social milieu of organizations have been redefined. There is now an emerging body of knowledge and experience enabling design and management problems of high-technology workplaces to be solved in an integrated way. Indeed, it has been argued that the progress of work automation has been so fast over the past decade that the pace has often outstripped the capacity of organizations to absorb new technology and to reap their potential benefits effectively. High-technology, moreover, is seen to be affecting the workplace in two different and complementary ways. Directly, it is being invaded by a whole new range of equipment, with new, and frequently conflicting environmental needs. Indirectly, it must change to adapt to the transformations of work processes and organizations that result from automation (Gourmain 1989).

The advent of the 'intelligent building' was a striking feature of the 1980s. Stimulated by the globalization of the financial services industry, with the accompanying cascade of terminals, cables, atria and dealing rooms, it coincided with a radical reassessment of building procurement, construction and management processes (Duffy 1991). Buildings must obviously be capable of accommodating new demands and be developed accordingly. They must also be managed as business assets showing an acceptable return.

The nature, form and effectiveness of the intelligent building has been the subject of much study, definition and debate since the mid-1980s. What seems to be required in the current market is adaptable low-cost space capable of delivering high levels of operationally networked performance providing an integrated environment for those involved. Put another way:

> The intelligent building straddles two vastly different, but essential demands made by the modern firm. Buildings must respond to changing demands effectively and quickly, and must support a high level of interworking by workers.
>
> (Robathan 1993)

The facilities manager

Opinions differ about the nature and scope of facilities management, and thus the role of the facilities manager. From a management perspective, it is suggested that facilities managers may be said to look after five key aspects of an organization:

- Shareholders: by maintaining the asset value – regular checks of fabric, etc.;
- Employees: by creating efficient working environments conducive to high morale and productivity;
- Customers: by maintaining and reinforcing the good image of the organization;
- Community: the impact of the organization on the environment and the local community;
- Suppliers: by ensuring the quality of suppliers and services.

(Powell 1990)

Barret and Baldry (2000) identify typical facilities management activities as follows.

Facility planning
- Strategic space planning
- Set corporate planning standards and guidelines
- Identify user needs
- Furniture layouts
- Monitor space use
- Select and control use of furniture
- Define performance measures
- Computer-aided facility management (CAFM).

Building operations and maintenance
- Run and maintain plant
- Maintain building fabric
- Manage and undertake adaptation
- Energy management
- Security

- Voice and data communication
- Control operating budget
- Monitor performance
- Supervise cleaning and decoration
- Waste management and recycling.

Real estate and building construction
- New building design and construction management
- Acquisition and disposal of sites and buildings
- Negotiation and management of leases
- Advice on property investment
- Control of capital budgets.

General/office services
- Provide and manage support services
- Office purchasing (stationery and equipment)
- Non-building contract services (catering, travel, etc.)
- Reprographic services
- Housekeeping standards
- Relocation
- Health and Safety.

From the above, it can be seen that the responsibilities of the facilities manager are remarkably wide-ranging.

Facilities management and property development

The need to provide premises in the right place, at the right time, with the right services, offering the right level of management and at the right price is paramount. Current user markets have done much to alter the attitude of building owners and developers.

Much lip-service is paid to landlords focusing on the needs of the end user, but because most property is built speculatively, the ultimate occupiers generally have to compromise their requirements or deal with severe restrictions imposed at the design stage. It is suggested that these restrictions fall into two categories: those imposed by the building shell and its plant and equipments; and those dictated by real estate procedures, that frustrate the efficiency of the occupier (Prodgers 1992). Tenants are becoming less and less willing to live with inadequacies in the original design of a building, and more demanding of a flexible and service-oriented approach by the landlord towards tenure than hitherto.

The message is perhaps a simple one: the future management of properties facilities, in the very widest sense, should be incorporated as part of development planning at the very earliest stage of the development process. It has been argued that the management of an organization's facilities, its built environment and its infrastructure must take into account the nature of the activities that take place within the building and which the facilities are serving. Moreover, it must be fitted not only to the formal goals of the organization, but also to the way that the organization is structured: its pattern of work and its pattern of decision-making. Therefore, an approach to facilities management that looks into the late 1990s and beyond should be aware of predicted trends and changes that are already taking place in the productive organization (Baldry & Pitt 1993).

Conclusion

We have seen many changes in office development. PFIs are here to stay and a corporate PFI is likely to be the way forward for many organizations (total property outsourcing incorporating both property and facilities management services). Serviced offices, enriched by understanding the ways in which hotel and business centres make most of their money (such as by selling services by the second rather than square feet by the year), have gained substantially in prominence. However, in terms of quality of office building, especially in relation to user priorities, as opposed to the more macro-level ways in which office development is financed and marketed, evidence of innovation and improvement is much harder to find (Battle 2003).

New ways of working, sustainability and productivity are the watchwords for the future. Office owners/developers will have to manage their developments and buildings they create and provide after-sales care. The real challenge faced by developers is to deliver guaranteed buildings tailored to the company's business plan priorities and reach the level of service attained by other suppliers. Gone are the days of 'let and forget' philosophy prevalent for so many years. Developers will have to compete. To do so they will need suitably qualified teams to manage the entire development process, challenge previous accepted norms and preconceptions, transfer experience, knowledge and innovation, enhance the value of advisers and reduce potential conflicts of interest to deliver commercially valuable cost-effective buildings.

17 Industrial development

Low unemployment and interest rates, changing industrial processes, new technology and new ways of working have all combined to require a reconsideration by both public and private sector agencies involved in the production of industrial and business development properties in respect of what they build, where and for whom. The 1980s witnessed a transformation in both the location and property requirements of modern industries because of decline in traditional manufacturing and growth in the service sector. The 1990s saw globalization and radical changes in information and communication technology. In the new millennium we are seeing a continued contraction of the manufacturing sector, the increasing dominance of the service sector, and major advances in the integration of information and communication technology in the manufacture, assembly, storage, sale and delivery of goods and services.

Figures for 2001–2 amply illustrate the changing patterns of employment (similar patterns are apparent for previous years) (Table 17.1).

The dominance of the service sector can also be seen in changes in the contribution to GDP (Index: 1995 = 100) (Table 17.2).

In this way, it has been projected that by 2005 the manufacturing workforce will have fallen to 4 million, having halved from 8 million in 1971. The industrial real estate market is on the threshold of revolutionary change. The efficiency of traditional distribution centre sizes, locations and designs will become increasingly questioned in a market where new logistics processes are allowing shorter product cycles, lower inventory levels and faster turn around (Jones Lang LaSalle 1999).

In terms of the broad characteristics of modern industry, research has concluded that:

- The shift in economic activity from manufacturing industry to the information and service sectors has changed the types of sites and buildings required for modern industry.
- These emerging sectors are concerned with mental skills – the applications of specialist knowledge – rather than manual skills. This loosens traditional ties and generates new demands – in particular to provide a 'people' rather than machine environment, resulting in a specification more akin to an office than a factory.
- To meet market demands and keep abreast of the latest technology these sectors are also concerned with producing limited product runs of

Table 17.1 Workforce by industry in December 2002
(change on December 2001)

Sector	'000s
Agriculture and construction	−48
Production	−161
Services	+254
Overall	+44

Source: *Labour Market Statistics 2003, National Statistics*

Table 17.2

Sector	1999	2002
Agriculture, forestry and fishing	103.1	92.4
Manufacturing	103.1	98.6
Distribution, catering and hotels; repairs	116.0	126.2
Transport, storage and communication	129.0	149.4
Business services and finance	121.8	135.7

Source: Quarterly national accounts: fourth quarter and year 2002, *National Statistics*

specific customized products. This requires the centralization under one roof of research and design, product assembly and customization, and marketing and consumer services. The building must have flexibility to vary the mix of uses within any part of the building as the organization and its products grow and adapt.

(DEGW 1985)

Thus, more than ever, it is essential that the property development industry has a greater understanding of the nature of the changes that are taking place within the economy, the general implications that these changes have for businesses, workers and local authorities, as well as on buildings and the kind of responses that will be needed.

This chapter explores the nature of industrial and business property development by examining the following issues:

- location for industry
- planning policy
- design and layout
- warehousing and distribution
- high-technology development
- estate management.

Location for industry

Conventional industrial location theory has assumed that firms behave in a rational and logical manner and are able to achieve their optimum locations.

Rational behaviour in location decision-making was felt to be determined by the aim of profit maximization. However, it has been pointed out that more recent theories of industrial location have abandoned the pretence of the optimal location and have acknowledged that locational decisions are often surrounded by uncertainty and personal preference. Land may be prevented from passing to the highest possible bidder by factors such as owners' expectations and behaviour, the cost of redevelopment and upheaval, or the existence of planning controls. As with other property sectors, because of substantial imperfections, land markets operate only at partial equilibrium. Supply and demand do not automatically equate, supply being determined primarily through the planning system, whereas demand depends upon private sector actions. This is said to make it extremely difficult to apply competitive market analysis to the industrial land market (Adams *et al.* 1993).

Basic factors of location

Although it remains broadly true that the combination of correct location and good design sells space everywhere, it has become increasingly clear since the late 1980s that the industrial development market is highly segmented, and different categories of user possess different locational requirements. Likewise, certain parts of the country enjoy strong competitive advantages over others. However, there are several basic factors that exercise a growing influence over the location and demand for industrial and business property. These can be summarized as follows:

- *Communications.* The need to have quick and ready access to clients, markets, suppliers, labour, services and complementary parts of the business is an absolute prerequisite to modern industry. Thus, motorway linkage and high carparking standards are crucial.
- *Flexibility.* A healthy firm has to be able to adapt quickly to changing requirements in respect of both the amount and the use of available space. Room to expand, and the capacity to reorganize methods of production and alter the nature of activities taking place within a building, are becoming more and more critical. Open flexible space, an easily extendable and convertible structure and low site coverage are, therefore, necessary ingredients.
- *Environment.* The image portrayed by the site and building chosen by a firm are increasingly important. So too is the internal working environment, and desired conditions in many industrial premises are fast approaching those demanded in offices. Semi-rural positions on the outskirts of town are proving most popular.
- *Design.* From the above it can be seen that modern industrial design must be not only stylish, creating an individual identity through character and quality, but also capable of conversion into offices, research, training and production space. Moreover, it must create a building that can accept electronic communications systems and be constructed to minimize running costs.

Many modern cities have an abundant stock of disused factory and ware-house buildings, which tend to occupy land in strategic urban locations with excellent accessibility to major transport routes and waterfronts.

Manufacturing was usually the initial magnet for urban growth, drawing in capital, labour and expertise from the surrounding regions and stimulating new economic activities in business and services.

However, when urban economies develop to a more advanced stage, economic restructuring inevitably leads to a shift from industrial into higher-value activities in finance, business and services. High urban land prices and space demands of manufacturers resulted in massive exodus of industrial activities from urban areas (Tang 2000).

An acceleration of this trend has been experienced since the mid 1980s.

With the decline of rail transport and the growth of car ownership, residential and working populations have become more dispersed. This is reflected in the decline of major cities, a process often called counter-urbanization. The 1980s and 1990s saw a decline in the population of large urban areas (such as inner and outer London, Birmingham, Manchester, and Liverpool), which can be compared with the growth of a selected number of smaller towns over the same period (such as Bracknell, Milton Keynes, Guildford, Solihull, and Bromsgrove).

As with office developments, there is what has been described as a 'push-me, pull-you' interplay of factors encouraging companies to locate either in or out of town. The push away from town centres involves increased congestion, rising costs and longer commuting times. Conversely, the out-of-town location may be able to offer cost savings, an attractive working environment, better carparking provision and generally greater accessibility. Against this, however, out-of-town sites often show certain disadvantages, such as inadequate amenities and facilities. The town centre might also have certain advantages in terms of accessibility to the public transport network and benefits from a variety of shopping and recreational activities. A survey of companies showed the relative importance of various locational factors. Proximity to motorways and environmental quality were stressed as of most importance, followed by access to markets, airports, the rest of the company, and staff availability, attraction and skills, all well ahead of the availability of public transport, leisure and housing (Debenham Tewson Research 1990).

Regional trends

The deep structural changes that have been taking place within the economy since the mid-1980s – whereby emerging industries are based upon information and communications more than raw materials and productive processes, with a workforce more dependent upon management and innovation than on handling and manufacturing – has means that such knowledge-based companies are increasingly mobile. As a result, the concentration of new industrial development upon the South East of England has accelerated throughout the 1980s and 1990s.

The much vaunted Golden Triangle, formed within the area marked by Hammersmith, Swindon and Guildford, has grown and changed shape to create a kind of Golden Trapezium bounded by lines joining Bristol to the west and Southampton to the south, as well as those connecting Guildford and Hammersmith. Within this area, demand to occupy industrial floorspace and pressure to release land have become especially focused along the Western Corridor created by the M4 leading again from Hammersmith to Heathrow, Reading, Swindon and Bristol. A premium can be discerned on sites within a 30 minute drive time of Central London and Heathrow, and to a lesser extent along the M1, M3 and, more recently, M40 motorways up to a distance of 75 to 100 miles. Much interest has been stirred by the implementation and proposed widening of the M25 orbital route around London, which has had a dramatic effect upon commercial and industrial location decisions.

Demand for new industrial space in the South East is generated from a variety of sources. There are large multinational and national companies decentralizing from Central London. Then there are major fast-growth companies already located in the South East but in need of new and larger premises. Smaller fast-growth companies, both home grown and from over-seas, are also actively seeking and occupying space. Probably the greatest demand for new industrial development since the mid-1980s has, in fact, come from abroad.

Globalization has meant that British labour has had to compete with Third-World countries where labour is a fraction of the cost. This has led Marks and Spencer, for example, to reduce the proportion of clothing it buys from the British textile industry from over a half to barely a third. With the decline of heavy industry and the coming of globalization, manufacturing has declined in the northern half of the country and the population has declined too in favour of the thriving south (Schiller 2000).

Relative economic success within the South East during the 1980s brought with it certain disadvantages that began to impinge upon the ability of existing firms to expand. Problems in the supply of suitably skilled and affordable labour, together with increased congestion and a slowdown in economic growth, resulted in oversupply of exclusively business-use accommodation in certain parts of the South East. This raised questions concerning the nature and location of new development. It encouraged, in part, a shift towards the provision of more traditional industrial premises and, in part, a shift in attention towards other regions within the UK. With regard to the business park type of development, the South West, East Anglia, North West, Yorkshire and Humberside regions all experienced significant increases in floorspace provision in the 1990s. This shift in development activity towards other regions should be seen as a long-term trend that is unlikely to challenge the predominance of the South East.

Major transportation infrastructure projects are natural catalysts for industrial and business developments. Another generative factor influencing development growth in the sector is the decision of a single substantial investor or producer to locate in a particular town, city or region. A prime example is in the Tyne & Wear region, where Nissan, the Japanese car manufacturer, has chosen to locate its 140 000 m² plant in Washington, near Sunderland. Known as the 'Nissan Effect', the massive investment has brought significant spin-off benefits, not only in terms of the immediate 3500 jobs directly created but also by generating renewed business confidence in the region (Mills 1992).

No examination of regional trends would be complete without some mention of the European dimension. Here it has been found, in a survey from the University of Cambridge, that the quality and size of the labour force is a key factor affecting company location decisions in Europe (Moore *et al.* 1991). As might be expected, the availability of regional development assistance was identified as being important for production companies and for companies relocating from abroad. However, the level of wage costs was generally less important than the quality and size of the labour supply. It is interesting that the quality of infrastructure did not rate highly, and neither did the level of rents, nor the attractiveness of the environment. On the evidence of the survey, preferred regions are those offering minimal costs, but also quality and supply of labour and good access to markets. This would suggest the run-down industrial areas of northern France, Belgium, the Netherlands and the Ruhr. In Britain it would point to the Midlands and the North. We have perhaps seen an indication of this with the location of Japanese car firms.

The industrial property market

In the current economic climate (early 2003) business investment is weak, confidence is fragile and user demand is flat. After a flurry of development activity in the late 1990s, there is likely to be an oversupply of space not because of over-development but because of expected corporate failures (RICS 2002).

Parts of the industrial sector are really booming. For example, three years ago the price of an acre of industrial land close to one of the Birmingham M6 junctions was typically around £250 000 per acre. This has risen to £450 000 per acre and even more. Agents have expressed concern that while land prices have risen dramatically rents have not and development does not seem financially feasible. However, many sites are not earmarked for development until at least 2004 when developers expect rents will have risen sufficiently to justify the land price (*Estates Gazette* 2002a).

New development only represents about 10 per cent of the available stock so much of the vacant property is made up of second-hand properties. Problems arise with these buildings where they have been adapted to the use of the operator and are not flexible enough for conversion to other users except at very high cost. Some very attractive tenant incentive packages are being offered on these by occupiers, attempting to cut costs and release themselves from long-term liabilities. Unfortunately, many such buildings may never be let, since they are inflexible, and offer poor access and high maintenance liability.

In the distribution sector there has been a noticeable increase in demand. However, distribution companies operate on the basis that the contracts being awarded to them are short-term and, therefore, often require break clauses in their leases. Choice for the occupier has previously been limited by the unwillingness of owners to bring land forward for this type of use, because of the low value released. There is a rising trend in the development of industrial property which has been evident since 2000. However, this is far short of the peak of 23 per cent in 1989 (King Sturge 2002). Improvements in handling methods with widespread use of computerized stock holding is leading to more intensive use of space and higher eaves height, increasing the efficiency of individual units.

With the concentration of supply in second-hand buildings, the upturn in the market is likely to lead to a shortage of modern well located buildings. At the larger end of the market – 4645 m^2 (50 000 ft^2) upwards – the demand is likely to be met by purpose-built developments.

At present, there is interest from investors in the industrial market, with funds perceiving a growth in rentals in the future. This interest provides opportunities for sale and leaseback, and funding of expansion space by pre-lettings on new development. The cost of renting is driving the freehold market, which is currently riding on the crest of a wave.

The choice of industrial location for the development of large manu-facturing units involves balancing the quality of the local labour force, the availability of strategic sites and of grants, and the quality of infrastructure. The North and the North East in particular have many attractions for the relocating industrialist.

Control over inflation, stable interest rates, the availability of a skilled labour force and greatly improved industrial relations since the mid-1980s make the UK attractive in the context of the European Union. Some major international industrialists have sought to establish themselves in the UK but, overall, growth in this area has been limited. It is likely that any further expansion by European businesses will depend upon the British govern-ment's attitude to the adoption of the Euro.

Types of industrial development

It has already been stated that the industrial development sector is highly segmented. An understanding of the different types of industrial development is important, because they invariably involve different user requirements, development agencies, sources of finance, design require-ments, and management policies. A useful classification has been devised, which identifies categories of traditional, new growth and innovation industries (Worthington 1982):

Traditional industry
- Community workshop: small workshops aimed at encouraging embryo enterprises by developing skills and providing equipment and administrative support. Located close to residential areas in old buildings.
- Flatted factory: multi-storey industrial buildings, with goods lift and corridor access to some small independent tenancies.
- Industrial estate: mixture of manufacturing and service uses. Industrial character where delivery areas predominate.
- Trading estate: warehouse uses with some office content. May attract retail warehousing and trade outlets.

New growth industries

- Working community: a group of independent small firms co-operating in sharing a building and joint services. The objective is to enjoy a scale of premises and facilities normally available only to larger companies. The group will normally have a policy of selecting compatible or complementary firms.
- Commercial/business park: having a high-quality low-density environment. Aimed at firms requiring prestige or high-calibre workforce. Mixtures of manufacturing, office and sales functions.
- Trade mart: a multiple tenanted building with office showrooms and centrally provided exhibition, conference areas, reception and support services. Normally developed around a theme.
- Research/innovation.
- Innovation centre: an individual building, immediately adjacent to a university campus, providing small units 30–150 m² (323–1615 ft²) for starter firms growing out of research projects within the university and drawing upon its facilities and support services.
- Research park: sites or advanced units for young or established firms in the field of research or development. Often close to a university and associated with university research laboratories and amenities. Such schemes are often joint ventures.
- Science/technology park: with universities and research institutions within a 30-mile catchment area. Attractive life-style, low-density development aimed at scientific or technology-orientated companies.
- Industrial park: aimed at clean manufacturing organizations with a landscaped setting and leisure amenities for staff.

Planning policy

Industrial development is now perceived as a major area of government responsibility in much the same way that public housing was some years ago. At central government level, a report by the Trade and Industry Select Committee in April 1994 told government to shrug off the vestiges of its *laissez faire* approach to industry. The report, in examining competitiveness, urged the government to enshrine the importance of manufacturing in economic policy, reflecting a widespread belief that the decline of Britain's manufacturing industry since the 1960s poses a serious threat to the country's ability to sustain economic growth. However it is now recognized that, although the industrial sector is important, warehousing and distribution activities to support the ever-growing service sector are now a vital focus of activity. At local level, many planning authorities are very progressive in their approach towards development proposals and supportive of initiatives, whereas others seem caught in a mesh of plans and policies a decade out of date. The effect of local authority planning can most conveniently be discussed by reference, on the one hand, to the exercise of their negative powers under development control and, on the other, the more positive attitudes that some of them adopt, which are demonstrated through an array of employment generation policies.

The national context

In a report produced in August 1994 by the Employment Policy Institute (EPI) it has been argued that a healthy manufacturing sector is important for the continuing prosperity of the country (EPI 1994). The report points out that rates of productivity growth in manufacturing at an average of around 4 per cent per annum are higher than in services and more than double the productivity growth rate of the economy as a whole. In practice, this means that manufacturing provides more jobs, despite the frequently repeated claim that services are more labour intensive. The EPI report also states that:

- The number of jobs sustained by the sector is not fully reflected by the number of people directly employed there. Some manufacturing and construction processes, for instance, rely on a wide range of outside goods and services.
- Government should consider the issues of new knowledge and product innovations, because industrial advances make an invaluable contribution to technological progress.
- Although manufacturing output only accounts for about 20 per cent of UK GDP it provides in excess of 60 per cent of UK exports, and it is important that this level is maintained.
- The government needs to change its approach radically to ensure the right economic environment for manufacturing to prosper.

In respect of the last point, criticisms have been made that the government's view of financial support is too short term; relies heavily on the interplay of market forces, which are not always attuned to the needs of certain businesses; tends to be more concerned about the City of London's financial services sector and large high-profile projects such as Toyota, Nissan and Samsung; and supports insufficient training initiatives to provide an effective skilled labour force. Both France and Germany are cited as examples of government commitment to the support of major industry.

A principal plank in government planning policy is laid down in PPG13, *Highways considerations in development control*, which encourages mixed uses in a bid to achieve sustainable development. Factories are considered juxtaposed with shops, offices and housing. This move back to mixing development activities is intended to reduce travel to work, cutting down on car use and promoting public transport, cycle routes and walking, with landscaped buffers, public open space and playing fields being used to separate employment and residential areas where appropriate. To accelerate the movement away from private to public transport, the Royal Commission on Environmental Pollution recommended substantial increases in the price of petrol, together with a major shift in public spending away from roads and into public transport. Nevertheless, although society might seem to be heading away from a heavy and growing dependence on cars, which will increase demand for mixed-use development schemes, it has been pointed out that it could be the manufacturers themselves who need the most convincing that it is in their interests to move with the times (Mills 1994).

One problem that has to be faced, given the predicted decline in the manufacturing workforce to around 4 million by 2005, is that of redundant and obsolescent industrial space. With an average floorspace per employee of around 44 m² (474 ft²) demand for industrial floorspace in the UK as a whole will be around 175 million m² (1884 million ft²), and it is clear that there will be much less demand for manufacturing floorspace than now. Much existing space will have reached the end of its physical and economic life, and as space is redeveloped it will be the best located, least polluted sites that will be creamed off for redevelopment for alternative uses, leaving a rump of contaminated, derelict land with little or no chance of change.

This, of course, assumes that the planning system allows the situation to develop. Too often the planning system is used to present entrenched opposition to changes in use. The perception is that, by retaining land for industrial development, this will in itself attract industrial employers. However, the planning system simply cannot hold out against the pressures for change caused by a shrinking manufacturing workforce. Pragmatic guidance is urgently required from central government as to the acceptance and control of alternative uses for redundant industrial land (Thomson 1994/5).

Another sector of the industrial property market deserving of government attention and guidance is that of storage and distribution. It can be argued that the planning system has not yet come properly to terms with the explosive nature of the distribution industry. The interests of the national economy might well be served if the ODPM were to issue more specific guidance to local planning authorities on the matter, distinguishing the sector from retail activities, otherwise an unproductive disarray might take place, similar to that which took place in the 1980s in respect of major out-of-town shopping centres.

Because of their economic importance, for example, the sanctity of certain strategic gaps and rural sites adjacent to the motorway interchanges should not be squandered unless there are very compelling environmental objections. As has been pointed out, through the years of the B1 (Business) office boom, most such key locations allocated for development have been mopped up for business campus uses, and warehousing has frequently been diverted to low-value sites remote from the communications network. As a result, heavy lorry traffic is often sucked through residential areas, with adverse environmental effects (Vail 1994).

On the question of traffic, a popular sentiment echoes around the property development industry that government lacks a coherent policy towards transport. PPG13 and other government edicts seek to limit car journeys. The distribution of goods throughout the country depends primarily upon heavy goods vehicles and, although many believe it is lorries that clog up the system, surveys have showed that such carriers typically account for no more than 15–20 per cent of traffic flows. Persuading passenger traffic to switch to public transport would greatly ease the movement of freight. The thorny issue of toll roads has bloodied a few hands in its time. Stephen Byers and John Prescott both lost their transport briefs as a result of wrestling with congestion on motorways. However, it is now widely accepted that toll roads and private intervention in motorway construction are the way forward. The first toll route in Britain – the Midland Expressway – is due to open before the end of 2003.

Local planning practice

The more detailed application of development control regulations as they apply to industrial property, especially the operation of the Use Classes Order 1987, is dealt with elsewhere (Chs 2 and 3). Suffice it to say that in a post-industrial society, such as that in the UK, distribution between factory-based employment and office-based employment is an artificial and largely unhelpful one. Increasingly this is recognized, but the fact remains that, for whatever reason, many local authorities fear creeping office use in what they ostensibly approved as industrial buildings. The B1 (Business) use class has greatly reduced this problem.

However, another circumstance where difficulties of mixed use emerge is the proposed combination of residential accommodation with workspace. Not only are planning authorities reluctant or unprepared to consider such proposals, but building regulations, in particular those relating to fire, render mixed-use developments of this kind extremely complex and expensive to design and build. Nevertheless, it is an interesting field of possible future invention.

A distinctive feature of local authority policy since the mid-1980s has been the concentration of effort upon the generation of employment, by both the encouragement of existing local industries and the attraction of more mobile ones from elsewhere. Among the initiatives that have been taken by councils to support the level of employment in their area and assist the development of industrial property are the following:

- *Development plans revision.* Amendments to structure plans and local plans or unitary development plans releasing additional land for industry or rolling forwards planned future allocations have been made by many authorities. Similarly, site specific planning and development briefs identifying potential industrial estates have become a popular means of attempting to stimulate private sector development.
- *Economic development units.* Under a variety of titles many local authorities have established special departments and appointed economic or industrial development officers responsible for employment generation. These offer a wide range of schemes covering both business advice and financial assistance.
- *Serviced sites and development.* In order to induce potential firms to come to their area, local authorities have frequently laid out the principal roads and services on selected sites, and sometimes have erected speculative units in advance of demand. Many councils have gone further and acted as developer. The early science parks at Warrington, with the well publicized Genesis Building, and Killingbeck, where Leeds City Council itself funded the first phase of the 12 ha (30 acre) estate, were among the most notable initial ventures.
- *Headleasing.* Where market uncertainty exists and, because of either doubts about the location of the site or the size and nature of the units,

private sector developers are wary about taking all the risks of letting and management entailed in a proposed scheme, it has become quite common for the local authority to take the head-lease of the property and subsequently to sublet the units to occupying firms. A variation to this agreement is typified by the agreement entered into by various councils, whereby they have undertaken to take a head-lease from a developer if the particular project is still unlet after a certain period of unsuccessful marketing.

- *Key worker housing.* In an attempt to overcome some of the problems experienced by firms in relocation to new premises, a few local authorities have provided subsidized housing or cheap building land for key workers. The conversion of high-rise flats into hostels for single people or young couples is another way of retaining or attracting desired workers.
- *Other initiatives.* It has been suggested, at one time or another, that local authorities might:

  - Introduce special long-term incentives on rates; these remain one of the greatest worries among the business community, which does not always benefit from the services provided.
  - Offer rental guarantees to developers and investors, possibly linked to some form of indexing. In this way, dubious investments let to relatively young companies or firms that are recovering from a recession, will immediately acquire a 'blue chip' quality.
  - Concentrate on improving the physical environment in existing and proposed new business areas through better roads, landscaping (hard and soft), refuse collection, lighting and the like.

Design and layout

Historically, the design of industrial buildings has been poor, often being more the preserve of the engineer than the architect. The adherence to strict zoning regulations tended until recently to constrain any serious consideration of the need for good design. It is really only since the late 1970s that employers and management have become concerned about the working environment of their labour force, realizing that pleasant and effective buildings are synonymous with high productivity and satisfactory returns. Moreover, with the relaxation of rigid industrial zoning policies and a movement away from the separation of industrial processes into large estates, it became obvious that many small industrial developments would have to be sympathetically moulded into existing urban areas, and other large industrial developments would have to be sited in exposed and sensitive rural locations, often close to motorways where they would be most apparent. The general quality of design for industrial development, therefore, has improved enormously, with such leaders in the architectural field as Terry Farrell, Nick Grimshaw and Norman Foster bringing a kind of respectability to what was previously a largely drab utilitarian approach. Nevertheless, a strong conservative influence survives among occupiers, and a degree of tenant reluctance to accept some of the more exciting modern design concepts is exemplified by the initial slow letting of certain notable quality estates.

Changing character

As never before, developers need to market their product largely through excellence of design and specification. Architects, therefore, are having to respond with flair and imagination, for they are being asked to devise new buildings that are economic to construct, suitable for new industries and trades, acceptable to institutions that still have half an eye to long-term flexibility, and are in themselves positive marketing and promotional statements. Not only must the buildings conform to newly established criteria, however, but the settings in which they are placed must generate an attractive and compelling business climate. Developers now demand estates that demonstrate upon entry an excellent working environment with genuine landscaping and full amenities. The main reason for this changing character can be summarized as follows:

- The industrial sector, as such, has given way to a business sector comprising retail, high-technology and office use as well as production and distribution.
- Since the economic recession of the early 1990s, the negotiating balance between landlord and tenant has tilted sharply towards the tenant.
- Businesses are much more mobile than in the past, and tend increasingly to seek a consolidation of their administrative activities with their productive operations.
- Employees are also mobile, with higher levels of car ownership and different perceptions of work opportunities.
- With changing business functions and different forms of productive process, the single-storey rule is disappearing.

Density and layout

Traditionally, an overall site cover of 45–50 per cent was always considered to be an appropriate density for modern industrial estate development. The trend over recent years has been for a lower site coverage, and it is likely that an acceptable average for the foreseeable future will be closer to 30–35 per cent. With certain special developments, such as science parks and office campuses, the average density can fall even lower to between 20 and 25 per cent and below. However, it must be remembered that a lower site coverage by no means implies a lower density, for many forms of modern industry it is perfectly acceptable to operate on two or more storeys. In fact, with some processes in both the light electronics and pharmaceutical fields, a 'layer cake' concept of factory design is most suitable, whereby the production area is laid out on the ground floor, and one or more levels of service or handling space are built above. Not multi-storey in the true sense, developments of this kind rarely suit a portal frame structure, for it is generally not sufficient to carry the loads involved. Nevertheless, the footprints of buildings across a site so developed can be quite scattered.

With regard to the overall layout of estate roads and parking facilities, changes in both the use of the private car, and in the size and nature of delivery vehicles, have dictated changes in the assessment of siting, road circulation, address and services. Not only is the general level of car ownership much higher these days, but the nature of many new industries creates a greater need for carparking facilities, because of the higher income group of employee, the increased level of office-type activity and the additional amount of visiting traffic from clients and other members of the company. As a guideline, most modern estates require one parking space for every person employed, or alternatively one space for every 23 m^2 (250 ft^2). An even higher level of provision is necessary if there is any retail warehouse element within the estate, whereas pure warehousing operations demand very much less. The advent of the juggernaut has meant that all industrial estates now need to cater for 15 m (49 ft) plus lorries. Access and forecourt roads need to be wider, longer and more substantial than hitherto, to allow for manoeuvrability. An incidental gain from this is that it produces large open areas for landscaping. Forecourt layouts and delivery parking facilities are critical if an estate is to be successful, and certain industrial activities and freight operators will require plenty of parking space for vehicles and trailers. Special trailer parking areas are also sometimes needed. Common open areas of concrete or tarmacadam can be laid out and marked for individual units, or segregated spaces with a physical barrier to prevent encroachment can be provided. Although it is important to supply loading and parking facilities to a high standard, it is also important these days to separate them from the office areas on an estate. The roads themselves can be of either a concrete or a tarmacadam finish. Concrete costs more initially, but tarmacadam is more expensive to maintain, leading to complaints from tenants and high service charges.

Design principles

Although the concept of dual capacity – whereby buildings on industrial estates are designed so that they can be adapted for both warehouse and production uses – in order that institutional investors and developers can cast their letting net as wide as possible, is now regarded as redundant, the keynote of good design remains that of flexibility. The following guidelines represent an attempt to describe good design practice that will retain flexibility of use without sacrificing the individual quality of buildings.

- *Floor slab.* This should be designed to ensure that an adequate loading capacity, say 227–340 kg (500–750 lb), can be offered through time to a wide range of uses. Once constructed there is very little that can be done to rectify any deficiency.
- *Eaves height.* Reference is often made to the institutional requirement for a 5.5 m (18 ft) eaves height, but in many ways this standard is too high for most modern factory buildings, too low for current warehousing needs and insufficient to allow for horizontal conversion. A clear height of 6.7 m to 7.3 m (21–24 ft) permits the inclusion of a mezzanine floor or the conversion into two-storey offices, and retains the possibility of

warehouse use. For purpose-built single-storey light industrial buildings, however, a clear height of 3.7 m to 4.6 m (12–15 ft) is much more popular than the traditional 5.5 m to 6.1 m (18–20 ft). Special high-bay warehouses require at least 10 m (33 ft) eaves height for a minimum 10 000 m² (107 639 ft²) floorspace at 45 per cent site cover.

- *Column spacing.* As a general rule, columns hinder flexibility. Where the structure, span and loads are such that they have to be provided, it is essential that correct column spacing is planned to allow for the possible need to provide extra support for mezzanine floors, subdivide into self-contained smaller units or facilitate pallet racking.

- *Cladding materials.* Once again the aim should be to achieve a reasonable degree of flexibility, not merely in the selection and design of cladding but also in respect of the provision of glazing, doors and bays. In attaining this, architects have benefited from the development of profiled metal sheeting with factory-bonded insulation. External finishes on profiled metal are virtually maintenance free. Advances have also been made in the use of glass-reinforced concrete and glass-reinforced plastic, which in sheet cladding form are said to offer a whole new range of design possibilities in both aesthetic and practical terms. All these insulated flexible skins can be produced in a variety of modular panel systems incorporating interchangeable door, window and service-bay openings so as to provide a range of sophisticated and highly adaptable facades. However, some doubts have been expressed regarding the extensive and exclusive use of demountable and interchangeable cladding panels. For example, great care is required in their selection, because the testing of new materials is not all it should be. The exclusive use of either glazing or cladding is not always popular with tenants and, although the notion of interchangeability is fine in theory, it is less likely to be adopted in practice, for some developers would say that it is often better to provide for internal flexibility within the building rather than in the structure itself.

- *Roofs.* Until recently it has probably been fair to say that absolutely flat roofs were not acceptable because of performance and maintenance problems, but nearly flat roofs could normally be achieved successfully. Now, however, it is feasible to produce a leak-proof flat roof by using a plastics-based membrane material. The object of obtaining as flat a roof as possible is to optimize the internal volume of the building. Nevertheless, it is commonly accepted that a slightly pitched steel trussed roof, which permits the ready attachment of tenants' equipment, is best, so long as the truss is constructed deep enough for the installation and maintenance of services to be easily effected. False ceilings are often installed to facilitate the introduction of additional services, as well as to create a better working environment and reduce energy consumption. In both walls and roofs it should always be recognized at the basic design stage that windows and roof lights might have to be added or subtracted at some future date. Likewise, both environmental and process services may have to come through either roofs or walls. Indeed, the very structure should be designed to carry these services, on top of any mechanical handling equipment a tenant may wish to install.

- *Building services.* Although an increasing emphasis is placed upon the provision of adequate internal services, there are a growing number of developers who prefer to construct a simple shell capable of accommodating a wide range of building services, but await an actual letting before the specified services are installed. One of the most effective means of supplying electrical services is by way of a ring main around the perimeter of the building. In respect of distribution across a building, building regulations in the UK insist upon the boxed trunking of electrical transmission, unlike the USA where taped carpet tiles can be employed, giving ultimate flexibility. With regard to lighting, good-quality daylighting factors are often required, and natural lighting to office standards is sometimes sought. Otherwise, artificial lighting to around 500 watts is normally sufficient, often to be found hung from a suspended ceiling. Air-conditioning is fast becoming a sought-after facility in many modern industrial estate developments, and is virtually obligatory in some of the more sophisticated high-technology schemes. In any event, consideration in design should be given to ensure that the basic structure and skin are suitable for power, heat and ventilation systems to be added later if required. Similarly, the fundamental design should aim at high standards of insulation, with an airtight skin, because good insulation can literally halve the heating costs of small units and substantially reduce those of larger ones.
- *Office content.* The traditional proportion of ancillary office space, at 10–15 per cent of total floorspace, still adopted as a standard by some local planning authorities, is no longer a reliable guide to real need. In fact, most occupiers of modern industrial premises are rarely satisfied with less than 20 per cent, and with certain high-technology operations as much as 50 per cent or more is required. At planning approval stage, a prospective developer would definitely be well advised to gain consent for around 30–40 per cent office use in any proposed estate development, or alternatively avoid any condition as to a fixed percentage. With regard to design, there is a growing desire on the part of potential occupiers, particularly in the South East of England, to create a headquarters building on an estate alongside their distribution operations. This creates a need for an individual or corporate identity for the firm to be created. At the very least, therefore, it is sensible for a developer to reserve land accordingly, or to make sure that certain buildings could be converted if need be. In the context of office space industrial buildings, it is now a common convention that buildings on industrial estates should not have a rear elevation as such, but rather that there should be a double-sided design, with a separate approach for office staff and visitors, preferably on the south side of the building, on the opposite side to the properly planned loading bays and goods handling facilities. It is also the case that a greater area of glazing to permit views and afford natural light for the workforce, or the ability to create it, is required nowadays.
- *Fire.* It is often argued that in the UK the cost of fire prevention and control is excessive. Nevertheless, such requirements remain an important consideration in all forms of development. Moreover, in the London area, what are known as Section 20 regulations provide that, in order to

avoid the need in larger units for complete compartmentalization, they must be served with sprinkler installations. Although some developers still do not supply such facilities, the extra cost and effort on the part of the potential tenant could easily tilt the balance against a letting if two or three possible premises have been short-listed. As a small point, it might be worth noting that the fire-proofing of steel structures has become more economical over recent years with the use of intumescent paints and coatings, which also have the added advantage that they are a more attractive finish than the normal concrete or dry lining.

- *Loading bays.* Not only should consideration be given to how many doors there should be, where they might be located and how vehicles will get to and from them, but some thought should be given to the provision of weather-protected, tailboard-height bays reached over carefully planned approach areas. For speculative developments it is advisable to provide floodlit unloading areas and adjustable levellers, and to ensure some kind of shelter from the bay to the inside of the building.

- *Office and amenity areas.* Provision should normally be made for such facilities as an attractive entrance hall and reception area; well finished and insulated curtain walling systems with double-glazed tinted window units; fully fitted carpets and good quality wallpaper; easy subdivision of open-space office area; suspended ceiling and recessed light fittings; perimeter skirting trunking for power, telephone and VDU installations; double-socket power outlets positioned in the ceiling voids; fully tiled spacious male and female toilets, possibly with shower units and dressing areas; central heating system; and drinking fountain, tea bar and cleaners' cupboards.

- *Energy conservation.* Some developers are beginning to give consideration to the incorporation of sophisticated energy-saving systems. One such approach is known as 'condition-based maintenance' that uses advanced technologies such as remote temperature sensors, electronic flue gas analysers and current injection test sets. The savings in running costs and reduction of town-time can be a good selling point in a tight market.

- *Others.* Special drainage facilities cannot always be added, particularly in heavy load-bearing floors, and it is often worthwhile providing a flexible facility, either by having a soft floor finish or by incorporating floor trenches at convenient intervals.

  Good toilet facilities are often forgotten by developers, although movable prefabricated toilet modules have been found to be a positive advantage in some industrial estate development schemes. Toxic waste disposal services might be demanded by prospective tenants, not merely those from more traditional noxious industries, but also from some of the newer high-technology firms. Likewise, advanced fume-extraction facilities might have to be incorporated.

Refurbishment of old industrial buildings

It has been estimated that there is well over 16 million m^2 (172 million ft^2) of floorspace left vacant in industrial buildings throughout the country, much of which is no longer needed for its original purpose (Thomson 1994/5). A great deal has been said and written about the need to re-use these old redundant buildings, and since the mid-1980s a growing number of successful refurbishment projects undertaken by a variety of development agencies have been implemented. Many of these fall outside the mainstream of conventional property development; but, equally, many opportunities exist for profitable commercial development to be tackled by entrepreneurs who understand the special factors that underlie the market.

All that is possible in this section is to list some of the more critical factors that determine whether or not a viable refurbishment of conversion can be effected. These can conveniently be summarized as follows:

- *Initial outlay.* This must be kept to a minimum, not merely in respect of the capital sum, carrying a debt charge, expended on the purchase of the building, or the head rent that has to be paid, but also with regard to the cost of works that have to be undertaken before all or part of the building can be let. Wherever possible, it is advisable to try to plan a gradual programme of upgrading, so that some of the costs can be funded from income.
- *Overheads.* In the same vein, most successful conversions of old industrial buildings take place where overheads have been reduced as far as possible. This invariably means that professional fees are minimized or avoided, with developers performing most of the professional tasks themselves. Similarly, contractors' and developers' profits are often absorbed in the same way, so that developer, contractor and project manager, and even agent at times, are all rolled into one, and a single slice of fees and profits is sought by that party.
- *Location.* Experience shows that buildings best suited to conversion are convenient for both staff and customers, say five minutes at most from the nearest public transport, are situated in an area of some existing and potential business demand and have good access off a main road on to a two-way street wide enough for parking.
- *Site coverage.* It is desirable to have 60 per cent or less site coverage and to possess good site access with off-street parking and delivery facilities.
- *Building configuration.* Evidence suggests that deep buildings with poor aspects should be avoided. Under 14–16 m (46–52 ft) depth is preferable, and in no circumstances should buildings over 18 m (59 ft) be considered if natural lighting and ventilation are to be exploited. Likewise, a three- or, better still, four-way aspect is best.
- *Structure and condition.* Obviously, a building possessing a superior initial construction, and where there is little need for major structural repair, is most attractive. At least the structure should be fairly sound and the building capable of being made wind-proof and watertight without too much trouble. Ideally, the building should be of fire-proofed frame construction and either brick or concrete. More than three storeys become problematical, and the ground floor should have a floor height of 2.5–4 m (8–13 ft) at most. It is also important that there are wide stairways and the facility for incorporating a goods lift if required.
- *Statutory.* It must not be too difficult or costly to have to comply with such statutory requirements as fire or public health, and it often helps if

there is no need to apply for planning permission for a change of use. Above all, perhaps, the single common factor that seems to characterize all successful conversions of old industrial buildings is the presence of a strong personality responsible for the development, who is thoroughly committed to the scheme.

As a last word on the subject of the refurbishment of old industrial buildings, where elsewhere so much professional attention is paid to the relatively simple, clean, large estates designed for established national and international organizations, it is worth noting the role that has still to be played by the small business sector of the economy. There is a shortage of very small premises of around 10–50 m² (108–538 ft²) in multiple tenanted accommodation, with shared access on flexible occupancy agreements and offering varying amounts of central support services. Therefore, enormous opportunities exist for the small developer with sufficient initiative and sympathetic funding.

Warehousing and distribution

A key feature of the property scene in the UK since the mid-1980s has been the phenomenal growth of the distribution industry and its consequent land-use and property requirements. Indeed, in a relatively stagnant commercial property market, the distribution industry represents one of the very few sectors of property growth with the demand for increasingly sophisticated warehousing premises.

The traditional concept of the warehouse as a crudely converted simple storage building situated in a run-down industrial area has undergone a fundamental change. There is now a widespread demand among distributors of goods for purpose-built, fully automated storage premises designed to satisfy their operational requirements, located on strategically identified sites within, and adjacent to, urban regions and throughout the country generally (Taylor 1993).

Research undertaken by DTZ Debenham Thorpe pointed to a period of sustained activity in the warehouse property sector throughout the 1990s, as major operators respond to the emergence of new markets. Distribution networks that were once viewed as effective and efficient are becoming less so as a result of the combined effect of lower rates of economic growth, the employment of 'just-in-time' methods (JIT) and automation in the warehouse, as well as the effect of existing and proposed legislation. Together, these elements are bringing about a major shift in the location and property requirements of many companies, a shift with implications for both developers and investors. The internet has raised consumer expectations about choice and efficiency and has created an assumption that immediacy of the virtual order can be matched by the speed of the actual delivery. This has implications for supply chain management, fluid vision for the design, style, location, size, and connectivity of distribution property in the years to come.

The distribution sector underpins all economic activity. It provides the link between suppliers, manufacturers and retailers in a complex network that is increasingly taking on a pan-European dimension. The warehouse lies at the heart of the supply chain, providing a buffer between fluctuations in supply and demand. However, throughout the 1990s, warehouses were increasingly viewed not simply as a place to store goods but as an integral element of the logistics network capable of making a positive contribution to corporate wellbeing or, negatively, acting as a major constraint on operational efficiency.

The increasingly widespread use of JIT means that warehouses perform a set of functions different from those undertaken in the past. Much greater emphasis is placed on stock rotation, trans-shipment activities and break-bulk, as well as a range of ancillary activities including repackaging and some light assembly. This range of emerging needs requires a comprehensive reassessment of the location and specification of premises deemed suitable in the late 1990s.

Major issues in warehouse and distribution development

Some major issues affecting the development of warehousing and distribution property over the next decade or so can be identified as described briefly below.

Europe

Manufacturers, retailers and other companies throughout Europe are considering their distribution needs on a pan-European basis, with the increasingly common phenomenon of a single distribution site with a super-warehouse servicing all of Europe. However, several sites are a more popular solution. Although northwest Europe has distribution facilities similar to the UK, including traditional estates and free-standing distribution centres, the region has seen developments rarely witnessed in the UK. They include groups of road-haulage depots on a single site and loose groupings of depots and warehouses offering a range of logistical services at one site, including model interchange. Strong competition, standardization and sophistication are destined to become the themes of European distribution development. Legislation regarding environmental taxes, the exchange-rate mechanism, the Social Chapter and operational constraints, will all have an effect on location.

UK regional distribution centres (RDCs)

An RDC is difficult to define according to size or function, but in very general terms it can be stated that manufacturers tend to be concentrated in the Midlands, whereas retailers are dispersed across the country. Most major retailers prefer no more than 2–2.5 hours between distribution depots. It is predicted that RDCs will grow in size and reduce in number, with significant restructuring of both industrial and distribution activities within the regions, probably favouring the Midlands. In addition, it is thought that road will continue to dominate rail networks for regional distributors, although some companies are now environmentally sensitive enough to prefer rail over roads. Generally owner occupied or pre-let, the RDC market is for units over

250 000 square feet. Sainsburys are averaging 600 000 square feet (Jones Lang LaSalle 2000).

Planning policy

To date, the attitude of planning authorities towards storage and distribution-related development has been relatively low key, with very few specific expressions of interest having been published at either national or local level. There is little to find on the subject in structure plans, local plans or unitary development plans, despite the importance to local as well as regional and national economies. Purely in design terms warehousing is unlikely to present any real issues or major conflicts with local planning authorities, whose prime concern in this respect should be satisfaction that environmental and amenity considerations are met. Despite the fact that the purpose-built warehouse is higher and larger than its single-storey predecessor, there is no reason why warehouses should not be designed to look pleasant. Locational factors are the ones most likely to concern planners. Traditional locations in urban areas are no longer attractive to distributors. They need a great deal of space, which cannot normally be found in built-up areas; rural areas, preferably near to motorway interchanges, are their preferred locations. However, it is at these locations, where planners are anxious not to allow development, that sustainability, environmental and countryside policies take preference. Taking the situation on an *ad hoc* basis, therefore, it is realistic to assume there would be planning opposition to developments of this nature on these sites, unless sites were identified by planners in advance within the context of a clear policy framework. Such a framework would certainly need to indicate sites for major distribution parks. This property form is seen in some distribution industry quarters as the answer to their property requirements and where planning objections can be overcome through well designed, well landscaped layouts (Taylor 1993).

Classification and specification

In an attempt to understand the various levels of warehouse requirement, a useful classification of operations into simple, medium and sophisticated storage can be made. Simple storage operations are those where the goods in question can be block-stacked to a limited height using ordinary counter-balanced fork lift trucks and need a clear height of up to 5.5–6.0 m (18–20 ft). Some of the traditional standard units, therefore, are suitable. Medium storage operations take place where goods are stored in racked pallets with wider aisles and handled by the use of reach or turret trucks. Clear heights of up to 8.0–8.5 m (26–28 ft) are required. Sophisticated storage operations imply the existence of an automated warehouse and thus a high commitment to mechanical handling equipment. Wire guidance systems, automatic stacker cranes and computer-assisted stock control are all features of such operations, and buildings with clear heights of up to 36 m (118 ft) have been constructed to accommodate demand. In fact there is a burgeoning growth in the development of high-bay warehouses. An early example of such a development was the Associated Biscuit factory at Worton Grange near the

M4 Reading junction where stacking to over 12 m (40 ft) occurs, and 40 per cent more storage capacity was created at only 18 per cent more cost than would have been incurred in the construction of a conventional warehouse. The reduced floor area can also mean lower land costs, and the new 6500 m² (70 000 ft²) building replaces a traditional multi-storey warehouse of 16 700 m² (180 000 ft²) floorspace. The basic object of modern warehouse design, therefore, is to maximize the amount of usable storage volume out of the gross volume of a building. Although costs of construction increase with height, the rate of increase falls, and produces what has been described as a lower cost of pallet aperture. Unlike industrial premises, it is important that offices should actually oversee the loading bays. A single-sided approach for cars and trucks is thereby created and consequently back-to-back development is possible. Another difference is that insulation to the skin may or may not be necessary, depending upon what is to be stored.

Distribution parks

The lack of large suitable sites for low-density development, the need for good motorway access and the trend towards 24-hour operations, coupled with the availability of both public transport and ancillary services and facilities are all factors likely to enhance the apparent attractiveness of dedicated distribution parks. Nevertheless, many potential occupiers are strangely suspicious about such developments, preferring stand-alone sites or a location on a more traditional industrial estate. This is probably because of the perceived costs associated with distribution parks and the possible lack of access to an adequate supply of skilled labour, as well as other ancillary facilities such as retail (Debenham Tewson Research 1990).

Europe's largest fully integrated national distribution centre, however, is being developed at Magna Park in Leicestershire. Started in 1988, 715 000 m² (7 696 188 ft²) was completed by 1998 and it is still growing today. Situated in the golden triangle of the country's road network, from this site nearly 92 per cent of the population of Great Britain can be reached with the return journey being undertaken on the same day. The scheme features high-quality designed structures with a distinct architectural style, steel portal-frame warehouses with eaves heights of 10 m or more, leases of 999 years allowing the use of positive covenants to control estate maintenance and management, superior landscaping provision, and a cost-effective centralized sewerage system. Since its inception, Magna Park has secured an impressive range of tenants and investment deals.

Freight villages

These are massive distribution centres located at strategic points around the country, providing integrated multimodal high-bay facilities based on rail as well as road networks, the rail link being used for long haul and the road service for collection and delivery. The EU has declared war on road freight and the British government is following its lead, with an alternative preference for long-haul, large-load freight movements by trains that carry the equivalent of 50 lorry loads. British Rail proposes nine such freight villages and the private sector more. Nervousness about rail technology, equipment and service, unavailability of information on possible pricing structures, a general lack of confidence in rail management, and a reluctance to be over-dependent upon rail operators – all militate against the ready acceptance of such schemes.

High-technology development

The term 'high tech' became the buzz word of the 1980s, but there seemed to be little or no common understanding as to the way it was used in the property world. It would often appear to have had as much to do with industrial marketing and architectural fancy as with the true needs of occupiers. The labelling of estates with colourful claddings, tinted glass and expensive landscaping as being high tech led one leading agent to observe, 'It is not entirely unreasonable to regard the high-tech chapter in industrial marketing as something of an elaborate self-deception by a number of architects and agents'.

   The growth of high-technology estate development has its roots in the USA where, although many early American business parks were actually poorly located, a more risk-conscious and responsive property industry led the way in the design and development of accommodation to suit high-technology based companies. The explosive growth that took place in Santa Clara County ('Silicon Valley') during the 1970s is now familiar. However, there were lessons for the UK to be learned because the rapid establishment of well over a thousand major companies across an area of 70 square miles eventually led to a state of over-development with a fall in environmental design standards, increasingly inadequate infrastructure services that became seriously overtaxed, and a massive rise in domestic house prices. Nevertheless, the strong trading links between US and UK companies means that high and selective standards of location and design are increasingly sought.

The definition of high-technology development

Perhaps too much time and effort has been expended upon worrying away at what is high tech and what is not. Everyone seems to become very excited about categories and definitions, but it is possible to wonder just how relevant is such sophism. For straightaway, one important distinction to make is that between high-tech buildings and high-tech users. Many high-tech users can happily operate in low-tech accommodation. Many high-tech buildings house very low-tech operations. What has really happened, is that there has been a response to the demand by a variety of industrial and commercial users for adaptable, high quality, comfortable and attractive buildings set in pleasant surroundings, which are well located and available on acceptable terms to potential occupiers. Nevertheless, for the purposes of this text, the term 'high-technology property' includes:

* buildings in an architectural style of design that has come to be known as 'high tech'

- buildings occupied or intended for occupation by high-technology companies
- modern buildings in which mixed and flexible uses of space (including administrative use, laboratory, business, assembly and storage) occur.

(Fletcher King 1990)

Since the introduction of the 1987 Use Classes Order, the term B1 has been rapidly adopted to imply the multi-use space that was previously described as high-tech, despite the fact that pure office buildings also fall under the B1 heading in planning terms. The high-tech definitions can now be seen as forming two distinct groups. The first is where there is academic involvement or where research and development is an important part of the occupiers' activities; the main group here is science parks, together with research parks, technology parks and innovation centres. The second cluster contains the main group of business parks and also the office parks group, which because of the misuse of the B1 (Business) Class description within the Use Classes Order can be seen almost as a specialized form of business park. These are dealt with elsewhere (Ch. 16).

The high-technology developments identified in the first group above have been defined as follows (Fletcher King 1990).

Science Park

A science park is a collection of high-technology companies or research institutes, situated in attractive surroundings developed to a low density, engaged in product research and prototype development, close to a tertiary education establishment with which there are significant opportunities for interaction and cross-fertilization of ideas. The term has suffered from imprecise use, but an attempt has been made to insist on a link with a tertiary education or research establishment in order to constitute a true science park.

Research park

Also known as a research science park and discovery park, a research park is a collection of high-technology companies or research institutes situated in attractive surroundings developed to a low density, engaged in product research and prototype development, close to a tertiary education establishment with which there are significant opportunities for interaction and cross-fertilization of ideas, and with conventional production and office activities specifically excluded. A research park is very similar to a science park, but with the specific exclusion of conventional production and office activities.

Technology park

A technology park is a collection of high-technology industrial companies situated in attractive surroundings developed to a low density, engaged in research and manufacturing, probably within a reasonable distance of a tertiary education establishment, but not dependent upon it.

Innovation centre

Also known as science nursery, seed-bed centre and enterprise centre, an innovation centre is a collection of newly formed companies, usually housed in an existing building or buildings, converted to form small units, engaged in developing commercial applications of academic research projects and situated within or alongside a tertiary education establishment.

Upgraded industrial estate

Also known as an industrial park, industrial mall and industrial area, an upgraded industrial estate is a development of industrial buildings with certain characteristics of high-technology property, which, although distinguishing it from other more traditional industrial estates, does not change its nature from being an industrial estate. These estates may be designed in a high-tech style or have more extensive landscaping than the previous generation of industrial estates, but despite marketing attempts they do not legitimately fall into any of the previous groups.

Another concept developed in the USA puts occupiers with a common business on one park. Thus, a 'medi-park' contains medical research and development tenants with private hospitals, rehabilitation centres and sports clinics. It would seem that a medi-park is a technology park with medicine common to the tenants. Similarly, tenants with other industries as the common denominator would attract a generic title; for example, a park based upon the food industry would constitute a Food Park (Fletcher King 1990).

The features of high-technology development

Although a great deal has been researched and written about high-technology developments, there would seem to be three basic ingredients common to all successful schemes, not always in accord with the definitions given above. These can briefly be described as follows:

Location

Location is critical, and certain locational factors can be categorized as essential, important and relevant. Those deemed essential are proximity to an international airport, a good road network with motorway access, pleasant residential and working environments, and the availability of a specialist skilled workforce. Those considered important are proximity to markets, proximity to the capital city, good rail links to the capital city, and the availability of support from a university or leading research establishment. Those thought relevant are proximity to suppliers, proximity to a domestic airport, good cultural and recreational amenities, and the existence of selective financial assistance (Williams 1982). Put another way, it has been stated that five factors have a significant influence on the location decisions of high-technology companies (Taylor 1985):

- the market for their product and the proximity of purchasers
- the availability of suitable premises and their cost
- a high-quality environment
- the accessibility of the motorway network
- the residence of directors and key personnel.

Flexibility

With regard to the type of buildings suitable for high-technology users, perhaps the most important factor is flexibility. There are several aspects to this:

- *Flexibility of use within the structure.* So that the various functions of research and development, production and offices can mix and match, change emphasis and grow or contract according to the needs of the company, a suitable layout might permit any of the three elements to be changed, with only the removal or fitting of carpets for certain types of space or thermoplastic tiles for others. Some true high-tech companies are working to state of the art specifications and do not know, almost from one month to another, exactly how they need to organize their space.
- *Flexibility for growth.* Many companies active in this sector are expanding at a rapid rate. In one study over 80 per cent of the firms interviewed planned to expand in the forthcoming five years, and about 30 per cent envisaged that their corporate expansion would involve occupying more accommodation. Thus, on the one hand, there is a need to allow for physical flexibility for expansion *in situ* and, on the other, for a flexibility of leasehold terms so that firms can move to alternative accommodation without undue constraint. A 25-year lease is a very long time for a company that can scarcely predict its own market for more than a year or two at a time.
- *Flexibility of covenant strength.* Many firms will be relatively new and exploring fresh markets, often without a track record, and sometimes without the necessary three years acceptable sets of accounts.

Design

Some of the emerging interior and exterior designs for high-technology developments rival many prime office headquarters buildings, and probably one of the most powerful motivations behind many moves to new technology parks is the desire for a strong and attractive corporate image. Nevertheless, there is a danger of building to specifications unrelated to consumer demand, as it is often the case that occupiers are perfectly happy to accept traditional exteriors – preferring to spend their money on better interior facilities. The likely truth is that the market comprises a wide range of potential occupiers with varying requirements and perceptions. However, there are a few special points of design worth noting:

- extensive carparking facilities are essential
- adequate underfloor space for cabling must be provided

- roofing must sometimes have to take loads of up to 100 lb per m^2
- reinforcement for dish aerials will normally be wanted
- cleanliness is occasionally a problem
- energy-efficient buildings are increasingly sought
- the facility to introduce air-conditioning should be allowed
- very high standards of landscaping must be provided
- a high level of security is often required
- a range of finishes should be on offer rather than the typical tenants' norm
- the preference for two-storey development could well extend to three storeys
- with larger schemes, a village centre with small retail and service outlets could be beneficial
- excellent voice and data communication infrastructure.

In the property context of high-technology developments, it should be appreciated that, because of the rapid changes that are taking place in the field and the relatively slow gestation period of development projects, a site being developed in phases over several years can start out in one form and then alter its nature in response to demand. For example, phase I of an upgraded industrial estate may be succeeded by phase II units of multi-use space, more specialist high-technology space or even office or business space, so that taken as a whole the character of the estate may change through time. Telecommunications companies have been eager occupiers of high-technology developments. However, the well-publicized problems with extreme bids for 4G licences and dwindling phone sales have meant that a substantial amount of their property is now vacant and to let.

Estate management

For many years, a large proportion of industrial estate development in Britain lacked even the most basic level of management services, which accounts for their general unsightly appearance. Apart from the New Town Development Corporations and a few notable private development companies such as Slough Estates and Brixton Estates, the management function was largely eschewed, and the burden of responsibility passed on to tenants. However, over more recent years a realization of the importance of good industrial estate management has dawned upon the property development industry. Most of the fundamental principles relating to the planning and design of estates have already been discussed, but other points are worthy of mention. These are as follows:

- *Image.* Not merely for initial marketing, but also for subsequent letting and rent review negotiations, it pays to establish and maintain an appealing corporate image for an industrial estate. The naming of an estate, the creation of a special logo, well designed name boards at access points, the construction of an attractive gateway building, and the publication of professionally presented marketing material all make for a sense of community and a successful letting record.

- *Tenant mix.* In the same way that there has been an appreciation of the importance of selecting the right mix of tenants in the management of planned shopping centres over the years, so a similar awareness is beginning to grow in the management of industrial estates. The correct identification of likely occupiers will help in planning estate layout and services, because freight operators, distribution centres, retail warehouses, light industry office and research-based users all dictate different buildings, service and traffic management solutions. Complementarity of use, which generates business between tenants, is also a consideration in small unit estates.

- *Signposting.* Although it may not seem to be a major aspect of industrial estate development and management, the careful selection and siting of directional signposts around an estate can greatly enhance the general appearance. The careful incorporation of tenants' logos with a corporate framework, both at the entrances to an estate and on the individual buildings, can also add to the overall impression of the development.

- *Landscaping.* What used to be regarded as an unnecessary and expensive luxury, often imposed as a condition of planning approval, is now usually seen as an essential attribute of any successful industrial development by investors, developers and occupiers alike. In fact, it is becoming quite fashionable to retain large striking natural features within an estate plan, or even to create artifacts such as an artificial lake or a folly type of building as a focal point to an estate. However, it should be remembered that even the selection and care of trees and shrubs is a relatively specialist affair. Effective landscaping will also attempt to avoid the fencing-in of industrial plots. As a corollary to this, it has been found that the imposition of positive covenants in the lease upon the tenant is rarely the best way of looking after the common landscaped areas of an estate. It is normally much better for a developer to arrange for the management of the estate as a whole at the outset, and recover the cost by way of a properly accounted service charge.

- *Security.* Even on the smallest estates, security is a matter of considerable concern to tenants. Control at gate houses, the entrances to the estate, is often required, and they should be sited for maximum visibility around the estate roads. On larger estates, or where there are special tenants' requirements, it will often be necessary to install cameras around the estate, or even to provide 24-hour security, which can cost around £75 000 a year for just a one-man operation. How much security is provided, of what kind and who pays, is obviously a matter of negotiation between landlord and tenant.

- *Power.* Some estate developers undertake the bulk purchase of oil and gas, which they make available on a metered supply. Slough Estates is perhaps exceptional in that it generates its own electricity at a privately operated 90 MW power station for its 300 tenants at Slough. It also supplies water and steam to the 700 000 m^2 estate. Central sprinkler installations are another facility commonly provided.

- *Refuse disposal.* Although on most estates this is normally looked upon as a tenant's responsibility, some developers have installed central compactors, where demand for such service is thought likely to be high. Otherwise, one of the main problems encountered in day-to-day industrial estate management is the monitoring and enforcement of conditions relating to the storage of rubbish and the placing of skips.

- *Personal services.* Increasingly, developers are conscious of the need to consider the possible provision of shopping, catering, health, banking, bus services, leisure and recreation facilities. Many of these services can now be accessed online, for example major supermarkets have experimented with delivery of groceries ordered over the internet to a number of high-profile business locations.
- *Tenants associations.* Although such organizations are comparatively rare on industrial estates, both landlords and tenants are slowly coming to recognize the mutual benefits that can be gained from the formation of a tenants association.

Conclusion

The problem for big warehouses hanging around the market has been that they are just not big enough for the requirements out there. The North West's speculative buildings, for example, got left behind at 100–200 000 square feet, while regional distribution centre requirements have mushroomed to the 250–400 000 square feet range (*Estates Gazette* 2002b). However, in this context the charge has been laid against developers and their advisers that, in the industrial and distribution sectors, specific working knowledge of functions and operations is all too often lacking. In a 1993 study by IBM Consulting Group, for example, only 2 per cent of British factories were deemed to be world class. It would seem that, although methods of manufacturing, storage and distribution have undergone revolutionary changes since the mid-1980s, suppliers of property have been slow to react to changing demand. It can be argued, therefore, that a much greater interest in, and deeper knowledge of, occupiers' requirements is needed. Post-occupancy evaluations should be conducted as standard practice in order to ensure that development practitioners are truly in tune with their clients, and that vital lessons can be learned that can quickly be translated into improved building and services. Thus, it has been opined that:

> He who puts the right product in the right place at the right time will profit. Listening to the needs and concerns of the end-user is the best way of finding out what and where. The firms that will be a force in the next upswing will be those that best understand the businesses of their clients.
>
> (*Estates Gazette* 1993)

18 Residential development

> Britain's programme of new house building is at its lowest level since 1924, yet developers are reported to have land banks equivalent to two million single-house plots. Builders are clear about why the mismatch occurs: long planning delays and demands for social housing and planning gain by local councils are making it harder to manage land, with the spectre of a slow residential sales market hanging over them.
>
> *(Estates Gazette* 2002)

Any examination of the many issues surrounding residential development will require knowledge of the detailed nature of design and layout in new-build housing or conversion of existing stock as well as knowledge of the wider debate surrounding the allocation of new housing land. This chapter will consider both issues and will raise contemporary issues relating to both new settlements and urban villages. This subject area is heavily influenced by the debate surrounding both regeneration and building on brown land. Reference therefore should also be made to Chapter 9 on Urban Renaissance and Regeneration.

This chapter is divided into four sections as follows:

- submitting planning applications for residential development
- housing land availability
- new settlements
- urban villages

The starting point for an examination of residential development issues is to be found in government guidance as set out in PPG3, which was revised in March 2000. This document deals with both design and layout issues and the allocation of housing land on green-field or brown-land sites.

Paragraph 2 states local planning authorities should:

- Plan to meet the housing requirements of the whole community, including those in need of affordable and special needs housing
- Provide wider housing opportunity and choice, and a better mix in the size, type and location of housing than is currently available, and seek to create mixed communities
- Provide sufficient housing land but give priority to re-using previously developed land within urban areas, bringing empty houses back into use

and converting existing buildings, in preference to the development of green-field sites
- Create more sustainable patterns of development by building in ways that exploit and deliver accessibility by public transport to jobs, education and health facilities, shopping, leisure, and local services
- Make more efficient use of land by reviewing planning policies and standards
- Place the needs of people before ease of traffic movement in designing the layout of residential developments
- Seek to reduce car dependence by facilitating more walking and cycling, by improving linkages by public transport between housing, jobs, local services and local amenity, and by planning for mixed use
- Promote good design in new housing developments in order to create attractive, high-quality living environments in which people will choose to live.

Paragraph 1 of PPG3 states:

> The government intends that everyone should have the opportunity of a decent home. They further intend that there should be greater choice of housing and that housing should not reinforce social distinctions. The housing needs of all in the community should be recognized, including those in need of affordable or special housing in both urban and rural areas. To promote more sustainable patterns of development and make better use of previously developed land, the focus for additional housing should be existing towns and cities. New housing and residential environments should be well designed and should make a significant contribution to promoting urban renaissance and improving the quality of life.[1]

This is a significant departure from the commitment in the previous version of this guidance to allow housing development, subject to the protection of both the urban and rural environment.

Government policy is committed to allowing housing development subject to the protection of both the urban and the rural environment. This would in theory restrict the erosion of agricultural and green belt land from development or the 'cramming' of new buildings within the urban area. However, with ever-increasing demands for new housing, some new land must be allocated, and although a debate rages about whether greater use should be made of existing derelict or under used land, it is almost inevitable that the objectives of PPG3 paragraph 1 will be compromised in an attempt to meet the housing needs of British society. Town planning represents the arbitrator, seeking to allocate new land for housing and determining planning applications for residential development. Arbitration is required between the housebuilding industry and those promoting the conservation of rural and urban environment whose detailed interests are articulated by lobbying and pressure groups (e.g. Friends of the Earth or the Council for the Protection of Rural England) or by the local politicians who compose the planning committees of local planning authorities. PPG3 (2000) establishes a national target that by 2008 60 per cent of new housing shall be provided on previously developed land and through conversions. This will be achieved by giving greater attention to the recycling of urban land and building on it at higher densities than previously.

Submitting planning applications for residential development

It is important to recall that planning consent will be required for:

*   operational development, including new buildings and structural alteration, rebuilding, additions to buildings and other operations normally undertaken by a person carrying on business as a builder (such as demolition)[2]
*   conversion of one dwelling into two or more dwellings.

Outline or full?

It is common practice for developers to submit an *outline application* when seeking planning permission for major residential development (10 or more dwellings). This establishes whether or not the *principle* of residential development is acceptable. An outline planning permission provides the developer with an element of certainty before drawing up detailed plans and may therefore enhance the valuation of the land prior to its potential sale. The outline application can be made with all 'reserved matters'[3] to be considered at a later stage, however, it is usually the practice to submit details of siting of the dwellings and means of access onto the highway. This allows the local planning authority to consider the safety of the access and relationship of the proposed dwellings to adjoining ones at the outline stage. Such issues may be vital in the consideration of whether or not to grant outline consent. Although nothing prevents the developer from submitting a full application, it is most commonly employed in preference to outline/reserved matters, when dealing with minor residential development (less than 10 dwellings) or applications within conservation areas. The smaller the site, the greater the potential for concern regarding the impact of the development on adjoining occupiers. For example, by reasons of 'loss of light' to habitable rooms in neighbouring properties or by appearing 'cramped' and out of character with the surrounding development because the plot is too small. Such smaller plots are mostly found within existing urban areas, where the need for new housing makes the development of small plots economically viable. Such town infilling (i.e. adding built development within the existing urban fabric) has been referred to as 'town cramming' by critics who argue that it results in an erosion of character and, despite control exercised by local planning authorities, results in a loss of amenity to adjoining occupiers. During the 1980s the rise in the value of residential property resulted in a dramatic increase of such infilling, especially within the existing London suburbs (Case Study 18.1). Many LPAs felt that the direction of government policy at the time meant they had insufficient grounds to refuse such applications. Some LPAs attempted to bolster their own policies by under-

---

Case study 18.1: Housing layout and backland development

Arcadian Developments acquire a house with a large rear garden located within outer London. They propose to demolish the existing house and run a road into the backland and to build a block of 10 flats. The site is large enough to satisfy all local plan policies regarding amenity space, car parking and separation from existing development. The new road width satisfies highway considerations in Design Bulletin 32 and incorporates a sufficient 'buffer' width on either side to allow for screen planting, so that the residents on either side are not affected by the movement of vehicles to and from the new development.

---

taking environmental appraisals of their residential areas in an attempt to resist such a tide of development.[4] Since 2000 all LPAs have been required to undertake urban housing capacity studies to assess the levels of land capable of recycling to meet government targets. Such infilling proposals could take several forms.

- *Infill.* To build one or two dwellings within the gap between existing dwellings and facing onto the same road (Fig. 18.1).
- *Backland.* To develop existing large back gardens (Fig. 18.2).
- *Tandem.* One house immediately behind another and sharing the same access. This is generally considered to be unacceptable, as the vehicular use of the access would result in a loss of amenity to the occupier of the frontage dwelling (Fig. 18.3).
- *Houses to flats.* Since the late 1960s, housebuilding has taken place at higher densities as a direct reflection of the increased cost of land with residential planning permission. Between the late 1960s and late 1980s the price of building land increased sevenfold (Cheshire 1993). Consider the following scenario (Fig. 18.4):

Developers purchase several houses, usually with spacious gardens, and apply to demolish and build a series of two- and three-storey flats (with the second-floor accommodation contained within the roof void). The relative size of the overall plot permits separation from neighbouring property, car parking, sizeable garden/amenity space to satisfy council provision and similar scale of development by maintaining predominantly a two-storey bulk. Permission is granted as the proposal satisfies many of the detailed development control criteria found in local plan policy, as well as meeting the demand for lower-cost one- and two-bedroom residential units. During the next five years many other such applications are submitted and granted. The overall result is that the character of an area has been changed from a low-density residential area to a medium- or high-density one.

This creeping incremental change was difficult to resist during the 1980s and the character of many suburban areas was dramatically altered during

Figure 18.1 An example of infill development.

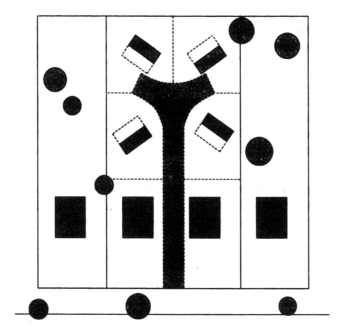

Figure 18.2 An example of backland development.

this period. As density policy has changed over the last 15 or so years, it is inevitable that new development will affect the character and appearance of the area in which it is located. It is the responsibility of the planning system to ensure that such change is appropriate.

Figure 18.3 An example of tandem development.

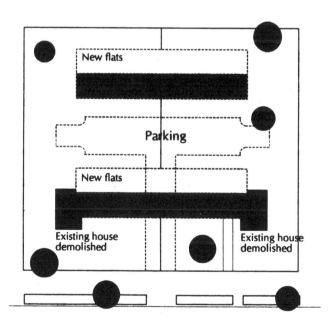

Figure 18.4 An example of flatted development on land previously occupied by houses.

Design and layout

In considering residential design and layout certain specific issues must be considered, as follows (summary as Table 18.1).

Table 18.1 Examples of residential town planning standards

Topic	Standard	Source
Overlooking	21 m minimum window to window	Local plan
Carparking	Varies, but usually one space per dwelling. In flatted developments a percentage for visitors is added.	Local plan
Roads	4.8–5.5 m width	Design Bulletin 32 *Places, Streets and Movement* (DETR 1998)
Amenity space	Flats 10 m² per habitable room. Houses 40 m² per two bedroom house and 15 for each additional bedroom.	Local plan
Density	Between 70 and 95 habitable rooms per acre.	Local plan
Conversions	To ensure some parking and/or amenity space is provided.	Local plan
Separation of development	Varies between 20 and 30 m (taken rear to rear/front elevation).	Local plan
Rear garden depths	Standards discouraged by government yet LPAs do include them at between 10 and 15 m depth in new development.	Local plan

Design

Design control as exercised by the LPA is limited. Matters such as the choice of brick colour or mortar detail, the design of a front porch or garage and the proposed fenestration[5] are for the developer to consider and not for the LPA to seek to control. In effect, the ultimate design of a residential development is a reflection of commercial judgement. A reason for refusal based solely on such a design issue would probably constitute unreasonable behaviour for which the LPA could be liable for an award of costs unless supported by clear planning policies and adopted supplementary planning guidance (see PPG3 (2000) Paragraph 63).

Within Conservation Areas, Areas of Outstanding Natural Beauty or in proximity to listed buildings, design control can be exercised more freely. Many Conservation Areas are principally made up of residential buildings and open spaces. Some may comprise fine period-housing layouts such as the Georgian properties in Bath; others may not be so impressive, yet it is important to maintain examples of twentieth-century development, for example, 'Metroland', 1930s suburban design as found in Harrow, Middlesex (Case Study 18.2).[6] In all these varied cases the role of design control over new development is widely accepted. Many LPAs employ specialist conservation officers to advise on such matters.

Case study 18.2: Housing development within a Conservation Area

Arcadia Developments seek outline planning permission to develop a pair of detached dwellings in the Sylvan Park Conservation Area.

The Sylvan Park area was developed between 1890 and 1910 for workers' homes by a local industrialist who was influenced by the writings of Ebenezer Howard. The local planning authority designated the Conservation Area to protect the town planning layout, incorporating deep rear gardens, cul-de-sac road layout and considerable tree planting on both the street frontages and in rear gardens.

The proposal satisfies Council residential standards for existing dwellings and carparking. However, it is considered to result in an erosion of the character of the Conservation Area. The 'form' of development is alien to the original layout, and planning permission is refused because:

> The proposal introduced a form of development which is not compatible with the layout of Sylvan Park and therefore harms the character of the Conservation Area.

If the site was **not** within a Conservation Area, the proposal would be considered as an acceptable form of development.

Scale, mass and bulk

The following terms are widely used by planning professionals, yet are poorly defined:

- scale refers to the overall size of development
- bulk refers to the volume of development
- mass refers to the height and width of elevations.

These concepts should not be confused with that of design. LPAs will seek to ensure that the scale of new development[7] is harmonious with existing development, that the bulk and mass do not result in any demonstrable loss of light or overshadowing of the neighbouring properties. No national planning guidelines exist for dealing with such issues and every site will be considered on its own merits against the judgement of the individual officer. Some guidance on overshadowing is provided by the Building Research Establishment (Littlefair 1991).

Overlooking

If an LPA were to refuse planning permission on grounds of overlooking, this overlooking would need to be material, that is to say result in a *demonstrable* loss of amenity. This is usually taken to be direct overlooking between habitable rooms. A distance of 21 m window to window is a common standard in many local plan policies, considered sufficient to prevent any serious overlooking.

Highways and carparking

Highway planning criteria have perhaps exercised the greatest impact over residential housing layouts in recent years. The configuration of a road layout effectively dictates the layout of plots and overall urban design of the scheme. The principal source of guidance on this is Design Bulletin 32 (1992), which details standards for road widths, pavement widths and visibility requirements at junctions. For example, the Design Bulletin requires a 5.5 m road width to allow all vehicle types to pass each other, a 4.8 m to allow a car to pass a service vehicle and 4 m for only single file traffic (Fig. 18.5).

Design Bulletin 32 is in itself a technical document prescribing a whole set of criteria dealing with traffic and pedestrian safety. It is widely transposed into practice at the local level by highway engineers, who advise planning officers on highway issues within individual residential applications. This results in little real discretion at the local level, as issues of highway safety predominate, in an attempt to accommodate the motor car within residential layouts. Therefore, the majority of layouts contain roads of 4–5.5 m width, some with a separate footway and others with no footway (where a shared surface serves both pedestrians and vehicles).

Such road configurations will shape the plot relationships and ultimately the form of the entire scheme. Concern that adherence to this 'roads first, houses later' approach was producing a poor quality of urban design in

Demarcation between users

Shared surface

Figure 18.5 Road layouts following criteria as stated in Design Bulletin 32.

residential environments led to the government issuing *Places, Streets and Movement: A Companion Guide to Design Bulletin 32* (DETR 1998). This promoted a more imaginative approach to matters of radii and visibility to improve the layouts produced by residential developers. Carparking standards are produced by the LPA usually in the local plan/unitary development plan or in supplementary planning guidance.[8] In most cases these standards distinguish between the various housing types (flats, houses, sheltered accommodation, hostels) and between parking within the curtilage of the property or within a shared parking area. PPG3 (2000) promotes the employment of reduced parking standards to a maximum provision of no more than 1.5 off-street spaces per dwelling. Cities like Edinburgh and York have been promoting 'car-free' development in areas well served by public transport and services. People are prevented from owning private vehicles by virtue of location (city centres with no kerbside parking) and by legal agreement (signing a covenant that is linked to a Section 106 Legal Agreement).

Dwelling mix/internal standards

Although internal alterations fall outside the definition of development and therefore planning control, the size of individual rooms in new development or resulting from conversion is a material planning consideration. The most complete set of minimum internal space standards were the Parker Morris Standards, which were employed in council house building during the 1960s and 1970s (Parker Morris Committee 1961); for example, a two-storey family dwelling should incorporate 72–92 m² (770–900 ft²) floorspace. Today no such standards exist for public or private sector, although compliance with Parker Morris was always voluntary. As with design issues, the government position is that such matters should be left to the judgement of the developer and not the LPA. The mixture of dwelling types is also of importance and some LPAs, most notably in inner London, will seek to control such dwelling types to meet sectoral needs such as to maintain family housing when faced with increasing pressure to convert existing stock into one- and two-bedroom flats.

Landscaping/amenity space

In similar tone to internal space standards, government guidance on garden sizes is that such matters are best left to the developer. Many LPAs will produce amenity space standards for new residential development or conversion, setting out minimum garden depths or required communal space provision per bedroom or habitable room.

In most major residential proposals the LPA will expect some form of landscaping proposal detailing new tree and shrub planting as well as existing trees/shrubs to be retained. In some schemes the developer may propose a communal play area. The ownership and maintenance may be passed on to the LPA by means of a planning obligation.

Affordable housing

There is no single and widely accepted definition of what constitutes affordable housing. Generally, the term refers to low-cost homes to either rent or buy. Considerable legal attention has also focused upon whether the concept of affordable housing can be considered as a legitimate town planning matter. In the decision of *Mitchell* vs *Secretary of State for the Environment and the Royal Borough of Kensington and Chelsea* (1994), the Court of Appeal reversed a previous decision of the High Court and held that affordable housing does constitute a material planning consideration and local planning authorities may pursue it in local plan policy and in deciding planning applications.[9] It will usually be sought in large-scale housing projects and both new settlements and urban villages enjoy potential for a proportion of all dwellings to be low-cost housing. The majority of such housing tends to be provided by housing associations who hold and/or manage such property with funding from central and local government or by their own finance, usually raised by market loans. Such provision is necessary in both urban and rural areas. Government Circular 6/98, *Planning and Affordable Housing*, establishes that a community's need for affordable housing is a material planning consideration and lays down guidance on suitable local plan policy for such provision.

Density

Density is a crude measure of the amount of housing development on a site. However, it is measured in a very exact way as follows:

$$\frac{\text{Habitable room}}{\text{Site area in hectares}} = \text{density, expressed as habitable rooms per hectare}$$

A habitable room is a bedroom, living room, dining room or kitchen (greater than 13 m²). Site area includes road frontages of the site, which are included to half of the road width. PPG3 (2000) heralded the beginning of an attempt to substantially raise density standards to between 30–50 dwellings per hectare net.

Housing land availability

The allocation of new housing land has exposed the many political tensions that underlie the British planning system. During the 1980s many LPAs sought to appease strong local opposition to new residential development by refusing permissions and fighting and losing appeals. Planning committees in several London boroughs refused planning permission against officer recommendation that permission be granted. A consortium of major housebuilders sponsored large-scale new settlements to accommodate such demand in major proposals to reduce pressure on existing urban areas. In the 1990s the problem did not go away, with some Councils seeking to resist further housing growth. There is real concern that the latest planning guidance outlined above will stifle development. In 2000 and 2001 completions of new houses were at their lowest level since 1946 (under 150000). Commentators are even warning that the dearth of houses in England could worsen as urban sites are switched back to office use and planning restrictions begin to take effect. The new settlements initiative has enjoyed only limited success and the urban villages have emerged as a new planning innovation. The housing pressures have resulted in the creation of two new acronyms NIMBYISM[10] (**n**ot **i**n **m**y **b**ack **y**ard) and BANANA (**b**uild **a**bsolutely **n**othing **a**nywhere **n**ear **a**nyone), reflecting the political impact on the planning system following the local backlash against increasing amounts of residential development. To understand this pressure we must examine the process of housing land allocation and the issues surrounding new settlements and urban villages.

In spite of the lack of a formal system of regional planning within Britain, the allocation of housing targets is the consequence of an 'informal' system of consultation between regions and the ODPM. Each regional area incorporates its own regional conference, comprising representatives of the constituent county councils and district/boroughs. These bodies are invited to submit advice to the Secretary of State for the Environment following their own consultations.[11] The ODPM will consider these views, together with a collection of statistical forecasts dealing with population and housing demand before issuing the housing target figures for the overall region. Such guidance (in the form of a Regional Planning Guidance Note) is issued by the Secretary of State, following preparation by the relevant regional planning body and local planning authorities. This 'RPG' will establish the level of housing provision for each region, for incorporation into the relevant Development Plans or the UDPs of the constituent Local Authorities. Implementation will be monitored by the regional planning body, annually, to assess likely under- or over-provision of housing units. The government have viewed this system as a flexible one, in which housing allocations may be 'planned, monitored and managed' over many years. When regional assemblies are created and assume planning responsibilities, they will take on these duties. The individual districts are expected to conform with these *targets* when producing their local plans. The LPA is encouraged to produce allocations on a site-by-site basis, and to set out the policies against which residential applications should be considered. Some allowance should be made for windfall sites up to one hectare in area, where sites are not individually allocated but which may unexpectedly become available and which make an important contribution to housing land supply.

The production of housing targets begins at the regional level, where regional planning conferences produce policy guidance in co-operation with regional government offices. Public comment (including that of landowners and developers) is sought and the guidance is tested by an 'Examination in Public' in which participants (drawn from those responding to the participation) are invited to comment on the guidance before an independent Chair. The Chair's report may lead to revisions before the document is presented to the Deputy Prime Minister for issue. The subsequently issued regional planning guidance provides the foundation for future housing allocations. Its introduction in 1999 replaced the previous regime in which the Secretary of State himself issued guidance, following consultation with regional planning bodies. This system is more inclusive and certainly less 'top–down', with the regional bodies driving the process. When regional assemblies are established they will embrace such responsibilities. As county councils will be stripped of their structure plan powers (as proposed in the 2001 Planning Green Paper), this regional focus will be given greater significance. Regional assemblies will thus link directly with (the proposed) Local Development Frameworks as produced by local planning authorities.

The individual LPA is encouraged to produce allocations on a site-by-site basis, and to set out the policies against which residential applications should be considered. This allocation at the local level is also the subject of review and consultation by public and developers via the Development Plan process. The Development Plan forms an umbrella title, covering both structure plan and local plan or unitary development plan (applicable to unitary authorities such as the London boroughs and the authorities in most conurbations). Structure plans set out a series of broad and strategically based policies such as housing targets (carved up from regional guidance), green belts, transport strategies, mineral workings, and tourism strategies. Local plans are much more site-specific, identifying particular areas as suitable for housing, industry, retail, or other uses. Unitary development plans (UDPs) combine both strategic vision and site specific allocations. The production of such documents involves a complex series of consultation and review (see Table 18.2). In both structure and local production, objectors are given significant opportunity to influence the content of the plan, in the Examination in Public (EIP) or local/UDP inquiry, respectively. The principal distinction between these is that the EIP takes place before an independent Chair and panel (who consider all public consultation and invite certain groups to present a case before them) while the local/UDP inquiry is presided

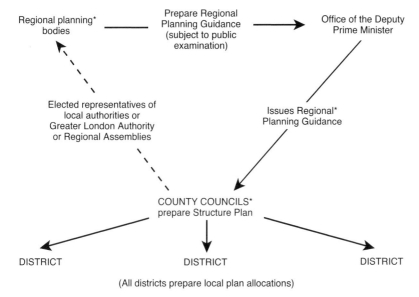

Regional planning* bodies — Prepare Regional Planning Guidance (subject to public examination) → Office of the Deputy Prime Minister

Elected representatives of local authorities or Greater London Authority or Regional Assemblies

Issues Regional* Planning Guidance

COUNTY COUNCILS* prepare Structure Plan

DISTRICT   DISTRICT   DISTRICT

(All districts prepare local plan allocations)

* This system is liable to change as Regional Assemblies take on regional planning responsibilities, which will make redundant Regional Planning Guidance issued by the Deputy Prime Minister. County councils are due to lose their planning powers and Regional Development Agencies are expected to become more involved in developing sustainable development and regeneration strategies.

Figure 18.6 Organization chart.

over by an Inspector (who considers all objections and representations made at the inquiry, with objectors enjoying the automatic right to appear before the Inspector and present a case). In both cases the EIP panel and Inspector will report back to the structure plan authority (county council) or local/UDP authority (district council or borough) with recommendations that may give rise to further modifications (and, therefore, additional opportunity for public comment). The respective planning authorities are *not* duty-bound to follow such recommendations, although if they disagree they must give reasons. The final stage involves the completed documentation being submitted for ultimate approval to the Secretary of State, who enjoys (rarely used) powers to intervene in the process and redirect the council to amend or otherwise modify the plan. Once all such stages have been completed the plan is formally 'adopted' and this carries full weight as a material consideration.

This entire process is due for a radical shake-up in the period 2003–5 as the government reviews Local Development Frameworks and seeks to streamline the adoption process by removing the inquiry component. Any democratic component in local planning policy will need to be accommodated at a much earlier stage, such as when policies are formulated.

During the production of Development Plans there is good deal of argument as to whether or not an adequate supply of land exists and whether

Table 18.2 Plan production chart

	Structure Plan	*Local plan or UDP*
Draft produced	Consultation of certain bodies to include Deputy Prime Minister and relevant LPAs	Consultation of interested groups prior to deposit (bodies determined at discretion of LPA)
Deposit	Plan published and subject to six-week period to object	Plan published and subject to six-week period to object
Revised Deposit Stage	↓	Opportunity to negotiate and amend plan to satisfy objectors
Review Stage	Examination-in-Public, with invited participants commenting on series of issues	Inquiry presided over by an Inspector, with objectors enjoying right to appear and present a case
Report Stage and Modification	EIP report issued ⟶ County council must respond on each recommendation and may make modifications (public consultation being required).	Inspector makes recommendations ⟶ LPA respond and may amend accordingly ⟶ Reasons given for failure to amend ⟶ Consultations on any modifications (review stage may be re-opened)
Secretary of State	Power to direct county council to modify*	Powers to direct LPA to modify the plan*
	ADOPTION	ADOPTION

* Usually for reasons of incompatibility with national or regional policy.

the sites identified by the LPA (in the local plan or the UDP) are economically capable of being developed and are free from any planning, physical or ownership constraints that would otherwise prevent implementation of a housing scheme. To avoid protracted disputes, the LPAs are encouraged to discuss the provision of such sites with representatives of the housebuilding industry. In the absence of a five-year supply the LPA should consider measures to increase provision, such as providing infrastructure to facilitate development or granting more planning permissions for residential development.

In 2000 the Secretary of State announced the end of 'predict and provide' in housing allocation and its replacement by a new orthodoxy, that of 'plan, monitor and manage'. This shift was subtle (although the DETR press release at the time described it as radical), as the fundamental principles of the system would remain in place. The Secretary of State told parliament: 'We have adopted a more flexible approach which will conserve green-field land and improve the quality and design of housing developments'. It was thus accepted that the process of allocation was more than an exercise in accommodating numbers of residential units (as may have been the case in past years). It was increasingly accepted by government that housing projections must be considered alongside regional economic needs and the wider environmental implications of location on, say, urban extensions or corridors. Further, regional planning bodies (which may subsequently become regional assemblies) were encouraged to monitor the level and distribution of housing supply on an annual basis. This will permit greater assessment of the success or failure of the 60 per cent target (and related matters such as improvements in density) and allow planners to reappraise strategies to make policy more pro-active in achieving sustainable development. This additional flexibility should, in future years, allow for a more accurate monitoring of policy, although it does not mean that new housing proposals on green-field sites will be any more acceptable to local residents or their elected politicians, merely that the process of allocations is more sensitive to meeting a growing sustainable agenda.

The notion of 'plan, monitor and manage' was designed to give greater encouragement to the absorption of new housing allocations within the existing urban fabric. PPG3 (2000) would establish a sequential model in which green fields would be developed only in the event that opportunities on brown land or other urban sites were exhausted. LPAs would be required to conduct urban capacity studies to assess the potential to accommodate additional housing within urban areas. The Secretary of State at the time, John Prescott, set great store by this new initiative, employing it to lower the figures for allocating green-field housing in South East England by 2020. John Prescott rejected the conclusions of the South East Regional Planning EIP (chaired by Professor Stephen Crow), which had concluded that 1.1 million new homes should be accommodated in the South East outside London (Rest of South East and ROSE). Prescott criticized this figure for its rigid adherence to a predict-and-provide approach without sufficient regard to urban capacity and sustainable growth. While the Secretary of State would countenance a number of growth areas (Milton Keynes, Ashford and Stansted) he was resolute that brown-field targets would have to be satisfied concluding 'I am determined that we should take as little green-field land as is necessary to provide the new homes that will be needed. Compared with Professor Crow, our proposals will save 42 square miles of countryside – enough to build a city the size of Manchester'. (Statement made to Parliament on 7 March 2000.)

The confrontation over housing allocations produced criticisms of the system. Housebuilders criticized some counties for seeking to 'cap' housing growth, some lobby groups criticized the planning system for seeking to restrict supply, thereby increasing the price of housing land and restricting access to the housing market by some groups, whereas others such as the CPRE criticized the system for not exercising enough control to prevent the loss of agricultural land.

The current system of land allocation involves an element of consultation but is largely a 'top-down' process as the ODPM issues target guidelines to counties, and counties allocate to districts (Case Study 18.3). At the local level the districts must allocate sites to provide a five-year supply. Demand for new housing units will continue to grow.[12] Any failure to meet the

Case study 18.3: Housing land availability in the South East region

The many political problems surrounding housing allocation within England are most polarized in the South East area. SERPLAN is the regional conference for the 12 South East counties* and 32 London boroughs. Looking at population and household trends (including a significant increase in households due to demographic trends such as more young people leaving home and a greater lifespan) SERPLAN predicted that 730 000 additional dwellings would be required between 1991 and 2001. Following consultation, the DoE pushed the projection downwards to a figure of 570 000 in February 1989. This figure was then divided among the counties, with an allowance made for London. These target agreements came at the end of the building boom of the 1980s with the considerable pressures to build at increased densities on housing land. Local opposition was reflected by district and county councillors and whether or not this was a NIMBY or BANANA reaction, the planners were facing increasing hostility to new housing allocation. The Council for the Protection of Rural England reported that since 1945 the urban area of the South East has grown by almost twice as much as any other region. During this period 188 000 ha of land have been developed for housing, commerce, industry and roads.[†]

Hampshire and Berkshire in particular have sought to confront their housing allocations figures by seeking lower targets. Berkshire proposed 37 000 new dwellings against a DoE target of 40 000. Berkshire had experienced considerable urbanization since the mid-1960s and the county's strategy was to slow this urbanization by restricting both new housing and industry.

In Hampshire the County proposed 58 000 dwellings between 1991 and 2001 against a DoE target of 66 500 dwellings. Such battles continued into the structure plan adoption process as developers sought to challenge and oppose such downward trends. Ironically, the outcome in Berkshire was that the structure plan panel, responsible for considering objections to the new housing policy, recommended a total of 48 000 new dwellings over the period 1991–2006, 8000 more than the DoE target figure.

* Hertfordshire, Bedfordshire, Kent, West Sussex, East Sussex, Surrey, Hampshire, Oxfordshire, Berkshire, Buckinghamshire, Essex and the Isle of Wight, represented by the London Planning Advisory Committee.
[†] Sinclair (1992).

regional targets will result in increasing pressure on the housing market with consequences for price, density and architectural quality. The question now is whether new initiatives to the existing allocation and implementation of housing have to be found. Two important policy initiatives seeking to provide new housing land have emerged from the 1980s and 1990s in the form of new settlements and urban villages.

New settlements

A new settlement is a private sector sponsored new town of between 2000 and 10000 dwellings.

The concept of building new communities away from existing urban areas is not a new phenomenon. The very origins of the British town planning movement and profession can be traced back to 1898, when Ebenezer Howard first published his ideas on the 'Garden City'. Letchworth and Welwyn Garden City were constructed on this model.

The New Towns Act of 1946 introduced a wave of post-war new towns to accommodate overspill housing from Britain's major conurbations. Between 1946 and 1950 a first wave of 14 such new towns were designated in England and Wales, there was one further designation between 1951 and 1961, and then in a second wave an additional 14 between 1961 and 1970. The final designations in the late 1960s included Milton Keynes (1967), Warrington (1968) and Central Lancashire (Leyland) in 1970. The post-war new town Policy was combined with a planned expansion of existing country towns around London during the 1950s and 1960s.

In 1985 a group of major housebuilders[13] formed Consortium Developments Limited (CDL) to submit planning applications for private-sector sponsored new communities or new settlements on several sites. The idea was seen by its promoters as preferable to the town extensions or infilling of existing settlements. This approach permitted a fresh start, with a planned integration of residential, industry–employment, retail and educational uses. New settlements would accommodate housing growth and reduce the pressure for new housing, which had been directed to town cramming within existing urban areas. The concept was in size many ways closer to the Garden City ideas of Ebenezer Howard than the post-war new towns, because it was sponsored by the private and not the public sector. The proposed size of settlement would be much smaller than Howard's population of 30 000 in each Garden City or 250 000 in the polycentric social city. CDL proposed a population of around 10 000 in each new settlement. The idea received favourable, if qualified support, among the planning community, notably the Town and Country Planning Association, an organization founded by Ebenezer Howard.[14] This support expressed a desire that such new settlements must be used to provide a form of balanced development in a good environment, taking pressure away from existing towns and villages and protecting existing countryside. Sites should be carefully chosen to be away from high-grade land while being integrated with existing transport infrastructure (Hall 1989).

It follows that such a new settlement would require careful thought and would be most effectively considered by sponsorship through the development plan process. Ironically, the most significant feature surrounding the early submissions of both CDL and non-CDL sponsored new settlements was that of conflict and not harmony with the planning system.

The three most prominent examples are:

- *Tillingham Hall, Essex.* Proposed 5000 dwellings. Refused planning permission and dismissed on appeal 1988 because of location within Metropolitan Green Belt.
- *Stone Bassett, Oxford (alongside Junction 7 of the M40).* Proposed 6000 dwellings. Refused planning permission and dismissed on appeal, 1990. The Inspector considered that the siting of a new settlement here would

result in an adverse impact on the character of this rural area and create growth and traffic problems. The proposal also conflicted with development plan policies seeking restraint in this part of the county, and no shortage of housing land existed to justify an exception. An application for an award of costs against CDL for unreasonable pursuit of appeal (i.e. no chance of success) was recommended by the Inspector but not accepted by the Secretary of State. This gave a signal to CDL that although such appeals may be dismissed, the government did not consider it unreasonable to pursue the matter to a Public Inquiry.

* *Foxley Wood, Hampshire.* Proposed 4800 dwellings. Refused planning permission and dismissed on appeal in 1989 following a change of Secretary of State for the Environment.

During 1990, two other non-CDL-sponsored new settlement proposals were rejected: at Great Lea near Reading (Speyhawk Developers) and Wymeswold Airfield in Leicestershire (Costain Homes). In all of these cases the planning authorities objected on the grounds of the significant visual impact of the proposals alongside conflict with existing development plan policies.

In both the Foxley Wood and the Stone Bassett decision letters, the government Inspectors acknowledged the harm caused to the character of existing urban areas by past policies of peripheral expansion and infilling. However, these were considered against and outweighed by ecological and environmental harm caused by such large-scale development in these locations. The Foxley Wood Inspector concluded:

> The major cost of the proposed development would be the loss of a significant ecological interest and the urbanization of an attractive rural area of value for its recreational opportunities . . .

As with such major development proposals, both Stone Bassett and Foxley Wood appeals were decided by the Secretary of State for the Environment, with the Inspector's report forming a recommendation. In Stone Bassett the Secretary of State agreed with the Inspector and dismissed the appeal. However, in Foxley Wood the Secretary of State, Nicholas Ridley, although agreeing with the Inspector's identification of the key issues, disagreed with the ultimate *balance* between environmental protection issues and housing need. Ridley considered that Foxley Wood provided an opportunity for much-needed housing provision within north-east Hampshire, about 42 per cent of all units anticipated being provided within the county between 1991 and 2001.[15] This would relieve housing pressure within the existing urban areas of Hampshire and provide for a 'planned' environment with social and physical infrastructure provision built into the proposal. Ridley announced that he was 'minded to allow' the appeal, but would await further comments on the matter from all parties. This provoked a mobilization of local opposition to the proposal in what was a solidly Conservative-supporting area of South East England. Such political opposition could not fail to reverberate within a Conservative government. A

Cabinet reshuffle during the autumn resulted in Nicholas Ridley being replaced by Christopher Patten. One of Christopher Patten's first decisions at the DoE came in October 1989 when he announced that he was 'minded' to accept the Inspector's recommendation and to dismiss the appeal. Following a further round of comments by parties to the appeal, it was dismissed later that year.

In reflecting upon the outcomes of Foxley Wood, Stone Bassett and Tillingham Hall, it is important to distinguish between political and town planning issues:

- *Political issues.* The importance of these cannot be overestimated. Foxley Wood and Stone Bassett were sited within areas of strong Conservative support. By allowing both proposals, a Conservative Secretary of State would run the risk of eroding local political support.
- *Town planning issues.* None of these proposals were sponsored within the development plan process. They were the subject of speculative planning applications, which were refused by the local planning authority and then considered at appeal. Tillingham Hall was located in green belt and contrary to government and local policy. Foxley Wood adjoined a Site of Special Scientific Interest, that would be affected by the proximity of such a large-scale development. Any new settlement proposal will result in significant impact on the local environment by affecting the highway network and local landscape. The significant outcome from this early wave of proposals was that such major development could be far more acceptably dealt with within the town planning system by the promotion within and agreement with the county and district Councils instead of by means of speculative applications and appeals. By 1992 184 new settlements had been proposed, with 60 of them in the South East resulting in a potential for 175 000 new homes if all the schemes had received planning permission.

At the Foxley Wood Inquiry, Hart District Council, the local planning authority for the application site made submissions to the effect that ad hoc appeals do not provide the best process within which to deal with issues of such strategic importance. Government planning policy has supported such a stance:

> The need to respect local preference means that specific proposals for New Settlements should normally only be promoted through the district wide local plan or UDP . . . local plan policies for New Settlements should address the need for social educational and community facilities and for a wide variety of house types including an element of affordable housing provision. The opportunity to start a New Settlement will be rare and should not be wasted.[16]

Despite such government policy support and the evident desire for such proposals to be the product of liaison between housebuilders and Councils, the subsequent story after 1990 only witnessed a limited improvement in the success of such proposals gaining planning permission.

Table 18.3 New settlements with planning permission

New settlement success	Details
Chafford Hundred, Grays (Essex)	5000 dwellings and commercial community buildings, 18-hole golf course and built on 234 ha (575 acres) of former chalk quarries
New Ash Green (Kent)	2000 dwellings on 174 ha (430 acres)
Chelmer Village, Chelmsford (Essex)	2500 dwellings and a retail park of 142 ha (350 acres) of land
Church Langley, Chelmsford (Essex)	3500 dwellings on 162 ha (400 acres)
Great Notley Garden Village, Braintree (Essex)	2000 dwellings, business park, shops, hotel and a country park on a former US Air Force Hospital
Dickens Heath, Solihull (West Midlands)	1100 dwellings on 49 ha (120 acres)
Peterborough Southern Township (Cambridgeshire)	5200 homes, retail centre and business park on 809 ha (2000 acres) of former brick claypits
Kettleby Magna, Melton Mowbray (Leicestershire)	1000 dwellings on former airfield
Martlesham Heath (Suffolk)	1200 dwellings
Bradley Stoke, Bristol	3500 dwellings
Haydonwick Farm, Swindon	3380 dwellings

New settlement success

In spite of a whole host of setbacks for the promotion of new settlements, both through planning appeals and by working within development plan and review, the concept has enjoyed some success (Table 18.3). Some schemes have received planning permission from the local planning authority and without the use of 'call-in' procedure by the Secretary of State.

Government support for the concept of new settlements remained luke-warm during the late 1980s and early 1990s. Despite support for the idea in PPG3 (2000) Paragraphs 72–5 and various ministerial pronouncements on the issue[17] (Case Study 18.4) the identification of such sites is not easy. A new settlement will occupy some 243 ha (600 acres) of land yet must be separated from existing settlements, avoid protected land and be located within an area of housing need, which, like the South East and West Midlands, is already heavily developed (Case Study 18.5). This, combined with local objections and the associated political problems, means that the progress of new settlements as an alternative to town cramming is hampered by a cocktail of political and planning problems that limit the role it will play in satisfying

Case study 18.4: New settlements and development plan promotion –
Cambridgeshire County Council

Cambridgeshire County Council incorporated the allocation of two new settlements within County structure plan policy. Planning professionals felt it was more a case of 'where' the new settlement should be located as opposed to 'if' a new settlement would be located.* A new settlement proposal also received support from the East Anglian Regional Planning Conference. Developers were understandably encouraged by this stance and three schemes were proposed in the corridor of land straddled by the A10 road and a further seven were proposed in the corridor of land straddled by the A45 road. Consideration of these matters was called in by the Secretary of State who appointed an Inspector to hear evidence and report back on the options. The Inspector found that one site on the A45 was acceptable but could not accept any on the A10 corridor. The Secretary of State did not agree with the Inspector's findings on the recommended scheme and rejected the proposal on the grounds that the business park component within the scheme was larger than that envisaged in the appropriate local plan. All proposals were subsequently rejected.

* Nigel Moor, *Housebuilder* (September 1990: 24).

Case study 18.5: New settlements and development plan promotion: Micheldever
in Hampshire

This new settlement, Micheldever Station Market Town of 5000 dwellings was as with Cambridgeshire A10 and A45 schemes promoted through the process of structure plan review, but unlike the Cambridge proposals the County Council (Hampshire) opposed the Micheldever proposal set against their own attempts to reduce housing land availability targets from 66 500 (in SERPLAN guidance) to 58 000. Eagle Star Properties, who owned the site, argued that not only is the county's lower figure inadequate to satisfy housing demand, but also that new settlements have distinct advantages over the alternatives of housing provision: relieving pressure on existing communities, minimizing the environmental impact of development, and providing increased access to affordable housing.*

* Micheldever Station Market Town. Representations by Eagle Star Properties 1993, to Hampshire County Structure Plan Review.

housing provision to the year 2008. Research proposed a major recommendation that larger-scale new settlements (up to 6000 or even 10 000 dwellings) will be required in future years to provide one of the most desirable forms of urban development.

Summary: New settlements

Problems/disadvantages	Benefits/advantages
'NIMBYISM' problems of considerable local opposition.	Comprehensive and co-ordinated way of providing for new housing with necessary infrastructure and diverting pressure for 'town cramming' away from existing urban areas or land with special value (AONB, SSSI or high-grade agricultural land).
Site assembly – requires some 234 ha (600 acres) of land, which is unlikely to be within one ownership.	Ability to provide for social housing and other forms of planning gain within/adjoining the new settlement.
Difficulty in obtaining planning permission by either speculative planning application (Tillingham Hall, Stone Bassett or Foxley Wood) or by promotion through the structure/local plan review process (A10 and A45 Cambridgeshire). Smaller new settlements (around 2000–3000 dwellings) or on brown land stand the best chances of gaining permission.	The potential to work with the planning system as Councils seek to promote the concept in their planning policy as they realize the benefits of new settlements.
Secretary of State for the Environment faced with problems of local feeling when considering considering various Inspectors' recommendations, however . . .	Government support for the idea has been published in planning policy advice (PPG3).

Urban villages

An urban village is a mixed-use mixed-ownership urban development based on public–private sector co-operation and covering about 2000 acres.

(Stubbs)

I am hoping we can encourage the development of urban villages in order to reintroduce human scale, intimacy and vibrant street life. These factors can help to restore to people their sense of belonging and pride in their own particular surroundings.

(HRH The Prince of Wales 1989)

There is already a move away from development monoculture: many developers, architects and planners have been promoting schemes both new-build and refurbishment, which integrate a number of uses into attractive local environments. There is evidence that these can be more stable and attractive and therefore in the longer term a better investment.

(Urban Villages Forum 1992)

In 1989 Prince Charles expressed his desire for both investigation and promotion into the concept of planned mixed-use and mixed-tenure developments that would enhance the quality of life for those people who lived and worked in them as well as creating a form of sustainable development. Late in the same year, the Urban Villages Forum was formed to promote the idea. The Forum was an amalgamation of various property-related professions who believed that a new approach was required when building urban areas. This new approach formed a reaction against many forms of post-war urban planning in which planners zoned separate areas for separate uses and developers built mass-volume housing estates on the edge of towns and offices in the centre. The housing lacked any sense of community or urban design and at night the town centres were 'dead', devoid of any life or activity. The commuting between the two resulted in a waste of resources. What was needed was a revitalized form of housing and employment land use to bring life back to cities, and new large-scale housing proposals.

The key features of the urban village are:

- Mixed-use buildings and areas comprising housing, small businesses, shops and social amenities. Although one of the key objectives is to provide housing, it is considered important that an urban village maintains a degree of 'community' in which people may live and work in the same area.
- Mixed ownership with rented and owner-occupied housing.
- A high standard of urban design to enhance the public spaces and quality of development.
- A total population of between 3000 and 5000 residents.
- A form of development suitable for redevelopment within existing urban areas, but also possible for new-build schemes on greenfield-sites. There is some overlap with new settlements because a new settlement could incorporate these urban village features.

A considerable obstacle to this initiative has been that traditionally financial institutions have been reluctant to lend money on buildings that involve a mix of uses on different floors, as this increases the cost of managing the investment and may reduce the future value of the building. For example, a building split into general office and residential results in separate tenants with exclusive tenancy terms and conditions. The letting of the office may be adversely affected by flats above, as occupiers perceive the flats as creating problems of security. This in turn may suppress the value of the offices and therefore the investment potential resulting from the scheme.

How to implement an urban village

The urban villages concept represents a challenge to the land use and development orthodoxy of recent years. This challenge during the 1990s and into the new century has manifested itself in both seeking to change perceptions of property development and by the implementation of schemes that both foster interest and demonstrate the commercial success of the idea.

Role of the planning system

The implementation of an urban village will be best served through its promotion within the existing development plan and development control system. Local plans should designate areas suitable for such development, detailing the necessary planning obligations or public sector contributions and should also detail the scale of expected development. Such areas should incorporate 40–80 ha (100–200 acres) in an area and a combined resident and working population of 3000–5000. Suitable locations would include brown land (vacant inner-city land), suburban or edge-of-town sites or greenfield sites. To engender social and economic integration, the urban village promoter[18] will be encouraged to provide not just a balance of uses but also a variety of housing tenures[19] and commercial freehold and leasehold tenures (Urban Villages Forum 1994, Lichfield 1995).

The urban village concept pushes the planning system towards the greater consideration of creating mixed-use urban neighbourhoods. This will require a rethink of some planning policy standards that prescribe requirements for parking and amenity space. The rigid application of such policies will inhibit the flexibility necessary to create an urban village. Further, as planners move away from the 'development monoculture' of single-use areas and towards mixed-use areas or buildings, a re-awakening of ideas and training will be required. Lord Rogers, in the *Urban Task Force Report* (1999) endorsed greater interdisciplinary training within the course content of university Built Environment courses, to promote greater awareness of the problems to be tackled to create sustainability across architecture, planning and land management disciplines.

Implementation of ideas

Some early examples of urban villages provide an encouraging vision for the further employment of this idea to provide housing and deliver environmental quality.

• *Crown Street, Glasgow: the redevelopment of a cleared 16 ha (40 acre) site in Glasgow formerly occupied by a 1960s high-rise housing estate.* A masterplan was devised, which established layout mix of unit types, including family accommodation and with a split of 75 per cent owner occupation and 25 per cent rented, elevational treatment and creation of a community trust to manage the development. The form of development recreates traditional Scottish tenement living with four storeys incorporating residential accommodation and shops, workshops and studios on the ground floor. Private amenity space would be created within the block. In this case the urban village promoter was a combination of housing developers: City Council, Glasgow Development Agency and a housing association.

- *Poundbury, Dorchester, Dorset: the new development of a 162 ha (400 acre) greenfield extension to the west of Dorchester on land owned by the Duchy of Cornwall.* The masterplan initially devised by Leon Krier involves an urban form with a medium-density layout with houses (including 20 per cent rented accommodation), offices, shops and industrial space. This mixed-use urban environment has been planned for implementation over many stages, with a development period stretching from 1994 to 2019. Work on the first phase of 61 houses was started in 1994.

- *Hulme, Manchester: the redevelopment of 1 km² of 1960s eight-storey deck-accessed concrete housing blocks.* Since construction in the early 1970s it has become notorious for its social, economic and health problems, irrespective of the inhuman architecture and planning of the estate.

   Redevelopment work began in 1992, involving the demolition of the housing blocks and the rebuilding of the area employing the principles of mixed-use high-density urban form of redevelopment with a strong element of urban design. The masterplan for redevelopment was a product of public consultation. It emphasizes the fact that merely rebuilding the physical form of an estate such as Hulme is not sufficient; attention is required to create a feeling of community. The Hulme regeneration involves a mix of uses within buildings and areas, as well as a mix of housing tenure and a projected population sufficient to sustain local school, businesses and community facilities into the longer term. The promoter incorporated both City Council, private housebuilder and housing association.

   By 2002 the project was substantially completed. Attention in Manchester would turn to a similar approach being adopted for a vast swathe of derelict land to the east of the city centre (partially regenerated by sites used for the 2002 Commonwealth Games) and areas like Ancoats, blighted by urban decay but incorporating an array of architecturally impressive yet derelict listed buildings.

- *Brindleyplace, Birmingham: a much-lauded Birmingham City Centre mixed use scheme comprising 6.88 hectares of offices, retail, leisure and residential uses.* The scheme incorporates a strong urban design element with the creation of public spaces linking the development to existing city and canal-side waterfront locations. The success (both commercial and physical) of Brindleyplace has spurred on other mixed-use projects in the city (most notably Birmingham Mailbox, the redevelopment of a former Royal Mail Sorting Office into hotel, retail, leisure and residential uses). A new pedestrian street was carved through the centre of the building and permeability further enhanced by linking the development to a new canal pedestrian footbridge.

- *Gallions Reach, Woolwich: redevelopment of a formerly vacant, and before that contaminated, site at Woolwich Arsenal, following a land reclamation project funded by English Partnership between 1997 and 2001.* Remediation of contaminated soil was completed on-site by means of a newly

Summary: Urban villages

Problems/disadvantages	Benefits/advantages
Traditional reluctance by funding institutions to become involved in mixed-use buildings.	Important and significant critique of monoculture of post-war British development, which focuses attention on a change in our approach to urban development and the funding of that development.
Only a few examples implemented during the early 1990s resulting in a small overall contribution to housing land supply.	Creation of a popular 'band-wagon' following the successful implementation (financial, social and environmental) of key schemes.
Important mechanism in recreating communities in depressed inner cities.	Few NIMBY problems associated with brownland schemes.
Increased perception of the concept and promotion among the planning community.	

developed soil washing technology. A spatial masterplan was developed on the lines of mixed uses and urban densities linked by Urban Design Strategies. The project will be implemented in stages from 2001 onwards and when completed will comprise around 700 homes, light industrial workshops, a commercial leisure centre, a refurbished Listed Building (for the Royal Artillery Museum), an ecological corridor of open space, and an 'eco-park' of energy-efficient houses. The whole project epitomizes the 'retrofit' approach of the Urban Task Force by linking to existing areas and adding around 3500 new residents to support existing services and enhance new ones. The site is close to central London but has been historically isolated by poor public transport linkages. This scheme brings the necessary economic power to justify better transport networks (a link to the Docklands Light Railway was proposed) and so benefit the wider area in which the project is located.

These examples incorporate ideas and concepts drawn from the increasing desire among property professionals to integrate social and economy activity when recreating (as in Hulme) or building afresh (as in Poundbury). The most significant problems facing urban villages as a means of satisfactory new housing targets are that, by 2000, the total number of units provided is small. The most tangible benefit is the attempt to refocus ideas towards the quality of urban environment.

The renaissance in city living

This chapter on residential development would not be complete without mention of the surge in residential development activity in our city centres over the last decade. City-centre living has enjoyed a massive increase in popularity and many developers have enjoyed a relatively smooth and profitable ride on its coat tails. In Manchester, for example, it is estimated that by 2005, 20 000 people will live in the city compared with just 1000 in 1990 (according to Manchester City Council). Encouraged by many LPAs as a means of helping to regenerate city centres, residential development and the concurrent focus on enhancing retail and leisure facilities has created a significant market. However, some are starting to argue that the undersupply of stock that pushed prices up when the trend for city centre living took hold has now been addressed.

Conclusions

Both new settlements and urban villages should not be viewed as mutually exclusive forms of development. It is conceivable that a new settlement could be developed on the principles of an urban village as promoted by the Urban Villages Forum. Both initiatives have predecessors in planning history, notably the works of Ebenezer Howard and the Garden City movement. The problem of housing demand exceeding supply will remain well into the next century because of the rising number of households. It appears doubtful that the targets for the South East will be satisfied and the planning system will play its part in controlling supply and increasing the value of land with residential permission. However, greater attention than in previous decades is being focused upon the residential quality of new environments. New settlements and urban villages will hopefully improve the quality of life for their inhabitants by utilizing the newly found enthusiasm for the quality design of urban spaces and reacting against the excessive separation of land uses in previous new town developments of the 1950s and 1960s. It is important that both new settlements and urban villages do create the quality of environment that they have set out to achieve and do not become mis-represented as mere marketing catch-phrases to conceal more volume housebuilding for the private sector. Planners and developers have become increasingly aware that new-build housing must form part of a wider mixed-use/mixed-ownership strategy to create a high-quality environment with a social and economic mix that fosters a sense of place or community among its inhabitants.

The initiatives of the Urban Villages Forum are to be welcomed, especially in their attempts to tackle negative perceptions regarding the funding of such projects. Yet, it is important that the idea is widely propagated and, more significantly, that it is widely implemented, otherwise the concept of the urban village will become just another 'good idea' in theory, marginalized in practice to a few inner-city redevelopment schemes or novel experiments with famous patronage, such as in Poundbury. By 2008 the urban village will be the key driver in focusing new housing in existing urban areas and pro-moting an urban renaissance.

Notes

1 Urban planning and real estate development: the context

1 *Report on the Sanitary Condition of the Labouring Population of Great Britain* (1842).
2 Published as *To-morrow: A Peaceful Path to Real Reform* and re-issued in 1902 as *Garden Cities of To-morrow*.
3 Strictly, this was the first planning legislation applied nationally with the very first such legislation dealing with 'town planning' being the Hampstead Garden Suburb Planning Act, passed in 1906.
4 A concept defined further in Chapter 6 'Planning gain and planning obligations'.

2 Policy and implementation of urban planning

1 This date is important in determining what is 'original', so that, when calculating permitted development tolerances, anything built before the appointed day is original and therefore not considered to be an extension.
2 Established in May 2002 and taking responsibility for policy areas from both the former Department for Transport, Local Government and the Regions and the Cabinet Office. A new and separate Department for Transport was also created.
3 A close interaction between transport and land use is guaranteed by the creation of regional transport strategies (linking with Regional Planning Guidance) and Local Transport Plans (linking with Development Plans). For more detail see PPG12: Development Plans (DETR 1999b) Chapter 5, which establishes that . . . 'the ultimate aim is to ensure that the overall planning and transport strategies are consistent . . . and integrated with one another'.
4 In Scottish regional councils (Borders, Dumfries, Highlands), all planning functions are implemented at regional level. No district authorities exist in the Island Regional Authorities, so all planning is undertaken by the island councils.
5 Non-elected Regional Chambers were established in eight English Regions in 2000. In 2002 a White Paper was published that reiterated a government commitment to establish elected regional assemblies in England within two or three years.
6 Section 54A of the Town and Country Planning Act 1990. Refer to the section entitled 'The decision-maker's duty'.
7 This legislation has been enacted across England, Wales and Scotland.
8 The panel is appointed by the Secretary of State and consists usually of three independent experts, usually one each from the Planning Inspectorate, the Office of the Deputy Prime Minister and an experienced planning solicitor or barrister. The panel tends to adopt the style of probing discussion of issues rather than a 'forensic' inquiry into the substance of objections raised. For more depth see Sections 31–35C of TCPA 1990 and commentary in Grant (2003).
9 'Shaping the nation', editorial opinion in *Estates Gazette*, 14 November 1992.

10 For example, Woking Borough Council in 1992 published a series of targets dealing with such matters as responding to letters and dealing with pre-application advice.

11 See the report on the practice adopted by Newbury planners in *Planning*, 12 February 1993.

12 Under provision of the General Development Procedure Order, Article 20, the LPA must give notice of a decision on a planning application within eight weeks of receipt. This period may be extended by written agreement between both parties. Office of the Deputy Prime Minister target figures aim for 80 per cent of all applications to be decided within this period. Adherence to this target is subject to wide fluctuations across the country, with some LPAs as low as 35 per cent within eight weeks while others exceed 80 per cent.

13 So that targets are separated for major commercial/industrial applications, minor commercial/industrial applications and all other applications.

14 Similar to Simplified Planning Zones of the 1980s, where specific types of development related to business use are exempt from planning permission.

15 The Planning and Local Government pages of The Office of the Deputy Prime Minister http://www.planning.odpm.gov.uk

16 Nick Raynsford, quoted in DTLR News Release 2002/0146, 8 April 2002.

17 See the section beginning the 'definition of development' in the following chapter.

18 To avoid any uncertainty regarding whether permission is required, an application can be made for a Certificate of Lawfulness of Existing or Proposed Use or Development; see section on enforcement in the next chapter.

19 See below for a discussion of material considerations.

20 Guidelines on planning conditions can be found in DoE Circular 11/95: *The use of conditions in planning permissions*, or in Scottish Office Circular 18/86 or Welsh Office 35/95.

21 See DoE Circular 15/92, *Publicity for planning applications*.

22 Introduced by the Planning and Compensation Act 1991, in which responsibility for publishing all planning applications was imposed on LPAs.

23 The LPA may impose conditions on a planning permission 'as they think fit'. Such planning conditions will need to be related to land-use planning as well as the development being permitted. In all cases they must be reasonable. Government guidance on the use of such conditions is contained in DoE Circular advice, which states that all conditions must be necessary, relevant to planning, relevant to 'the development' enforceable, precise and reasonable. Further Guidance on Planning conditions can be found in Circular 11/95, *The use of conditions in planning permissions*.

24 DoE Circular 8/93, *Award of costs incurred in planning and other proceedings* (para. 9 of Annex 3) EGCS 9 and *Regina* vs *Selby District Council, ex parte Oxton Farm* (1997) ECGS 60.

25 Contained in DoE Circular 14/85, *Development and employment*, which was cancelled in 1990.

26 See *Enfield London Borough Council* vs *Secretary of State for the Environment* (1975), JPL 155, and *Chelmsford Borough Council* vs *Secretary of State for the Environment and Halifax Building Society* (1985) JPL 555.

27 For some case law on this refer to *St Albans District Council* vs *Secretary of State for the Environment* [1993] PLR 88 and *Jones* vs *Secretary of State for the Environment* (1997).

28 See *Stringer and Minister of Housing and Local Government* (1970) 1 WLR 1281 and comments of Justice Cooke.

29 Legal references are cited as follows:
P&CR: Property, Planning and Compensation Reports
JPL: Journal of Planning and Environment Law
All ER: All England Law Reports
WLR: Weekly Law Reports
PLR: Planning Law Reports

AC: Appeal Cases

EGCS: *Estates Gazette* Case Summary

30 To check the current list of PPGs reference should be made to The Encyclopaedia of Planning Law and Practice (Grant 2003) and to the website of The Office of the Deputy Prime Minister at www.planning.odpm.gov.uk/ppg/index. The Green Paper of 2001 indicated that such policy statements were too prescriptive and tended to overburden the system with detail. All PPGs would be reviewed with an initial focus on a number of key ones, including PPG1 which provides headline guidance for the system. They will become PPSs.

31 Section 220 of the Town and Country Planning Act 1990 and Town and Country Planning (Control of Advertisements) Regulations 1995. Also see PPG19 (1992), *Outdoor advertising control*, and DoE Circular 5/92, *Town and country planning* (Control of Advertisement) Regulations 1992.

32 Section 336 of the Town and Country Planning Act 1990.

33 Ombudsman powers are found in the Local Government Act (1974: part III).

34 Annual statistics published by the Ombudsman reveal that housing issues constitute the largest number of complaints at 35–40 per cent, with planning second at 20–25 per cent of all complaints.

35 In the remaining cases the Ombudsman found no maladministration had occurred, or that there was maladministration with no injustice, or that the investigation had been discontinued.

36 See Chapter 9, Urban Renaissance.

37 See detailed section on the Ombudsman in this chapter.

38 For example, officers who are members of the Royal Town Planning Institute are bound by a code of professional conduct that requires members to 'impartially exercise their independent professional judgement'.

39 Each council, since May 2002, must publish its own code of conduct covering the behaviour of elected members and officers and the creation of a Standards Committee for each authority.

40 Part III of the Local Government Act 2000.

41 *Report of an Independent Inquiry into Certain Planning Related Issues in Bassetlaw to the Bassetlaw District Council* (1996).

42 Commentary on Nolan Third Report in 'Current Topics', *Journal of Planning and Environment Law* (1997), September, p. 795.

43 Local Government Act 1999.

44 SI 1999/3251 Local Government England Local Government Wales: The Local Government (Best Value) Performance Plans and Reviews Order 1999.

45 Circular 10/99 Local Government Act 1999: Part I Best Value.

3 Town planning law and regulation

 1 Agriculture is defined by Section 336(1) of the TCPA 1990 as including horti-culture, fruit and seed growing, dairy farming, market gardening, grazing land, meadow land and nursery land.

 2 Definition provided in Section 290, Town and Country Planning (Minerals) Regulations 1971. Also see Minerals Planning Guidance Notes (MPGs), Town and Country Planning (Minerals) Act 1981 and Schedule 14 of the Environment Act 1995.

 3 *Cambridge City Council* vs *Secretary of State for the Environment and Another* [1991] *JPL* 428. Demolition control is described by Sir Desmond Heap (1991) as 'a ghost which haunted planning law. The time has now come for the ghost to be laid to rest' (p. 114).

 4 Please refer to sections on Listed Buildings and Conservation Area in Chapter 7.

 5 For more guidance, see the *Town and country planning (demolition – description of buildings) Direction* 1995 and DoE Circular *Guidance on planning controls over demolition*.

6 *Burdle* vs *Secretary of State for the Environment* [1972] 1 WLR 1207.
7 This is not to be confused with the Town and Country Planning (General Development Procedure) Order 1995 (SI 419), which deals with procedural matters relating to the submission of a planning application, e.g. it establishes the eight-week period for the determination of an application.
8 Served under Article 4(1) of the Town and Country Planning (General Permitted Development) Order 1995.
9 DoE Circular 13/87 *Change of use of buildings and other land: town and country planning (Use Classes) Order* 1987.
10 Such breaches of planning control are established by Section 171A of the TCPA 1990.
11 Interest in Land means a legal or equitable interest such as ownership or the grant of a tenancy or lease. A PCN may also be served on an occupier who is carrying out operations or uses such as a builder. Refer to subsections 171C and D of the TCPA 1990.
12 This appeal must be made against one or more of seven specific grounds. Reference should be made to Section 174(2) of the TCPA 1990.
13 See Chapter 4.
14 Served under Section 183 of the TCPA 1990. Certain activities cannot be prohibited by a stop notice, namely use of a building as a dwelling, or to stop operational development that has been carried out for a period exceeding four years.
15 Served under Section 187A of the TCPA 1990.
16 Refer to subsections 191 and 192 of the TCPA 1990.
17 I.e. the four-year immunity does not start to run until the operational development has been largely finished.
18 Similar powers were previously available under the Local Government Act 1972 but were introduced specifically to town planning by this section. Section 3 of the Planning and Compensation Act 1991 introduced a new section, 187B, into the TCPA 1990.

4 Planning appeals

1 Refer to the judgement of Justice Forbes in *Seddon Properties Ltd* vs *Secretary of State for the Environment* (1978), legal reference [1978] JPL 835, in which it was established that the courts when exercising Statutory Review were not concerned with matters of planning merit but instead with the question of legality in decision-making.
2 See the Planning Inspectorate *Annual report and accounts* for a yearly update. This document is published towards the end of each year in question.
3 Refer to the judgement of David Widdicombe QC in *Pound Stretcher Ltd* vs *Secretary of State for the Environment* (1988), legal reference 3 PLR 69.
4 Sir Frank Layfield in *Barnet Meeting Room Trust* vs *Secretary of State for the Environment*, legal reference 3 PLR 21.
5 Legal reference 65 P&CR (1992) 137–147.
6 Following recommendations of W. S. Atkins (planning consultants), December 1993, to the Planning Inspectorate (1993b).
7 Usually contained in Statutory Instruments, e.g. the Town and Country Planning (Appeals) (Written Representations Procedure) Regulations 2000 (SI 1628), the Town and Country Planning (Hearings Procedure) (England) Rules 2000 (SI 1626), the Town and Country Planning (Inquiries Procedure) (England) Rules 2000 (SI 1624), and the Town and Country Planning Appeals (Determination by Inspectors) (Inquiries Procedure) (England) Rules 2000 (SI 1625).
8 See *Ricketts & Fletcher* vs *Secretary of State for the Environment and Salisbury District Council* [1988] JPL 768, on how the Inquiry method may be considered as a direct, effective and efficient means by which evidence can be tested.

9 Every year the Planning Inspectorate publishes its *Annual report*, which includes statistical analysis of appeals allowed for each appeal method. (See www.planning-inspectorate.gov.uk)

10 In the late 1990s this was around £800 per written appeal.

11 That 80 per cent of all Written Representations will be handled within 22 weeks.

12 Town and Country Planning (Appeals) (Written Representations Procedure) Regulations 1987 (SI 701). Also see DoE Circular 11/87 on *Written representation procedure*.

13 See Planning Inspectorate (1993a).

14 Planning Inspectorate, *Annual reports and accounts*, 1993.

15 Planning Inspectorate 1993b.

16 Legal reference [1998] JPL 778.

17 See Annex 2(i) and 2(ii) to DETR Circular 5/00.

18 The Secretary of State may disagree, because new evidence or matters of fact have been taken into account or because he differs from the Inspector on a matter of opinion on which a conclusion or recommendation has been based.

19 For guidance on the detailed content of proofs of evidence and statements of common ground see (DETR) Circular 5/00 Planning Appeals: Procedures (DETR 2000i).

20 Refer to Royal Institute of Chartered Surveyors, *Surveyors Acting as Expert Witnesses*, Practice Statement and Guidance Notes.

21 Royal Town Planning Institute, *Chartered Town Planners at Inquiries*, Practice Advice Note (Number 4).

22 This legislation is applied to town planning appeals by virtue of section 320 of the Town and Country Planning Act 1990. The modern system governing such awards was established by an influential report in the 1960s, *Report of the Council on Tribunals on the Award of Costs at Statutory Inquiries* (1964), Cmnd 2471 1964.

23 Section 320(2) and Schedule 6 of the TCPA 1990. Similar provisions are to be found in Section 89 of the Planning (Listed Buildings and Conservation Areas) Act 1990 and Section 37 of the Planning (Hazardous Substances) Act 1990.

24 Discussion of this threshold is contained in the judgement of Justice Auld in *R vs Secretary of State for the Environment ex parte North Norfolk District Council*, legal reference [1994] 2 PLR 78.

25 The Advisory Panel on Standards for the Planning Inspectorate publish an annual report of their work. That of 2002 was the eighth such report.

26 Although the government has stated that it will make the award of costs available in Written Representations as soon as resources allow. By the mid-1990s this had not been introduced.

27 *Estates Gazette*, editorial, 2 July 1994, p. 43.

28 *Financial Times*, 18 December 2000.

5 The future for dispute resolution in planning

1 Paper published as C. Shepley (1997) Mediation in the Planning System. *Planning Inspectorate Journal*, Spring, no. 7, pp. 9–15.

2 This flyer stated that in a mediation . . . 'A solution . . . is produced by the parties themselves with the help of the mediator'. It established that mediation is 'confidential, voluntary' and that the mediator is a neutral party 'who helps the parties find an acceptable solution.'

3 Government planning policy guidance (PPG2) accepts the principle of replacement dwellings in green belt locations where the new dwelling is comparable in size and site coverage to the one that it is replacing.

4 DETR news release 385/30 May 2000.

5 Mediations were employed in the Examination in Public of the East Midlands *Regional Planning Guidance* (2000) and Barnet Unitary Development Plan (2001–2).

6 Providing such a challenge was deemed admissible by the European Commission in Strasbourg.

7 See Human Rights Act 1998. *Home Office Core Guidance for Public Authorities: A New Era of Rights and Responsibilities.* London, Home Office.

8 Article 1 of the UN Economic Commission for Europe Convention on Access to Information, Public Participation in Decision Making and Access to Justice on Environmental Matters, agreed at Aarhus, Denmark, June 1998.

9 Public Authority as defined by section 6 of HRA covers (in planning) Government Minister and Department (e.g. DETR). Local Authorities (e.g. LPAs), Courts, Tribunals (e.g. Public Inquiry) and any organization that carries out some function of a public nature (e.g. Planning Inspectorate, National Rivers Authority, English Heritage).

10 Challenge is made in High Court by way of judicial review of public law (which includes planning) and by civil action.

11 Section 174(f) of Town and Country Planning Act 1990.

12 For details of such an approach refer to *Sparkes* vs *SETR* in *Journal of Planning and Environment Law* (2000), pp. 1090–1091 and see Purchas and Clayton (2001), p. 137.

13 Referred to as the Alconbury case. Legal reference (2001) 1 PLR 58 and see *The Times*, 24 January 2001.

6 Planning gain and planning obligations

1 Planning gain, community gain, community benefit, planning advantage, planning requirements, planning obligations, planning agreements, developer's contribution, legal arrangements, improvements and additional facilities, community impacts, environmental impacts.

2 Housing. Town Planning Etc. Act 1909 followed by Section 34 of the TCPA 1932.

3 Advisory group composed of property professionals, independent of government.

4 Although a little confusing, the 1991 Act amended the 1990 Act. Therefore, the reforms came into force in 1991 on the basis of a statute of 1990.

5 By injunction against failure to comply.

6 Provides power to do anything that will facilitate the discharge of their functions.

7 See DoE Circular 11/95, *The use of conditions in planning permission.*

8 Introduced by Section 12 of the Planning and Compensation Act 1991.

9 Section 106A and 106B of 1990 Act.

10 Under provision of Section 84 of the Law of Property Act 1925.

11 Betterment refers to an increase in land value caused by public action (such as the granting of planning permission) as opposed to private action (the effort or investment of the owner or occupier). See Grant (1992).

12 Relying on a separate research report commissioned by the Task Force, see Punter (1999).

13 [1988] AC 578.

14 [1993] EGCS 113.

15 [1995] 1 WLR 759, [1995] AUER 636.

16 The practice of impact fees in the United States, unpublished paper presented to Royal Institution of Chartered Surveyors Conference 'Impact Fees: Could They Work Here?', March 1999.

7 Specialist town planning controls

1 Legislative provision can be found in Section 1(1) of the Planning (Listed Buildings and Conservation Areas) Act 1990. In Scotland refer to the Town & Country Planning (Scotland) Act 1972.

2 Around 3000 requests to spot list are received every year by English Heritage.

3 A fourth grade of 'local interest' identified by the LPA but not the Secretary of State is now obsolete and carries no statutory significance.

4 The six are The Ancient Monuments Society, The Council for British Archaeology, The Georgian Group, The Victorian Society, The Society for the Protection of Ancient Buildings, and The Royal Commission on Historical Monuments (England). Also refer to Circular 14/97 Planning and the Historic Environment – Notification and Directions by the Secretary of State, paragraph 15.

5 Such an appeal may be lodged on the grounds that the building is not of special interest and should be removed from the list. In deciding upon such an appeal, the Secretary of State or Inspector may find that it should remain on or be removed from the list.

6 Served under Section 38 of the Planning (Listed Buildings and Conservation Areas) Act 1990.

7 Requires the consent of the Secretary of State and represents a reserve power designed to achieve a longer-term preservation of the building.

8 See discussion in 'Taking action to stop Britain's heritage going to rack and ruin', *Chartered Surveyor Weekly* (1 October 1992, p. 26).

9 For a discussion of the merits of such post-war listing, see English Heritage (1992b).

10 A government-funded agency and 'think tank' vested with responsibility to promote good design in architecture and the built environment. CABE, unlike English Heritage, have no formal (i.e. statutory) powers of intervention in the protection of listed buildings, but are often consulted by local planning authorities and advise on post-war listed buildings.

11 This is the dictionary definition. The relevant Act provides no definition of 'special' in the context of Conservation Areas.

12 Section 72 of Planning (Listed Building and Conservation Areas) Act 1990. In Scotland reference should be made to the Town & Country Planning (Scotland) Act 1972.

13 [1992] 1 All ER 573 and [1992] 2 WLR 204.

14 [1989] *JPL* 259.

15 By Town and Country Amenities Act 1974.

16 PPG15, *Planning and the historic environment* (1994: para. 4.27).

17 From 30 March 1994, LPAs were given additional powers to withdraw selective permitted development rights without the need for an Article 4 Direction. No authority would be required from the Secretary of State. These 'selective' works would include insertion of new doors, windows and roofing materials.

18 Order served under Town and Country Planning (Control of Advertisements) Regulations 1992 SI No. 666.

19 Section 211 of the TCPA 1990. Also refer to DoE Circular 36/78.

20 Views expressed by the British Property Federation in the early 1990s.

21 Introduced by DoE Circular 22/80, *Development control – policy and practice*.

22 PPG1, issued 1988 and revised in 1992, *General policy and principles*, Annex on design considerations. For a critique of this approach see N. Taylor, 'Aesthetic judgement and environmental design: is it entirely subjective?', *Town Planning Review* 65(1), 21–58, 1994. A new PPG1 was issued in 1997 with further revisions affecting aesthetic matters anticipated during a review of this guidance in 2003–4.

23 1993 figure, published in PPG2 (1995) 14/84.

24 PPG2, *Green belts* (issued 1995). In Scotland similar guidance can be found in Scottish Office Circular 24/85, *Development in the countryside and green belts*.

25 Surveys of derelict land in England, Wales and Scotland.

26 Extract from PPG2, *Green belts* (1995: para. 2.10).

27 The Cambridge Green Belt makes for an interesting study in itself, as the Local Planning Authority themselves countenanced an enlargement of the city by sustainable urban extensions within the proximity of the inner green belt boundary. Such 'erosion' of the inner boundary coupled with extension of the

outer boundary is arguably a more sustainable option than 'leapfrog' development. This illustrates the tensions between green belts and sustainable development (Cambridge City Council 1999).

28 See PPG7, *The Countryside: Environmental Quality and Economic and Social Development* (para. 4.2) and §61 of Part III, Environment Act 1995.

29 The Norfolk Broads Act was designated by Act of Parliament in 1988 and New Forest Heritage Area designated by government and relevant local authorities, in 1994. In both cases their status and duty to conserve natural beauty with public enjoyment and recreation are the same as any other National Park Authority. The New Forest becomes a National Park in 2004.

30 Under powers in section 28 of the Wildlife and Countryside Act 1981.

31 Designation under provision within the Wildlife Countryside Act 1981.

32 Countryside Act 1968 in England and Wales, or Countryside (Scotland) Act 1967.

33 Under Section 1 of the Ancient Monuments and Archaeological Areas Act 1979.

34 See PPG16, *Archaeology and planning* (1990: paras 8 and 27).

8 Sustainable development

1 By the UK Climate Change Impacts Review Group.

2 Referred to as the 'Earth Summit'.

3 *The Earth Summit: Press Summary on Agenda 21*. United Nations Conference on Environment and Development, Rio de Janeiro, 3–14 June 1992.

4 *Sustainable Development – The UK Strategy 1994* (Cmnd 2426) London: HMSO.

5 *Climate Change: The UK Programme 1994* (Cmnd 2424) London: HMSO.

6 *Biodiversity: The UK Action Plan 1994* (Cmnd 2428) London: HMSO.

7 *Sustainable Forestry: The UK Programme 1994* (Cmnd 2429) London: HMSO.

8 Agenda 21 strategies comprise local action plans for sustainable development, prepared with the broad involvement of the local community.

9 In part by reducing VAT for listed buildings that are places of worship.

10 Via tax relief for the costs of converting redundant space over shops into residential accommodation.

11 Via reducing the level of VAT charged on conversion and renovation of residential property.

12 In 1988 Department of Environment statistics estimated that some 60 000 ha of vacant or derelict land existed in England, Scotland and Wales. Other estimates by environmental campaigners have been far higher. Stephen Joseph puts the figure at 110 000 for England and Wales (Joseph 1987).

13 For more details on this debate refer to DoE (1994c: ch. 11) and to Urban Task Force findings (DETR 1999), Part Three.

14 In 1990 carbon dioxide emissions in Britain were calculated at 158 million tonnes expressed as carbon. By the year 2000, projections range between 157 and 179 million tonnes.

15 A political agreement on the 1998 Kyoto Protocol was eventually reached in Bonn in July 2001. A total of 180 countries agreed both to cut various emissions and to provide funds to developing countries for climate change related activities.

16 Other ozone depleting chemical include carbon tetrachloride 1.1.1, hydrobromo-fluorocarbons (HBFCs) and hydrochlorofluorocarbons (HCFCs).

17 Montreal Protocol on substances that deplete the ozone layer, held in 1987.

18 Extract of a speech by the Secretary of State for the Environment, John Gummer, to the Town and Country Planning Association, January 1994.

19 The government published 15 'headline' indicators by which objectives of sustainable development could be measured. The government department vested with responsibility for their appraisal (DEFRA) publishes an annual report every Spring, with appraisal of delivery measured against each target.

20 *Conservation of Natural Habitats and of Wild Fauna and Flora*, EC Council Habitats Directive 92/43.
21 EC Council *Birds Directive* 79/409.
22 Article 6 of the Habitats Directive, 92/43.
23 More detailed consideration of the impact of parking on urban design is considered in Chapter 8.
24 See *Gateshead District Council* vs *Secretary of State for the Environment and Northumbrian Water* (1994) JPL B8.
25 Refer to PPG23, 1994, *Planning and pollution control and the comments of Lord Justice Glidewell in Gateshead MBC* vs *Secretary of State for the Environment and Northumbrian Water Group PLC* (1994) EGCS 92, where it was accepted that pollution was a material planning consideration.
26 *Bolton MDC* vs *Secretary of State for the Environment* (1994) JPL B37. While this decision was later overturned, these comments remain valid.
27 Section 54A of the TCPA 1990, introduced by the Planning and Compensation Act 1991. See Chapter 2.

9 Urban renaissance and regeneration

1 Contained in *Design Bulletin* 32 (DoE 1992).
2 City Challenge involved the competitive bidding by cities for regeneration funding. A total of 31 equally funded partnerships were implemented for a five-year period.
3 The SRBs were established to allocated funding towards a mix of economic, social and physical regeneration for any period up to a maximum of seven years. By the late 1990s 600 SRBs were established, replacing the City Challenge, which terminated in 1998.
4 DETR response to House of Commons (1999–2000) *Environment, Transport and Regional Affairs Select Committee Report on the Proposed Urban White Paper*.
5 In other words, to avoid setting long-term housing targets to be met by councils, in favour of a more flexible system of shorter-term targets, adjusted in the light of continuous review.
6 Development plans should follow a sequence of site identification for housing, starting with re-use of previously developed land, then urban extension and finally around nodes in public transport corridors.

12 Development valuation

1 The examples used in this chapter, and some of the associated text, are taken from the chapter on development valuation by John Ratcliffe & Nigel Rapley in *Valuation: Principles into Practice*, W. A. Rees (ed.) (London: Estates Gazette, 4th edn, 1993).

16 Office development

1 Extract from property sales brochure produced by Greycoat Estates, 1984.
2 This section is drawn from an article by Martin Simmonds (Chief Planner for the London Advisory Planning Committee) in *Property Review* 4(7), 213–17, 1994.
3 Extract from the draft town centre plan for Kingston, London Borough of Kingston, 1983.

18 Residential development

1 From PPG3 2000 *Housing*.
2 Section 55 of the 1990 Act, refer to section called 'The decision-maker's duty' in Chapter 2.

3 Refer to the section in the 1990 Act.

4 The London Borough of Harrow, an outer suburban local authority, commissioned Wootton Jeffreys (planning consultants) to undertake an environmental assessment of all the borough's residential areas to enhance its chance of winning planning appeals on residential development. Since 2000 greater attention has been paid to such matters of townscape importance in government guidance, see PPG3 (2000) Paragraph 56.

5 Fenestration refers to the arrangement of windows in a building.

6 Some outer London boroughs have designated certain inter-war suburban roads as conservation areas.

7 PPG3 (2000) *Housing*, states in Paragraph 56 that planning policies should 'create places and spaces which are attractive, have their own distinctive identity but respect and enhance local character'.

8 Supplementary guidance is not a part of development plan policy and will carry weight as a material consideration only if it has been the subject of some public consultation.

9 See Case report in *Journal of Planning and Environment Law*, October 1994, 916–19.

10 First used by the late Nicholas Ridley to describe forceful local opposition to the building boom of the late 1980s.

11 Refer to PPG12 *Development Plans*, Paragraphs 1.1 to 1.9 and Circular 07/99 *Town and Country Planning (Development Plans) and Consultation (Departures) Directions 1999*.

12 Especially so as a result of the increase in the number of households, projected to the end of the century.

13 Barratt, Beazer, Bovis, Ideal, Laing, Lovell, McCarthy and Stone, Tarmac, Wilcon and Wimpey.

14 It was suggested by the former Director of the Town and Country Planning Association, David Hall, that about one dozen substantially new towns of 75 000–100 000 are required in the South East and the southwest Midlands regions of England.

15 Northeast Hampshire housing target was adjusted to 11 550, Foxley Wood providing 4800.

16 Refer to PPG3, *Housing* (1992: Paras 34 and 35). Now cancelled and replaced by PPG3 (2000).

17 Such as in a speech by the Housing Minister, George Younger, in December 1993.

18 Housebuilders, developers and local investors rather than institutions.

19 Owner occupation, rent, equity sharing or retirement.

Bibliography

Legal citations
The following citations are referred to in the text when citing sources of relevant case law:

AC	Appeal Cases
All ER	All England Reports
EGCS	*Estates Gazette* case summaries
JPL	*Journal of Planning and Environment Law*
P & CR	Property Planning and Compensation Reports
PLR	Planning Law Reports
WLR	Weekly Law Reports

Abel, R. 1982. The Contradictions of Informal Justice. In *The Politics of Informal Justice*, R. Abel (ed.). New York: Academic Press.

Acland, A. 1990. *A Sudden Outbreak of Common Sense*. London: Hutchinson Business Books.

——1995a. Mediation Goes Green. *Family Mediation*, Vol. 5(3), pp. 11–12.

——1995b. Simple Negotiations. *Legal Action*, November, pp. 8–9.

——1995c. *Resolving Disputes Without Going to Court*. London: Century Business Books.

Acton, J. 1998. Planning Gain Risks our Reputations, *Planning*, 9 January, 11.

Adams, C. D., L. Russell, C. S. Taylor-Russell 1993. Development Constraints: Market Processes and the Supply of Industrial Land. *Journal of Property Research* 19(1), 49–61.

AIREA 1979. *What to Look for in an Appraisal*. Chicago: American Institute of Real Estate Appraisers.

Anderson, F. 1985. Structural Engineering. In *Office Development*, P. Marber and P. Marber (eds), 177–203. London: *Estates Gazette*.

Armon-Jones, C. 1984. Revealing the Art of Estate Agency. *Estates Times* (March).

Ashworth, W. 1954. *The Genesis of Modern British Town Planning*. London: Routledge.

Association of Metropolitan Authorities 1990. *Costs Awards at Planning Appeals*. London: Association of Metropolitan Authorities.

Astot, H. and C. Chinkin 1992. *Dispute Resolution in Australia*. Sydney: Butterworths.

Atkinson, R. and G. Moon 1994. *Urban Policy in Britain*. London: Macmillan.

Auerbach, J. 1983. *Justice Without Law*. Oxford: Oxford University Press.

Audit Commission 1992. *Building in Quality: A Study of Development Control*. London: HMSO.

——1999. *Local Authority Performance Indicators in England*. London: The Audit Commission.

Avis, M., V. Gibson, J. Watts 1989. *Managing Operational Property Assets*. Department of Land Management and Development, University of Reading.

Bailey, N. with A. Barker and K. MacDonald 1995. *Partnership Agencies in British Urban Policy*. London: UCL Press.

Barnard, L. 1993. The Concept of Sustainable Development and its Impact on the Planning Process. *Property Review* 2(9), 394–7.

Baldry, C. and D. Pitt 1993. *Building for the New Organisation*. In *Facilities Management 1993*, K. Alexander (ed.), 78–91. London: Haston Hilton.

Bannock, G. & Partners 1994. *Property in the Boardroom – A New Perspective*. London: Hillier-Parker.

Barret, P. and D. Baldry 2000. *Facilities Management: Towards Best Practice*, 2nd edn. London: Blackwell.

Barrett, V. and J. Blair 1982. *How to Conduct and Analyze Real Estate Market and Feasibility Studies*. New York: Van Nostrand Reinhold.

Bater, J. 1980. *The Soviet City*. London: Edward Arnold.

Battle, T. (ed.) 2003. *The Commercial Offices Handbook*. London: RIBA Enterprises.

Baum, A. and D. Mackmin 1989. *The Income Approach to Property Valuation*, 3rd edn. London: Routledge.

BCO 1994. *Specification for Urban Offices*. London: British Council Offices.

Beckwith, D. 1987. ADR in Australia. *Arbitration*, Vol. 53(3), pp. 213–14.

Bell, R. 1999. British Food Retailing – A Comparative Analysis, *European Retail Digest*, Issue 21, pp. 687–96.

Bentley, I. *et al.* 1985. *Responsive Environments – A Manual for Designers*, Oxford: Architectural Press.

Bentley, I., S. McGlynn, G. Smith and A. Alcock 1985. *Responsive Environments*. Oxford: Architectural Press.

Berkley, R. 1991. Raising Commercial Property Finance in a Difficult Market. *Journal of Property Finance* 1(4), 523–9.

—— 1992. Funding Review. *Journal of Property Finance* 2(4), 517–19.

Bernard Thorpe and Oxford Institute of Retail Management 1990. *Who Runs Britain's High Streets?* London: Bernard Thorpe [chartered surveyors].

Bevan, A. 1992. *Alternative Dispute Resolution: A Lawyer's Guide to Mediation and Other Forms of Dispute Resolution*. London: Sweet and Maxwell.

—— 2000. Mediation: Lifting the Veil – the Concepts of Privilege and 'Without Prejudice' in Mediation. *Solicitors' Journal*, p. 948.

Blackhall, J. C. 1990. *The Award of Costs at Public Inquiries*. Newcastle: Nuffield Foundation and University of Newcastle upon Tyne.

—— 1993. *The Performance of Simplified Planning Zones*. Working Paper 30, Department of Town and Country Planning, University of Newcastle upon Tyne.

Blake, J. 1995. Energy Policies and Planning. Paper presented at the Town and Country Planning Association Annual Conference, London, April.

Blowers, A. 1993. *Planning for a Sustainable Environment: A Report by the Town and Country Planning Association*. London: Earthscan.

Bourne, F. 1992. *Enforcement of Planning Control*, 2nd edn. London: Sweet & Maxwell.

Boys, K. 1983. Bridging the Communication Gap. *Chartered Surveyor Weekly* (15 September).

Bramson, D. 1992. Joint Ventures and Partnership Funds Today: The Art and Practice of Financing Property. Paper presented at Henry Stewart Conference, London.

Brindley, T., Y. Rydin, G. Stoker 1989. *Remaking Planning*. London: Unwin Hyman.

Briner, R. (1997) The Role of Lawyers in ADR. In *Global Law in Practice*, J. Ross-Harper, J. (ed.). The Hague: Kluwer Law International.

British Council for Offices 2000. *BCO Guide 2000: Best Practice in the Specification of Offices*. London: BCO.

British Government Panel on Sustainable Development 2000. *Sixth Report*. London: HM Stationery Office.

Brown, C. 1990. Retail Property: Development in the 1990s. *Estates Gazette* (9004), 20–24.

Brown, H. and Marriot, A. 1993. *ADR Principles and Practice*. London: Sweet and Maxwell.

Brownhill, S. 1990. *Developing London's Docklands: Another Great Planning Disaster?* London: Paul Chapman.

Bruggeman, W. and L. Stone 1981. *Real Estate Finance*. Homewood, Illinois: Irwin.

Bruton, M. J. and D. J. Nicholson 1987. *Local Planning in Practice*. London: Hutchinson.

Bullock, H. 1993. *Commercial Viability in Planning*. Occasional Paper 21, *Journal of Planning and Environment Law*.

Burgess, K. 1982. Long-term Mortgages are Back in Favour. *Chartered Surveyor Weekly* (9 December).

Burns, A. 1992. A Break from Tradition Helps Settle Disputes. *Chartered Surveyor Weekly*, 41: 3, 54.

Burton, J. 1988. *Conflict Resolution and Prevention*. London: Macmillan.

Butler, J. 1982. Making the Most of your Marketing. *Estates Times Review* (October).

Byrne, S. 1989. *Planning Gain: An Overview – A Discussion Paper*. London: Royal Town Planning Institute.

Cadman, D. and L. Austin Crowe 1983. *Property Development*, 2nd edn. London: Spon.

Cadman D. and Topping R. 1995. *Property Development*, 4th edn. E. & F. N. Spon.

CALUS 1974. The Property Development Process. *The Future of the Office Market*. Derby: The College of Estate Management.

Cambridge City Council 1999. *Cambridge Green Belt: Towards 2016*, Cambridge: Cambridge City Council.

Carnwath Report 1989. *Enforcing Planning Control*. London: HMSO.

Case, J. 1985. Building Services. In *Office Development*, P. Marber and P. Marber (eds), 283–315. London: *Estates Gazette*.

CB Hillier Parker 2000. *The Sequential Approach to Retail Development: Report on a National Research Project for the National Retail Planning Forum, British Council of Shopping Centres, Department of the Environment, Transport and the Regions*. London: CB Hillier Parker.

CBI/RICS 1992. *Shaping the Nation: Report of Planning Task Force*. London: Royal Institution of Chartered Surveyors.

CEC 1990. *Green Paper on the Urban Environment*. London: HMSO.

CEC Directorate General for Regional Policy 1991. *Europe 2000: Outlook for the Development of the Community's Territory*. Luxembourg: Office for Official Publications of the European Communities.

CEC Directorate General for Environment, Nuclear Safety and Civil Protection 1992a. *A Community Programme of Policy and Action in Relation to the Environment and Sustainable Development*, Vol. II: *Towards Sustainability*. Brussels: Commission.

—— 1992b. *The Impact of Transport on Environment – a Community Strategy for Sustainable Mobility*. Brussels: Commission.

Centre for Dispute Resolution 1977. *Mediator Training Course Handbook*, London: CEDR.

Chapman, H. 1995. Tomorrow and Beyond: Office Occupiers. *Property Review* 5(2), 34–6.

Charlesworth-Jones, S. 1983. Promoting the Corporate Image. *Estates Gazette* 265, 942–4.

Choreneki, G. 1997. Mediating Commercial Disputes. In *Rethinking Disputes: The Mediation Alternative*, J. MacFarlane (ed.). London: Cavendish.

CIOB 1992. *The Code of Practice for Project Management for Construction and Development*. Ascot: Chartered Institute of Building.

Cheshire, P. 1993. Why NIMBYism has gone BANANAs. *Estates Gazette* (9321), 104–5.

Clark, R. 1991. Refinancing. *Journal of Property Finance* 1(3), 435–9.

Cleavely, E. 1984. The Marketing of Industrial and Commercial Property. *Estates Gazette* 217, 1172.

Cole, H. 1993. The Irresistible Rise of the Superstore. *Estates Gazette* (9301), 73.

Commission for Architecture and the Built Environment (CABE), University College London and Department of Environment, Transport and The Regions 2001. *The Value of Urban Design: A Research Project Commissioned by CABE and DETR to Examine the Value Added by Good Urban Design*. London: Thomas Telford.

Commission for Local Administration in England 1994. *Annual Report for the Local Government Ombudsman 1993/94*. London: The Commissioner.

Committee on Standards in Public Life 1995. *Standards of Conduct in Parliament, the Executive and Non-departmental Public Bodies*. London: HM Stationery Office.

—— 1997. *Standards of Conduct in Local Government in England, Scotland and Wales. Vol I: Report*. London: HM Stationery Office.

—— Third Report 1997. *Standards of Conduct in Local Government in England, Scotland and Wales*. London: HM Stationery Office.

Council for National Parks 1997. *National Parks for Life: An Agenda for Action*. London: Council for National Parks.

Council for the Protection of Rural England 1994. *Green Belts – A Response by the Council for the Protection of Rural England to the Department of the Environment's Draft Revised Planning Policy Guidance Note 2*. London: Council for the Protection of Rural England.

Coupland, A. 1992. *Docklands: Dream or Fisaster?* in A. Thornley (ed.) *The Crisis of London*, 149–62. London: Routledge.

Coupland, A. (ed.) 1997. *Reclaiming the City – Mixed Use Development*. London: E. & F. N. Spon.

Court, Y. and Z. Southwell 1994. Town Centre Management: Are the Initiatives Effective? *Estates Gazette* (9436), 138–9.

CPRE 1992. *Where Motor Car is Master*. London: The Council for the Protection of Rural England.

Crow, S. 1997. Planning Fain: A Time for Change. *Planning*, 31 October, 10.

Cullen, G. 1961. *Townscape*. London: Architectural Press.

Curle, A. 1990. *Tools for Transformation*. Stroud: Hawthorn Press.

Damesick, P. 1994. The Major Provincial Office Centres: Offices Opportunities, Values and Trends. Paper presented at 'Offices' (Henry Stewart Conference, London).

—— 2003. A Growth Platform on Shifting Sands. 15 February 2003.

Dana, D. 1990. *Talk it Out*. London: Kogan Page.

Davies, H. W. E. and D. Edwards 1989. *Planning Control in Western Europe*. London: HMSO.

Davies, H. W. E., J. A. Gosling, M. T. Hsia 1993. *The Impact of the European Community on Land-use Planning in the United Kingdom*. London: Royal Town Planning Institute.

Debenham, Tewson & Chinnocks 1988. *Planning Gain: Community Benefit or Commercial Bribe?* London: Debenham, Tewson & Chinnocks.

Debenham Tewson Research 1990. *Development Trends*. London: Debenham, Tewson & Chinnocks.

—— 1991. *Business Parks*. London: Debenham Tewson.

DEGW 1983. *ORBIT: Office Research on Buildings and Information Technology.* London: DEGW.

DEFRA 2002. *Departmental Report of the Department for Environment, Food and Rural Affairs*. London: Stationery Office.

—— 1985. *Meeting the Needs of Modern Industry*. London: DEGW.

Dennis, C., L. Harris and B. Sandhu 2002. From Bricks to Clicks: Understanding the e-consumer. *Qualitative Research: An International Journal*, Vol. 5, No. 4, pp. 281–90.

Department for Culture, Media and Sport 2001. *The Historic Environment – A Resource for our Future*. London: Department for Culture, Media and Sport.

Department of the Environment 1992. *Design Bulletin 32. Residential Roads and Footpaths*, 2nd edn. London: HM Stationery Office.

—— 1993. *Enquiry into the Planning System in North Cornwall District*. London: HM Stationery Office.

—— 1995. *Urbanization in England. Projections 1991–2016. Department of the Environment Planning Research Programme*. London: HM Stationery Office.

—— 1996a. *Indicators of Sustainable Development for the United Kingdom*. London: HM Stationery Office.

—— 1996b. *Household Growth. Where Shall We Live?* London: HM Stationery Office.

—— 1997. *The Use of Density in Land Use Planning. A Practice Manual*. London: HM Stationery Office.

—— 1998a. *Land Use Change Statistics*. London: HM Stationery Office.

—— 1998b. *Parking Standards in the South East*. London: HM Stationery Office.

—— 1998c. *Planning for Sustainable Development: Towards Better Practice*. London: HM Stationery Office.

—— 1998d. *Places, Streets and Movement. A Companion Guide to Design Bulletin 32: Residential Roads and Footpaths*. London: HM Stationery Office.

—— 1998e. *Planning for the Communities of the Future*. London: HM Stationery Office.

—— 1999a. *A Better Quality of Life. A Strategy for Sustainable Development for the United Kingdom*. London: HM Stationery Office.

—— 1999b. *Development Plans* (PPG12). London: HM Stationery Office.

—— 2000a. *Planning Policy Guidance Note 3*. London: Department of the Environment, Transport and the Regions.

—— 2000b. *Our Towns and Cities. The Future – Delivering an Urban Renaissance* (Urban White Paper). London: Department of the Environment, Transport and the Regions.

—— 2000c. *The State of English Cities*. London: Department of the Environment, Transport and the Regions.

—— 2000d. *By Design – Urban Designing the Planning Process: Towards Better Practice*. London: DETR and Commission for Architecture and the Built Environment.

—— 2000e. *Mediation in the Planning System*, Michael Welbank in Association with Nick Davies and Ian Haywood. London: Department of the Environment, Transport and Regions.

—— 2000f. *Environmental Court Project – Final Report*. London: Department of the Environment, Transport and Regions.

—— 2000g.*Sustainable Development: Local Quality of Life Counts*. London: HM Stationery Office.

—— 2000h. *Housing* (PPG3). London, HM Stationery Office.

—— 2000i. *Circ 5/2000 Planning Appeals; Procedures*. London: HMSO.

—— 2001a. *Reforming Planning Obligations: A Consultation Paper*. London: Department of Environment, Transport and the Regions.

—— 2001b. *Strategic Gap and Green Wedge Policies in Structure Plans – Final Report*. London: Department of the Environment, Transport and the Regions.

—— 2001c. *Transport* (PPG13). London: HM Stationery Office.

—— 2001d. *Land Use Change in England Bulletin No.16*. London: Department of the Environment, Transport and Regions.

—— 2001e. *Planning: Delivering Fundamental Change*. London: Department of Environment, Transport and the Regions.

Department of Environment, Transport and Regions and Commission for Architecture and the Built Environment 2000. *By Design – Urban Design in the Planning System*. London: Department of the Environment, Transport and the Regions.

Department of National Heritage 1996. *Protecting Our Heritage – A Consultation Document on the Built Heritage of England and Wales*. London: Department of National Heritage.

Derby City Council 1991. *Sir Francis Ley Industrial Park – Simplified Planning Zone: The First Three Years*. Derby: Derby City Council.

Design Bulletin 32 1992. *Residential Roads and Footpaths*. London: HMSO.

Detoy, C. and S. Rabin 1985. Office Space: Calculating the Demand. In *Readings in Market Research for Real Estate*, J. Vernor (ed.), 243–57. Chicago: American Institute of Real Estate Appraisers.

Development Systems Corporation 1983. *Successful Leasing and Selling of Property*. Chicago: Real Estate Education Company.

Dixon, T. 2003. Buy into Better Cities. *Estates Gazette*, 22 March 2003.

DoE 1988. *Town and Country Planning Assessment of Environment Effects: Regulations*. London: HMSO.

—— 1990a. *This Common Inheritance: Britain's Environmental Strategy* [Cm 1299]. London: HMSO.

—— 1990b. *The Urban Programme Management Initiative: A Consultation on Proposal Changes*. London: Department of the Environment/HMSO.

—— 1991. *Circular 16/91. Planning and Compensation Act 1991. Planning Obligations*. London: HMSO.

—— 1992a. *The Use of Planning Agreements*. London: Department of the Environment/HMSO.

—— 1992b. *Development Plans and Regional Guidance* [PPG12]. London: HMSO.

—— 1993a. *Town Centres and Retail Developments* [PPG6]. London: HMSO.

—— 1993b. *Alternative Development Patterns: New Settlements*. London: HMSO.

—— 1993c. *Reducing Emissions through Planning*. London: HMSO.

—— 1994a. *Transport* [PPG13]. London: HMSO.

—— 1994b. *Roads to Prosperity*. London: HMSO.

—— 1994c. *Sustainable Development – The UK Strategy*. London: HMSO.

—— 1994d. *Planning and Pollution Control* [PPG23]. London: HMSO.

—— 1995. *A Guide to Better Practice* [PPG13]. London: HMSO.

Dobry, G. 1975. *Review of the Development Control System*. London: HMSO.

Dower, M. 1995. What Change for the Countryside? Town and Country Planning Association Annual Conference. London, April.

DTZ Debenham Thorpe 1995. *Special Report on Shopping Centre Refurbishment* (June).

Duffy, F. 1991. *The Changing Workplace*. London: Architecture Design and Technology Press.

—— 1994. The Future of Work: Renaissance of the City. *Property Review* 4(1), 7–10.

Dyker, D. A. 1992. *Restructuring the Soviet Economy*. London: Routledge.

Dukes, E. 1996. *Resolving Public Conflict*. Manchester: Manchester University Press.

Eames, R. 1993. *'The Enabling Council': Planning for Recovery*. London: Sweet & Maxwell.

Early, J. 1994. Urban Regeneration: A Developer's Perspective. *Property Review* 4(5), 158–60.

Edwards, M. and J. Martin 1993. Planning Notes. *Estates Gazette* (9313), 106–7.
—— 2003. Get to Grips with the Bill. *Estates Gazette*, Planning Notes, 11 January 2003.
Edwards, R. 1991. *Fit for the Future*. Cheltenham: Countryside Commission.
Eldred, G. and R. Zerbst 1985. A Critique of Real Estate Market and Investment Analysis. In *Readings in Market Research for Real Estate*, J. Vernor (ed.), 133–42. Chicago: American Institute of Real Estate Appraisers.
Elliott, D. 1996. Med:Arb – Fraught with Danger or Ripe with Opportunity? *Arbitration*, Vol. 62(3), pp. 175–183.
Elson, M. 1986. *Green Belts: Conflict Mediation in the Urban Fringe*. London: Heinemann.
—— 1990. *Negotiation for the Future: Planning Gain in the 1990s*. Gloucester: ARC Ltd.
Elson, M., S. Walker, R. MacDonald, J. Edge 1993. *The Effectiveness of Green Belts*. London: HMSO.
Elson, M. and A. Ford 1994. Green Belts and Very Special Circumstances. *Journal of Planning and Environmental Law*, 594–601.
Elson, M., C. Steenberg and N. Mendham 1996. *Green Belts and Affordable Housing – Can We Have Both?* Bristol: The Policy Press.
Elson, M., C. Steenberg, and L. Nichol 2000. *Strategic Gap and Green Wedge Policies in Structure Plans*. Oxford: Oxford Brookes University School of Planning, Planning Policies Research Group.
Elvin, D. and J. Maurici 2001. The Alconbury Litigation: Principle and Pragmatism. *Journal of Planning and Environment Law*, August, 883–902.
English Heritage 1990. *The Conservation Areas of England*. London: English Heritage.
—— 1992a. *Buildings at Risk: A Sample Survey*. London: English Heritage.
—— 1992b. *A Change of Heart*. London: English Heritage.
—— 1995a. *Monitor Report*. London: English Heritage.
—— 1995b. *Developing Guidelines for the Management of Listed Buildings*. London: English Heritage.
—— 1995c. *English Heritage Grants for Buildings at Risk*. London: English Heritage.
—— 1998. *Conservation-led Regeneration*. London: English Heritage.
—— 1999. *The Heritage Dividend – Measuring the Results of English Heritage Regeneration*. London: English Heritage.
—— 2001a. *Annual Report and Accounts*. London: English Heritage.
—— 2001b. *Buildings at Risk. The Register 2001*. London: English Heritage.
EPI 1994. *Why Manufacturing Still Matters*. London: Employment Policy Institute.
Essex County Council 1973. *Design Guide for Residential Areas*. Chelmsford: Essex County Council.
Estates Gazette 1990. Focus on Business Parks. *Estates Gazette* (9026), 65–157.
—— 1993. Focus on Marketing: 'Posting your Way to Success'. *Estates Gazette* (9302), 76–7.
—— 1999. Industry Slams Planning Consents. *Estates Gazette*, 1 May, 35.
—— 2002. Stock Up ub the Lockup. *Estates Gazette*, 12 January 2002.
—— 2002. How to Improve Your Aim. 29 June 2002.
—— 2002a. The Big Gamble, Focus. *Estates Gazette*, 26 October 2002.
—— 2002b. Northern Exposure, Focus. *Estates Gazette*, 19 October 2002.
Evans, A. W. 1988. *No Room! No Room! The Costs of the British Town and Country Planning System*. London: Institute of Economic Affairs.
Evans, D. 1997. *A History of Nature Conservation in Britain*, 2nd edn. London: Routledge.
Faludi, A. (ed.) 1973b. *A Reader in Planning Theory*. Oxford: Pergamon.
Fisher, R. and W. Urry 1997. *Getting to Yes. Negotiating an Agreement Without Giving In*. London: Arrow Business Books.

Fletcher King 1989. *Retail Warehousing*. London: Fletcher King [chartered surveyors].
—— 1990. *Business Parks*. London: Fletcher King [chartered surveyors].
Foley, D. 1960. British Town Planning: One Ideology or Three? *British Journal of Sociology* 11(2), 211–31.
Folger, J. and T. Jones (eds) 1994. *New Directions in Mediation*. London: Sage.
Franks, D. 1957. *Report on the Committee on Administrative Tribunals and Inquiries*. London: HMSO.
French, R. A. and F. E. Hamilton 1979. *The Socialist City: Spatial Structure and Urban Policy*. Chichester, England: John Wiley.
Fryer, D. 1994. Viewpoint – The European Council of Town Planners. *Town Planning Review* 65(2), iii–iv.
Garner, J. and B. Jones 1997. *Countryside Law*, 3rd edn. Crayford, Kent: Shaw & Sons.
Genn, H. 1998. *The Central London County Court Pilot Mediation Scheme: Evaluation Report No. 5/98*. London: The Lord Chancellor's Department Research Secretariat.
Gerald Eve Research 1995. *Whither the High Street?* London: Gerald Eve.
Gibson, B. 1999. Beyond Shopping Centres – e-Commerce. British Council of Shopping Centres Conference.
Gibson, V. 1995a. Is Property on the Strategic Agenda. *Chartered Surveyor Monthly* 4(3), 34–5.
—— 1995b. Is Property on the Strategic Agenda. *Property Review* 5(1), 104–9.
Giles, G. 1978. *Marketing*, 3rd edn. Plymouth: MacDonald & Evans.
Glasson, J., R. Therivel, A. Chadwick 1994. *An Introduction to Environmental Impact Assessment*. London: UCL Press.
Gourmain, P. (ed.) 1989. *High-technology Workplaces*. New York: Van Nostrand Reinhold.
Graaskamp, J. 1981. *Fundamentals of Real Estate Development*. Washington DC: Urban Land Institute.
Grant, M. 1989. *Permitted Development: the Use Classes Order 1987 and General Development Order 1988*. London: Sweet & Maxwell.
—— 1992. Planning Law and the British Planning System. *Town Planning Review* 63, 3–12.
—— 1993. Planning Gain: the Legal Question. *Housebuilder* 52(3), 26–27.
—— (ed.) 1995a. *Encyclopedia of Planning Law and Practice* [6 vols]. London: Sweet & Maxwell.
—— 1995b. Planning Obligations: What's Going On? *Property Review* 5(2), 50–2.
—— 2000. Human Rights and Due Process in Planning. *Journal of Planning and Environment Law*, December, 1215–1225.
—— 2001. Alconbury: Human Rights or Planning? *Encyclopedia of Planning Law and Practice*, Monthly Bulletin, May, 1–6. London: Sweet & Maxwell.
—— 2003. *Encyclopaedia of Planning Law and Practice*. London: Sweet & Maxwell.
Gregory, T. 1989. So We've Found Another Roman Palace. *Estates Gazette* (8922), 20–2, 62–4.
Grime, K. and V. Duke 1993. A Czech on Privatisation. *Regional Studies* 27(8), 751–7.
Hall, D. 1989. The Case for New Settlements. *Town and Country Planning* 58(4), 111–14.
Hall, P. 1975. *Urban and Regional Planning*. London: David & Charles.
—— 1988. The Industrial Revolution in Reverse? *The Planner*, 74, 1, 1988.
—— 1992. *Urban and Regional Planning*, 3rd edn. London: Routledge.
—— 1993. Forces Shaping Urban Europe. *Urban Studies* 30(6), 883–98.
—— 1995. Planning Strategies for Our Cities and Regions. *Property Review* 5(10), 302–5.
Hammond, B. 1989. Keys to Success. *Estates Gazette* (8945), 95–9.

Harding-Roots, S. 1998. Finding Fault with Listing Process. *Planning*, 29 May 1998, p. 7.

Harris, J. 1980. *Legal Philosophies*. London: Butterworths.

Harrison, J. 1997. Environmental Mediation: The Ethical and Constitutional Dimension. *Journal of Environmental Law*, Vol. 9(1), pp. 81–102.

Hart, D. 2000. The Impact of the European Convention on Human Rights on Planning and Environmental Law. *Journal of Planning and Environment Law*, February, 117–133.

Harvey, D. 1973. *Social Justice and the City*. London: Edward Arnold.

Harwood, E. 2000. *England: A Guide to Post-War Listed Buildings*. London: Ellipsis.

—— 2001. This is Tomorrow: The History of Post-War Architecture in England. In *Preserving Post-War Heritage: The Care and Conservation of Mid-Twentieth Century Architecture*, Macdonald, S. (2001) (ed.). Bath: Donhead Publishing.

Havard, T. 2002. *Contemporary Property Development*. London: RIBA Enterprises.

Hawking, H. 1992. Checkout Superstores. *Estates Gazette* (9205), 146, 170.

Hawkins, S. 1990. Using your Solicitor Correctly. *Estates Gazette* (9005), 26, 63.

Hayward, R. and S. McGlynn 1993. *Making Better Places: Urban Design Now*. Oxford: Butterworth.

Healey, P. 1983. *Local Plans in British Land-use Planning*. Oxford: Pergamon Press.

—— 1991. Models of the Development Process. *Journal of Property Research* 8(3), 219–38.

Healey, P., P. McNamara, M. Elson, A. Doak 1988. *Land-use Planning and the Mediation of Change*. Cambridge: Cambridge University Press.

Healey, P. and R. Nabarro (eds) 1988. *Applied Property Research UK 2000: An Overview of Business Parks*. London: Applied Property Research.

Healey, P., M. Purdue, F. Ennis 1993. *Gains from Planning? Dealing with the Implementation of Planning*. York: Joseph Rowntree Foundation.

Healey, P. and R. Williams 1993. European Urban Planning Systems: Diversity and Convergence. *Urban Studies* 30(415), 701–20.

Healey, P. and A. Baker 1986. *National Office Design Survey*. London: Healey & Baker.

—— 1989. *Serviced Offices in Central London*. London: Healey & Baker.

Heap, Sir Desmond 1991. *An Outline of Planning Law*, 10th edn. London: Sweet & Maxwell.

Heilbron, H. 1994. Civil Justice on Trial. *ADR Law Journal*, Vol. 2(3), pp. 83–90.

Henney, A. 1983. *Tomorrow's Office for the 1980s*. London: Town and City Properties.

Higgins, J. 1997. Mediation: The Training Component In *Rethinking Disputes: The Mediation Alternative*, J. MacFarlane (ed.). London: Cavendish.

HMSO 1983. *Streamlining the Cities: Government's Proposals for Reorganising Local Government in Greater London and Metropolitan Counties* [Cmnd 9063]. London: HMSO.

—— 1994a. *Climate Change: The UK Programme* [Cm 2424]. London: HMSO.

—— 1994b. *Sustainable Forestry: The UK Programme* [Cm 2429]. London: HMSO.

—— 1994c. *Biodiversity: The UK Action Plan* [Cm 2428]. London: HMSO.

—— 1994d. *Sustainable Development – The UK Strategy* [Cm 2426]. London: HMSO.

Holdaway, E. and G. Smart 2001. *Landscapes at Risk? The Future for Areas of Outstanding Natural Beauty*. London: Spon Press.

Holden, R. 1986. Business Parks and Science Parks. *Estates Gazette*, 278, 684–6.

Holgate, D. and I. Gilbey 2001. Business as Usual. *Estates Gazette*, 19 May 2001, 218.

Home, R. 1989. *Planning Use Classes: A Guide to the 1987 Order*, 2nd edn. Oxford: Blackwell Scientific.

Houghton, G. and E. C. Hunter 1994. *Sustainable Cities*. London: Regional Studies Association.

Houghton, J., B. Callender, S. Varney (eds) 1992. *Climate Change*. Cambridge: Cambridge University Press.

House of Commons 1999. *Environment, Transport and Regional Affairs Select Committee Seventeenth Report, Housing: Planning Policy Guidance Note 3*. London: London Planning Advisory Committee.

——1999–2000. Environment, Transport and Regional Affairs Committee. Thirteenth Report. *The Planning Inspectorate and Public Inquiries*, Vol. 1, Report and Proceedings of the Committee. London: HM Stationery Office.

Howard, M. 1989. Planning Applications, Appeals and Development Plans, *Journal of Planning and Environment Law*. Proceedings of Oxford Law Planning Conference, Occasional Papers No. 16.

HRH The Prince of Wales 1989. *A Vision of Britain*. London: Doubleday.

Isaac, D. 1996. *Property Development: Appraisal and Finance*. Basingstoke: Macmillan.

Jacobs, J. 1961. *The Death and Life of Great American Cities*. New York: Random House.

Jenks, C. 1988. *The Prince, the Architects and New Wave Monarchy*. London: Academy Editions.

Jenks, M. *et al.* 1996. *The Compact City: A Sustainable Urban Form*. London: E. & F. N. Spon.

Jennings, R. 1984. *The Role of the Developer*. London: Henry Stewart.

Jolly, B. 1979. *Development Properties and Techniques in Residual Valuation*. Property Valuation Handbook B1, College of Estate Management, Reading.

——1995. Retailing in the 1990s. *Property Review* 5(5), 148–50.

Jonas, C. 1994. Property in the European Economy. *Property Review* 4(1), 11–17.

Jones, P. and D. Hillier 2000. Changing the Balance – the 'Ins and Outs' of Retail Development. *Property Management*, Vol. 18, No. 2, pp. 114–26.

Jones Lang LaSalle 1999. *Bricks and Clicks: The Future of Distribution Property*. London: Jones Lang LaSalle.

——2000. *Wired for Profit*. London: Jones Lang LaSalle UK Property Research, September 2000.

——2000. *Bricks and Clicks II – Sheds in the New Economy: New Distribution Networks, New Sheds?* London: Jones Lang LaSalle.

Jones Lang Wootton 1990. *The City Office Review 1980–89*. London: Jones Lang Wootton.

Joseph, S. 1987. *Urban Wasteland Now*. London: Civic Trust.

Jowell, J. 1977. Bargaining in Development Control. *Journal of Planning and Environment Law*, 414–33.

Keeble, L. 1969. *Principles and Practice of Town and Country Planning*. London: Estates Gazette.

——1985. *Fighting Planning Appeals*. London: Construction Press.

Kendrick, R. 1995. Finding an Alternative Way. *Legal Executive*, January, pp. 50–1.

Key, T., T. Key, F. Zarkesh, B. MacGregor, N. Nanthkumaran 1994. Understanding the Property Cycle. *Property Review* 4(2), 61–3.

Kee, D. 1990. *Europe's International Retailers*. Shopping Centre Horizons No. 18. Reading: College of Estate Management.

King Sturge 2002. *Industrial and Distribution Floorspace Today*. London: King Sturge Research.

Knutt, E. 2001. Fortress Under Fire. *Estates Gazette*, 14 July 2001, 53–57.

Kolb, D. 1983. *The Mediators*. Cambridge, MA: MIT Press.

Lavers, A. and B. Webster 1990. *Practice Guide to Town Planning Appeals*. London: Estates Gazette.

Lawless, P. 1989. *Britain's Inner Cities*. London: Paul Chapman.

Lawson, D. 2003. All the Fun of the Shopping Centre, *Estates Gazette*, 1 March 2003.

Layfield, F. 1993. *A Retrospect: Planning Inquiries.* Occasional Paper 20, *Journal of Planning and Environment Law.*

Lichfield, N. 1989. From Planning Gain to Community Benefit. *Journal of Planning and Environment Law,* 68–81.

—— 1995. Economics of Urban Villages. *Property Review* 5(2), 42–5.

Littlefair, P. J. 1991. *Site Layout Planning for Daylight and Sunlight – A Guide to Good Practice.* Watford: Building Research Establishment.

Lizieri, C., C. Ward, S. Palmer 2002. *Financial Innovations in Property Markets: Implications for the City of London.* Corporation of London and RICS Research Foundation.

Llewelyn-Davies and the Association for the Protection of Rural Scotland 1998. *Green Belts – Frames or Fragments? A Study of the Edinburgh Green Belt.* Edinburgh: Association for the Protection of Rural Scotland.

Low, F. 1994. Development in the 1990s: A Developer's Perspective. *Property Review* 4(3), 82–5.

Lowe, P. 1995. National Trust Centenary Conference, September 1995.

Lowes, V. 2000. See that Rights are Protected. *Estates Gazette,* 26 August, 80–81.

LPAC 1994. *Advice on the Revision of RPG3 1989.* London: London Planning Advisory Committee.

McCollum, W. 1985. Basic Research Procedures. In *Readings in Market Cesearch for Real Estate,* J. Vernon (ed.), 183–206. Chicago: American Institute of Real Estate Appraisers.

McCoubry, H. 1990. *Effective Planning Appeals.* Oxford: Blackwell Scientific.

MacDonald, R. 1991. *The Use of Planning Agreements by District Councils.* Report of research findings, School of Planning, Oxford Polytechnic and Association of District Councils.

MacEwen, A. and M. MacEwen 1987. *Greenprints for the Countryside – The Story of Britain's National Parks.* London: Allen & Unwin.

MacFarlane, J. (ed.) 1997. *Rethinking Disputes.* London: Cavendish.

McGlynn 1993, in R. Hayward and S. McGlynn, *Making Better Places: Urban Design Now.* Oxford: Butterworth.

McKee, W. 1994. The Image of the Property Market. *Property Review* 2(11), 466–9.

McLoughlin, J. B. 1969. *Urban and Regional Alanning: A ystems Approach.* London: Faber.

McNamara, P., A. Jackson, S. Mathrant 1985. *Appellants' Perceptions of the Planning Appeal Aystem: Final Report to DoE.* Departments of Town Planning and Estate Management, Oxford Polytechnic.

MacRae, J. 1993. Rail freight. *Estates Gazette* (9346), 157–8.

Mackie, K. 1997. Mediation Futures. In *Rethinking Disputes: The Mediation Alternative,* J. MacFarlane (ed.). London: Cavendish.

Mackie, K., Miles, D. and Marsh, W. 1995. *Commercial Dispute Resolution: An ADR Practice Guide.* London: Butterworths.

Marber, P. 1985. Project Managing Office Development. In *Office Development,* P. Marber and P. Marber (eds), 177–201. London: *Estates Gazette.*

Marriott, O. 1989. *The Property Boom.* London: Abingdon Publishing.

Marshall, P. and C. Kennedy 1993. Development Valuation Techniques. *Journal of Property Valuation and Investment* 11(1), 57–64.

Martin, P. 1982. *Shopping Centre Management.* London: Spon.

—— 1993. Review of Planning Obligations. *Estates Gazette* (9306), 98–100.

Maynard, P. (Jones Lang Wootton) 1990. Contribution During International Council of Shopping Centres. Helsinki 1990.

Meadows, H. 1972. *The Limits to Growth: A Report for the Club of Rome's Project on the Predicament of Mankind.* London: Earth Island.

Michalik, A. 1990. Breathing Life into B1. *Estates Gazette* (9026), 110–12.

Miles, M., E. Malizia, M. Weiss, G. Berens, G. Travis 1991. *Real Estate Development: Principles and Process.* Washington DC: Urban Land Institute.

Miller, M. 1989. *Letchworth: The First Garden City.* Chichester: Phillimore Press.

Mills, L. 1992. Nissan Still Drives the Market. *Estates Gazette* (9242), 70–1.

—— 1994. Planning: A Mixed Outlook. *Estates Gazette* (9446), 124–5.

Ministry of Agriculture, Fisheries and Food 1997. *Agricultural Land Classification of England and Wales.* London: Ministry of Agriculture, Fisheries and Food.

Ministry of Transport 1963. *Traffic in Towns: A Study of the Long-term Problems of Traffic in Urban Areas* [Reports of the Steering Group and Working Group appointed by the Minister of Transport]. London: HMSO.

Moore, B., P. Tyler, D. Elliot 1991. The Influence of Regional Development Incentives and Infrastructure on the Location of Small and Medium-sized Companies in Europe. *Urban Studies* 28(6), 1001–26.

Moore, C. 1996. *The Mediation Process.* San Francisco: Jossey-Bass.

Moore, V. 1997. *A Practical Approach to Planning Law*, 7th edn. London: Blackstone Press.

Morgan, P. and S. Nott 1988. *Development Control: Policy into Practice.* London: Butterworth.

Morphet, J. 1995. *The Planning System: Broken or Fixed?* Town and Country Planning Association Annual Conference, London (April).

Moss, N. and M. Fellows 1995. A Future for Town Centres. *Estates Gazette* (9506), 141–3.

Murdoch, J. 1993. Property Misdescription: Staying Afloat. *Estates Gazette* (9313), 85–8.

Mynors, C. 1999. *Listed Buildings, Conservation Areas and Monuments*, 3rd edn. London: Sweet & Maxwell.

Nairn, I. 1955. *Outrage.* London: Architectural Press.

National Audit Office 1990. *Regenerating the Inner Cities.* London: HMSO.

Naughton, T. 1992. Mediation in the Land and Environment Court of New South Wales. *Environmental and Planning Law Journal*, Vol. 9(3), pp. 219–24.

Newell, M. 1989. Development Appraisals. *Journal of Valuation* 7(2), 123–33.

Newman, P. 1996. ADR Class. *Construction Law*, Vol. 7(1), pp. 9–12.

Norris, S. and P. Jones 1993. Retail Impact Assessment. *Estates Gazette* (9304), 84–5.

Northen, I. 1977. *Shopping Centres: A Developer's Guide to Planning and Design.* College of Estate Management, Reading.

O'Connor, P. 1992. Alternative Dispute Resolution: Panacea or Placebo? *Arbitration*, Vol. 58(2), pp. 107–115.

Office of the Deputy Prime Minister 2002. *Guidance Note: Best Value Performance Plan and Reviews.* London: Office of the Deputy Prime Minister.

—— 2003. *Sustainable Communities: Building for the Future.* London: ODPM.

Oliver, P., I. Davis, I. Bentley 1981. *Dunroamin: The Suburban Semi and its Enemies.* London: Barrie & Jenkins.

PA Cambridge Economic Consultants 1987. *An Evaluation of the Enterprise Zone Experiment DoE Inner Cities Research Programme.* London: HMSO.

Parfect, M. and G. Power 1997. *Planning for Urban Quality.* London: Routledge.

Parker Morris Committee 1961. *Homes for Today and Tomorrow.* London: HMSO.

Parker, A. 1994. Town Centre Management: A New Urban Panacea. *Property Review* 4(5), 161–3.

Parker, B. 1995. *Planning and Transport – The Key Relationship.* Town and Country Planning Association Annual Conference, London (April).

Parliament of New South Wales 1991. 57th Report of the Public Accounts Committee. *Hansard Report 57.* Sydney: New South Wales Government.

Parnell, L. 1991. *A Project Manager's Companion Guide*. Paper 3, Project Strategy. RICS Diploma in Project Management, College of Estate Management, Reading.

Pearce, B. 2000. Mediappeal: A New Kind of Appeal Procedure? *Journal of Planning and Environment Law*, December, 1240–1245.

Pearce, D. 1994. *Blueprint 3: Measuring Sustainable Development*. London: Earthscan.

Pennington, M. 2002. *Liberating the Land*. London: Institute of Economic Affairs.

Pharoah, T. 1992. *Less Traffic, Better Towns*. London: Friends of the Earth.

Planning Inspectorate, The 1993a. *Customer Survey: Study of the Appellants' Experience of the Written Representation Appeal System*. Epsom, Surrey: W. S. Atkins.

—— 1993b. *Customer Survey: Study of Appellants' and Local Authorities' Experience of the Hearings System*. Epsom, Surrey: W. S. Atkins Planning Consultants.

Powell, C. 1990. *Facilities Management: Nature, Causes and Consequences*. Ascot: CIOB Technical Information Service.

Prince's Foundation 2000. *Sustainable Urban Extensions: Planned Through Design*. London: The Prince's Foundation.

Prior, J. 1993. *BREEAM: New Offices Version 1/93. Environmental Assessment for New Office Designs, Buildings Research Establishment Report*. Watford: Building Research Establishment.

Prodgers, L. 1992. Facilities Management: Facing up to Responsibilities. *Estates Gazette* (9238).

Property Advisory Group 1980. *Planning Gain*. London: HMSO.

Property Week 2002. Pretty Vacant, Sector Profile: Business and Science Parks. *Property Week*, 3 May 2002.

Pugh, C. 1992. The Globalisation of Finance Capital and the Changing Relationships Between Property and Finance – 2. *Journal of Property Finance* 2(3), 369–79.

Punter, J. 1993. *Development Design Skills for Development Controllers*. In *Making Better Places: Urban Design Now*, R. Hayward and S. McGlynn (eds), 10–18. Oxford: Butterworth.

Punter, L. 1999. *The Future Role of Planning Agreements in Facilitating Urban Regeneration*. London: Department of Environment, Transport and the Regions.

Purchas, R. and Clayton, J. 2001. A Field Day for Crackpots? The Human Rights Act Development Projects and Control. *Journal of Planning and Environment Law*, February, 134–149.

Purdue, M. 1991. *Planning Appeals – A Critique*. Buckingham: Open University Press.

Raggett, B. 1993. Implications of the New PPG6. *Estates Gazette* (9330), 78–9.

Rawson-Gardiner, C. 1993. Where Next for Relocation. *Estates Gazette* (9344), 106–7.

Redcliffe-Maud Report 1969. *Report of the Royal Commission on Local Government in England* [Cmnd 4040]. London: HMSO.

Redman, M. 1991. Planning Gain and Obligations. *Journal of Planning and Environment Law*, 203–18.

—— 1993. European Community Planning Law. *Journal of Planning and Environment Law*, 999–1011.

Reeves 2001. Plain Speaking. *Estates Gazette*, 8 December 2001.

Regional Studies Association 1990. *Beyond Green Belts – Managing Urban Growth in the 21st Century*. London: Regional Studies Association.

RICS 1999. Planning Policy Guidance 6 (PPG6: Town Centres and Retail Development). *Public Policy*, RICS, 12 March 1999.

—— 2002. Report Into the Industrial Property Sector. *RICS News*, 20 June 2002.

RICS Foundation 2002. *Red Man, Green Man. Indicators for Urban Sustainability*. London: RICS Foundation.

RICS and English Heritage 1993. *The Investment Performance of Listed Buildings*. London: RICS and Investment Property Databank.

Ringer, M. 1989. Is the Shopper Really King? *Estates Gazette* (8945), 109–12.

Robathan, P. 1993. The Intelligent Building. In *Facilities Management*, K. Alexander (ed.), 50–3. London: Haston Hilton.

Roberts, S. 1995. Litigation and Settlement. In *Reform of Civil Procedure*, A. Zuckerman and R. Cranston (eds.). Oxford: Oxford University Press.

Robertshaw, P. and J. Segal 1993. The Milking of ADR. *Civil Justice Quarterly*, Vol. 12, pp. 23–38.

Roger Tym and Partners 1984. *Monitoring Enterprise Zones Reports*. London: HMSO.

—— 1993. *Merry Hill Impact Study* [final report for West Midlands Planning and Transportation Subcommittee, Wyre Forest District Council and DoE]. London: HMSO.

Rogers, R. and Power, A. 2000. *Cities for a Small Country*. London: Faber.

Ross-Goobey, A. 1992. *Bricks and Mortals: The Dream of the 80s and the Nightmare of the 90s, the Inside Story of the Proper World*. London: Century Business.

Royal Commission on Environmental Pollution 1994. *Transport and the Environment*. Oxford: Oxford University Press.

Royal Institution of Chartered Surveyors 1995. *RICS Appraisal and Valuation Manual*. London: RICS.

Royal Town Planning Institute 1991. *Planning – Is it a Service, and How Can it be Effective?* London: Royal Town Planning Institute.

—— 1993. *The Character of Conservation Areas*. London: Royal Town Planning Institute.

—— 1997. *The Role of Elected Members in Plan Making and Development Control. A Summary of the Study Commission from the School of Planning, Oxford Brookes University*, London: The Royal Town Planning Institute.

Rydin, Y. 1993. *The British Planning System: An Introduction*. London: Macmillan.

Saggess, J. 1993. *Shopping Centre Management: The Way Forward, Shopping Centre Progress 1993–94*. London: British Council of Shopping Centres.

Salata, A. 1990. The Starting Grid. *Estates Gazette* (9026), 122–3.

Samuels, A. 2000. Planning and Human Rights, *Solicitors Journal*, 972–975.

Sands, D. 1993. Service with Style. *Estates Gazette* (9341), 66.

Save Britain's Heritage 1999. *Buildings at Risk*. London: Save Britain's Heritage.

Satterthwaite, D. 1999. *The Earthscan Reader in Sustainable Cities*. London: Earthscan.

Savills 1990. *Financing Property*. London: Savills.

Saxon, R. 1993. Seeking a Consensus. *Estates Gazette* (9318), 70.

Scanlon, K., A. Edge, T. Willmott 1994. *The Economics of Listed Buildings*. MS, Department of Land Economy, University of Cambridge.

Schiller, R. 1983. Shopping Trends as they Affect the Investor. *Estates Gazette* 267, 420.

—— 2001. *The Dynamics of Property Location*. London: Spon Press.

Scruton, R. 1996. Under Scrutiny. *Perspectives on Architecture*, February/March, p. 89.

Sharp, T. 1942. *Town Planning*. London: Penguin.

Shayle, A. 1992. Deep Discount Bonds, Convertible Mortgages, Participating Mortgages: The Art and Practice of Financing Property. Paper presented at Henry Stewart Conference, London.

Sheail, J. 1998. *Nature Conservation in Britain – The Formative Years*. London: The Stationery Office.

Shilston, A. 1996. Why Not Arb-Med? *Arbitration*, Vol. 63(3), pp. 161–163.

Simmie, J. (ed.) 1994. *Planning London*. London: UCL Press.

Simmonds, M. 1994/5. Planning for Office Development: A Strategic Approach. *Property Review* 4(7), 213–16.

Sinclair, G. 1992. *The Lost Land: Land-use Change in England 1945–1990*. London: Council for the Protection of Rural England.

Smith, N. 1994. The End of Grants as we Know Them. *Property Review* 4(5), 152–5.

Smith-Morris, E. 1997. *British Town Planning and Urban Design – Principles and Policies.* Harlow, Essex: Longman.

Society for Advanced Legal Studies 1998. *Report on Planning Obligations,* London: The Advanced Legal Studies Planning and Environmental Law Reform Working Group.

Solesbury, W. 1974. *Policy in Urban Planning.* London: Pergamon Press.

Somers, B. 1984. The Role of the Contractor. Paper presented at the Property Development Workshop. Henry Stewart Conference, London.

Steelcase Strafor 1990. *The Responsive Office.* Streatley on Thames: Polymath Publishing.

Stewart Hunter, D. 1983. Property Marketing: The Impending Revolution. *Estates Gazette,* 265, 86.

Street, L. 1992. The Courts and Mediation. A Warning. *Judicial Officers' Bulletin,* Vol. 3(1), pp. 10–11.

Stubbs, M. 1994. Planning Appeals by Informal Hearing: An Appraisal of the Views of Consultants. *Journal of Planning and Environment Law,* 710–14.

—— 1997. The New Panacea? An Evaluation of Mediation as an Effective Method of Dispute Resolution in Planning Appeals. *International Planning Studies,* 2: 347–364.

—— 1999. Informality and Fairness: Unlikely Partners in the Planning Appeal? *Dyason* Mediation and Informality, *Journal of Planning and Environment Law,* February, 106–112.

—— 2000. When Councillors Overturn the Chief Planning Officer – Do Costs Follow? *Journal of Planning and Environment Law,* November, pp. 1102–1104.

—— 2001. Councillors and Costs: The Vulnerability of Member-led Planning Refusals to an Award of Costs at Planning Appeal in England and Wales. *Planning Practice and Research,* Vol. 16(2), pp. 121–141.

Stubbs, M. and A. Lavers 1991. Steinberg and After. *Journal of Planning and Environment Law,* 9–19.

Stubbs, M. and J. Cripps 1993. Planning Obligations and Future Prospects. *Property Review* 2(3), 102–5.

Suddards, R. and J. Hargreaves 1996. *Listed Buildings,* 3rd edn. London: Sweet and Maxwell.

Syms, P. 1997. *Contaminated Land: The Practice and Economics of Redevelopment.* Oxford: Blackwell Science.

Talbot, J. 1988. Have Enterprise Zones Encouraged Enterprise? Some Empirical Evidence from Tyneside. *Regional Studies* 22, 507–14.

Tang, B. and R. Tang 1999. Industrial Property, Market Initiative and Planning Policy: Restructuring Obsolete Industrial Properties in Hong Kong. *Journal of Property Management,* Vol. 17, No. 2, MCB University Press.

Tanner, J. 2001. More than an Ad Hoc Tool. In K. Tasso, *Estates Gazette,* Professional Articles, 13 October 2001.

Tasso, K. 2001. More than an Ad Hoc Tool. *Estates Gazette,* Professional Articles, 13 October 2001.

Taussik, J. 1992. Surveyors and Pre-application Inquiries. *Estates Gazette* (9221), 96–100.

Taylor, R. 1985. New High-technology Survey. *Estates Gazette* 275, 20.

Taylor, T. 1993. Shedding Light on Storage. *The Valuer* 62(5), 23.

Thame, D. 1992. From the Ppast to the Future. *The Valuer* 61(6), 14–15.

Thomson, R. 1994/5. Manufacturing Floorspace Demand. *Property Review* 4(7), 237.

Thorne, J. 1994. Green Belts and Institutions Standing in Extensive Grounds. *Journal of Planning and Environment Law,* 308–13.

Thornley, A. 1991. *Urban Planning Under Thatcherism: The Challenge of the Market.* London: Routledge.

—— 1993. *Urban Planning Under Thatcherism,* 2nd edn. London: Routledge.

Todd, E. 1993. Offices Head for Home. *Estates Gazette* (9318), 98.

Tugnett, T. and M. Robertson 1987. *Making Townscape*. London: Mitchell Publishing.

Twining, W. 1993. Alternative to What? Theories of Litigation Procedure and Dispute Settlement. *Modern Law Review*, Vol. 56(3), pp. 380–92.

Unit for Retail Planning Information 1980. *Pedestrian Flows at Selected Retail and Service Business*. Reading, England: Unit for Retail Planning Information.

United Kingdom Round Table 1999. *Fifth Annual Report*. London: HM Stationery Office.

Urban Task Force 1999. *Towards an Urban Renaissance*. London: Department of Environment, Transport and the Regions and Thomas Telford Publishing.

Urban Villages Forum 1992. *Urban Villages: A Concept for Creating Mixed-use Urban Development on a Sustainable Scale*. London: Urban Villages Forum.

—— 1994. *Economics of Urban Villages*. London: Urban Villages Forum.

URBED 1994. *Vital and Viable Town Centres: Meeting the Challenge*. London: URBED and Comedia Consultants/DoE.

Vail, J. 1994. The Ills of Over-intensive Development. *Estates Gazette* (9414), 118.

Verdict 2002. *Verdict on Electronic Shopping 2002*. London: Verdict Research.

Walker, T. 1990. *Design Revolution in the 1990s*. London: *Estates Gazette*.

Ward, S. 1994. *Planning and Urban Change*. London: Paul Chapman.

Wates, N. 1999. *Action Planning*. London: Prince of Wales's Institute of Architecture.

Watt, D. and J. Valente 1991. Tenant Mix – Retailers' Views. *Estates Gazette* (9143), 82–3.

—— 1995. Invest at Leisure. *Property Review* 5(7), 220–5.

Watts, R. 1982. Marketing for a Pre-let. Paper presented at Henry Stewart Conference, London.

Welbank, M. 1995. Planning and Uncertainty. *Property Review* 5(7), 204–7.

White, A. 1995. The Future of Offices. *Property Review* 5(5), 138–40.

Wilks, D. and H. Brown 1980. Selling Techniques Have Become More Vital. *Estates Times Review* (October).

Williams, J. 1982. *A Review of Science Parks and High-technology Developments*. London: Drivers Jonas [chartered surveyors].

Williams, R. 1990. ADR: Salvation or Chimera? *Arbitration*, Vol. 56–7(2), May, pp. 101–9.

Winter, R. and R. Vergine 2000. Planning and Human Rights. *Solicitors' Journal*, pp. 972–5.

Wood, C. and G. McDonic 1989. Environmental Assessment: Challenge and Opportunity. *The Planner* 75(11), 12–18.

Woolf, L. J. 1996. *Access to Justice: Report to the Lord Chancellor on the Civil Justice System in England and Wales*, London: Lord Chancellor's Department.

World Commission on Environment and Development [Brundtland Report] 1987. *Our Common Future*. Oxford: Oxford University Press.

Worthington, J. 1982. Changing Industrial Environments. *Architects Journal* 175(16), 80.

Worthington, J. and A. Kenya 1988. *Fitting Out the Workplace*. London: The Architectural Press.

Index